The Italian Wine Guide

The Definitive Guide to Touring, Sourcing and Tasting

Touring Club Italiano
President and Chairman: Roberto Ruozi
General Manager: Guido Venturini

Touring Editore
Managing Director: Alfieri Lorenzon
Editorial Director: Michele D'Innella

International Department
Fabio Pittella
fabio.pittella@touringclub.it

Editor: Paola Pandiani
Texts: Francesco Soletti
Translation: Studio Queens
Maps: Touring Club Italiano
Editing and paging: Studio editoriale Selmi – Twister, Milano

Advertising Manager: Carlo Bettinelli
Local Advertising: Progetto
www.progettosrl.it – info@progettosrl.it

Typesetting and color separations: Twister, Milano
Printing: Grafiche Mazzucchelli – Settimo Milanese (MI)
Binding: LEM – Landriano (MI)

Distribution
USA/CAN - Publishers Group West
UK/Ireland - Portfolio Books

Touring Club Italiano, corso Italia 10, 20122 Milan
www.touringclub.it

Code K7G
ISBN 88-365-3085-0

Printed in September 2004

Summary

How to Use this Guide

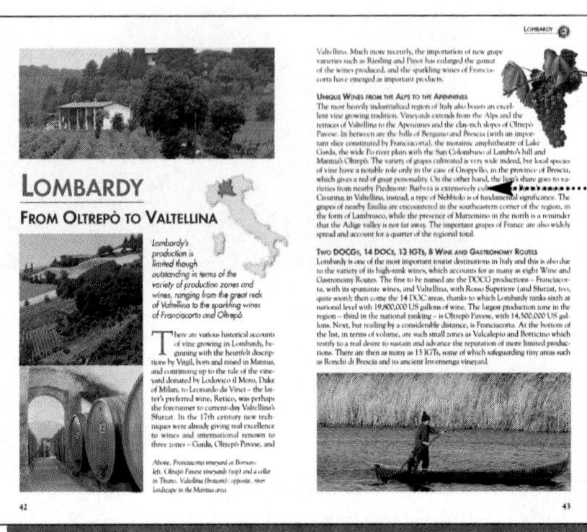

Regional introductions

This guidebook is divided into 18 regional chapters, each commencing with a presentation of the local vine-growing, providing a brief description of its distinctive traits: tradition, production, current legislation, and present trends.

Regional maps

The regional introductions are followed by a map, on one or two pages, that schematically highlights the areas covered by a DOCG and DOC Denomination of Origin. The legend also contains the IGTs (Typical Geographic Indication).

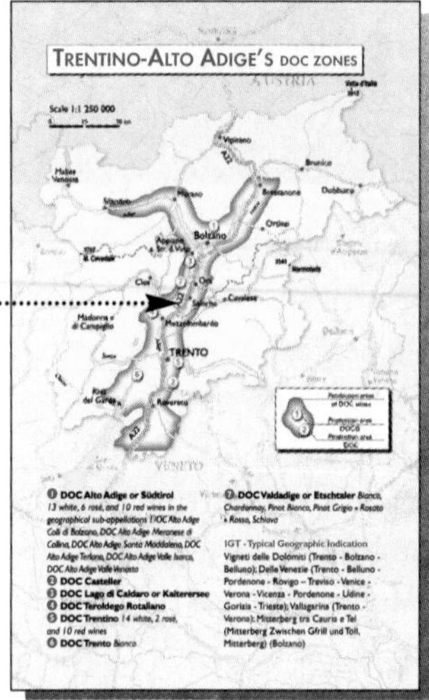

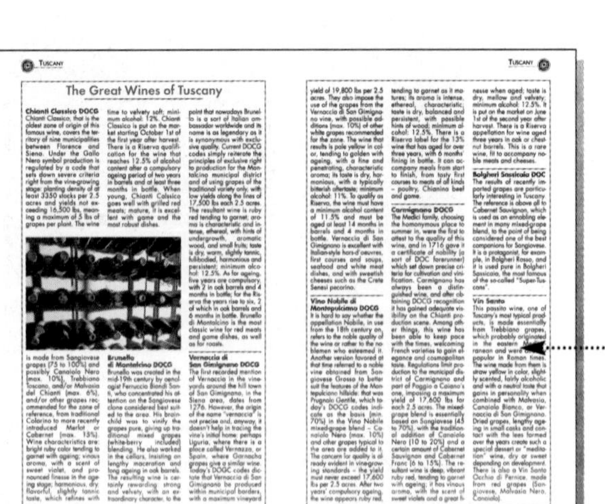

Wines

The description of each region includes one or more pages devoted to the "great" regional wines. For each one, after a few historical notes, it specifies the blends of grapes, indicates the distinctive organoleptic characteristics and identifies the most appropriate gastronomical combinations.

Provincial sections

The regional chapters are divided into sections on single wine-producing districts or groups of adjacent districts, thus lending continuity to the description of DOCs that cover large areas.

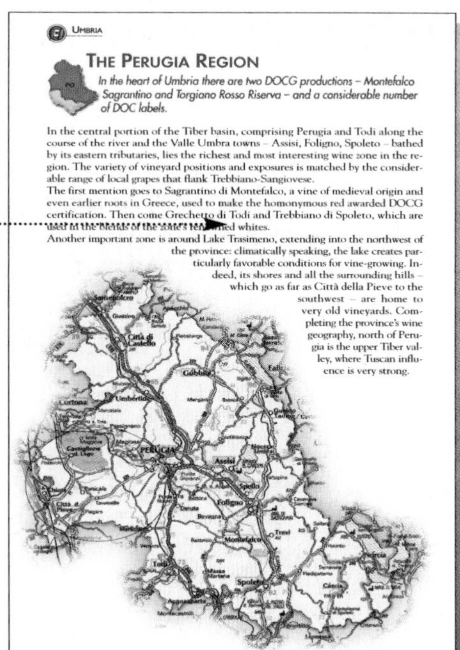
Umbria

The Perugia Region

In the heart of Umbria there are two DOCG productions – Montefalco Sagrantino and Torgiano Rosso Riserva – and a considerable number of DOC labels.

In the central portion of the Tiber basin, comprising Perugia and Todi along the course of the river and the Valle Umbra towns – Assisi, Foligno, Spoleto – bathed by its eastern tributaries, lies the richest and most interesting wine zone in the region. The variety of vineyard positions and exposures is matched by the considerable range of local grapes that flank Trebbiano-Sangiovese.
The first mention goes to Sagrantino di Montefalco, a vine of medieval origin and even earlier roots in Greece, used to make the homonymous red awarded DOCG certification. Then come Grechetto di Todi and Trebbiano di Spoleto, which are used in the blends of the zone's renowned whites.
Another important zone is around Lake Trasimeno, extending into the northwest of the province: climatically speaking, the lake creates particularly favorable conditions for vine-growing. Indeed, its shores and all the surrounding hills – which go as far as Città della Pieve to the southwest – are home to very old vineyards. Completing the province's wine geography, north of Perugia is the upper Tiber valley, where Tuscan influence is very strong.

206

Theme boxes

The provincial section pages include special boxes highlighting the institutions that promote awareness of the wine – from museums to schools and Regional wineries – or they address food and wine themes flanking the main arguments.

Da Donnas a Morgex

Grappa, Genepy, and Ratafià

First and foremost is grappa, or more precisely marc brandy, which ranges from the most aromatic varieties such as Muscat, also available in the flétri (passito) version. Grappa is most commonly used in making Valle d'Aosta-style coffee, served as part of the friendly grolla ritual that involves passing a characteristic wooden bowl from hand to hand and sipping from one of the many spouts. Next are the productions of grape brandies, made directly from the fruit itself, and the traditional William's pear distillate. The herb liqueurs include Genepy: in the Savoy dialect the name refers to a certain group of small herbs which mountain folk believe to be a cure against all ills. What is actually used to obtain this distinctive greenish-tinted liqueur with a pleasantly bitter taste are some types of Artemesia (mugwort), gathered at high altitudes or even grown. The production of traditional liqueurs also includes ratafià, made by letting wild or sour cherries steep in marc brandy and then adding lemon peel and sugar or syrup. Spirit lovers will be keen to meet growers and producers: in some instances the distilleries are part of wine firms, such as La Crotta di Vegneron in Chambave or La Cave des Onze Communes in Aymavilles; in other cases they are specialist companies like Ottoz from Saint Christophe and La Valdôtaine from Saint-Marcel.

Donnas. This long-time capital of the Bassa Valle region lies along Via delle Gallie, an ancient Roman road full of remains, and is lined with beautiful period houses. Long a wine-growing town, it uses Nebbiolo, which flourishes in the sandy ground, to produce the valley's oldest and most heavily produced DOC wine. The Caves Coopératives de Donnas, set up in 1971, safeguard the production and marketing of local wines.

• Arnad. Situated on the plain of the same name in the lower section of Valle d'Aosta, this was an important place in the Middle Ages, as can be seen from its three castles. There still is an 11th-century parish church and the picturesque sanctuary of Machaby, buried away in thick chestnut woods at a height of 2300 feet. Arnad is also the headquarters of the La Kiuva farm cooperative, whose members are wine-growers and farmers from seven different municipalities.

Media Valle. Along the 28 miles of the Media Valle, vineyards are located in all kinds of different settings: from the heavily farmed and sheltered Saint-Vincent basin to the stretch of land beyond Châtillon, which is so dry and sun-baked that there is even Mediterranean vegetation; from the Aosta plain, where the valley is at its widest before rising up across vine-covered slopes, to the wide open tree-lined prairies covered with vineyards on the slopes to the north of Sarre; from the ridges of Saint-Nicolas,

A typical Valle d'Aosta arbor

7

Itineraries

These offer wine-lovers a brief exploration of the area and when possible follow the trails traced by the Wine Routes, specifically created for the purpose. The suggested visits are divided into 'stops' and describe the tourist attractions of the most important places.

Production zones

The provincial sections describe the wine districts and those of interest to wine-lovers, and they introduce one or more possible visits.

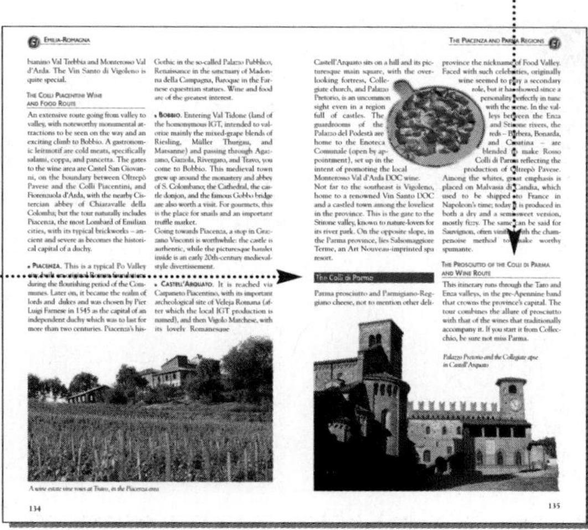
Emilia-Romagna

The Piacenza and Parma Regions

The Colli Piacentini Wine and Food Route

The Colli di Parma

The Prosciutto of the Colli di Parma and Wine Route

Palazzo Pretorio and the Collegiate apse in Castell'Arquato

A wine estate vine rows at Travo, in the Piacenza area

134

135

INTRODUCTION

A few years after its first presentation to the English-speaking public, *The Italian Wine Guide* edited by Touring Club of Italy is once more available in a new, improved version, updated and – if possible – even more useful for wine tourists.

The subject matter is still divided by region and by provincial wine-producing districts. Whenever possible, the tours follow the Wine Routes that are gradually appearing in Italy, the expression of a new way of combining a love of travel with wine tasting, exploring the territory and discovering good food, environmental attractions, and organized tourism.

This guide provides essential information – precise and not too technical – on food and wine theme tours that do not hesitate to branch out and appreciate the natural, artistic, and historical attractions of which Italy abounds. Attention focuses immediately on the wines, on the "great wines" that stand out on the highly variegated panorama offered by the many (20) different Italian regions. Where can I drink or buy them?

Along with the descriptions, you will find small boxes entitled "Wineries". These will send you to the final section of the book and the list of wine cellars selected town by town (although we should say hill by hill) by the Seminario Veronelli, one of the most prestigious institutions in the world of Italian wines.

Grape harvest, mosaic work in the Santa Costanza mausoleum, Rome, 4th century

NOT JUST BAROLO AND BRUNELLO DI MONTALCINO

Getting down to specifics as quickly as possible, it is important to point out that the prestige which is now attached to the names of Italy's finest wines, sought and requested in all of the world's markets where fine wine is consumed, should not be allowed to overshadow the single most important aspect of Italian wine: its astonishing variety. Unlike other major producing countries, where viticulture is confined to specific areas, often separated from others by great distances, the vine is cultivated everywhere in Italy, from the Alps bordering Austria and Switzerland to the southeastern corner of Sicily, at a more southern latitude than the city of Tunis in Tunisia. In addition to the very significant climatic differences which inevitably result, the geography of the country, famously hilly, has created an undulating topography with an undescribable richness of specific vineyard situations.

Above, Nicolas Regnier, Soldier Raising a Flask, *Modena, Galleria Estense, 18th century (top) and Joan Miró,* Wine Bottle, *Barcelona, Fundació Joan Miró (bottom). Opposite (top), Greek amphora, Rome, Museo di Villa Giulia, 6th century B.C.*

The variety of soils and microclimates is perhaps even exceeded by that of the grapes cultivated in Italy's vineyards, many hundreds in number. The time span they represent is astonishing in and of itself: some date back to ancient civilizations, those of the Etruscans or the first Greek colonists in Italy's south, while others, introduced only a few decades ago, are already demonstrating important results. It is only logical that non-Italian observers be most impressed by the new level of excellence attained by Nebbiolo- or Sangiovese-based wines, but the fact of the matter is that they represent only the tip of the iceberg in the overall context of Italian wine. There are dozens, scores, of interesting, enjoyable, and rewarding wines currently being produced in Italy, in all of the country's various regions. Intelligent and informed consumers will seek out not only the best known names, but also the richness of a viticultural production which spans three millenia and now, at the beginning of the fourth millenia of its systematic cultivation of the vine, is offering more intriguing and satisfying wines than ever before.

A Few Words on Wine

With the advice and assistance of the Enoteca di Siena, a rapid course in enology and related matters, prepared for the novice wine tourist.

Before departing on a trip in search of wine, with cellars and enotecas as preferred destinations, it is a good idea to master a few basic concepts of winemaking. The pleasure of discussions with grower-producers or with sommeliers will notably increase, particularly when the conversation turns to specific matters of blends or of winemaking and aging techniques. The following brief summary has been prepared by the experts of the Enoteca Italiana di Siena, the public institution which has been given the official task of promoting Italy's quality wines.

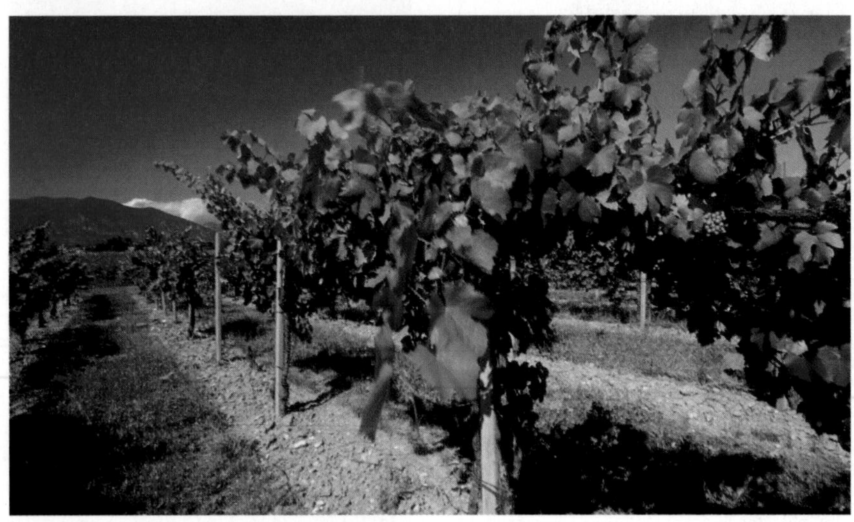

White, Red, Rosé...

THE FUNDAMENTALS OF ENOLOGY

Not all wines are prepared in the same way. Vinification and ageing techniques vary substantially according to the type of wine which the producer wishes to obtain. In the case of white wines, for example, grapes are crushed in horizontal presses equipped with perforated cylinders which rotate on a horizontal axis and with screw-driven plates which move towards the center of the cylinder and crush the grapes between them. The must falls through the holes in the cylinder into tanks below the press and ferments without contact with the grape skins. This is the classic white wine fermentation, and can also be used for certain types of red grapes when the aim is to obtain either musts with little color or a light pink hue. The former type of must, almost colorless, is used for sparkling wines (many famous Champagnes, for example, have a percentage as high as two thirds of Pinot Noir, a red grape). The latter, instead, is utilized to produce rosé wines, which are consequently not a blend of white wines and red wines, but the result of particular vinification techniques.

Opposite, Franciacorta's vineyard (Lombardy); above, Apulian vigneron at work

From the Contact with the Skins, the Character of the Wine

Matters – and equipment – change entirely in the case of red wine. The grape skins are broken and opened in destemmer-crushers which separate the grapes from the stalks before crushing them. Must and skins ferment together for periods which vary according to the grape variety and the type of wine desired. For light and fragrant wines such as Bardolino and Chianti, a few days of contact with the skins are sufficient. In the case of austere and powerful wines such as Barolo or Brunello di Montalcino, the period of skin contact can be as long as 20-30 days. But this type of fermentation for red wines – in systematic contact with the skins – is rarely used for white wines, only when one is aiming for a rustic, traditional type of product. (Skin contact for a few hours at low temperatures is sometimes used for aromatic white wines, and in this case the technique helps trasfer to the must aromatic substances found in the grape skins and not in their pulp). After the wine has been run off its skins, it is placed in wooden containers – casks or barrels – of various sizes and remains there for the period of time prescribed by the DOC production rules (in the majority of cases, for two or three years for wines of a certain level).

A recently planted vine

ABBREVIATIONS WHICH IDENTIFY THE WINES: IGT, DOC...

Italian wine production, as established by law 164 of the year 1992, is divided into categories, or denominations, which together form a kind of quality pyramid. At the base of the pyramid are the *vini da tavola* or table wines, ordinary products which only need a minimum alcoholic content of 10% and no supplementary descriptions may be added to their name. IGT (Indicazione Geografica Tipica), ample appellation (which at times include an entire region) wines form the next level. Their production rules regulate the grape varieties which can be used and maximum yields per acre, just to give two examples, and the vintage year may be put on the label. The central feature of the framework legislation enacted by law 164 of 1992 concerns DOC (Denominazione di Origine Controllata) wines. They are now approximately 700 in number and cover a large part of the country's territory. Each *denominazione* or appellation contains precise rules prescribing the exact geographical area from which the grapes of DOC wines must come, the manner and period of the ageing of the wines, and certain basic minimum chemical parameters (alcohol, acidity, dry extract), and even the maximum yield in juice from the grapes. DOC wines can indicate their vintage date and, where permitted by the rules of the individual appellation, the grape varieties used in the blend.

Spumante wine bottles declined in the pupitres

DOCG: TOP QUALITY

DOCG (Denominazione di Origine Controllata e Garantita) wines represent, instead, the peak of the quality pyramid. There are, at the present moment, just over 20 (and they are all "aristocrats") by law "wines of special quality": Albana di Romagna, Asti Spumante, Barbaresco, Barolo, Brunello di Montalcino, Chianti, Chianti Classico, Franciacorta Brut, Vernaccia di San Gimignano, Vino Nobile di Montepulciano. A DOCG is a sort of super DOC: production rules are more rigorous, and both chemical and tasting controls are envisaged each and every time a certain quantity of wine is bottled.

DOCG wines carry a strip – pink for red wines, green for white wines – which is a kind of seal of approval of the Italian state, numbered and granted to the single producer according to the amount of wine which has satisfied the required tests and controls.

The Professionals of Wine

Less poetry and more science – this is the trend of modern wine. Cellars are modern and spotlessly clean, and they are now populated by men in white jackets working in laboratories where analyses and controls are carried out. The true protagonists in this sector, by now, are trained oenologists, men and women with either a diploma or a doctorate. They guarantee that all phases of vinification are executed as well as possible. But to produce quality wine, it is necessary to have first-rate grapes. And it is therefore necessary that the vineyards be planted in the proper places and that they be properly cultivated. And thus there is a second professional figure in winemaking operations, that of the agronomist, with either a diploma from a specialized school or a doctorate in agronomy with a specialization in fruit-bearing plants.

From the Cellar to the Table

At the end of the production cycle, the wine is released and goes onto the market and, at this point, it needs to make a name for itself. It is also essential to know how to store it, to serve it, and to match it with various types of food. Sommeliers are the professionals involved in this aspect of wine, but other professionals also take part: restaurateurs, owners of enotecas and wine shops, waiters specializing in wine service, managers of important hotels, buyers for supermarket chains. The Association of Italian Sommeliers (AIS) organizes courses for the training of professionals, with a whole series of levels of instruction. One can become a real sommelier only after passing the examination of the third course, and those already involved in wine as part of their work can add the word "professional" to the title of sommelier.

The Grape Harvest Festival in Merano

A WINE FOR EVERY OCCASION
PRINCIPLES OF MATCHING WINE TO FOOD

Matching wine to the dishes which have been served is only apparently a simple operation. General rules do exist, and these will be explained in the pages which follow, but, as in all matters of taste, rigid rules cannot and do not exist. One simple observation should suffice: a specific wine is never the same, it changes according to its age and vintage, and even two bottles of the exact same wine often show slight differences. And, in just the same way, a recipe will never give identical results on different occasions, even when executed by the same cook. The experience, the advice of experts, the texts of the classic works of gastronomy are, together with regional traditions, obviously helpful, but, in the final analysis, it is the individual opinion which counts.

CONTRAST AND BALANCE

A classic way of matching food to wine is that of seeking an overall harmony by way of contrast. If, for example, a dish is fairly rich, a dry wine can be served, perhaps sparkling or semi-sparkling, so that the palate remains clean and refreshed, ready for a new mouthful. A classic example: that of dry Lambrusco with a cooked sausage, a typical regional match in Emilia-Romagna. Whereas a soft white wine goes better with a dish prepared with lemon or vinegar, with a certain perceptible acidity to its flavors. A final consideration: dishes with persistent flavors should be matched with wines with a long finish and aftertaste, an aged Parmesan cheese, for example, with an aged red wine or an elegant and mature sparkling wine. Pasta, rice, or crepes dilute and lighten flavors and require wines with more delicate flavors than their sauce.
Other simple observations derive from experience: the tannins of red wines clash with the delicate flavors of fish, which is therefore accompanied by white wine, more stuctured when the dish comes with an elaborate sauce or preparation. But even in this case there are some exceptions: a tasty fish soup, perhaps slightly spicy, goes very well with a light, soft red wine, best served fresh and cool. Red wine goes best with meat, but the type varies according to the importance of the dish. Matching wine to cheese is a fascinating subject: light and fresh cheese

Gastronomy fair in Piedmont

goes best with a white wine of good acidity, but sweet or dessert wines are the preferred match for soft, full-flavored cheese, particularly blue cheese. The principle of contrast is not valid with desserts, and sweet wines are the best accompaniment; the flavors of creamy desserts can often best be cleaned from the palate by sparkling wines, while fortified wines, of a greater or lesser sweetness, are an excellent accompaniment to petits fours.

Pasta and Rice: it Depends on the Sauce

For a good match with pasta and rice, the sauce is the essential factor to take into consideration. Just as one example, let us analyze the ingredients of the famous and frequently encountered meat sauce of Bologna. In this sauce there are both fatty elements such as butter and several kinds of meat, and an acidic element as well, tomatoes. The softness of the flavors, in any case, accentuated when the sauce accompanies egg pasta, is quite evident even when used to flavor spaghetti or maccheroni. The wine to accompany this sauce, therefore, needs to have certain characteristics which will attenutate the fattiness, a certain level of tannin whose astringence will provide the requisite balance. A Sangiovese di Romagna might be a good solution, but there are other possibilities as well: Barbera d'Alba, a Valpolicella Classico, a Merlot from the Collio zone of Friuli, or a Torgiano Rosso from Umbria.

From the Sea to the Woods and the Garden

The same logic applies when the sauce is based on products from the sea, as in the case with spaghetti with clam sauce or rice with seafood. White wine is the indicated accompaniment in both cases, lighter and more acidic with the former dish, a Gavi, a Verdicchio dei Colli di Jesi, or a Fiano d'Avellino, more aromatic and full bodied with the latter, a Sauvignon from the Collio zone of Friuli or a Riesling from the Alto Adige. Mushrooms, instead, are sworn enemies of tannins and of acidity, both of which tend to damage their delicate fragrance. Rosé wines are therefore an excellent solution with pasta or rice dishes with mushroom sauces: a Rosato di Bolgheri, an Alezio Rosato, a Bardolino Chiaretto, a Lagrein Kretzer. In conclusion, for pasta or risotto seasoned with vegetables, increasingly popular in today's cuisine, soft white wines are a good match, perhaps from Italy's center-south: a Locorotondo, an Alcamo, a Vermentino di Gallura. Vegetable soups with pasta or rice are a different story. Young red wines are suggested in this case: Chianti, Rosso di Montepulciano, Cabernet Franc from the Grave del Friuli area.

For Meat, Red Wines of Character

Let us begin with the simplest dishes of all, those cooked directly on the fire with a total absence of supplementary fatty materials, be they butter or oil. The prince of wines to accompany grilled meat, white or red, is a young Chianti Classico.

Monferrato wine bottles

Good alternatives are other Sangiovese-based wines such as Rosso di Montalcino, Torgiano Rosso, Sangiovese di Romagna, Velletri Rosso, Chianti Rufina, or Rosso Piceno. Another fairly simple dish is a pot-au-feu, or mixed boiled meats. There are wonderful Italian wines to accompany this dish: Dolcetto d'Alba or Dolcetto di Dogliani, Barbera d'Alba or Barbera d'Asti, Bonarda from the Oltrepò Pavese, or Valpolicella Classico Superiore. Red meat with a long preparation, stewed or cooked in a sauce, need wines with a notable ageing capacity such as Barolo, Barbaresco, Gattinara, Amarone, Brunello di Montalcino, Vino Nobile di Montepulciano, or Taurasi. Some final thoughts on such cold dishes as chicken in aspic, chicken salad, veal with a tuna fish sauce, or cold roast beef, all of which can be accompanied by a Sylvaner from the Alto Adige or a Gewürztraminer from the same region.

FISH, SHELLFISH, AND SEAFOOD

Fish with white flesh, steamed or grilled, prepared without additional fats and with little fat of their own, are best suited to delicate white wines, without excessive roughness and with medium alcoholic strength: a Chardonnay from Trentino, a Ribolla Gialla from Friuli's Collio, a Vermentino di Sardegna, a Lugana, or a Bianco di Custoza. Seafood, instead, can go well with lightly aromatic white wines, even those with a slightly bitter aftertaste which balances the sweetness of their flesh. An Alto Adige Sauvignon, a soft Malvasia Istriana from the Carso in Friuli, a Verdicchio dei Castelli di Jesi will all do the trick very nicely. A plate of mixed fried fish can be matched to a classic, bottle-fermented Spumante, but goes equally well with a Gavi, a Collio Ribolla Gialla, a Verdicchio di Matelica, or a Greco di Tufo. Oven-baked fish dishes or blue fish such as sardines, fresh anchovies, or mackerel need a white wine of a certain body or a flavorful rosé: Soave Classico Superiore, Vernaccia di San Gimignano, Fiano d'Avellino, Corvo Colomba Platino, Montepulciano Cerasuolo. Last on the list, fish soup or broth: here too, white wines or rosés of a certain body are required. But a light red wine can also be a good match, a Novello, a Colli del Trasimeno Rosso, a young Chianti. These should be served cool, almost as though they were white wines.

MUSHROOMS AND VEGETABLES, TOUGH CUSTOMERS

Mushrooms, in general, are delicate in flavor and can only be matched with soft wines, white or rosé, rarely red wines and if so only with Merlot. Suggestions include Schiava from the Alto Adige, Trentino's Marzemino, Bardolino or Garda Bresciano Chiaretto, Montecarlo Bianco, Collio Tocai Friulano. Only in unusual cases can vegetables be precisely matched to specific wines. Medium bodied red wines such as Chianti or Valpolicella go well with vegetable soups; a rustic Gragnano, a lively wine from the hinterland behind Naples, is a good accompaniment to Parmesan-style eggplant. And then there are the classic matches of specific regional cuisines: in Rome or in Latium, one cannot avoid drinking a Frascati or a Marino with *carciofi alla giudia*, artichokes prepared according to the traditions of Rome's Jewish population, while in Friuli a Sauvignon from the Grave del Friuli zone is a natural accompaniment to the white asparagus of the same area.

With Cheese, Depending on How It Has Been Aged

Some cheese is so strongly flavored that it risks overpowering the palate after a few mouthfulls. A well matched wine avoids this risk. This means that lengthly aged and tasty cheeses such as Grana or Asiago should be had with a red wine of real structure. Important Nebbiolo-based wines from Piedmont such as Barbaresco, Barolo, and Gattinara are a good choice, as are such classy Tuscan wines as Vino Nobile di Montepulciano or Chianti Classico Riserva. A Salice Salentino or a Cirò Classico Rosso go equally well with *caciocavallo* from Sicily or a savory *provolone* from Cremona. If, instead, the cheese is a delicate and fresh one, a *stracchino* or a mozzarella, the wine should be light and fragrant: a white wine from Grave del Friuli, a Greco di Tufo, a Bianco di Custoza, or even a Verdicchio dei Castelli di Jesi, despite its reputation as a wine for fish. A surprising match is that of certain salty and highly flavored cheeses such as *pecorino romano* or *pecorino sardo* with sweet and alcoholic red wines. Another unusual but successful match is that of a blue cheese such as *gorgonzola* and a long and persistent dessert wine: an Amarone della Valpolicella or a Marsala Vergine.

Reds and Rosés for Ham and Salami

The world of salami is a universe of flavors in Italy, and great sensitivity is required to match them well with wine. Fattier ones such as cooked salami, the *salama da sugo* of Ferrara, or Modena's *cotechino* go best with the wines of their native regions: a Barbera d'Asti or a lively Barbera del Monferrato, a Bonarda of the Oltrepò Pavese, a Lambrusco Grasparossa di Castelvetro or a Lambrusco Salamino di Santa Croce. Spicy salami (the sausages of Calabria or salami with peppercorns) go well with the rosé wines of Apulia's Salento, soft and alcoholic, an Alezio or a Squinzano, and with rosés from Calabria's Cirò zone as well. Matching wine to salted pork products, in particular to hams such as *prosciutto*, is anything but simple. Delicate wines from the Alto Adige such as Lago di Caldaro, Schiava, or Santa Maddalena are a good choice with *speck*. A rosé from Bolgheri, a Cerasuolo from Abruzzo, or a Morellino di Scansano are good alternatives.

A selection of Italian cheeses

THE END OF THE MEAL: DESSERTS AND THEIR WINES

A good place to begin is with soft and creamy desserts: mousse, Bavarian cream, or semifreddo-style ice creams. A certain level of alcohol is needed, from wines such as Moscadello di Montalcino Passito, Moscato di Cagliari, or Malvasia delle Lipari Dolce Naturale. If the dessert contains bitter chocolate, the wine needs to be even sweeter and a Passito di Pantelleria is a good choice. Cakes with leavened dough such as *panettone*, *pandoro*, or *colomba*, traditional fare at Christmas or Easter, have an ideal match in Asti Spumante and Moscato d'Asti or, alternatively, with the Moscato Fior d'Arancio of the Colli Euganei and Moscadello di Montalcino. Fruit tarts (but not those made with fruit jams), and such pastry classics as *strudel*, not excessively sweet, need equally delicate dessert wines without excessive

The Evolution of the Wine Market in the USA

In the last 35 years the U.S. wine market has been basically characterized by a big expansion that began in the early 70's and lasted for 15 years, till 1985, followed by a period of recession from 1986 to 1993 and by a new expansion from 1994 to the end of 2003.
The cycle that started the biggest and longest boom after the end of the prohibitionism in the 30's began in 1970 when the total yearly wine consumption in the United States was approximately 10 million hectoliters.
In those times, wine was little known to the large masses of consumers in the United States and consumption was limited especially to ethnic groups immigrated to the United States from Europe.
Wines from California were considered products of a lower quality, consisting mostly of "jug wines", produced with mixed grapes and marketed in glass containers of one gallon each (approx. 3.785 liters). The U.S. wine market was practically in the hands of a few wineries (one of them controlled over 50% of the U.S. wine market).
The imported wine market was controlled instead by the French wines (especially Bordeaux and Burgundy), which were considered by far the best available in the U.S. and held almost a 35% share of the imported wine market.
Italian wines (mostly Chianti and Veronese wines) were in third position, considerably behind the French wines and slightly behind the Portuguese wines (mostly Porto). They were considered fair quality wines, but certainly of a lower quality than the French wines. They held less than a 19% share of the U.S. imported wine market.
The U.S. import of Italian wines in 1970 had reached approximately 143,000 hectoliters with a value of less than 14 million dollars, against imports of 253,000 hectoliters and 43.3 million dollars for the French wines. Total imports of wines in the U.S. in that year were approximately 773,000 hectoliters valued at 91 million dollars.
Among the fad wines, Porto from Portugal and Sangria from Spain had gained a great popularity among U.S. consumers.
Lambrusco, in the meantime, had been introduced to the U.S. market. In 1970 approximately 40,000 cartons (3,600 hectoliters) were imported from Italy. Sweet and slightly sparkling, it had an immediate appeal to the American consumers, especially younger men and women who were approaching wine for the first time.
In the next 10 years imports of Lambrusco into the United States had a spectacular increase, reaching 270,000 hectoliters in 1975, 900,000 hectoliters in 1980 and almost one million hectoliters in 1981.
In the wake of Lambrusco, most Italian wines (especially Soave, Bardolino and Valpolicella from the Verona area, Verdicchio dei Castelli di Jesi from the Marche region, Frascati from Latium and Corvo wines from Sicily) had great success on the U.S. market. Imports of Italian wines in fact increased almost 1,500%, reaching a record amount in 1983, with over 2.4 million hectoliters.
From 1985 to 1993 American consumers lost their interest in wines and consumption fell constantly for nine straight years. During those years, total

residual sugar. A classic combination of this type is Picolit or Verduzzo with apple tart. Crusty fruit pies often create virtually insurmountable problems. There is not a large number of possibilities in this case, but a Brachetto d'Acqui or a Malvasia Rossa di Castelnuovo Don Bosco are a possible solution, but only when the pies are made with strawberry or wild cherry jam. The great creamy desserts of haute cuisine such as a charlotte or a millefeuille, if prepared without liqueur, go well with moderately sweet wines but ones with a good level of alcohol, and Recioto di Soave or Recioto di Gambellara are quite suitable. Very few wines can stand up to chocolate desserts such as a Sacher-Torte, and Italy has only Sicily's Ala and Sardinia's Anghelu Ruju to offer. No wines go well with ice cream or sherbet: the cold anaesthetizes the taste buds and damages the wines' flavor.

imports of wines into the U.S. fell more than 60%, from 4.5 million hectoliters to 1.95 million hectoliters. In the same period, imports of Italian wines fell more than 66%, from 2.4 million hectoliters to 754,000 hectoliters and French wines fell 42%, from 1.06 million hectoliters to 552,000 hectoliters. Consumption of American made wines also fell more than 27,5%, from 16.7 million hectoliters to 12.1 million hectoliters.
The main reasons for the decline was a general loss of interest in all alcoholic beverages by the American consumers; a persistent campaign at all levels of government - federal, state and local - against consumption of alcohol and drunk driving; various campaigns to emphasize the evil effects of alcohol drinking on human health; and the long period of economic recession, especially from 1989 to 1993.
In addition, imports of Italian wines were also affected by the absence of a large scale promotional campaign at the institutional level in the United States which, instead, had been intensively conducted in the years from 1975 to 1985.
In fact, during the big expansion of the U.S. wine market, sales of Italian wines had constantly increased not only because of a natural interest in all wines by the American consumers, but also thanks to the huge promotional campaign that was conducted at all levels of distribution and consumption, in all the publicity media, mainly radio, television and press.
The new expansion of the U.S. wine market began in 1994, at the end of the economic recession. The revival of wine consumption, however, was due not only to the new economic boom that officially lasted for almost eight years, but also to a new climate surrounding consumption of alcoholic beverages.
During that time, in fact, there was an almost total absence of negative campaigns against alcoholic beverages. In addition, in the case of wine, the frequent publication of medical studies on the beneficial effects of a moderate wine consumption on the human health was also very helpful.
Probably the most effective of such reports was the so called "French Paradox" which revealed that French people, even with their traditional diet of fatty foods, were less subject to heart attacks because of a substance contained in red wines, which they consumed abundantly.
In the last 10 years, U.S. wine imports have almost tripled, from 1.96 million hectoliters and 650.6 million dollars in 1993, to 5.5 million hectoliters and 2.6 billion dollars in 2003.
Similarly, imports of Italian wines during the same period have increased from 754.000 hectoliters and 186.3 million dollars in 1993, to 1.94 million hectoliters and 822.8 million dollars in 2003.
Even though the U.S. wine market, after 10 years of constant expansion, is currently starting to show some signs of slowing down, it represents a very strong outlet for Italian wines in the years to come.
Wines represent one of the leading category of products exported to the United States from Italy, and should remain in top position in the future.
Italy is the largest wine producer in the world and produces such a variety of quality wines that it can fully satisfy the demand of the American consumers.

Italian Wine & Food Institute

What is the Touring Club of Italy?

Benvenuti al **Touring Club Italiano**

www.touringclub.it

Long Tradition, Great Prestige

For over 110 years, the Touring Club of Italy (TCI) has offered travelers the most detailed and comprehensive source of travel information available on Italy. The Touring Club of Italy was founded in 1894 with the aim of developing the social and cultural values of tourism and promoting the conservation and enjoyment of the country's national heritage, landscape and environment.

Advantages of Membership

Today, TCI offers a wide rage of travel services to assist and support members with the highest level of convenience and quality. Now you can discover the unique charms of Italy with a distinct insider's advantage. Enjoy exclusive money saving offers with a TCI membership. Use your membership card for discounts in thousands of restaurants, hotels, spas, campgrounds, museums, shops and markets.

↘ JOIN THE TOURING CLUB OF ITALY

How to Join

It's quick and easy to join. Apply for your membership online at www.touringclub.it Your membership card will arrive within three weeks and is valid for discounts across Italy for the entire year. Get your card before you go and start saving as soon as you arrive.

$25 Annual Membership fee includes priority mail postage for membership card and materials. Just one use of the card will more than cover the cost of membership.

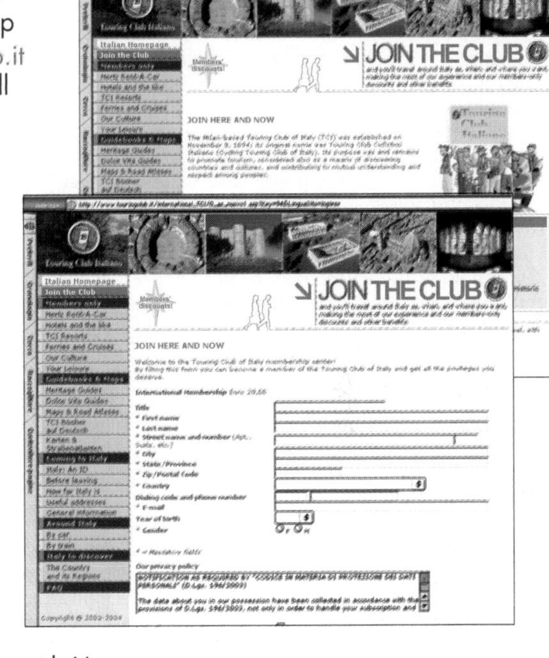

Benefits

- Exclusive car rental rates with Hertz
- Discounts at select Esso gas stations
- 20% discount on TCI guidebooks and maps purchased in TCI bookstores or directly online at www.touringclubofitaly.com
- Preferred rates and discounts available at thousands of locations in Italy: Hotels - B&B's - Villa Rentals - Campgrounds -TCI Resorts - Spas - Restaurants - Wineries - Museums - Cinemas - Theaters - Music Festivals - Shops - Craft Markets - Ferries - Cruises - Theme Parks - Botanical Gardens

The Authors

The Author:
Francesco Soletti
Originally from Lake Como, he is an adopted son of Veneto and so poised between Sforzato della Valtellina and Amarone della Valpolicella. Having grown up within the ranks of Touring Club of Italy, he is now 45 years old and in charge of the food and wine series. One of his most recent works is the *Guida all'Italia del Caffè* (2004) and new projects include a guide to distilled liquors and spirits.

Seminario Veronelli
The name of Luigi Veronelli, a great connoisseur and 'lover' of Italian wines, a forerunner of the contemporary food and wine culture in Italy, is well known to all enthusiasts. The publisher of one of the leading Italian wine guides, Veronelli promotes various cultural initiatives, including the Seminario Permanente, wich has accompanied Touring in the new edition of this guide. The spirit underlying this collaboration is basically that of a shared goal. Every stress and recommendation made in the food and wine tours herein is in keeping with the ideals of quality and the food and wine culture championed by Veronelli.
The Seminario Permanente Luigi Veronelli was established in Bergamo on 7 April 1986 at the initiative of a discriminating group of vinedressers and today numbers the most prestigious names in the Italian food and wine world. Its aim is to promote quality food and wine through the study, propagation and creation of a "culture of quality".
The Seminario is based in one of Bergamo's old streets (Via Pignolo 78) and has a beautiful 17th-century reception room. It promotes meetings, roundtables, presentations, and seminars on the new developments in vine growing and winemaking, in collaboration with the leading university faculties and the most prestigious research institutes in Italy and abroad. It also organizes tasting and sensorial analysis courses for enthusiasts and operators as well as regular expert tasting sessions for wines, spirits, olive oils, coffees and other foods.
Quarterly it publishes a technical-scientific journal, *Il consenso*. The website www.seminarioveronelli.com presents all members divided by category: companies, restaurants, artisans, and wineries. For further information please send an e-mail to: info@seminarioveronelli.com

The Italian Wine & Food Institute
The Italian Wine & Food Institute, headquartered in New York, is a nonprofit organization, founded in 1983 for the enhancement of the image and prestige of Italian wines, gastronomy, and food products in the United States.
To this end the Institute organizes educational and promotional events and carries out public relation activities to educate the American consumers about the high quality of Italian wines, food products, and gastronomy.
The promotional activities of the Institute consists in a series of initiatives directed at the professional media, the operators in the specific sectors, at every level of distribution, the opinion leaders and the most qualified American consumers.
The promotional activities of the Institute comprise seminars and tastings; it provides detailed information on the Italian gastronomy and wines; it distributes information materials and gives press interviews for the American radio and television; it carries out an intense public relations program; it participates in the most important local promotional activities and events; it maintains contacts with the American and Italian authorities in this sector; it carries out market research and surveys and publishes a bimonthly newsletter, *Notiziario*, about the American market.
The Institute has in addition published a book on Italian cuisine and booklets on Italian wines and food products such as *Discovering Italian Wines* and *Gala Italia* with the goal to educate the American consumers. The institute publishes, moreover, detailed information on its various initiatives on its Web Page.
The President of the Institute, Dr. Lucio Caputo, has been active in the promotion of Italian wines and gastronomy for over twenty years, first in his position as Italian Trade Commissioner, and later as the President of the Italian Wine & Food Institute, of the European Wine Council, of the International Trade Center, and of the Italian Representative Group-G.E.I. and as US representative of the Verona Fair Authority.

Touring for Wine in Italy

Valle d'Aosta

Rare and Heroic Wines

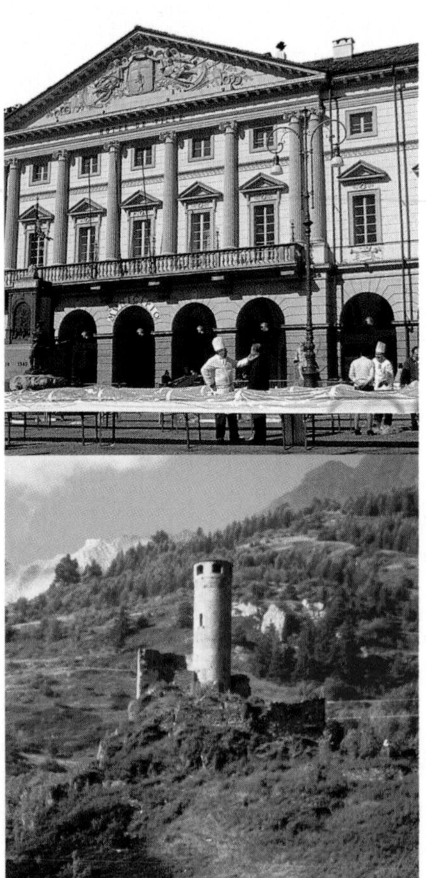

In the Alpine valley of the Dora Baltea river, the cultivation of the vine extends to the very foot of Mont Blanc. The never-ending, laborious struggle between local growers and their mountainous environment gives rare – indeed unique – wines, there to be discovered along the valley's Wine Route.

In the land of strong contrasts which corresponds to the deep furrow cut by the Dora Baltea, the vine has been bound to confront a process of difficult acclimatization to local conditions since Roman times. Its habitat begins at Pont Saint-Martin, at 1000 feet above sea level, where the rocky soil reflects the intense solar rays, and extends as far as Morgex, at 4000 feet, where grapes ripen among the firs and larches of Mont Blanc.

Above, Torrette vineyards; left, Aosta, piazza Chanoux (top) and one of Valle d'Aosta's castles (bottom); opposite, Alta Valle landscape

The principal characteristic of the valley's viticulture, in fact, is the necessity of adapting to a far from generous terrain; success is always linked to particular and specific conditions. Above all, vineyards are almost exclusively confined to what is locally called the "adret", that is the mountain side directly exposed to the sun. But there are other limiting factors as well: those which restrict vineyards to positions best protected from winds and with adequate sources of water – the valley, closed off by mountains which block the arrival of clouds, is one of the least rainy parts of all of Italy. These are indeed choice spots, often with a natural absence of fungal diseases so common elsewhere, sparing the vineyards from regular spraying, a necessary part of vine growing elsewhere.

The Human Element in the Valle d'Aosta Miracle

There is a miraculous quality to the production of these Alpine wines, and much credit must be given to the human factor, the knowing work of man which has taken advantage of every square inch of available soil and, in a series of terraces, has even redesigned the landscape. The walls of piled stones, originally conceived to protect the slopes from erosion and enlarge the cultivatable surface, are also functional to the vine's vegetative cycle: the stones capture and absorb the sun's heat, mitigating the sharp temperature swings from day to night, while columns and pergolas aid the vine in its ceaseless struggle with the wind. The agronomical skills of local residents is also seen in their keen selection of grape varieties particularly resistant to mountain climes. The absolute champion is Blanc de Morgex, which manages to ripen at record altitudes, but there are many other local varieties, which still have a significant place in the region's oenology. Production codes indicate 22 different grapes, both indigenous and imported, and these give rise to a large gamut of different wines.

A Sole DOC Appellation for a Region of Important Wines

A part of the local production has been grouped under the officially recognized appellation name of Valle d'Aosta DOC or Vallée d'Aoste, the latter a homage to the region's bi-lingual tradition. Some wines can be produced in any of the areas specifically suited to viticulture, others only in specific sub-zones. Wines in the first group are named after the valley itself with either the specification of "Bianco" (white), "Rosso" (red), and "Rosato" (rosé) or the added name of the varietal. Wines in the second group, on the other hand, are named after the specific areas where they are produced: Donnas, Arnad-Montjovet, Chambave, Nus, Torrette, Arvier, and Morgex-La Salle. Notwithstanding the large variety of wine types, their quantities are indeed limited. In a word, little but rare and high-quality wine.

The Great Wines of Valle d'Aosta

Valle d'Aosta Petit-Rouge - Valle d'Aosta Torrette - Valle d'Aosta Enfer d'Arvier - Valle d'Aosta Chambave

The Petit Rouge, an autochthonous grape variety presumably derived from the vines imported by Roman colonizers, is grown across almost a third of Valle d'Aosta's vineyards. Cultivation yields its best results in the mid-valley, between Saint-Vincent and Avise. The premier wine from this area is Valle d'Aosta Petit-Rouge DOC, which is made from over 85% Petit Rouge grapes. Same percentage for Enfer d'Arvier; 70% for Torrette and Chambave Rosso wines. The high proportion of Petit Rouge gives these wines a ruby-red color, sometimes with mauve highlights, a dog-rose and violet nose with a touch of almond after ageing. The alcohol content (11.5-13%) is reasonably high and the wines have a medium-bodied velvety dry taste with a slightly tannic finish. They are at their best accompanying red and roasted meats or game. In fact, they go well with any meal provided the menu starts with one of the local soups containing *fontina* and includes sliced cured meats and mature cheese.

Valle d'Aosta Arnad Montjovet - Valle d'Aosta Donnas

These two geographical denomination wines have a basis of Nebbiolo, the famous Piedmontese grape variety found in the lower valley in an ecotype locally known as Picoutener. This kind of grape, which is responsible for a third of the region's wine production, is found in the minimum quantities of 85% in Donnas, which is understandably known as "Mountain Barolo", and 70% in Arnad-Montjovet (Dolcetto and Freisa, highly recommended in wine-making blends, also come from Piedmont). The greater the percentage of Picoutener, the more the wines are similar to the great reds from the Langhe: a ruby color, with garnet highlights depending on the production year and on ageing; a fine, vinous bouquet with complex aromas acquired during fining (spices, chocolate, and toasted hazelnut), an alcohol content between 12 and 13%, and a velvety dry taste with a lasting tannic flavor. It is ideal with chamois dishes, most game and mature cheese.

Valle d'Aosta Blanc de Morgex et De La Salle

This white wine is made from pure Prié Blanc grapes. The origin of this vine variety is unknown; it might have been imported in the early 17th century from Valais or Savoy, or have formed spontaneously from natural mutations. It fares well in the upper valley thanks to its late sprouting and early ripening, and it is grown up to 4000 feet opposite Mont Blanc, using very low pergolas to absorb all the warmth coming from the soil. This wine is either straw yellow or pale green with a distinctly mountain grass and recently-cut-hay nose. The flavor is very delicate and dry, with fruity notes and agreeable acidity. It is a superb accompaniment to delicate hors d'oeuvres or fish, especially trout. It comes in both the still and sparkling varieties. Vendemmia Tardiva Chaudelune is rather special: this passito wine is made from grapes left to ripen on the vine-branches until the first frost arrives – the same as for Eiswein in the Rhine Valley.

A vineyard in Valle d'Aosta with its distinctive drywalls

VALLE D'AOSTA'S DOC ZONES

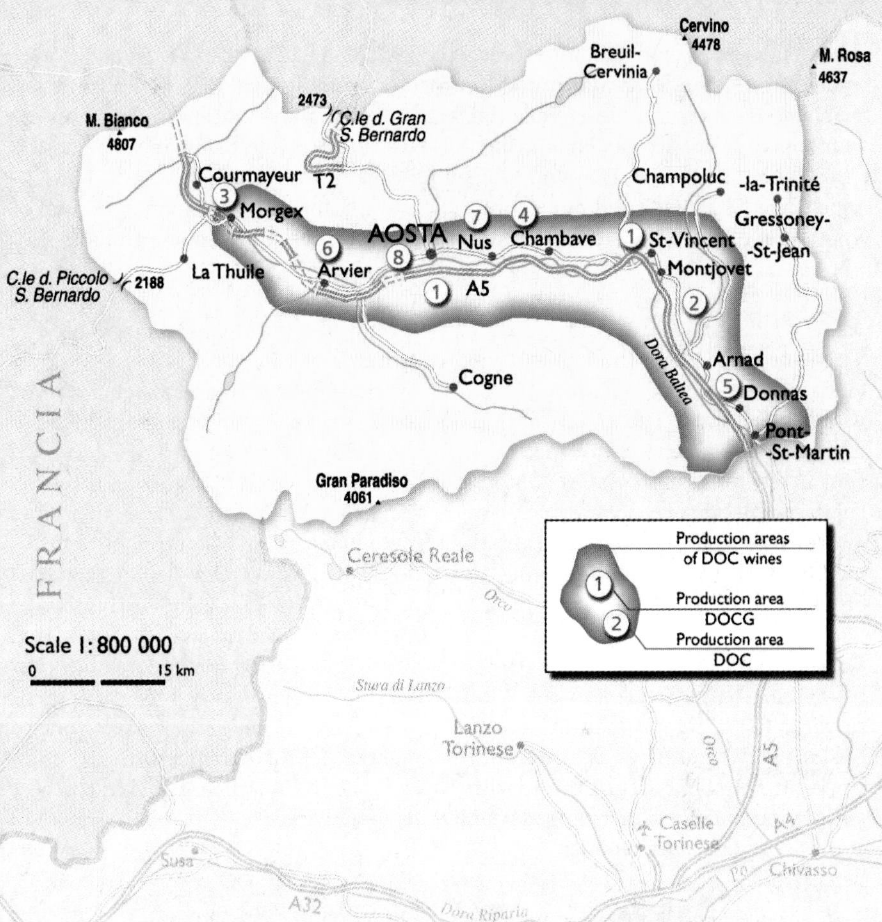

❶ **Doc Valle d'Aosta / Vallée d'Aoste**
Bianco (Blanc), Chardonnay, Müller Turgau, Peit Arvine, Pinot Grigio (Pinot Gris), Pinot Nero (Bianco/Blanc) ▪ Rosato (Rosé), Premetta ▪ Rosso (Rouge), Fumin, Gamay, Petit Rouge, Pinot Nero (Rosso/Rouge)

❷ **Doc Valle d'Aosta / Vallée d'Aoste**
Arnad-Montjovet

❸ **Doc Valle d'Aosta / Vallée d'Aoste**
Blanc de Morgex et de La Salle

❹ **Doc Valle d'Aosta / Vallée d'Aoste**
Chambave *Moscato (Muscat), Moscato Passito (Muscat Flétri) ▪ Rosso (Rouge)*

❺ **Doc Valle d'Aosta / Vallée d'Aoste**
Donnas

❻ **Doc Valle d'Aosta / Vallée d'Aoste**
Enfer d'Arvier

❼ **Doc Valle d'Aosta / Vallée d'Aoste**
Nus *Malvoise, Malvoise Passito (Flétri) ▪ Rosso (Rouge)*

❽ **Doc Valle d'Aosta / Vallée d'Aoste**
Torrette

IGT - Typical Geographic Indication
No IGTs in Valle d'Aosta

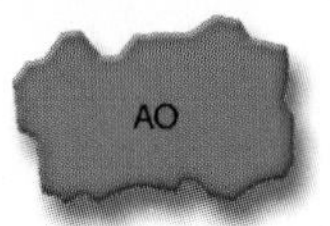

FROM DONNAS TO MORGEX

A variety of different grapes are found right along the valley: red ones like Nebbiolo, Petit-Rouge, and Vien-de-Nus and white ones like Petite Arvine and Blanc de Morgex.

The region may be divided into three wine-producing areas: the Bassa Valle (lower valley) from Pont-Saint-Martin to Montjovet, where the local Picoutener variety of Nebbiolo is grown; the Media Valle (mid-valley), from Saint-Vincent to Arvier, mainly producing Petit-Rouge, Fumin, Vien-de-Nus, and Moscato di Chambave; and the Alta Valle (upper valley), around Morgex-La Salle, with the highest vineyards in Europe (over 3300 feet asl), known for its exclusive Blanc de Morgex vines. A total of 1600 acres of vineyards are to be found here, mainly on sharply sloping ground.

THE WINE ROUTE

The wine route winds through the vineyards producing the region's 20 DOC wines. It follows the 26 and 27 national roads and then some minor roads. The tour is scattered with Caves Coopératives, members of cooperative winegrowers' associations, that also provides meeting places for promoting wines and other local products.

Bassa Valle. The first 15-mile stretch, from Pont-Saint-Martin to the Montjovet defile, is set against the stunning backdrop of the Alps: the mountain slopes are covered with terraced vineyards, vine branches are wrapped round stone columns and wooden beams, and several important castles dominate the surrounding landscape. Nebbiolo, known locally as Picoutener or Picotendro, is the main grape variety. Inseparably linked to the Piedmont region, it is used in both Donnas and Arnad-Montjovet, the area's two major wines. Most of the other vines have black grapes, like the autochthonous Neyret and Freisa-bleu. Around Arnad and Montjovet the cultivation of Vien-de-Nus and Cornallin, two local vines anticipating the upper valley production, begins. Lastly, it is worth mentioning that Donnas was the first wine to receive DOC certification in Valle d'Aosta and is still considered the best regional wine.

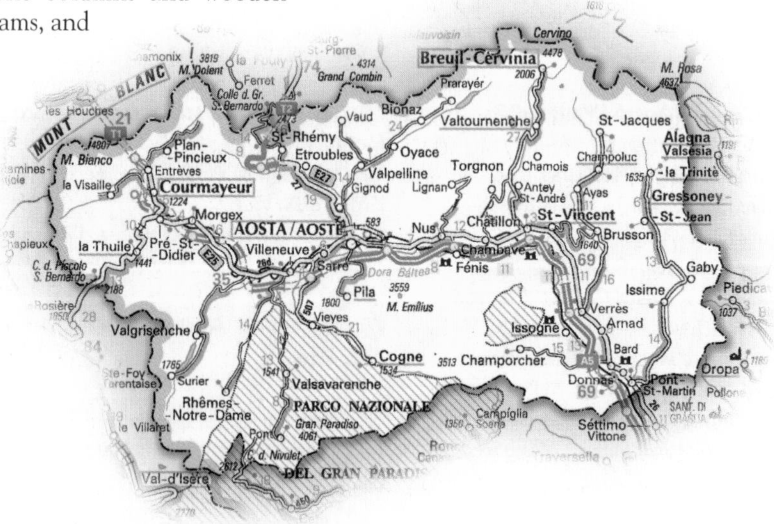

GRAPPA, GENEPY, AND RATAFIÀ

First and foremost is grappa, or more precisely marc brandy, which ranges from the most aromatic varieties such as Muscat, also available in the *flétri* (passito) version.
Grappa is most commonly used in making Valle d'Aosta-style coffee, served as part of the friendly *grolla* ritual that involves passing a characteristic wooden bowl from hand to hand and sipping from one of the many spouts.
Next are the productions of grape brandies, made directly from the fruit itself, and of the traditional Williams pear distillate.
The herb liqueurs include Genepy: in the Savoy dialect the name refers to a certain group of small herbs which mountain folk believe to be a cure against all ills. What is actually used to obtain this distinctive greenish-tinted liqueur with a pleasantly bitter taste are some types of Artemesia (mugwort), gathered at high altitudes or even grown.
The production of traditional liqueurs also includes *ratafià*, made by letting wild or sour cherries steep in marc brandy and then adding lemon peel and sugar syrup.
Spirit lovers will be keen to meet growers and producers: in some instances the distilleries are part of wine firms, such as La Crotta di Vegneron in Chambave or La Cave des Onze Communes in Aymavilles; in other cases they are specialist companies like Ottoz from Saint Christophe and La Valdôtaine from Saint-Marcel.

▪ **DONNAS.** This long-time capital of the Bassa Valle region lies along Via delle Gallie, an ancient Roman road full of remains, and is lined with beautiful period houses. Long a wine-growing town, it uses Nebbiolo, which flourishes in the sandy ground, to produce the valley's oldest and most heavily produced DOC wine. The Caves Coopératives de Donnas, set up in 1971, safeguard the production and marketing of local wines.

▪ **Arnad.** Situated on the plain of the same name in the lower section of Valle d'Aosta, this was an important place in the Middle Ages, as can be seen from its three castles. There still is an 11th-century parish church and the picturesque sanctuary of Machaby, buried away in thick chestnut woods at a height of 2300 feet. Arnad is also the headquarters of the La Kiuva farm cooperative, whose members are wine-growers and farmers from seven different municipalities.

Media Valle. Along the 28 miles of the Media Valle, vineyards are located in all kinds of different settings: from the heavily farmed and sheltered Saint-Vincent basin to the stretch of land beyond Châtillon, which is so dry and sun-baked that there is even Mediterranean vegetation; from the Aosta plain, where the valley is at its widest before rising up across vine-covered slopes, to the wide open tree-lined prairies covered with vineyards on the slopes to the north of Sarre; from the ridges of Saint-Nicolas,

A typical Valle d'Aosta arbor

exploited for tree-growing, to the spectacular terraces of Arvier, known as Enfer (Hell) due to the intense summer heat. The most common grape in this area is Petit-Rouge, a variety also grown in Envers, which represents the north-facing side. Its grapes are also used to produce Torrette wine, famous since the 17th century, and Enfer d'Arvier, one the region's leading wines. Vien-de-Nus is another important local vine grown downstream from Quart. Other red grapes from the area include the indigenous Fumin and Neyret, as well as other important varieties like Gamay, Pinot Nero, Dolcetto, and Freisa. There is an equally impressive production of white grapes, though no major local varieties. The main grapes are Pinot Bianco and Grigio, Petite Arvine (imported from Valais with some success), Müller Thurgau, Moscato Bianco, and Chardonnay.

▪ **CHAMBAVE.** Surrounded by vineyards as early as Roman times, this small town along old Via delle Gallie is the home of the famous Moscato wine. The Cave Coopérative La Crotta di Vegneron is almost entirely responsible for managing the production of local small vineyards, with an average of 200 thousand bottles a year and 13 different qualities of wine. A lovely Grape Festival is held here on the last Sunday in September.

▪ **AOSTA.** The region capital, known in ancient times as *Augusta Praetoria*, stands in a strategic position at the crossroads of routes leading down from the Piccolo San Bernardo and Gran San Bernardo passes. There are still numerous relics from Roman times, such as the Augustan Arch, the walls, and an amphitheater. The collegiate church named after Sant'Orso, dating back from before the year 1000, is the site for an arts and crafts fair which, legend has it, is almost as old as the collegiate.

The *bataille des reines* (battle of queens), fought head-to-head to decide the proudest animal, is celebrated every September when the cows come down from their mountain pastures.

The Enoteca Regionale (wine shop and bar) and the Institut Agricole Régional are two prestigious institutions, one serving promotional and the other educational purposes in the wine producing sector. The Enoteca, or Taberna ad Forum, stands in Piazza della Cattedrale, the old city centre in Roman times, and combines wonderful architecture and ar-

CROSSING THE VALAIS BORDER

Here is a nice idea for a short trip into Switzerland. From Aosta the road climbs up to Colle del Gran San Bernardo – a picturesque place brimming with history – and then drops down into Vallée d'Entremont before continuing on to Martigny, a lovely little town on the Rhone, the real hub of the Valais wine district (www.swisswine.ch, www.vinsduvalais.ch). Covering 12,800 acres of land, stretching for about 60 miles and featuring about fifty varieties of wine, this is the most important Swiss wine district: these mountainous vineyards yield almost 40% of the national wine production. This warm and sun-baked valley is highly complex in geological terms – granite, limestone, slate, bits of rock –, giving the wines some unusual characteristics. The most important wines are: Fendant (Chasselas), Johannisberg (Sylvaner), Petite Arvine, Chardonnay, Malvoise (Pinot Grigio), Amigne, Muscat, Ermitage (Marsanne Blanche), and Païen, for white wines; Pinot Noir, Gamay, Humagne Rouge, Syrah, Cornalin, and Diolinoir, for the reds. There are 700 wineries. The best known appellations are: Fendant and Dole.

The best locations or so-called 'grand crus' are: Vétroz, St-Léonard, Salquenen, Fully, and Conthey. The region curio: 'Le vin du glacier', glacier wine, produced in the Sierre area ever since ancient times and left to age in natural cavities in the upper Val d'Anniviers; repeated annual top-ups make it rather like Madera wine.

Aymavilles Castle, not far from Aosta

chaeology with an almost full range of wines; local produce can also be tasted here. The Institut Agricole Régional is a real school for mountain wine growing: this is where the up-and-coming cattle farmers and wine-growers from the valleys get their training – excellent wine is also produced here.

▪ **AYMAVILLES.** This winter sports and summer resort stands at the entrance to Valle di Cogne in the shadow of an old crenellated castle. It is the home to the Cave des Onze Communes, a cooperative of wine producers from 11 municipalities in the surrounding district. It houses a small museum about local wine-producing. Visitors to the Les Cretes winery can taste plenty of fine wines.

Alta Valle. This area is also known as Valdigne and, by convention, starts at the Pierre Taillée gorge, just before Avise, and ends by the slopes of Mont Blanc. In terms of vineyards, interest focuses solely on a section of the main valley between Morgex (3028 feet) and La Salle (3261 feet), where the slope is less steep and the valley floor widens for about 1.5 miles. Only one type of vine, Blanc de Morgex or Valdigne, the pride of the valley, actually manages to grow in the Alta Valle at heights above 3300 feet. There are less than 50 acres of vineyards shared between Morgex and La Salle. The planting area is confined to the alluvial lands around the confluence of the tributary streams into River Dora.

▪ **MORGEX.** A small village set in a charming plain surrounded by mountains. Ever since ancient times it has been the administrative hub of the valley – it is called the "heart of Valdigne". The church of the Assunta, rebuilt in the 17th century, has an original Romanesque bell tower and some 14th-15th-centuries frescoes. The village is also the headquarters of the Cave du Vin Blanc de Morgex et de La Salle, a cooperative involved in processing and marketing wines coming from over 50 acres of vineyards in the area. The cooperative huge high-tech chalet, furbished with a tasting room and restaurant, holds the unusual record of being the highest production plant in Europe. A handful of quality wine producers is spread around the district.

Wineries *pp. 344-345*
Aosta, Arnad, Aymavilles, Challand-Saint-Victor, Chambave, Donnas, Introd, Morgex, Quart, Sarre, Villeneuve.

▪ Specialties in Valle d'Aosta ▪

VALLE D'AOSTA CAN BOAST a variety of local food and wine which other regions, in relation to their sizes, cannot even dream of. First mention must go to *fontina*, a cheese made from full-cream milk produced by Valle d'Aosta's stocky little dappled cows; it has an incomparable aroma of mountain flowers, which is further enhanced by its being left to mature in caves. Traditionally it is washed down with a natural rosé like Prëmetta (Prié Rouge) or a medium-bodied red like Nus. When used in a fondue (melted *fontina* sauce served with brown toast), it is usually accompanied by a full-bodied white wine like Pinot Gris. Other seasoned cheeses include *fromadzo* and *toma*, to be eaten with a strong red like Donnas, Enfer d'Arvier Arnad-Montjovet, or Torrette. 
The most well-known preserved meats are *Jambon de Bosses*, ham cured in a *malga* (mountain cabin), Arnad lard, with a rich array of aromas, which is best eaten with black bread and a drop of honey, and *mocetta*, a processed goat's or chamois's leg, the most traditional of the various preserved meats. Pinot Noir, Gamay, and Nus are the ideal wines to accompany these specialties.

THE DISH THAT epitomizes old-times local cuisine is soup, combining all the different mountain tastes and flavors: rye bread, cheese, meat, potatoes, cabbage and other home-grown vegetables. It should be eaten with a well-bodied and medium-aged red wine produced from Petit Rouge or Vien de Nus grapes. Other starters include barley soup, polenta seasoned with butter and cheese, and gnocchi with *fontina*. Next come the meat dishes, combined with cheese in the famous *cotoletta alla valdostana* (or Val d'Aosta chop, which is best accompanied by Gamay wine); otherwise, meat can be marinated, if not actually cooked, in red wine with a dash of juniper berries or some another mountain flavor – this is the case of *carbonade*, "sweetened" with onion (Chambave), or of game, with tasty roe buck and chamois top of the list (Donnas).

WHITE WINES are generally served with hors d'oeuvres, trout-based dishes (Blanc de Morgex et de La Salle, Chardonnay) or white meats (Müller Thurgau, Nus Malvoise, Petite Arvine).
Towards the end of the meal, apples and chestnuts are a key parts of the delicious sweets, mainly cakes and other desserts. This is the time to serve wines like Chambave Muscat Flétri or Nus Malvoise Flétri. Be sure to taste the little Martin Sec pears cooked in red wine. To complete the meal, *caffè alla valdostana*: Val d'Aosta-style coffee with added grappa.

PIEDMONT

REGION OF GREAT REDS

The Langhe and the Monferrato hills are the two aces in the hand of a region which has combined the defense of its tradition and the renewal of its winemaking technology and know-how. Exceptional opportunities for the wine-loving visitor.

With 43 DOC and 7 DOCG wines, Piedmont is one of the most prestigious wine-producing regions of Italy and, according to many, the best in terms of quality. This is a territory where wine is synonymous with culture, with commitment to hard work, and with a centuries-old artisan tradition. And where, at the beginning of the third millennium, there is the ambition to build, with its wines as the foundation, new opportunities for economic development and preservation of the environment.

Above, Barolo vineyards; left, view of La Morra (top) and Carema's pergola vineyard (bottom)

VINEYARDS WHICH EXTEND FROM THE PREALPS TO THE APENNINES

The fundamental basis of the success of Piedmont's viticulture is the particularly favorable environment offered to the vine, that is the hills which cover a third of the region's territory. Production can be divided, a bit schematically, into two major areas. The most important can be found in the southeast and extends from the Monferrato hills, on the right side of the River Po, to the Langhe, bisected by the Tanaro, and includes the provinces of Asti and Alessandria as well as part of the province of Cuneo. The second is in the foothills of the Alps, from Cuneo across the provinces of Turin, Biella, Vercelli, and Novara up to Verbania. These areas differ in terms of their geological origins and, consequently, in the character of their soil. The Monferrato and Langhe hills were generated by the gradual rising of the bottom of the ancient sea which occupied the Po valley and are characterized by sedimentary deposits which are an actively present factor for viticulture. The Prealps foothills, like the peaks which surround them, are rocky, or, in certain cases, where valleys open out, of morainic origin, and are suited to vine-growing only in certain select spots.

THE TERRITORY OF BAROLO AND BARBARESCO

Soil and climate combine in the Langhe and the Monferrato hills to create wines of an exceptional level: red wines such as Barolo, Barbaresco, and Nebbiolo d'Alba and white wines, with Asti Spumante as a leading example. An analysis of the cultivation of the grape, dividing it into three distinct zones, can only underline the extreme versatility of this part of Piedmont. The warmest part extends from the plain of the Tanaro to an altitude of 1000-1300 feet and is most suitable for the cultivation of varieties with a long ripening cycle and much need of heat: Barbera, Nebbiolo, and, to a lesser extent, Grignolino. This is the area of long-ageing wines. At altitudes of 1000-1300 feet, with larger temperature swings from day to night and lesser humidity, fruity and aromatic red and white varieties are planted; this is the area of cultivation for Moscato d'Asti, Dolcetto, Brachetto, Cortese, and Favorita. Moscato, Brachetto, and Dolcetto vines resist in the very highest zones (1500-2000 feet), where there are large temperature differences from day to night during the spring and late summer.

THE HILLS OF GHEMME AND GATTINARA

Sub-alpine viticulture, in contrast, takes place in a very extensive area of hillsides characterized by warm temperatures, great luminosity, and ample temperature swings

from day to night. It is a more selective environment, to be sure, where truly favorable zones for viticulture are rarer but where results, in compensation, are excellent. We are dealing with zones such as Caluso, Carema, Gattinara, and Ghemme which – and it is no accident – have given their name to important, and in some cases superlative, wines.
It is interesting to note how this contrast – excellent results on a geographically limited scale – is reflected in patterns of entrepreneurship in a context where the average vineyard property is a mere 4 acres in size. There is a more specialized approach in the southern part of this area, with wine-producing firms of a certain importance, while, in areas more to the north and closer to the mountains, family farms where viticulture is a more marginal and part-time activity tend to dominate.

Nebbiolo and Its Entourage

The viticulture of Piedmont is essentially based on local grapes, cultivated for centuries and by now perfectly adapted to the specific conditions of the region: new varieties have been introduced only more recently to enlarge the gamut for markets looking for important wines but also more affordable ones. Seventy per cent of the vineyards are planted to red grapes, thirty per cent to white. Nebbiolo, its existence already documented in the Middle Ages, is, by definition, the great grape of Piedmont and it gives birth to such famous Piedmontese wines as Barolo, Barbaresco, Gattinara, and Ghemme, all DOCG. The most widely planted variety is Barbera, which accounts for 50% of the total regional acreage. Next in importance among the reds are Dolcetto, Freisa, Grignolino, Bonarda, Brachetto, and Malvasia, all wines with an enthusiastic public. Moscato predominates among white grapes, with an unchallenged position thanks to the 80 million bottles of Asti produced annually. Other traditional white varieties are Cortese, Erbaluce, and Arneis, while Pinot Bianco, Pinot Grigio, Riesling Italico and Riesling Renano, Chardonnay, Sylvaner, and Müller Thurgau are of more recent date.

Classic Piedmont landscape of hills and vines

A REGION OF APPELLATION WINES

Piedmont distinguishes itself for its constant search for quality, and this is felt both at the regulating and the practical level. An ample number of DOC wines, often with a very limited production, has been supplemented by appellations with a large sweep in terms of the territory they cover; these have eliminated a myriad of table wines and IGTs. These four wide-ranging appellations are Piemonte, Langhe, Monferrato, and Colline Novaresi and they regulate, and insure the quality of, 75% of the red wines and 90% of the white wines produced in the region. This commitment to formal controls over wine production is matched by an equally strong one for steady quality improvement based on low yields per acre and major investments in new winemaking technology and marketing campaigns. Two significant examples confirm this commitment. The first is the growth of the total area under vines despite an EEC policy of incentives for uprooting vineyards to prevent overproduction. New plantings have enlarged total acreage, above all in the most prestigious zones of all, the ones which give the greatest renown to the region's $700 million annual production. The second example concerns Barbera, historically a fundamental part of Piedmont's production, which now has more than compensated for certain production excesses of recent times. The individual producers have rolled up their sleeves both in the vineyard and in the cellar, introducing new techniques such as barrique ageing and creating a wine more in line with contemporary international taste.

ENOTECHE AND BOTTEGHE DEL VINO

Piedmont has given a key place to the vine and to wine in a strategy of greater visibility to and awareness of its territory. Part of this strategy is the system of public Enoteche and Botteghe del Vino, which has no equals in other parts of Italy. The difference between the two types of sales and exhibition points are in their size and overall aims: the public Enoteche, often housed in historic buildings, promote the wines of an entire zone; the Botteghe del Vino, the direct expression of a producers' consortium, have a more specialized approach and reflect the production of a single municipality. Both express Piedmont's keen awareness of the role of wine, which also takes the concrete form of membership in the Associazione delle Città del Vino (Association of the Cities of Wine) – 64 of the region's municipalities are members of the Association – and in the Movimento del Turismo del Vino (Movement for Wine Tourism) – with 120 cellars open to the public.

A EUROPEAN FUTURE

Piedmont's prompt adherence, in a proposed regional law, to the EEC programs creating Wine Roads and Wine Districts, and its interest in ecologically sound viticulture, now practiced in 65,000 of the region's 150,000 acres of vineyards, are both signs of real dynamism. Another important project is that of the Enoteca Regionale del Piemonte which, it is hoped, will be housed in a prestigious site in Turin, one capable of receiving a large and constant stream of visitors. As for private commitment, suffice it to cite the Tenimenti di Barolo and Fontanafredda's initiative: the two historic wineries have issued the so-called Buoni Ordinari del Barolo (BOB – Barolo Bonds), so that it is possible to invest on wine bottles as on any other stock exchange good – the newest financial approach for a centuries-old product.

The Great Wines of Piedmont

Barolo DOCG
"The king of wines and wine of kings", the old slogan goes. The most famous wine from Nebbiolo grapes (see Nebbiolo DOC further on) is a blend of the sub-varieties Michet, Lampia, and Rosé. The wine is garnet red with orangey highlights, intense characteristic aroma with hints of fruits and spices, austere but velvety taste, and great texture. Regulations envision alcohol content of a minimum 13% and three years of obligatory ageing, which rise to five for the Riserva. The Barolo Chinato denomination is for the wine aromatized to follow the old Italian tradition of tonic beverages.
The production zone, in the Langhe, covers the entire territories of the municipalities of Barolo, Castiglione Falletto, Serralunga d'Alba, and part of Monforte d'Alba, Novello, La Morra, Verduno, Grinzane Cavour, Diano d'Alba, Cherasco, and Roddi. About 3100 acres are registered for the DOCG, producing an average of 7.5 million bottles a year. The accompaniments to this most famous representative of Piedmont oenology are at the summit of taste intensity: *bagna cauda* (crudités served with a mainly garlic dip) and similar hors-d'oeuvres; *agnolotti* and all pasta courses seasoned or filled with braised meat; important dishes of stewed meats, especially in wine sauces, such as *brasato al Barolo* or *lepre in civet*; aged Langhe cheeses, such as Murazzano or Toma.

The countryside around Asti

Barbaresco DOCG
A wine of ancient glory, Barbaresco was so famous that the eponymous village was symbolized in Alba's Cathedral as a chalice dripping with grapes. The wine is made from Nebbiolo grapes in the sub-varieties Michet, Lampia, and Rosé. It is garnet in color, with intense and characteristic aroma, dry, full and complex taste. Minimum alcohol: 12.5%. Obligatory ageing is for two years, four for the Riserva. The production zone covers the entire territory of the municipalities of Barbaresco, Neive, Treiso, and the San Rocco Seno d'Elvio part of the Alba municipality, in the province of Cuneo. About 1250 acres are registered for the DOCG, producing just less than 3 million bottles a year.

Gattinara DOCG
Gattinara is a famous old red, born in the homonymous municipality in the province of Vercelli and made from Nebbiolo (Spanna) grapes with possible small additions of Vespolina and Bonarda di Gattinara. The wine is garnet red tending to orangey, with a violet reminiscent aroma when lengthily aged, and a dry, harmonious and typically bitterish taste. Minimum alcohol: 12%. Regulations dictate three years of obligatory ageing and at least four for the Riserva (the latter's minimum alcohol content must be 13%). Production is rather limited since only 250 acres are planted with pertinent vines.

Ghemme DOCG
Similar to Gattinara for lengthy history and limited production (only 125 acres of vineyards), this wine is produced in the homonymous municipality and neighboring Romagnano Sesia, in the province of Novara, from Nebbiolo (Spanna) grapes (minimum 75%) with additions of Uva Rara and Vespolina. It is ruby red with garnet highlights, fine and characteristic aroma, full, dry and slightly bitterish taste and alcohol content of 12%.

PIEDMONT'S DOC ZONES

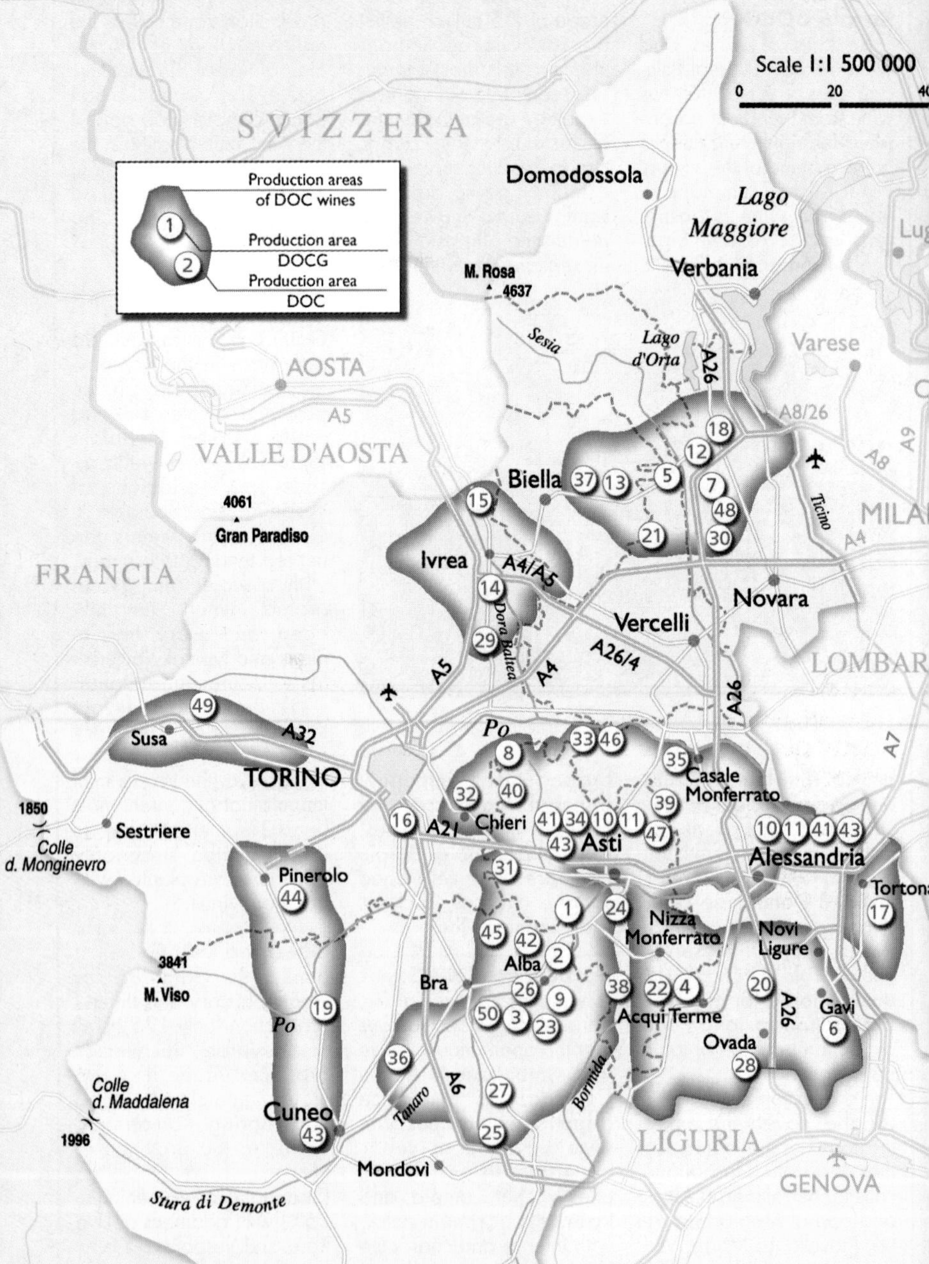

1 **DOCG Asti** *Moscato and Spumante*
2 **DOCG Barbaresco**
3 **DOCG Barolo** *Chinato*
4 **DOCG Brachetto d'Acqui or Acqui**
5 **DOCG Gattinara**
6 **DOCG Gavi or Cortese di Gavi**
7 **DOCG Ghemme**

8 **DOC Albugnano**
9 **DOC Barbera d'Alba**
10 **DOC Barbera d'Asti**
11 **DOC Barbera del Monferrato**
12 **DOC Boca**
13 **DOC Bramaterra**
14 **DOC Canavese** *Bianco ▪ Rosato ▪ Rosso, Barbera, Nebbiolo*
15 **DOC Carema**
16 **DOC Collina Torinese** *Rosso, Barbera, Bonarda ▪ Malvasia, Pelaverga or Cari*
17 **DOC Colline Novaresi** *Bianco ▪ Rosso, Barbera, Croatina, Nebbiolo or Spanna, Uva Rara or Bonarda, Vespolina*
18 **DOC Colline Saluzzesi** *Rosso or Rosato, Pelaverga, Quagliano*
19 **DOC Colli Tortonesi** *Bianco, Cortese ▪ Chiaretto ▪ Rosso, Barbera, Dolcetto*
20 **DOC Cortese dell'Alto Monferrato**
21 **DOC Coste della Sesia** *Bianco ▪ Rosato ▪ Rosso, Bonarda or Uva Rara, Croatina, Nebbiolo or Spanna, Vespolina*
22 **DOC Dolcetto d'Acqui**
23 **DOC Dolcetto d'Alba**
24 **DOC Dolcetto d'Asti**
25 **DOC Dolcetto delle Langhe Monregalesi**
26 **DOC Dolcetto di Diano d'Alba or Diano d'Alba**
27 **DOC Dolcetto di Dogliani**
28 **DOC Dolcetto di Ovada**
29 **DOC Erbaluce di Caluso**
30 **DOC Fara**
31 **DOC Freisa d'Asti** *Secco and Amabile*
32 **DOC Freisa di Chieri** *Secco and Amabile*
33 **DOC Gabiano**
34 **DOC Grignolino d'Asti**
35 **DOC Grignolino del Monferrato Casalese**
36 **DOC Langhe** *Bianco, Arneis, Chardonnay, Favorita ▪ Rosso, Dolcetto, Freisa, Nebbiolo*
37 **DOC Lessona**
38 **DOC Loazzolo**
39 **DOC Malvasia di Casorzo d'Asti**
40 **DOC Malvasia di Castelnuovo Don Bosco**
41 **DOC Monferrato** *Bianco, Casalese Cortese ▪ Chiaretto ▪ Rosso, Dolcetto, Freisa*
42 **DOC Nebbiolo d'Alba**
43 **DOC Piemonte** *Chardonnay, Cortese, Moscato, Moscato Passito, Spumante, Pinot Bianco Spumante, Pinot Grigio Spumante, Pinot Nero Spumante ▪ Barbera, Bonarda, Brachetto, Grignolino*
44 **DOC Pinerolese** *Rosso, Barbera, Bonarda, Dolcetto, Doux d'Henry, Freisa, Ramie*
45 **DOC Roero Arneis**
46 **DOC Rubino di Cantavenna**
47 **DOC Ruché di Castagnole Monferrato**
48 **DOC Sizzano**
49 **DOC Valsusa**
50 **DOC Verduno** *Pelaverga or Verduno*

IGT - Typical Geographic Indication:
No IGTs in Piedmont

Grape harvesting

Obligatory ageing is for three years, four for the wines that, reaching an alcohol content of 13%, are intended to vaunt the Riserva label. It goes with the same foods as Gattinara: pasta dishes with robust seasonings or fillings; red meat and game dishes and *tapulon*, the local mule stew; aged cheeses, starting with Toma Piemontese DOP.

Brachetto d'Acqui DOCG

At the present time, Brachetto (whose ancestor was a *Vinum Aquense* praised as early as Roman times) is grown in 18 municipalities in the Asti and 8 in the Alessandria provinces, including Acqui Terme. In all, there are about 1350 acres producing 2.5 million bottles per annum. In addition to dictating exclusive use of Brachetto grapes, DOCG codes list the qualities of the resultant wine: ruby red tending to garnet or roseate; subtle and musky characteristic aroma; sweet, delicate taste; fine and persistent perlage in the spumante version. It goes well with baked desserts and especially with red-fruit tarts and sweets based on strawberries or peaches.

Nebbiolo DOC

The name is that of a vine documented since the 14th century and probably originating in the Langhe, specifically in the environs of Alba. The term may derive from the pruinose grape skin, which look as though mist ("nebbia") had condensed on it. The wine, obtained by pure vinification, has many good qualities: fine amounts of alcohol and good acidity, which predispose it to ageing; aroma and fine taste which evolve in very interesting ways. Nebbiolo grapes are the base of many celebrated Piedmont reds – Barolo, Barbaresco, Gattinara, and Ghemme, to cite only the DOCGs – but are also used in specific productions (Nebbiolo del Piemonte DOC, Nebbiolo del Monferrato DOC, Nebbiolo delle Langhe DOC, Nebbiolo d'Alba DOC). In the Novara area it goes by the name of Spanna.

Barbera DOC

The most popular Piedmont wine comes from a grape that probably originated in the Monferrato area, getting its name from the striking grape acidity which is similar to that of the berries of a hedge shrub, *Berberis vulgaris*. Vinified pure, Barbera is ruby red, vinous in aroma and dry in taste, severe but at the same time fine if acidity (which aids in ageing) is well controlled. A mass-consumption wine, it has risen in esteem after a reduction in yield highlighted its finer qualities. It is also appreciated in the easy-to-drink semi-sweet and fizzy versions.

Dolcetto DOC

It is made from a grape autochthonous to Monferrato, which takes its name from the sweetness of its pulp. The wine, more or less deep ruby red, with pleasant aroma, is dry in taste or only slightly semi-sweet, with characteristic notes of licorice and bitter almond. Depending on the zone and on how the wine is made, it can be austere and important or fresh and easy to drink. Its reduced acidity advises drinking it within the year or after limited ageing. It is very common both in Monferrato and in the Langhe; particularly renowned productions are Acqui's, Dogliani's, and Ovada's.

Grignolino DOC

The land of origin of this wine and of the grapes it is made from are the Monferrato hills between Asti and Casale. The name appears to derive from the many seeds, in dialect *grignolé*, contained in the grapes. Vinified pure, it is a pale ruby wine with orangey highlights, it has a floral aroma with notes of spices (specifically pepper), dry and very tannic taste. On the whole a well-endowed wine but hard to balance, making it best when blended with Barbera and Freisa, which add harmony. There are two specific DOCs: Grignolino d'Asti and Grignolino del Monferrato Casalese.

Moscato d'Asti DOCG and Asti Spumante DOCG

Between the Alto Monferrato and the Langhe lies the great vineyard of Moscato Bianco, a variety unmistakable for its so-called "musky" aroma, also described as an overlaying of fruity notes (apricot, peach) with floral ones (wisteria, linden, acacia, black-berried elder, orange) and essences (sage, bergamot). A very common variety in the Mediterranean area, it has found a favorable habitat in the Piedmont hills. It is used to make sweet, intensely aromatic wines, still (Asti DOCG) or more often fizzy, spumante (Asti Spumante DOCG) and even passito (Loazzolo DOC) ones. The DOCG wines are produced in 52 municipalities in the provinces of Asti, Alessandria, and Cuneo, for a total of over 22,000 acres of vineyards registered in the DOCG lists, 80 million bottles produced a year and 7000 producers.

The Moscato d'Asti denomination indicates the still or sometimes fizzy wine with the following characteristics: more or less deep straw-yellow color; fragrant, characteristic aroma; sweet, aromatic, varietal taste. It goes well with rich desserts flavored with dried or candied fruit, beginning with *panettone*, but also with white-fruit tarts and lemon cakes.

The Asti or Asti Spumante denomination is instead for the wine obtained through natural fermentation in the bottle or in autoclave, featuring fine and persistent perlage and brilliant clarity. It goes well with baked desserts in general, especially the lighter ones such as *pandoro*, and is also excellent in cocktails.

Gavi DOCG

Documented in Piedmont since the 18th century, it may have originated in the southeastern part of the region, between Alessandria, Tortona, and Novara, where it is still very common. Vinified alone, it gives a straw-yellow wine tending to greenish, with delicate aroma and dry, fresh, light taste with a distinctive note of bitter almond. The most renowned production is Gavi or Cortese di Gavi DOCG. The zone covers Gavi and 9 neighboring municipalities in the southern part of the Alessandria province, nearly bordering on Liguria. This white wine is made from pure Cortese grapes, which are locally called Courteis. About 2500 acres are registered DOCG, producing an average of 7.5 million bottles a year. The wine, which comes in the Tranquillo, Frizzante, or Spumante versions, is more or less intense straw yellow in color, it has delicate and characteristic aroma, dry and harmonious taste, fresh in the still version and full in the spumante one. Minimum alcohol: 10.5%. All types go well with hors-d'oeuvres, especially of seafood, and light first courses such as delicate risottos, or fresh cheeses like local *robiola*.

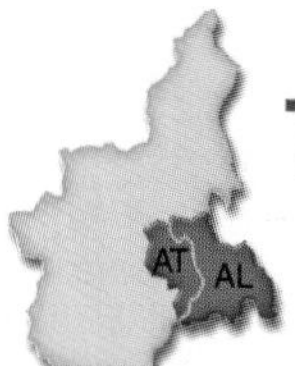

THE MONFERRATO REGION

The name of this picturesque stretch of hills is traditionally linked with three fine Piedmont wines: Barbera, Grignolino, and Moscato d'Asti.

Monferrato is a vast hilly region stretching across the southeastern part of Piedmont in the arc formed by the River Po, where it runs between Chivasso and Casale Monferrato, and, roughly speaking, the border between the Asti and Cuneo provinces. Another internal border splits this land in two, as if to acknowledge certain differences in character and environment that are also reflected in wine production: Basso (Lower) Monferrato is more open and friendly, while Alto (Upper) Monferrato is more austere. To make it simple, the border line between the two areas corresponds to the imaginary line passing through Chieri, Asti, and Alessandria, which initially follows the path of the Padana Inferiore road and then, more precisely, the lower course of the Tanaro river. The Asti hills, a world apart in terms of wine making and production, are wedged between the two areas.

Basso Monferrato

Contrary to what one might expect, Basso Monferrato is the northern part of this huge wine district, where the tallest hills lie and peaks are as high as 2300 feet. The average height, however, is around 1150 feet, making it ideal for vine growing. This area lies between the towns of Casale Monferrato and Asti, and its main wines are Barbera and Grignolino, whose cheerful character makes them stand out in the rather austere company of Piedmont reds. These are the two most outstanding wines from a land that is proud of its traditions but certainly not conservative, as recently demonstrated by its willingness to comply with new market trends. This is a reference to barrique wines produced to cater for "younger" and more international tastes; but it applies also to some fine though "lesser" wines, such as Malvasia di Casorzo and Ruché di Castagnole.

History and Wine

The following places lie in a zigzag line across the hills and vineyards of Monferrato – among Barbera and Grignolino d'Asti grapes, you might even say – from Casale to the outskirts of Asti, taking a detour to the west towards the Turin hills and the lands of Freisa. The countryside offers a wide range of tempting food and wine and is also very interesting from a historical point of view.

■ **Casale Monferrato.** Lying along the right bank of the River Po on the Castle side, the old town center is a treasure trove of historical memories, mainly from the 18th century, the Middle Ages and the Renaissance. For a long time Casale was actually the capital of Monferrato and one of the best equipped and most fought over strongholds in Europe until its fortifications were dismantled in the late 17th century. The Cathedral, Town Hall Tower, Municipal Museums (paintings and plaster casts, arranged in what used to be the convent of Santa Croce), and the Synagogue are the main tourist attractions.

■ **Serralunga di Crea.** The sanctuary of Crea stands on a rise not far from this little town built around a majestic me-

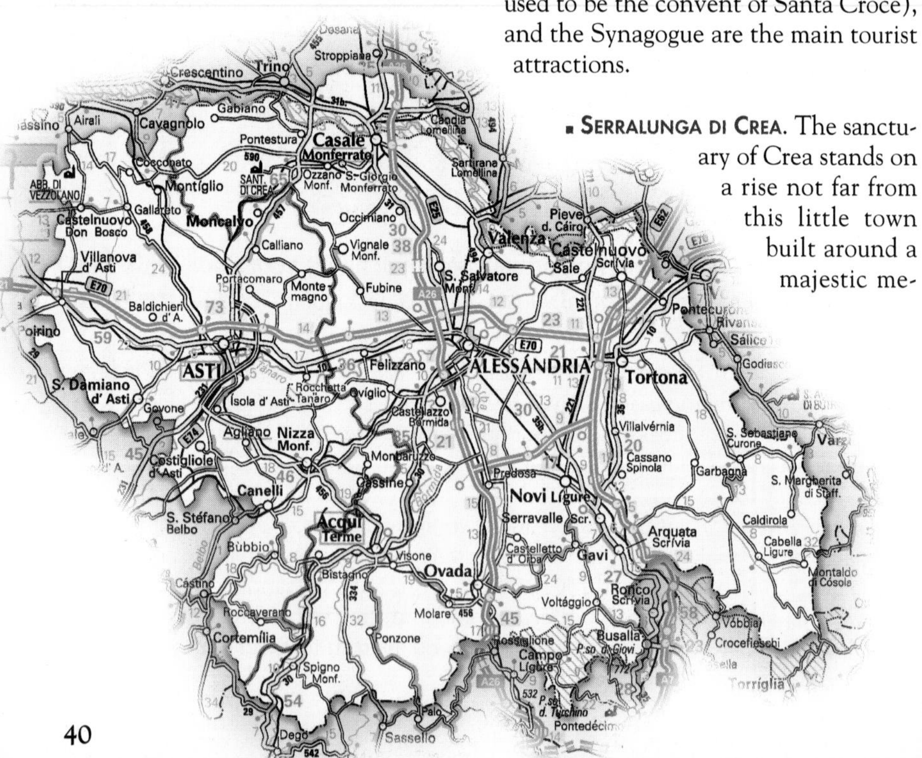

The vineyards around Galliano, in the Asti province

dieval castle (and a fine winery). The monumental religious complex was first built in the 12th century and then modernized several times in different styles; it has 23 chapels scattered in the woods.

▪ **Moncalvo.** Overlooking Monferrato and the lowland plains from a hill, this is the "smallest town in Italy". This title was awarded in 1705 and is corroborated by a wealth of buildings and churches that testify to Moncalvo's former importance, also in military and strategic terms. The church of S. Francesco (13th-14th C) stands in the old ramparts. The main wines here are Grignolino, Barbera del Monferrato, Barbera d'Asti, and Freisa. Truffles are also on the menu.

▪ **Vignale Monferrato.** This farming town is also on a hill and features the Enoteca Regionale del Monferrato, housed in the striking Palazzo Callori, with its wine cellars, known as "infernotti", excavated in the tufa rock. There is also an adjoining restaurant. In addition to other wineries, the town is also renowned for its Town Hall Tower, the church of the Addolorata (a Gothic-Lombard building dating from 1496-1505), and the 18th-century parish church of S. Bartolomeo.

The Secret of Vermouth

There is no question that Piedmont's most famous product is Vermouth, the aperitif. Modern-day production of this drink, a descendant of aromatized wines from olden times, is generally acknowledged to have been started by Antonio Benedetto Carpano, who in 1786 had his own shop in the heart of Turin, beneath the porticos of Piazza Castello. The name comes from the German word Wermuth or absinth, a reference to the aromatic herb that plays a key part in fortifying its alcoholic base, consisting mainly in Moscato wine, to which it adds a distinctive slightly bitter taste. The Cora brothers were the first to try exporting it to America in 1838. In the wake of their success, all the main wine producers started making it: Gancia, Martini, and Cinzano, to mention merely the best known, each with its own secret recipe for the special blend of herbs and spices, ranging from yarrow and ginger to coriander, gentian, and rhubarb. The regulations currently in force set certain standards: an alcohol content of at least 17.5% and varieties ranging from Bianco Secco or Dry, Bianco Dolce, and Rosso.

A wine-production center in Costigliole d'Asti

■ **PORTACOMARO.** As an indication of its undisputed supremacy with Grignolino, the town's historical old tower – remains of the medieval *ricetto* (fortress) – houses the Bottega del Grignolino, where you can taste and purchase wine or simply enjoy a meal at the neighboring inn. Other local DOC wines include Barbera d'Asti and Barbera Monferrato, Ruché di Castagnole and Freisa d'Asti.

■ **CHIERI.** The home of Freisa wine, one of the oldest and most famous reds from Piedmont, also available in a sparkling version, stands in the western part of Monferrato, bordering on the lush Turin hills. The old town center has a distinctive architectural imprint, with some quite remarkable religious and civil buildings. The Cathedral and churches of S. Domenico and S. Giorgio feature beautiful Gothic forms. The Martini e Rossi winery is based in the hamlet of Pessione; in the adjoining Museum of Wine Making History are outstanding exhibits such as the wagons once used for transporting the grapes after they had been picked, featuring some marvelous wine-related carvings. Other DOC wines from the area are Malvasia di Castelnuovo Don Bosco (an aromatic red wine), Albugnano (made from Nebbiolo grapes), Gabiano, and Rubino di Cantavenna (made from Barbera grapes).

■ **MONCUCCO TORINESE.** Winding scenic roads lead to Moncucco, whose 15th-century castle now houses the Town Hall. The wine cellars of an 18th-century building are the home of a Bottega del Vino (wine shop) with an excellent trattoria; diners can enjoy the wines of Castelnovese – Freisa d'Asti, Malvasia di Castelnuovo, and Albugnano – as well as food specialties from the Chieri area. Out in the vineyards, just a few miles away, you can visit the Vezzolano Abbey, one of the most important examples of late Romanesque Piedmont art.

The Asti Hills

A wine growing and production area of exceptional interest lies to the south of the province's main center, encompassing the towns of Canelli and Nizza Monferrato. The natural setting is full of vines, most notably vineyards of Moscato and Barbera d'Asti, but it is also outstanding for its wide range of alternating weaves and colors thanks to the different crops grown in the humid valley bottoms and to the surviving woodlands on the northern slopes. The area's most distinc-

tive feature, however, is its spumante, invented a century ago and still produced here more than anywhere else; this is the scene of a unique wine-making process. Smaller productions include Loazzolo DOC, a sweet wine made from pure vinification of Moscato grapes.

THE BARBERA AND SPUMANTE ROUTE

This route, lined with wineries and cellars, stretches between the Tanaro and Belbo rivers from Asti, one of Italy's wine capitals on the border between the two Monferrato zones, to the expanse of Moscato vines bordering the Langhe. This is a veritable paradise for wine-lovers.

■ **ASTI.** It would take more than a few lines to describe Asti, a city of art with a truly human dimension. To really appreciate its magic, just wander through the old town center, with its red brick and yellow tufa houses and truncated medieval towers that stand among austere baroque façades. Outstanding monuments include the medieval Rotonda di S. Pietro, the Cathedral and the church of S. Secondo, both Romanesque-Gothic in style. Discovering that this is the spumante and Barbera capital is a fundamental part of the visit. The key event on the wine calendar is the Duja d'or, which takes place in the first two weeks of September, a festival of ancient origins that is named after a terracotta jug used for pouring wine and is now associated with a national competition for DOC wines. The Festival delle Sagre takes place on the second Sunday of the same month, when 40 municipalities in the Monferrato and Langhe areas show off the best of their food and wine.

■ **COSTIGLIOLE D'ASTI.** A lovely town built on a rise, where the municipal winery is inside the imposing Gothic town castle; wine tasting and events such as the auction of Barbera wines from historical vineyards (end of May) are held here.

■ **CASTAGNOLE DELLE LANZE.** The chestnut trees mentioned in the place name have now given way to quality vineyards up in the hills of the Tinella valley. This little town, with its old center at the top, is renowned for its Bottega del Vino (Barbera d'Asti, Moscato, Dolcetto d'Alba, Grignolino, Cortese, and Chardonnay), a lovely little shop beneath the old colonnade, and for its tiny Folk Museum.

■ **NIZZA MONFERRATO.** This charming town, which holds a sub-zone of Barbera d'Asti, hosts numerous events along its narrow porticoed streets, where the magnificent medieval Town Hall Tower catches the eye. Wines, cattle, and qual-

A beautiful farmstead between Rosignano Monferrato and Terruggia

TURIN, A CITY OF GREAT GASTRONOMY

The Lingotto fair complex in Turin (www.lingottofiere.it) has been the home of the Salone del Gusto (food and drink fair) since 1996. This biennial event held around the end of October turns the city into one of the European capitals of food and drink, offering everything from traditional regional dishes and drinks to the widest range of ethnic products.

In mid-November, there is the more specifically wine-oriented Salone del Vino (wine fair) devoted to producers and other experts in the sector. Apart from this extremely popular event, Turin provides a unique setting for fine Piedmont cuisine with its Savoy buildings, porticos and memorable bars and restaurants, which still have the same charm as a hundred years ago. The shop windows filled with delicacies are a mesmerizing sight: traditional chocolates – Gianduiotti, Cremini, Alpini and, Grappini – , all kinds of delicate pastries and rum-flavored chocolate pralines, not to mention candies and sweets, marrons glacés and candied violets, zabaglione and *bicerin* – a delicious mixture of coffee and cocoa.

All the famous old cafés are a magical blend of charm and elegance. A good place to set off on a 19th-century tour through velvet upholstery and mirrors might be Piazza Castello, opposite the Regio theatre. Walking beneath the porticoes, you come to the Mulassano café (1907) and the Baratti & Milano (1875) pastry shop; the Fiorio café-ice cream parlor (1780) is in nearby Via Po and slightly farther on is the pastry shop-confectioner's Abrate (1866); in Piazza S. Carlo is the pastry shop-confectioner's Stratta (1836) and the Torino restaurant-café (1903); the Del Cambio restaurant-café (1757) is in Piazza Carignano, the Al Bicerin café-confectioner's (1763) is in Piazza della Consolata and the Platti café (1875) is in Corso Vittorio Emanuele.

ity fabrics – together with its favorable location in Valle del Belbo on the Turchino road – made it a popular market place with people from Piedmont, Liguria, and Lombardy back in the 16th century. Products from the hills form the basis of a truly exceptional selection of food and wine – still its strong point. A Bottega del Vino, also known as the Vineria della Signora in Rosso, does the local honors: situated in the 18th-century Palazzo Crova's cellars, in the town center, it lays on wine-tasting and themed food evenings. The Folk Museum has an unusual collection of wine-related prints and objects dating from the 17th century to the present day and stands next to the Bersano & Riccadonna - Antiche Cantine Conti della Cremosina winery. The outdoor section, displaying presses, wine carts and all kinds of equipment, has been extended with a Museum of Prints, featuring everything from valuable ampelography to the most unusual labels. The Confraternita della Bagna Caôda, which in autumn awards the Paisan Vignaiolo prize to leading exponents of Italian culture, is also based in the museum.

The local gastronomy pride is the *bovino della coscia* (local cattle breed), the main attraction at the Fiera del Bue Grasso, a festival which takes place in early November, closely followed by a special day devoted to truffles, bent cardoons, and Barbera.

▪ **MOMBARUZZO**. The medieval Clock Tower and the beautiful Gothic church of S. Antonio Abate evoke times gone by, when the village already had its own laws governing wines and trade. The wine cooperative established in 1887 was a forerunner and is still in business (producing Barbera d'Asti and Moscato). The summer is a time of festivals, and at the height of the season, in August, you can dine out under the stars, enjoying the wines and famous *amaretti* (almond cakes).

▪ **CANELLI**. The Belbo valley, where vines flourish, is the crowning glory of the capital of spumante. The Gancia Castle, which looms over this old town center, provides it with a worthy home. All around you can see signs of well-known producers; their miles-long wine cellars, excavated in the tufa hillside, produce almost 80 million bottles a year. On every street corner there is a chance to taste the most famous Italian wine in the world and other excellent products from the same soil, such as Cortese, Barbera, Dolcetto, and Freisa. The Enoteca Regionale di Canelli e delle Terre d'Oro promotes them all with great competence and equity. It also offers the opportunity to taste wines and other local products. Tours into the Asti hills and visits to the main wine producers are also organized; a wine bar is open on Friday, Saturday, and Sunday evenings, offering live music.

▪ **CALAMANDRANA**. This isolated village, with an imposing castle that was once an outpost for the Marquises of Monferrato against the people of Asti, now has a late 17th-century appearance. Nearby, the Romanesque parish church of S. Giovanni delle Conche is also worth a visit. A Bottega del Vino, a wine cooperative, and important private producers also await wine-lovers.

▪ **MANGO**. The town stands on the ridge between the Tinella and Belbo valleys. Busca Castle houses the Enoteca Regionale Colline del Moscato, that offers about 150 types of wine, cakes, and other typical local products; there is also an adjoining restaurant.

▪ **CASTIGLIONE TINELLA**. A peaceful farm town in the hills commanding an incredible view across the Bassa Langa region and the Moscato wine lands. The sanctuary of Madonna del Buon Consiglio is situated in the Tinella valley. There is a busy Bottega del Vino at the Osteria Verderame, in the town center.

Alto Monferrato

As already mentioned, despite the closeness to the Apennine ridge and despite what its name suggests, the southern part of the Alessandria province is actually

Villages and vines in the Basso Monferrato region

An old Piedmont winery

lower than Basso Monferrato. As a contradiction within the contradiction, the ground is also more rugged, with steeper slopes and deeper valleys. It is interesting to note the effects of these geological peculiarities on the wine. Apart from obvious similarities, mainly in the case of Barbera del Monferrato and Moscato d'Asti, the main focus of interest is on certain vines widely held to be autochthonous. Most notably, Cortese, known locally as Courteis, has come to be the most important white-berried variety in Piedmont. Although they are also grown elsewhere, the grapes produced here are of incomparable quality. The main production center is the town of Gavi, which lends its name to a DOCG wine. The second mention must go to Dolcetto, whose fine quality grapes flourish in an even more beneficial habitat than the nonetheless favorable soils of nearby Langhe. Acqui and Ovada, which both hold their own DOC zones, are the main local production centers. Rounding off the trio of fine wines from Alto Monferrato is Brachetto, actually more popular and more widely drunk than Moscato in times gone by, but now confined to no more than 100 acres of vineyards around Strevi – almost a collector's item.

CORTESE, BRACHETTO, AND DOLCETTO

The wine map around Alto Monferrato is divided into three sections, all boasting first-rate cuisine, too: the lands of Cortese, around Gavi and Novi Ligure; Brachetto country, that extends through the hills and villages from Acqui Terme in the direction of Nizza Monferrato; and, lastly, the terrain where Dolcetto grows, stretching west from Ovada to Dogliani and crossing into the Langhe.

▪ **GAVI**. Set in the gently rolling countryside of the Lemme valley in the Monferrato region, this small town is not far from the Bocchetta Pass that has always linked the Po Valley and Genoa – the proximity to Genoa explains the distinctly Ligurian features of this center and its ideal climate for vineyards. A Genoese fort looms over the town, where the exquisite Romanesque parish church of S. Giacomo catches the eye. For at least a thousand years, local vine dressers have been producing a valuable wine from Cortese grapes, which even has a feast named after it on the last Sunday in June. Truffles are on the menu in autumn.

▪ **NOVI LIGURE**. Situated in the lowlands around Alessandria, at the entrance to the Scrivia valley, both its name and the design of its beautiful buildings evoke centuries of Genoese rule. This busy little town is surrounded by lovely hills embellished with vineyards, castles, and villages – the tower in the castle park affords a splendid view over them. It is renowned for its wine and sweets, notably its great tradition for homemade chocolate.

▪ **ACQUI TERME**. Renowned since ancient times for its spas and baths, it still has important Roman relics (in the Archaeology Museum) and medieval vestiges from the time when it was the capital of Alto Monferrato. It is the home of the Enoteca Regionale del Brachetto housed in the wine cellars of 15th-century Palazzo Robellini, but it also owes its fame to a Dolcetto wine awarded a DOC label.

▪ **STREVI**. This town, with a delightful old center built on the slope of a hill and striking views down the valley, has an old castle and a number of fine villas. The famous sweet and fizzy Brachetto red wine, rather overshadowed by dry white sparkling wines, is coming back into fashion thanks to the local vine dressers. They also produce a full-bodied Dolcetto left to age in barrels.

▪ **QUARANTI**. This little town to the north of Acqui has just 200 inhabitants (the smallest wine town!), but plenty of events are staged for wine-lovers. The Bottega del Vino inside the Folk Museum is the real hub of activity, promoting the work of the 80 local wine makers and producers: a splendid wine-tasting evening is organized on the night of 10 August (St Lawrence's Night).

▪ **CASSINE**. Set on the left side of the Bormida valley, where the Alessandria lowlands open into rolling slopes covered with vineyards, this is one of the most interesting places in Alto Monferrato, with scenic squares and important buildings such as the church of S. Francesco, founded in the 13th century, and Palazzo Zoppi, frescoed with courtly scenes (15th century).

▪ **OVADA**. This town, with a picturesque Ligurian-style old center, stands at the foot of the Apennines, where the Orba river flows into the Stura to create a sort of narrow peninsula. The highway leading to the coast at Voltri now skirts the town. This place is famous for its truffles and biscuits, as well as for wine, of course. The climate, affected by the proximity to the sea, gives Dolcetto such an unusual taste that is has been awarded its own DOC label.

▪ **DIANO D'ALBA**. Beyond the Bormida and Belbo rivers, a scenic route leads to this very old town that long rivaled Alba for strategic importance and is dominated by

Vineyards producing Gavi's famous wine along the road to Novi Ligure

REGIONAL *ENOTECHE*

Enoteca del Piemonte
This association represents the 10 regional wineries operating in the area. It is based at the Lingotto complex in Turin, where some of the major Italian food and drink fairs are held. It publishes an annual directory about the 800 syndicated companies and can be found on the web at: www.enotecaregionaledelpiemonte.com. Innovative on-line services include a price list (prices are ex the regional winery) to help consumers with their purchases.

Enoteca Regionale Acqui "Terme e Vino"
Located in Acqui Terme, in the Alessandria province, in the majestic setting of Palazzo Perbellini, this focuses on Brachetto and Dolcetto d'Acqui. It has 82 members.

Enoteca Regionale del Barbaresco
Based in the municipality of the same name in the Cuneo province, this is housed in what used to be the church of S. Domenico. It has 94 members.

Enoteca Regionale del Barolo
Based in Barolo Castle, in the Cuneo area, where the Marquises of Falletti used to have their home, now converted into a history museum. As well as Barolo, other wines offered for tasting include Barbera d'Alba and Dolcetto d'Alba. It has 150 members.

Enoteca Regionale del Monferrato
Based in the historical Palazzo Callori in Vignale Monferrato (Asti), this promotes Grignolino del Monferrato Casalese, Barbera del Monferrato, Freisa, and Malvasia. There is a restaurant inside the winery. It has 48 members.

Enoteca Regionale "Colline del Moscato"
Housed in Busca Castle in Mango (Cuneo), in addition to Asti and Moscato d'Asti it boasts a wine selection from the Langhe, Roero, and Monferrato regions. It has a restaurant serving local food and drinks. It has 155 members.

Enoteca Regionale del Roero
Housed in a building in the old town center of Canale (Cuneo), this promotes local wine production, most notably Arneis and Rosso del Roero. It has a restaurant serving local food and drinks. It has 131 members.

Enoteca Regionale della Serra
Housed in Roppolo Castle (Biella), on Lake Viverone, its main wines are Erbaluce di Caluso, Carema, Lessona, Bramaterra, Gattinara, Coste della Sesia, Boca, Fara, Sizzano, Colline Novaresi, Colline del Canavese, and Pinerolese. The tower displays a range of passito wines and distillates. It has a restaurant serving local food and drinks. It has 340 members.

Enoteca Regionale di Canelli e dell'Astesano
Housed in Canelli (Asti), in the Palazzo di Corso Libertà's wine cellars; the wine bar is open from Thursday to Sunday in the evening and serves food and wine. Local wines are Asti and Moscato d'Asti, Barbera and Dolcetto d'Asti, Brachetto d'Acqui. It has 59 members.

Enoteca Regionale di Gattinara e delle Terre del Nebbiolo Nord Piemonte
Housed in 19th-century Villa Paolotti, this promotes Gattinara and other wines made from Nebbiolo grapes: Ghemme, Fara, Sizzano, Lessona, Boca, Bramaterra, Coste della Sesia. It has 45 members.

Enoteca Regionale Piemontese "Cavour"
Housed in the castle that used to belong to the great statesman Camillo Benso Cavour in Grinzane Cavour (Cuneo), this can boast one of the finest ranges of local wine production from 105 wineries and 12 distilleries. The building also contains a history museum and a restaurant serving food and drinks from the Langhe region. The winery hosts the well-known "Grinzane Cavour" literary prize and regular auctions of Barolo, Barbaresco, and white truffles.

a fortress that commands an unforgettable view of the Langhe. As well as a certain amount of Barolo, a rightly famous Dolcetto is produced here, often known quite simply as Diano, to which the best vines have been allocated. Its fame stems from a policy of enhancing the best vine-growing areas, which have been registered and now lend their name to the highest quality wines.

Autumn vines in Diano d'Alba

▪ **DOGLIANI.** The final stop on the route is an elegant, aristocratic town that has recently been closely associated with Dolcetto wine. Luigi Einaudi, the first president of the Italian Republic (1948-55) even made some of this wine (so everybody called it the "President's Dolcetto"). The pride of the town is its public winery called the Bottega del Vino Dolcetto, a wine producers' association housed in one of the Town Hall cellars. A pleasant trip can be made to Mondovì: starting from the picturesque Piazza Maggiore in the upper medieval part of the town, with its baroque monuments, this takes visitors into the underground levels of a period building for a stop at a wine bar with a panoramic terrace that offers a splendid scenic view of the Langhe.

Wineries *pp. 345-370*
Acqui Terme, Agliano Terme, Albugnano, Alice Bel Colle, Asti, Brignano-Frascata, Bubbio, Calamandrana, Calliano, Calosso, Camino, Canelli, Capriate d'Orba, Casorzo, Cassinasco, Castagnole delle Lanze, Castagnole Monferrato, Castel Boglione, Castello di Annone, Castelnuovo Belbo, Castelnuovo Don Bosco, Castel Rocchero, Cerro Tanaro, Cocconato, Corsione, Cossombrato, Costa Vescovato, Costigliole d'Asti, Cuccaro Monferrato, Frassinello Monferrato, Gavi, Incisa Scapaccino, Isola d'Asti, Lerma, Loazzolo, Moasca, Mombaruzzo, Mombercelli, Moncalvo, Mongardino, Monleale, Montegrosso d'Asti, Morbello, Morsasco, Murisengo, Nizza Monferrato, Novi Ligure, Ottiglio, Ovada, Ozzano Monferrato, Portacomaro, Prasco, Quargnento, Ricaldone, Rocca Grimalda, Rocchetta Tanaro, Rosignano Monferrato, San Martino Alfieri, San Marzano Oliveto, Sarezzano, Scurzolengo, Serralunga di Crea, Strevi, Tagliolo Monferrato, Tassarolo, Turin, Tortona, Treville, Vesime, Vignale Monferrato, Vinchio.

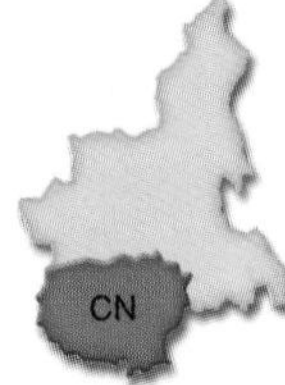

THE LANGHE AND ROERO REGIONS

Barolo and Barbaresco make this one of the most famous wine growing and production districts in the world, and one of the most popular destinations with wine-lovers.

The Langhe are an extensive range of hills stretching, roughly, between the Ligurian Alps and Monferrato, with which they share the same origins (raising and folding of the water bed of the Po Valley sea in primitive times), geological nature (various kinds of sedimentary material), and an ideal climate for vine growing. The height of the ridges that form the landscape, the so-called "Langhe", varies between 1300 and 2600 feet, with considerably higher average heights than the Monferrato region. The path of the Belbo river divides the land into two distinct parts: the Bassa (Lower) Langa or "cultivated" Langa to the north, so lovingly described by novelist Cesare Pavese, and the Alta (Upper) Langa or "wild" Langa to the south; the former is full of vines and not unlike the neighboring Monferrato area, while the latter is landscaped with woods, pastures, and much simpler farming.

The Langhe

This area falls within the province of Cuneo and its main wine growing and production center is Alba. It owes its worldwide fame to two smaller towns, Barolo and Barbaresco. This is where Nebbiolo, a vine that also grows quite effectively in other parts of Piedmont, gives its most luscious grapes, used to produce Barolo and Barbaresco, the first wines in Italy to be awarded DOCG certification in 1981. The Langhe's range of wines is completed by a first-rate Moscato d'Asti, a collection of excellent red wines including Nebbiolo and Barbera d'Alba, and four different Dolcetto reds associated with four well-known places.

The Marquises of Barolo's estate in Barolo

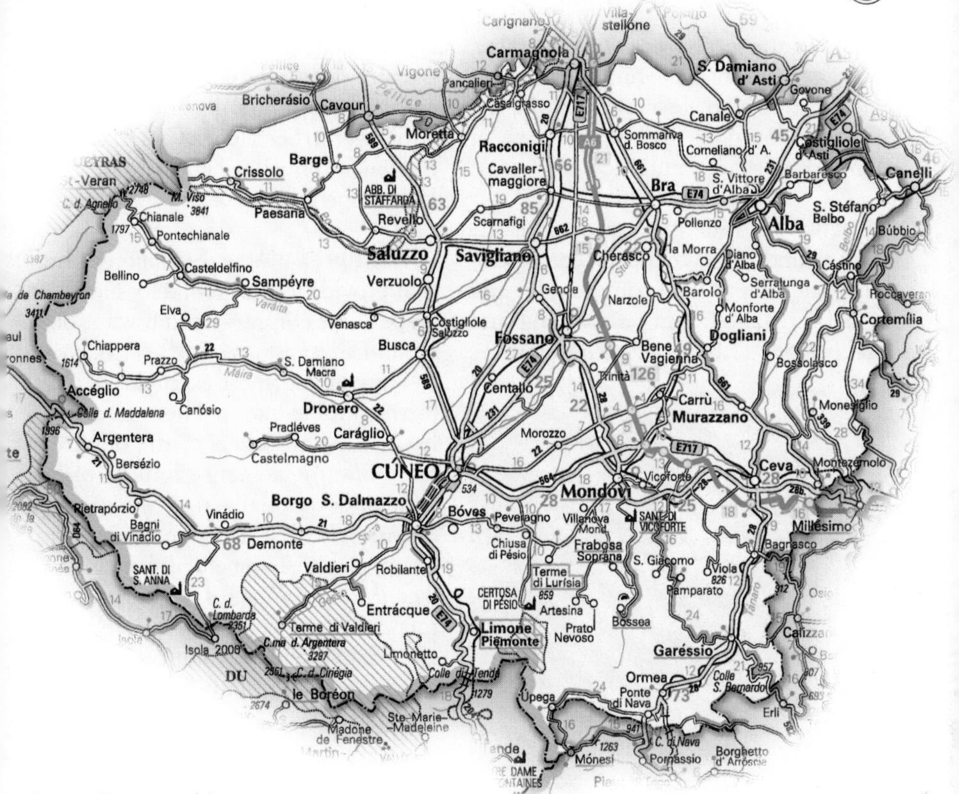

IN THE REIGN OF NEBBIOLO

"Wandering through the Langhe" among vines and castles: this might well be the slogan of a trip through one of the magnificent Italian wine-growing lands, full of carefully ordered vineyards and offering scenic views from the roads along the ridges. Various routes depart from Alba and pass through the various wine-growing centers – all close to each other –, but you must resist the temptation to keep stopping along the way.

▪ **ALBA**. At the triangular intersection where the Cherasca stream flows into the Tanaro, a circle of ramparts still surrounds the medieval town, filled with towers and tower-houses, that features Romanesque-Gothic and baroque monuments. The rolling hills of the Bassa Langa rise all around, quite familiar to food and drink lovers for their quality wines and prestigious white truffles. For both, the trading and moral capital of this piece of paradise provides extremely important events: Vinum, a wine fair mainly devoted to ready-to-drink products, takes place in the latter half of April; the last three weeks in October are the date of the national Truffle Fair. It is hardly surprising to find that the local cuisine has extraordinary pleasures in store.

▪ **BAROLO**. Upstream from Alba, the Tanaro river runs around the delightful hills that surround a small town full of narrow streets and quaint little corners: the small but striking capital of a unique wine district. It stands in the shadow of the castle owned by Marquis Falletti. The manor house, renovated in the early 19th century, is the home of the Enoteca Regionale del Barolo, which presents the new vintage in early May. Of all the wine-related events held in town, mention must be made of the Barolo Festival staged in the second week in September, with gastronomic evenings and pavement artists who cleverly transform the feelings conjured up by the "wine of kings" into shapes and colors.

■ **CASTIGLIONE FALLETTO.** A medieval castle with cylindrical corner and central towers stands impressively on the ridge and can be reached along a winding and steep road. There is also an adjoining parish church and the Confraternita dei Battuti. The square commands a view across the rolling hills of the Langa of Alba over to Serralunga Castle; the municipal wine cellar beneath the Town Hall is open on Sundays.

Vine-covered hills

■ **SERRALUNGA D'ALBA.** Set amongst hills that provide fertile ground for Nebbiolo grapes, this ellipse-shaped town is built around an impressive 13th-century castle, one of the finest examples of a hill fortress in Piedmont. The wine store is housed in the cellars of the old Town Hall, offering a chance to taste or buy wine; it occasionally hosts wine-related events. The first mention of wine producers goes to Tenimenti di Fontanafredda e Barolo: 175 acres of vineyards surround the wine cellar that used to be Vittorio Emanuele II's hunting lodge and twenty families still live in the surrounding houses.

■ **MONFORTE D'ALBA.** The town, which has a medieval layout, extends up the hillside in a maze of narrow streets to an old bell tower. The Sette Vie chapel, with its 15th-century fresco, and Palazzo Scarampi, once a medieval castle, both catch the eye. The Horszowksy auditorium stands in front of the church and is where an important program of symphony music is on stage in July-August. As for wine, this is one of the Langhe sanctuaries, with at least twenty quality wine producers.

■ **NOVELLO.** Built on a hill on the right bank of the Tanaro river, this little town with its neo-Gothic manor house and baroque parish church flanked by a Romanesque tower stands amid the hills favored by Alba's vacationers for their charming beauty and fine climate. The Bottega del Vino in the middle of the town is, rather unusually, in the crypt of what used to be the church of S. Sebastiano.

BAROLO CHINATO

Barolo Chinato is an aromatized wine obtained from room-temperature maceration of cinchona-bark, rhubarb and gentian roots, with a final addition of spices, including cardamom. Barolo Chinato was first made in the 19th century and quickly gained fame for its medicinal properties, believed to be a cure-all for minor ailments, especially colds. In popular credence, drunk as mulled wine, hot and invigorating, it had antipyretic and digestive properties. In an era when beverages with a cinchona-bark base were in vogue, Barolo Chinato became the ideal drink to offer guests; more recently, it has been rediscovered as a "conversation wine". Its truly unique organoleptic qualities combine the structure of the noblest of Piedmont reds with the aromatic complexity of spices; outstanding among its gifts is its exceptional affinity with chocolate, even the darkest varieties.
Production is submitted to the code of Barolo DOCG and foresees 20 days' maceration at 85°F, at least two years' stabilizing in oak casks and another year of ageing in bottles.

▪ **LA MORRA.** This old little town, spread like a fan, offers astonishing views across the Langhe and the Alps and boasts interesting monuments. Wine-lovers must visit the municipal winery, set in a historical location. Its range of wines – Barolo, Nebbiolo, Dolcetto, and Barbera – come from over 40 producers; in addition to wine tasting and selling, it also has plenty of books and information. Those interested in finding out more about local wines can visit the Alba Wine Museum beside the Renato Ratti - Antiche Cantine dell'Abbazia dell'Annunziata winery: set in a wonderful location, it also has a collection of vine working tools, vessels, wine presses, and period prints.

▪ **VERDUNO.** This small town is known as the "sentry of the Langhe" because of its position and medieval castle, but its name is more familiar to wine-lovers for the exclusive DOC wine of the same appellation, also named after the Pelaverga vine stock, of ancient origins. It boasts lovely views of the florid Langhe vineyards just across the Tanaro river.

▪ **GRINZANE CAVOUR.** Plenty of wine-lovers gather inside the walls of the majestic castle (13th C., renovated in the 17th C.) of this little town situated in the Barolo area. The manor house, which also acts as Enoteca Regionale with an adjoining restaurant and History-Ethnography Museum, is the favorite location for the activities of the Maestri della Confraternita dei Cavalieri del Tartufo e dei Vini d'Alba. It also hosts a well-known literary prize at the end of May, plus round tables and conventions. The wines available for tasting include Barolo, Barbaresco, Dolcetto, Barbera, Nebbiolo, Arneis, and Favorita, as well as various distillates.

▪ **CHERASCO.** Situated where the Stura di Demonte flows into the Tanaro, this is a handsome town with wide porticoed

Wineries *pp. 345-370*
Alba, Barbaresco, Barolo, Bastia Mondovì, Bra, Canale, Castellinaldo, Castiglione Falletto, Castiglione Tinella, Clavesana, Corneliano d'Alba, Diano d'Alba, Dogliani, Farigliano, Govone, Grinzane Cavour, La Morra, Mango, Monforte d'Alba, Montà, Montelupo Albese, Monteu Roero, Neive, Neviglie, Novello, Piobesi d'Alba, Priocca, Roddino, Rodello, Santa Vittoria d'Alba, Santo Stefano Belbo, Serralunga d'Alba, Treiso, Trezzo Tinella, Verduno, Vezza d'Alba.

streets and fine works of architecture. The surviving Visconti Castle evokes its past as a military stronghold of the House of Savoy. The Romanesque church of S. Pietro and baroque S. Maria del Popolo are both of interest. Cherasco, which produces Barolo, Barbera, and Nebbiolo, is also known as the "Italian snail capital" – plenty of variations on this particular dish are available.

▪ **BARBARESCO**. It is almost embarrassing to talk about such a famous and prestigious name – it actually speaks for itself. Wine-lovers cannot but be impressed by the endless expanse of vineyards, which literally seem to have small towns and villages floating among them. The Bricco Tower is as tall as a lighthouse. This landmark for the entire municipality is a majestic remnant from the times when it was fought over by the inhabitants of Asti and Alba. The church of S. Donato, which no longer serves as such, now houses the Enoteca Regionale, which represents the various wines from the four municipalities producing Barbaresco DOCG; it has a display of ethnographic materials and is open for wine-tasting/sales.

▪ **NEIVE**. The town is built in concentric circles around the ancient *ricetto*, a fortress which, when need be, protected local people and their crops against intruders. The Bottega del Vino, housed in the 18th-century premises of a central building, is eloquently named the House of Four Wines: Barbaresco, Moscato d'Asti, Barbera, and Dolcetto d'Alba. The churches of the Confraternita di S. Michele and Ss. Pietro e Paolo date from the mid-18th century.

Roero: Arneis and Favorita

Roero is a wine producing district that has managed to maintain its own identity comprising twenty or so municipalities situated on the left bank of the Tanaro river, opposite Alba, and is named after the family that ruled over it for centuries. The main towns are Bra and Canale. Like the Langhe region, it is given over to Nebbiolo grapes, although its growing fame is actually due to two white-berry grapes: Arneis and Favorita (the local name for Vermentino from Liguria). These grapes were once used to add character to reds, but now they are vinified pure with excellent results.

Arneis vineyard in Canale d'Alba on Bric Renesio, the hill that lends its name to the vine

The cooper's shop reconstructed in the museum of the Enoteca Regionale di Grinzane Cavour

THE ARNEIS HILLS

This route starts from Bra and runs through the small towns and villages that straddle the Tanaro and Borbore valleys, passing historical places, castles, scenic views, and wineries.

▪ **BRA**. Built around the year 1000 when the townsfolk of the nearby Roman town of Pollentia took shelter there, this is now a baroque town offering visitors a tempting range of food and wine, as well as plenty of cultural attractions. It is notably worth visiting the sumptuous church of S. Andrea, built in 1682, and Gothic Palazzo Traversa, with its History and Art Museum.

▪ **SANTA VITTORIA D'ALBA**. This picturesque little town built on a scenic ridge overlooking the wide Tanaro valley notably features a watchtower, the church of the Assunta, and the frescoed chapel of the Confraternita di S. Francesco. A visit to the Cinzano plant is a must: "Fiery red, blue blood" has been this famous company's motto ever since 1757, when Cinzano used to have its headquarters in the so-called Villa Storica, previously a royal hunting lodge. The surrounding manufacturing plant still handles 80% of production, ranging from spumante wines to most famous vermouths and aperitifs. The underground wine cellars are startling for their size and style, covering 3600 square yards in the heart of the Santa Vittoria hill. The permanent exhibition of the Francesco Cinzano history archives displays advertising materials and documents that formed part of this famous brand's 200-year history as it conquered markets worldwide. The so-called Glass Collection includes 140 goblets and glasses ranging from Roman times to the great English school of design.

▪ **CASTELLINALDO**. Tightly huddled around its 13th-century castle, this old-looking little town lies in the picturesque setting of hills that separate the waters of the Tanaro from those of the Borbore. The local Bottega del Vino is housed in a 15th-century hall in the castle; it is equipped for wine tasting and selling as part of theme evenings and promotional events.

■ **CANALE D'ALBA**. Situated in the upper Borbore valley along the road up the Cadibona hill, this little town is renowned for its Enoteca Regionale del Roero, housed in a specially refurbished building in the charming porticoed town square. An outstanding event held here is Porté Disné, at the end of May. It is a roving lunch that travels from hill to hill and concludes with strawberries for everybody in the central square. The town is also famous for its peaches.

■ **CISTERNA D'ASTI**. Situated on the south-western Monferrato hillside, it has an interesting castle of medieval origin hosting a historic Arts and Crafts Museum. The Bottega del Vino, housed in an old building close to the town square, offers a chance to taste Bonarda and all the other local products.

The Saluzzo Hills

The Colline Saluzzesi (Saluzzo hills) DOC production comprises the rolling hills around a bend in the River Po near lovely Saluzzo, set at the foot of Mt Monviso. As well as Barbera and Nebbiolo grapes, the vineyard also grows red Pelaverga and Quagliano, which are vinified pure to make two wines of the same names.

THE ENVIRONS OF SALUZZO

Saluzzo, the ancient capital of a marquisate of the same name, is surrounded by a landscape of low hills and vineyards cut across by two streams, Varaita and Bronda. This isolated area provides a wonderfully charming setting for the production of fine wines.

■ **SALUZZO**. Saluzzo was a miniature capital in the 16th century and conserves its somewhat Lombard-Gothic and Renaissance feel, set as it is against the impressive mountain backdrop of Monviso. In the old part of town, nestling below the castle with winding streets, flights of steps and 15th-century brick houses, the attractions include: the Cathedral (1491-1501); the Cavassa House, a late-15th century home full of furniture and works of art and offering a scenic view of the city; the Gothic church of S. Giovanni; and the castle itself (or Castiglia), with a picturesque path leading to it past old decorated houses.
A short diversion beyond the River Po leads to Revello, which used to be owned by the Marquises of Saluzzo and conserves a late-Gothic part, and to the Cistercian abbey of Staffarda, one of the region's main monuments.

■ **MANTA**. A straight road out of Saluzzo leads south to Manta, situated at the foot and on the ridge of a highland plain. Apart from a few ancient houses, the reason for the visit is the 14th-century Manta Castle, or rather the famous courtly frescoes (ca 1420) that decorate the baronial chamber, portraying "men of valor" and romantic heroines.

Frescoes in Manta

THE VINEYARDS OF THE PREALPS

The Nebbiolo vines that grow on the foothills in the provinces of Biella, Novara, and Vercelli produce two wonderful red wines: Ghemme and Gattinara. The Turin province has two interesting wine producing areas in the Ivrea hills and in the valley that climbs to Bardonecchia.

The foothills stretching east of Biella towards Lake Maggiore give further proof of how well Nebbiolo vines grow in the Prealps. The peculiarity of local production stems from the nature of the ground, also ideal for Bonarda Novarese and Vespolina, which give a distinctive flavor to local wines made from Nebbiolo grapes. The range of reds includes Croatina, even more common in the Oltrepò Pavese region; white-berry grapes such as Greco (the local name for Canavese Erbaluce) and Malvasia are also present.
The Prealps in the Turin province can, in turn, boast two good DOC wines in the Canavese and Valle di Susa areas. The best red wines again come from Nebbiolo grapes, together with local varieties that are gradually returning to the fore, but there is also a rare and refined white grape variety called Erbaluce grown in the Caluso area.

Eastern Prealps

This wide strip of Piedmont hills skirting the plains produces plenty of DOC wines, two of which are truly first class. The first is a red called Gattinara, famous since ancient times when Cardinal Mercurino Arborio, chancellor to the court of Charles V, sang its praises. Such a noble past has been confirmed by DOCG certification, forcing wine makers to focus much of production on single crus. Ghemme, another favorite with wine-lovers, received the same certification in 1997.

GATTINARA, GHEMME, AND MUCH MORE

Attention inevitably focuses on the two towns situated on opposite banks of the Sesia river that lend their names to prestigious DOCG wines made from Nebbiolo grapes. There is, however, plenty of ground to cover between Ivrea and Lake Maggiore, mostly clad with vineyards that produce other

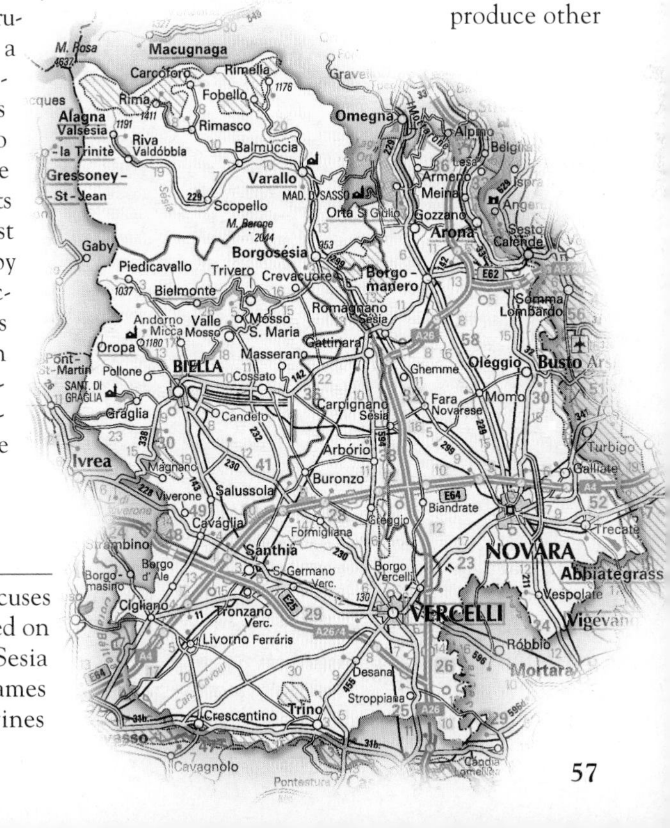

Rice fields in the Novara district

well-known Piedmont DOC wines, ranging from Boca and Bramaterra to Fara, Lessona, and Sizzano.

▪ **GATTINARA.** It is situated on the right bank of the Sesia river, on the edge of the flatlands and with the easternmost Biella hills behind it, where vines were planted by the Romans in the 2nd century AD. The checkerboard layout of this small town dates from when it was founded by the people of Vercelli in 1242. The 15th-century parish church of S. Pietro stands out in the town center with its fine terracotta decorations and Renaissance cloister. Nebbiolo wine making influences every aspect of village life, and it is a real pleasure to visit the wine shops and bars. The Enoteca Regionale del Gattinara is housed in the renovated Villa Paolotti, where the Istituto Terre del Nebbiolo del Nord Piemonte promotes wines from this vast area.

▪ **GHEMME.** This small town, located between the flat rice fields and the Prealps, has an intriguing medieval appearance and enjoys a peculiar combination of climatic features that enhances the vines. This must have been known since ancient times, as Pliny himself referred to the location as the home of a fine wine. There are an imposing baroque church and the remains of a *ricetto*.

The Canavese Region

Wine production mainly affects the northeastern part of the Turin province, and the very best results come from the area between the Valle d'Aosta national road and the border with Biella. The wine district around the town of Caluso is particularly renowned and stretches up towards the morainic hills of Ivrea, brightened by the lakes of Candia and Viverone. The predominant autochthonous white-berry variety is Erbaluce, which produces a passito wine with a long tradition and an extremely delicate white wine. The second jewel in the Canavese district's crown is the Carema area, where the Dora Baltea river enters Piedmont. The habitat is similar to Valle d'Aosta's, with crystalline rocks alternating with morainic and alluvial deposits. The terraced vineyards with drystone walls and columned arbors supporting the vine shoots are similar to those in Valle d'Aosta, too. The main variety of vine here is Nebbiolo, which produces one of Piedmont's finest reds.

ERBALUCE AND NEBBIOLO

From Caluso to Carema, the undisputed wine capitals of the area, our journey takes us from south to north along the banks of the Dora Baltea river, occasionally drifting out in search of wines, lakes, and castles.

▪ **CALUSO.** This small town hidden amidst the vineyards on the southern slopes of a low-lying morainic hill still has the remains of the old town walls and the ruins of a castle on a hilltop. There is a marvelous view across Candia and its lake, partly surrounded by woody hills, lowlands, and the Alps. The Erbaluce white wine is the main attraction (notably at the September festival).

■ **AGLIÈ**. The main attractions are Erbaluce di Caluso and the Canavese DOC wines. This little town is built around its magnificent 18th-century ducal castle, but there are also plenty of historical churches and buildings to be seen.

■ **IVREA**. The main city in the Canavese district stands on the banks of the Dora Baltea river, set amongst green morainic hills and with a Cathedral and Castle of great charm. The two monuments can be reached on a delightful path along the Dora that then crosses the town's main streets, Via Arduino and Via Palestro, and their lovely squares.

■ **ROPPOLO**. Roppolo Castle stands on the east bank of Lake Viverone. It is currently the headquarters of the Enoteca Regionale della Serra, strategically placed between the Canavese and the Ghemme and Gattinara areas and offering their best products. The Enoteca Regionale has its own hotel and restaurant and hosts concerts in summer.

■ **CAREMA**. Set in a sunny basin, this has always been a border town since olden times. Before the year 1000, it marked the border with the Kingdom of Burgundy and it is now the last municipality in Piedmont before entering Valle d'Aosta, whose basic characteristics and distinctive features it shares. This applies not only to its landscape of strikingly high terraced vineyards but also to its customs. It is hardly surprising that the Grape Festival in September-October also provides a chance to commemorate the Battle of Queens, a hard fought contest between cows for the title of "queen" of the valley. There is a well-stocked Bottega del Vino for those interested in tasting Carema DOC wine.

Valsusa and the Pinerolo Area

The Valsusa DOC area comprises vineyards that rise from the Dora di Bardonecchia river basin to a height of 3300 feet, partly upstream of the main town of Susa. This is a mountain vine growing area – apparently dating from before Roman times – that relies on traditional grape varieties such as Avanà and Neretta Cunese. The terraced vineyards have been planted on sunny slopes that enjoy particularly favorable microclimates. On the western border of the

Vineyards around Novara

Turin province is a wide stretch of foothills where Pinerolese DOC vineyards crown the town of Pinerolo at the entrance to the Chisone valley. The selection of local wines includes lesser known names such as Neretto, Doux d'Henry, Avanà, and Averengo.

Wineries *pp. 345-370*
Agliè, Borgone Susa, Brusnengo, Crevoladossola, Fara Novarese, Galliate, Gattinara, Ghemme, Ivrea, Lessona, San Giorgio Canavese, Suno.

West of Turin

A route leading up the Val di Susa to Turin and then through Colle delle Finestre into the neighboring Chisone area brings together lands famous for both their works of art and their fine wines.

■ **Avigliana.** Charming medieval town at the entrance to the Val di Susa, overlooking a picturesque morainic basin. Its setting attracts visitors to the nearby Sacra di San Michele, whose Gothic (and panoramic) abbey church is one of the region's most spectacular monuments.

■ **Susa.** This town at the crossroads of the memorable Moncenisio and Monginevro mountain routes has lent its name (through the valley) to a new DOC wine. The Roman Arch of Augustus and the Cathedral named after S. Giusto (founded in the 11th century) stand out against the backdrop of a ring of rugged mountains.

■ **Pinerolo.** The upper part of the town is built on the S. Maurizio hill, at the entrance to the Chisone valley, while the modern city is down in the plain. It used to be the capital of the tiny kingdom of the Acajas and then an insolated French outpost in Piedmont. Its traditionally mild climate, sheltered from the north, is ideal for growing vines that produce wines with the same DOC label.

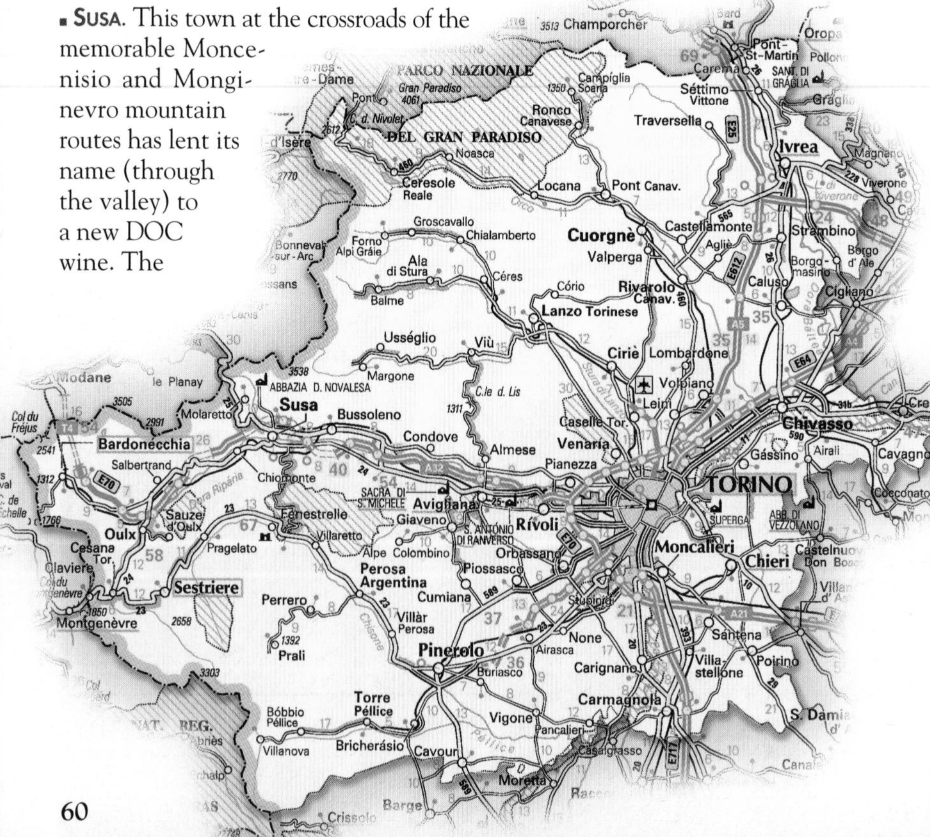

Specialties in Piedmont

WHEN PEOPLE MENTION Piedmont, you either think of Turin, with its relics from the House of Savoy in the shadow of the Mole Antonelliana, or the Langa and Monferrato hills, with their vineyards and castles. Facts and figures confirm that most tourists and wine-lovers are interested in an area comprising Turin and the cities of Asti, Alessandria, and Cuneo. This is an impressive area that begins on the right bank of the River Po and extends up to the Apennines and the Alps. The setting includes everything from vegetable gardens and fruit orchards in the valley bottoms to vineyards on the best-exposed slopes and to almost inaccessible pasture lands. The wide variety of raw materials adds luster to the local rustic cuisine, which becomes sumptuous when passing in the hands of manor-house chefs.

A GLANCE THROUGH a typical local menu shows what a wide range of dishes is on offer. A special mention among hors d'oeuvres must go to two sauces: *bagna cauda* and *finanziera*. The former is made with olive oil and salted anchovies brought from Liguria along the old Salt Route and completed with vegetables grown in Monferrato, notably bent cardoons, which are dipped in the sauce raw. The second sauce is a combination of simple ingredients such as chicken giblets and livers and fancy titbits that made it popular with Turin's bankers. Both are ideally washed down with a glass of Nebbiolo. Next come egg pastas, a real test of the cooking skills of local housewives - first and foremost *tajarin*, garnished with a roast-meat sauce or given added flavor by white truffles, a fine finishing touch to many Piedmont dishes; stuffed pasta shapes have simple fillings, either spinach or stewed meat. They are always served with red wines, ranging from Dolcetto to Nebbiolo. Special mention ought to go to rice, the lowland area's main contribution to local cuisine: risotto is served with creamy garnishing and added with truffles.

PRIDE OF PLACE among the meats goes to Langhe's "large-legged" beef: this is the main ingredient in mixed boiled meats and unforgettable pot roasts (Barbera d'Alba). Then comes the game, hare first and foremost, cooked in red wine and with vegetables – accompanied with wines made from Nebbiolo grapes (Barolo, Barbaresco). Meat dishes such as Marengo chicken and rabbit, garnished with a flourish of peppers (Dolcetto di Ovada, Dolcetto di Dogliani), are also popular. Another famous dish is *fritto misto* – a mixture of fried meats and vegetables as well as apples and amaretto biscuits (Barbera d'Asti). Frogs and snails add a rather unusual touch to the menu. Cheeses inevitably conjure up names such as Bra, Castelmagno, Murazzano, Raschera, and Roccaverano, which have recently come to the fore. Soft cheeses go with white Gavi wine, while stronger ones are ideally matched with Dolcetto, Grignolino, Barbera, and Ghemme or Gattinara for the ripest and strongest. Last but not least come the desserts: Asti is served with oven-baked desserts and there is a very special Brachetto for tarts and pies; there is also surprisingly tasty Barolo Chinato for chocolate-based desserts.

Lombardy

From Oltrepò to Valtellina

Lombardy's production is limited though outstanding in terms of the variety of production zones and wines, ranging from the great reds of Valtellina to the sparkling wines of Franciacorta and Oltrepò.

There are various historical accounts of vine growing in Lombardy, beginning with the heartfelt descriptions by Virgil, born and raised in Mantua, and continuing up to the tale of the vineyard donated by Lodovico il Moro, Duke of Milan, to Leonardo da Vinci – the latter's preferred wine, Retico, was perhaps the forerunner to current-day Valtellina's Sfurzat. In the 17th century new techniques were already giving real excellence to wines and international renown to three zones – Garda, Oltrepò Pavese, and

Above, Franciacorta vineyard at Bornato; left, Oltrepò Pavese vineyards (top) and a cellar in Tirano, Valtellina (bottom); opposite, river landscape in the Mantua area.

Valtellina. Much more recently, the importation of new grape varieties such as Riesling and Pinot has enlarged the gamut of the wines produced, and the sparkling wines of Franciacorta have emerged as important products.

Unique Wines from the Alps to the Apennines

The most heavily industrialized region of Italy also boasts an excellent vine growing tradition. Vineyards extends from the Alps and the terraces of Valtellina to the Apennines and the clay-rich slopes of Oltrepò Pavese. In between are the hills of Bergamo and Brescia (with an important slice constituted by Franciacorta), the morainic amphitheatre of Lake Garda, the wide Po river plain with the San Colombano al Lambro's hill, and Mantua's Oltrepò. The variety of grapes cultivated is very wide indeed, but local species of vine have a notable role only in the case of Groppello, in the province of Brescia, which gives a red of great personality. On the other hand, the lion's share goes to varieties from nearby Piedmont: Barbera is extensively cultivated in Pavia's area, as is Croatina; in Valtellina, instead, a type of Nebbiolo is of fundamental significance. The grapes of nearby Emilia are encountered in the southeastern corner of the region, in the form of Lambrusco, while the presence of Marzemino in the north is a reminder that the Adige valley is not far away. The important grapes of France are also widely spread and account for a quarter of the regional total.

Two DOCGs, 14 DOCs, 13 IGTs, 8 Wine and Gastronomy Routes

Lombardy is one of the most important tourist destinations in Italy and this is also due to the variety of its high-rank wines, which accounts for as many as eight Wine and Gastronomy Routes. The first to be named are the DOCG productions – Franciacorta, with its spumante wines, and Valtellina, with Rosso Superiore (and Sfurzat, too, quite soon); then come the 14 DOC areas, thanks to which Lombardy ranks sixth at national level with 19,800,000 US gallons of wine. The largest production zone in the region – third in the national ranking – is Oltrepò Pavese, with 14,500,000 US gallons. Next, but trailing by a considerable distance, is Franciacorta. At the bottom of the list, in terms of volume, are such small zones as Valcalepio and Botticino which testify to a real desire to sustain and advance the reputation of more limited productions. There are then as many as 13 IGTs, some of which safeguarding tiny areas such as Ronchi di Brescia and its ancient Invernenga vineyard.

LOMBARDY'S DOC ZONES

Scale 1:1 250 000

0 15 30 km

1 **DOCG Franciacorta** *Spumante ▪ Spumante Rosé*

2 **DOCG Valtellina Superiore** *with geographic denomination: Grumello, Inferno, Sassella, Valgella*

3 **DOCG Sforzato di Valtellina**

4 **DOC Botticino**

5 **DOC Capriano del Colle** *Bianco or Trebbiano ▪ Rosso*

6 **DOC Cellatica**

7 **DOC Garda** *Chardonnay, Cortese, Garganega, Pinot Bianco, Pinot Grigio, Riesling, Riseling Italico, Sauvignon, Tocai, Frizzante ▪ Barbera, Cabernet, Cabernet Sauvignon, Corvina, Marzemino, Merlot, Pinot Nero*

8 **DOC Garda Colli Mantovani** *Bianco, Chardonnay, Pinot Bianco, Pinot Grigio, Sauvignon, Tocai Italico ▪ Rosato or Chiaretto ▪ Rosso, Cabernet, Merlot*

9 **DOC Lambrusco Mantovano** *Rosso, Rosato, Viadanese-Sabbionetano Rosso, Viadanese-Sabbionetano Rosato, Oltrepò Mantovano Rosso, Oltrepò Mantovano Rosato*

10 **DOC Lugana** *also liquoroso*

11 **DOC Oltrepò Pavese** *Chardonnay, Cortese, Malvasia, Moscato, Pinot Grigio, Pinot Nero, Riesling Italico, Riesling Renano, Sauvignon, Spumante ▪ Rosato ▪ Rosso, Barbera, Bonarda, Buttafuoco, Cabernet Sauvignon, Sangue di Giuda*

12 **DOC Riviera del Garda Bresciano** *Bianco ▪ Chiaretto ▪ Rosso, Groppello*

13 **DOC San Colombano al Lambro**

14 **DOC San Martino della Battaglia**

15 **DOC Terre di Franciacorta** *Bianco ▪ Rosso*

16 **DOC Valcalepio** *Bianco, Moscato Passito ▪ Rosso*

17 **DOC Valtellina**

IGT - Typical Geographic Indication

Alto Mincio (Mantua); Benaco Bresciano (Brescia); Bergamasca (Bergamo); Collina del Milanese (Milan - Lodi - Pavia); Montenetto di Brescia (Brescia); Provincia di Mantova (Mantua); Provincia di Pavia (Pavia); Quistello (Mantua); Ronchi di Brescia (Brescia); Sabbioneta (Mantua); Sebino (Brescia); Terrazze Retiche di Sondrio (Sondrio)

The Great Wines of Lombardy

Franciacorta Docg

Never called spumante, this is simply known as "Franciacorta" or, informally, as "Bollicine" (bubbles). It was certified as DOCG, the highest classification of quality, in 1995, a fitting climax to one of the most interesting wine-making enterprises undertaken in Italy in recent decades: the aim was to produce a wine that could vie with Champagne in the minds of the public. Franciacorta is made from Chardonnay, Pinot Bianco and Pinot Nero grapes and is left to ferment on lees in bottles for 18 months; the entire process takes at least 25 months from harvest to marketing. It is straw-yellow in color with green or gold highlights. It has a slight yeast (bread crusts) aroma, soft though strong, with hints of dried fruits and nuts (almonds, hazelnuts, figs) as well as spices (cloves). In descending order of intensity, the six types are: Non dosato (Pas Dosé, Dosage Zéro, and Nature); Extra Brut; Brut; Extra Dry; Sec; Demisec. There is also the rather special Franciacorta Satèn, made mainly from Chardonnay grapes with added Pinot Bianco. The name comes from the silky delicacy of its perlage and its smoothness on the palate, together with a distinctive feature of ripe fruits. Another specialty is Franciacorta Rosé, made from Chardonnay and Pinot Bianco grapes with the dosed addition of Pinot Nero, that can clearly be smelt in the bouquet. Special consideration must go to Franciacorta Millesimato, only produced in the most favorable years and left to age at least 37 months, 30 of which inside the bottles on lees. The specialty of this product is in the way wines from the same year are blended together – unlike traditional cuvées, which are balanced with different vintage wines.

Valtellina Superiore DOCG and Sfursat DOCG

Vine cultivation in Valtellina apparently dates back to before Roman times, when the area was inhabited by Ligurians and Etruscans. In centuries past, the red wine from Valtellina was made from typical local grapes – Rossola, Pignola, and Brugnola among others – which were gradually replaced by Nebbiolo from Piedmont, known locally as Chiavennasca, as vines were gradually replanted in the wake of the destructive Phylloxera epidemic that struck in the late-19th century. The production code for Valtellina Superiore DOCG indicates the use of pure Nebbiolo grapes or, alternatively, 10% recommended red grape varieties. This high-quality production, awarded DOCG certification, relates to four sub-zones – Sassella, Grumello, Inferno, and Valgella – mentioned on the labels. The resulting wine is ruby-colored, turning slightly garnet-colored with ageing; it has a distinctive, lasting aroma and a dry, slightly tannic flavor that tends to turn velvety and rather austere. Before being sold it must be left to age for two years (three for the Riserva), of which one year in oak barrels. It is ideally served with palatable local dishes from the Valtellina region and ripe cheeses. Sforzato (Sfursat) is made from selected Nebbiolo grapes left to ripen and dry out in fruit cellars for about three months. This wine has a high alcohol content (14%), intense color and flavor. It ought to be drunk with tasty cheeses or between meals – ideal as a "meditation wine".

Garda Classico Chiaretto DOC

This famous claret wine, the praises of which were sung by ancient travelers visiting Lake Garda, originally comes from the hilly lands of

the Valtenesi region, between Desenzano and Salò, the so-called "classic" area. Local Groppello grapes are used pure to produce a red character-wine, with a well-rounded flavor and distinctive chestnut aroma. The rosé, on the other hand, is made from a blend of Barbera (10-20%), Marzemino (5-30%) and Sangiovese (10-25%) grapes. This blend produces a wine varying in color from petal pink to dull cherry, with floral and fruity aromas, a dry distinctly salty flavor and almond aftertaste, if any. There is also a spumante version called Garda Rosé.

Oltrepò Pavese Rosso DOC

This wine sums up the ampelographic vocation of the main wine growing district in Lombardy: it is actually produced by combining Barbera grapes from Piedmont and native Croatina (with the possibly consistent addition of local Uva Rara and Vespolina) together with Pinot Nero, widely used in the area for making spumante wines. A similar combination of grapes – but higher in specific percentages – is also used to produce Oltrepò Pavese Barbera DOC and Oltrepò Pavese Bonarda DOC (another name for Croatina). Other local products are Buttafuoco, a dry full-bodied wine, still or slightly fizzy, to be consumed with palatable dishes, and Sangue di Giuda, a rather sweet sparkling wine that is served with desserts.

Oltrepò Pavese Spumante DOC

The leading wine-growing district in Lombardy is also renowned for its quality spumante wines. The distinctive feature is their unmistakable texture, given by the high percentage of Pinot Nero grapes (sometimes over 85%), which makes them a suitable accompaniment to a much wider variety of fish and meat dishes.

Moscato di Scanzo

This is a real curio among wines, made from a red grape variety of ancient origins: Roman settlers probably brought it to Scanzorosciate, in Valcalepio (Bergamo area), the only place where it is still grown. Over-ripe grapes produce a ruby-colored dessert wine with garnet-colored highlights, which is notable for its deep, rich and lasting rose aroma.

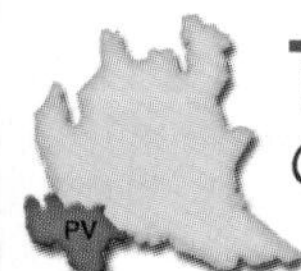

THE OLTREPÒ PAVESE REGION

One of Italy's leading wine-growing districts, appreciated by all wine-lovers for the quality and variety of its products.

When referring to the wines from the Oltrepò Pavese ("across the River Po") region – the name itself helping to place its geographical context – we are actually talking about the hills that run along the basin of the River Staffora at a height of 330-1600 feet, a triangular plot of Lombardy wedged between Piedmont and Emilia, more specifically between Alessandria and Piacenza, with all that this entails in terms of wine-producing influences. Grapevine cultivation, which was introduced here more than a thousand year ago, now involves a good 39,500 acres of land spread over 42 municipalities. It is aided and abetted by the nature of the land, generally made of limestone and clay, and by the weather, as cool breezes blow in from Liguria, keeping the temperature down.

Red grape vines are prevailing in this ideal setting of sun-kissed low hills. Most spread are the red grapes varieties of Barbera and Croatina (known locally as Bonarda), used unblended for varietals or like basis for several blended-grapes full-bodied red wines, including the famous Buttafuoco and Sangue di Giuda, given extra flavor through the addition of Vespolina and Uva Rara. White-berry grapes cultivation is sensibly spreading out on east facing slopes, where changes in temperature are more marked. Outstanding amongst local wines is Riesling Italico. There is also a remarkable range of spumante wines, mainly obtained from white vinification of Pinot Nero grapes as well as from plenty of Chardonnay, Pinot Bianco, and Pinot Grigio. Moscato is also produced in large quantities. A total of 14,5 million US gallons of DOC wines are produced in the region – the third largest production in Italy after Chianti and Asti. Quantity is matched by the universally acknowledged quality, thanks also to gradual replanting of the vines in high-density patches exploiting cutting-edge crop-growing techniques.

THE OLTREPÒ PAVESE WINE AND GASTRONOMY ROUTE

Pavia, a town of art and fine cuisine, necessarily marks one of the stops on five itineraries crisscrossing the Padana Inferiore national road, running up and down the hills along quiet backcountry roads and setting off from Voghera, Casteggio, Broni, and Stradella (twice). The high density of wineries here is matched by astonishing gastronomic opportunities, not least of which is the tasting of white truffles.

▪ **PAVIA.** The town exudes the warm colors of Lombardy terracotta and a medieval atmosphere – old towers, tiny squares, and quiet streets – all woven into the opulent setting of the 18th-19th century town center. The churches of S. Pietro in Ciel d'Oro and S. Michele are illustrious examples of Italian Romanesque style, and the Visconti Castle evokes the subsequent period of lordly rule that gave Pavia its *studium*, the present-day University. The River Ticino, featuring the distinctive covered bridge that leads to Borgo Ticino on the other side, and the Naviglio Pavese, which flows into it, evoke the busy days of river trading and gives modern visitors charming sights of the luscious Lombardy countryside.

Slightly further north from Pavia, on what used to be the outskirts of a huge park surrounding the Visconti Castle, stands the magnificent Renaissance Certosa (charterhouse) of Pavia in its entire splendor.

To the northwest, beyond the River Ticino, Vigevano is mainly popular for its famous Piazza Ducale (1494), one of Italy's great squares.

Vineyards around Canneto Pavese

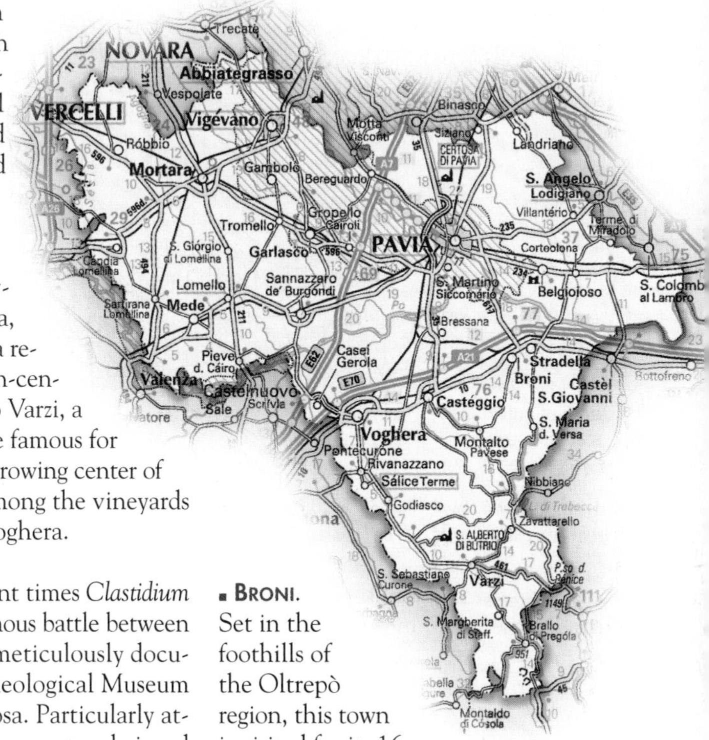

▪ Voghera. The town center shows both Lombard and Piedmontese architectural features; the porticoed low buildings around the town square are overlooked by the Collegiate and the Visconti Castle. Traveling up Valle Staffora, past Salice Terme (spa resort with a lovely 19th-century air), you come to Varzi, a quiet little old village famous for its salami. The wine-growing center of Torrazza Coste lies among the vineyards to the southeast of Voghera.

▪ Casteggio. In ancient times *Clastidium* was the scene of a famous battle between Romans and Gauls, meticulously documented in the Archaeological Museum at Palazzo della Certosa. Particularly attractive are the old town center, designed along medieval lines around a hillock; the surrounding rolling country, concealing architecturally intact villages (such as Fortunago); and a tempting abundance of white truffles.
Slightly to the south, a scenic road leads to a splendid sweeping view of vineyards in Montalto Pavese, which also has a beautiful 16th-century castle.

Wineries *pp. 370-379*
Borgo Priolo, Broni, Canevino, Canneto Pavese, Casteggio, Corvino San Quirico, Godiasco, Montalto Pavese, Montebello della Battaglia, Montecalvo Versiggia, Montù Beccaria, Mornico Losana, Pietra de' Giorgi, Retorbido, Rocca de' Giorgi, Rovescala, San Damiano al Colle, Santa Giuletta, Santa Maria della Versa, Torricella Verzate, Zenevredo.

▪ Broni. Set in the foothills of the Oltrepò region, this town is visited for its 16-century collegiate with baroque-style interiors. Cotechino (boiled pork sausage) dishes and traditional cakes are washed down with local wines. Farther south, Valle Scuropasso winds through a picturesque landscape of hilly vineyards, farmlands and woodlands, spattered with old manor centers (such as Pietra de' Giorgi and Rocca de' Giorgi) with a long wine-making tradition. Even older is the wine-making tradition in the village of Santa Giulietta, just off the Padana Inferiore national road in the direction of Casteggio.

▪ Stradella. Skirting the River Po and the last spurs of the Apennines, Stradella still features the crenellated tower of what was once a 14-century fortress and could be described as the town of bread (the *miccone* is a large loaf of crumbly bread), of wine (Oltrepò Pavese DOC) and of accordions (the first modern ac-

Certosa of Pavia, the pergola with monumental vineyard

cordion was made here in 1876). The Valle Versa road, heading south, passes through a number of other important wine-producing centers: Canneto Pavese, which received an award for its red wines as early as the beginning of the 20th century and is almost the sole producer of Buttafuoco and Sangue di Giuda DOC wines; Montù Beccaria; Santa Maria della Versa, which has a 17th-century sanctuary of the same name and where white truffles are to be found among the vineyards. Other important wine producing centers, renowned for their Bonarda and Barbera productions, such as San Damiano al Colle and Rovescala, are situated along the right bank of the Versa stream, at the border with Emilia.

BS

FROM FRANCIACORTA TO GARDA BRESCIANO

A paradise for tourists interested in wine, with unique spumante wines, plus Chiaretto and Garda Classico DOC reds.

The province of Brescia can boast two of Italy's leading wine-making areas and a number of smaller production zones. Vineyards cover the strip of hills which separates the Prealpi mountains from the plain.
The wine-making district of Franciacorta in the west occupies the rolling morainic hills which frame the south banks of Lake Iseo, more or less from the border of the Bergamo area to the outskirts of Brescia. This area has a great wine-making tradition, but has really won international acclaim only over the last few decades with its range of Franciacorta Spumante DOCG wines; its still wines bear the Terre di Franciacorta DOC label.
The so-called Garda Bresciano district, to the east, corresponds to the Lombard portion of the Lake Garda morainic amphitheater; it has an age-old wine-making tradition and has been fully discovered by tourists in recent times. The Garda DOC quality denomination includes the Garda Classico DOC.
Around the provincial capital are also a number of small wine-producing areas, set in the Colli Bresciani (Brescia hills): Botticino, Cellatica and Capriano del Colle DOCs, and Montenetto di Brescia and Ronchi di Brescia IGTs.

Franciacorta

Franciacorta is the name of the morainic amphitheatre situated to the southeast of Lake Iseo bordering with the Orfano and Alto mountains and the Oglio and Mella rivers. The district takes its name from the Latin *francae curtis*, a reference to the tax privileges enjoyed by the old monastic courts which once farmed these lands. This is an exceptional area for wine production, thanks to its mild climate, gentle breezes and loose soils ideal for growing a wide variety of vines.

The Franciacorta Wine Route

The Franciacorta wine and gastronomy route gets going just a few miles from Brescia, as the road heads up into the hills stretching out to Lake Iseo. This is a gently winding 50-mile tour through quiet places, where wine-lovers can find plenty of interesting opportunities. For any further tourist information visit the website www.stradadelfranciacorta.it.

■ **BRESCIA.** Summing up all the interesting features of Brescia, a multi-faceted art town, is hard indeed. It would be better to just point out some of the possible themed tour to be made in the shade of the 16th-century style castle: the "Roman Town", whose hub is the Capitoline Temple; the "Romanesque and Communal Town", with its Rotonda and Broletto; the "Venetian Town", embodied by Piazza della Loggia; the "Longobard and Early-Medieval Town", with the monastery of S. Giulia (and adjoining museum) and the basilica of S. Salvatore; the "Art Town", with the masterpieces of the Tosio Martinengo Art Gallery and Titian's paintings in the church of Ss. Nazaro e Celso.

A real curio for wine-lovers, the Pusterla vineyard, located up on the Cidneo hill, at the foot of Brescia castle, can claim to

Wineries *pp. 370-379*
Adro, Capriolo, Cazzago San Martino, Coccaglio, Cologne, Corte Franca, Erbusco, Monticelli Brusati, Passirano, Provaglio d'Iseo, Rodengo Saiano, Rovato.

The sweeping vineyards of Franciacorta

be the largest in-town vineyard in the world; old Invernenga grapevines are grown here, producing a white passito wine labeled Ronchi di Brescia IGT.
Brescia vineyards stretch across the surrounding hills, all well exposed and showing a wide range of geological features, whose clay and marl soils are ideal for vine-growing. Botticino, to the east of the town, and Capriano del Colle, to the south, are famous old wine-making centers which have now their own DOC label and are key destinations along the Colli Longobardi (Longobard hills) wine route.

▪ **ERBUSCO.** This is the wine-making heart and soul of Franciacorta (headquarters of wine safeguard consortium). A number of medieval buildings have survived in the old town center, up on the hill, notably the 13th-century Pieve; beautiful 17th-18th century villas (Villa Lechi is the most significant) are legacies of the aristocrats from Brescia and Milan who used to vacation here.
Traveling a few miles through the vineyards into the gently sweeping morainic hills of Sebino, you find wine-producing centers like Adro, Corte Franca, Provaglio d'Iseo (with the remains of the Cluniac monastery of S. Pietro in Lamosa), and also Capriolo and Paratico. From the steep bank of Lake Iseo you can leave for a pleasant trip to Monte Isola and take the opportunity to taste oven-baked stuffed tench.
Further inland stand the striking old wine-making town of Rovato, from where it is just a short trip up Monte Orfano to the convent of SS. Annunziata with its refined 15-century cloister; Cazzago San Martino, with its manor houses and castles; Passirano, where is to be found the most imposing of the Franciacorta castles (a fortified medieval enclosure with tall walls, swallowtails and towers, hosting today a winery's cellars); and Rodengo Saiano, home to the abbey of S. Nicola, which best testifies of the Benedictine-Cluniac monastic order presence in Franciacorta and features three cloisters and paintings by Romanino.

The Garda Bresciano

This wine-producing district envelops the morainic hills running along the south bank of the lake. The mild, wind-swept climate is ideal for vineyards. Three main DOC wines are produced here: Garda, San Martino della Battaglia, and Lugana. Already boasting a centuries-old wine-making tradition, local wineries have wit-

nessed a real boom in the recent decades which has taken them to the very top in terms of quality and targeted tourism.

THE GARDA BRESCIANO WINE ROUTE

This is a long circular tour through the vineyards and olive-groves along the Benaco southwest bank, stretching from the well-known views of Desenzano and Sirmione to the picturesque inland setting of Valtenesi, dotted with villages and castles. Encompassing all three DOC areas, this route is extremely interesting for the variety of wines and the importance of wine-makers. For further information visit the website www.stradadeivini.it.

▪ **SIRMIONE.** This picturesque town is set in the south Garda region, on the narrow peninsula stretching out into the lake, amidst olive trees and oleanders. Old churches, the 13th-century Della Scala Fortress, the Catullo Caves (actually the remains of a Roman villa dating from the Imperial Age), and the dry elegance of Lugana white wines, all await visitors to the area. The just mentioned DOC wine's name is connected to a small site near Sirmione called Santa Maria di Lugana, a sort of enclave producing a renowned white wine from Trebbiano grapes, also available in the spumante version; the peculiarity of this wine is due to an age-old grape selection and to the pedoclimatic features of the area, right inland of the lake.

Wineries *pp. 370-379*
Bedizzole, Calvagese della Riviera, Cazzago San Martino, Desenzano del Garda, Lonato, Manerba del Garda, Moniga, Polpenazze del Garda, Pozzolengo, Puegnago del Garda, San Felice del Benaco, Sirmione.

▪ **SAN MARTINO DELLA BATTAGLIA.** The Tower (museum and charnel-house) commemorating a battle fought in 1859 during the Italian War of Independence overlooks the wide open scenery of morainic hills in the Garda inland. The town lends its name to a DOC white wine, shared with Veneto, made from pure Tocai grapes or with just little additions, dry tasting but also available in a liquoroso wine version; the stony ground brings out the best in the Tocai vine which originally came from Friuli.

View of Lake Garda

▪ **LONATO**. The imposing dome of the 18th-century Cathedral can be seen from as far as the highway, standing alongside the Visconti Fortress and the splendid Podesta's house. This latter building, restored in 15th-century style, was the 19th-20th century home of senator Ugo da Como, a collector and bibliophile, and its antique furniture, picture gallery and valuable library are still in perfect condition.

▪ **DESENZANO DEL GARDA**. Facing onto the sweeping basin of the lower lake, Desenzano's old town has a genuine Venetian flair, with its overlooking castle, the old harbor and nearby Duomo (the Cathedral, displaying a *Last Supper* by G.B. Tiepolo), and the delightful lake front.
Further along the coastal road lie the picturesque towns of Moniga del Garda, the home of Chiaretto wine, with its crenellated medieval fortress, and Manerba del Garda, an ideal stopping place to taste a twaite shad or bleak fried in DOP (protected origin denomination) Garda extra virgin olive oil.

▪ **SALÒ**. Past San Felice del Benaco, which, in addition to the lovely view, boasts some valuable works of art in the sanctuary of Madonna del Carmine (1452, votive frescoes inside) and the parish church (displaying an altar piece by Romanino), you get to the town of Salò, rich in history and appreciated by tourists for its healthy climate. In the pleasant setting of the old center stand out the late-Gothic Duomo and the 16th-century Palazzo Fantoni.
The route leads on from Salò into the Valtenesi region, a land of wines, valuable olive oils and charming panoramic views across nearby Lake Garda: the route leads through some important wine-producing centers, notably Puegnago del Garda and Polpenazze del Garda.

▪ **GARDONE RIVIERA**. The town faces onto the shore of the lake's mid-basin, along which a series of villas, hotels, and gardens stand close to one another; its name evokes the dazzle of the belle époque and D'Annunzio's "deads", since it is here, in the magnificent Vittoriale villa-estate, that the poet spent the last 17 years of his life until he died in 1938. The various buildings (mausoleum, home, open-air theater, reconstruction of part of a ship) spread across the picturesque park are rich in history and biographic references.

The countryside around San Felice Benaco in the Garda Bresciano area

VALTELLINA

The upper valley of the River Adda is a marvelous example of mountain wine-growing, producing wines of truly outstanding quality and character from Nebbiolo grapes.

The province of Sondrio can boast one of the most distinctive and highly appreciated wine-making districts in Lombardy: Valtellina, where the River Adda makes its upper course from its sources to its final destination (Lake Como at Colico) through the Stelvio mountains. The most interesting area in wine-making terms is actually downstream from Tirano, where the valley faces from east to west and its northern slopes, bathed in sunshine, are almost completely covered with terraced vineyards. The main vine is Nebbiolo, known locally as Chiavennasca. It is used to make full-bodied and long-ageing red wines, together with traditional grapes, like Brugnola, Pignola, and Rossola, or more recent ones, such as Merlot or Pinot Nero. The area is the home of two DOC denominations: Valtellina DOC and Valtellina Superiore DOCG (with its five geographical sub-zones: Maroggia, Sassella, Grumello, Inferno, and Valgella). Sfursat, a passito wine made from selected grapes, is also produced in good years. Terrazze Retiche di Sondrio IGT is produced down in the valley, a little farther from the area just mentioned.

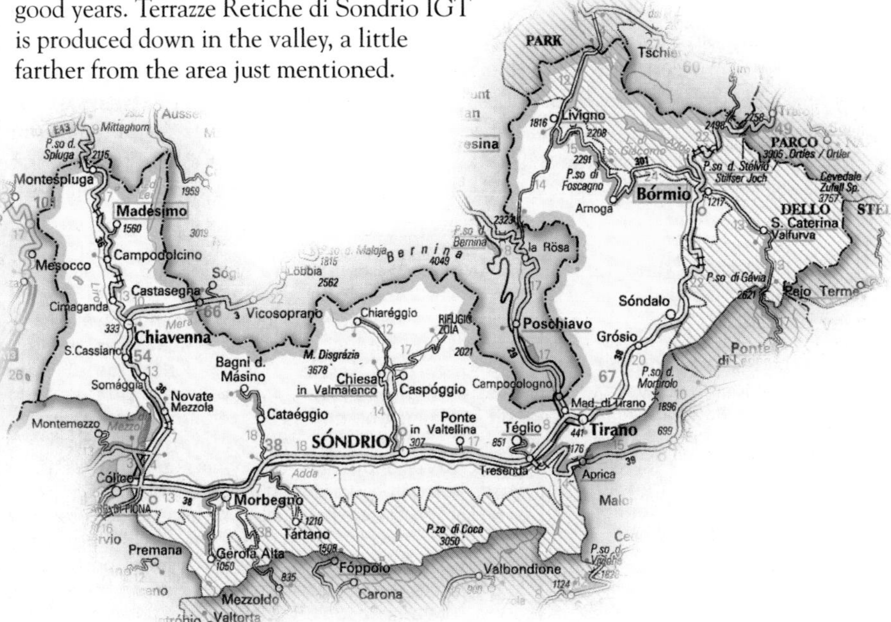

The Valtellina Wine and Gastronomy Route

This tour runs along the bottom of the Adda valley – providing striking views and the chance to visit some ancient settlements – and on the Rhaetian side, where a scenic mid-coastal road passes through the terraced vineyards. In addition, some alternative circular tours into classic wine-production areas (Maroggia, Sassella, Grumello, Inferno, Valgella, Baruffini) have been planned. The fine local cuisine offers a rich variety of traditional dishes and products: *bresaola* (air-dried fillet of beef), *violino* (made from goat's meat), and other types of dressed meat; Bitto and Casera cheese; *pizzoccheri* and other mountain specialties.

Wineries *pp. 370-379*
Chiuro, Mese, Sondrio, Teglio, Tirano, Villa di Tirano.

▪ **SONDRIO**. This is the real heart of the Valtellina tour, located at the mouth of Val Malenco. Gastronomy is probably the main temptation here, with succulent local dishes like *pizzoccheri*, buckwheat tagliatelle served with vegetables and garnished with butter and mountain cheese; but there are also some noteworthy historical landmarks, like the 16th-century Town Hall, the Ss. Gervasio e Protasio collegiate (18th C.), the Carbonera House, and Masegra Castle.

▪ **TEGLIO**. This old village features one of the most magnificent stately homes in the area, the 16th-century Palazzo Besta. The whole surrounding area is consecrated to wine-making, on the south-facing slopes right to Tirano.

▪ **TIRANO**. The sanctuary of the Madonna, in the little hamlet of Madonna di Tirano, is a sort of Renaissance apparition amidst the rugged Valtellina mountains; not far away, a narrow-gauge railway line leads to Saint Moritz, in Switzerland. In the old town center the Conti Sertoli Salis firm, based in a sumptuous 16th-century building which testifies of the exploits of one of the valley's most illustrious families, offers a superb blend of art and fine wines.

Outside Tirano, there is more wine drinking than wine growing, but it is worth continuing along upper Valtellina to the winter sports resorts of Bormio, at the foot of Stelvio National Park, and Livigno.

VILLAS ON LAKE COMO AND MERLOT WINE FROM CANTON TICINO

The imaginary triangle traced around the heart of Lake Como marks the limits of a true wonderland: Villa Melzi in Bellagio, Villa Carlotta in Tremezzo, and Villa Monastero in Varenna. We could also add Villa Balbianello in Lenno (www.fondoambiente.it), provided you get there across the lake: built in the 18th century as a sort of pleasure resort, it has a magnificent terraced garden and a belvedere that offers twin views across the peninsula ridge.
The inevitable trip across the lake can be matched with an interesting wine-tasting experience just across the Swiss border, in Canton Ticino, well worth the effort due to the quality of the wines and the fact it is easy to get to (30-60 miles, all by highway, setting off from Milan; and about 19 miles from Menaggio to Lugano). The vineyards in Canton Ticino cover about 2500 acres in the Sotto Ceneri and Sopra Ceneri areas; from Mendrisio and Lake Lugano to Ascona, Locarno, and Bellinzona; around Lake Maggiore to Biasca; and in the Levantina and Blenio valleys. Merlot is the leading wine here, first brought to the area in 1905 and developed into a top-ranking product in recent years. The vocation for this Bordeaux grape is so strong here that it is also made into white and spumante wines. In typically Swiss fashion, the Ticinowine Association has drawn on the "Ticino Chessboard" a map of the 43 producers, 69 restaurants and 5 wine shops involved in the project; wines and facilities are arranged in hierarchical order like chess pieces ranging from the "King" to "Pawns" according to the products and services on offer. This is backed up by the traditional tour of *grotti* – rustic buildings set up in cool locations for seasoning cheeses and treated meats, but also used as wine bars in summertime – the ideal place where food and wine meet most spontaneously. No wonder, the local specialty is salmi of beef cooked in wine.

THE COLLI BERGAMASCHI

The production of DOC wines in Valcalepio, a graceful valley stretching down towards Lake Iseo, is the pride of grape-growers.

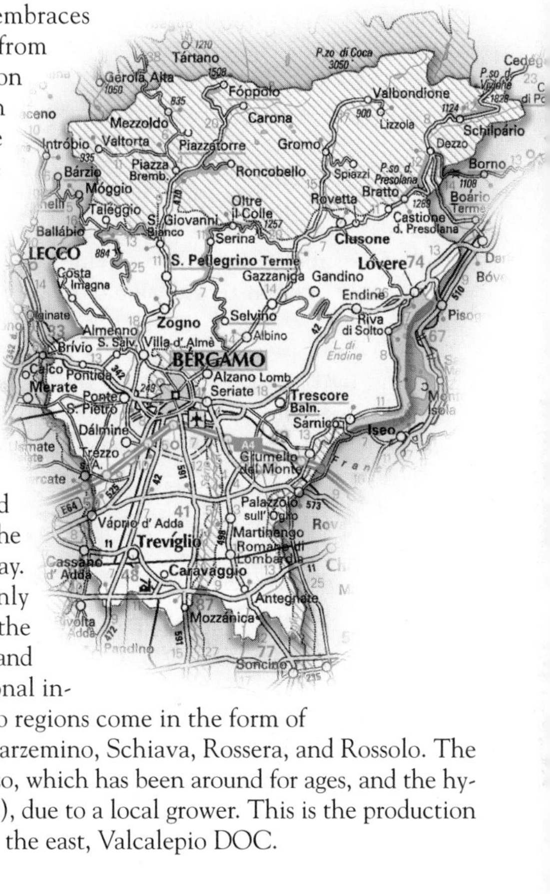

The Bergamo vine growing area embraces a semicircle of foothills stretching from Almenno to Grumello and Sarnico on Lake Iseo. Valcalepio is the main wine-making area, situated along the right bank of the River Oglio, to the east of Bergamo, but other vineyards can be found in Val Cavallina, at the entrance to Val Brembana and Val Seriana, and in part of Val San Martino.

The Bergamo hills, where vineyards grow at heights between 1000 and 1600 feet, may be divided into two pedological areas: from Bergamo to Lake Iseo, to the east, the soil is made up of limestone and clay; and from Bergamo to the River Adda, to the west, it is rich in silica, schist, and clay. Most of the vines are imported, mainly Merlot and Cabernet Sauvignon for the reds and Pinot Bianco, Pinot Grigio, and Chardonnay for the whites. Traditional influences from the Brescia and Trento regions come in the form of red-berried grapes like Groppello, Marzemino, Schiava, Rossera, and Rossolo. The local specialties are Moscato di Scanzo, which has been around for ages, and the hybrid Terzi (Barbera x Cabernet Franc), due to a local grower. This is the production area of Bergamasca IGT and, over in the east, Valcalepio DOC.

The Valcalepio Wine and Gastronomy Route

The tour focuses on Bergamo, whose upper part is a real gem, rich of art treasures and culture with distinctly Venetian traits, and surrounded by a nature reserve. Fine quality food and wine provides a foretaste of what is on offer in the Bergamo valleys: celebrated cheeses, meats, and game are inevitably served with polenta.

Wineries *pp. 370-379*
Carobbio degli Angeli, Cenate Sotto, Foresto Sparso, Gandosso, Grumello del Monte, Scanzorosciate, Sorisole, Torre de' Roveri, Trescore Balneario.

■ **BERGAMO**. Not big at all, though it's one of Italy's great art centers. The most picturesque part of the town is Bergamo Alta, wedged between the medieval (Palazzo della Ragione, S. Maria Maggiore, the Baptistery) and Renaissance (Colleoni

Chapel) masterpieces of Piazza Vecchia and Piazza del Duomo. Not far away is the museum devoted to Gaetano Donizetti, the famous musician from Bergamo. Major works of Venetian and Lombard painting are on display just outside town (S. Agostino), in the Carrara Academy Art Gallery. Take the cable railway up Colle S. Vigilio to get a spectacular view over the entire town.

Just to the east of Bergamo, up in the hills strewn with historical villas, Scanzorosciate has a noteworthy old rustic center and the even more remarkable Moscato Passito di Scanzo, whose vine was probably brought to Valcalepio by Roman settlers.

■ **TRESCORE BALNEARIO.** In Trescore Balneario, situated at the opening of Val Cavallina, you can admire the baroque Villa Terzi, with its beautiful park, and rare frescoes by Lotto in the 14th-century church of S. Barbara.

A trip into the valley takes you past vineyards to Entratico's medieval buildings and to Bianzano Castle, dominating Lake Endine.

■ **GRUMELLO DEL MONTE.** This medieval village, overlooked by the manor house first owned by Colleoni and then by the Gonzaga family, is the historical capital of wine-making in Valcalepio. The vineyards cover a picturesque semicircle of hills.

■ **SARNICO.** The village is set out in a semicircle around the church of S. Paolo; the art noveau style Villa Faccanoni, designed by G. Sommaruga in 1912, overlooks the banks of Lake Iseo, otherwise known as "Sebino".

THE COLLINA MILANESE

Lodi's wineries produce a character red wine from Barbera, Croatina, and Uva Rara as well as fresh and light white wines from Verdea and Malvasia grapes.

This little wine district is peculiar in two ways. Firstly, in geographical terms, because set on an Apennine-like hill right in the middle of a plain used for forage growing and dairy production. Secondly, from an administration viewpoint, since the municipality of San Colombano al Lambro, the hub of wine production, is a Milanese enclave right in the heart of the new province of Lodi. Hence the historical name Collina Milanese (Milanese hill), also used for regulative reasons when referring to the DOC and IGT certifications of its wines.

The range of wines is clearly influenced by the nearby vineyards of the Pavia area, as shown by the tern made up of Barbera, Croatina, and Uva Rara, which form the basis of a fine red wine. The white wines interestingly include Verdea, an old Lombard wine also known as Uva d'Oro, used for producing a fresh and fruity wine. More recently a number of international vine varieties have been introduced (Riesling, Pinot Bianco and Nero, Chardonnay), which are bearing excellent fruits.

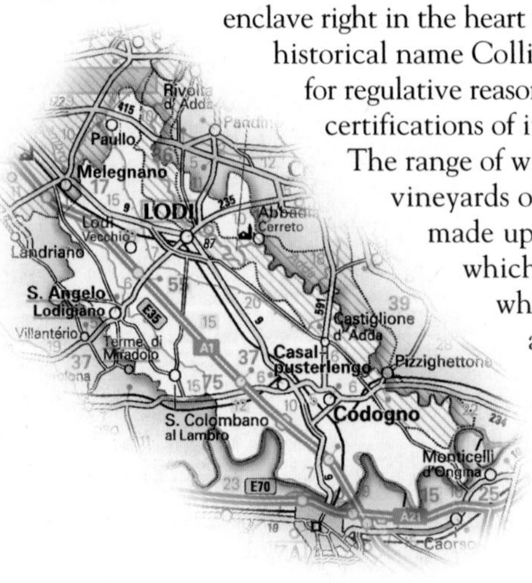

THE SAN COLOMBANO WINE AND LODI GASTRONOMY ROUTE

Tourists set off from Milan, stop off at the Cistercian abbey of Chiaravalle and then make their visit to Lodi, a town with numerous cultural and culinary resources, renowned for its cheeses and local cuisine. The fairly small-sized wine growing district (about 35 miles) can be comfortably covered in a day.

■ **LODI.** Founded anew in 1158 by Frederick Barbarossa on the right bank of the River Adda, after *Laus Pompeia* (Lodi Vecchio) had been repeatedly destroyed, Lodi embraces a vast area of farmland and offers a delicious cuisine. History and art are tied in with its remarkable monuments – the medieval Duomo and Broletto, the Renaissance sanctuary of Incoronata displaying magnificent paintings by Bergognone – listed among Lombardy's finest architectural achievements.

Wineries *pp. 370-379*
San Colombano al Lambro

Leaving Lodi, the route heads off into the luscious countryside of the Lower Po Valley, passing Sant'Angelo Lodigiano, with its renovated Visconti castle (housing the Lombard Museum of Agricultural History and the Museum of Bread), and Miradolo Terme.

■ **SAN COLOMBANO AL LAMBRO.** A river port back in Roman times, this town takes its name and vineyards from the Irish monk who stopped here in the 6th century. The small medieval village still preserves some old towers and remains of the castle walls. The castle courtyard is the home of a wine shop stocked with local DOC wines; the restaurants serve delicious *raspadura* – Grana Padano cheese expertly sliced into flakes which literally melts in the mouth – with the accompaniment of either red or white wine. Looking down from the hill stretching above the town, you can gaze across the plains strewn with canals as far as the Alpine ridge and the first spurs of the Apennines.

San Colombano, the castle courtyard

THE MANTUA REGION

The province of Mantua is set between two regional boundaries: its Lambrusco testifies to its links with Emilia, while other wines mark the passage from Brescia to Verona.

Mantua borders on both the Veneto and Emilia-Romagna regions, a peculiarity which has a fundamental influence on its vineyards. The northern part of the province, wedged between Brescia and Verona, encompasses the lower edge of the morainic amphitheater of Lake Garda, where typical local wines are produced with a distinct preference for Veneto grapes. The wines are classified specifically as Garda Colline Mantovane DOC and generically as Garda DOC, plus those of the Alto Mincio IGT area.
The vineyards in the southern part of the province are split in two areas: to the west, Viadanese Sabbionetano, that is the lands contained between the Oglio and Po rivers, where the first flows into the second bordering the province of Parma; and the Oltrepò Mantovano district to the east, right next door to Modena. The entire area produces Lambrusco Mantovano DOC, the most popular local wine; Sabbioneta and Quistello IGTs provide some added variety.

From Lake Garda to Viadanese and the Oltrepò Region

This circular route has Mantua as starting point and passes through sections of the Po Valley of striking beauty and unexpected wine-growing resources: Lambrusco Mantovano DOC is produced in the two areas known as Viadanese and Oltrepò Mantovano. The area's culinary attractions are all typical dishes of the Lower Po Valley region, enriched by the delicious aroma of white truffles.

MANTUA WINE AND GASTRONOMY ROUTE

There are three basic itineraries for ex-

Landscape of Garda Colli Mantovani

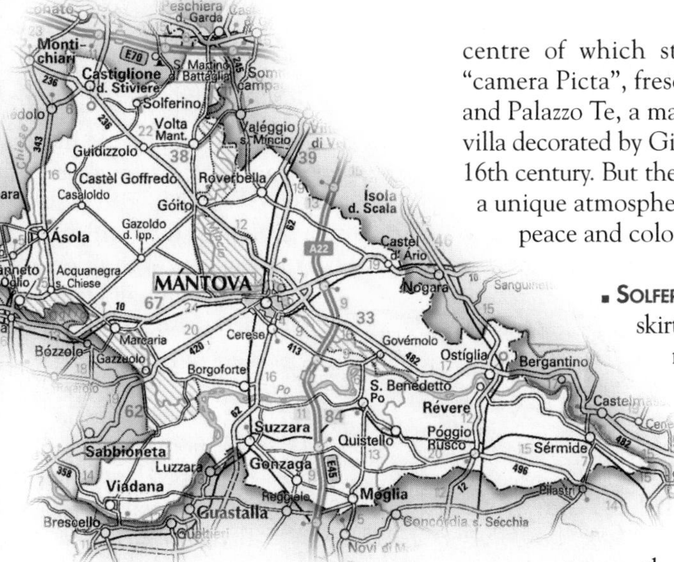

ploring the Mantua wine-growing districts. The first, to the north of Mantua, embraces the lands of Garda Mantovano and sets off from the picturesque river setting of Ponti sul Mincio, near the lake, and heads on to Mantua along the river; the second itinerary, in the Viadanese-Sabbionetano region, stretches from Mantua to Viadana; while the third stretches through the Oltrepò Mantovano from Mantua to San Benedetto Po, Quistello and the River Po along the River Secchia valley.

Wineries *pp. pp. 370-379*
Monzambano.

■ **MANTUA**. An illustrious town for history (as the old capital of the state ruled for centuries by the Gonzaga family), art, cuisine and even geographical setting, amongst the picturesque Mincio lakes. The main attractions on the city tour are the church of S. Andrea, designed by Leon Battista Alberti, a fine example of Italian Renaissance architecture; Palazzo Ducale, a town within the town divided into buildings, churches, inner squares, gardens and porticoes, at the centre of which stands the dazzling "camera Picta", frescoed by Mantegna; and Palazzo Te, a magnificent suburban villa decorated by Giulio Romano in the 16th century. But the entire town exudes a unique atmosphere which combines peace and color.

■ **SOLFERINO**. Set on the outskirts of the magnificent morainic amphitheater of Lake Garda, the town's Risorgimento Museum provides a testimony of the battles fought between the Piedmont armies and the Austrians here and at nearby San Martino in June 1859. Via Castellaro Lagusello – castle and walled town center with a picturesque pond – and Monzambano, you soon come to the River Mincio and to Goito, a checker-shaped village where other battles were fought during the Italian Risorgimento (19th century).

■ **SABBIONETA**. This "ideal town", Renaissance jewel perfectly set within the star-shaped enclosure of its walls, lies across the River Oglio, out in the neat farmlands; visitors can enjoy Palazzo Ducale, Teatro Olimpico designed by Scamozzi, and Palazzo del Giardino with its Galleria degli Antichi. Lambrusco is the most popular local wine.

■ **SAN BENEDETTO PO**. This Oltrepò Mantovano town developed around the abbey of Polirone, whose lands were effectively reclaimed as early as the Middle Ages. The remarkable basilica of S. Benedetto still survives, rebuilt by Giulio Romano between 1539 and 1547. Not so far away, along the banks of the Secchia river, the town of Quistello lies in the heart of a magnificent rural and fluvial setting of high-water beds, poplar groves and canals.

Specialties in Lombardy

LOMBARDY IS A TAPESTRY of sceneries and flavors, unrivalled anywhere else in Italy: a central region in the geography and history of northern Italy, whose heart and soul lies in Milan but can boast a whole range of attractions right across all ten surrounding provinces. In a bird's eye view, the region stretches from the lands of the Po Valley up to the hills around the lakes and into the Alps, but our food trip is bound to begin in Milan, where tradition still holds sway at chosen places despite all the new trends.

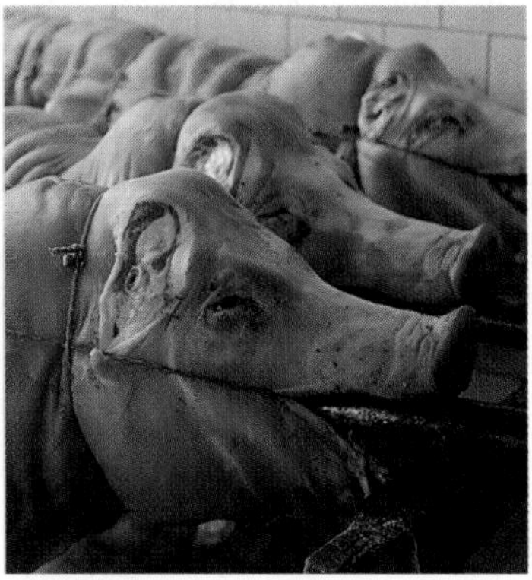

WHEN EATING IN MILAN, you cannot help but start with cold sliced meats – salami from Brianza and Varzi, *bresaola* from Valtellina and cured ham – matched by a variety of wines, from Chiaretto del Garda or fizzy Lambrusco Mantovano to full-bodied reds. This is inevitably followed by a *risotto alla Milanese*, a delicious rice dish (yellow-colored due to the saffron it contains) which probably has Spanish origins, to be accompanied by a glass of Franciacorta DOCG or of Oltrepò Pavese Pinot Grigio. Risotto is a popular dish outside Milan as well, made in a wide range of recipes: garnished with savoy cabbage, pumpkin, sausage, fish, and even frogs. There is also abundance of tasty stuffed pasta like *casonzei* from Bergamo or pumpkin tortelli from Mantua. Meat is next on the menu: *cotoletta alla milanese*, a peculiar breaded veal chop fried in sizzling butter, a popular dish with the wealthy back in the days of the Hapsburg (Terre di Franciacorta Rosso); *ossobuco*, marrowbone in a creamy sauce given extra flavor by a dash of lemon, often served on a bed of yellow rice (Oltrepò Pavese Barbera): *cassoeula*, a country dish popular in winter with pork stewed with savoy cabbage and served with polenta, another ever-present recipe in traditional Lombard cuisine (Oltrepò Pavese Rosso). That leaves the fish dishes from up in the lakes area, requiring white wines for fried or grilled fish and red ones for stewed dishes.

CHEESES, A REAL PRIDE of the region, are another "must" in traditional local cuisine. First and foremost, lowland specialties like Grana Padano and blue-veined Gorgonzola (to be tasted with a passito wine like Oltrepò Pavese Moscato or the rare Moscato di Scanzo); the cuisine offers also a rich variety of cheeses from the Alpine pastures, such as Taleggio and Furmai de mut in the Bergamo area, Bitto and Casera in Valtellina. They are used in various combinations in some of the best-known dishes from the Lombardy mountains, such as *pizzoccheri* (Valtellina Superiore DOCG) and *polenta taragna*.

Trentino-Alto Adige

Wine and Tradition

Touring the valley of the Adige river, from the vineyards of Trentino to those of Alto Adige, means discovering a centuries-old tradition of high quality wine-making, reflected in the very varied DOC wines of today.

The Adige valley was already renowned for its wines in Roman times, when its vineyards, as a result of the different climatic conditions compared to those of today, were far more extensive and at notably higher altitudes. In the Middle Ages, production of wines became the monopoly of important monastic centers of Bavaria and of Swabia, which owned lands south of the Brenner Pass where they were the only ones to grow Schiava grapes up to the

Above, a view of Val di Fiemme; left, Trentino's pergolas (top) and a cellar in Termeno (bottom)

Napoleonic era. The Istituto Agrario of San Michele all'Adige was then founded in 1874 and has become a mainstay in the oenology of the zone in recent years, when mountain wine-growing has became increasingly important. Specialized wine production, based on over 22,000 acres of vineyards in the province of Trento and 9400 acres in the province of Bolzano, is still a fundamental force in the local economy. High costs create certain difficulties for the sector, but favorable conditions for the vine allow to focus energies on the search for maximum quality, with a gamut whose ampleness is rarely matched elsewhere. Anyway, wine quality and natural beauties call for an increasingly high number of tourists specifically interested in wine and gastronomy, and this is a major contribution to the local tourism industry as a whole.

THE GRAND VINEYARD OF SCHIAVA

The overall ampelographic picture is very varied: the region's ancient varieties have been joined more or less recently by many others from beyond the Alps – from France but also from Germany, which is typical of this region. Monoculture tends to dominate in Alto Adige, where vine-growing has become a more specialized activity, whereas the more tradition-oriented growers of Trentino frequently cultivate mixed varieties. The vineyard is dominated by typical single and double pergolas. Schiava (either Grossa or Gentile) is the dominant grape, accounting for 37.2% of the regional total, with the many imported varieties trailing at a considerable distance. Among the other major native varieties are Teroldego, almost a monopoly of the Piana Rotaliana between Mezzolombardo and Mezzocorona, which gives Trentino's best known wine; Marzemino, whose birthplace is often given as Isera and which has found an almost perfect habitat in Vallagarina; and Nosiola, the typical grape of the Sarca valley which gives, with the proper care and attention, a renowned Vino Santo.

RECORD QUALITY AND VARIETY

The fourth region in Italy in terms of production of quality wine, but the first in terms of the percentage (70%) of DOC wines compared to the overall regional total, Trentino-Alto Adige shares its largest DOC area, Valdadige, with neighboring Veneto and divides its production into two provincial denominations, Alto Adige and Trentino (ninth and tenth respectively in the national ranking). "Alto Adige" groups together the entire production of the province of Bolzano (over 30 different wines) and gives special recognition to such high level sub-zones as Santa Maddalena and Collina di Merano. The only exception is the Lago di Caldaro DOC, giving independent status to a particularly relevant production. The Trentino DOC follows the same pattern, with the Casteller, Teroldego Rotaliano, and Trento sub-zones – the latter relates to champenoise-method spumante wines. From the entrepreneurial point of view, both provinces are characterized by wineries associations, whose collective productions reach high quality levels rarely to be found elsewhere.

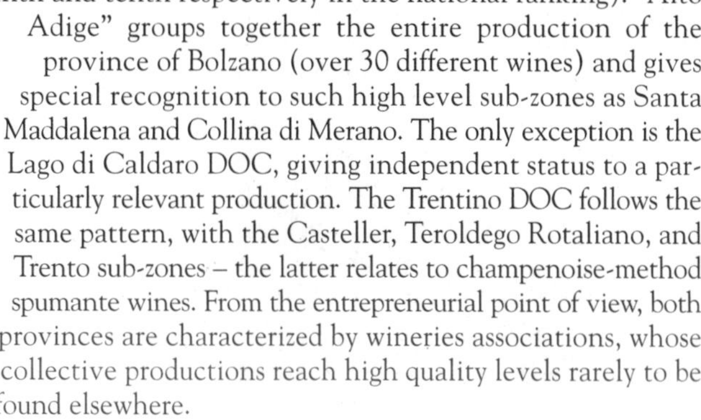

The Great Wines of Trentino-Alto Adige

Trentino Wines

Chardonnay

This wine is produced from the most common grape in the region, with a marked prevalence in the Trento province, where, with Pinot Grigio, Pinot Bianco, Pinot Nero, and Meunier, it is the basis for excellent spumante production. Vinified pure, it has unmistakable characteristics: outstanding apple aroma, which evolves into notes of Artemisia and toasted hazelnut; fine, elegant, and velvety taste.

Müller Thurgau

This white wine is named from the oenologist and Swiss canton responsible for the birth of a hybrid between Riesling Renano and a variety recently identified as Chasselas. In Trentino this new variety grows best in Val di Cembra, but also fares in the Sarca valley. The wine is pale yellow in color, it has a fruity aroma with sage hints, and it is dry and slightly tart in taste.

Teroldego

Notwithstanding its probable Verona origin, this red wine is the almost exclusive pride of the Piana Rotaliana, a plain area north of Trento. It is bright ruby red, vinous in aroma with a special note of violet, dry and slightly tannic taste. It ages well but can also be drunk as a new wine.

Marzemino

This comes from a grape that may have originated in Carinthia (Austria) and that is widespread in northeastern Italy since ancient times. In Trentino it has an excellent production zone in Vallagarina (Isera, Volano). The wine is deep ruby red, has a fruity aroma, characteristic taste (with a note of violet) and good alcohol content.

Vino Santo Trentino

This is a passito wine as famous as it is rare. It comes from Nosiola grapes, a presumably autochthonous variety, now grown mainly in the valley of the Sarca river. The wine is usually straw yellow in color, with greenish highlights, a delicately fruity aroma, and dry, fresh taste with a characteristic note of hazelnut. When the grapes are used dried, the color turns amber and the aromatic notes are enhanced on a sweet background.

Moscato Giallo

This is the least known of the white-berry grape Moscato wines. It is found in northeastern Italy thanks to the Venetians, who probably imported it from Greece. In Trentino it is noteworthy in the valley of the Sarca river. In Alto Adige it is known as Goldenmuskateller.

Alto Adige Wines

Lago di Caldaro, Santa Maddalena, Meranese di Collina

The most famous Alto Adige reds come from Schiava grapes. The vine probably came to Italy from Slavonia, today's Croatia, brought by the Lombards. The wine is generally pale ruby red, with considerable aroma and characteristic taste (clear note of bitter almond). Some productions, such as Santa Maddalena, are more concentrated.

Lagrein

This wine is produced in both Trento and Bolzano provinces, although the oldest documents refer to Alto Adige. As to its origin, recent investigations have confirmed the Greek ancestry suggested by the name Lagara, an ancient Ionic colony.

The wine is a vibrant but not deep red in color, with pleasant aroma and a dry, full-bodied taste.

Traminer Aromatico

Also called Gewürztraminer, it comes from a grape variety of Central European origins (perhaps from the Rhine area), but it is undeniable that in Termeno/Tramin it has given unique results.

This very alcoholic wine has more or less vibrant color, an intense aroma of rose, and velvety, pleasantly bitterish taste. The grapes lend themselves to late harvesting.

Sylvaner Verde

The vine originated in Austria, in Styria to be exact, and is grown primarily in the Isarco valley. The wine is straw yellow, tending to greenish, with characteristic aroma, velvety, dry and bitterish taste. A good combination of alcohol and acidity makes it suitable to ageing.

Moscato Rosa

From Greece to Dalmatia and then to the Tyrol: this is probably how the vine got to the region. More than to the color of the grapes, the name refers to the wine's deep flowery aroma. The local appellation is Rosenmuskateller.

TRENTINO-ALTO ADIGE'S DOC ZONES

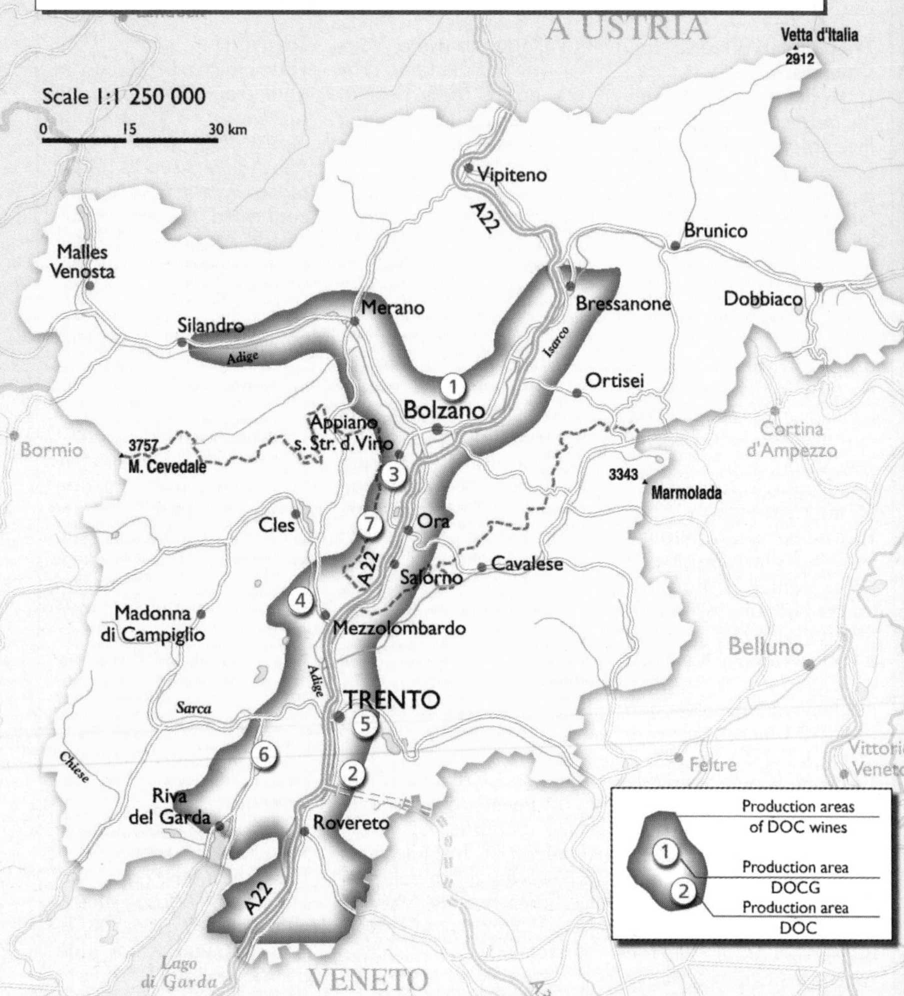

❶ DOC Alto Adige or Südtirol
13 white, 6 rosé, and 10 red wines in the geographical sub-appellations DOC Alto Adige Colli di Bolzano, DOC Alto Adige Meranese di Collina, DOC Alto Adige Santa Maddalena, DOC Alto Adige Terlano, DOC Alto Adige Valle Isarco, DOC Alto Adige Valle Venosta

❷ DOC Casteller

❸ DOC Lago di Caldaro or Kalterersee

❹ DOC Teroldego Rotaliano

❺ DOC Trentino *14 white, 2 rosé, and 10 red wines*

❻ DOC Trento *Bianco*

❼ DOC Valdadige or Etschtaler *Bianco, Chardonnay, Pinot Bianco, Pinot Grigio ▪ Rosato ▪ Rosso, Schiava*

IGT - Typical Geographic Indication

Vigneti delle Dolomiti (Trento - Bolzano - Belluno); Delle Venezie (Trento - Belluno - Pordenone - Rovigo – Treviso - Venice - Verona - Vicenza - Pordenone - Udine - Gorizia - Trieste); Vallagarina (Trento - Verona); Mitterberg tra Cauria e Tel (Mitterberg Zwischen Gfrill und Toll, Mitterberg) (Bolzano)

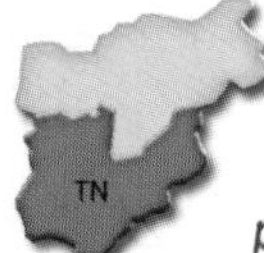

THE TRENTINO VINEYARDS

An extraordinarily varied wine-growing scene, rising from the Veneto plain and Lake Garda: the star of the cellars is famed Marzemino.

The core of the Trentino wine district is in the Adige valley, from the border with Veneto to the border with Alto Adige, the latter marked by the Salorno narrows. Two distinct production areas branch off toward Valsugana and Val di Cembra, while a zone apart is the Sarca valley above Lake Garda. Local vineyards are like a mosaic of grape varieties which combine traditional stocks, such as Marzemino and Teroldego, with imported ones – Pinots and Cabernets were taken to the region in the late 19th century, Chardonnay was introduced in the 1960s by the Istituto Agrario of San Michele all'Adige to rejuvenate the range of whites. From the normative standpoint, Trento province production is protected mostly by broad territorial denominations.

Vallagarina and the Trento Hills

The southern portion of the Adige valley, from the Rivoli lock in the Verona province to the Calliano narrows, just north of Rovereto, is called Vallagarina. This Pre-alpine land has the great oenological merit of having given birth, in Isera it would seem, to Marzemino, a red character-wine with a delicate aroma of sweet violet, praised by Mozart. Alongside it (and also in the rest of the Adige valley) grow vines of Pinot Grigio, Lagrein, Cabernet Franc and Sauvignon,

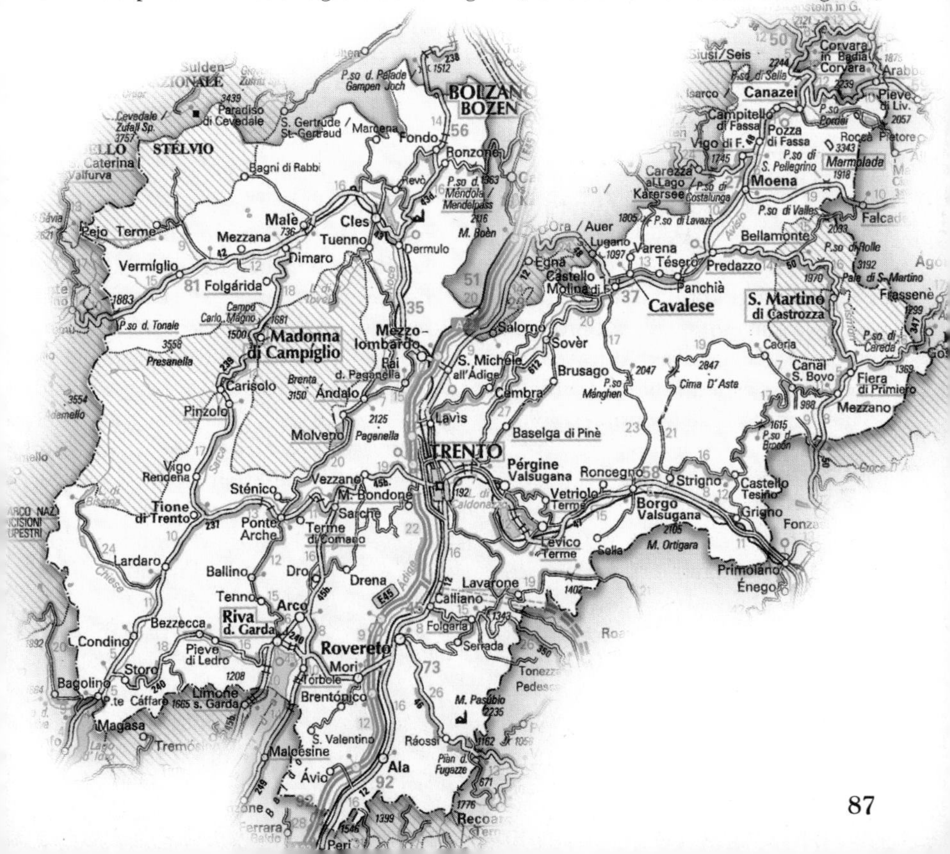

Vineyards in San Michele all'Adige's environs

and Merlot, which make a substantial contribution to the fame of the big Trentino reds.

On the hills surrounding the provincial capital is instead produced what since the 17th century has been known as the "Trento wine" par excellence. Today the production zone extends to a broader section of the Adige valley, from Avio to Lavis, and even to a part of the lands washed by the Sarca river in the area of Lake Toblino and further south around Arco. Casteller vineyards alternate on the valley bottoms with those of the Trentino DOC, more traditional in composition: Schiava grapes prevail, but protagonists are also Merlot and jagged-leaved Lambrusco (here called Enantio) which give wine unmistakable body and color.

THE VALLAGARINA WINE AND GASTRONOMY ROUTE

This route goes up the Adige valley from the Verona plain to Trento, departure-point for further itineraries. It criss-crosses an intensely cultivated vineyard area – a splendid sea of green from spring to harvest time –, taking visitors to castles and wineries; the itinerary can also be completed by bicycle, on protected lanes, taking advantage of train service when needed (Information office: APT Rovereto e Vallagarina, Corso Rosmini 14, Rovereto).

▪ **AVIO**. The town, immersed in vineyards, is dominated by a very beautiful castle built in 1053 and until recently the property of the most important local noble family (it now belongs to FAI - Italian Environment Fund). The castle contains frescoes on the themes of war and love, painted by an unknown Verona master of international Gothic.

▪ **ROVERETO**. A city of fine architecture (some with Venetian accents) and very noteworthy cultural traditions that have won it the title of "Trentino Athens". Above the Leno stream rises the castle housing Italy's largest and most interesting World War I museum. Not far from it is the

Galleria Depero, devoted to the many-talented Futurist artist. The recent opening of the MART (Trento and Rovereto Museum of Modern and Contemporary Art) – a huge, ultra-modern structure designed by Italian-Swiss architect Mario Botta – has endowed the city with an art and cultural venue of extraordinary importance, especially for the study of Futurism.

■ **ISERA.** The ruins of a Roman villa, with fragments of mosaics and frescoes, testify to the ancient origins of this town, known as the cradle of Marzemino: such an important role is underlined by the presence of the Casa del Vino della Vallagarina, where local products can be tasted and bought.

■ **VILLA LAGARINA.** This farming town of ancient origins boasts the striking monumental church of the Assunta, with remarkable French-flavored stuccowork in its baroque 17th-century interior. Higher up, among the vineyards, you can see the Noarna castle, with interesting frescoes and annexed farming estate.

Trento's Buonconsiglio Castle: the Cycle of the Months (detail)

■ **TRENTO.** The provincial capital, full of art and history, lying among the mountains enclosing the Adige valley, is hard to describe in just a few words. Bathed by the river, it is located where the various Trentino valleys converge and it still has the severe appearance and fine architecture of the ancient times of Prince-Bishops' rule. The tour starts from Piazza del Duomo – with its lovely Romanesque-Gothic cathedral surmounted by a ponderous bell tower – and, going up elegant Belenzani and Manci streets, whose buildings have frescoed façades, it culminates in the Buonconsiglio Castle and frescoed Aquila Tower, a masterpiece of international Gothic. The historic Trautmannsdorf Palace is the home of the Istituto dei Vini Trentini (Trentino Wine Institute).

The Sorni Hills and Val di Cembra

Inside the Trentino DOC area, the slopes of Mount Corona between Giovo, Lavis, and San Michele all'Adige form the Sorni geographical sub-zone, where Schiava and Nosiola grapes are equally protagonists on opposite hill sides. Other grapes grown here are Sylvaner and Müller Thurgau, whose cradle is in neighboring Val di Cembra. Worth separate mention are the Pinots, cultivated between Lavis and San Michele all'Adige: together with Chardonnay, and nowadays Pinot Nero Meunier, too, they are the basis for first-rate spumante production.

VAL DI CEMBRA

■ **LAVIS.** The name is a contraction of "Villa d'Avisio": Avisio is the name of the stream that crosses the area but it is also and foremost the ancient denomination of the local vineyards. Thus, it is

VINO SANTO AND GRAPPA IN THE VALLEY OF THE LAKES

The Valley of the Lakes, overlooking the Trentino Upper Garda, is extraordinary for its scenery and oenological vocation. As it has already been said, a special role in the vineyard is played by Nosiola grapes, which, according to ancient tradition, are used to make Vino Santo. The only six producers to keep this tradition alive – Toblino, Gino Pedrotti, Marco and Stefano Pisoni, Francesco Poli, Giovanni Poli, Pravis di Lasino – are grouped in the Vignaioli Vino Santo Trentino DOC association in order to safeguard a product as rare as it is imitated.
Another pride of the Valley of the Lakes is grappa, which here has its most authoritative distillery in the name of Tullio Zadra's, master in stills fabrication, who in the 1950s perfected a discontinuous double-boiler system which is still deemed as the best.

not surprising that this town at the mouth of Val di Cembra, realm of Müller Thurgau, occupies an important place in Trentino oenology. Around Pressano you can find some of the best vineyards in Trentino.

■ **CEMBRA.** You follow the Avisio upstream for a visit to the main center in the Müller Thurgau valley, which has a narrow bottom but opens up to vineyards and woods higher up. Worth a visit in Cembra are the churches of S. Maria Assunta (16th century) and of S. Pietro (older than the former one). Attractions in the environs are picturesque Lago Santo and the Segonzano Pyramids, unusual earthen pinnacles often topped by boulders which are the symbols of the valley.

■ **SAN MICHELE ALL'ADIGE.** A wine town on the left bank of the Adige, on the edge of the Piana Rotaliana where the Val di Non road branches off. This is the site of an ancient settlement, from 1145 home to an Augustinian monastery that was closed in 1810. It conserves some historical buildings, but the greatest draw is the Trentino Folk Museum, located in the former monastery, which also houses the already mentioned Istituto Agrario with wine estate, one of Italian oenology "academies" (and also producer and vendor of excellent wines, such as Castel San Michele and Rebo, along with its own grappas and fruit and grape brandies).

The Piana Rotaliana

"Europe's most beautiful grape garden": such is the description given for the Piana Rotaliana, and in actual fact the great vineyard that stretches from Mezzolombardo to Mezzocorona, the so-called Piana Rotaliana (under the benevolent eye of San Michele all'Adige) is one of the loveliest wine environments in the region, if not in all Italy. Part of the charm lies in its being the birthplace to Teroldego, a robust red wine with a delicate raspberry aroma, traditional emblem of local production.

IN THE HOMELAND OF TEROLDEGO

■ **MEZZOCORONA.** A place of primary interest because of the historical Cantine Mezzocorona, founded in 1904. From the parent company came the Cantina Rotari, one of Europe's most important producers of champenoise-method spumante; and from it comes renowned Talento Trento Rotari DOC.

Wineries *pp. 379-389*
Ala, Aldeno, Avio, Calavino, Calliano, Cermes, Civezzano, Faedo, Isera, Lasino, Lavis, Mezzocorona, Mezzolombardo, Nogaredo, Nomi, Roverè della Luna, Rovereto, San Michele all'Adige, Trento, Vezzano, Volano.

▪ **MEZZOLOMBARDO**. From a historical point of view, this is the most important center in the Piana Rotaliana and in the immense vineyard amidst the mountains already known to the Romans for its Teroldego – the area boasts today another six Trentino DOC wines. The little town sits on the border with Tyrol established in 1271, whence the appellation "Lombard", meaning "Italian" (Mezzocorona, across the border, was originally called "Mezzotedesco", since "tedesco" in Italian means German).

▪ **ROVERÈ DELLA LUNA**. In view of the Salorno narrows, natural border with Alto Adige, you come across this wine town overlooking the right bank of the Adige river, lying under a rocky ledge at the opening to Valle dei Molini.

The Valley of the Lakes

The valley of the Sarca river is renowned for the cultivation of autochthonous Nosiola, one of the most typical and widespread of Trentino vines, whose wine is characterized by delicate fruit and hazelnut hints. A portion of these grapes – selected at harvest time from the bunches with fewer grapes that are better exposed to the sun – are dried for a long time on racks and pressed during the week before Easter: after three years of ageing Trentino Vino Santo is ready. Broad in aroma and extraordinarily mellow in taste, it has been called the flower of Trentino's oenology. The production of spumante, mostly made from Chardonnay grapes, is also typical to the area.

AMIDST THE AROMAS OF NOSIOLA

A truly unique route links the Adige valley to Lake Garda, from Trento to Arco, through landscapes dotted with lakes and castles. Interest in wine goes hand in hand with that for seasonal produce, from Dro plums to Drena chestnuts, also used as ingredients for special preparations.

▪ **CALAVINO**. The town's noteworthy church of S. Maria Assunta (with frescoes) and castle (just out of town) were both commissioned in the 15th century by Trentino nobles. The municipality also includes the lovely Lake Toblino, with a castle on one shore and the Maso Torresella, today prestigious headquarters of the Ca' Vit wine firm, on the other, amidst avant-garde vineyards.

▪ **DRENA**. The main attraction is the castle, an ancient fortification reduced to ruins by the French in the early 18th century; from the donjon there is a splendid view of the valley and peculiar *marocche* (boulder heaps) along the way down to Dro and Arco.

▪ **ARCO**. A fascinating town on the Sarca plain behind Lake Garda, it has always been favored by a temperate climate (olive trees, oleanders, and even palms are proofs of that) and in the past was the haunt of Hapsburg nobles in search of Mediterranean elegance. The scenic castle on the cliff was immortalized by Dürer in one of his watercolors. A few miles ahead, on the lake shore, Riva del Garda is another exclusive resort of great atmosphere.

Drena, in the Valley of the Lakes

THE ALTO ADIGE VINEYARDS

A spectacular viticultural scene accompanies the Adige valley, from the Salorno narrows to Silandro, and the Isarco valley up to Bressanone.

In Alto Adige vines are planted on hilly terrain and the first band of valley slopes, from the Salorno narrows up to Merano, on the sunny side of the Val Venosta up to Silandro and between Bolzano and Bressanone on the Isarco banks. Not many acres are covered with vineyards, but it is significant that almost all of them are registered DOC. Following ancient custom, most of the production is exported to Switzerland, Germany, and Austria. As a whole, the autonomous Bolzano province is the site of the Alto Adige DOC production which incorporates several older DOCs, now considered as varietal or geographic sub-denomination wines. Production is broad-ranging and traditionally characterized by the use of Schiava red grapes, which have been prominent in Alto Adige oenology since the Middle Ages. Latest-generation wines are Pinot Nero and Cabernet, more and more often aged in barriques. This is also the case with the whites, with Pinot keeping tradition high and Chardonnay, aided by careful cellarwork, expressing trendier tastes. From the normative standpoint there are a DOC (Alto Adige) and some provincial IGTs (Mitterberg tra Cauria e Tel, Vigneti delle Dolomiti), along with other DOCs (Caldaro, Terlano) for local wines of major importance.

The Oltradige and the Caldaro Lake

Passing through the Salorno narrows, you come to a wine district stretching through the Adige valley to beyond Bolzano. The premier wine here is Lago di Caldaro DOC; grown mainly on the left slope of the valley, it gets its name from the small lake that is an indubitable climatic boon to viticulture. On the slopes surrounding it there is a predominance of Schiava grapes, grown with Pinot Nero on steeper stretches and with Lagrein on the few flat areas. Epicenters of the reds made from these grapes are Caldaro/Kaltern, capital of what Bolzano inhabitants simply call Oltradige, and Appiano/Eppan, a little further north. The Classico zone is traversed by a wine route of consolidated fame, thanks to the seven municipalities found along it which have added to their original names "an der Weinstrasse", "sulla Strada del Vino" – "along the Wine Route".

THE SALORNO TO BOLZANO WINE ROUTE

This itinerary follows the traditional Oltradige Wine Route, which winds for 26 miles from Salorno to Bolzano in a sequence of truly exceptional wine-growing landscapes. The welcome is first-rate, starting with the taverns that participate in the rite of the Törgellen, an end-of-harvest celebration protracted until the first snowfall, during which the stars of the table are black bread and speck (smoked Tyrol ham), barley soup, sausages and sauerkraut, and chestnuts.

▪ **MAGRÈ/ MARGREID.** A few miles from Salorno, Magrè surprises visitors with its architecture embellished with arches, balconies and flowered loggias. Unusual assets of the town are the centuries-old vines planted next to the houses to celebrate births and marriages and lovingly cared for from one generation to the next.

■ **TERMENO/TRAMIN**. Home of the highly aromatic Gewürtztraminer (for which an annual international fair is held), this is a town of noble appearance: the high pinnacle of the Gothic parish church contrasts with the soft shapes of the Castellaccio hill, where the church of S. Giacomo in Kastelaz has splendid Romanesque frescoes in its apse. An excursion along the left bank of the Adige river can lead from here, or from Cortaccia, to the vineyards and wineries of Ora/Auer and Egna/Neumarket, with its lovely portico-lined main street.

■ **CALDARO/KALTERN**. We are in the home of the most famous Alto Adige wine, that *vinum de Caldaro* cited as early as 1220. With its beautiful lake, the town welcomes visitors with hotels and ancient residences along its main street. In the center, at the old Di Pauli winery, you can visit the important

Alto Adige vineyards

Alto Adige Wine Museum. Schiava is celebrated with its own festival.

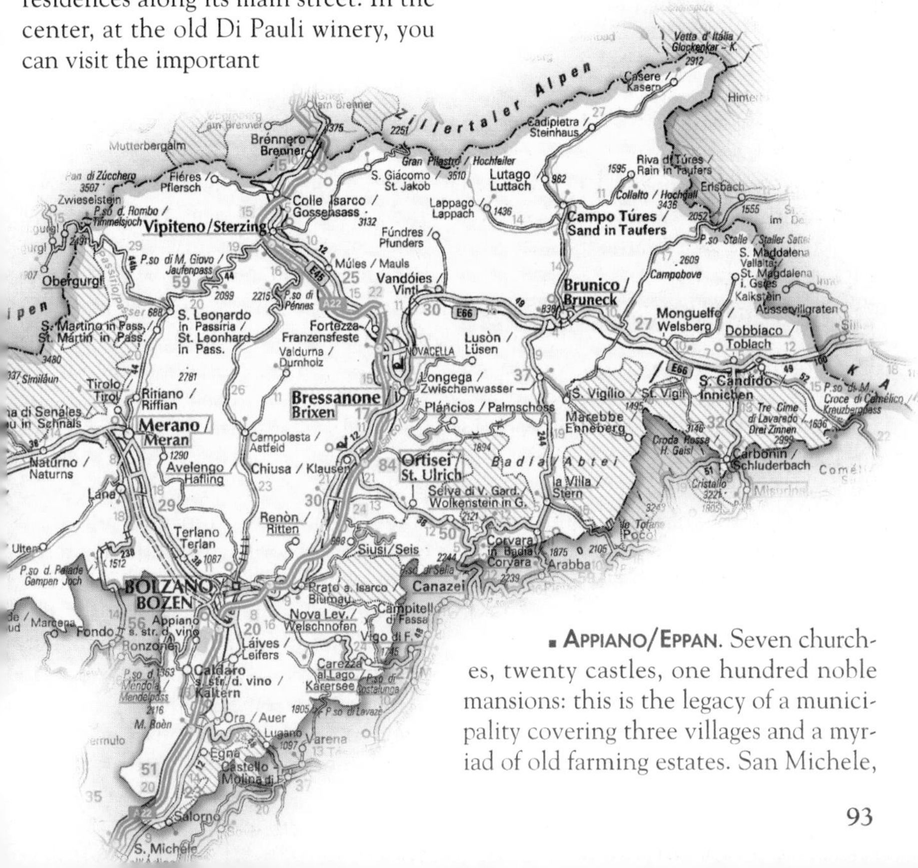

■ **APPIANO/EPPAN**. Seven churches, twenty castles, one hundred noble mansions: this is the legacy of a municipality covering three villages and a myriad of old farming estates. San Michele,

CALDARO, THE WINE TOWN

In itself it is a dream of a place: an Alpine lake with an extraordinarily mild climate, on whose banks prosper not only vines but also fig trees, oleanders, and strawberry trees.
Making it unique in the already wondrous scenery of the Weinstrasse (Wine Route) is a project which, under the logo "wein.kaltern" unites dozens of wine and tourism operators in an offer peerlessly organized in terms of variety and level.
First of all, the wines: the focus of attention is Lago di Caldaro Scelto, or Kalterersee-Auslese if you prefer, made from Schiava grapes selected according to criteria based on strict vineyard zoning and worked with the precise aim of excellence. A significant detail: tastings at consortium wineries and restaurants are always done with the same type of wineglass (from the famous Riedel glassworks in Kufstein) to better highlight the features of the wine. The assortment then broadens to Alto Adige classics, from Gewürztraminer to Goldenmuskateller, up to full-bodied Cabernet Sauvignons. Among the first-class wineries, two big cooperatives – Erste & Neue and Viticoltori Caldaro – are outstanding, and are alongside one another in critics' praise as well as in actual premises.
The tourism offer first concerns the "wine path", the so-called wein.weg: a 8-shaped itinerary with the cross point passing through the town center, running along the lake promenade and then immersing itself in the vineyards. The path is scattered with big slabs of marble bearing the names of historic crus; at intervals there are stone tables with bronze plaques describing the wines or the special features of the place; noteworthy buildings are also marked – especially the farmsteads housing wineries – as well as restaurants, farm holiday sites, and hotels.
The level of information is excellent: visitors can learn about the area from an extraordinary map of the vineyards in the Caldaro Lake basin, from the wein.kaltern.magazin (mailed on request), and from the web site www.wein.kaltern.com, which offers an extensive overview of the project.

the main center, is an obligatory stop for its excellent wineries and the noble 16th- and 17th-century mansions in Oltradige style. Also worth a visit is San Paolo, with its late-Gothic parish church that looks like a city cathedral.

The Bolzano Hills and Terlano

Traveling up the valley you reach Bolzano, truly embraced by vineyards. The wine-producing centers of Bronzolo and Vilpiano, which almost spread as wide as the horizon, are the cardinal points of a zone whose two former DOC productions – Colli di Bolzano and Santa Maddalena – are now geographical sub-zones of the Alto Adige appellation. From the ampelographic viewpoint, the area is characterized by the dominance of Schiava, along with Pinot Nero and Lagrein grapes. Santa Maddalena is one of the greatest and most famous wines in the whole Alto Adige, rich in history, which in the past used to be shipped to Central Europe. The Classico zone, which includes the homonymous town and a few other villages, has a vineyard landscape of rare beauty. Upriver from Bolzano, on the left bank of the Adige, you encounter the pretty town and summer resort that lends its name to the Terlano DOC. In a region of prevalently red wines, here is an oasis of whites. The undisputed star in the vineyard is Pinot Bianco, which here finds one of its finest Italian habitats. Along with it are good amounts of Sauvignon and moderate ones of Chardonnay (excellently acclimatized here), Riesling, with a marked prevalence of the Italico over the Renano variety, Müller Thurgau, and, last, Sylvaner. Production is concentrated in the area between Settequerce and Vilpiano, but also includes other important centers in the Oltradige area.

The Merano Hills and Val Venosta

Merano lies in a sunny basin ringed with hills and covered with vineyards and orchards – the kingdom of Schiava grapes, in its different sub-varieties that are vinified pure to make the renowned Meranese di Collina. The production zone runs precisely from the southern slopes of Mount Murra right to the town, then elongates in two thin branches, one of which descends on the left bank of the Adige river to Tésimo and the other on the right one as far as the outskirts of Gargazzone. In any case, the hub of production is Merano, where in October a grandiose Grape Festival is held, with lots of folklore floats and plenty of libations. Beyond Merano you enter Val Venosta, the upper part of the Adige valley, which is, for a good stretch, oriented east to west and thus well exposed to the sun. This is a green and open valley, with gently rising meadows and fields and forests further up. Vines prosper on the sunny side that runs for about 20 miles from the Merano basin to Silandro.

THE BOLZANO HILLS, THE MERANO AREA, AND VAL VENOSTA

After a wine-tourism stop in Bolzano, you follow the main Alto Adige wine route to Merano, cradle of Schiava grapes and a tourist attraction of refined Central European imprint.

▪ **BOLZANO/BOZEN.** What is striking about this pretty city located where the Isarco and Talvera rivers meet the Adige is the Gothic appearance of the old town, with its picturesque Via dei Portici and Duomo. Its commercial vocation is underlined on the portico-lined main streets, full of shops and department stores, and a magnet for shoppers during the Christmas Flea Market. There are two wine routes, pleasant in any season, starting from the central Piazza Walther.
The first leads to the hills around the city, amidst the vineyards of Santa Maddalena. Going through Piazza delle Erbe you walk along the Lungotalvera promenade that quickly brings you within sight of Castel Mareccio, surrounded by vineyards. The S. Antonio bridge is the departure point for the S. Osvaldo walk leading to Santa Maddalena, a pretty little town set among the wine estates.
The second itinerary, devoted to Lagrein, ideally starts from the two renowned wineries overlooking Piazza Greis. You continue along the Guncina promenade with a magnificent view of the city and various opportunities for wine tasting.

A view of Lake Caldaro

▪ **TERLANO/TERLAN.** A resort and wine center, famed for centuries for its whites and now given a specific sub-denomination, it is also renowned for its asparagi, that between April and May are the protagonists of a food fair. The Gothic parish church with two bell towers holds 15th-century frescos by Hans Stotzinger.

▪ **LANA/LANA.** A town divided into three historical wards, on a plain rich in vineyards and orchards where the Val d'Ultimo and Adige valley converge. It is famed for its apples, to the point of being the site of the Alto Adige Fruit Farming Museum. The Gothic church of S. Maria Assunta has a big altar carved by Johann Schnatterpeck (early 16th century).

▪ **MERANO/MERAN.** A green basin filled with vineyards, orchards, and castles; a ring of mountains; the Gothic Duomo; promenades along the Passirio and fine mansions; thermal baths and a race course; cafés and shops along Via dei Portici; Tyrolean tastes and Austro-Hungarian reminders and atmosphere – all this is fascinating, cosmopolitan Merano, where today as in the past you can enjoy grape-therapy.

▪ **NATURNO/NATURNS.** A stop amidst the vineyards and orchards of Val Venosta for a taste of one of Alto Adige's less known wines. In Naturno the sun shines an average of 315 days a year. The archaic frescos (dated 8th-11th C.) in S. Procolo, are masterworks by unknown Lombard artists.

Valle Isarco and Bressanone

North of Bolzano, following the major tributary of the Adige, you enter the Alto Adige Valle Isarco DOC zone. The vineyard cloaks the steep mountainous slopes from Fiè allo Sciliar to Bressanone, offering scenery of rare beauty in the already extraordinary Alto Adige panorama. Vines are planted up to an altitude of 2600 feet and require special forms of cultivation, including pergolas, to capture even the slightest ray of sun. White grapes reign here, with Sylvaner just ahead of Müller Thurgau.

FROM MERANO TO BRESSANONE

This is an itinerary rich in cultural attractions in the heart of the third-ranking Alto Adige wine district. The wines are all waiting to be discovered, especially the whites, which get character from the big changes in temperature between night and day.

▪ **CHIUSA/KLAUSEN.** Between the river and the convent of Sabiona lies a little

Missiano, near Appiano

Wineries *pp. 379-389*
Andriano, Appiano sulla Strada del Vino, Bolzano, Bressanone, Caldaro sulla Strada del Vino, Castelbello Ciardes, Cermes, Chiusa, Cornedo all'Isarco, Cortaccia sulla Strada del Vino, Cortina sulla Strada del Vino, Egna, Fiè allo Sciliar, Magrè sulla Strada del Vino, Marlengo, Meltina, Merano, Montagna, Nalles, Naturno, Ora, Parcines, Salorno, Silandro, Terlano, Termeno sulla Strada del Vino, Tesimo, Varna, Villandro.

square and an old-time road, just wide enough for a stagecoach. The 13th-century Capitano tower looms over the ancient houses of the town, with their bay windows and portals.
A DOC wine is produced here with a specific denomination, Klausner Laitacher, made from Schiava, Lagrein, and Portoghese grapes.

▪ **BRESSANONE/BRIXEN.** This city of Prince-Bishops, built where the Isarco and Rienza rivers meet, charms you with its ancient sights and a truly delightful welcome. You can stroll along Via dei Portici Maggiori, amidst shops and picturesque houses with bay windows, and visit the famous cathedral cloister.
A must (for wine tourists, too) is the Abbazia di Novacella/Neustift in Varna, founded in 1142 and since then active in viniculture, with holdings in the finest wine-growing areas in the valley and cellars of exceptional historical value.

HOW A GREAT WINEGLASS IS BORN

A visit to Kufstein, in the Austrian Tyrol, is certainly worth the journey of 60 miles from the Brenner Pass along the highway to Munich. The attraction is not so much the wine – although Austria has considerable surprises in store – as the wineglass most suitable for tasting it. In fact, the destination is one of the most famous wineglass manufacturers in the world, Riedel, a centuries-old, 11-generation concern begun in Bohemia – thousands of workers and a leader in so-called technical glass – and transferred to Tyrol after World War II to specialize in wineglasses. Today it turns out 8 million pieces, nearly a million of them hand-worked. Its past thirty years' history is worth recounting in detail to learn how the current owner, Georg Riedel, applied the functionalist theory to wineglass design, calculating curves on the basis of organoleptic properties. If content determines shape – this is the conclusion – then every wine will have its own specific glass. The principle on which whites need a tulip glass and reds need volumes and curves proportional to their personality thus evolves into infinite versions, achieved through consultation with wine producers who know their products' most intimate traits. Riedel recently designed a wineglass for the Consorzio del Prosecco of Conegliano Valdobbiadene: it is anything but the usual flute and you can really note the difference. Given all this, a tour of the Kufstein glassworks offers a spectacle unique of its kind: a catwalk above the work stations of the master glassmakers, almost all of them from Bohemia, gives you a close-up view of how, in just seven minutes, a bubble of incandescent glass is turned into a perfect crystal wineglass. Accompanying the visit is an intriguing multimedia show titled "Sinn-fonie", a play on words meaning "symphony of the senses". This is an almost amusement-park route to discovering the mechanisms behind sensorial perceptions of wine. Then you can go to the head-whirling sales area, set up also to demonstrate Riedel's theories: the same wine is poured into different, but not very different glasses, and you will be amazed at how it changes. Finally, the wine shop, truly international. And how much does a Riedel glass cost? The answer is obvious: as much as the wine it is meant to hold. And there is truly one for every pocketbook.

▪ Specialties in Trentino-Alto Adige ▪

ON EITHER SIDE of the Salorno narrows, the Trento and Bolzano regions have two cultural matrixes: the Po-Valley, in the part that broadens into the Verona and Lake Garda plain, and the Tyrolean, of Austrian ancestry, in the valleys approaching the divide. A duality that is also found in food, with pasta and beans a staple on the tables of the Veneto mountains (Marzemino), contrasting with the *knodeln*, big bread dumplings variously seasoned with meat or vegetables (white Traminer or Terlano or red Lago di Caldaro, depending on the recipe); local milk-stewed beef (Merlot) are countered by goulash, a spicy stew recalling Hungary and the Hapsburgs' time (Santa Maddalena); polenta (or potatoes in certain cases) versus rye bread in its numerous forms. In any case, above and beyond these differences, this is mountain cuisine, unified by the raw materials coming from the valley-bottom orchards, hillside terraced vineyards and tilled plots; from the rivers, the streams and the woods; from the farms and mountain pastures.

GREATLY RENOWNED are the region's berries – strawberries, raspberries, blueberries – and apples, which form the basis for a huge amount of pastries; cheeses, like Grana Trentino and Puzzone di Moena (Teroldego); and cold meats like speck and Alto Adige würstel (Meranese di Collina). One province may be more famous than the another for a certain type of product, but this detracts nothing from the lesser-known specialties, which can actually become a pretext for getting to know the place better: this is the case with the so-called *carne salada*, typical of Valsugana, eaten with beans in a dish of ancient tradition (Sorni Rosso); or Graukäse, a cheese from the Val Pusteria, characteristic for its gray rind and sharp taste (Lagrein). Not to mention certain rare specialties, such as the olive oil from the upper Lake Garda, the northernmost oil area in Italy, which enhances fish from the lake (Chardonnay, Nosiola, Müller Thurgau), or the pastries of Viennese tradition, beginning with strudel (Moscato Giallo, Moscato Rosa, Vino Santo Trentino), which is one of the attractions of Alto Adige resorts.

MENTION SHOULD ALSO BE MADE of the fine level of accommodation that the two provinces share, whose lovely venues range from the cities (severely medieval Trento, worldly Bolzano) to small towns, where romantics are free to choose between the farmsteads dotting the meadows or the little inns lost in the woods. Also praiseworthy are the restaurants, whether traditional or champions of the traditional revised (with results of absolute excellence). It is hard to make a choice between summer and winter: so many are the occasions for a special holiday that tourism has by now become one of the major headings in regional economy.

VENETO

CHAMPION WINES

Among Italy's DOC wines, the Veneto holds three national records: almost 53 million US gallons produced, 20 officially recognized zones, and 4 of the top ten appellation wines in terms of volume. Yet, despite all of this, the wines are better known in foreign markets than in Italy.

From the area around Verona to Marca Trevigiana, vineyards are a constant feature of the Veneto landscape. The credit must be given to the monastic orders that worked during the Middle Ages to reclaim and farm the land between the Adda and Piave rivers, bringing back the cultivation of the vine and restoring it to the vigor it had known in Roman times. A driving force in the economy during the Age of the Communes and when the great villas were be-

Above, Vicenza's Rotonda; left, a view of Lake Garda (top) and the towers of the Montagnana castle (bottom)

ing built under the rule of the Serenissima, which was able to import new grapes from its colonies, the vine underwent a thorough renewal in the 19th century with the introduction of French varieties. Today, it is one of the pillars of the region's economy and one of the most reliable resources for development.

FROM THE GARDA RIVIERA TO THE TREVISO REGION

The first specific natural environment for the vines in the Veneto is a prolongation of Lombardy's one, on the shore of Lake Garda and on the gentle slopes of the morainic hills to the south of the lake. Beyond the valley carved out by the Adige river over the course of time and which represents the southern extension of the vineyards of Trentino, there is a grand sweep of vineyards located on mountain foothills and stretching all the way to the border with Friuli. This territory begins in the west with the Monti Lessini – or Recioto hills, in honor of the most typical wine of the zone – on whose calcareous slopes are located first the vineyards of Valpolicella, then those of Soave and Gambellara.

On the last slopes of the Monti Lessini, astride the border which divides the provinces of Verona and Vicenza, is located the Durello zone, while the vineyards of Breganze are to be found to the south of the Asiago plateau. This arc of foothills continues towards Montello and then the Colli Asolani, while beyond the river Piave are the Colli di Conegliano, famous for Prosecco wine. Two greatly different zones are located in flatter areas. The first consists of the low hills silhouetted against the horizon of the Po river plain: the Colli Berici, to the south of Vicenza, and the Colli Euganei, to the south of Padua. The second wine-growing zone of the plain, instead, has been formed by the alluvial deposits of the Piave river and offers a first glimpse of what will be the typical landscape of Friuli.

THE GRAND VINEYARD OF MERLOT

In terms of the varieties cultivated, the leading grapes are Merlot, which by itself covers 30% of the overall regional vineyard surface, along with autochthonous Garganega and Prosecco, which add another twenty plus percent. Local Corvina Veronese and Rondinella are also significant grapes, as are imported varieties such as Chardonnay, Pinot Bianco, Pinot Grigio, Riesling, and Sauvignon among the white grapes, Cabernet Franc, Cabernet Sauvignon, an Pinot Nero among the reds. As far as DOC overall production is concerned, the Veneto is in first place among Italy's regions with almost 53 million US gallons.

The province of Verona – another startling figure – produces as much DOC wine as all of Piedmont and more than Tuscany. There are twenty individual DOC zones (second in the rating of Italy's regions), yet another confirmation of the size and extension of Veneto wine-growing. Of these 20 DOC zones, fifteen belong solely to the Veneto, while five are shared either with Lombardy, Trentino-Alto Adige, or Friuli-Venezia Giulia. Four of the former fifteen zones, yet another record, are numbered among the top ten in Italy and are, in the order of their respective importance, Soave, Valpolicella, Prosecco di Conegliano, and Bardolino. There are also 9 IGTs productions, six of which are exclusive to the region, such as the "Veneto" indication. The volume of wine exported is another significant figure: 70% of the total produced, a fact which demonstrates that these wines are better known outside of Italy than in the domestic market, where they would deserve to be better promoted.

The Great Wines of the Veneto

Valpolicella DOC - Recioto della Valpolicella (Amarone)
This famous red wine from Verona is based on three autochthonous grapes: Corvina (40 to 70%), Rondinella (20 to 40%), and Molinara (5 to 25%). The resulting wine must have: vinous, delicate, characteristic bouquet, sometimes reminiscent of bitter almond; a dry or velvety taste, robust, slightly bitter but harmonious; minimum alcoholic content of 11% and 12% for the Superiore. Noteworthy is the old practice of *ripasso*, that is the addition of slightly dried grape to the must for a second fermentation that enhances the fruity wild cherry flavor typical of the blend.
As for Recioto, this extraordinary wine gets its name from the *recie*, the "ears" of the bunches or the outermost clusters most exposed to the sun and therefore richest in sugary substances. These parts, selected during harvesting, are put to dry for 20 to 90 days; grape must fermentation takes place during the winter with a process very different from the usual one, leading to the characteristic features that have made this wine a success. In particular, the difference between sweet and dry Recioto depends on drawing-off timing: if it is done early, before the sugars have partially or completely turned to alcohol, the result is sweet Recioto; if delayed, Recioto is dry, as in the case of renowned Amarone.

Bardolino DOC
The eastern shore of Lake Garda is home to this red of great (almost legendary) and centuries-old tradition. The most typical Veronese grapes are used in the blend: Corvina, Rondinella, and Molinara. The resulting wine has the following characteristics: ruby red color tending to garnet when aged; delicate, characteristic aroma; dry, full, slightly bitter taste, harmonious and featuring a hint of wood if aged in wooden barrels or barriques; minimum alcohol: 12%. Since 2002 Bardolino has been able to vaunt the pink band of DOCG in its Superiore and Superiore Classico productions. The production code also includes Chiaretto and Novello.

Prosecco
Vine-species researchers are uncertain about the origins – in the Veneto or Friuli – of this grape, which some historians associate with legendary Pucino wine, praised by Roman Empress Livia. On the other hand, there is no doubt about the fact that vine-growers of the Marca Trevigiana have taken full advantage of its potential. Vinified pure or with moderate additions of other local grapes, it gives a wine that can be still or fizzy, dry or, sometimes, semi-sweet, for the table or for desserts, depending on the type. Constant quality features are: pale straw yellow color; slightly vinous and outstandingly fruity aroma, with hints of wisteria and acacia; robust flavor with a characteristic vein of slight bitterness. If the wine is produced in the area of San Pietro di Barbozza (near Valdobbiadene), called Cartizze, it can be labeled Superiore di Cartizze.

Soave DOC and Recioto di Soave DOCG
The vineyards surrounding the walled town of Soave are practically monopolized by Garganega grapes, with long, alate bunches. The wine in question is made from Garganega grapes (70 to 100%) with possible additions of Pinot Bianco, Chardonnay, and Trebbiano di Soave. The result is straw yellow in color, tending at times to green-

Vineyards in the Veneto hills

VENETO'S DOC ZONES

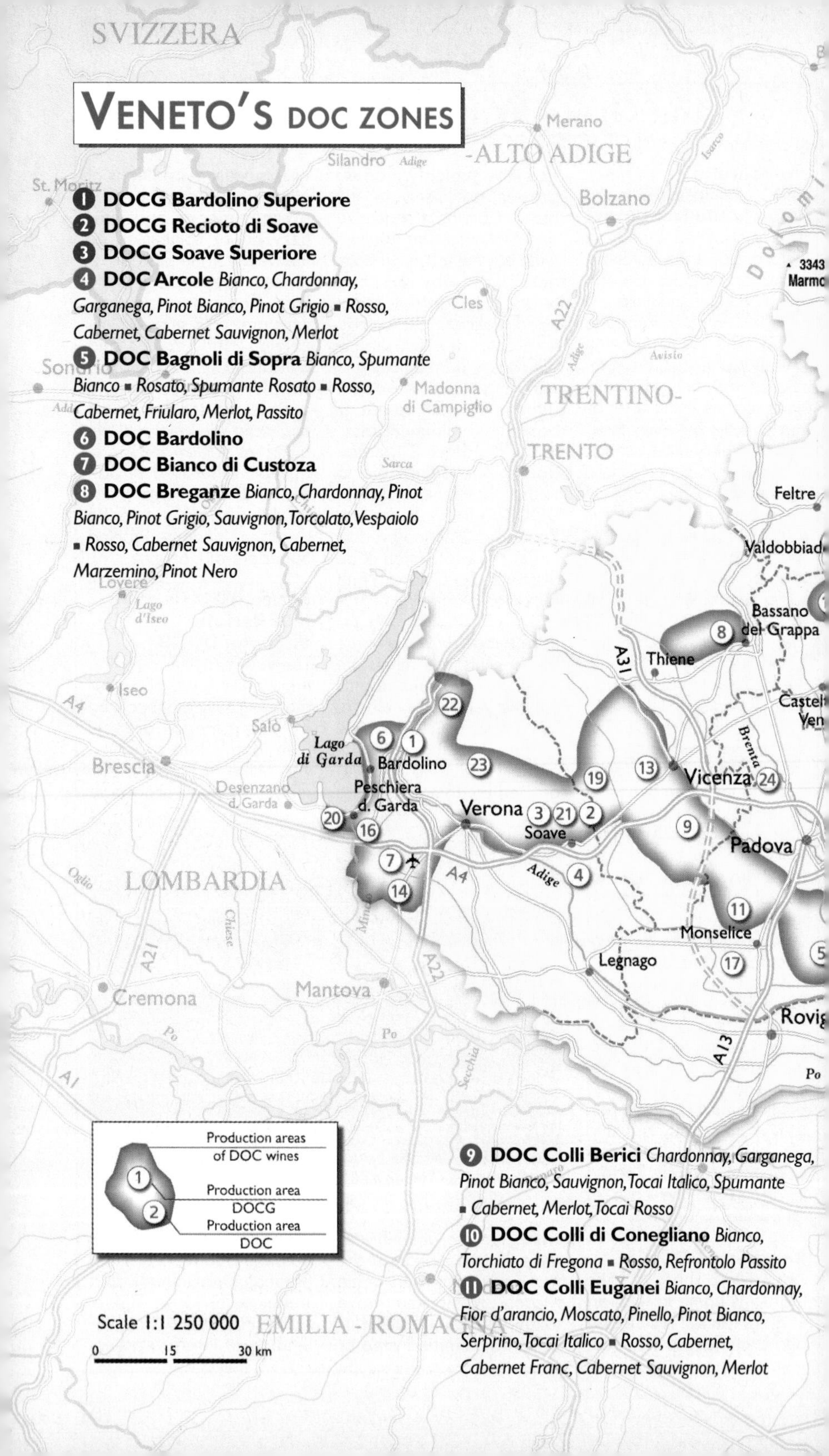

❶ **DOCG Bardolino Superiore**
❷ **DOCG Recioto di Soave**
❸ **DOCG Soave Superiore**
❹ **DOC Arcole** *Bianco, Chardonnay, Garganega, Pinot Bianco, Pinot Grigio* ▪ *Rosso, Cabernet, Cabernet Sauvignon, Merlot*
❺ **DOC Bagnoli di Sopra** *Bianco, Spumante Bianco* ▪ *Rosato, Spumante Rosato* ▪ *Rosso, Cabernet, Friularo, Merlot, Passito*
❻ **DOC Bardolino**
❼ **DOC Bianco di Custoza**
❽ **DOC Breganze** *Bianco, Chardonnay, Pinot Bianco, Pinot Grigio, Sauvignon, Torcolato, Vespaiolo* ▪ *Rosso, Cabernet Sauvignon, Cabernet, Marzemino, Pinot Nero*

Production areas of DOC wines
Production area DOCG
Production area DOC

Scale 1:1 250 000
0 15 30 km

❾ **DOC Colli Berici** *Chardonnay, Garganega, Pinot Bianco, Sauvignon, Tocai Italico, Spumante* ▪ *Cabernet, Merlot, Tocai Rosso*
❿ **DOC Colli di Conegliano** *Bianco, Torchiato di Fregona* ▪ *Rosso, Refrontolo Passito*
⓫ **DOC Colli Euganei** *Bianco, Chardonnay, Fior d'arancio, Moscato, Pinello, Pinot Bianco, Serprino, Tocai Italico* ▪ *Rosso, Cabernet, Cabernet Franc, Cabernet Sauvignon, Merlot*

⓬ **DOC Conegliano Valdobbiadene**
⓭ **DOC Gambellara** *Recioto, Vin Santo*
⓮ **DOC Garda** *see Lombardy*
⓯ **DOC Lison-Pramaggiore** *Bianco, Pinot Bianco, Riesling Italico, Riesling, Sauvignon, Tocai or Lison, Verduzzo ▪ Rosso, Cabernet, Cabernet Franc, Cabernet Sauvignon, Malbech, Merlot, Refosco dal Peduncolo Rosso*
⓰ **DOC Lugana**
⓱ **DOC Merlara** *Bianco, Malvasia, Tocai ▪ Rosso, Cabernet, Cabernet Sauvignon, Marzemino, Merlot*
⓲ **DOC Montello e Colli Asolani** *Chardonnay, Pinot Bianco, Pinot Grigio, Prosecco ▪ Rosso, Cabernet, Merlot*
⓳ **DOC Monti Lessini** *or Lesini Bianco, Durello, Spumante ▪ Rosso*
⓴ **DOC San Martino della Battaglia**
㉑ **DOC Soave**
㉒ **DOC Valdadige Terra dei Forti** *Chardonnay, Pinot Bianco, Pinot Grigio, Sauvignon ▪ Rosso, Cabernet Franc, Cabernet Sauvignon, Enantio*
㉓ **DOC Valpolicella and Recioto della Valpolicella** *Amarone, Recioto della Valpolicella*
㉔ **DOC Vicenza** *Bianco, Chardonnay, Garganego, Manzoni Bianco, Moscato, Pinot Bianco, Pinot Grigio, Riesling, Sauvignon ▪ Rosato ▪ Rosso, Cabernet, Cabernet Sauvignon, Merlot, Pinot Nero, Raboso*
㉕ **DOC Vini del Piave** *Chardonnay, Pinot Bianco, Pinot Grigio, Tocai Italico, Verduzzo ▪ Cabernet, Cabernet Sauvignon, Merlot, Pinot Nero, Raboso*

IGT - Typical Geographic Indication

Alto Livenza (Treviso - Pordenone); Colli Trevigiani (Treviso); Conselvano (Padua); Delle Venezie (Trento - Belluno - Padua - Rovigo - Treviso - Venice - Verona - Vicenza - Pordenone - Udine - Gorizia - Trieste); Marca Trevigiana (Treviso); Provincia di Verona or Veronese (Verona); Vallagarina (Trento - Verona); Veneto (Belluno - Padua - Rovigo - Treviso - Venice - Verona - Vicenza); Veneto Orientale (Venice - Treviso); Vigneti delle Dolomiti (Bolzano - Trento - Belluno)

ish, with a vinous aroma, deep and delicate and evoking elder-berry flowers and violets; its taste is dry, medium-bodied and slightly bitter; minimum alcohol: 10.5%. Soave DOC also includes Brut and Dry Spumante.
Selecting the riper bunch clusters (the so-called *recie*) and drying them on racks for four to six months, the same grape mixture results in Recioto di Soave DOCG, a golden yellow dessert wine, intensely fruity and semi-sweet or sweet, velvety on the palate, which through time develops interesting scents of dried fruit and honey, with a hint of wood if aged in barriques. Minimum alcohol: 14% – at least 11.5% developed. There is also a spumante version of Recioto di Soave DOCG.

Merlot
Originally from Bordeaux, this is a variety of extraordinary quality, which can be vinified both pure – producing a red character wine, fruity and full-bodied, velvety even young and with a bitter-almond aftertaste after its brief ageing – and in a blend with Cabernet Sauvignon and Cabernet Franc, giving absolutely excellent results in terms of texture and elegance. In Italy it was initially acclimatized here in the Veneto.

Cabernet Franc - Cabernet Sauvignon
The Veneto vine-growers have great esteem for Cabernets and are rewarded with excellent results. Used alone, Cabernet Sauvignon gives wines bright red in color, tannic and with good body, suited for long ageing; in them, the youthful aromas of vegetables (green bell pepper) evolve with maturity into more complex and pleasing aromas (violet). Cabernet Franc is a similar variety, but with more outstanding traits: it is vinified pure primarily in the Veneto and Friuli. Excellent results are also gotten from the classic Bordeaux-style blend of Cabernet with Merlot.

Tocai Italico
This variety, a standard-bearer of Friuli oenology but also quite common in the Veneto, gives a wine that is colored straw yellow tending to greenish, with a delicate, dry, fresh aroma and a typical bitter note of almond and hay. The name Tocai is a matter of international dispute with Hungary, which claims exclusive rights to it. Recently, Tocai Friulano was identified as Sauvignonasse, a variety that has disappeared from France but is still widely grown in Chile.

Torcolato di Breganze
This famous passito wine comes from the Vespaiola grape specific to the Breganze DOC zone, which gets its name from the wasps attracted by its sugary juice. Vinified immediately after harvesting it produces a dry white wine with characteristic flavor. On the other hand, dried grapes produce Torcolato, a wine with a warm, golden or amber color, honey and raisins aroma, and taste that is slightly sweet or sweet, velvety, and enhanced by lengthy ageing.

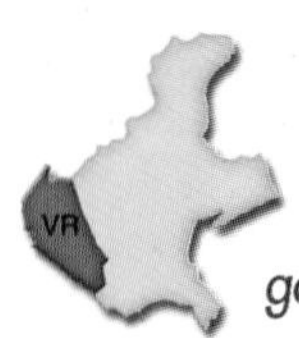

THE VERONA REGION

From Lake Garda to Monti Lessini the province offers wines that go from long-ageing reds to refined spumante.

Verona is one of the great protagonists of Italian viticulture: tradition, quality and high production levels are the elements of a success which, taking advantage of the territory's lovely scenery and cultural attractions, has created first-class wine tourism. The provincial wine scene is a sequence of hillside zones quite different in positioning and history. It opens on Lake Garda, with the Bardolino zone at the feet of Mount Baldo, and goes on to the morainic hills on the southern edge of the lake, where we find the Bianco di Custoza, Lugana, and San Martino della Battaglia DOC zones, the two latter shared with Lombardy, along with the more generic Garda denomination. Then come the gravelly stretches of the Valdadige DOC, which reach the plain down from Trentino-Alto Adige. Finally, the calcareous Monti Lessini, with their DOC areas: Valpolicella, at the heart of the range of hills; Soave, on its south-

ern edge, with Recioto di Soave DOCG production; Lessini Durello, on the boundary with Vicenza; and the small Arcole DOC on the plain south of Soave.
The Provincia di Verona or Veronese IGT is tasked with safeguarding all the wines that, because of the place of production or of the choice of wine-growers, are not part of the DOC zones.

The Adige Valley

The Adige valley is home to an inter-regional DOC zone lying in the provinces of Verona, Trento, and Bolzano. Veneto production refers to four valley-bottom municipalities lying between the Baldo chain to the west and the Monti Lessini to the east. Concentrated in the initial portion of the Val Lagarina are the fortresses once defending what was for a long time the main route through the Alps. Hence the nickname "Land of the Forts" for a zone with outstanding traits even where wine is concerned, characterized by alluvial soil and the coexistence of Veneto and Trentino grapes. The area has an outstanding vocation for Pinot Grigio and takes special pride in its Enantio, an autochthonous red of ancient origin.

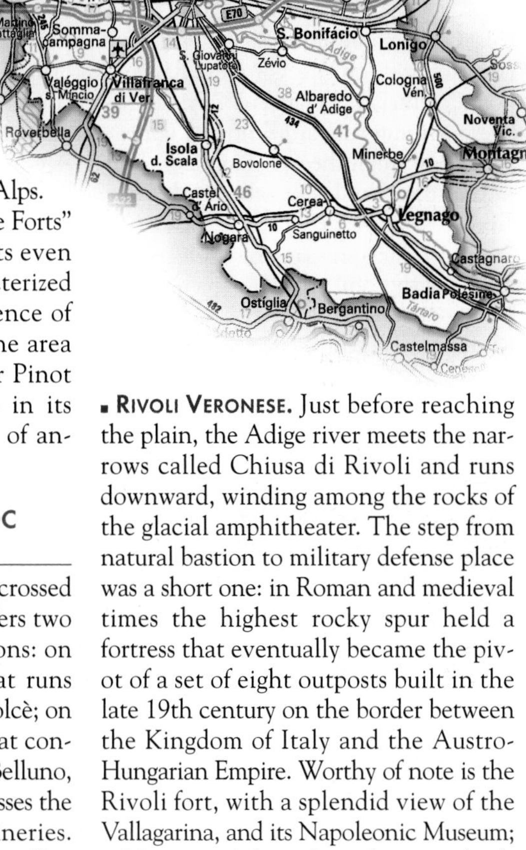

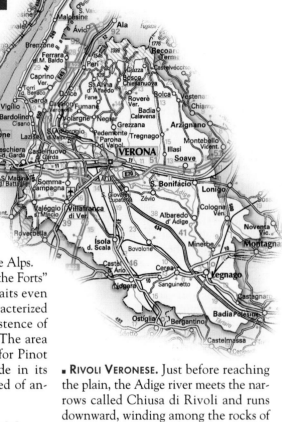

THE VALDADIGE-TERRA DEI FORTI DOC WINE ROUTE

The bottom of the Adige valley, crossed by the Brenner highway, also offers two rather more relaxing route options: on one side, the national road that runs through the various hamlets of Dolcè; on the other, the provincial road that connects Rivoli Veronese, Brentino Belluno, and Avio. The wine route crisscrosses the valley, linking the associated wineries. Well organized is the gastronomy offering marking the passage from Trentino to the Veneto.

▪ **RIVOLI VERONESE.** Just before reaching the plain, the Adige river meets the narrows called Chiusa di Rivoli and runs downward, winding among the rocks of the glacial amphitheater. The step from natural bastion to military defense place was a short one: in Roman and medieval times the highest rocky spur held a fortress that eventually became the pivot of a set of eight outposts built in the late 19th century on the border between the Kingdom of Italy and the Austro-Hungarian Empire. Worthy of note is the Rivoli fort, with a splendid view of the Vallagarina, and its Napoleonic Museum; a 20 minutes' drive from the town leads to the Orto botanico del Baldo (botanical gardens, 3946 feet above sea level).

■ **DOLCÈ**. This municipality, which is also Città del Vino (wine town), stretches over the eastern slope of the valley with its five little villages. The first on the way up is Volargne, enriched with the 16th-century Villa Dal Bene; then comes Ceraino, near the Chiusa di Rivoli and therefore with various fortifications, followed by Dolcè, whose historical center contains some noble mansions and lovely rustic courts. Further on are Peri and Ossenigo, part of which lie in the Lessinia Regional Park. Continuing up the Adige valley, one meets the Trentino border in Avio, where the splendid local castle is well worth a visit.

The Garda Veronese

Lake Garda confirms its exceptional wine vocation also on the Veronese Riviera, from Peschiera del Garda to Torri del Benaco – home to Bardolino red wine – and in the amphitheater of morainic hills surrounding the lake to the south – the land of Bianco di Custoza. Added to these productions are the DOC zones shared with Lombardy: Lugana and San Martino della Battaglia, right on the regional border, and Garda, which infiltrates the Verona district well past the province capital city.

THE BARDOLINO ROUTE

This is a ring route winding over the hills separating the shores of Lake Garda from the Adige valley. The reference points are the six centers of Bardolino Classico, with various detours to the rest of the production area. A leaflet with a detailed description of the itinerary is distributed locally.

■ **BARDOLINO**. This little town overlooks the lake in the typical "comb" configuration of lakeside villages. Outside its walls are the important churches of S. Zeno (one of the most beautiful reminders of the Carolingian period in Italy) and of S. Severio, Romanesque in origin. A lovely excursion leads to the court of S. Colombano and to the picturesque Camaldolensian hermitage.
A must for wine tourists are the stops at the Enoteca del Bardolino, housed in Villa Carrara Bottagisio and run by the tutelary consortium (which organizes local wine tastings), and at the Wine Museum at the Zeni estate.

Wine estate near Cavaion Veronese

■ **LAZISE.** A former port of the Venetian Republic, it still possesses the castle (at whose feet lay the military port), the turreted walls, the customs building, and a few ancient churches.

■ **GARDA.** Looking out over the lake between the imposing fortress and the outline of San Vigilio Point, this is a little town with a lovely atmosphere. In the middle is the harbor, still crowded with fishing boats; in the square behind it stands the Venetian-style Palazzo dei Capitani. The nature trail that runs along the bay amidst evergreen underbrush is very pleasant.

■ **TORRI DEL BENACO.** This evenly laid out village of Roman origins, with its beautiful lakeside promenade, lies between the marina on Garda's blue waters and the 14th-century Della Scala Castle that dominates it; the castle conserves archeological finds and local history documents.

GARDA'S MORAINIC HILLS AND CUSTOZA'S WINERIES

This is a wine and gastronomy tour which starts in Sommacampagna, tangential to the Serenissima highway, and which then, heading southwest, goes up to the Garda shore. In addition to Bianco di Custoza, local wineries offer tasting of interesting wines from the Bardolino, Soave, Garda, and Lugana DOC areas, the latter shared with Lombardy.

■ **SOMMACAMPAGNA.** Particularly attractive is this Risorgimento town with quality modern wineries. The name evokes the beautiful view across the morainic hills of Lake Garda. In the Custoza country ward, topped by impressive Villa Ottolini, you can visit the Ossuary – this was the site of two crucial battles in the Italian War of Independence.

■ **VILLAFRANCA DI VERONA.** Founded in 1185 as a Verona military outpost on the border with Mantua, its focus is the Della Scala Castle that housed a sequence of armies, lastly in the Napoleonic and Risorgimento periods, and today is a museum and host to cultural events.

Typical malga *on Monte Baldo*

■ **VALEGGIO SUL MINCIO.** The river with its imposing Ponte Rotto and the watermills of Borghetto; the castle and the Sigurta Park: these and more are the attractions of this little town with lovely atmosphere and fine food.

■ **PESCHIERA DEL GARDA.** Roman in origin, in the Middle Ages it became an important stronghold: you can note the Venetian influence on the town and the additions made under Napoleon and Austria rules.

The Recioto Hills

The broad band of limestone hills lying at the feet of the Monti Lessini crosses the Verona province from the bed of the Adige river to beyond the border with Vicenza.

VERONA AND VINITALY

"There is no world without Verona walls", says Shakespeare's Romeo, and it's believable. In the city bathed by the Adige, where many tourists from beyond the Alps have their first contact with Italy, the seasons and ages of the past create an unforgettable scenario. Great opera is performed at the Arena, and in the Romanesque church of S. Zeno you are astonished by the beauty of the Mantegna altarpiece. Crossing the crenellated bridge to Castelvecchio you reach Piazza dei Signori and stroll in the shadow of Verona's mansions and arches. Also attractive is the modern part of the city, which every year in the third week of April offers wine tourism an exceptional event: Vinitaly, the international wine and spirits fair. This is Italy's premier wine fair, drawing over two thousand producers, and thus a major occasion for getting acquainted with different national and international products. Exhibitors satisfy the curiosity of dealers and simple aficionados alike, never denying them a tasting. Five hectic days, but well worth it, if only to watch the show of wine people, from the gruff Alto Adige vine-grower to the noble Tuscan wine merchant.

Coming from the west, you cross the huge Valpolicella vineyard, Italy's fourth largest DOC in terms of output, where the red grapes earlier encountered around Bardolino prevail. This is an area extraordinarily dense in oenological presences and traditions: villages that grew up around very old parish churches; villas in the center of great estates; vineyards that stretch from the plain to terraced hills. Here we enter the lands around the lovely walled town of Soave, where white-berry grapes, first and foremost the autochthonous Garganega (also a protagonist in Gambellara, in the Vicenza province) dominate. Characterizing overall production on the Verona hillsides are the Recioto wines made from dried grapes – red in Valpolicella, white in Soave – which are famous even abroad.

Wineries *pp. 389-400*
Bardolino, Castelnuovo del Garda, Cavaion Veronese, Colognola ai Colli, Fumane, Illasi, Lazise, Marano di Valpolicella, Mezzane di Sotto, Montecchìa di Crosara, Monteforte d'Alpone, Negrar, Peschiera del Garda, San Bonifacio, San Martino Buon Albergo, San Pietro in Cariano, Sant'Ambrogio di Valpolicella, Soave, Sommacampagna, Sona, Valeggio sul Mincio, Verona.

IN THE LAND OF VALPOLICELLA CLASSICO

The points of reference along the Valpolicella Wine Route are the centers of the Classico production zone, but many detours can be taken to other places of interest for wine and food. A rich calendar runs from the cherry to the chestnut seasons, from olive oil time to that of new wine and to those of Monte Veronese cheese, of truffles and of snails, multiplying the good reasons for a visit.

▪ **SANT'AMBROGIO DI VALPOLICELLA.** Historically a marble production center, this little town also boasts some of the finest vineyards in the zone. From the main square two paths lead to the hillside villages of Gargagnano (site of Villa Serego-Alighieri, a lovely complex of buildings from various epochs immersed in the vineyards) and San Giorgio, with a medieval and Renaissance imprint and a very beautiful old parish church.

▪ **SAN PIETRO IN CARIANO.** A town of ancient nobility, as testified to by the noteworthy church of S. Floriano (12th C.) and the many patrician dwellings scattered through the area: the most impressive is Villa Serego Boccoli, in Pedemonte, designed by Palladio and featuring massive rusticated columns.

▪ **FUMANE.** The superb Villa della Torre, with uncertain but noble paternity (designed by Sanmicheli or Giulio Romano) is certainly worth a visit, so as the Parco delle Cascate (waterfall park), one of the loveliest places in Lessinia. A must for wine tourists is a stop at the Enoteca della Valpolicella, which combines the zone's finest labels with seasonal dishes.

▪ **NEGRAR.** A very large municipality that unites, between hillside and mountain, many of the villages located in the homonymous valley and a multitude of villas scattered through it: one of the most outstanding is Villa Bertoldi, nicknamed the Palazzo, one of the most scenic examples of portico-and-loggia constructions in the entire province.

THE SOAVE ROUTE, AMIDST CASTLES AND OLD PARISH CHURCHES

This route connects the main wine centers in the three valleys of Mezzane, Illasi, and Alpone, in the part of the Monti Lessini area sloping down to the plain. The tour was ideated by the Associazione Strada del Vino Soave, which unites 42 wineries listed in a brochure prepared by the tutelary consortium.

Soave's castle

▪ **SOAVE.** A delightful medieval town located on the lowest spurs of the Monti Lessini, with still intact four sided walls that go up to the castle. Here and there are bits with Venetian flavor. A beautiful view unfolds from Piazza dell'Antenna (where the Venetian flag of St. Mark once waved): on one side there is the ancient Hall of Justice, on the other the Gothic Palazzo Cavalli and, close by, the parish church of S. Lorenzo, founded in the 14th century. All around, the green of the vineyards on rolling hills.

Panoramic view of Monti Lessini

▪ **COLOGNOLA AI COLLI.** At the entrance to the Illasi valley lies this pretty village of Roman origin, which conserves traces of the layouts of the parish church and of some villas. In the direction of Verona is a smallr village that grew up around the Romanesque church of S. Maria della Pieve, surrounded by the vineyards of a wine estate headquartered in a villa with shed and rustic outbuildings.

▪ **ILLASI.** This is an aggregate of various noble residences; outstanding among them are the Palladian Villa Carlotti, in the center of town, and the grandiose Villa Peres Pompei Sagramoso, whose parkland extends to the top of the hill hosting the ruins of the Della Scala Castle. Across vineyards, olive and cypress trees you can catch glimpses of Soave and the distant Colli Berici-Euganei.

▪ **MONTECCHIA DI CROSARA.** This village is the real heart of the Alpone valley. In the Castello neighborhood stands the Romanesque church of S. Salvatore, with a crypt on columns bearing lovely capitals and embellished by splendid frescoes. Not far away is Bolca, one of the world's most famous fossil-bearing deposits; there is a Paleontology Museum annexed.

THE VICENZA REGION

VI

The foothills, from the Monti Lessini to Mount Grappa, and the Colli Berici district offer a panorama of wines that includes also passito and spumante ones.

There are two distinct wine zones in the Vicenza province. North of the provincial capital are the foothills that run from the final spurs of the Monti Lessini to the hills that are a prelude to the Asiago plateau and to Mount Grappa. To the south, the Colli Berici rise from the plain like a limestone island, where a Mediterranean climate prevails. In the former zone white grapes are the stars, and are also used to make the province's renowned sweet and passito wines; in the latter the reds are dominant. The Vicenza province embraces four DOC areas; one is province-wide, the others relate to the Colli Berici, Breganze, and Gambellara districts.

The Colli Berici

Since ancient times, good climate and soil have been boons to viticulture on these gentle hills, which medieval chronicles described as already covered with vineyards. The vine varieties found here are those typical of the region, with a preponderance of Merlot and Cabernet among the reds and of Pinot Bianco and Garganega among the whites. However, the best oenological find here is a vine presented as Tocai Rosso until some years ago, and more recently identified as a member of the celebrated Grenache family; the Berica Riviera offers a light and aromatic red wine, Barbarano, which might be the real discovery of the tour.

THE COLLI BERICI DOC WINE ROUTE

This route winds through vineyards and farmland along the line where hills meet the plain. Villas and historic villages provide a cultural alibi for a memorable wine and gastronomy tour. The reference points along the way are Barbarano (headquarters of the tutelary consortium for red Barbarano DOC) and Lonigo, the two wine towns that serve as the eastern and western entrances to the area.

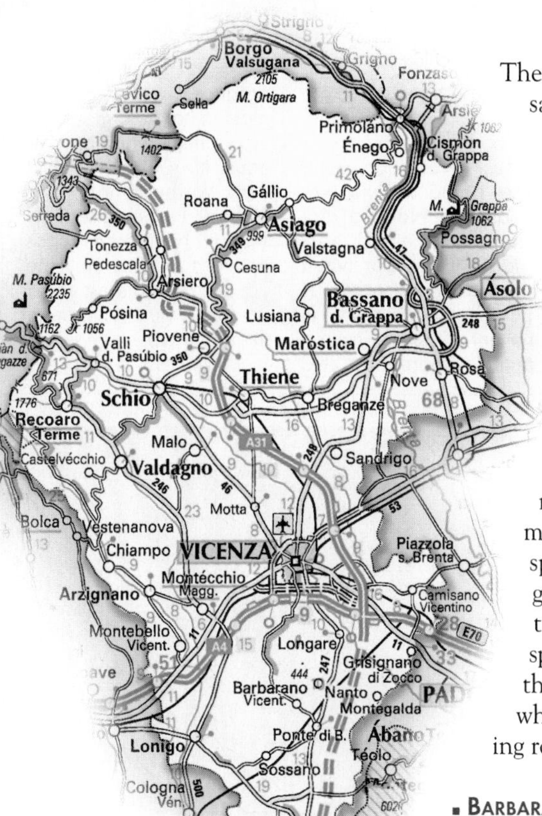

The ring is cut in half by the "Dorsale", the road that climbs the hills from Vicenza to the sanctuary of Mount Berico, offering lovely vistas and a chance to stop at first-rate trattorias and restaurants.

▪ **LONGARE.** Leaving Vicenza, first on stage is the most famous of Palladio's villas, La Rotonda. The Berica Riviera then reaches Costozza, an ancient town rich in noteworthy architecture that marks the start of the zone more specifically dedicated to wine-growing. Among other attractions is Villa Da Schio, with spectacular stepped gardens and the headquarters of a wine estate whose cellars are carved from living rock.

▪ **BARBARANO VICENTINO.** An important wine town – in the heart of the area producing the most typical of the Colli reds –, though more than that. Fine architecture includes the Venetian-style

The Colli Berici landscape

Vicenza, City of Palladio (and more)

The architectural works of Andrea Palladio – the Basilica and Olympic Theater, Palazzo Chiericati, and Villa La Rotonda (the most important of an extraordinary series of villas) – has given Vicenza a place on UNESCO's World Heritage list, but the city is also a mini wine-and-food capital.
A must event for wine lovers is the Salone Nazionale del Novello (national new wine fair), held in early November when the first bottle of the year is officially uncorked: this is an event unique of its kind that unites more than 200 producers and allows you, glass in hand, to make tasting comparisons hard to equal elsewhere.
Also worthy of note is the Biblioteca Internazionale La Vigna, an important repository of books on vineyards, containing over 35,000 volumes, many of them antique.

Palazzo dei Vicari and the 18th-century parish church containing paintings by Maganza and Palma il Giovane; also significant is the 18th-century Villa Godi Marinoni.

▪ **Noventa Vicentina**. Passing through Villaga, hosting Villa Piovene (headquarters of a wine estate), the road winds through the Val Liona, where you find another historic winery at Villa Dal Ferro Lazzarini (designed by Sanmicheli), and on to Orgiano, noted for spectacular Villa Fracanzan Piovene, with its interesting museum describing life in a Veneto villa. Finally, Noventa Vicentina, in the southernmost part of the province, has a striking porticoed square, at the center of which is sumptuous Venetian-style Villa Barbarigo. Close by is Villa Pojana, one of Palladio's most singular works.

▪ **Lonigo**. Lying at the extreme southwestern part of the Colli Berici, this ancient town was once the stronghold of Verona's ruling Della Scala family and then hub of the possessions of the Venetian Pisanis, builders of La Rocca, a lovely villa designed by Scamozzi that dominates the town.

The Palladian Basilica of Vicenza (detail)

The Foothill Vineyards

The band of hills crossing the upper part of the province has three wine districts with different traits. From the wine and food standpoint, worth a mention is the Asiago plateau, with its cheeses, alpine specialties, and distillates.

The Durello Route

This wine route follows three itineraries: an inter-provincial one (to which the places described in full farther on belong), that goes through the heart of the production zone, and two provincial ones, that take in the outermost wine-making centers (Monteforte d'Alpone, Soave, and Illasi in the Verona area; Valdagno, Schio, and Malo in the Vicenza province). The tutelary consortium, with offices in Soave, distributes a brochure with maps and recipes from restaurants ensuring tasting of the finest labels.

▪ **Montecchio Maggiore.** The route starts at Villa Cordellina, with its famous frescoes by Tiepolo. On the hills forming the backdrop to the town are the castles known as Romeo's and Juliet's, in honor of the most illustrious son of Montecchio, Luigi da Porto, who wrote the famous short story that inspired Shakespeare.

▪ **Arzignano.** The geographical center of the DOC zone is noteworthy for its castle, with walls and turrets carved from living basalt rock, and for a sun-filled church with a Neoclassical interior. From here you can fan out to the wine centers in the furthest parts of the province, such as Valdagno and Schio, site of a museum devoted to industrial archeology, unique of its kind in Italy.

▪ **Roncà.** This is a small wine town in the province of Verona committed to Soave and, above all, it is the Durello's historical capital. Monte Veronese cheese is produced in its higher districts. Widening the spoke, you proceed towards Montecchia di Crosara and Monteforte d'Alpone in the Soave Classico zone, and climb towards Bolca, famous for a fossil deposit unique in the world.

The Magnificent Recioto di Gambellara Route

First this route passes through the Soave Classico area and then goes as far as the edges of the DOC zone, with possible extensions. The Cantina Sociale di Gambellara offers informative material about the wine route.

▪ **Gambellara.** On the border with the province of Verona, this would seem to be a quiet country village surrounding its parish church, were it not for the wine produced by Italy's largest private winery, Casa Vinicola Zonin. Here you can examine interesting wine collections destined for the civic museum currently being built. A lovely road winds uphill to the panoramic ridge between Val Fonda and Val di Selva, in the heart of the Classico zone, then descends to Selva di Montebello, where excellent wineries can be found.

The Casa Zonin's collections in Gambellara

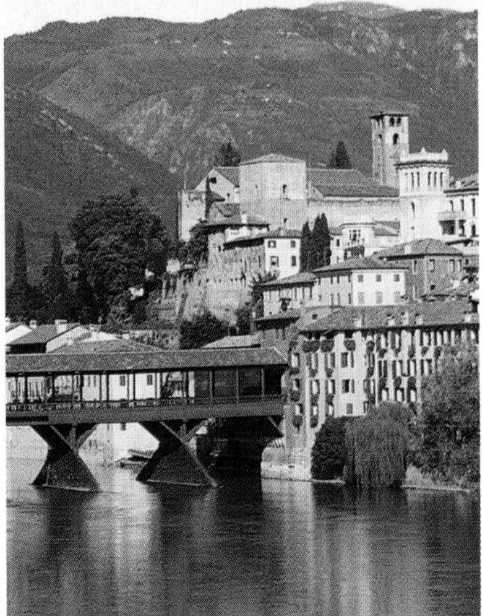

River view of Bassano del Grappa

Wineries *pp. 389-400*
Bassano del Grappa, Breganze, Cornedo Vicentino, Gambellara, Longare, Montebello Vicentino, San Germano dei Berici, Villaga.

The Breganze DOC Route

This route begins from Piovene Rocchette, arrival point of the Valdastico highway, and then runs between plain and hills in the immediate vicinity of Breganze, with a stop at Bassano del Grappa to taste its famous spirits.

▪ **Thiene.** At the center of this town, located on the western boundary of the DOC zone, stands Villa Da Porto Colleoni, a late Gothic building also called the Castle for its towers and showy crenellations. In October, the adjacent central squares are the venue for the appealing Fiera Franca, a costume re-evocation of a Renaissance market.

▪ **Breganze.** In antiquity it was a fortified town along the road to the Altopiano dei Sette Comuni (plateau). Relics of this are the many towers (now used as dovecotes) still in existence (not surprisingly, the local gastronomy specialty is young pigeon grilled on a spit). Briganze is the home to a well-known cooperative winery and a private one of international fame.

▪ **Marostica.** This is a still-intact medieval village, girded with crenellated walls connecting its two castles. The legend of the lovely Lionora is re-enacted every two years in the chess game played with living pieces in the main square. In addition to grapes, celebrated cherries are also grown on its hills.

▪ **Bassano del Grappa.** Crossing the Brenta river to the east you enter one of the most picturesque provincial Italian towns: millenarian Bassano, with its houses hugging Ponte Vecchio, its castle and Cathedral higher up, and Mount Grappa in the background. Among the reasons to visit are its famous spirits produced by historic distilleries.

Bassano and Grappa

Apropos of the term "grappa": the European Community has ruled that it can be used solely for marc brandy produced in Italy. In any case, speaking of grappa you think of Bassano, which holds no special secrets but rather a peerless heritage of grappa history, tradition, and artisan skills. Symbol of the sector is the well-known Nardini distillery, based since 1779 near the famous Ponte Vecchio; but the province is also given luster by other grappa makers, many of whom have been operating for centuries. Highly recommended is a visit to Jacapo Poli, whose distillery is in Schiavon, near Marostica, but who also has a shop and museum near the Ponte Vecchio in Bassano. Nor are Gianni Capovilla's fruit distillates to be missed: the company is in Rosà but its products can be found (together with extraordinary chocolates) at the Al Ponte restaurant in Bassano.

THE PADUA REGION

The Colli Euganei, with the Dominio di Bagnoli and Conselvano vineyards, are the core of Padua's oenology.

The highest expression of this province's oenology can be found in the Colli Euganei wineries, direct heirs to Venice's mainland dominions. Adjacent to them is the Bagnoli di Sopra DOC, whose vineyards extend into the lower Padua plain stretching towards the Venetian lagoon. More internally, the Montagnana area is home to the recently instituted Merlara DOC. In the portion southwest of the Colli Euganei the Conselvano IGT is also to be found.

The Colli Euganei

Nature has created a favorable habitat for vines on these hills, with soil that is volcanic in origin (as can be seen in the conical shape of the hills and the presence of many hot-springs).

Vineyards, documented as early as Roman times, today include 3200 acres of specialized plantings and a good 13 DOC productions. The grapes are primarily Tocai, Merlot, and Cabernet, but there are also more specific varieties. Outstanding is the presence (the sole in the Veneto) of Moscato, both Giallo (yellow) and Bianco (white), denominated in the Fior d'Arancio zone. There is also the indigenous Pinella grape, traditionally used as a blending grape for white wines but lately vinified alone with good results. Another special vine variety is Serprino, of uncertain origin but considered similar to Prosecco and likewise used for fizzy wines, especially dessert ones. The production zone is concentrated around Arquà Petrarca, Galzignano, and Torreglia, with extensions into 14 neighboring centers.

THE COLLI EUGANEI WINE ROUTE

This route begins just outside Padua, taking the so-called Strada delle Terme Euganee along the eastern side of the hills and then swinging to the southernmost limit of the wine zone, looping back to include the centers on the opposite slope: Cinto Euganeo, Vò Euganeo, and Teolo. It should be noted that most of the DOC zone lies within the borders of the Colli Euganei Regional Park.

■ **ABANO TERME.** Renowned as a spa resort, it retains the appearance of a 19th-century ville d'eau, with eclectic, flowery architecture works

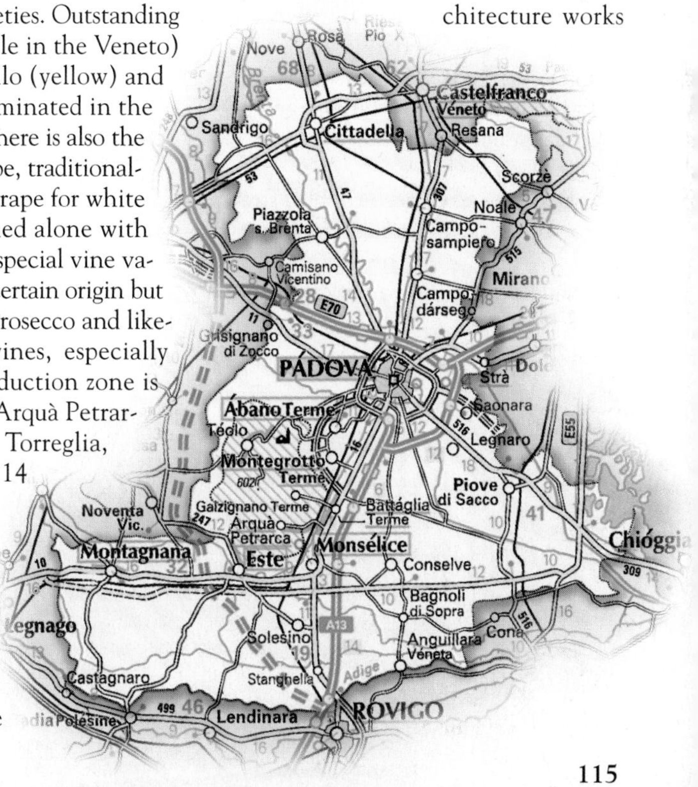

Wineries *pp. 389-400*
Bagnoli di Sopra, Cinto Euganeo, Monselice, Selvazzano Dentro.

such as the neoclassical Hotel dell'Orologio. Nearby are the sanctuary of the Vergine di Monteortone, with important 15th-century frescoes, the convent of S. Daniele in Monte, with its hillside panorama, and, just a little farther south, along the national road, Montegrotto, another historical hot-springs resort. Worth visiting is the nearby Benedictine abbey of Praglia, built in the 15th and 16th centuries.

▪ **GALZIGNANO**. You continue on towards Torreglia and Luvigliano, a village dominated by the 16th-century Villa dei Vescovi, now the home of a well-known winery. At Valsanzibio, not far from Galzignano, there is the stunning Italian-style garden of Villa Barbarigo, dating from 1669; its monumental entrance (also known as Diana's Bath and formerly a river-landing) opens out into a marvelous park full of fountains, statuary and geometrically laid out greenery.

▪ **ARQUÀ PETRARCA**. Steep cobbled streets, stone houses, and small Gothic-style buildings bring to mind the great poet of Arezzo, Petrarch, who spent his last years and died here. Timeless is the cultivation of the jujube, a shrub imported from Asia in Venetian times that has olive-like fruit used to make sweets and a liqueur according to an ages-old recipe.

▪ **ESTE**. The first thing you see is the medieval castle girded by walls and rebuilt by the Cararesi family in 1339-40. Este was founded much earlier than that, though; eloquently testifying to this is the Archeological Museum, which documents the pre-Roman past of the town when it was the principal center in the Veneto. The town is famed for its artistic pottery and cold meats.

▪ **SELVAZZANO**. Nearly back in Padua after a complete tour of the hills, you come upon Villa Emo Capodilista, a stately home with a square layout and identical portico-and-loggia façades which, in the 16th century, was annexed to the medieval castle standing on the Montecchia hill. The oldest part of the complex is home to a first-class winery.

The Dominio di Bagnoli

Tangential to the Colli Euganei zone, in the southeastern part of the Padua plain,

Padua's Prato della Valle

lies the vineyard that was once a mainland "dominion" of the Venetian Republic. It is not well known but is significant for its traditions and the caliber of the historic wine estate in its midst.
The pride of the vineyard, planted mostly with red-berried grapes, is Friularo, an autochthonous member of the Raboso vine family that also produces wines in the Vendemmia Tardiva (late-harvest) and Passito versions.
Alongside of it are Merlot, Cabernet, and Carménère, an ancient and aromatic variety of Cabernet Franc, which have been grown here for more than a century.

Petrarca's statue at Arquà

THE STRADON (ROUTE) DEL VIN FRIULARO

This wine and gastronomy route starts in Padua, takes in Bagnoli di Sopra along the Conselvana road (the "Antico Stradon del Vin Friularo") and continues in a ring linking the most significant places in the DOC zone. A description of the itinerary can be gotten at the office of the Dominio di Bagnoli tutelary consortium.

▪ **BAGNOLI DI SOPRA.** The so-called Dominio di Bagnoli was founded in 964 A.D. and was owned by the Benedictine monks who first planted vines in the alluvial soil of the Conselvano. In the 17th century, under Venice, the dominion passed to the Widmann family, which transformed the abbey into the sumptuous complex that bears the architectural mark of Longhena's design: a villa with adjacent church, stables, cellars, and enormous granaries. Along with its historical importance, the place has literary echoes, as a host to Goldoni and other literati.

▪ **MONSELICE.** A pretty medieval little town on a slope, with concentric streets and access ramps. Here you can visit the Duomo Vecchio, the sanctuary of the Seven Churches contained within the precincts of scenographic Villa Duodo, and the castle, rising on the cone of trachyte – the isolated *Mons silicis* ("flintstone mountain") – which gives the place its name.

▪ **BATTAGLIA TERME.** This lovely riverside town relives its river-trading past in the Museo del Burchio, devoted to the barge, the most characteristic of ancient Venetian transport boats. Great patrician dwellings, such as the Cataio (a singular "place of delights") and Villa Selvatico Capodilista are reminders of Venetian splendors.

View of Este's castle

THE TREVISO REGION AND THE EASTERN PLAIN

TV
VE

Between Valdobbiadene and Conegliano you find one of the champions of Italian oenology, Prosecco, while the vineyards of the Bassa (lower plain) border on Friuli

The eastern part of the region, crossed by the Piave river as it issues from Val Belluna, has two well-defined wine districts. The first consists of the band of foothills which falls within the Treviso province and aligns the Asolo Hills and the Montello area with, across the river, the gentle rises linking Conegliano with Valdobbiadene. The second district encompasses the alluvial terrain of the lower Treviso plain and of the Venetian hinterland, and is a prelude to the Friuli's Grave. In addition to the DOC labels, on the provincial level there is also the Marca Trevigiana IGT.

The Land of Prosecco

However different the soil may be on either side of the Piave, the foothills find homogeneity in the cultivation of Prosecco, a vine whose grapes are ideal for spumante production. This is a first-rate wine district and one of international fame.

THE COLLI ASOLANI AND THE MONTELLO AREA

The tutelary consortium, with headquarters in beautiful Villa Barbaro in Maser, has worked out a wine and gastronomy route that winds through territory thick in attractions – one of the most picturesque in the province.

■ **NERVESA DELLA BATTAGLIA**. Reached from Treviso on the Pontebbana national road, Nervesa was witness to important events during World War I, as attested to by the memorial monument on the lower slopes of nearby Montello. Not far from here is Selva, with the huge Loredan shed, now home to a winery, and also Venegazzù, noted for the 18th-

Hills and vineyards at Conegliano

century Villa Loredan Gasparini, home to another wine producing firm.

▪ **MONTEBELLUNA**. Formerly the Roman *Mons Bellonae*, today it is one of the province's busiest manufacturing centers, especially of sports shoes, as can be seen in the Boot Museum housed in 16th-century Villa Zuccareda-Binetti. Quite close by is Caerano San Marco, an ancient village featuring the turreted façade of Villa Benzi-Zecchini.

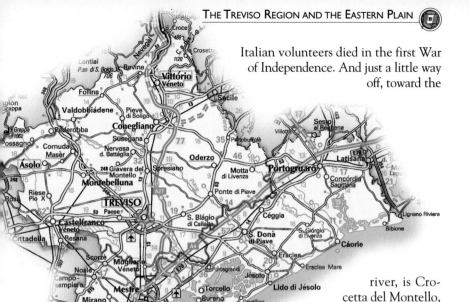

▪ **CORNUDA**. A village guarding the mountain pass into the Piave valley; not far from the sanctuary of S. Maria della Rocca is an ossuary built in memory of the Italian volunteers died in the first War of Independence. And just a little way off, toward the river, is Crocetta del Montello, with Villa Sandi, in Palladian style and adorned with statues, today the home to an important winery.

▪ **MASER**. A tranquil hill town renowned as the site of Villa Barbaro, one of Palladio's finest works enriched with a large set of frescoes by Veronese and stuccowork by Vittoria. Standing out along the road is the so-called Tempietto, Palladio's version of the Pantheon; worth visiting are the Carriage Museum, housed in a nearby outbuilding, and the villa's underground vaulted wine cellars, built in the 19th century.

▪ **ASOLO**. This splendid town – praised for centuries by travelers and poets and surrounded by olive and cypress trees and a countryside scattered with villas – can be fully appreciated from the fortress dominating medieval buildings, fountains, and flower-adorned windows.
Not far away is Possagno, birthplace of Canova, where the artist's childhood home can be visited along with the annexed museum containing original plaster models and drawings of his works. Here, too, is the great Temple, built from 1819 to 1830 and designed by Canova himself.

THE CONEGLIANO VALDOBBIADENE PROSECCO DOC ROUTE

A very pleasant, linear route connecting the two main cities of the Alta Marca Trevigiana. The beauty of the countryside and a strong wine tradition have favored the development of first-class restaurants and wine-gastronomy tourism. This wine route was the first to be inaugurated in Italy, in 1966.

■ **CONEGLIANO**. One of the busiest entrepreneurial cities in the province, it still conserves the imprint of a medieval fortress; the Duomo holds a Madonna on a Throne by Cima da Conegliano, and, climbing the Castelvecchio esplanade, or, even better, looking out from the Torre della Campana, the vista embraces the Marca Trevigiana from the plain to the hills. Descending towards the Piave river you come to Susegana and the castle of S. Salvatore, a fortified village girt by a double circle of walls. On the border with Pieve di Soligo is the castle of Collalto, similar in structure but damaged and now home to an important winery.

■ **SAN PIETRO DI FELETTO**. A scattered hillside municipality, it gets its name from the millenniums-old Romanesque church of S. Pietro, filled with admirable frescoes. Not far away is Refrontolo, one of the best known places in the Marca for having given its name to a special passito wine made from Marzemino grapes.

■ **PIEVE DI SOLIGO**. This is the hub of the Quartier del Piave, in the heart of the Prosecco production zone; its historical center contains delightful Venetian-style buildings and a Neoclassical parish church with a lovely 16th-century altarpiece. At Solighetto, in a charming park overlooking the valley, sits 18th-century Villa Brandolini d'Adda, among other things home to a small museum devoted to opera star Toti Dal Monte and to the Prosecco tutelary consortium. It is a quick climb to Follina, a village with lovely 16th-century houses that grew up around the Cistercian abbey of S. Maria. You then continue through the "Conca d'Oro", so called for its extraordinary wine vocation.

■ **VALDOBBIADENE**. Lying at the feet of the Cesen massif, this town appears through hills carpeted with vineyards. San Pietro di Barbozza is the center of reference for the small production zone of Cartizze Superiore, in which most Prosecco produc-

Brenta Riviera near Dolo

Rural buildings at Lison, in Portogruaro's municipality

ers are concentrated. Of great prestige is the National Spumante Show, held each year in early September at Villa dei Cedri.

The Eastern Plain

The vast plain running from Treviso to the border with Friuli is an area of well-drained alluvial soil very suitable to viticulture. It is home to the Piave and Lison-Pramaggiore DOC zones, the latter shared with the Pordenone province in Friuli. The two IGTs, Alto Livenza and Veneto Orientale, complete the panorama of safeguarded wines.

On Both Sides of the Piave

Conegliano is also the departure point for a red wine route (Raboso wine in the first place), which goes through the south-eastern territory.

▪ **Oderzo**. In a landscape marked by an abundance of water, in which poplars alternate with vineyards, you pass through Vazzola (the main wine center of the Piave DOC), San Polo di Piave (one of the Veneto's largest wine towns), and Ormelle, a village with old-fashioned atmosphere and lovely churches, finally reaching Oderzo, the ancient *Opitergium*. The beauties of Roman mosaic work can be seen in the Civic Museum and found in the Duomo, built over an early Christian basilica. The historical center is a delight, with noble mansions with porticos as mementos of a long and felicitous Venetian period. From here the route continues on to Livenza, at the eastern edge of the DOC, with significant stops at Motta di Livenza (an old river port) and San Stino di Livenza, a point of contact with the Lison-Pramaggiore DOC.

▪ **Portobuffolè**. Located a few miles north of Oderzo, this is a still-intact, charming 16th-century town that until that century served important military functions and was a go-between in trading between Venice and Germany. The Venetian era lives on in the public buildings of Piazza Maggiore, and the town's fluvial history in the tiny Borgo dei Barcaroli, beyond a dry branch of the Livenza.

Across the Vineyards of the Doges

The tutelary consortium protecting the Lison-Pramaggiore DOC, with headquarters at the Enoteca Regionale di Pramaggiore, has prepared three itineraries distinguishing the Classico zone from those running seaward along the Livenza river to the west and along the Tagliamento to the east.

- **PORTOGRUARO**. A city crossed by the Lemene river, it was linked for centuries to water-based activities, as the mills and picturesque Pescheria can attest to. Its historical center, rich in medieval and Renaissance mansions, also contains the Gothic-style Loggia del Comune.
Nearby, where ancient Via Postumia and Via Annia intersect, is the site of the former *Julia Concordia*, today Concordia Sagittaria, where Roman ruins can still be seen as well as the remains of an early Christian cathedral. Witness to another phase of history is the beautiful church of S. Maria Maggiore in Sumaga, a reminder of the Benedictine abbey that brought viticulture to the zone.

- **SAN STINO DI LIVENZA**. A river town enriched with villas and pretty churches (S. Marco, Madonna della Salute), it dates from the Venetian domination that be-

The bell tower of Caorle's Cathedral

Wineries *pp. 389-400*
Annone Veneto, Conegliano, Crocetta del Montello, Fossalta di Piave, Fossalta di Portogruaro, Gorgo al Monticano, Mansuè, Maser, Nervesa della Battaglia, Pieve di Soligo, Refrontolo, Roncade, Salgareda, San Fior, Santo Stino di Livenza, Spresiano, Valdobbiadene, Vidor, Vittorio Veneto, Volpago del Montello.

gan in the 15th century after long disputes between Venice and Aquileia, which had fortified the town. From here it is worth a side trip to Corbolone, with the frescoed 16th-century church of S. Marco, and further on to Caorle, an Adriatic port with a fine historical center and excellent food, especially fish (Livenza eels are a specialty).

- **ANNONE VENETO**. The town takes its name from the Latin *ad nonum*, or the "ninth mile" along the Via Postumia, and lies between Oderzo and Concordia Sagittaria. It is worth a stop for its winery, famous for organic production and housed in a villa with annexed wine gallery.

- **PRAMAGGIORE**. The Venetian Republic considered this as its own "wine reserve" and even today it stands out in the Venetian hinterland as a possessor of DOC wines, as well being the site of the tutelary consortium and annexed Enoteca Regionale, plus an interesting Folk Museum housed in the 15th-century Belfiore water-mill on the banks of the Loncon.

- **SESTO AL REGHENA**. A dip into Friuli to admire the treasures of the Benedictine abbey of S. Maria in Silvis, which in the Middle Ages had jurisdiction over an ample part of the interior; quite lovely is the Romanesque-Byzantine basilica with crypt and extensive frescoes.

Specialties in the Veneto

IN THE NORTHERN Italian panorama, the Veneto is the region with most varied natural environments: from the Adriatic lagoons to the Dolomites, from Lake Garda to the Colli Berici and Euganei. Equally varied is its food scene: cheeses (starring Asiago); cold meats, with a special soft salami called *soppressa* and the Berico-Euganeo prosciutto; produce, with red Treviso radicchio (in salads and cooked) and the Lamon beans of the Belluno area, prime material for *pasta e fagioli*. And then Garda olive oil, an exceptional complement to freshwater fish; the rice from the lower Verona plain and Polesine, which goes so well with vegetables, herbs, meats, and cold meats; Marano corn, the base for traditional polenta.
And what to say of Venice, so particular a place? Seafood, from the lagoon and the Adriatic sea, is the star of the table, without forgetting game from the valleys and produce from coastline farms. Unmistakable is the use of raisins and spices – such as in the typical *sarde in saor* (sweet-and-sour sardines) – that can be traced to ancient trading with the Levant.

IN THE INTERIOR, Padua, Treviso, and Rovigo each put their own accents on the passage from sea to plain: on the banks of the Bacchiglione the princely dish is risotto, enriched with the meat of local praised chickens; in the city bathed by the Sile river, the protagonists are eels and red radicchio; along the Po, the country-bred guinea hen *in tecia* is a counterpoint to the fish and game of the delta valleys. Further inland, Vicenza stands out for an unexpected specialty, *baccalà* (dried cod), prepared in a very special amalgam of milk, oil and anchovies, while Verona is divided between Lake Garda, with its fish and Mediterranean accents, and the lower plain, with its *pastissada de caval* (horsemeat or beef stewed in wine) and its mixed boiled meats with *pearà*. In the mountains between the two provinces, from the Asiago plateau to the Lessinia valleys, the ethnic niche of the Chimbrians offers flavors of Teutonic descent: potato dumplings with ricotta, spicy pork sausage with sauerkraut, and apple fritters. Finally, Belluno and the Piave valley are the most properly alpine, first with pasta and beans, then with barley minestrone, great game and the typical Ladin dishes in the Ampezzo area.

AS FOR WINES, the choice is the widest possible. Whites of exceptional character accompany hors-d'oeuvres and first courses but also entire meals, when fish is on the menu: famous, like Prosecco or Soave, but also pleasant discoveries like the Lison-Pramaggiore Tocai or Bianco di Custoza. A fine match for cold meats are Bardolino Chiaretto and Tocai Rosso dei Colli Berici. For cooked meats there is a crescendo from Valpolicella to "French" Merlot and Cabernet to Amarone, which is great with game. And a sweet grand finale, with lots of bubbles: Recioto di Soave or di Gambellara; Moscato Fior d'Arancio from the Colli Euganei; Refrontolo, Torchiato di Fregona, and Torcolato di Breganze for the tastiest pastries. After the meal, a great "meditation" wine is Recioto della Valpolicella.

FRIULI-VENEZIA GIULIA

FROM GRAVE TO CARSO

Despite its limited geographical area, this region has a major place in the overall panorama of Italian wine-making, and the credit goes to its vine-growers, who have managed to reconcile tradition and modern concern for quality.

"A vineyard called Friuli" is the slogan coined by the region to promote wine tourism. This is not a snappy phrase, created just to produce a momentary effect, but is intended to serve as an introduction, brief and lapidary as it may be, to a solidly based productive system. The praises of the vineyards of Aquileia and Cividale, like those of Istria, were sung by ancient chroniclers and the present day wines confirm the validity of such judgments.

Above, Friuli vineyards; left, a modern farm at Codroipo (top) and a winery in Punta di Pordenone (bottom)

A UNIQUE CONTEXT FOR WINE

The reasons for this predestined role for viticulture are various and begin in the physical characteristics of the region: the drier upper plains give way to the lower-lying land strip bordering on the Venetian lagoons and the sea, watered by underground springs, while the calcareous ledges of Carso contrast with the fields bathed by the fragrant breezes from the Adriatic Sea. Friuli is a region of men and women of true character, with a great attachment to the soil and the culture of their rural areas, proud of their fine gastronomic products such as San Daniele prosciutto. Fortunately, this region still has a dense network of taverns, the perfect spots where to quench one's thirst with a glass of wine or one's hunger with a dish of tripe or cotechino.

San Floriano del Collio's Wine Museum

FROM MERLOT TO TOCAI

The vineyards of Friuli, 70% in the plain and the rest on the hillsides, are dominated by Merlot, which, on its own, covers over half (54%) of the total vineyard surface. It is followed, though trailing far behind, by Tocai, with 11%; the real banner of local oenology, Tocai is also the bone of contention of a legal battle being waged on the Community level between Hungary, which claims exclusive rights to the Tokaj denomination, and Friuli, which has no intention of relinquishing its own. While the nation of the Carpathians puts forth as evidence the city for which the wine was named, Friuli submits not only the genetic difference between the two varieties but also the difference in the wines: the Italian is dry, while the Hungarian is sweet, the first comes from a mono-varietal grape, while the second from several blended grapes. Currently, Hungary's reasoning has won out, and Italian production is soon destined for a new denomination, Friulano or Furlan. However, there is talk of appeals, and, given the enlargement of the European Union, a review of the question is making headway.

ONE DOCG AND NINE DOC ZONES WITH A HIGH QUALITY VITICULTURE

Trailing behind the two leading vine stocks is a large group of imported varieties such as Cabernet Franc, Pinot Bianco, and Pinot Grigio. Local varieties are Refosco dal Peduncolo Rosso, Verduzzo Friulano, Malvasia Istriana, and rare Picolit. Though not particularly prolific, these are all quality-oriented and worthy of the renown which the region's typical viticulture enjoys. An analysis of overall quality, which can be measured by the ratio of appellation production to overall production, shows that Friuli is one of Italy's vanguard regions. Almost three-quarters of the local vineyards, some 32 thousand acres, are officially registered to appellation areas. Overall production, some 15,800,000 US gallons, amounts to 6.75% of the national total and is seventh among Italian regions'. There are one DOCG appellation, recently granted to Ramandolo, and nine DOC zones: Carso, Collio, Colli Orientali del Friuli, Friuli Annia, Friuli Aquileia, Friuli Grave, Friuli Isonzo, Friuli Latisana, and Lison-Pramaggiore, the last of these shared with the bordering Veneto region.
A future project is the extension of appellation status to the entire area under vines and a further zonal breakdown of the vineyards in order to even more firmly cement the ties between the wines – which never cease to amaze for their variety and character – and the territory which gives birth to them.

FRIULI-VENEZIA GIULIA'S DOC ZONES

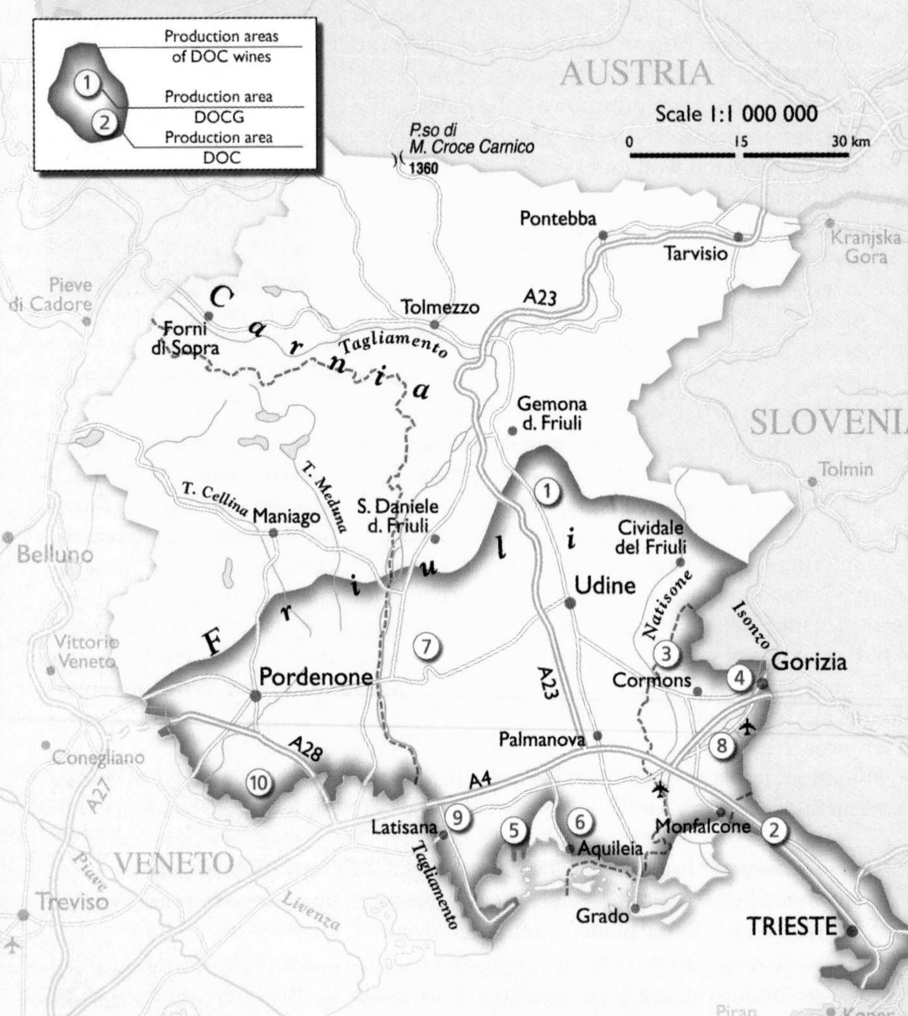

❶ **Docg Ramandolo**
❷ **Doc Carso** *6 white and 6 red wines*
❸ **Doc Colli Orientali del Friuli** *19 white, 1 rosé, and 15 red wines*
❹ **Doc Collio Goriziano** *13 white and 6 red wines*
❺ **Doc Friuli Annia** *9 white, 1 rosé, and 5 red wines*
❻ **Doc Friuli Aquileia** *11 white, 1 rosé, and 6 red wines*
❼ **Doc Friuli Grave** *10 white, 1 rosé, and 7 red wines*
❽ **Doc Friuli Isonzo** *14 white, 1 rosé, and 6 red wines*
❾ **Doc Friuli Latisana** *10 white, 1 rosé, and 7 red wines*
❿ **Doc Lison-Pramaggiore** see *also* Veneto

IGT - Typical Geographic Indication
Alto Livenza (Treviso - Pordenone); Delle Venezie (Trento - Belluno - Padua - Rovigo - Treviso - Venice - Verona - Vicenza - Pordenone - Udine - Gorizia - Trieste); Venezia Giulia (Pordenone - Udine - Gorizia - Trieste)

The Great Wines of Friuli-Venezia-Giulia

Ramandolo

Friuli's first DOCG was given to a dessert wine made from Verduzzo Friulano grapes grown in a small area of the Colli Orientali DOC zone called Ramandolo, lying between Tarcento and Nimis. The grapes come from a native vine stock of centuries-old tradition, especially in the Udine area. The wine made from them is golden yellow, sometimes deep in color, with an intense fruity aroma; it is robust and rather tannic to the palate, often with high alcohol content, and tends to be semi-sweet, with evident notes of honey. From dried pure Verduzzo grapes come semi-liqueur dessert wines.

Ramandolo's history is a prestigious one (this was one of the wines served to Pope Gregory XII at the Council of 1409). Its specificity, attributable to very particular soil and climatic conditions, is linked to greater aroma intensity and more accentuated grape acidity. Typically, the wine is golden in color, especially when settled in casks. Production is about 150,000 bottles a year. Its aroma has uncommon notes of dried apricot and chestnut honey, and its flavor is full-bodied, with a slight hint of aromatic herbs, pleasingly sweet. A classic "meditation wine", it usually accompanies sweet biscuits and dried fruit. In its zone of origin it is also served with San Daniele prosciutto and figs, with Montaperta lard and Nimis salami, with Montasio cheese, hazelnuts and honey, with smoked trout from Cornappo and Torre, and with the typical Cividale cake, *gubana*. To be served at 53.5-57 °F.

Picolit

Picolit's origins are uncertain, but one finds citations praising the goodness of this sweet wine from as early as the 17th century. The name would seem to refer to the smallness of the grape and bunches, also very sparse due to flower abortion. The very little amount of wine therefore possible to produce has led to near extinction of the vine, whose cultivation is by now limited to a very few acres in the Colli Orientali. However, this detracts nothing from the wine's extraordinary quality: its color is deep golden yellow, especially when aged or stabilized in wood; its aroma – very fine and intense – is floral, fruity, quite complex; its taste is sweet, velvety, harmonious. Alcohol content is generally fairly high. Its characteristics make it a "meditation wine", difficult to be matched with any food and preferably enjoyed by itself. Serving temperature is 53.5 to 57 °F.

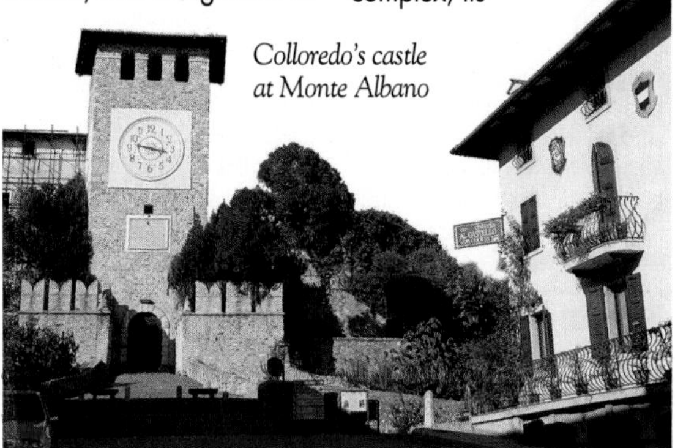

Colloredo's castle at Monte Albano

Cabernet Franc

Together with Veneto, Friuli is the principal zone in which, instead of being classically blended with Cabernet Sauvignon and Merlot, Cabernet Franc is vinified pure with excellent results. The resultant wine is ruby red, tending to purple; its aroma is intense, distinctly herbaceous and vinous; its flavor is full, tannic, and generally not very alcoholic. Drunk young it goes well with red meats and roasts; somewhat aged it is good with wildfowl dishes and aged cheeses.

Merlot

Friuli is one of the prime zones in which this famous Bordeaux vine has taken root in Italy. It is deep ruby red in color and its aroma is full and fragrant, slightly herbaceous, with hints of wild cherry and woodland berries. After the brief ageing that becomes it, it takes on spicy notes. Its taste is dry, structured and strong. It is a wine that goes well with red and white meats, roasts and medium-aged cheeses.

Refosco dal Peduncolo Rosso

An ancient Friuli vine, it produces a robust wine, ruby red tending to purple; its aroma is intense, with hints of blackberry, raspberry, and red currant; its flavor is strong, slightly tannic and

Vineyards in the Colli Orientali area

bitterish. It gives excellent results with ageing. The grapes are traditionally grown on hillsides but also in DOC zones on the plains. It is a fine accompaniment to fatty meats and the rustic dishes of Friuli cuisine.

Schioppettino
Production is limited but traditionally very important. Schioppettino is red in color, tending to purple; its aroma is typical of woodland berries – wild blackberries, raspberries, and blueberries; its flavor is full-bodied, deep, and rather sharp. It goes well with home-style Friuli fare, red meats, game dishes, and medium-aged cheeses. To be served at 61-64.5 °F.

Tocai Friulano
This dry, velvety white wine is the emblem of this region's oenology. Documented with this name since the 18th century, it has been the protagonist of a legal dispute with Hungary, which claims exclusive rights to the Tokaj denomination. The victim of years of over-production, disruptive to its reputation, Tocai Friulano is now finding redress in a return to traditional varieties that give the wine typical notes of bitter almond and hay. It is excellent as an aperitif, especially to accompany San Daniele prosciutto; it is also good with first courses, white meats, and fresh cheeses.

Pinot Bianco
A variety of exceptional quality, it produces velvety wines with enough alcohol content and acidity to allow considerable development over time. When young it has apple, apricot and Artemisia aromas; with ageing it acquires notes reminiscent of ripe fruit, dried fruit, and aromatic herbs. It is an aperitif wine suited to a vast array of lean hors-d'oeuvres, soups, and dishes based on eggs or fish.

Pinot Grigio
This medium-sized grape produces well-structured varietals with a good bent for ageing. Their color varies in intensity – coppery in the case of lengthier contact with the peels – its aroma is reminiscent of acacia flowers and its taste is dry, typically slightly bitter. It goes well with ham, fresh cheeses, first courses with tomato sauces, and white meats.

Sauvignon
A white wine with fairly intense color, it is unmistakable for its heady aroma of yellow flowers and ripe fruit or, in certain situations, of fig leaves, sage, mint, tomato, bell pepper. It has a velvety, full-bodied taste, and thanks to its good acidity it takes little ageing to evolve well. It is an aperitif wine but also a good accompaniment to cream soups and vegetable soups, medium-aged cheeses, and ham.

Malvasia
Historical sources cite the presence of a variety of this originally Greek vine in Friuli and even earlier in Istria, giving it the name of Malvasia Istriana – the variety that has come down to us. The wine made from these grapes is straw yellow with green highlights and has a delicate aroma; it is moderately alcoholic, light, and thirst quenching. Excellent as an aperitif, especially with lean hors-d'oeuvres, it is also suitable for first courses based on vegetables and dishes made with eggs or fish.

Ribolla Gialla
A wine with a straw yellow color, tending to greenish; floral, fragrant aroma; dry, fresh, and light to the palate. It goes well with cold hors-d'oeuvres, vegetable-based soups, and velvety creamed soups. To be served at 50-53.5 °F.

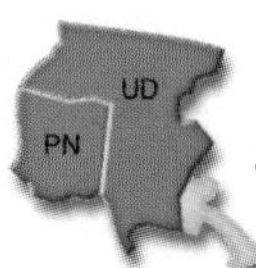

FRIULI

Seven DOC areas, almost all of them in the provinces of Udine and Pordenone, make for one of Italy's major wine zones.

The name Friuli derives from the Latin *Forum Iulii*, the ancient name for Cividale, a city founded by Julius Caesar. Today the term refers, with good approximation, to the territories of the Pordenone and Udine provinces. The Friuli wine-producing district is found on the plain crossed by the Tagliamento river, with the Livenza and Isonzo rivers as outer limits, and on the surrounding hills that follow the curve of the easternmost part of the Alps.

From the Tagliamento to the Isonzo

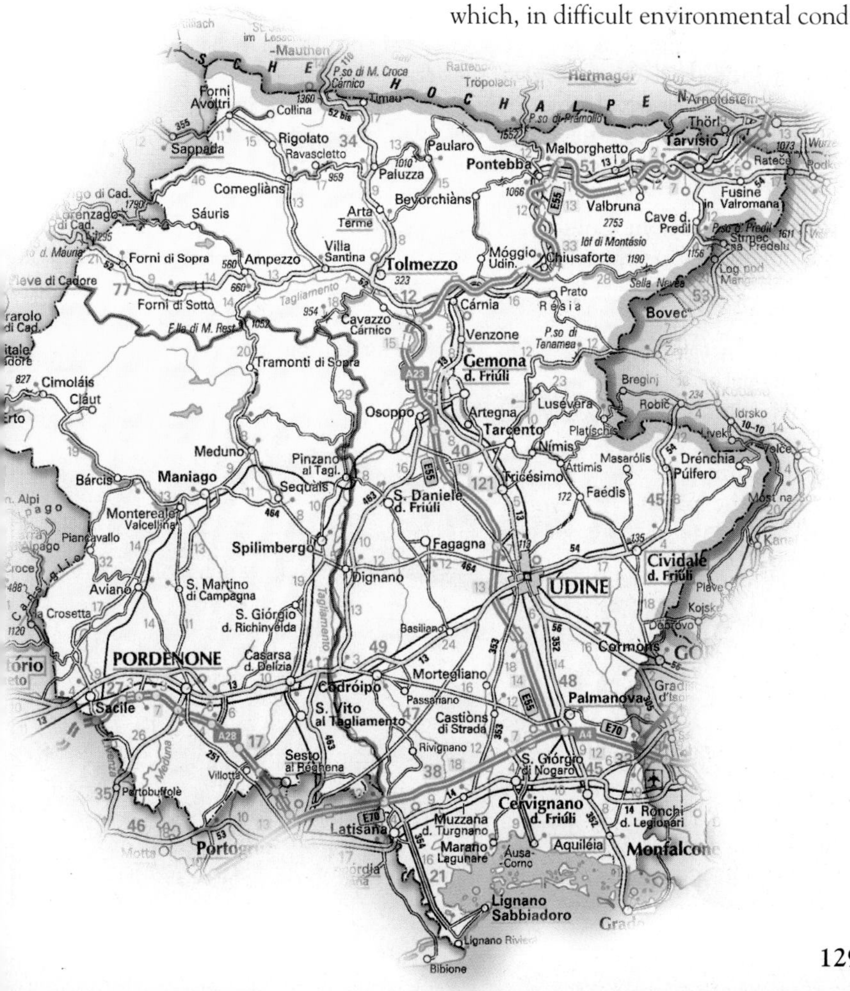

The alluvial deposits carried by the rivers crossing the plain have created a wide band of loose and permeable soil that follows the whole arc of the Friuli hills, from the border with Veneto to the Colli Orientali. Surface water is scarce in this area and vegetation has a hard time growing, hence the barren landscape of *magredi*. Paradoxically, this poor type of soil is an excellent home for the vine, which, in difficult environmental conditions, bears little but high-quality fruit. From a pedological point of view, the zone is divided into the upper plain, where the deposits are coarse, and the lower plain, where finer soil prevails. Climatically, there are two zones: to the west, the Pordenone area, with continental weather, and to the east the Udine area, which has a milder climate. Of oenological interest are the following subzones: Azzano Decimo, Casarsa della Delizia, Castelnovo del Friuli, Codroipo-Risano, Magredi, Le Castella di Sacile, San Foca-San Quirino-Roveredo in Piano. There was a similar alluvial genesis for the soil on the Isonzo plain, in the Gorizia province, east of the Judrio river. The particularity of this little zone lies in its closeness to the sea as well as in the composition of its soil, found at the foot of the marly-sandstone Collio hills and of the limestone Carso plateau.

IN THE GRAVE VINEYARDS

This itinerary follows a long diagonal path across the Friuli plain, going from the banks of the Livenza river to those of the Natisone. The road is the Pontebbana national road no. 13, from which one makes a specifically gastronomic detour to San Daniele.

▪ **SACILE.** A lovely town on the Livenza river, with portico-lined streets and buildings overlooking the water, emphasizing its Venetian character.

▪ **PORDENONE.** The name derives from *Portus Naonis*, "port on the Naone" (today's Noncello), in remembrance of times in which the city had river trade with the coastal lagoons. Corso Vittorio Emanuele, the old city's main street, is lined with palaces and churches built by Venetians at the time of the Serenissima Republic. Just outside the city, Azzano Decimo is home to the Principi di Porcia e Brugnera winery, which has marked the province's wine history since the 13th century.

▪ **CODROIPO.** Passing through Casarsa della Delizia, a town of ancient origins lying on the Postumia consular way, one arrives at Codroipo, on the border between the spring-rich lands of the lower plain and the upper dry ones. A must is a detour to Passariano to admire splendid 16th-century Villa Manin, often a venue for exhibits and events.

Casarsa's castle

WINE SPOTS

Udine: Casa della Contadinanza
The history and charm of this provincial capital, halfway between Venice and the Alps, can be seen in the splendid Piazza della Libertà, a most singular square in appearance, blending Gothic and Renaissance elements with masterful touches by Palladio and young Tiepolo in the nearby Archbishop's Palace. The oenological venue is Casa della Contadinanza, in Piazzale del Castello, the reconstruction of an ancient tavern in a 16th-century building: it is both wine exhibit and wine-bar, where DOC Friuli wines can be matched with the region's most typical products and tasted with dishes like soups, *gnocchi col frico* (potato dumplings with crunchy cheese and onions) and *baccalà mantecato* (minced cod sautéed with tomato sauce and oil).

Gradisca d'Isonzo: Enoteca Regionale La Serenissima
At the end of the 15th century the Venetians transformed Gradisca into a such a mighty fortress to resist not only the advance of the counts of Gorizia but also raids by the Turks, and it was at that time that Francisco Tren commissioned the Palazzo dei Provveditori Veneti: a jewel-case of a building now housing the town's mementos. It is also home to the Enoteca Regionale La Serenissima, with its permanent display of the wines, spumante wines, grappas, and other premium food products of the region. Covering about 11,000 sq. ft., it continually hosts high-level events and selections of products, outstanding among which are grappas, spumante wines, and honeys; the "Noè" is a strict selection of wines carefully chosen to become part of the permanent exhibit. Along with wine and allied product tasting, the Enoteca also offers an assortment of foodstuffs, starring San Daniele prosciutto, Montasio cheese, and sweets typical of the region.

▪ **SPILIMBERGO.** Climbing up from the Tagliamento, one finds this town, situated on a natural terrace looking out over Grave with its vineyards and orchards and the untilled lands of *magredi*. The Duomo is a lovely example of Gothic architecture, while the side of the castle overlooking the courtyard is richly decorated.

▪ **SAN DANIELE DEL FRIULI.** A name on everyone's lips thanks to the splendid tradition of the prosciutto "with hoof", but also a place with architectural dignity and cultural traditions, to be discovered by strolling through its ancient center, high on a hill. San Daniele is the departure point for the so-called Castles and Prosciutto Route, which, from hill to hill, leads to Udine.

Lower Friuli

Here we are in a land of karst springs, with sandy-clayey soil, that benefits climatically from its proximity to the sea, transformed into an environment quite favorable to vines after a century of reclamation. Most of the vines are red grapes varieties, with Merlot, Cabernet, and Refosco dal Peduncolo Rosso in the forefront. Whites include Tocai Friulano and Pinot.

TOURING THE VINEYARDS OF THE DOGES

This tour follows the arc ideally connecting Lignano and Grado, passing through the Latisana, Annia, and Aquileia DOC zones.

▪ **LATISANA.** The town Cathedral, located on the reclaimed lands along the Tagliamento, houses an authentic jewel: the *Baptism of Christ* by Veronese.

▪ **PALMANOVA.** It is worth a side-trip to admire this marvel of 17th century urban planning: a mighty fortress designed and built as a nine-pointed star by the Venetians, who adorned it with palaces and churches.

▪ **AQUILEIA.** With its conspicuous ruins of a Roman river port and the splendid mosaics of its early Christian basilica, it is visited as one of Italy's most fascinating archeological sites.

▪ **GRADO**. Founded by the inhabitants of Aquileia in defense against the Huns, it has a well preserved ancient nucleus, with alleys, small squares, and the early Christian basilica of S. Eufemia, charmingly located on an island between the lagoon and the sea.

The Colli Orientali

This wine zone includes the low hills of the eastern part of the Udine province, a thin but valuable strip of rolling land running from Tarcento to Nimis and from Cividale to Buttrio and Ramandolo. It is varied in soil composition and micro-climatic conditions (especially in relation to the variable distance from the sea), but in any case vine-friendly and home to seven areas of traditional excellence: Buttrio in Monte, Cialla, Cividale del Friuli, Corno di Rosazzo, Ronchi di Ipplis, Ramandolo, and Rosazzo. Vineyards are typically terraced.
White wines prevail, and among them Tocai Friulano, Sauvignon, and Pinot Grigio. There is a tiny but very prized harvesting of Picolit, the true banner of Friuli vine-growing. Merlot dominates among the reds, trailed by Cabernet and Refosco dal Peduncolo Rosso.
And not to be forgotten are two native vine varieties, Pignolo and Tazzelenghe, intelligently kept from decline and extinction.

TOURING THE COLLI ORIENTALI

The main roads of this itinerary are national roads no. 356, between Tarcento and Cormons, and no. 56, between Udine and Gorizia; around these axes are all the centers of wine interest in the Colli Orientali DOC area. The tour has its natural continuation in the Collio Goriziano itinerary (see further on).

▪ **NIMIS.** A community comprising lovely rural hamlets such as Ramandolo, possessor of the only DOCG in the region.

▪ **CIVIDALE.** High above the Natisone river, crossed by the scenic Ponte del Diavolo, this is a jewel-case of Lombard treasures, with a lovely central square adorned by the Duomo and the ancient Palazzo dei Provveditori, which houses the Archeological Museum.

▪ **PREMARIACCO**. Here one can admire the Roman bridge and two worthy testimonials to medieval times: the frescoed church of S. Silvestro and Rocca Bernarda, an

Cividale del Friuli

ancient fortress now owned by the Sovereign Military Order of Malta.

▪ **San Giovanni al Natisone.** Past Buttrio, whose very high bell-tower features the oddity of a clock with a reversed dial, and Manzano, "the chair capital", one turns east to reach this ancient post-station along the Roman way between Aquileia and Cividale.

▪ **Corno di Rosazzo.** This ancient little town is linked to the medieval Abbey of Rosazzo, praised as early as the 15th century for its "very perfect wines". Worthy of note are the Gramogliano castle tower and the 16th-century Villa Torriani.

Wineries *pp. 400-410*
Bagnaria Arsa, Bertiolo, Buttrio, Cervignano del Friuli, Cividale del Friuli, Corno di Rosazzo, Gonars, Manzano, Nimis, Palazzolo dello Stella, Pavia di Udine, Porcia, Pravisdomini, Premariacco, Prepotto, Sacile, San Giorgio della Richinvelda, San Giovanni al Natisone, San Lorenzo Isontino, San Martino al Tagliamento, San Quirino, Spilimbergo, Talmassons, Torreano, Villa Vicentina.

Venezia Giulia

In the narrow stretch between Gorizia and Trieste lies a wine zone characteristic not only for its landscape but also for its typical vine-growing.

The term Venezia Giulia stands for the narrow territory remaining to the provinces of Gorizia and Trieste after land was ceded at the end of World War II to what was then Yugoslavia. From the wine standpoint, the zone marks the transition from the Friuli context, with the vast Isonzo plain and the soft rises of Collio, to that of Istria, with the bleak highlands of the Carso overlooking the Adriatic Sea. Production, all high-level, is part of the Collio Goriziano, Friuli Isonzo and Carso DOC, and the Venezia Giulia IGT.

A Famed Name throughout the World

The Collio zone covers the hills extending from Gorizia to Dolenga, along the border with Slovenia. It is an area contiguous with and geologically similar to that of Friuli's Colli Orientali, but something makes the wines of these lands inimitable and justifies their fame: a gentleness and a delicacy of bouquet rarely found elsewhere.
In a framework of overall excellence we can pinpoint six "historical" vineyards: Capriva del Friuli, Cormons, Dolenga del Collio, Farra d'Isonzo-Villanova di Farra, Oslavia, and San Floriano. A land of great whites, Collio boasts as its primary pro-

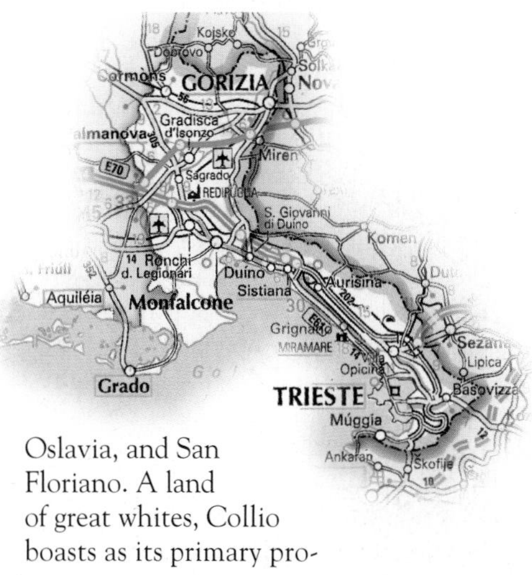

Wineries *pp. 400-410*
Capriva del Friuli, Cormons, Dolegna del Collio, Duino-Aurisina, Farra d'Isonzo, Gorizia, Gradisca d'Isonzo, Mariano del Friuli, Sagrado, San Canzian d'Isonzo, San Floriano del Collio.

ductions Pinot, Tocai Friulano, and Sauvignon, while Ribolla Gialla and Picolit are native, white-berry varieties whose grapes are vinified pure. Cabernet, Merlot, and Pinot Nero are the bases of red wine production.

TOURING THE COLLIO, ALONG THE SLOVENIAN BORDER

This itinerary ideally connects with that of Friuli's Colli Orientali, starting from Cividale. The provincial road on the border with Slovenia leads to Cormons, main center in this area, and then to Gorizia, focus of the last part of the route.

▪ **DOLEGNA DEL COLLIO.** At the northernmost end of the district, this town is crossed by the Judrio river, which a little farther on marks the border with Slovenia. In the immediate surroundings one can visit excellent wineries and the Ruttars and Trussio castle centers.

▪ **CORMONS.** Founded in pre-Roman times, it still has part of its medieval walls and distinguished buildings from the 17th and 18th centuries, including the cathedral of S. Adalberto. It is the capital of Collio and home to the Cantina Produttori di Cormons winery, famous for its Wine of Peace, artistically bottled and presented as a sign of goodwill to heads of state; and the Enoteca di Cormons, housed in a wing of Palazzo Locatelli. Cormons prosciutto is also renowned.

▪ **CAPRIVA DEL FRIULI.** Girded to the north by vineyard-covered, terraced hills, its urban texture is a reminder of its vicissitudes under Venice and Austria. Places of exceptional oenological importance are the hilly amphitheater of Spessa and the Russiz Superiore plateau.

▪ **GORIZIA.** The city, dominated by Borgo Castello (with the castle that was home to the counts of Gorizia), rises amidst the last spurs of the Julian Alps, where the Isonzo river reaches the plain. Worth a visit is the elegant town center, of Central European imprint. Nuova Gorica is nearby.

▪ **SAN FLORIANO DEL COLLIO.** We are again on the border, as the World War I Ossuary reminds us. Two castles remain as testimonials to the strategic role this small town played in a long-ago past: among other things, the Formentini Castle houses an historic winery and, in its cellars, a wine museum.

Carso: Just Waiting to be Discovered

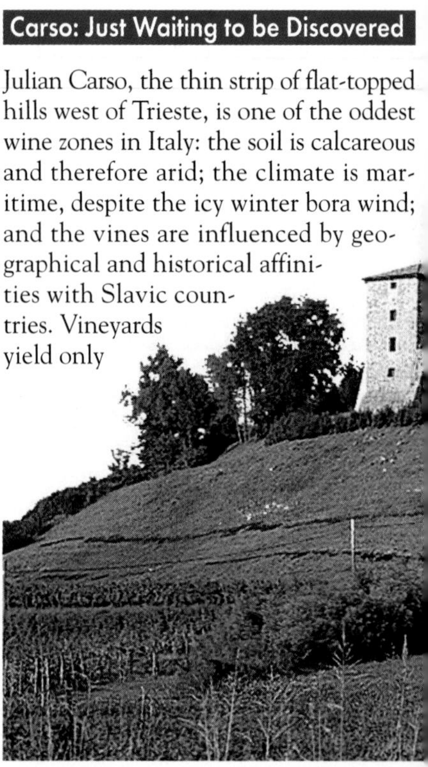

Julian Carso, the thin strip of flat-topped hills west of Trieste, is one of the oddest wine zones in Italy: the soil is calcareous and therefore arid; the climate is maritime, despite the icy winter bora wind; and the vines are influenced by geographical and historical affinities with Slavic countries. Vineyards yield only modest amounts, but possess intelligently preserved old native vines such as Terrano (red-berry grapes) and, prevailing among the whites, Malvasia Istriana and Vitouska. Other varieties included in the DOC list are Cabernet Franc and Sauvignon, Merlot, Pinot Nero, and Refosco dal Peduncolo Rosso; Pinot Grigio, Sauvignon, and Traminer.

THE TERRANO ROUTE

This itinerary begins in Gorizia, crosses the Isonzo Valley, enters deep into the unmistakable Trieste landscape, and reaches the regional capital by way of roads parallel to the main ones.

▪ **GRADISCA D'ISONZO.** Its origins as a fortress, built in the 15th century by the Venetians, are evident in the walls, bastions, gates, and towers that gird the historical center, home to the picturesque Palazzo dei Provveditori Veneti and the Enoteca Regionale La Serenissima. Also worthy of note are Palazzo Torrani (designed by Palladio and today the home of the Gallery of Modern Art) and the ancient castle, modified by the Austrians.

▪ **DUINO-AURISINA.** Once a fishing village, its chief adornment is the Castello Nuovo (new castle); the ruins of the old castle, destroyed by the Turks, can be seen on a headland. From here the road follows the coast to Sistiana, a seaside resort encircled by woods; then it heads inland, along the so-called Terrano Route, from Visogliano to Opicina, with stops at the many traditional recommended trattorias. Premium local products are Carso prosciutto and cheese from Mount Tabor.

▪ **TRIESTE.** Its seafaring, mercantile, and cosmopolitan atmosphere gives Trieste – scenically located between the sea and the hill of San Giusto – unique charm. Among the many attractions of this city, home to novelist Italo Svevo, are the old cafés (Pirona, San Marco, Tommaseo, Torinese, Degli Specchi) that were formerly the sites of literary disputes and political ferment, or the buffet in the heart of town that offer steaming-hot sausages to be washed down with beer or Terrano wine. When dining, plum dumplings, goulash, and Sacher Torte revive memories of the Austro-Hungarian Empire.

Ruttars castle center near Dolegna del Collio

■ Specialties in Friuli-Venezia Giulia ■

WE ARE IN THE FAR northeastern corner of Italy, delimited by the Carnic and Julian Alps that gently slope into foothills and the plain, first dry then verdant, running towards the Adriatic lagoons. There are two provinces in Friuli, Udine and Pordenone, once among the most appraised mainland dominions of Venice; and two in Venezia Giulia, Gorizia and Trieste, still vibrant with Austro-Hungarian atmosphere and nerve centers of contact with Central Europe.

ALL THIS NATURALLY reflects on food. From the Latin sphere come the flavors of the plain, with risotto and polenta served with all sorts of garnishing, and seafood, with the Levantine touch typical of Venetian *sarde in saor*. Of Central European origin are the dishes one can eat at the buffet in the port of Trieste, such as goulash and sausages served on steaming-hot sauerkraut. Finally, typically Slovene are the spicy flavors of skewered meats and certain seafood dishes. Should we need to prove the region's exceptional vocation for wine and food, the first mention would go to the hills, dotted with castles, where the vines offers their finest products and livestock raising provides that star of Italian cold meats, San Daniele prosciutto.

CARNIA IS A WORLD APART, with Carinthian-accented alpine flavors: great products are the cheeses (especially Montasio) and Sauris smoked ham; typical dishes are barley and bean soup, meat ravioli called *cialzons*, and game seasoned with spices evoking Austrian cuisine. As for restaurants, in an overall outstanding context special mention should be given to the osterie (taverns), still largely in existence and genuine in character. In these sanctuaries of tradition, the daily rite – sacred to most of the inhabitants – is that of the *tajut*, a glass of white to wash down a bit of *cotechino con la brovada*, in which the flavor of spiced pork sausage and the tartness of turnips combine in a wonderful way as a prelude to the specialties of local cuisine.

AS FAR AS WINE is concerned, the range of whites provides a generous accompaniment to hors-d'oeuvres and first courses, especially fish dishes: trout from the Natisone, grilled seafood, seafood risotto, and fish broth are combined in growing intensity with Tocai Friulano, Pinot Bianco, Ribolla Gialla, Sauvignon, and Pinot Grigio. This last wine also goes well with prosciutto and white meats cooked in sauces. Cold meats, spicier first courses, fish in tomato sauce, white meats and medium-aged cheeses call for Merlot. The two Cabernets, Franc and Sauvignon, plus Refosco and Schioppettino come on the scene with red meats and more aged cheeses. Game dishes are the province of Cabernet, with roebuck in the forefront. An interesting case is that of the two most famous dessert wines, Ramandolo and Picolit, which can also accompany liver pâté and cheese streaked with green mold. Another eclectic wine is Verduzzo: dry, it goes well with fish; semi-sweet with pumpkin tortelli and Venetian-style liver-and-onions; sweet, with desserts.

LIGURIA

THE VINES AND THE SEA

Ligurian viticulture is inextricably linked to the image of the Cinque Terre vineyards, carved into the face of the mountains by centuries of unceasing toil. Today, new and equally interesting zones have begun to attract the attention of connoisseurs.

The cultivation of the vine in Liguria is at the mercy of two opposing forces: a maritime climate which is exceptionally favorable to agriculture and a rugged terrain which is anything but generous in terms of arable spaces. Topographically, this is a mountainous region, with peaks which descend almost to the sea and slopes which are almost prohibitively steep. In spite of that, a grand passion for their work and the certitude that other elements are work-

Cinque Terre: above, a view of Manarola; left, typical terraced vineyards (top) and Riomaggiore (bottom)

ing in their favor are enough to convince vignerons to continue the toil of maintaining the terraced vineyards which are a dominant feature of an ample part of the coast. Subjected as it is to these objective limits, the wine production has long been, and remains, a limited part of the local economy, characterized by very few specialized vineyards. Over the past few years, with the creation of several new DOC zones, there has been a re-launching of Ligurian wines, but it is, nonetheless, still difficult to find them outside their native region.

A Large Number of Grape Varieties and Two Outstanding Wines

One of the major features of Ligurian viticulture is the large number of different grapes which are grown. Until recently, 85 different types of wine, mostly white, were produced from a large variety of blends (over 100 grape varieties were grown in the vineyards). This is a common characteristic of maritime regions, where commerce by sea, and subsequently overland commerce as well, contributed to the diffusion of a multitude of grape varieties from many different countries. Vermentino apparently arrived from Spain by way of Corsica, while Dolcetto descended from Piedmont through the mountain passes; Tuscany contributed Canaiolo, Ciliegiolo Nero, Trebbiano Toscano, and Vernaccia del Chianti. Of other varieties, such as Rossese of the Dolceacqua DOC and Bosco and Albarola of Cinque Terre DOC, little is known except for their centuries-old presence in the territory.
The DOC rules have drastically reduced the number of grapes which are cultivated, to the benefit of a more constant quality – but not without some apprehension for the ampelographic patrimony of the region.

An Enological Patrimony with 7 Doc Zones

Two historical DOC wines, Cinque Terre and Rossese di Dolceacqua, at opposite ends of the arc-shaped coastline, characterize the regional production panorama. Five others, notably newer, have joined them: Colli di Levanto, Colli di Luni, Golfo del Tigullio, Riviera Ligure di Ponente, and Valpolcevera. IGT (Typical Geographic Indication) rules regulate other production areas: Golfo dei Poeti, Spezzino, and Colline Savonesi. Despite this praiseworthy reorganization of the territory, Liguria's image is still closely linked to a limited number of wines which, though produced in small quantities, have gained a notable fame in the rest of Italy as a result of a reputation gained by centuries of high quality.
The most typical product of the region is Sciacchetrà, a sweet wine indissolubly linked to the Cinque Terre landscape. The name derives from the fusion of two dialect words: "sciac", or crush, and "trà", put aside, a clear reference to the long ageing which the wine undergoes. The grapes, hung up to dry for two to three months, are pressed and then drawn from the fermenting vats after a mere 24 hours. The must passes immediately into the barrel, it is poured out three times on the average and is bottled in April. With this process, the percentage of residual sugar remains very high and gives the wine its desired sweetness. Rossese di Dolceacqua is the next most important wine in terms of fame, and is likewise linked to a particular landscape, the area just inland from Ventimiglia. It is Liguria's sole red wine with a strong personality.

The Great Wines of Liguria

Cinque Terre Sciacchetrà

This is the Ligurian wine on everyone's lips, partly for the charm of its origin place and partly for its rarity. Sciacchetrà is made primarily from Bosco grapes (min. 40%), with additions of Albarola and Vermentino (max. 40%) and other local grapes. The bunches are generally dried on shaded racks in ventilated positions so that the sugary juice concentrate slowly. By law, pressing cannot begin before November 1st. The resulting wine ranges in color from golden yellow to amber and has an intense scent of passito, with hints of honey, fruits, and spices; taste varies from slightly sweet to sweet, is well-bodied and has an almond aftertaste. Alcohol: 17%, at least 13.5% of which developed. Minimum refinement is for a year, rising to three for the Reserve. Sciacchetrà was born as a dessert wine and is excellent with traditional Ligurian pastries like Genoa's *pandolce* or *canestrelli* cookies, but also with delicacies like candied bitter-orange rind. It should also be tried with the stronger cheeses streaked with green mold, as well as with *pecorino.*

Vermentino

Everything leads to the belief that Vermentino came to Liguria from Spain several centuries ago by way of Corsica. This grape variety gives a wine that is straw yellow in color with greenish highlights; it has a delicate aroma and a dry, bitterish taste that improves with some ageing. Vermentino is also suited to producing passito and liquoroso wines as well as good-quality spumante. Protagonist in a number of mixed-grape blends, it has its own specific label in the Colli di Luni, Golfo del Tigullio, Riviera Ligure di Ponente, and Valpolcevera DOCs. Recent studies have shown a basic similarity between Vermentino and Pigato, also produced with a specific label in the Riviera Ligure di Ponente DOC.

Rossese

This vine of unknown origins has been grown for more than a century in the hinterland of Imperia. The result is a superior wine, suitable for ageing, of ruby red color tending to garnet when aged, with delicate and characteristic aroma and aromatic, mellow, alcoholic taste. Protagonist in the Rossese di Dolceacqua DOC, it also has a specific label in the Riviera Ligure di Ponente DOC.

Ormeasco

This wine comes from Dolcetto grapes imported from Piedmont and cultivated in the highest part of the Ponente Ligure vine-lands. It is a ruby red wine with garnet highlights, it has a woodland berries and violets aroma with hints of vanilla and pepper; its taste is dry, with a bitterish aftertaste, and its texture and alcohol content are significant.

Vines high above the sea at Vernazza

LIGURIA'S DOC ZONES

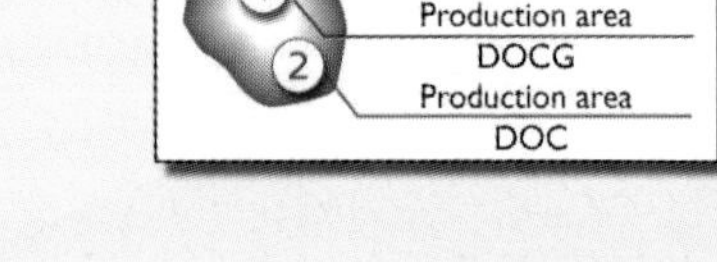

Scale 1:1 250 000

0 15 30 km

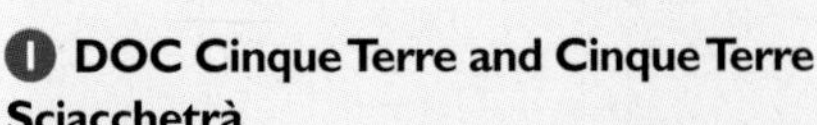

❶ **DOC Cinque Terre and Cinque Terre Sciacchetrà**

❷ **DOC Colli di Luni** *Bianco, Vermentino* ▪ *Rosso*

❸ **DOC Colline di Levanto** *Bianco* ▪ *Rosso*

❹ **DOC Golfo del Tigullio** *Bianco, Bianco Passito, Bianchetta genovese, Moscato, Moscato Passito, Vermentino, Spumante* ▪ *Rosato* ▪ *Rosso, Ciliegiolo*

❺ **DOC Riviera Ligure di Ponente** *Pigato, Vermentino* ▪ *Ormeasco, Ormeasco Sciacchetrà, Rossese*

❻ **DOC Rossese di Dolceacqua**

❼ **DOC Valpolcevera** *Bianco, Bianchetta Genovese, Coronata, Passito, Vermentino* ▪ *Rosato* ▪ *Rosso*

IGT - Typical Geographic Indication

Colline del Genovesato (Genoa); Colline Savonesi (Savona)

THE RIVIERA DI LEVANTE

The terraced vineyards of Cinque Terre reveal all the charm of a region lying between mountains and sea.

The wine fame of the Riviera di Levante (Eastern Riviera), running from Genoa to La Spezia, comes almost exclusively from the output of the Cinque Terre DOC, instituted in 1973 to protect the wine district at the end of the arc of Liguria's coast, as small as it is significant in oenological terms. In 1995 this DOC was joined by Colline di Levante on one side and Colli di Luni on the other (the latter shared, if only in three municipalities, with Tuscany) to form the widest La Spezia wine district. More recently, the Golfo del Tigullio and Valpolcevera DOCs were created, covering the wine land in the Genoa province.

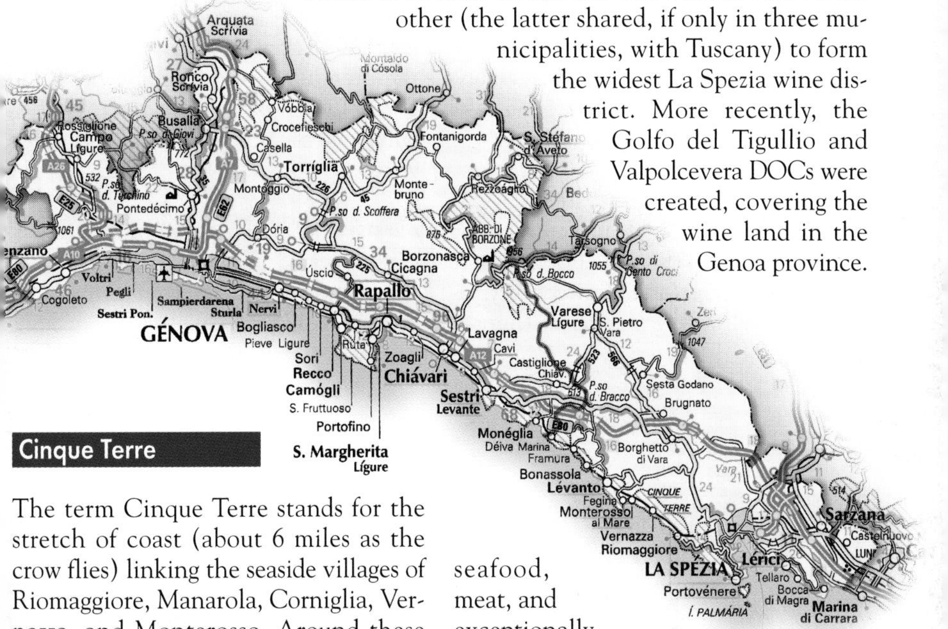

Cinque Terre

The term Cinque Terre stands for the stretch of coast (about 6 miles as the crow flies) linking the seaside villages of Riomaggiore, Manarola, Corniglia, Vernazza, and Monterosso. Around these centers, on the sloping coastline, are terraced vineyards that cannot but arouse admiration and amazement. The wines that result (with imaginable efforts) have been praised in every epoch: they include a legendary Sciacchetrà, a rarity that is today very much imitated.

LEVANTE WINERIES

This route runs from Genoa to La Spezia, exploring the Riviera's five DOC zones. It passes through places so famous they need no introduction, but also goes inland into rural zones of surprising beauty. It could also be described as a gastronomy route, where seafood, meat, and exceptionally tasty produce abound; one begins with the uniqueness of the region capital city, which sums up all of Liguria's cuisine traditions, and then lingers over special accents at places which have always been influenced by nearby Emilia and Tuscany.

▪ **GENOA.** A great Mediterranean port and metropolis, very rich in history, charm, moods and tastes. Part of the city is medieval, around the Cathedral dedicated to S. Lorenzo and the fascinating Piazza S. Matteo, and part is mannerist and baroque, as shown by extravagant patrician dwellings and monumen-

tal buildings – see Via Garibaldi. Modern additions are to be found, for instance, in the old port's tourist attractions, such as the splendid Aquarium (Europe's largest), the panoramic cable car that runs above the sea, and the ancient port buildings converted to public use according to Renzo Piano's design.
For seekers of wine finds, Coronata marks the start of the Valpolcevera DOC, which here has a specific geographical mention. You then go inland, to Sant'Olcese and even higher, to taste, among other things, cheeses and cold meats of renown.

▪ **CHIAVARI.** The capital of the Golfo del Tigullio DOC is notable for its charming portico-lined streets parallel to the shore and its many 17th and 18th-century patrician dwellings. From here, there is much to choose from. Tourists and sea-lovers are drawn to Santa Margherita Ligure, an elegant town on the Tigullio Bay famed for its road or sea excursions to Portofino. The oenological "circuit" takes you inland to the farming zones of Val Fontanabuona, luscious with vineyards, orchards, olive groves, and hazelnut trees. At the bottom of the valley the Ponte Vecchio crosses the Lavagna stream along an ancient trade route heading to Lombardy. The vignerons of the premium Casarza area grow Bianchetta Genovese grapes which, vinified pure, give the homonymous DOC white wine.

▪ **SESTRI LEVANTE.** The town historical center, with typical Ligurian seafaring traits, rises on a promontory romantically set between Baia delle Favole, a bay opening

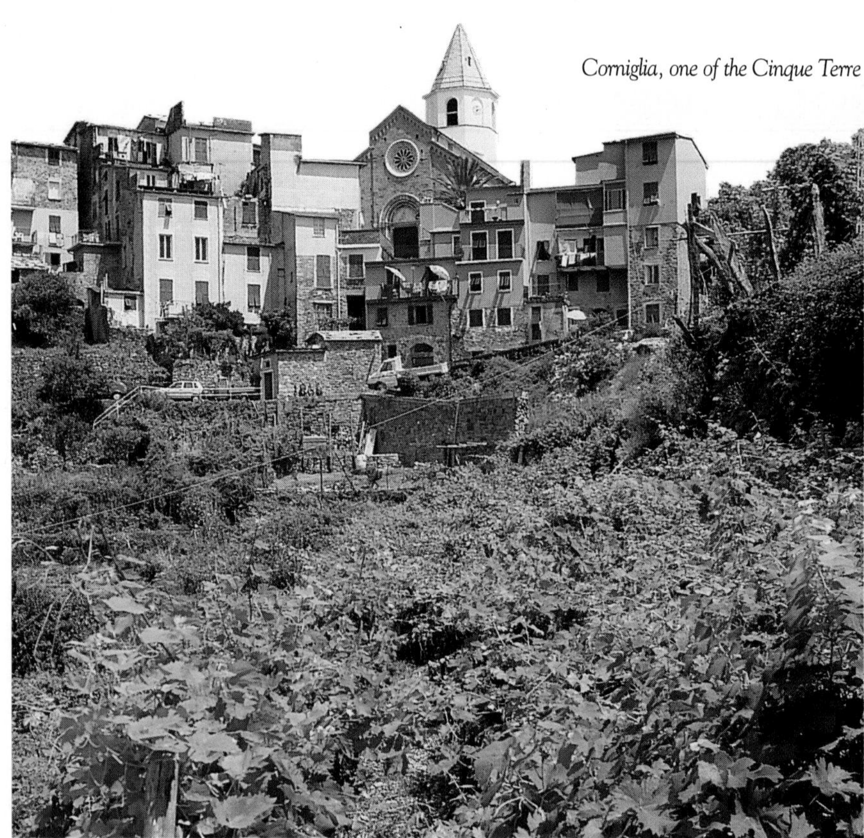

Corniglia, one of the Cinque Terre

Wineries *pp. 410-412*
Castelnuovo Magra, Chiavari, Ortonovo, Riomaggiore, Sarzana.

on to the Tigullio, and Baia del Silenzio, more secluded among the rocks. Lovers of good food will be seeking wine – we are in one of the main centers of the Golfo del Tigullio DOC – but also cheese and cold meats.

▪ **LEVANTO.** Enclosed in a natural amphitheater of vineyards and olive groves, this former fishing village (and now seaside resort) is the prime place of reference for the homonymous DOC.

▪ **RIOMAGGIORE.** With its tall, abutting houses, winding lanes, and tiny squares, this town lies between a mountainside carpeted with vineyards on one side and cliffs that drop to the sea on the other – dividing-line is the railway. Riomaggiore – the Cinque Terre easternmost town – and nearby Vernazza offer the most thrilling pictures of an ancient and laborious viticulture that add prestige to the homonymous DOC. From Riomaggiore departs the Via dell'Amore, a romantic promenade high above the sea that leads to the handful of houses at Manarola, a vignerons' village overlooking a natural amphitheater of vineyards and produce gardens. Farther on is Corniglia, high on a steep ledge, and even further Monterosso al Mare; these two villages lie in a basin with sandy beaches backed by the hills.

▪ **PORTOVENERE.** A picturesque carugio (lane) crosses this intensely Ligurian town, beloved of Byron, with a spectacular waterfront of houses and a great view of Cinque Terre. Its peninsula, along with the nearby island of Palmaria, forms the Gulf of La Spezia; Lerici (and other Mediterranean enchantments) awaits on the opposite shore.

▪ **SARZANA.** Past Vezzano and Arcola, medieval villages on either side of the Magra river, you reach Sarzana, Lunigiana's capital. Partly encircled by Genoese walls, it contains important relics of an arms-and-trading past; outstanding among them is the Romanesque-Gothic Cathedral. All around are the hills that embrace the ancient town of Luni, from whence the name of the local DOC. Not far away is Castelnuovo Magra, an ancient village built around the parish church (with a *Crucifixion* by Pieter Brueghel the Younger) and the castle, dating from the 13th century. The wine tourist is awaited at the Enoteca Pubblica della Liguria e della Lunigiana.

ENOTECA PUBBLICA DELLA LIGURIA E DELLA LUNIGIANA

It is located in the historical heart of Castelnuovo Magra and, together with the tourism office, has premises in the ancient Ingolatti-Cornello palace.
The display is set up in the vaulted cellars of the 18th-century building and concerns the entire region's oenological output, from the two Rivieras, with special attention to local Colli di Luni production; Tuscan wines from the Candia dei Colli Apuani DOC are also presented; this enlargement was logically suggested not only by the fact that the Val di Magra vineyards are shared between the La Spezia and Massa-Carrara provinces, but also by the grape "osmosis" which through the centuries has seen Sangiovese and Ciliegiolo seep into Liguria, and Vermentino into Tuscany.
The Enoteca Pubblica is the venue for many events: traditional ones – like the Goods and Livestock Fair in early September and the Pace di Dante, a procession re-evoking an historical event – and wine-and-gastronomy festivals, devoted to wine and olive oil.

THE RIVIERA DI PONENTE

A wine of great tradition, Rossese di Dolceacqua, is the jewel in the crown of the provinces of Savona and Imperia.

The Riviera di Ponente (Western Riviera), which covers the provinces of Savona and Imperia, is famous for its olive oil but also has some rather interesting wines: in a region of whites, here, on the border with Piedmont, the reds stand out: Dolcetto, locally called Ormeasco, and Rossese, made from a grape grown here from time immemorial. From the normative standpoint, the western portion of the region has two DOC productions: Rossese di Dolceacqua, circumscribed by the Nervia valley right on the border with France, and Riviera Ligure di Ponente, covering a good part of the Savona and Imperia provinces.

Between Savona and Imperia

Where the spacious territory of the Riviera Ligure di Ponente DOC is concerned, regulations define four production sub-zones, recognizing the different results the same grape can give within this vast area: Riviera dei Fiori, between Cervo and Ventimiglia, where the star is Vermentino, imported centuries ago from Spain; Ormeasco, inland from Imperia and Ventimiglia, colonized by Piedmont's Dolcetto; Albenganese, in the hinterland of Albenga and Andora, where Pigato and Rossese di Albenga predominate; and Finalese, between Noli and Borghetto Santo Spirito, land of Lumassina (or Buzzetto) and Vermentino.

THE WINE AND OIL ROUTE FROM THE ALPS TO THE SEA

This long itinerary covers the territory of the three mountain municipalities of Alta Valle Arroscia, Ingauna, and Pollupice and passes from the Savona province to Imperia's. As the name of the route indicates, it goes through a sequence of variegated landscapes, all rich in natural, historical, and artistic charm as well as in inviting wines and food.

Wineries *pp. 410-412*
Albenga, Camporosso, Chiusanico, Chiusavecchia, Diano Castello, Dolceacqua, Finale Ligure, Imperia, Isolabona, Ortovero, Pieve di Teco, Pontedassio, Quiliano, Ranzo, Soldano, Vendone.

▪ **SPOTORNO.** In addition to seaside bathing, the town offers nice walks along the lanes of its historical center, crowded with shops, lovely buildings, and loggias adorned with mullioned apertures.

▪ **FINALE LIGURE.** Beyond Noli, one of Liguria's best-preserved ancient towns (see the scenic remnants of the castle), you come to this lively seaside resort with three historical centers. The collegiate church of S. Biagio, with a 15th-century octagonal bell tower, and the picturesque Castel Gavone are architecturally outstanding. The hinterland is characterized by a series of highlands, where cultivated fields alternate with patches of Mediterranean countryside. Interesting medieval remains can be seen at Orco-Feglino.

▪ **LOANO.** Passing through Pietra Ligure (with a medieval castle), among vegetable gardens and Vermentino vineyards, you come to Loano, a town with

An alley in ancient Verezzi

remains of the old fishing village and historical settlement; today, it is better known for a very long sandy beach with a palm-lined promenade. Immediately past it comes Borghetto Santo Spirito, rich in medieval flair.

■ **ALBENGA.** This town has the most intact historical center in the Riviera di Ponente – Roman in layout and medieval in appearance. Monuments (such as the early-Christian Cathedral and Baptistery) and museums (with Roman finds) invite to an extended visit. On the surrounding plain, hothouses alternate with historical-artistic attractions such as Cisano sul Neva, a town partially girded by ancient walls, and the nearby Renaissance castle (once belonging to the Del Carretto family) and Romanesque church of S. Calogero.

■ **PIEVE DI TECO.** Following the Valle Arroscia national road – past Villanova, an interesting fortified medieval town, Ortovero, and Ranzo's country wards (in the Imperia province), scattered among chestnut woods, vineyards, olive groves, flower and herb cultivations – you come to Pieve di Teco. In this nearly intact ancient village that grew up along the Salt Road going to Piedmont are many noble residences and 15th-century buildings, such as the church of Madonna della Ripa and the Augustinian convent with the largest cloister on the Riviera di Ponente.

The vineyards of the Alta Valle Arroscia, guarded by five Savoy forts, belong to Pornassio's five country wards: the largest cultivated part (Ormesasco di Pornassio DOC) is shared by Villa and San Luigi, the valley main centers.

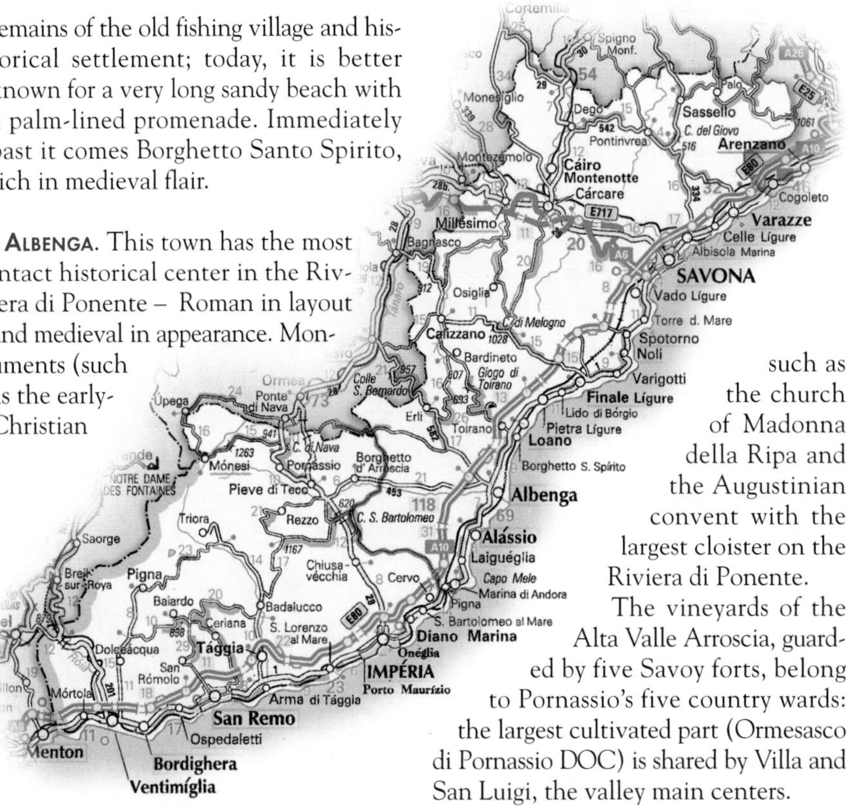

The Imperia Hinterland

The Rossese di Dolceacqua DOC, instituted in 1972, takes it name from a picturesque medieval village dominated by the ruins of a medieval castle. Production covers the areas inland from Bordighera and Ventimiglia, which have managed to conserve a lively wine industry, unlike the neighboring Cote d'Azur, devoted to tourism body and soul. This is the land of choice for the Rossese variety with its typical alate bunches and purple grapes. Other vines in Liguria bear the same name but only this one is capable of giving a wine of great finesse.

In the Dolceacqua Valley

While one of Italy's smallest, the province of Imperia has no inferiority complex. As for wine, Rossese invites you to explore the valley of Nervia and Dolceacqua, the hub of the proposed itinerary. Oil is also a star, with famous Taggiasca olives and Oneglia's oil-mills. Even the cuisine has a special character, midway between sea and mountain, enriched with an unmistakable accent of Provence.

▪ **Imperia**. This city, named from the stream that crosses it, was created in 1923 by the merger of two sea ports, Oneglia and Porto Maurizio, still distinct in appearance. The first, although older in foundation, has a 18th and 19th-century architectural imprint; Porto Maurizio is more picturesque: its historical center – perched on a promontory jutting into the sea – has retained its medieval flavor and significant works of art. One of the prime products of the area, olive oil, is documented in the Museo dell'Olivo dei Fratelli Carli in Oneglia.

▪ **Dolceacqua**. In the verdant landscape of the Nervia valley you quickly come across the ancient village of Camporosso. Just further on is Dolceacqua, an intact medieval center with its lovely Terra quarter and, across the single-arched bridge on the Nervia river, the Borgo quarter. Higher up, on rock spur, streets of strong medieval flavor rise to the Doria castle. Descending to Vallecrosia you come to Perinaldo and then get to the sea at Soldano and San Biagio della Cima, a scenic spot straddling the watershed between the two Rossese valleys.

The bridge on the Nervia stream at Dolceacqua

Specialties in Liguria

FROM A GEOGRAPHICAL point of view, Liguria is unique on the Italian scene, marked as it is by the Apennine range whose initial stretch runs for 155 miles just inland from the coast. United in a single sweep, you can often see the sea, bristling with schools of bluefish and big deep-sea fish, together with a steep (when not cliff-like) coastline, where vineyards and vegetable gardens have been planted on laboriously terraced plots, and a verdant interior, where olive groves are soon replaced by chestnut trees and an unexpectedly pastoral economy.

THIS WIDE RANGE of landscapes is reflected in Liguria's food and produce, primarily Mediterranean: olive oil and Taggiasca eating-olives; vegetables and basil, which becomes sublime in *pesto*, the most celebrated Ligurian sauce; La Spezia clams and salted anchovies. Going hand in hand with these are the inland flavors, from the cheese of Santo Stefano d'Aveto to the salami of Valpolcevera, from the white beans of Pigna and Conio and to Gabbiana chestnuts from Val Bormida. As to fine dining, first of all comes seafood, which sometimes, as with dried cod, is reminiscent of seafaring days. Exceptional are the vegetable dishes, including the famous *torta pasqualina*, which the very mild climate gives accents impossible to reproduce elsewhere. Awaiting to be discovered are the hinterland specialties, from filled pasta to goat stew.

GENOA SUMS UP THE BEST of Ligurian cuisine: from the *focaccia* sold by street vendors to *trenette al pesto*, true gastronomical emblem; from rabbit with olives and pine nuts – a Mediterranean dish par excellence – to *capon magro*, which, substituting capon meat with vegetables and fish, is a great surrogate of banquet dishes of the past. In such a small region, there are noticeable influences from beyond its borders. In the long stretch neighboring on Piedmont, just across the divide, you smell the Langhe aromas, from truffles to mushrooms, and taste Piedmont-style splendid boiled meats; on the Riviera di Ponente, from Imperia on, the Provençal influence can be felt in highly seasoned dishes, while on the Riviera di Levante, Chiavari's cuisine betrays Emilia's influence and Lunigiana anticipates robust Tuscan tastes.

WINE CONTRIBUTES to the gastronomic "state of grace" that characterizes a stay in Liguria. A range of first-class whites accompanies seafood: Cinque Terre and Vermentino are the most famous, Pigato and Bianco dei Colli di Luni among those to be discovered. Seasoned stewed fish, white meats, and medium-aged cheeses go well with Rossese or Ormeasco, which, slightly aged, are also fine accompaniments for grilled meats or rabbit in casserole. For red meat and game dishes (not particularly common in Liguria) the choice falls to the Superiore and Riserva reds.
At dessert time the inevitable selection is Cinque Terre Sciacchetrà, a passito wine ideal with pastries and tarts, but also with a cheese board full of well-aged and tasty delights.

Emilia-Romagna

From Lambrusco to Sangiovese

An endless vineyard stretches from the Apennine hills to the banks of the Po river and the shores of the Adriatic sea, and offers renowned wines, the symbol of a region where the pleasures of the table and of good company are an essential part of daily life.

Via Emilia, the spinal column of the region stretching its entire length, offers visitors an easy, if somewhat schematic, way of grasping the region's geography: on one side the Apennines, whose first rolling hills are a most favorable environment for vines, both in terms of slope and of climate; on the other side the Po river plain and the Adriatic coast, both far more suited to

Above, the Po delta; left, Apennines foothill landscape (top) and the Marecchia valley (bottom)

viticulture than one might expect. This linear geographical articulation of the territory finds its precise expression in four production zones, defined according to their wine-making traditions and to the vine varieties. The first consists in the hills of Piacenza and Parma, where the prevalence of Barbera and Bonarda clearly demonstrate the influence of neighboring Lombardy and of its Oltrepò Pavese vineyards. Directly adjacent is Lambrusco territory, which extends from the hills to the plain in the provinces of Reggio Emilia and Modena. Just a short distance away are the Colli Bolognesi and the lower valley of the Reno river, traditionally an area of white wines; the eastern end of the region, Romagna, is a zone of extensive cultivation of Sangiovese, Trebbiano, and Albana. The overall regional picture closes with the vineyards of the province of Ferrara, planted with Fortana on the sands of the River Po delta.

THE GRAND TREBBIANO AND SANGIOVESE VINEYARD

The overall composition of the Emilia-Romagna vineyards (almost 150,000 acres) is well delineated. Two sole varieties account for almost a half of the regional total: Trebbiano Romagnolo, a white-grape vine, with 31.8%, and Sangiovese, a red variety, with 14.6% – particularly spread in Romagna. Lambrusco, in its various forms, Ancellotta, Barbera, and Bonarda reinforce the position of red grapes, which are slightly prevalent. Albana, instead, swells the percentage of white varieties and gives the region's only DOCG wine. Other grapes of real, if more local, interest are Montù, grown in the lower Reno valley, and Malvasia Bianca di Candia (Parma and Piacenza).

ONE DOCG (ALBANA DI ROMAGNA) AND 20 DOC ZONES

Overall vineyard surface amounts to close to 150,000 acres, two-thirds in the plain and the other third on hillsides. Pride of place goes to the region's one DOCG wine, already-mentioned Albana di Romagna, which is joined by 20 DOC zones and ten IGTs. The overall production of DOC wines is fifth among Italy's regions, with two zones, Colli Piacentini and Reggiano, among the top twenty in terms of volume. It is worth noting that, of this total, twice as much red wine is produced than white. Less comforting is the fact that the regional production – over 180 million US gallons – is only partially regulated, 25% by DOC rules and 40% by IGT rules. In the near future, however, there is likely to be a substantial increase in these figures in a region which puts such great store in the traditions of its wine and food. That the sector is a dynamic one is indisputable and is proven by the polemical, often indignant, reception given to the marketing of some of the region's wines in cardboard containers. The market has responded well to this type of packaging, even if some consider it near blasphemy, and it has had a role in bringing wine to the younger generation and to social classes intimidated by the high price of many bottled products. The next step will be to convince these groups to move on to better and more important wines.

Talking about wine tourism, which Emilia-Romagna is specially suited to thanks to its beautiful sceneries, precious art treasures and welcoming vocation, as many as 11 wine and gastronomy routes crisscross the region and avail themselves of an extensive network of fine accommodation and food services which is unique in Italy.

EMILIA-ROMAGNA'S DOC ZONES

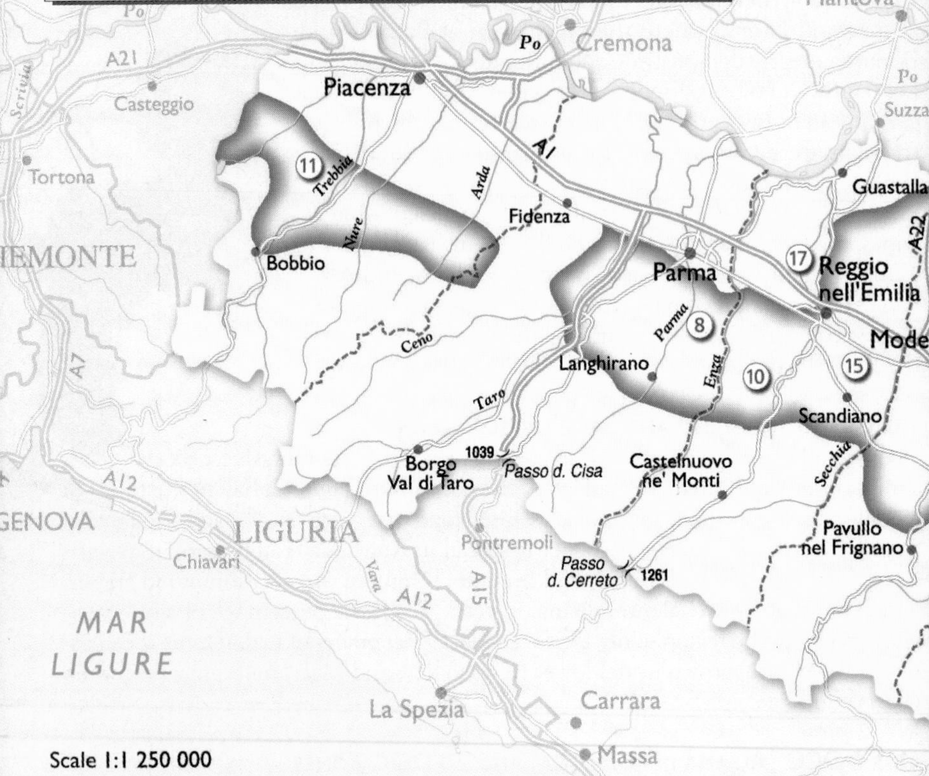

Scale 1:1 250 000

0 15 30 km

❶ **DOCG Albana di Romagna**

❷ **DOC Bosco Eliceo** *Bianco, Sauvignon ▪ Fortana, Merlot*

❸ **DOC Cagnina di Romagna**

❹ **DOC Colli Bolognesi** *Bianco, Chardonnay, Pignoletto, Pinot Bianco, Riesling Italico, Sauvignon ▪ Barbera, Cabernet Sauvignon, Merlot ▪ Colline di Riosto, Colline Marconiane, Colline Oliveto, Monte San Pietro, Serravalle, Terre di Montebudello, Zola Predosa*

❺ **DOC Colli Bolognesi Classico Pignoletto**

❻ **DOC Colli di Faenza** *Bianco, Pinot Bianco, Trebbiano ▪ Rosso, Sangiovese*

❼ **DOC Colli d'Imola** *Bianco, Chardonnay, Pignoletto, Trebbiano ▪ Rosso, Barbera, Cabernet Sauvignon, Sangiovese*

❽ **DOC Colli di Parma** *Malvasia, Sauvignon ▪ Rosso*

❾ **DOC Colli di Rimini** *Bianco, Biancame, Rebola ▪ Rosso, Cabernet Sauvignon*

❿ **DOC Colli di Scandiano e di Canossa** *Bianco, Chardonnay, Malvasia, Pinot, Sauvignon ▪ Cabernet Sauvignon, Lambrusco Grasparossa, Lambrusco Montericco, Malbo Gentile, Marzemino*

⓫ **DOC Colli Piacentini** *Chardonnay, Malvasia, Malvasia Passito, Monterosso Val d'Arda, Ortrugo, Pinot Grigio, Pinot Spumante, Sauvignon, Trebbianino Val Trebbia, Val Nure, Vin Santo, Vin Santo di Vigoleno ▪ Barbera, Bonarda, Cabernet Sauvignon, Gutturnio, Pinot Nero*

⓬ **DOC Colli Romagna Centrale** *Bianco, Chardonnay, Trebbiano ▪ Rosso, Cabernet Sauvignon, Sangiovese*

⓭ **DOC Lambrusco di Sorbara**

⓮ **DOC Lambrusco Grasparossa di Castelvetro**

⑮ **DOC Lambrusco Salamino di Santa Croce**
⑯ **DOC Pagadebit di Romagna**
⑰ **DOC Reggiano** *Bianco Spumante ▪ Rosso, Lambrusco, Lambrusco Salamino*
⑱ **DOC Reno** *Bianco, Montuni, Pignoletto*
⑲ **DOC Romagna Albana** *Spumante*
⑳ **DOC Sangiovese di Romagna**
㉑ **DOC Trebbiano di Romagna**

IGT - Typical Geographic Indication
Bianco di Castelfranco Emilia (Bologna - Modena); Emilia or dell'Emilia (Ferrara - Modena - Parma - Piacenza – Reggio Emilia - Bologna); Forlì (Forlì-Cesena); Fortana del Taro (Parma); Provincia di Modena or Modena (Modena); Ravenna (Ravenna); Rubicone (Forlì-Cesena - Ravenna - Rimini - Bologna); Sillaro or Bianco del Sillaro (Bologna – Forlì-Cesena - Ravenna - Rimini); Terre di Veleja (Piacenza); Val Tidone (Piacenza)

The Great Wines of Emilia-Romagna

Albana
"Potent wine of noble taste, easily preserved and medium subtle": such was Albana wine according to a 13th-century treatise, which added "that this kind of grape is better than anywhere else in Forlì and all of Romagna". Unmistakable for its elongated bunches and golden yellow grapes, Albana is distinctive for its sugar content that forms the basis for exceptionally fine vinification.
Italy's first white wine to get DOCG recognition, it is today the pride of the Bologna, Ravenna, and Forlì-Cesena provinces, which share 37,500 acres of specialized vineyards. Production codes include various types: Secco (dry, 11.5% alcohol), straw yellow in color, tending to golden with ageing, with characteristic aroma and dry, slightly tannic, warm, and harmonious taste; Amabile (semi-sweet, 12%) and Dolce (sweet, 12%), which differ in intensity of fruity notes and rounded flavor; Passito (15.5%), amber in color, with deep aroma and velvety, full taste. Its aptitude for ageing increases proportionately to its alcohol content – from 2 to 3 years for the dry wine and ten or more for the passito.
In its dry version Albana goes well with seafood in general and especially with crustaceans, fish soups and broths, but it is also a fine match for white meats (especially chicken in aspic) and foie gras. The semi-sweet and sweet are eclectic dessert wines, traditionally served with Romagna's typical ring-shaped cake. The passito wine is usually served with pastries and dried fruit, but also with cheeses streaked with green mold, even sharp, or enjoyed alone as a "meditation" wine.

Sangiovese
This is the most cultivated vine in Italy; according to experts it crossed the Apennines from its native Tuscany to become a protagonist in Romagna's vineyards, especially in the hills. In the valleys between Imola and Rimini, soil, climate, and vine evolution over the centuries have originated a ruby red wine, sometimes with purple highlights; it has a delicate aroma with hints of violets and a dry, harmonious taste with a bitterish finishing.

Trebbiano Romagnolo
This is a member of the large Trebbiano family, with Middle Eastern origins and cited as early as the 14th century. Cultivation is widespread in Romagna, especially in the provinces of Ravenna and Forlì, both in the plain and in the hills; it is less frequent in the Bologna area and only sporadic in various other zones of Emilia.
It is used mainly for still wines but also for spumante, and is the basis for some of Italy's best-known brandies and for the balsamic vinegar traditional to Modena and Reggio Emilia. Also present in the region are the Modenese and Toscano varieties.

Gutturnio
This red wine typical of the Piacenza province comes from a blend of Barbera (55 to 70%), of Piedmont origin, and indigenous Croatina (30 to 45%). The resulting wine is bright ruby red varying in intensity, with a characteristic aroma and dry or semi-sweet taste; it comes in the still or fizzy versions and it can be drunk throughout the meal; the Superiore and Riserva are best with red meat and game dishes. The new wine is fine as an aperitif, especially to accompany cold meats.

Lambrusco
This is a denomination that can be applied to a wide variety of red grapes, already known to Pliny and Virgil and probably deriving from wild vines. Production, concentrated in the provinces of Reggio Emilia and Modena, concerns eminently fizzy wines with a fragrant aroma, strongly violet scented, and a tart, fresh taste that makes them ideal companions for cold meats (especially the cooked ones) and rich Emilian preparations in general.
Lambrusco Grasparossa di Castelvetro, Lambrusco Salamino di Santa Croce, and Lambrusco di Sorbara, common in the plain, have acquired autonomous DOCs.

Pignoletto
Recent molecular analyses have pointed out the similarity of this vine – common mainly in the Bologna hills – with Grechetto, indigenous of Umbria. The wine made from this grape has greenish highlights, moderate acidity and a delicate fruity aroma, with a characteristic note of pear; it can be dry or semi-sweet, still or fizzy.

THE PIACENZA AND PARMA REGIONS

Passing from Oltrepò Pavese to the lands of Lambrusco, the vineyard first offers Barbera and Bonarda, then aromatic Malvasia.

From the border with Lombardy to the provincial boundary between Parma and Reggio Emilia, the northern slopes of the Tuscan-Emilian Apennines form a fairly homogeneous wine zone in which vineyards are found from 500 to 1500 feet asl and contain red grapes as well as white. Varietal composition is influenced by the proximity to Oltrepò Pavese, through which various red Piedmont grapes, primarily Barbera, have filtered; but there are also historical factors involved, such as the long rule over Parma and Piacenza by the Farnese family (Roman in origin), which probably introduced Malvasia grapes, and the Napoleonic domination, bringing in French varieties. From the normative standpoint, the Colli Piacentini DOC, as well as the Val Tidone and Terre di Veleja IGTs, cover the province of Piacenza, while Parma is home to the Colli di Parma DOC and Fontana del Taro IGT. Both provinces also fall under the Emilia IGT.

The Colli Piacentini

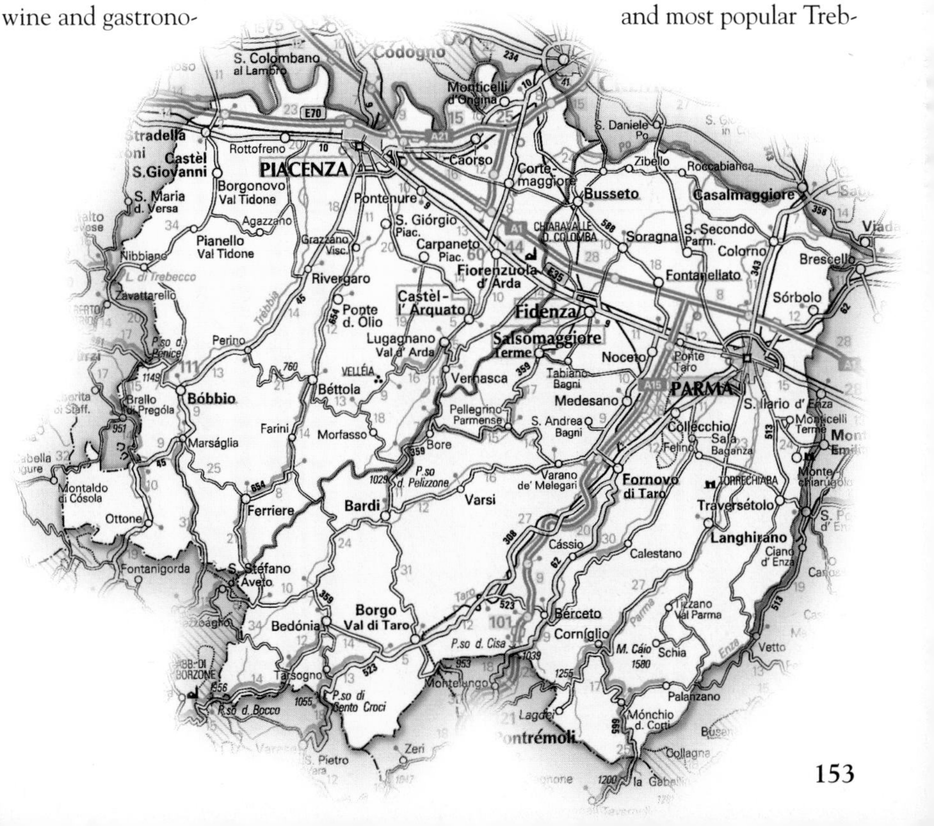

Piacenza's wines are enjoying considerable success, doubtless due to their excellent price/quality ratio but also to a recent demand for fizzy wines. Furthermore, wine and gastronomy tourism is being actively promoted. The most representative wine of this area is red Gutturnio, perfect accompaniment to the equally famous local cold meats: salami, *coppa*, and *pancetta*. Standing out among the whites are native Ortrugo and most popular Trebbianino Val Trebbia and Monterosso Val d'Arda. The Vin Santo di Vigoleno is quite special.

THE COLLI PIACENTINI WINE AND FOOD ROUTE

An extensive route going from valley to valley, with noteworthy monumental attractions to be seen on the way and an exciting climb to Bobbio. A gastronomic leitmotif are cold meats, specifically salami, *coppa*, and *pancetta*. The gates to the wine area are Castel San Giovanni, on the boundary between Oltrepò Pavese and the Colli Piacentini, and Fiorenzuola d'Arda, with the nearby Cistercian abbey of Chiaravalle della Colomba; but the tour naturally includes Piacenza, the most Lombard of Emilian cities, with its typical brickworks – ancient and severe as becomes the historical capital of a duchy.

▪ **PIACENZA**. This is a typical Po Valley city, built on original Roman foundations during the flourishing period of the Communes. Later on, it became the realm of lords and dukes and was chosen by Pier Luigi Farnese in 1545 as the capital of an independent duchy which was to last for more than two centuries. Piacenza's historical Gothic in the so-called Palazzo Pubblico, Renaissance in the sanctuary of Madonna della Campagna, Baroque in the Farnese equestrian statues. Wine and food are of the greatest interest.

▪ **BOBBIO**. Entering Val Tidone (land of the homonymous IGT, intended to valorize mainly the mixed-grape blends of Riesling, Müller Thurgau, and Marsanne) and passing through Agazzano, Gazzola, Rivergaro, and Travo, you come to Bobbio. This medieval town grew up around the monastery and abbey of S. Colombano; the Cathedral, the castle donjon, and the famous Gobbo bridge are also worth a visit. For gourmets, this is the place for snails and an important truffle market.
Going towards Piacenza, a stop in Grazzano Visconti is worthwhile: the castle is authentic, while the picturesque hamlet inside is an early 20th-century medieval-style divertissement.

▪ **CASTELL'ARQUATO**. It is reached via Carpaneto Piacentino, with its important archeological site of *Veleja Romana* (after which the local IGT production is named), and then Vigolo Marchese, with its lovely Romanesque

Vine rows at Travo, in the Piacenza area

Castell'Arquato sits on a hill and its picturesque main square, with the overlooking fortress, Collegiate church, and Palazzo Pretorio, is an uncommon sight even in a region full of castles. The guardrooms of the Palazzo del Podestà are home to the Enoteca Comunale (open by appointment), set up in the intent of promoting the local Monterosso Val d'Arda DOC wine. Not far to the southeast is Vigoleno, home to a renowned Vin Santo DOC and a castled town among the loveliest in the province. This is the gate to the Stirone valley, known to nature-lovers for its river park. On the opposite slope, in the Parma province, lies Salsomaggiore Terme, an Art Nouveau-imprinted spa resort.

The Colli di Parma

Parma prosciutto and Parmigiano-Reggiano cheese, not to mention other delicacies, have given the province the nickname of Food Valley. Faced with such celebrities, originally wine seemed to play a secondary role, but it has showed since a personality perfectly in tune with the scene. In the valleys between the Enza and Stirone rivers, the reds – Barbera, Bonarda and Croatina – are blended to make Rosso Colli di Parma reflecting the production of Oltrepò Pavese. Among the whites, great emphasis is placed on Malvasia di Candia, which used to be shipped to France in Napoleon's time; today it is produced in both a dry and a semi-sweet version, mostly fizzy. The same can be said for Sauvignon, often vinified with the champenoise method to make worthy spumante.

THE PROSCIUTTO OF THE COLLI DI PARMA AND WINE ROUTE

This itinerary runs through the Taro and Enza valleys, in the pre-Apennine band that crowns the province's capital. The tour combines the allure of prosciutto with that of the wines that traditionally accompany it. If you start it from Collecchio, be sure not to miss Parma.

Palazzo Pretorio and the Collegiate apse in Castell'Arquato

Culatello, *a Po valley delicacy*

■ **PARMA**. This is a city of vigorous Po Valley architecture, with outstanding medieval and 16th-century buildings, unadulterated flavors and refined cultural (particularly musical) tastes (its Teatro Regio is famous for opera performances). At the absolute summit of Italian painting are the frescoes by Correggio in the dome of the Romanesque Cathedral and inside S. Giovanni Evangelista church, in addition to those by Parmigianino in the church of Madonna della Steccata. Other masterpieces can be viewed at the Galleria Nazionale, home to the splendid Farnese Theater (1617-18).

■ **FORNOVO DI TARO**. Along the rise climbing to the Cisa Pass there are a lovely Romanesque church and reminders of pilgrimages along Via Francigena. The scenery is noteworthy, from the sunny banks of the Taro River Park to the shaded paths through the Carrega Woods. Ascending towards the "high" towns of the Val Taro you can follow the Strada del fungo porcino di Borgotaro (porcino mushroom road), of eminently gastronomic interest.

■ **CALESTANO**. Skirting Felino, famous mainly for its celebrated salami, you get to this little town whose historical center is full of stone buildings from the 15th-18th centuries; worth a visit are Palazzo Coruzzi, the church of S. Lorenzo, and the Archeological Museum. Outstanding in the environs are the Ravarano Castle and the "Devil's Drops", spires and pinnacles that cut the narrow Baganza valley in two. For lovers of good food, we are in the land of black truffles, which abound primarily around the charming village of Fragno.
The last stop on this tour is Langhirano, famous for its Parma prosciutto production.

THE CULATELLO OF ZIBELLO ROUTE

Following the Po River and Via Emilia through the so-called Bassa Parmense (Lower Parma region), the tour takes in mouth-watering specialties, ancient fortresses, and places tied to the life of opera composer Giuseppe Verdi (1813-1901). If you have time, make a stop in Fidenza, a lovely town on the edge of the route: in the Duomo, with splendid sculptures by Antelami, there are reminiscences of the life of martyr Donnino and of the medieval pilgrims who rested here prior to crossing the mountains.

■ **COLORNO**. This is a "little Versailles", once the summer residence of the Dukes of Parma, famous for its palace surrounded by a superb, French-style garden; also worth seeing are the ducal Orangery (an 18 th-century hothouse for citrus trees), site of the Folk Museum, and the churches of S. Liborio and of S. Margherita, Gothic in origin.

■ **ZIBELLO**. Home of choice to exquisite *culatello* (a variety of cured meat), this little town is built along the Po bank and conserves relics from the 15th and 16th centuries, namely the parish church, the cloister of the former Dominican monastery, and the portico of Palazzo Pallavicino.

■ **BUSSETO.** This is the capital of Verdiland: a sumptuous bronze statue of the Maestro stands in the central square, right in front of the 13th-century fortress that houses the Teatro Verdi. Also tied to the memory of this great composer are Palazzo Orlandi, Barezzi House, and the beautiful Villa Pallavicino, site of a museum full of relics. Also worthy of note are the church of S. Maria degli Angeli, a Franciscan complex built in 1470-74, and the collegiate church with its precious Treasury. Just southeast of Busseto, in Roncole, are the birthplace of opera composer Giuseppe Verdi and the church of S. Michele (16th-17th C.) where he was christened, with the organ on which he practiced as a child.

Wineries *pp. 412-417*
Borgonovo Val Tidone, Collecchio, Gazzola, Langhirano, Nibbiano, Piacenza, Ponte dell'Olio, Rivergaro, Travo, Vigolzone, Ziano Piacentino.

THE REGGIO AND MODENA REGIONS

Prejudice against "easy" wines like Lambrusco is hard to overcome, but time itself has rendered justice to this eclectic wine.

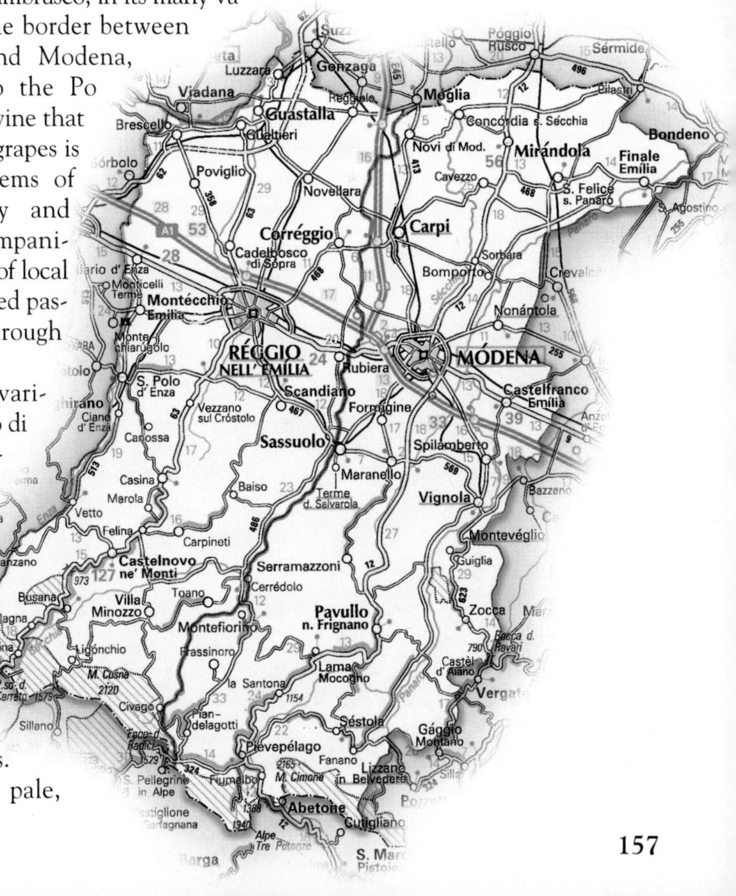

The vineyards of Lambrusco, in its many varieties, straddle the border between Reggio Emilia and Modena, from the hills to the Po lands. The foamy wine that comes from these grapes is one of the emblems of Emilian oenology and finds perfect accompaniment in the dishes of local tradition, from filled pasta to *zampone* through desserts.
The three main varieties are Lambrusco di Sorbara and Lambrusco Salamino di Santa Croce, grown on the plain, and Lambrusco Grasparossa di Castelvetro, grown on the hills. Sorbara produces pale,

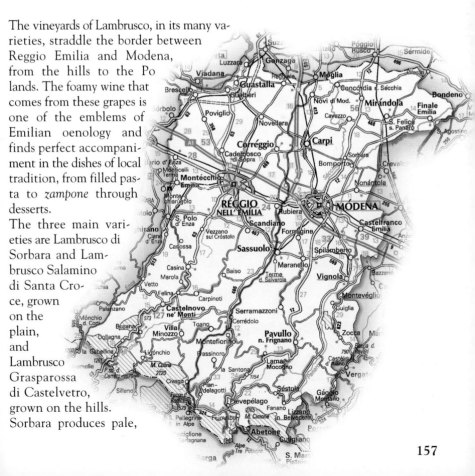

very fragrant wines that tend to be dry and average about 11% alcohol. Salamino di Santa Croce is deeper in color and slightly more alcoholic (11.5%), a trait that makes it easier to preserve. The Grasparossa di Castelvetro grape is the most prized, thanks to its environment and low yield per acre: structured and full-bodied, with an outstanding aroma of cherries and woodland berries, it is dry to slightly sweet, somewhat tannic, with 12% or more alcohol content.
Despite its great popularity here and elsewhere, for a long time Lambrusco was considered a second-class wine. Now this is no longer true, thanks not only to a boost in quality but also to more objective judgments by critics. From the normative standpoint, the Reggio Emilia province is covered by the Reggiano and Colli di Scandiano e Canossa DOCs; the province of Modena, instead, contains three DOC areas: Lambrusco di Sorbara, Lambrusco Salamino di Santa Croce, and Lambrusco Grasparossa di Castelvetro, as well as the Modena and Bianco Castelfranco Emilia IGTs. Finally, the entire district falls within the Emilia IGT.

Lambrusco and Much More

The Reggio wine district goes from the fairly broad plain to the hills behind the provincial capital that Baedeker described as "one of Italy's most beautiful" cities. Wine is produced throughout the district, from the Po river to the Apennine foothills, where Lambrusco is given not only a generic label and a varietal one (Salamino), but is also produced from a blend of Ancellotta grapes, unusually white-vinified to obtain a spumante. In this sea of Lambrusco there is an island of white: in addition to omnipresent Malvasia, the most interesting variety is Sauvignon, the basis for a wine of great tradition. Among the permitted reds are Marzemino and Malbo Gentile, very old local varieties now making a come-back.

The Colline di Scandiano e Canossa Wine and Gastronomy Route

The route winds for about 100 miles, linking 15 municipalities in the plain

Vine cultivated countryside between Reggio Emilia and Modena

BETWEEN REGGIO AND MODENA, IN THE LANDS OF BALSAMIC VINEGAR

Deserving specific mention is another noble child of the vine, Aceto Balsamico Tradizionale DOP, shared by Reggio Emilia and Modena in a production unrivalled worldwide.
Not to be missed is a tour of a vinegar-factory, with its amazing array of many-sized casks used to age the precious nectar. It is important to emphasize the fact that, in order to deserve the appellation "traditional", balsamic vinegar must be made from grape must concentrated through boiling over a direct flame (and not made from wine, as the cheaper versions are). Also to note is the fact that, unlike what the vinegar's color would lead you to believe, the grapes most used are Trebbiano, therefore white, although portions of red grapes (Lambrusco and others) are also added. The liquid resulting from this preparatory work has to mature by means of slow, natural acetification, and to finally be given refinement that entails at least 12 decantings per year into casks of different woods – oak, chestnut, cherry, juniper, and mulberry – exposed in attic storerooms to the changes in temperature that favor absorption of the wood noble tannins.
Aceto Balsamico Tradizionale di Reggio (www.acetobalsamicotradizionale.it) comes in three types – Aragosta (lobster red), Argento (silver), and Oro (gold - Extravecchio, aged for more than 25 years), with correspondingly colored labels – which, with increasing age, contain more and more sugar; they are generically used as a condiment for meat and cheese or even to garnish desserts.
Aceto Balsamico Tradizionale di Modena (www.balsamico.it), bottled in the unique round vial with a rectangular base designed by Giugiaro, also has an Extravecchio denomination (golden capsule). Vinegars aged for so long are even appreciated for tasting, sipped from a spoon or a glass.

and in the first low hills south of Via Emilia. The tour starts from the provincial capital and becomes particularly scenic in the area of the Canossa erosion furrows. In the extraordinary Emilian cornucopia, two high-caliber specialties stand out: traditional balsamic vinegar and Parmigiano-Reggiano cheese.

▪ **REGGIO EMILIA.** A hexagon of avenues marks the perimeter of the vanished walls: inside are the winding, narrow medieval streets of Reggio's historical center, opening on to the Piazza del Duomo and the Town Hall and offering artistic views from the various epochs, distributed with skillful balance. Just out of town, in one direction you can see the first hills, in the other the vast plain stretching to the Po.

▪ **SAN POLO D'ENZA.** From Sant'Ilario d'Enza, a pretty little spot filled with archeological remains and sumptuous patrician villas, you take a detour to Bibbiano, traditionally considered the cradle of Parmigiano-Reggiano cheese, until you reach San Polo d'Enza. A majestic tower introduces an ancient portico-lined street leading to the main square and the imposing fortress that overlooks the valley.
Do not miss the climb to Canossa: the castle that housed penitent King Enrico IV is in ruins, but the lunar landscape of erosion furrows is worth the effort.

▪ **SCANDIANO.** On the backdrop of the rolling Apennine foothills stand out the Rocca dei Boiardo (where poet Matteo Maria Boiardo was born) and the ancient towers of the little town, a wine center which co-owns a DOC. Worth visiting are the pretty churches and the home of scientist Lazzaro Spallanzani, another eminent "favorite son".
A bit to the northeast, on the border with the Modena region, Rubiera conserves its Ospitale, one of the most important medieval shelters for pilgrims and travelers and present-day venue for cultural events.

Modena and its Lambrusco Wines

There are three varieties of Lambrusco elevated to DOC status that monopolize Modena's viticulture. Each includes production of a fizzy red and fizzy rosé. Lambrusco di Sorbara is produced on the plain between the Panaro and Secchia rivers, in the environs of the homonymous town along the road to Mirandola. Lambrusco Salamino di Santa Croce vineyards stretch from the fields northwest of the city to the lower plain; the vine is named after a locality in the Carpi municipality. Lambrusco Grasparossa di Castelvetro comes from the band of vineyards lying between the hills and Via Emilia and its reference point is the pretty little town on the Via dei Castelli (castle road).

AMIDST CITIES, CASTLES, AND CHERRY TREES

This route running for about 125 miles amongst the hills links Modena to Bologna, winding along the so-called Via dei Castelli. Here only the stretch around Modena, amidst the vineyards of Lambrusco Grasparossa di Castelvetro, is taken into account; the Bologna hills part is dealt with in the following section. Keeping high the honor of Modena's food products are some exceptional ones: Aceto Balsamico Tradizionale, Parmigiano-Reggiano cheese, and Modena prosciutto.

▪ **MODENA**. Via Emilia separates the medieval city, built up in concentric circles around Piazza del Duomo, from the city of the Este family, traced in broad straight lines. On one side the Cathedral, among the masterpieces of Italian Romanesque architecture, and the Ghirlandina Tower; on the other, Palazzo Ducale, today the home of the Military Academy. The Este Library and Gallery hold treasures of culture and art.

▪ **SPILAMBERTO**. Of the ancient fortress guarding the Panaro river only remain the stronghold and a big tower, set among churches and portico-lined buildings. Villa Fabriani houses the Consorteria and the Museum of Traditional Balsamic Vinegar, dedicated to the most renowned local specialty.

Wineries *pp. 412-417*
Bomporto, Castelvetro di Modena, Sant'Ilario d'Enza.

▪ **VIGNOLA**. In springtime the hills in the Panaro valley are cloaked in white cherry blossoms; equally spectacular is the countryside tinged with autumn colors at grape harvest time. The village features an imposing fortress with towers on its corners.

▪ **CASTELVETRO DI MODENA**. In the Middle Ages this was a castle town at the crossroads between the foothills and the road climbing up into the Apennines. You will want to linger in the square with its charming Renaissance architecture, where in late September a checkers game is played with living pieces. The Casa dei Lambruschi in the nearby castle of Levizzano is worth a visit.

A bird's eye view of Modena

THE FERRARA REGION

The city of the Este family and the Po delta lands offer wines made expressly to accompany typical local dishes such as salama da sugo *and eel.*

The Ferrara-area production falls within the Bosco Eliceo DOC, which historically refers to the work of the Benedictine abbey of Pomposa and presently to the production zone along the Adriatic shoreline between the mouths of the Goro Po and of the Reno river. The denomination refers to the Gran Bosco della Mesola, called Eliceo from *elce*, another name for the ilexes that grow there. The local so-called "sand wines" are produced from vines traditionally trained in low cordons on the loose terrains just inland of the coast. The particular combination of soil and climate gives the grapes considerable color and intensity of aroma.

Twixt River and Valleys

The main vine of the zone is Uva d'Oro, also found elsewhere and called Fortana. Tradition would have it that this red-grape variety was imported from the Burgundy Côte d'Or by Renée of France, bride of Ercole II, Este Duke. It gives a red wine of modest alcohol content, to be drunk young with Ferrara cold meats or fish from the valleys. Regulations for the Bosco Eliceo DOC also include a white made primarily from Trebbiano Romagnolo and, in addition to Fortana, two varietal wines, Sauvignon and Merlot.

THE FERRARA PROVINCE WINE AND GASTRONOMY ROUTE

This itinerary covers the entire province and takes in three routes: "The Great River", with an exceptional epilogue at the Pomposa abbey; "The Este Courts", centered on Ferrara; and "The Delta", with Comacchio as a reference. Wineries are few but you will have plenty of opportunities to taste their wines at first-class restaurants.

The gastronomic component of the tour seesaws between the cold meats of Emilian tradition and fish dishes from the Comacchio valleys and the Adriatic.

▪ **FERRARA.** It is hard to describe Ferrara briefly: striking are its superb monuments – the medieval castle and Cathedral, the Renaissance Palazzo dei Diamanti, venue to art exhibitions –, but even more

Typical hut in the vineyards of Pomposa

striking is the overall quality of the city and the atmosphere that recalls the three centuries – from the 13th to the end of the 16th – during which the refined Este court reigned. Among the most outstanding historical sights are Palazzo Schifanoia and the Marfisa house. Dining is exceptional, with first courses and the famous *salama da sugo* (pork sausage in sauce) as stars of the cuisine.

▪ **Pomposa.** The bell tower of the celebrated abbey rises among a cluster of cypresses above the low lands of the Po, crossed by the Romea road. A must for lovers of art, Pomposa is also of great interest for the Bosco Eliceo DOC wines, named from one of the abbey's first holdings.

▪ **Mesola.** The castle, lying where the Romea road meets the Goro Po, used to be the home to the Este family during the deer hunts once held in the surrounding forests. The Gran Bosco della Mesola, the forest lining the road, is a lovely reminder of that time.
Leaving the Romea road you follow the banks of the Po, entering the reclaimed valleys until you reach Goro and Gorino: you are in the Regional Po Delta Park (150,000 acres), one of the most beautiful nature reserves in Italy.

▪ **Comacchio.** A charming fishing village crossed by the canals that connect the lagoons, the so-called "valleys" converted through the centuries to aquaculture. Gastronomically speaking, this is the Italian home to the eel, served in soups, grilled, or on the spit. In the town, after climbing the steps of the Trepponti (the most unusual of the bridges linking the 12 inhabited islets), you find ancient churches and towers. Worth visiting in the environs are the old salt-works, the Etruscan necropolis of Spina, and the fascinating lagoon environment of the Bertuzzi valley, just north of Comacchio.

The Colli Bolognesi and the Reno Plain

Just outside Bologna, between hill and plain, two ancient white-grape vines, Pignoletto and Montù (or Montuni) rejuvenate an old tradition.

Between Lambrusco-land and Romagna lie Bologna and its province, whose panorama, as far as viticulture is concerned, goes from the limestone formations – called Gessi Bolognesi – of the Apennine foothills to the plain cut through by the Reno and its tributaries.
South of Via Emilia, vineyards are separated into two districts: the Colli Bolognesi, around the city, and the Colli d'Imola, in the eastern valleys. The protagonist in the Colli Bolognesi area is Pignoletto, an autochthonous variety that gives fine whites. In the Colli d'Imola the oenological transition from Emilia to Romagna is marked

from Albana vineyards first and Sangiovese's predominance then. Completing the wine picture is the Reno zone, down in the plain, and its local star, Montù white wine.
On the whole, this is a territory with noteworthy scenery and history, which invites to excursions out of town. From the normative standpoint, the zone is covered by the Colli Bolognesi, Colli d'Imola, and Reno DOCs, and nearly all of it by the Emilia IGT; by the Bianco di Castelfranco IGT on the border with Modena and by the Sillaro IGT on the border with Ravenna.

The Colli Bolognesi

This production zone lies in the hills surrounding the regional capital, between the Panaro and the Idice rivers. Vineyards are planted at an average 330 to 1000 feet above sea level, on alternating loose and clayey soil. The wine town of reference is Monte San Pietro. Mostly white-grape vines are grown, the list including Chardonnay, Pinot Bianco, Riesling Italico, and Sauvignon, but a note of originality comes from an autochthonous vine of ancient history, Pignoletto, for quite some time the focus of a re-launch campaign that has included creating a Classico zone. Among the reds are Barbera, which boasts a long tradition, Merlot, and Cabernet Sauvignon, the latter with notable peaks of quality. In 1995, seven high-quality micro-zones were defined (Colline di Riosto, Colline Marconiane, Colline Oliveto, Monte San Pietro, Serravalle, Torre di Montebudello, and Zola Predosa), in which production is subject to particular restrictions on grape and wine yield per acre.

AMIDST CITIES, CASTLES, AND CHERRY TREES (2)

This route (previously described in its Modena stretch) links Bologna to Modena along the so-called Via dei Castelli, heading to Vignola but also touching the prettiest places in the area. The gastronomic attractions are part of Bologna's classic cuisine: from freshly-made pasta to cold meats, with autumnal acmes in Savigno's white truffles and Apennine foothills mushrooms.

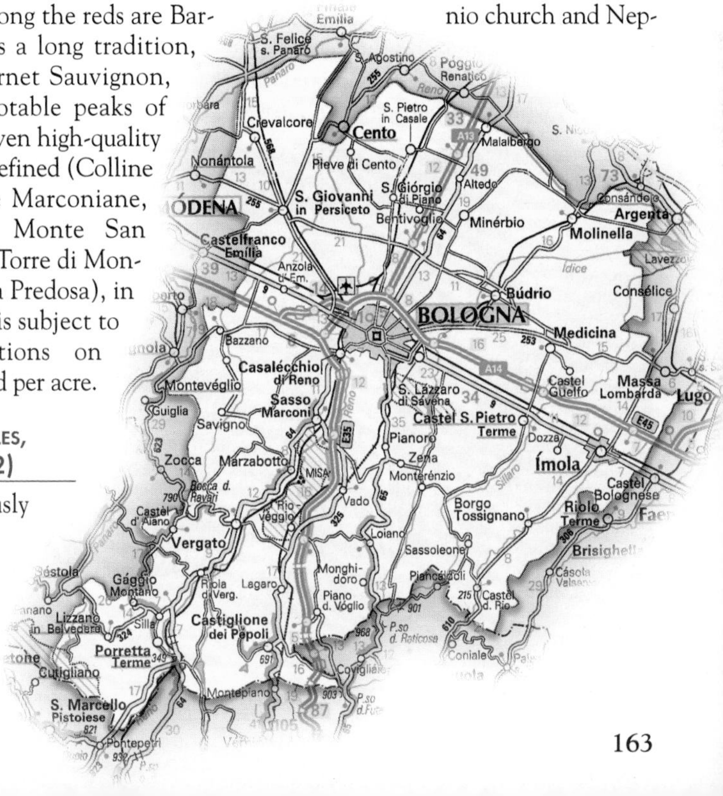

■ **BOLOGNA.** A city warm and convivial in atmosphere and ancient in culture (its university was the first to be founded in Italy). Though the two leaning towers (remains of a large medieval settlement) can be considered as the local symbols, city tours usually begin at Piazza Maggiore – with its Gothic S. Petronio church and Neptune Fountain –, which is the hub of Bolognese life. The charming character of this lively city can be felt in its portico-lined streets, where the red of typical Po Valley brickworks prevail, and at its many wine and food venues. Outstanding among old churches are S. Stefano and S. Domenico, while great Bolognese (and other) artistic masterpieces can be admired in the Pinacoteca Nazionale.

▪ **MONTEVEGLIO.** This little town is reached via Monte San Pietro, a small wine center that is presently the hub of a micro-zone in the Colli Bolognesi DOC. Monteveglio offers visitors an admirable abbey rising on a hill and a countryside landscape of ancient beauty, with small valleys, rural hamlets, and vineyards, all safeguarded by the recent institution of a regional park. San Teodo is headquarters to the consortium protecting local wines, slated also to become an enoteca and wine shop.

▪ **CASTELLO DI SERRAVALLE.** A charming little town atop a scenic knoll, surrounded by sloping vineyards and the vestiges of a castle. Its name comes from an old fortification which the gate, the 1523 tower, and 13th-century Town Hall are the remains of.
Not far away is Savigno, a medieval village lying along the road that leads to the Samoggia valley, land of mushrooms and truffles.

The Colli d'Imola

The certified vineyard lies in the eastern part of the province, stretching from the Colli Bolognesi to the border with Ravenna and following Via Emilia to lap on the Tuscan boundary. This is a land of transition between Emilia and Romagna, both from the historical and the oenological point of view. Here begins the production zone for the region's most prestigious wine, Albana di Romagna, but the Colli d'Imola DOC also includes a white, a mixed-grape blend red, and some wines with varietal labels: Chardonnay, Pignoletto, and Trebbiano; Barbera, Cabernet Sauvignon, and Sangiovese.

THE COLLI D'IMOLA WINE AND GASTRONOMY ROUTE

This tour runs for about 60 miles through the rolling valleys of the Santerno, Sil-

Inside a cellar in Monte San Pietro

THE ENOTECA REGIONALE DELL'EMILIA-ROMAGNA

"Good wine improves life and a healthy environment improves wine. Safeguard nature, safeguard wine" runs the slogan chosen by the Enoteca Regionale dell'Emilia Romagna (www.enotecaemilia romagna.it) which is housed in Dozza's Rocca Sforzesca – about 6 miles from Imola.
The headquarters location is not a random choice, since Dezza is the meeting-point of the two hearts – historical and oenological – of the region. In its cellars is a permanent display covering over 1000 sq yards, with a choice of more than 800 labels on sale selected by an in-house committee representing 200 associated producers and consortiums. The exhibition is organized on the basis of food accompaniment, which enables the visitor to scan an ideal wine list. It starts with fizzy whites and spumante wines for aperitifs and goes on to light, still whites for fish-based first courses, to structured whites for heavier first courses and second courses of white meats. Then come young reds for grilled meats and aged reds for roasts, game and aged cheeses, to end up with sweet and passito wines for desserts. The display also includes other products from the vineyard: balsamic vinegar from Reggio Emilia and Modena, spirits and liqueurs – brandies and grappas among the former and Nocino and Sassolino among the latter –, plus special conserves like the traditional *sapa*, made by cooking grape must. Only one exception is made, though it is very much in line with the vineyard products: extra-virgin olive oil from two appraisable zones – Brisighella, in the Ravenna hills, and Rimini's hinterland. The Enoteca has also devoted two small rooms to a wine bar, where on Friday and Saturday nights and Sunday afternoons you can order glasses of the "vins du jour" listed on the blackboard, with the precious assistance of professional sommeliers.
Evenings with theme tasting, tasting booths, tasting courses, and courses on combining wines and food are periodically organized.

laro, and Sellustra rivers. It ranges from Castel Guelfo, in the plain, to Castel del Rio, up in the Apennines, and leads to the discovery of Romagna specialties like *piadina* (flat bread), eaten with runny, fresh *squacquerone* cheese, and mutton.

▪ **CASTEL SAN PIETRO TERME.** This town on the Sillaro river was founded in the Middle Ages by the Bolognese to defend the Romagna border. The ancient atmosphere still lingers, but passing time has made the town's fame as a spa prevail. Authentic jewels of local gastronomy are *squacquerone* and Castel San Pietro cheese.

▪ **IMOLA.** Founded by the Romans along Via Emilia, its most significant icon is its fortress, designed by Leonardo da Vinci for one member of the Sforza family. Also of interest is the Agricultural Museum housed in Palazzo Tazzoni and devoted to wheat, hemp, and grape farming. In November it hosts the National Sangiovese Week. Not far from here is Dozza, site of the Enoteca Regionale (see box).

▪ **FONTANELICE.** This is a farming town in the Santerno valley, with a very pretty square guarded by the Torre dell'Orologio. Further up is Castel del Rio, for centuries owned by the Alidosi family, which also built the Palazzo, now Town Hall and museum, and the 15th-century mule-back bridge that crosses the Santerno just outside town. Chestnut woods cover the area, providing excellent harvests of marrons.

Wineries *pp. 412-417*
Casalecchio di Reno, Castello di Serravalle, Castel San Pietro Terme, Imola, Monte San Pietro, Monteveglio, Sasso Marconi, Zola Predosa.

The Reno Valley

The wine zone is located along the lower stretch of the river, that is from the last spurs of the hills to the semicircle of plain running north from Bologna nearly to Pieve di Cento.
Local characteristic feature is the white-grape Montù (or Montuni), a vine of ancient tradition also to be found in the neighboring provinces of Modena and Ravenna; protecting it has led to a good re-launch. Regulations envision a white wine, made primarily from Albana and Trebbiano Romagnolo grapes, and two varietal wines, Montuni and Pignoletto. The hub of production is Calderara di Reno.

ROMAGNA

Behind the Adriatic Riviera stretches a busy wine district, whose most outstanding product is Albana DOCG.

For those following Via Emilia, Romagna begins not far from Bologna, in Castel San Pietro, where the Sillaro river once marked the border with the Papal States. The land once ruled by the Pope roughly corresponds to the modern provinces of Forlì-Cesena, Ravenna, and Rimini, plus the Bolognese territory of Imola. Here vineyards are planted in the area that, from the middle-high hills (with mostly calcareous-clayey soil) runs into the Ravenna plain down to Lugo. An indubitable star of Romagna's viticulture is Sangiovese, one of the most common red-grape vines in Italy. Among the whites, Trebbiano Romagnolo is important in volume terms. Romagna is also home to Albana, the star of the region's only DOCG, which, according to tradition, would be the descendent of a variety imported in Roman times. Completing the grape panorama are other local vines that conservation has saved from decline: red Cagnina, a descendent of Terrano del Carso, which gives a

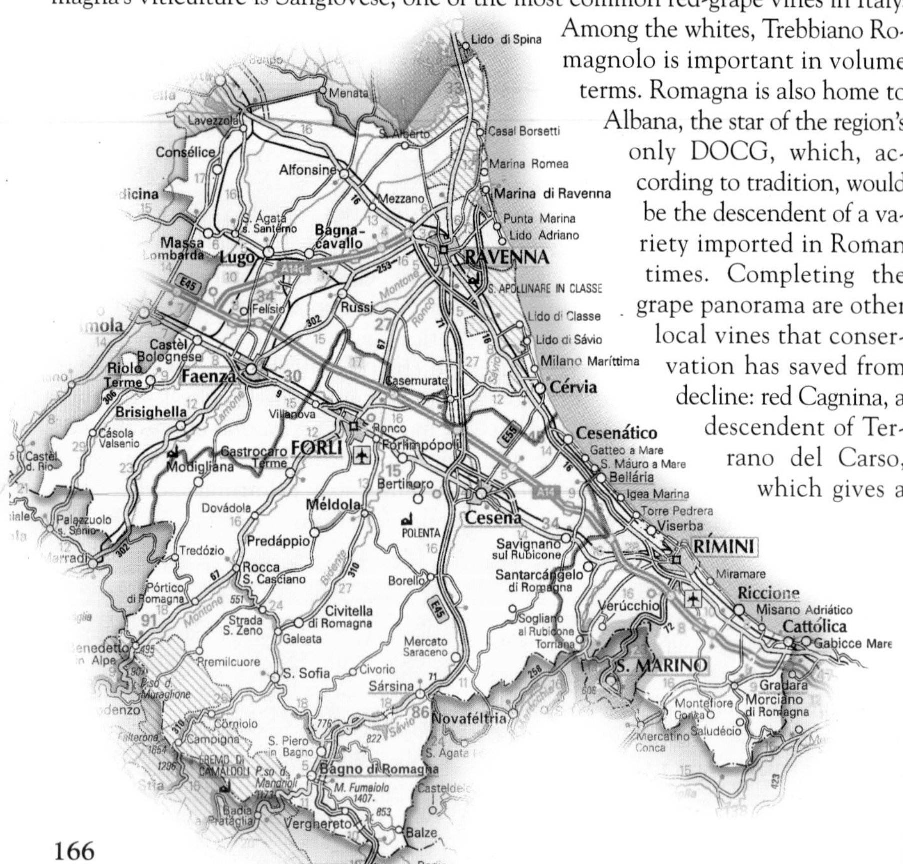

The Basilica of S. Apollinare in Classe of Ravenna

sweet wine of rare quality, and white Pagadebit, proverbial for its generosity. From the normative standpoint, in addition to the Albana DOCG the district boasts the Sangiovese di Romagna, Trebbiano di Romagna, Pagadebit di Romagna, Cagnina di Romagna, Romagna Albana Spumante DOCs and the Sillaro and Rubicone IGTs. Overlapping these denominations are others of a provincial nature: the Colli d'Imola, Colli di Faenza, Colli di Romagna Centrali, Colli di Rimini DOCs and the Forlì and Ravenna IGTs.

The Ravenna Province

The Ravenna vine-lands, among the region's most productive, stretch from the Apennine valleys to the Adriatic. In addition to the Albana DOCG and the Romagna DOCs and IGTs, they include two specific denominations. The Colli di Faenza DOC is in the hills and produces a white mainly from Chardonnay with additions of Pignoletto and other grapes, plus two varietal wines made from Pinot Bianco and Trebbiano Romagnolo. On the red front, a first wine is produced from Cabernet Sauvignon with additions of Sangiovese and Ancellotta among others, while Sangiovese pure vinification results in a varietal wine.

THE COLLINE DI FAENZA SANGIOVESE AND GASTRONOMY ROUTE

This itinerary takes in the valleys of the three rivers – Senio, Lamone, and Marzeno – that cut through the Ravenna Apennines. The focus of the tour is Faenza, but not to be missed is a visit to Ravenna, a city that was the capital of the Western Roman Empire for 150 years and still bears evidence of that in the extraordinary mosaics of its churches. The provincial capital is also home to a lovely enoteca, Cà de Vèn, run by the Ente Tutela Vini Romagnoli. Among the elements of gastronomic interest are not only the Apennine meats and cheeses but also the fine Brisighella DOP extra-virgin olive oil, among the absolute best.

ROMAGNA, HOME TO ITALIAN BRANDY

"The brandy that creates an atmosphere" runs the slogan of an historical Bolognese distillery, Buton, which has carved in collective memory the image of Romagna as the home to Italian brandy. Like Cognac and Armagnac, brandy is gotten from wine distilled in beakers similar to those used for grappa (which instead comes from wine dregs). In Romagna the base is Trebbiano, which proves to be especially suited to the purpose because of its features: white, not very aromatic, with low alcohol content and good acidity, resistant to oxidation. The distillate coming from it has the following characteristics: alcohol content of 40 to 43%; pale golden color with amber highlights; delicate but well-defined aroma, appropriately alcoholic, with hints of vanilla and tobacco; harmonious taste, with primary and secondary aromas of aquavit and tertiary aromas of the wood it was aged in (generally Slavonian oak, for at least one year). As for the producers, the past two decades have seen the birth of small but highly qualified distillers who offer brandy over 17 years old.
A selection of labels can be found at the Enoteca Regionale dell'Emilia-Romagna (see relevant box).

▪ **FAENZA**. This is the city of ceramics, with a famous museum illustrating their history and masterpieces: production was splendid in the 15th and 16th centuries and Faenza, *faïence* in French, became synonymous with ceramic-work per se. But it is also nice to linger in the spacious Piazza del Popolo, with its Town Hall and Cathedral (bits of the Middle Ages and Renaissance, respectively), or stroll under the porticos lining Via Mazzini.

▪ **RIOLO TERME**. From Castel Bolognese, which marks the beginning of the Colli di Faenza DOC along Via Emilia, you head to Riolo Terme, the first important town in the Senio valley, with a medieval center and a Renaissance fortress; near the river, the thermal baths building is Art Nouveau in style. Shallots, a typical local product, add flavor to a surprising number of preparations.

▪ **BRISIGHELLA**. This center is reached via Casola Valsenio, the Italian medicinal herb capital with its magnificent Herb Garden.
Brisighella is the main town of the lower Lamone valley, right at the foot of three big spurs of selenite on which stand the Torre dell'Orologio, the fortress and a sanctuary dedicated to the Virgin. Recent fame comes from local olive oil production, which has won a DOP – but the wines are no less good.

The Forlì-Cesena Province

Wine production is framed within the many DOC/IGT Romagna zones, which are overlapped by specific provincial denominations. Important wine towns are Bertinoro, for its Albana, and Predappio, for its Sangiovese. The Colli della Romagna Centrali DOC refers to the hills where, in addition to the classic Sangiovese and Trebbiano, Chardonnay and Cabernet Sauvignon are the protagonists.

THE COLLI DI FORLÌ AND COLLI DI CESENA WINE AND GASTRONOMY ROUTE

Almost 185 miles of Albana-land, up and down six valleys and 15 municipalities, including first-rate art cities and Castrocaro's spa resort. On the gastronomic front, a high point is *formaggio di fossa* (cave-aged cheese) made in Sogliano sul Rubicone.

▪ **FORLÌ**. Coming into town, Via Emilia opens on to two squares: one, named for the Ordelaffi, former lords of the place, hosts the Cathedral; the other, named from Aurelio Saffi, a follower of Mazzini, is the site of the Town Hall and the basilica of S. Mercuriale – with its ponderous bell tower, symbol of the city. The best places for gourmets are the Montone and Rabbi valleys.

▪ **PREDAPPIO**. Whoever visits the church of S. Cassiano in Pennino, in the Rabbi valley, will have a hard time ignoring the annexed cemetery where Benito Mussolini is buried. The visit continues to Predappio Alta, with its castle and Enoteca Ca' de Sanzves, where the host – should anyone have doubted it – is Sangiovese.

▪ **BERTINORO**. Past the gates you enter a town of medieval flavor and lovely vistas on the hillside vineyards and the sea. An old anecdote greets tourists: in the 13th century the families of the place put up a column in the square, and each attached a ring to it: a traveler would tie his horse to one of the rings and be the guest of the family it belonged to. Today Bertinoro has lost its walls but not its atmosphere or its welcoming character; as far as tasting is concerned, nothing surpasses the Enoteca Ca' de Be'.

▪ **CESENA**. Before crossing the Savio river, Via Emilia winds around a hill topped by the fortress of the Malatesta, the lords who exercised enlightened dominion on these lands in the 15th century. Present-time Cesena is a commercial city, with a welcoming and lively atmosphere; the codices in the Biblioteca Malatestiana testify to a splendid past.
Following Via Emilia farther on and taking a detour southward, you come to Longiano, a hill town close to the Adriatic with vineyards of ancient tradition. The Malatesta castle contains an important collection of contemporary art.

The Rimini Province

The province of Rimini lies on the southeastern border of Romagna and finds its continuation, even from an oenological viewpoint, in the Marches' Montefeltro area. Added to district denominations – Albana, Cagnina, Pagadebit, Sangiovese, and Trebbiano Romagnolo DOC, plus Rubicone IGT – is the provincial appellation. The group of Colli di Rimini DOC wines includes a white from Trebbiano Romagnolo and a

A wine estate in Bertinoro

Wineries *pp. 412-417*

Bagnacavallo, Bertinoro, Brisighella, Castel Bolognese, Civitella di Romagna, Coriano, Faenza, Meldola, Modigliana, Predappio, Russi, Savignano sul Rubicone.

red that is prevalently Sangiovese, enhanced through the addition of Cabernet Sauvignon. Varietal wines are Biancame and Rebola (Pignoletto) and Cabernet Sauvignon.

THE COLLI DI RIMINI WINE AND GASTRONOMY ROUTE

Inland from the worldliest town on the Adriatic Riviera, the ancient Strada Romagna (Romagna Road) leads to exploring the Marecchia and Conca valleys, once the realm of the Malatesta family. The gastronomic panorama goes from fish to meat and, in addition to *piadina*, the flat bread eaten with cheese and cold meats, stars olive oil, truffles, and chestnuts.

▪ **RIMINI.** Vacation center par excellence, it also has much else to offer: the historical center and hinterland are just waiting to be discovered, especially in off-season. Of the greatest interest are the Tiberius bridge and Augustus arch, from Roman times, the Sigismondo castle, the famous Malatesta temple (1447-1460), designed by Leon Battista Alberti, and – why not – the Grand Hotel of Fellini's remembrances.

▪ **SANTARCANGELO DI ROMAGNA.** The old part, with its winding streets and very old houses, lies on the Mount Giove knoll, which also hosts the Malatesta fortress; the new part, along Via Emilia, is a busy commercial center.

▪ **VERUCCHIO.** Dominated by an imposing Malatesta fortress which, some say, was the site of the tragic love of Dante's Paolo and Francesca, the town is an important archeological center (see the finds in the Civic Museum) and has beautiful churches like the collegiate and the parish church of S. Martino.

▪ **SAN CLEMENTE.** This fortified village, set in a dominating position, is the primary farming center of the Conca valley, on the border between Romagna and the Marches. It boasts premium wine production, especially Sangiovese.

SAN MARINO'S VINEYARDS

The Republic of San Marino vaunts a centuries-old wine tradition that finds expression in about 500 acres of vineyards in the area best suited for them – on the Adriatic side of Mount Titano (9 miles from the sea), at 330-1650 feet above sea level. About 300 producers belong to the Consorzio Vini Tipici di San Marino.
The vines that are cultivated are primarily Sangiovese (65%), followed by Biancale (Bianchello, 28%), Moscato Bianco (6%), and other white-grape varieties – Ribolla (Pignoletto), Canino, and Cargarello. Recently, Chardonnay, Pinot Bianco, and Pinot Nero have been introduced significantly. The most representative wines with the Identificazione d'Origine (the same as DOC) certification are: Brugneto, based on Sangiovese (min. 85%); Biancale (min. 85%); Moscato Spumante.
Along with these go some table wines: San Marino Riserva, with a Sangiovese base, aged in barriques; Sangiovese dei Castelli Sammarinesi; Rosato dei Castelli Sammarinesi; Bianco dei Castelli Sammarinesi; white Moscato, both still and sweet; Grilèt, a fizzy white from Biancale, Chardonnay, and Sangiovese grapes, vinified white; Riserva del Titano, a charmat-method brut spumante. Production also includes a brandy from Moscato Bianco distilled with the discontinuous double-boiler method devised by Tullio Zadra.

▪ Specialties in Emilia-Romagna ▪

LOOKING AT IT on the map, Emilia-Romagna is a sort of trapezoid contained within the course of the Po and the Apennine watershed, diverging slightly towards the Adriatic coast. Inside it two other axes are defined: lengthwise runs Via Emilia, the ancient Roman road separating the plain from the hills; on the other hand, across the region, roughly at the height of Imola, runs the historical boundary which, at the fall of the Western Roman Empire, divided Emilia (which entered the barbarian sphere) from Romagna (which continued to be part of the Latin world). These are the geographical and historical elements at the source – and what a source!– of regional cuisine. In fact, Emilian cooking has northern European ancestry, based on pig-raising and the use of animal fats; Romagna traditions are instead Mediterranean, tied to sheep and goat raising and olive oil.

SUBSTITUTES OF BREAD can be *gnocco fritto* (pan-fried dough) and, on the other hand, *piadina*, cooked on a hot-plate. An extraordinary range of cold meats is complemented by *pecorino* cheese that gains vigor with singular ageing in caves. Emilia's cooking is rich and suave, Romagna's is more vigorous and sanguine. Coming down from the north, the first stop is at Piacenza: great cold meats from the Apennine area (*coppa*, salami, *pancetta*) and, given its bordering position, a cuisine with Lombard, Piedmont, and Ligurian accents. Then comes Parma, home to Parmigiano-Reggiano cheese, Parma prosciutto, and *culatello* of Zibello. Then it is the turn of Reggio, where the Parmigiano-Reggiano cheese reign ends and the balsamic vinegar starts to rule. In the Modena area pork products star again, with prosciutto and *zampone*. The zenith of Emilian cooking is found in Bologna, where egg-based pasta in the form of *tagliatelle*, *tortellini*, or *lasagne* is the banner and *ragù* (Bolognese meat sauce) the anthem that accompanies it. Farther north is Ferrara, with its sumptuous *salama da sugo*. Castel San Pietro marks the start of Romagna, divided between Adriatic and Apennine flavors: Ravenna, with its gem of Brisighella olive oil; Forlì and Cesena, where the Apennine component prevails, with meat and game dishes that recall Tuscany; and finally Rimini, with its broth dense with tomato and spicy with vinegar and pepper, forerunner of the notes of central-southern Italy, and a produce-based cuisine that will find its full expression in the Marches' Montefeltro area.

AS FOR WINES, Albana, Pignoletto, Trebbiano, and refined whites like Pinot Bianco dei Colli Piacentini accompany hors-d'oeuvres, light first courses and all kinds of seafood. The flavorful first courses typical of the place go well with reds like Gutturnio. Both white and red are traditional with cold meats: Malvasia Colli di Parma or Fortana. With *zampone* and other spicy cooked pork sausages, only Lambrusco will do. Meats and Parmigiano-Reggiano cheese go well with Sangiovese, in all its varieties and intensities, and with good-vintage Barbera and Cabernet Sauvignon. When dessert is served, the choice is between semi-sweet and fizzy versions of Albana or a very special red, Cagnina.

Comune di Castelvetro di Modena

Tel. +39 059 758880 - Fax +39 059 790771

TERRITORY

Castelvetro has a very extensive surface area that sweeps from the flat meadows to the hills and finishes up by grazing the mountain feet.

Two waterways criss-cross the area: the Nizzola River and the Guerro River. The land is particularly fertile and is therefore suited for agricultural use

HISTORY OF THE NAME

Toward 150 B.C. Roman legions came to the area to set up a military outpost in the hills area, also known as a CASTRUM (military camp). Hence, the name of Castelvetro derives from CASTRUM (military camp) and VETUS (old, antique). Today, we can still see the remnants of the CARDO, DOCUMANUS, INSULE, and FORTRESSES, etc.

Later on, in the middle ages, in the year 988, Castelvetro is also called "CASTROVETERE". Only much later, in the 1500s, was Castrovetere mentioned in the annals under its current toponym CASTELVETRO, crossed "in the valley" by the GHERLO River, later called GUERRO.

THE ENOTECA COMUNALE

The Enoteca Comunale (municipal cellar) is located in the gallery of the Castle of Levizzano Rangone, originally constructed as a defensive rampart against the Hungarian invaders in the 9th century and later expanded by Bonifacio di Toscana (father of Matilde di Canossa), and by the Levizzani and Rangoni families.

The cellar gathers together the products of the member wineries of the "Terre di Castelvetro" and was founded on the initiative of several producers and the municipal government. In addition, all the farms of the Castelvetro territory have the opportunity to show off their products. In the splendid backdrop of Castle Matildico is the restaurant where visitors can sample the "Lambrusco Grasparossa di Castelvetro DOC", as well as other typical local products: Parmigiano Reggiano, traditional balsamic vinegar of Modena, "Torta Ducale", macaroons, local honey and "Nocino" (a walnut-flavoured liqueur).

EVENTS AND HAPPENINGS

MERCURDO – Month of June, on even years

This is the festival of the absurd that takes places in the squares and in the streets of the antique hamlet of Castelvetro. In every corner of the town are spectacles, entertainment, shows, stands, and booths marked by the hilarious, the bizarre and the original. Of course, there are always plenty of stands for passers-by to sample the culinary delights and refreshments, inspired by the local culinary tradition.

GRAPE AND MODENESE LAMBRUSO FESTIVAL – September

Castelvetro celebrates its wines, its land and its products with shows dedicated to produce and handicrafts, featuring folkloristic, cultural and sporting events. In addition, stands are set up for tasting typical products made by the main local producers which guide the visitor in search of our very best products.

THE 16TH CENTURY AND ITS SUGGESTIONS: HISTORIC PAGEANT AND LIVING DRAUGHTS GAME

The event (which is held on even years) centres around the historic pageant that re-enacts the arrival of the poet Torquato Tasso in Castelvetro and on the living game of draughts played on the draught-board square in the hamlet. Hundreds of figurines in splendid Renaissance costumes participate in the revelry.

THE 16TH CENTURY AND ITS SUGGESTIONS: FESTIVAL IN THE CASTLE

The event is held on odd years and consists in the re-enactment of a 16th-century banquet in costume, animated by games, tightrope walkers, and gypsies. There are also plenty of "commoners" hired to serve food and wine to the aristocratic guests.

TOURIST INFORMATION

For any additional information, contact the CASTELVETRO V.I.T.A. consortium (Integrated Valorization of Territory and Environment) which is involved in promoting and maximising the value of Castelvetro land and products and is assisted in this by the Castelvetro Shopping Association.

Tel. +39 059 758880 - Fax +39 059 790771

E-mail: turismo@comune.castelvetro-di-modena.mo.it

Sito Internet del comune: www.comune.castelvetro-di-modena.mo.it

Provincia di Modena
Assessorato
Agricoltura e
Alimentazione

The Lands of Lambrusco

Vineyard has been a part of the landscape of the province of Modena for many centuries.

Lambrusco, historic, strong and yet at the same time indulgent vine, has adapted as well to hillside planting as it has to the chilly and damp climate of the plain, always showing its very aspects, whether it is grown close together with elm or, as in contemporary practices, in specialized vineyards. The **Lambrusco wine** that is obtained from the grape of the same name is one of the most beloved and certainly one of the best-known in the world. Few other wines can take pride in the loyal following that Lambrusco enjoys.

In 1970, **Lambrusco di Sorbara, Lambrusco di Salamino di Santa Croce, and Lambrusco Grasparossa di Castelvetro** were granted the coveted DOC recognition **(Controlled Appellation of Origin)**.

Lambrusco can be made in red and rosé versions, either dry, demi-sec, suave or sweet and the minimum alcohol content is set at 10.5°.

DOC Lambrusco wines

Lambrusco di Sorbara

Also known as Lambrusco della Viola for its distinctive floral bouquet, Lambrusco di Sorbara was already a member of the elite class of Italian wines, which were fashionable in the 19th century. Its most distinguishing sensory characteristic is its brilliant colour, which can range from ***a rose-pink to light ruby red*** and effervescent froth with blush undertones and deep notes to the nose, while the flavour is light and delicate on the palate, full-bodied yet never overpowering.

Lambrusco Salamino di Santa Croce

The Salamino vine is arguably the most widely planted Lambrusco in the Modena area. It is extremely robust and provides an abundant and consistent production, harvest after harvest.

The sensory characteristic that most distinguishes Lambrusco Salamino di Santa Croce is the ***rose-pink to ruby red colour*** loaded with dramatic violet-tinged nuances. On the palate, it is crisp, flavourful, harmonious and moderately tannic, traits that make it supremely drinkable. It is ideal served with any meal.

Lambrusco Grasparossa di Castelvetro

Together with its sister grapes, Sorbara and Salamino, the Grasparossa vine was well-known and valued in the last century, as proven by historic documentary evidence.

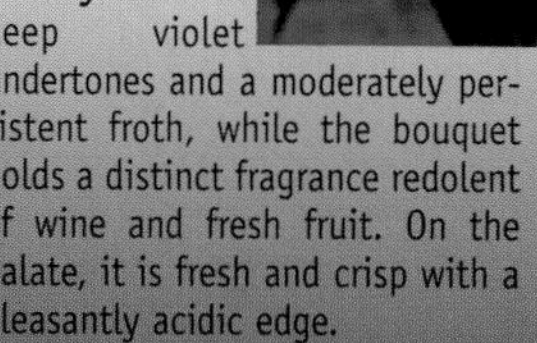

Extraordinarily elegant and well-balanced, but fuller bodied and more complex than the other types of Lambrusco, its colour can range from ***rose pink to ruby red*** with deep violet undertones and a moderately persistent froth, while the bouquet holds a distinct fragrance redolent of wine and fresh fruit. On the palate, it is fresh and crisp with a pleasantly acidic edge.

Where to go to taste and pu

Az. agr. GUERZONI ADRIANO
via Taglio, 26
41033 Concordia s. Secchia (Mo)
Tel. 0535/56561
info@guerzoni.com
www.guerzoni.com
produzione biodinamica

Az. vitivinicola PANCALDI
via Griduzza, 1/e
41012 Carpi (Mo)
Cell. 339/4485210
mpancaldi@tin.it

Az. Agr. PALTRINIERI GIANFRANCO
via Cristo, 49
41030 Sorbara di Bomporto (Mo)
Tel. 059/902047
cantina.paltrinieri@tiscalinet.it
www.cantinapaltrinieri.it

Az. Agr. GARUTI ELIO ed EREDI GARUTI ROMEO
via per Solara 6
41030 Sorbara di Bomporto (Mo)
Tel. 059/902021
az.agrgaruti@tiscalinet.it

Az. Agr. PEDRONI
via Risaria 2/4
41015 Rubbiara – Nonantola (Mo)
Tel. 059/549019
info@acetaiapedroni.com

Az. Agr. FOLICELLO
via Sparate 16
41010 Manzolino di Castelfranco E. (Mo)
Tel. 059/939045
folicello@inwind.it

Az. Agr. GIANELLI URBANO
via Lunga 28
41014 Castelvetro (Mo)
Tel. 059/790171
gianurb@libero.it

Az. Agr. BERTANI M. ASSUNTA
via Randelli 543
41050 Torre Maina – Maranello (Mo)
Tel. 0536/947943
azagrbertani@libero.it
www.ilmulinoditorremaina.it

Az. Agr. BELLEI AURELIO
via Ravarino Carpi 103
41030 Sorbara di Bomporto (Mo)
Tel. 059/909273

Az. Agr. CA' BERTI dei F.lli Vandelli
via Spagna 60
41010 Levizzano di Castelvetro (Mo)
Tel. 059/741025
info@caberti.com
www.caberti.com

Az. Agr. CANTINA BARBOLINI di M.Buffagni
via Fiori 40
41041 Casinalbo di Formigine (Mo)
Tel. 059/550154
barbolini@msw2.com

Az. Agr. CASTELVETRO
via Belvedere 8
41014 Castelvetro (Mo)
Tel. 059/3163311
azienda.agricola@chiarli.com

Az. Agr. MALETTI
via Canale 39
41019 Soliera (Mo)
Tel. 059/563876
info@lambruscomaletti.it
www.lambruscomaletti.it

Az. Agr. MESSORI GIANCARLO di Messori Andrea
via Viazza di Ramo 113
41010 Cittanova (Mo)
Tel. 059/848196

Az. Agr. NAVIGLIO F.lli Carafoli
via Cantina 85
41017 Ravarino (Mo)
Tel. 059/909102
carafoli.vini@tiscalinet.it

Az. Agr. PEZZUOLI di Pezzuoli e Venturelli
via Vignola 136
41053 Maranello (Mo)
Tel. 0536/948800
info@pezzuoli.it

Az. Agr. TENUTA PEDERZANA di Francesco Gibellini
via Palona 12/A
41014 Castelvetro (Mo)
Tel. 059/799677
francesco.gibellini@tin.it

Az. Agr. VEZZELLI FRANCESCO
via Canaletto Nord 878/A
41100 Modena
Tel. 059/318695

Az. Agr. VILLA DI CORLO
strada Cavezzo 200
41040 Baggiovara (Mo)
Tel. 059/510736
info@villadicorlo.com
www.villadicorlo.com

Az. Agr. vitivinicola CORTE MANZINI
via Modena 131/3
41014 Castelvetro (Mo)
Tel. 059/702658
cortemanzini@tiscali.it
www.cortemanzini.it

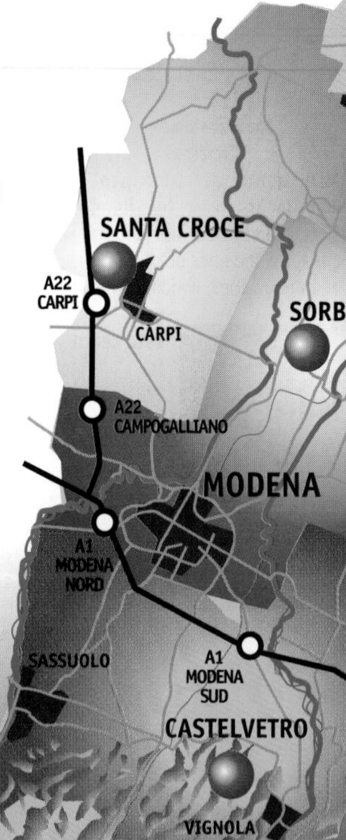

ase D.O.C. Lambrusco wines

Az. Agr. ZUCCHI DAVIDE
via Viazza 66
41030 S.Prospero (Mo)
Tel. 059/908934
info@vinizucchi.it
www.vinizucchi.it

Az. vinicola FIORINI
via Nazionale per Carpi 1534/5A
41010 Ganaceto (Mo)
Tel. 059/386028
fiorini@fiorini1919.com

Az. vitivinicola
FATTORIA MORETTO
di Altariva Fausto
via Tiberia 13/B
41014 Castelvetro (Mo)
Tel. 059/790183
az.moretto@tiscali.it

Cantina
CIV&CIV di Castelvetro
via Lingua Lunga 9
41050 Solignano di Castelvetro (Mo)
Tel. 059/702781
civcv@tin.it

Cantina
CIV&CIV di Sorbara
via Nazionale 70
41030 Sorbara di Bomporto (Mo)
Tel. 059/902053
civsorb@virgilio.it

Cantina
CIV&CIV di S.Marino di Carpi
via Provinciale Motta 79
41012 S.Marino di carpi (Mo)
Tel. 059/686248
civcarpi@virgilio.it

Cantina Sociale di CARPI
via Cavata 14
41012 Carpi (Mo)
Tel. 059/686120
cscarpi@libero.it

Cantina Sociale di FORMIGINE
via Pascoli 4
41043 Formigine (Mo)
Tel. 059/558122
info@lambruscodoc.it
www.lambruscodoc.it

Cantina Sociale di LIMIDI
SOLIERA E SOZZIGALLI
via Carpi-Ravarino 529
41010 Limidi di Soliera (Mo)
Tel. 059/561612

Cantina Sociale di S.CROCE
S.S. 468 di Correggio 35
41012 S.Croce di Carpi (Mo)
Tel.059/664007
cantinasantacroce@tin.it
www.cantinasantacroce.it

Cantina Sociale di SETTECANI
via per Modena 184
41014 Castelvetro (Mo)
Tel. 059/702505
cantssc@tin.it
www.cantinasettecani.it

Cantina Sociale di SORBARA
via Ravarino-Carpi 116
41030 Sorbara di Bomporto (Mo)
Tel. 059/909103
css@cantinasocialedisorbara.com
www.cantinasocialedisorbara.com

Cantina Sociale
LA PEDEMONTANA
viale Po 6
41049 Sassuolo (Mo)
Tel. 0536/804115
lapedemontana@tin.it

Cantina Sociale
MASONE-CAMPOGALLIANO
via Nuova, 7
41011 Campogalliano (Mo)
Tel. 059/526905
info@cantinamasonecampogalliano.com
www.cantinamasonecampogalliano.com

Cantine
CAVICCHIOLI U. & FIGLI
piazza Gramsci 9
41030 S.Prospero (Mo)
Tel. 059/812411
cantine@cavicchioli.it
www.cavicchioli.it

CHIARLI 1860 – Pr.I.V.I.
via Manin 15
41100 Modena
Tel. 059/3163311
chiarli@chiarli.com
www.chiarli.com

GAVIOLI ANTICA CANTINA
via Vittorio Veneto 65/A
41015 Nonantola (Mo)
Tel. 059/222014
info@gaviolivini.com
www.gaviolivini.com

GIACOBAZZI GRANDI VINI
via Provinciale Ovest 57
41015 Nonantola (Mo)
Tel. 059/540711
giacobazzi@giacobazzi.it
www.giacobazzi.it

ZANASI AZIENDA AGRICOLA
via Settecani Cavidole 53
41051 Castelnuovo R. (Mo)
Tel. 059/537052

info:

www.provincia.modena.it
www.agrimodena.it
www.lambrusco.net
info@lambrusco.net

wineries receive visitors only by booking.

In a locality in the Romagna, in the historical centre of Sogliano al Rubicone, the Mengozzi family has always used the travertine stone cavities, also known as "Antiche Fosse", on its property to bury its very finest local cheeses, keeping them protected underground for three months. Uncovering them after aging, the result is a sublime product known as the "Formaggio di Fossa". This special cheese releases a fragrance and flavour that was believed to have been lost forever with the passing of time. The special environmental conditions, the jealously guarded, labour-intensive method of preparation, and the experience, attention, and enthusiasm put forth by the owners of the "Antiche Fosse", inheritors of the Mengozzi family and keepers of the century-old tradition, make the "Formaggio di Fossa" a unique product that can only be found right here.

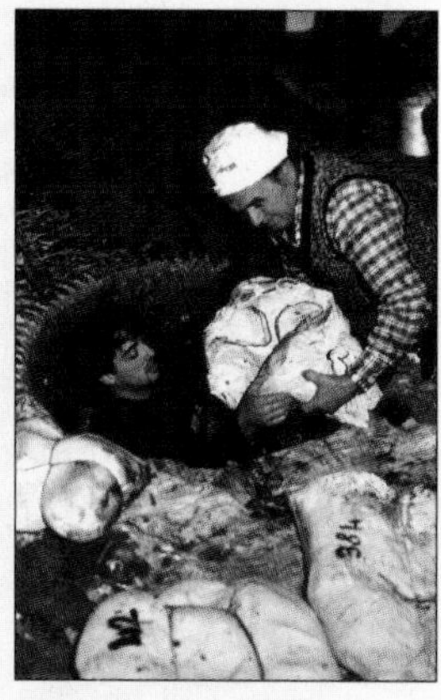

Once out of the stone cavity, the remodelled forms emerge with an oily sheen and a bit misshapen, but enveloped in an unmistakable and intoxicating aroma. The compressed cheese has an off white colour or a slightly yellow cast. Its distinctive crumbly texture melts in the warmth of the mouth, filling the palate with a robust flavour yet is sweet and delicate at the same time, infused with a slight pungency, tending toward sharpness. The "Antiche Fosse" makes its unique "Formaggio di Fossa" available for sale wholesale and retail buyers starting in the third week in November; traditionally, this product is removed from its hole in celebration of the feast day of St. Catherine, on November 25th. Batches of the "Formaggio di Fossa" cheese are also available in the spring and summer, especially aged for these periods. Considering the large demand and the limited quantities of the product, reservations are recommended. Arrangements can be made for home delivery of the cheese, even in small quantities. The owner of the "Formaggio di Fossa" Sas company, management of the "Antiche Fosse", is happy to provide additional information and clarifications.

"FORMAGGIO DI FOSSA" SAS

di Rossini Dr. Gianfranco & C.
Via G. Pascoli, 8 - 47030 Sogliano al Rubicone (FO)
Tel. and Fax +39 0541 948687

Ravenna intorno
Verde, Azzurro, Oro

Grapes and wine in the Province of Ravenna

The age-old tradition of viticulture in Ravenna and its surrounding area is confirmed by facts and figures that place the Province of Ravenna in the top spot for vineyards in the Emilia Romagna region and among the top ten across the country. Due to the predominance of vineyards on the flatlands, until just a short time ago, Ravenna was often associated only with quantity production.

Recently, things have changed quite a bit and Ravenna winemaking can also take pride in wines that are distinguished by an excellent quality/price ratio, and even some sparks of brilliance.

A historic moment in this quality turnaround was in 1962 when the Romagna Wine Protection Body was created, which opened the way to improvements to quality of modern Ravenna grape-growing and winemaking. This approach was consolidated with the conception and development of the Centro di Tebano, in the hills of Faenza, which still remains a standard for winemaking, regionally and nationally. It can also take pride in a university degree course in viticulture and oenology.

The province can be divided into three macro-areas in terms of its historic, technical and environmental and landscape characteristics: the hill and foothill area includes the district south of Via Emilia with a few offshoots toward the north, which includes the DOCG Albana di Romagna, the DOC "Colli di Faenza" and part of the DOC Romagna areas. The production in the area includes the Vena dei Gessi and the ravines of Brisighella, and is characterised by Albana, the first white wine to be awarded prestigious DOCG recognition (controlled and guaranteed appellation of origin). The wine is made with Albana grapes and achieves excellence as a sweet wine. Sangiovese is the standout in the DOC Romagna area. It is the most widespread grape and the pride and joy of the area. We also find Trebbiano Romagnolo, Cagnina and Pagadebit. Of the younger DOC Colli di Faenza wines, we remember Sangiovese, the Chardonnay-based white with an enhancement of Trebbiano Romagnolo or Sauvignon, Pinot Bianco and the delicious "reds", Cabernet Sauvignon and Merlot.

The seaside area starts from the boundary with the Province of Ferrara and covers the zone between the SS16 Adriatica and the sea, up to the border with the Province of Forlì-Cesena. It is part of the DOC "Bosco Eliceo" and its wine trail traverses the valleys and pine woods of the Ravenna portion of the Po Delta Park to reach Cervia. In addition to the classic Fortana (Golden Grape) we find "Bianco del Bosco Eliceo," a blend of Trebbiano Romagnolo and Malvasia di Candia, plus the white Sauvignon and the red Merlot.

The central plains area is the third and final region, tucked in between the other two areas described above: it is the undisputed land of the Trebbiano Romagnolo, still the most planted vine in the province. In recent years, this area has been seeking an identity, coupling production of Trebbiano Romagnolo with other grapes, such as the red Merlot and the Longanesi grape. The latter, also known as "Bursan" is demonstrating its attention-getting potential.

HISTORY AND NATURE IN PERFECT SYNCH

The hills known as the birthplace of the wireless telegraphy inventor are the ideal habitat for a diversified wine production, attentive to innovations and tradition

Located at the gateway of the Tuscan-Emilian Apennines, in a charming valley cleaved by the waters of the Reno and Setta rivers, between hills, woods and chestnut coppices, and criss-crossed by major connecting roads (including the A1 motorway and the Bologna - Porretta railway), Sasso Marconi is a mandatory stop for tourists visiting this part of the country, as well as a strategically important commercial and industrial hub. Thanks to a careful and specific development of the land, our countryside has grown gradually to become an extraordinary tourist attraction, which today represents the main engine for development of the entire region. Relyng on the holiday farm business, the wine and culinary trails, footpaths, and open air sports and by taking advantage of the historic and natural resources (the breathtaking cliffs, the Pliocene spur, river front park, Gothic and Resistance-era architecture, the Renaissance Palazzo de' Rossi, the 18th-century village of Colle Armeno, the numerous churches and parishes, the aristocratic manors and villas, including Villa Griffone, and the museum residence where Guglielmo Marconi conducted his earliest experiments with wireless telegraphy, all represent an invaluable artistic and cultural heritage), the region can present itself today as a tourist destination. A new economic and commercial infrastructure is slowly creating, based on the use of the hills and their bounty. As it can rely on an orography varying from 76 to 650 meters above sea level, Sasso Marconi is characterised by the sheer variety of its products, which include exceptional chestnuts, wine and olive oil. The local grapes grown most widely are Sauvignon, Pinot, Pignoletto, Cabernet-Sauvignon, Chardonnay, Merlot and Barbera: with its wine cellars and its vineyards, our lands are part of the "Cities of Wine" circuit. For several years, increasing and promoting planting, have re-launched the cultivation of olives, which had been abandoned centuries ago (the first local olive oil was produced in 2002). A well-established circuit of first-rate restaurants, small inns, and holiday farms offers the opportunity to appreciate the products of the local food and wine culture: truffles and mushrooms, combined with traditional specialities, such as tortellini, roasted meats, and S. Giuseppe ravioli also. The historic and cultural heritage and long-standing tradition also represent a living resource which can still characterise these lands: Sasso Marconi plays host to important events, based on the history and the popular folk culture which have become eagerly-awaited appointments for residents and visitors, such as the Fira di Sdaz on 8 September (a traditional folk festival that has been replicated every year for 330 years), and Tartufesta (one of the most eagerly awaited culinary events of the region, held in late October - early November).

Among the producers in Sasso Marconi, we are citing the ones that have a wine cellar and store and which visitors can tour.

AZIENDA AGRICOLA CAPPUCCI
via Moglio, 44 - tel. +39 051 846745

FATTORIA DI MONTECHIARO
via Montechiaro, 50 - tel. +39 051 6755140

FLORIANO CINTI
via Gamberi, 48 - tel. +39 051 6751646

ILDEBRANDO VALMORI
via Angonella, 7 - tel. +39 051 6755135

MARIO ZURLA
via Mandriolo, 13 - tel. +39 051 6755086

Città di Sasso Marconi

Piazza dei Martiri, 6 • Tel. 800-273218

E-mail: atuxtu@smarconi.provincia.bologna.it • Sito web: www.comune.sassomarconi.bologna.it

TUSCANY

THE WINE RENAISSANCE

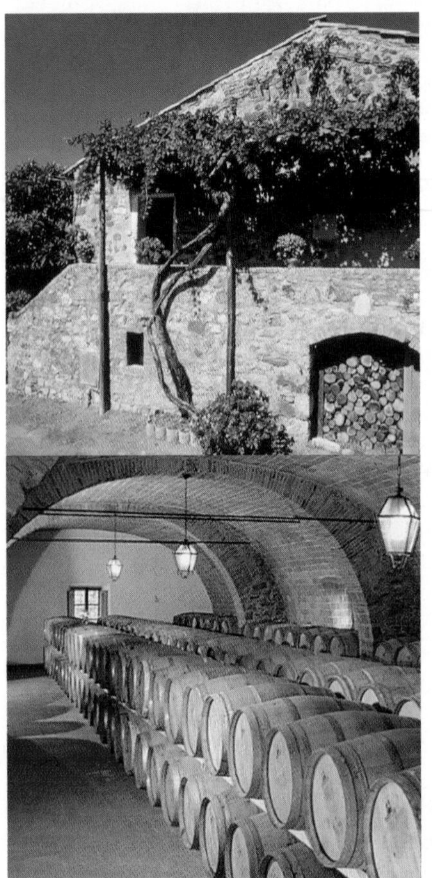

Chianti and Brunello di Montalcino are the champions of a region which, in terms of wine, has no equals in the rest of the world, the merit, to be sure, of its producers, but also of ideal growing conditions and a millenia-old culture.

When speaking of Tuscany, it is almost inevitable, sooner or later, to refer to Lorenzetti and his "Good Government" fresco in the Town Hall of Siena, where a well cultivated countryside and an industrious city are depicted. This citation could not be more natural in a book about wine and wine tourism, where the role of the cultivator in the protection of the environment and of the enhancement of hu-

Above, Volpaia Castle in Radda in Chianti; left, a winery (top) and a big cellar (bottom) in the Montalcino area

man and natural resources is of central importance. This is a valid general consideration, but it is of immediate relevance in a region where the countryside and many cities still bear a major resemblance to the landscape of the Lorenzetti fresco. And where the fruits of the vine and of the olive tree, together wiht other typical products, are at the center of a Renaissance of fine cuisine.

In the Realm of Chianti, with Much Else to Discover

Cypresses and broom, olive groves and vineyards... just open a window onto the Tuscan countryside, as long as you are not in the middle of the Apennines, and the Mediterranean colors will fill your eyes. Statistics confirm that hillsides are the chosen environment for the vine (67%), though vineyards are also widespread in the plain. Chianti, produced in Italy's largest single viticultural district, is the major protagonist: its perimeter goes far beyond the area of high hills which originally gave it its name and now, scattered over a large stretch of regional territory, involves over 100 municipalities and six provinces. It begins between Siena and Florence, the two provinces which share the Chianti Classico area and also offer a multitude of other sights and scenes: from the hills of the Arno valley to the undulating Crete Senesi, from Mount Albano to Valdichiana. Then comes the northern provinces, Massa-Carrara, Lucca, and Pistoia, a homogenous stretch which marks the transition from the Ligurian Apennines to those which divide Tuscany from Emilia. Pisa and Livorno make their presence felt along the coast, an area once dominated and influenced by the Etruscans, with its rolling hills facing the Tyrrhenian Sea and the unique Elba Island. Grosseto closes out this panorama, with its volcanic soils around Mount Amiata and vineyards which announce the nearby presence of Latium.

Sangiovese and Trebbiano, the Great Tuscan Couple

Tuscany is a region of great red wines, though also of white wines well worthy of note. This proportion is reflected in the region's top wines: of the six DOCGs, five are red while one is white. The statistical record speaks clearly: Sangiovese, with 72.4%, and Trebbiano, with 11.4%, are the dominant varieties planted. Brunello (1.8%) follows behind (but this is just another type of Sangiovese) together with Ciliegiolo, with 1.2%. No other variety – Vernaccia, Vermentino, Ansonica, Malvasia del Chianti, Malvasia Bianca, and Biancone di Portoferraio among the white grapes; Prugnolo Gentile (another type of Sangiovese), Merlot, and Pollera Nera among the red grapes – manages to reach 1%.

As far as the two leading varieties – both of ancient Tuscan origin – are concerned, they have shared a common fortune over time, particularly outside of their own regional territory. Mixed together in the highly successful Chianti blend invented by Baron Ricasoli in the 19th century, they have found many other uses. Sangiovese has conquered territory in every part of Italy, from the Alps to Sicily, thereby becoming the number one variety on a national scale with 10% of Italy's vineyard area. The same can be said of Trebbiano, whose name derives from the *Trebulanum* of the ancient Romans, long valued for its reliably abundant yields in the vineyard: rather paradoxically, it is now more widely planted in the north than in the center of the peninsula but, nonetheless, with 7% of the total vineyard area, it is the country's number one white variety. As far as vineyard training systems are concerned, the picture is rather varied: single or double pen arched cane, along with spurred cordon training, dominate, and expansive horizontal systems are almost entirely absent, a fact which testifies to the traditional commitment to quality.

A Region at the Vanguard of Quality

The production trends of the last few years evidence a drop in overall volume (to almost 71 million US gallons) and an increase in DOC wines to over 33.5 million US gallons. These figures indicate a percentage of quality production of over 47.5%, second in Italy only to Trentino-Alto Adige. These data in themselves give a clear picture of a region which for some time has been following the philosophy of "total quality" by creating new DOC zones in areas with a more recent tradition and, above all, by modifying existing DOC regulations to create new types of wines more in demand on the market. This particularly concerns red wines, with an increasing request that corresponds to changing tastes, and varietal wines, linked to grapes with strong personalities and seen as a valid response to standardization and international competition. Against the background of the six DOCG zones, 34 DOCs and 5 IGTs which currently exist, a proposal for an overall Tuscan DOC is now being advanced, an umbrella appellation for all DOC production: many of those active in the sector see this as the best way to give a specific connotation to the region's wines, a name known all over the world as a synonym for art, natural beauty, and fine cuisine.

Wine Routes: the Countryside Right at Hand

Tuscany has been a pioneering region for farm holidays, based on the splendors that we all know: stone houses, farms, and even castles, all open to visitors seeking rural hospitality and country cooking. Those who foresaw, with some optimism, a "second harvest" for the Tuscan countryside underestimated the phenomenon: by now the farming sector seems more oriented to hospitality than to agriculture. The new frontier of rural tourism is represented by wineries, only minimally accessible to the general public, and it is no surprise that the Movimento

Brolio Castle at Gaiole in Chianti

Turistico del Vino (Movement for Wine Tourism) had its debut in Tuscany in 1993 with the first edition of Open Cellars. Today, with this enjoyable springtime festivity extended to hundreds of cellars all over Italy, the new challenge, awaited with some impatience, is that of Wine Routes. In this case as well, Tuscany has shown itself open to the winds of change by approving a new law, the first and still the sole legislation of its type in Italy, which regulates the creation and functioning of these tourist itineraries. These are not intended to be roads simply for automobiles, but which ramify out into the surrounding territory to include wineries, restaurants, wine shops, monuments and whatever else might interest those who wish to make wine part of their vacation or free time. Fourteen of these routes have already been approved: Carmignano, Chianti Colli Fiorentini, Chianti Rufina and Pomino, Colli di Candia and Lunigiana, Colli di Maremma, Colline Lucchesi and Montecarlo, Colline Pisane, Costa degli Etruschi, Montecucco and Terre di Arezzo, Monteregio di Massa Marittima, Montespertoli, Vernaccia di San Gimignano, Vino Nobile di Montepulciano. Just a few, if one considers that such important names as Chianti Classico and Brunello di Montalcino are missing; but many, if one considers the complex work of organizing them.

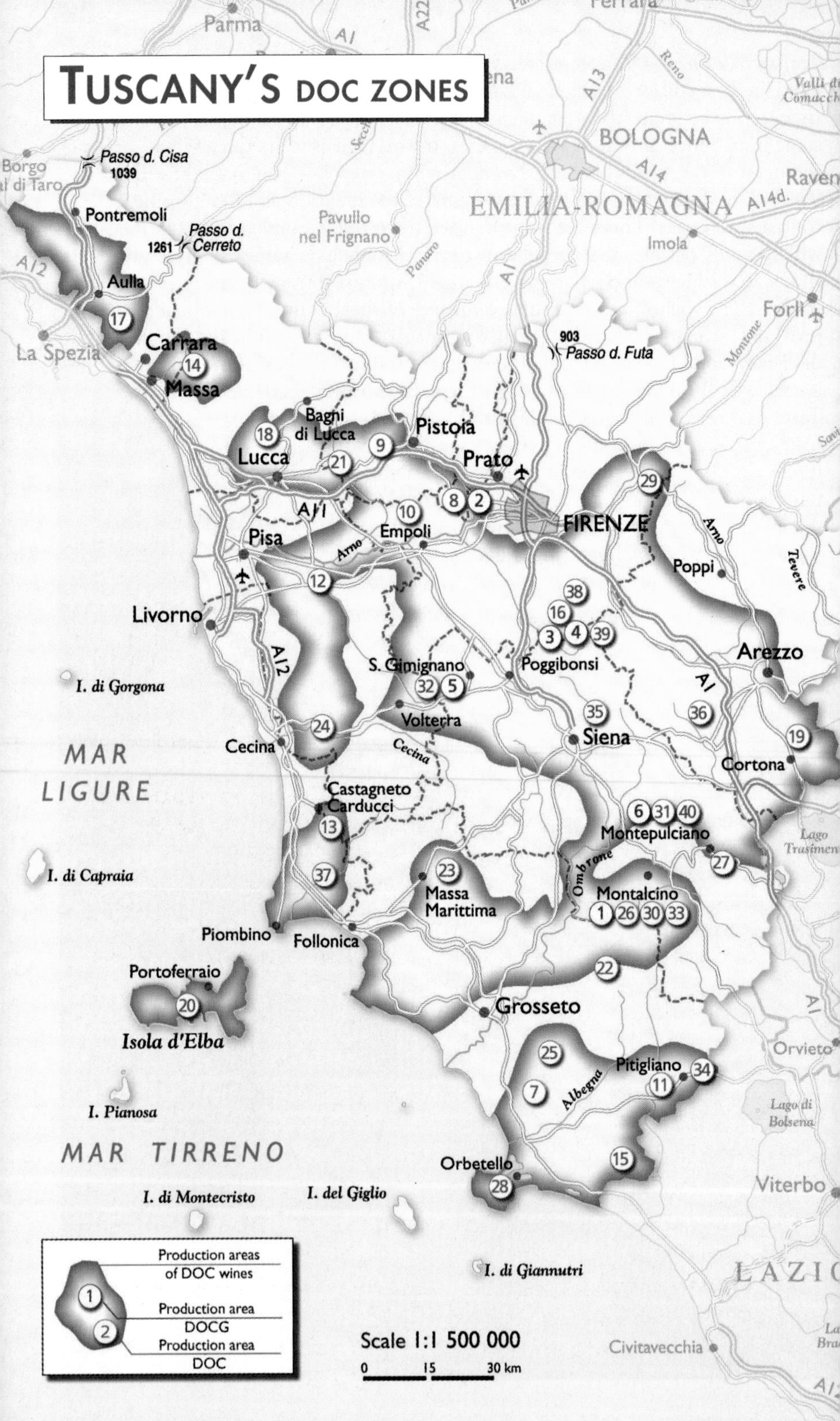
TUSCANY'S DOC ZONES
Parma
Ferrara
BOLOGNA
EMILIA-ROMAGNA
Passo d. Cisa
1039
Borgo
Pontremoli
Passo d.
1261 Cerreto
Pavullo
nel Frignano
Imola
Aulla
Forlì
La Spezia
Carrara
Massa
903
Passo d. Futa
Bagni
di Lucca
Pistoia
Lucca
Prato
FIRENZE
Pisa
Empoli
Poppi
Livorno
Arno
Tevere
S. Gimignano
Poggibonsi
Arezzo
I. di Gorgona
Volterra
Siena
Cecina
Cortona
MAR
LIGURE
Castagneto
Carducci
Montepulciano
Lago
Trasimeno
I. di Capraia
Massa
Marittima
Montalcino
Ombrone
Piombino
Follonica
Portoferraio
Grosseto
Isola d'Elba
Orvieto
Pitigliano
Albegna
I. Pianosa
Lago di
Bolsena
MAR TIRRENO
Orbetello
Viterbo
I. di Montecristo
I. del Giglio
I. di Giannutri
LAZIO
Production areas
of DOC wines
Production area
DOCG
Production area
DOC
Scale 1:1 500 000
0 15 30 km
Civitavecchia

1 **DOCG Brunello di Montalcino**
2 **DOCG Carmignano**
3 **DOCG Chianti**
4 **DOCG Chianti Classico**
5 **DOCG Vernaccia di San Gimignano**
6 **DOCG Vino Nobile di Montepulciano**
7 **DOC Ansonica Costa dell'Argentario**
8 **DOC Barco Reale di Carmignano**
Rosato di Carmignano ▪ *Vin Santo di Carmignano* ▪ *Vin Santo di Carmignano Occhio di Pernice*
9 **DOC Bianco della Valdinievole**
Vin Santo
10 **DOC Bianco dell'Empolese** *Vin Santo*
11 **DOC Bianco di Pitigliano**
12 **DOC Bianco Pisano di San Torpè**
Vin Santo
13 **DOC Bolgheri** *Bianco, Sauvignon, Vermentino* ▪ *Rosato, Vin Santo Occhio di Pernice* ▪ *Rosso, Sassicaia*
14 **DOC Candia dei Colli Apuani** *Bianco, Vin Santo*
15 **DOC Capalbio** *Bianco, Vermentino, Vin Santo* ▪ *Rosato* ▪ *Rosso, Sangiovese, Cabernet Sauvignon*
16 **DOC Colli dell'Etruria Centrale**
Bianco, Vin Santo ▪ *Rosato, Vin Santo Occhio di Pernice* ▪ *Rosso*
17 **DOC Colli di Luni** see *Liguria*
18 **DOC Colline Lucchesi** *Bianco, Sauvignon, Vermentino, Vin Santo* ▪ *Vin Santo Occhio di Pernice* ▪ *Rosso, Merlot, Sangiovese*
19 **DOC Cortona** *Bianco, Grechetto, Pinot Bianco, Riesling Italico, Sauvignon, Vin Santo* ▪ *Rosato, Occhio di Pernice* ▪ *Cabernet Sauvignon, Gamay, Merlot, Pinot Nero, Sangiovese, Syrah*
20 **DOC Elba** *Bianco, Ansonica, Moscato Bianco, Vin Santo* ▪ *Rosato, Vin Santo Occhio di Pernice* ▪ *Rosso, Aleatico*
21 **DOC Montecarlo** *Bianco, Vin Santo* ▪ *Vin Santo Occhio di Pernice* ▪ *Rosso*
22 **DOC Montecucco** *Bianco, Vermentino* ▪ *Rosso, Sangiovese*
23 **DOC Monteregio di Massa Marittima** *Bianco, Vermentino, Vin Santo* ▪ *Rosato, Vin Santo Occhio di Pernice* ▪ *Rosso*
24 **DOC Montescudaio** *Bianco, Chardonnay, Sauvignon, Vermentino, Vin Santo* ▪ *Rosso, Cabernet, Merlot, Sangiovese*
25 **DOC Morellino di Scansano**
26 **DOC Moscadello di Montalcino**
Vendemmia Tardiva
27 **DOC Orcia** *Bianco, Vin Santo* ▪ *Rosso*
28 **DOC Parrina** *Bianco* ▪ *Rosato* ▪ *Rosso*
29 **DOC Pomino** *Bianco, Vin Santo* ▪ *Rosso*
30 **DOC Rosso di Montalcino**
31 **DOC Rosso di Montepulciano**
32 **DOC San Gimignano** *Vin Santo* ▪ *Rosato, Vin Santo Occhio di Pernice* ▪ *Rosso, Sangiovese*
33 **DOC Sant'Antimo** *Bianco, Chardonnay, Pinot Grigio, Sauvignon, Vin Santo* ▪ *Vin Santo Occhio di Pernice* ▪ *Rosso, Cabernet Sauvignon, Merlot, Pinot Nero*
34 **DOC Sovana** *Rosato* ▪ *Rosso, Aleatico, Cabernet Sauvignon, Merlot, Sangiovese*
35 **DOC Val d'Arbia** *Vin Santo*
36 **DOC Valdichiana**
37 **DOC Val di Cornia** *Bianco, Ansonica, Vermentino* ▪ *Rosato* ▪ *Rosso, Aleatico Passito, Ciliegiolo, Merlot, Cabernet Sauvignon, Sangiovese, Suvereto*
38 **DOC Vin Santo del Chianti**
39 **DOC Vin Santo del Chianti Classico**
40 **DOC Vin Santo di Montepulciano**

IGT - Typical Geographic Indication
Alta Valle della Greve (Florence); Colli della Toscana Centrale (Arezzo - Florence -Pistoia - Prato - Siena); Maremma Toscana (Grosseto); Toscano or Toscana (Arezzo - Florence - Grosseto - Livorno - Lucca - Massa-Carrara - Pisa - Pistoia - Prato - Siena); Val di Magra (Massa-Carrara)

The Great Wines of Tuscany

Chianti Classico DOCG

Chianti Classico, that is the oldest zone of origin of this famous wine, covers the territory of nine municipalities between Florence and Siena. Under the Gallo Nero symbol production is regulated by a code that sets down severe criteria right from the vine-growing stage: planting density of at least 3350 stocks per 2.5 acres and yields not exceeding 16,500 lbs, meaning a maximum of 5 lbs of grapes per plant. The wine is made from Sangiovese grapes (75 to 100%) and possibly Canaiolo Nero (max. 10%), Trebbiano Toscano, and/or Malvasia del Chianti (max. 6%), and/or other grapes recommended for the zone of reference, from traditional Colorino to more recently introduced Merlot or Cabernet (max. 15%). Wine characteristics are: bright ruby color tending to garnet with ageing; vinous aroma, with a scent of sweet violet, and pronounced finesse in the ageing stage; harmonious, dry, flavorful, slightly tannic taste, which refines with time to velvety soft; minimum alcohol: 12%. Chianti Classico is put on the market starting October 1st of the first year after harvest. There is a Riserva qualification for the wine that reaches 12.5% of alcohol content after a compulsory ageing period of two years in barrels and at least three months in bottle. When young, Chianti Calssico goes well with grilled red meats; mature, it is excellent with game and the most robust dishes.

Brunello di Montalcino DOCG

Brunello was created in the mid-19th century by oenologist Ferruccio Biondi Santi, who concentrated his attention on the Sangiovese clone considered best suited to the area. His brainchild was to vinify the grapes pure, giving up traditional mixed grapes (white-berry included) blending. He also worked in the cellars, insisting on lengthy maceration and long ageing in oak barrels. The resulting wine is certainly rewarding: strong and velvety, with an extraordinary character, to the

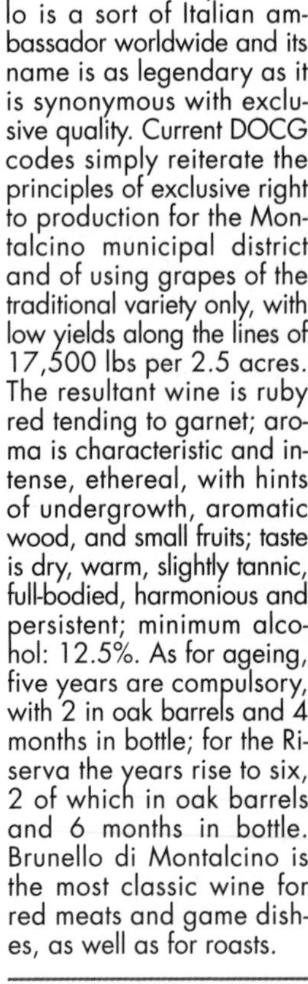

point that nowadays Brunello is a sort of Italian ambassador worldwide and its name is as legendary as it is synonymous with exclusive quality. Current DOCG codes simply reiterate the principles of exclusive right to production for the Montalcino municipal district and of using grapes of the traditional variety only, with low yields along the lines of 17,500 lbs per 2.5 acres. The resultant wine is ruby red tending to garnet; aroma is characteristic and intense, ethereal, with hints of undergrowth, aromatic wood, and small fruits; taste is dry, warm, slightly tannic, full-bodied, harmonious and persistent; minimum alcohol: 12.5%. As for ageing, five years are compulsory, with 2 in oak barrels and 4 months in bottle; for the Riserva the years rise to six, 2 of which in oak barrels and 6 months in bottle. Brunello di Montalcino is the most classic wine for red meats and game dishes, as well as for roasts.

Vernaccia di San Gimignano DOCG

The first recorded mention of Vernaccia in the vineyards around the hill town of San Gimignano, in the Siena area, dates from 1276. However, the origin of the name "vernaccia" is not precise and, anyway, it doesn't help in tracing the vine's initial home: perhaps Liguria, where there is a place called Vernazza, or Spain, where Garnacha grapes give a similar wine. Today's DOGC codes dictate that Vernaccia di San Gimignano be produced within municipal borders, with a maximum vineyard yield of 19,800 lbs per 2.5 acres. They also impose the use of the grapes from the Vernaccia di San Gimignano vine, with possible additions (max. 10%) of other white grapes recommended for the zone. The wine that results is pale yellow in color, tending to golden with ageing, with a fine and penetrating, characteristic aroma; its taste is dry, harmonious, with a typically bitterish aftertaste; minimum alcohol: 11%. To qualify as Riserva, the wine must have a minimum alcohol content of 11.5% and must be aged at least 14 months in barrels and 4 months in bottles. Vernaccia di San Gimignano is excellent with Italian-style hors-d'oeuvres, first courses and soups, seafood and white meat dishes, and with sweetish cheeses such as the Crete Senesi *pecorino*.

Vino Nobile di Montepulciano DOCG

It is hard to say whether the appellation Nobile, in use from the 18th century on, refers to the noble quality of the wine or rather to the noblemen who esteemed it. Another version favored at that time referred to a noble vine obtained from Sangiovese Grosso to better suit the features of the Montepulciano hillside: that was Prugnolo Gentile, which today's DOCG codes indicate as the basis (min. 70%) in the Vino Nobile mixed-grape blend – Canaiolo Nero (max. 10%) and other grapes typical to the area are added to it. The concern for quality is already evident in vine-growing standards – the yield must never exceed 17,600 lbs per 2.5 acres. After two years' compulsory ageing, the wine appears ruby red, tending to garnet as it matures; its aroma is intense, ethereal, characteristic; taste is dry, balanced and persistent, with possible hints of wood; minimum alcohol: 12.5%. There is a Riserva label for the 13% alcohol-content wine that has aged for over three years, with 6 months' fining in bottle. It can accompany meals from start to finish, from tasty first courses to meats – poultry, Chianina beef, and game.

Carmignano DOCG

The Medici family, choosing the homonymous place to summer in, were the first to attest to the quality of this wine, and in 1716 gave it a certificate of nobility (a sort of DOC forerunner) which set down precise criteria for cultivation and vinification. Carmignano has always been a distinguished wine, and after obtaining DOCG recognition it has gained adequate visibility on the Chianti production scene. Among other things, this wine has been able to keep pace with the times, welcoming French varieties to gain elegance and cosmopolitan taste. Regulations limit production to the municipal district of Carmignano and part of Poggio a Caiano's one, imposing a maximum yield of 17,600 lbs per 2.5 acres. The mixed-grape blend is essentially based on Sangiovese (45 to 70%), with the traditional addition of Canaiolo Nero (10 to 20%) and a certain amount of Cabernet Sauvignon and Cabernet Franc (6 to 15%). The resultant wine is deep, vibrant ruby red, tending to garnet with ageing; it has vinous aroma, with the scent of sweet violets and a great finesse when aged; taste is dry, mellow and velvety; minimum alcohol: 12.5%. It is put on the market on June 1st of the second year after harvest. There is a Riserva appellation for wine aged three years in oak or chestnut barrels. This is a rare wine, fit to accompany noble meats and cheeses.

Bolgheri Sassicaia DOC

The results of recently imported grapes are particularly interesting in Tuscany. The reference is above all to Cabernet Sauvignon, which is used as an ennobling element in many mixed-grape blend, to the point of being considered one of the best companions for Sangiovese. It is a protagonist, for example, in Bolgheri Rosso, and it is used pure in Bolgheri Sassicaia, the most famous of the so-called "Super-Tuscans".

Vin Santo

This passito wine, one of Tuscany's most typical products, is made essentially from Trebbiano grapes, which probably originated in the eastern Mediterranean and were already popular in Roman times. The wine made from them is straw yellow in color, slightly scented, fairly alcoholic, and with a neutral taste that gains in personality when combined with Malvasia, Canaiolo Bianco, or Vernaccia di San Gimignano. Dried grapes, lengthy ageing in small casks and contact with the lees formed over the years create such a special dessert or "meditation" wine, dry or sweet depending on development. There is also a Vin Santo Occhio di Pernice, made from red grapes (Sangiovese, Malvasia Nera, Canaiolo).

THE CHIANTI REGION

The Chianti hills, which stretch between Florence and Siena, are the core of a production which is by now region-wide.

Chianti wine has an ancient history and probably conserves some of the features of the Vermiglio wines praised in the Middle Ages. Actually, the name first appeared in the late 14th century, but the modern mixed-grape blend – a Sangiovese base enriched with additions of Canaiolo, Trebbiano, and other grapes – was created and codified by Bettino Ricasoli in the mid-19th century. Today, with production of 26.5 million US gallons, Chianti is the premier Italian DOC wine and undoubtedly one of the most popular on international markets.

The Chianti name refers to a precise geographical location – the group of hills stretching from Florence to Siena – but the production area is much larger: as early as 1726 a proclamation by the Grand Duke of Tuscany included territories far beyond the specific zone, while a royal decree of 1932 gave actual production prominence over geographical provenance, although pinpointing a "zone of older origin", Chianti Classico, extended to 9 municipalities on the border between Florence and Siena. DOC recognition, awarded in 1967, only confirmed this imprint, and today's enlarged district encompasses six provinces, corresponding to seven geographical sub-denominations: Colli Aretini, Colli Fiorentini, Colline Pisane, Colli Senesi, Montalbano, Montespertoli, and Rufina. Given its production distribution, Chianti can be considered a regional wine, justifying the decision to market it without individual provincial distinctions.

For the sake of completeness it has to be added that the Chianti DOCG area is also home to three other DOC labels: Colli dell'Etruria Centrale (which concerns production outside the "excellence" range), Vin Santo del Chianti, and Vin Santo del Chianti Classico.

In the Land of Chianti Classico

Limiting discussion to the Classico zone, Chianti's tourism offer is contradictory: while exuberant and highly qualified (the number of excellent wineries is impressive) it has not yet been officially framed into a wine route. The following is a simple list of the Chianti Classico municipalities, meant to be useful in drawing up an itinerary.

SIENA'S CHIANTI

■ **CASTELLINA IN CHIANTI.** An historic border town between Siena and Florence, it conserves the appearance of an ancient, wall-girded village dominated by the Rocca, a fortress with a 14th-century tower and a 15th-century castle keep. The typical Chianti countryside – vineyards, olive groves, and Etruscan ruins – is scattered with farmhouses converted into villas. The panorama of highly qualified wineries starts here.

■ **RADDA IN CHIANTI.** High on a knoll separating the Pesa and Arbia valleys, this town along the Chiantigiana road is Etruscan in origin, and it experienced the vicissitudes of a castle vied for by Florence and Siena. The medieval town center features lovely buildings from the 15th and 16th centuries.

▪ **GAIOLE IN CHIANTI.** The name is linked to the scenic Brolio Castle, once the home of Baron Bettino Ricasoli, a powerful and much-discussed minister of the Kingdom of Italy as well as the "inventor" of modern Chianti wine. The lovely landscape in the environs is full of country churches and castles.

▪ **CASTELNUOVO BERARDENGA.** Lying on the southern boundary of the Chianti Classico zone, this small town has strong traditions not only in wine-growing but also in the art of wrought iron; however, it is the surrounding countryside that strikes visitors most, rich as it is in broad vistas and historic dwellings.

▪ **POGGIBONSI.** Once a stopping-place for pilgrims and merchants along Via Francigena (or Cassia), today it is a reputed center for wine (on the western rim of the Classico zone) and for furniture. At the time of the Medici, an imposing fortress was built on the hill of Poggio Imperiale, a jewel of military architecture and prototype of Renaissance fortifications. The town also features the ancient church of S. Lorenzo.

Wineries *pp. 417-441*
Barberino Val d'Elsa, Castellina in Chianti, Castelnuovo Berardenga, Gaiole in Chianti, Greve in Chianti, Poggibonsi, Radda in Chianti, Rufina, Tavarnelle Val di Pesa.

FLORENCE'S CHIANTI

▪ **SAN CASCIANO IN VAL DI PESA.** A town along Via Cassia (national road no. 2) between the Greve and Pesa valleys, with ruins of ancient fortifications. A fine Museum of Sacred Art is housed in the church of S. Maria del Gesù; there are also many noteworthy wineries and beautiful parish churches in the environs.

▪ **TAVARNELLE VAL DI PESA.** A centuries-old center of transit and commerce with Val d'Elsa, it has a lovely Museum of Sacred Art in the nearby church of S. Pietro in Bossolo. Chianti is made here and used, among other things, to steep a variety of local peach (*pesca cotogna del Poggio*).

▪ **BARBERINO VAL D'ELSA.** High on a hill, the town has preserved its ancient traits:

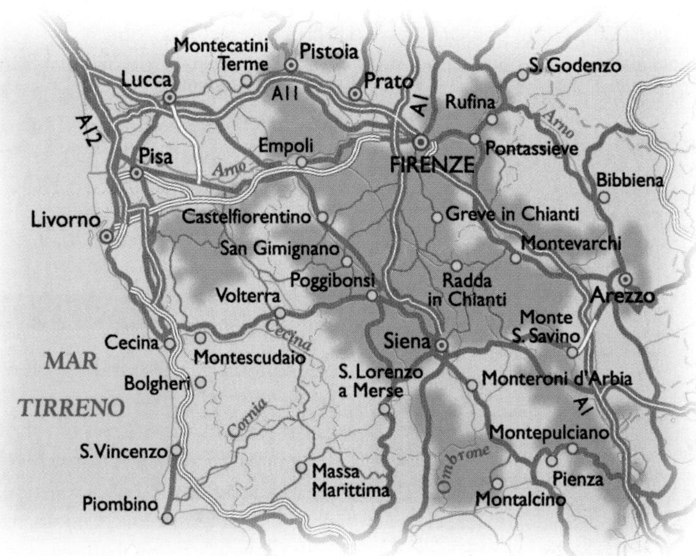

the elliptic walls, the street running from gate to gate, Palazzo Pretorio with the coats of arms of its regents in the central square. The church of S. Bartolomeo contains the fragments of a fresco from the 13th-14th centuries. Various wineries of interest are found here.

■ **GREVE IN CHIANTI.** An ancient market town on the Chiantigiana road, it features a lovely triangular square in its center, with terraced porticos that converge like a funnel towards the neoclassical church of Santa Croce, with a monument to Amerigo Vespucci.
Here, glass in hand, you can visit a host of wineries in and outside town, such as in the village of Panzano, which also boasts an important hand-embroidery tradition.

THE SIENA AND AREZZO REGIONS

Vineyards and famous wine estates dot a landscape where reality surpasses imagination.

Siena is the most prolific province in Tuscany as far as wine-growing is concerned: five out of six regional DOCG wines are produced here, as well as 12 DOCs, highlighting a consolidation of reds and a noteworthy development of whites. Siena's wine geography is clearly outlined by its main products' areas of influence: the Chianti Classico DOCG, covering the southernmost portion of the most traditional zone (shared with Florence), and Chianti DOCG, with its Colli Senesi sub-zone; the Brunello di Montalcino DOCG, in the district of the homonymous municipality, bordering on Grosseto; the Vernaccia di San Gimignano DOCG, in the northwestern part; the Vino Nobile di Montepulciano DOCG, in Valdichiana (with a production offshoot in the Arezzo area), which also has a specific Chianti sub-zone. Alongside these superb productions are the complementary DOC zones (Colli dell'Etruria Centrale, Moscadello di Montalcino, Rosso di Montalcino, Rosso di Montepulciano, San Gimignano, Sant'Antonio, Val d'Arbia) created to offer ready-to-drink wines made from the same mixed-grape blends as the lengthy-ageing ones, to provide an outlet for white grapes where reds prevail (and vice-versa), or to offer special products such as the celebrated Vin Santo (Vin Santo del Chianti, Vin Santo del Chianti Classico, Vin Santo di Montepulciano). Completing this picture of southeastern Tuscany is the province of Arezzo, with its specific production, Chianti Colli Aretini, and its two DOC zones, Valdichiana and Cortona.

Racks of bottles in Siena's Enoteca Italiana

The Colli Senesi

The landscape surrounding Siena is the loveliest imaginable for wine tourists: medieval towns and wineries of renown line the route, which starts running through the Chianti Classico DOCG zone, in the territories of Castellina, Gaiole, and Radda in Chianti's municipalities, and in part

of Castelnuovo Berardenga and Poggibonsi's. The itinerary then sheers off into the Chianti DOCG territory, more precisely into the Colli Senesi sub-zone. Complementary to the cited DOCGs are the Colli dell'Etruria Centrale, Vin Santo del Chianti Classico, and Vin Santo del Chianti DOCs.
The recently instituted Arbia DOC, instead, pays tribute to what was once called "White Chianti", made from Trebbiano Toscano and Malvasia del Chianti grapes – traditionally found in the huge Sangiovese areas – with modern additions of Chardonnay as an ennobling element. The same grapes are also used for a Vin Santo. This wines are produced in a wide area embracing Siena from north to south, covering the zones of Chianti Classico and Chianti Colli Senesi.

FROM THE CHIANTI HILLS TO THE CRETE SENESI

This route forms a sort of double loop centered on the provincial capital and based on Via Cassia: to the north are the Sienese centers of Chianti Classico, to the south the wine towns that form part of the incomparable landscape of the Crete.

■ **SIENA**. It is impossible to try to sum up Siena: you have to see it. Some years ago the Prince of Wales called it the "ideal city". And it certainly is for wine tourists, whose primary reference is the Enoteca Italiana, housed in the bastions of the Medici Fortress. Actually, wine is not only presented and promoted in Siena but it is also produced within its municipal borders. For the rest, you cannot help but immerse yourself in the unique urban atmos-

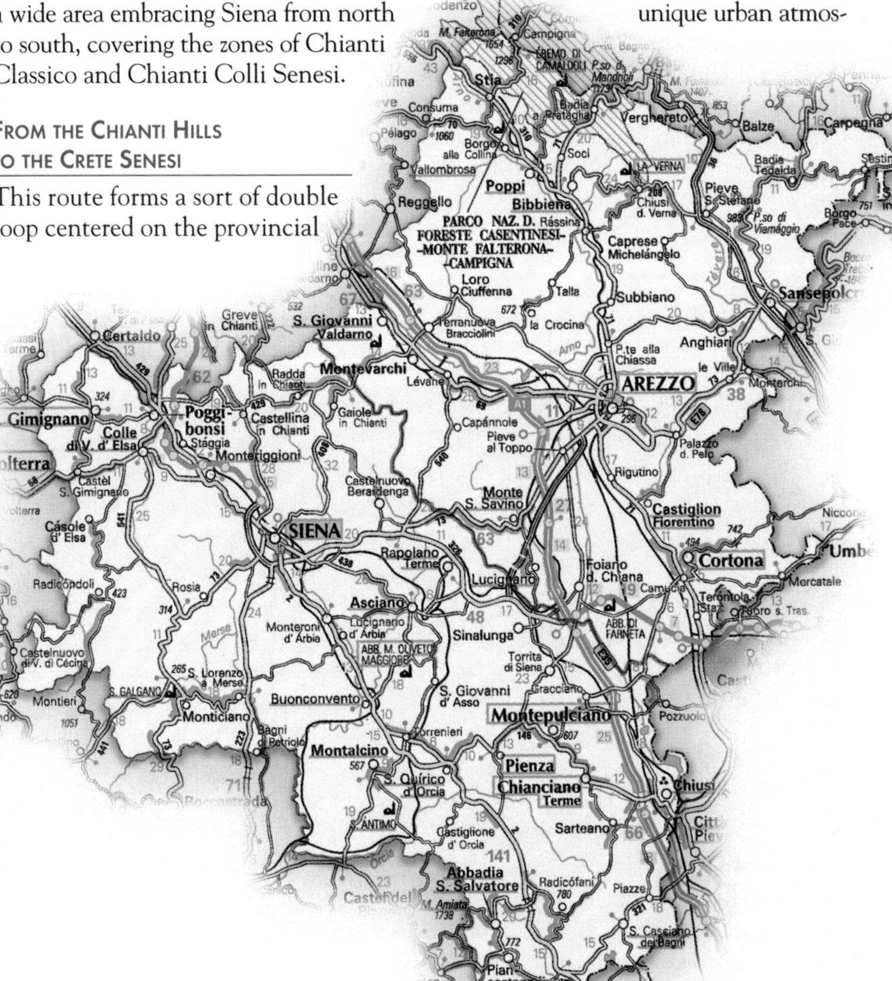

phere crystallized in a handful of decades (from the late 13th to mid-14th centuries) into a still-intact portrait of the Middle Ages. Piazza del Campo with its Palazzo Pubblico and Torre del Mangia, the Civic Museum with its masterpieces by Simone Martini and Ambrogio Lorenzetti, the splendid Duomo with the Piccolomini Library frescoed by Pinturicchio, the formidable array of Sienese School paintings at the Pinacoteca Nazionale – all are musts to visit.

■ **CHIANTI CLASSICO.** Heading north from Siena you enter the Chianti Classico area, with its enchanting landscape of woods, farmlands, olive groves, sloping vineyards, and rows of cypresses leading to estates and villas. The towns encountered – Castelnuovo Berardenga, Castellina in Chianti, Poggibonsi, Gaiole in Chianti, Radda in Chianti (cited in order of their distance from Siena) – has already been mentioned in the preceding itinerary. Here we merely add that, along Via Cassia, you also come across the "circular parapets" of Monteriggioni, a medieval town that has remained intact since Dante's time.

■ **RAPOLANO TERME.** This is the first stop on the route southwards of Siena, across and around the fascinating landscape of the Crete. This place is renowned for its sulfur springs and travertine extraction and working.

■ **CHIUSI.** A town perched on a tufa knoll amidst olive groves on the edge of the Valdichiana. Relics of the time in which it was the Etruscan *Chamars* can be seen in the National Archeological and the Cathedral Museums. Its historical center is Roman in layout, based on the previous Etruscan one, with various fine buildings from the medieval and Grand Duchy periods.

■ **CETONA.** A remote settlement on the slopes of Mount Cetona, it has retained the appearance of an ancient village with medieval charm. The Archeological-Nature Park of Belvedere-Biancheto pleases both lovers of pre-historical ruins and of beautiful scenery.

■ **SAN CASCIANO DEI BAGNI.** To the south, almost on the border with Lazio and in a gently rolling landscape lies this ancient

A farmstead surrounded by vineyards at Colle di Val d'Elsa

ENOTECA ITALIANA - SIENA

The Enoteca Italiana of Siena is a unique of its kind public institution founded in 1950. Its main purpose is to present to the public the finest Italian wines, selected by a special in-house tasting committee. The Enoteca is located in the very heart of Siena, in the lovely setting of the 16th-century Medici Fortress bastions, whose spacious, brick-vaulted rooms are simply equipped for wine exhibiting and tasting led by professional sommeliers. Each wine is presented in the most appropriate way, with mentions to how and at what temperature it is to be served, and is accompanied by ample information on its characteristics. There are over a thousand wines collected here, as well as fine grappas, liqueurs, and other typical products, such as, in particular, extra-virgin olive oils. This allows more than 400 producers, mainly small to medium-sized, to get in touch with a wider public.
Particularly attractive are the terraces, which in the summer months host cultural events, including the traditional Wine Week in early June.

village with a centuries-old fame for its mineral-water springs.

▪ **MURLO**. An isolated village in Val d'Arbia, crowned with houses bordering its walls and overlooked by Palazzo Vescovile. The Archeological Museum conserves important finds from the Etruscan complex of Poggio Civitate.

Montalcino

The small Montalcino area can be considered the inner sanctum of Tuscan oenology. In addition to prized Brunello, three DOC wines are produced here. The first is Rosso di Montalcino, created to give the market an annual wine with the same aromas as Brunello and to provide an outlet for the grapes not destined for superior production. The second is Moscadello di Montalcino, a long-famous wine made from Moscato Bianco grapes in the Tranquillo, Frizzante, and Vendemmia Tardiva varieties. Eclipsed by the extraordinary success of Brunello, it has lately been successfully launched anew. Finally, Sant'Antimo DOC, whose name refers to the famous abbey on Via Francigena, just a few miles from Montalcino. Protagonists, both in mixed-grape blends and with specific labels, are Chardonnay, Pinot Grigio, and Sauvignon; Cabernet Sauvignon, Merlot, and Pinot Nero.

▪ **MONTALCINO**. The fortress of Montalcino rises 1850 feet above the Orcia valley and tells of bellicose medieval events, when the ancient village became the last stronghold of Siena's defense against Florentine advance. A (religious) story apart is the abbey of S. Antimo's (founded in the 9th century), a splendid example of Romanesque architecture built along Via Francigena to assist pilgrims on their way to Rome. Still other stories are those of the local vine-growers, who have become famous worldwide thanks to Brunello wine. There are so many wineries that there is no need for a wine route: you simply wander from one place to the other: Altesino, Poggio alle Mure, Barbi, Castel Giocondo, Camigliano, Sant'Antimo.

Marvelous Vernaccia

Wine tourists come to the charming old town of San Gimignano seeking the most famous of the Vernaccias, for centuries a favorite of popes and princes and the first in Italy to be given DOC, and then DOCG, recognition – it is the only Tuscan white wine having been granted the highest quality seal. This absolute excellence production, which is part of a wider area (Chianti Colli Senesi DOCG, Chianti DOCG, Colli dell'Etruria Centrale DOC), is completed by another local denomination, San Gimignano DOC. In the realm of Vernaccia there is also room

The ancient borgo *of San Gimignano, with its medieval tower dwellings*

for other types of wine: a red based on Sangiovese, also in a Novello (new wine) version, plus a rosé and a Vin Santo Occhio di Pernice; among the whites, Vin Santo from Malvasia del Chianti, Trebbiano Toscano, and Vernaccia di San Gimignano.

The Vernaccia di San Gimignano Route

The Vernaccia route covers a good part of the municipal territory of San Gimignano, with four itineraries that spoke off from the picturesque medieval town and 75 participating producers.

• To the north, the route forms a loop that climbs almost to Certaldo;

• to the east, towards Poggibonsi, it divides into two branches, one leading to Cusona and Ulignano and the other to Villa Pietrafitta;

• to the south, a main road leads to Castel San Gimignano and Castelvecchio, while two sub-itineraries branch off from San Gimignano to Santa Lucia and Montauto;

• to the west, an arc path reaches Cellole's church, Lamiano, and Libbiano, with a detour to Pancole and Villa del Monte.

▪ **San Gimignano.** A flourishing center on Via Francigena as a resting-place for pilgrims en route to Rome and a marketplace for the surrounding countryside, San Gimignano has been favored by history in outstandingly conserving its medieval appearance. Around the two central squares – Piazza della Cisterna and Piazza del Duomo – crowd the towers (15 of the original 72), which were built as a symbol of the wealth of local notables and have since become the distinctive peculiarity of this very special place even in the rich panorama of Tuscan medieval towns.

However, San Gimignano means not only towers, art treasures, and museums: it also means, obviously, Vernaccia wine, on offer at many excellent wineries, and saffron. This praised golden powder, gotten from the crocus, was already exported in ancient times; a revival of interest has spurred production.

Montepulciano and the Colli Aretini

Vino Nobile di Montepulciano DOCG comes from the hills surrounding the homonymous town in the center of the

Siena province, straddling Val d'Orcia and Valdichiana. From this hub, where excellence is attained, production extends into the province of Arezzo. In addition to Chianti DOCG, also coming in the Colli Senesi and Colli Aretini sub-denominations (each with their Vin Santo), the following are worth mentioning: Rosso di Montepulciano DOC (a complement to the prestigious Vino Nobile production, making it possible to market a similar but ready-to-drink wine), and the Orcia, Valdichiana, and Cortona DOCs.

THE VINO NOBILE DI MONTEPULCIANO ROUTE

This itinerary concerns the territory of Montepulciano – in particular the low rises bordering the Chiana river – and is divided in two: the first part is devoted mainly to the town's visit, with history and art highlights, and the second (along three sub-itineraries) to scenic and oenological attractions in the town's environs.

• The first of these three circuits leaves town from Porta al Prato and leads to Madonna delle Grazie, Gracciano, and Abbadia; after passing under the railway twice, it goes back via Montepulciano Stazione and Nottola;

• the second forms a loop, which, running by the town's eastern walls, leads to Madonna delle Querce, Cervognano, and Acquaviva, passes over the highway twice and returns via Argiano, Villa la Cappella, and Sant'Albino;

• the third loop is on the town's opposite side and takes in the immediate environs of the Valiano country ward.

▪ **MONTEPULCIANO.** Built on the crest of a hill, this lovely town is full of noble buildings and winding lanes; on one side flows the Orcia river, on the other the Chiana, whose landscapes change with the light. The architectural imprint of this ancient-times atmosphere town is Renaissance, with mansions and churches lining the way from Porta al Prato to Piazza Grande. From the Town Hall tower you can see the great cupola of S. Biagio's church, a masterpiece by Sangallo, located on the town edge. The wine reference point is the Enoteca del Consorzio del Vino Nobile di Montepulciano, housed in the restored rooms of Palazzo del Capitano; among the events held there is the end-of-August Bravio delle Botti, in which the eight *contrade* vie with one another at rolling huge barrels through the town streets.

THE TERRE DI AREZZO WINE ROUTE

Starting from the provincial capital, the route forms a wide loop to include the major wine and tourism attractions between Valdarno and Valdichiana.

View of Montepulciano

Wineries *pp. 417-441*
Arezzo, Bucine, Castiglione d'Orcia, Cetona, Chianciano Terme, Chiusi, Colle Val d'Elsa, Cortona, Foiano della Chiana, Montalcino, Montepulciano, Monteriggioni, Monte San Savino, Montevarchi, Murlo, Rapolano Terme, San Casciano dei Bagni, San Gimignano, Sarteano, Siena, Sinalunga, Sovicille, Terranuova Bracciolini, Torrita di Siena.

▪ **AREZZO**. The town is admirable for its medieval buildings but also for its Etruscan and Roman remains; an extraordinary art legacy can be found in its churches and museums. Outstanding is the fresco cycle painted between 1453 and 1466 by Piero della Francesca in the church of S. Francesco; titled the *Legend of the Cross*, it is among the masterpieces of European art. The church of S. Maria is one of the most noteworthy examples of Romanesque architecture in Tuscany.

▪ **CASTIGLION FIORENTINO**. A scenic town, whose medieval structure has been well preserved; through the 15th-century arches of the loggia (said to be by Vasari) the main square looks out over the Valdichiana.

▪ **CORTONA**. This sandstone-colored town slopes down a steep buttress on the edges of the Valdichiana, filling only a part of the ancient Etruscan walls. Traces of its origins are preserved in the Museo dell'Accademia; the mansions and houses defining its current appearance are from the Middle Ages. Not far away, amidst cypresses and olive trees, lies the sanctuary of the Madonna del Calcinaio, a Renaissance jewel by Francesco di Giorgio Martini.

▪ **SAN GIOVANNI VALDARNO.** Passing through Lucignano and Monte San Savino – medieval hill towns overlooking the Valdichiana and the Esse valley respectively – and the ancient, scenic village of Civitella in Val di Chiana, you come to San Giovanni Valdarno.
Now an industrial center, long ago it was the birthplace of Masaccio. Lining the square bearing the name of this "favorite son" are the noblest buildings: the basilica of S. Maria delle Grazie, the church of S. Lorenzo, the so-called Palazzaccio.

The interior of a Tuscan cellar

The Colli Fiorentini and the Montalbano Region

Just outside the City of the Lily, Medici villas and first-rate wines are to be found.

Chianti is the main wine production in the Florence area, which includes the province of Prato. In order of importance, the first zone to be listed is the Florentine part of the Chianti Classico DOCG, south of the city, comprising the entire municipal territory of Greve in Chianti and portions of Barberino Val d'Elsa, San Casciano, and Tavarnelle Val di Pesa's. Production then widens out into the Chianti DOCG's local sub-zones: Colli Fiorentini, Chianti Rufina (on the doorstep of Mugello), Chianti Montespertoli (around the homonymous town southwest of Florence), and Chianti Montalbano (around Prato).

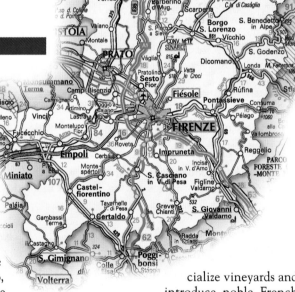

From Chianti to Pomino

In the province of Florence lie the northern portion of Chianti Classico (see the preceding pages) and three sub-zones with geographical denominations: Chianti Colli Fiorentini, Chianti Rufina, and Chianti Montespertoli. The real oenological pearl of the Florentine area is Pomino, produced in one of the smallest DOC zones in Tuscany, on the high hills of Val di Sieve. Production is limited to the homonymous country ward in the Rufina municipality, where approximately 225 acres of vineyards produce about 132,000 US gallons of wine. Despite small output, this is a very fine wine-producing zone, considered one of Tuscany's best since the early 18th century. Merit goes to the land, but also to the vine-growers, among the first to specialize vineyards and introduce noble French vines. Today's production is made up of whites (from Pinot Bianco, Chardonnay, Trebbiano Toscano), reds (from Sangiovese, Canaiolo, Cabernet Sauvignon, Cabernet Franc, Merlot) and white and red Vin Santo: limited quantity but excellent quality.

▪ **Florence.** In a marvelous position straddling the Arno river and surrounded by hills, this is a magical, beautiful city, par-

FINE WINES IN FLORENCE

Among the many wine and food attractions that Florence has on offer, you should include the shops of the *vinai*, the former taverns where market laborers and merchants from the city center gathered to pass the time over a glass of "the good stuff". The new-generation wine-sellers have kept the old premises but updated the offer, broadening the range of both wines and snacks. Served with famous and less famous (but always interesting) labels are well-selected cheeses and cold meats, plus *crostini* and typical fare like *ribollita*. Among the many *vinai* we can cite two that are direct outlets of excellent wineries: the Cantinetta dei Verrazzano (Via de' Tavolini 18) and the Cantinetta Antinori (Piazza degli Antinori 3). On a whole other level for menu and prices are two world-famous restaurants offering exceptional wines: Cibreo and Enoteca Pinchiorri.

adigm of the Italian Renaissance and the Tuscan art of construction. Rather than list the churches, palaces, and museums that make up a formidable concentration of art, we prefer to mention two celebrated belvederes, commanding views of the city from the south and the north respectively: Piazzale Michelangelo, on the far side of the Arno, and Fiesole (cited further on), just a few miles to the north.

THE CHIANTI RUFINA AND POMINO WINE ROUTE

This is a well-trodden route, divided into four itineraries, with 15 wineries and various farm holiday venues along the way. Proximity to Florence makes it possible to organize day trips taking in churches, castles, and wines (Consorizio del Chianti Rufina, Viale Duca della Vittoria 7, Rufina, www.chiantirufina.com).

▪ **PONTASSIEVE.** The Upper Valdarno road leads to this town with lovely wineries, an animated place of transit where the Arno and Sieve rivers meet; the rural landscape is charming, dotted with farms and stately dwellings. Beyond the Arno is the historical abbey of S. Maria in Rosano.

▪ **RUFINA.** Further upstream in Val di Sieve, this is the farming center on the doorstep of the Apennines that lends its name to the Chianti sub-zone. Standing out in a landscape of hills covered with

The charming square of the town of Greve in Chianti, on the way from Florence to Siena

The Wine Route at Montespertoli

vineyards and olive groves is the Renaissance Villa di Poggio Reale, with a Vine and Wine Museum and an enoteca.

▪ **PELAGO**. On the way back the tour reaches as far as Pomino, with its ancient church of S. Bartolomeo, and Pelago, where you can visit the picturesque Nipozzano Castle, the 14th-century manor house of an enormous estate.

THE CHIANTI COLLI FIORENTINI WINE ROUTE

This is an extensive itinerary whose four routes encompass the suburbs of Florence and the southeastern section of the province (Consorzio Vini Chianti, Viale Belfiore 9, Florence, www.chianti-colli-fiorentini.it).

• Westward, a double-theme tour (wine and handicrafts, especially pottery) touches Scandicci, Lastra a Signa, Montelupo Fiorentino, and Malmantile;

• to the southwest, a panoràmic route takes in Cerbaia, Montagnana, San Quirico in Collina, Romita, and, from there, Tavernelle Val di Pesa and Barberino Val d'Elsa (Florentine centers of Chianti Classico – see the preceding pages), Marcialla, Montespertoli (see further on), and Baccaiano;

• to the south and southeast, the route enters the gentle Florentine hills, making a sort of double loop: from Oltrarno it rises to Impruneta via Galluzzo and Tavernuzze and descends through San Gersolè and Grassina to Bagno a Ripoli. Here it heads to the Arno passing by San Donato in Collina, Bombone, Petriolo, and Rosano, it crosses the river before reaching Sieci, it climbs to Vetta le Croci and goes back to Florence via Fiesole;

• still further east, linking up with and extending the previous route, the fourth itinerary goes from Rignano sull'Arno through San Ellero to Reggello, Figline Valdarno, and (along the river) Incisa in Val d'Arno.

▪ **LASTRA A SIGNA**. An ancient outpost of Florence, this town still has its 1377 layout and walls. The Ospedale di Sant'Antonio features a lovely 15th-century loggia.

▪ **MONTELUPO FIORENTINO**. Founded as a marketplace where the Pesa and Arno rivers meet, it has become a flourishing center of ceramics production since the Middle Ages, as still attested to by many inviting pottery shops and an Archaeology and Ceramics Museum.

Vinci's castle

■ **IMPRUNETA.** It was built up around the sanctuary of the Madonna dell'Impruneta, consecrated in 1060 and renovated several times through the 17th century. In mid-October the main square hosts the agricultural fair of S. Lucia, whose origins are remote, and in September a grape festival with a parade of carts.

■ **SIECI.** On the banks of the Arno, you can visit the church of S. Giovanni in Remole (12th C.) with a soaring bell tower and ancient paintings.

■ **FIESOLE.** It was founded earlier than Florence, which it became part of later (1125). Luscious countryside, Etruscan and Roman ruins (in the archeological area), and sacred art (see Mino da Fiesole's sculptures in the Cathedral and nearby Badia Fiesolana) make a unique blend.

■ **REGGELLO.** Here you are on the slopes of Pratomagno, famed for Chianti wine as well as for olive oil. The church of S. Pietro a Cascia (1073) holds the first known work by Masaccio, the *Triptych of S. Giovenale*, a fascinating example of Italian painting.

■ **FIGLINE VALDARNO.** In the lovely scenery of the Arno valley, which widens up here, this town of stormy history (it was destroyed by the Florentines and sacked by the Pisans) has an interesting historical center with many ancient buildings.

THE MONTESPERTOLI WINE ROUTE

In recognition of Montespertoli as a subzone of the Chianti DOCG, a wine route was instituted that has many participants among wineries, restaurants, and enoteche (Town Hall of Montespertoli, Piazza del Popolo 1).
The town is the departure point for the Via di Castiglioni, an itinerary of about 2 miles through a farmed landscape, for a series of alternative routes within municipal boundaries, and for trek paths in the surrounding region. The background to all of them is the enchanting Chianti landscape, full of vineyards, olive groves, woodlands, cypresses, and Middle Ages remains scattered through the countryside and in villages.

■ **MONTESPERTOLI.** High on a knoll, 19 miles southwest of Florence, stands this little town that also expresses its agricultural vocation in a host of wine and food events: late May marks the lively Chianti

CHIANTI CLASSICO AND KOSHER WINE AT VILLA BRANCA

In San Casciano Val di Pesa you find Villa Branca (375 acres, 125 of which planted with vines and 40 with olive trees), dominated by a charming 14th-century turreted building that serves as offices and a scenic farm holidays venue. Wine production concentrates on Chianti Classico DOCG (also Riserva), with a mixed-grape blend enriched by the addition of Cabernet Sauvignon. Also first-class is the extra-virgin olive oil, stored in an ancient, underground oil-jar cellar. Of special oenological interest is the estate's production of kosher wine, strictly according to the dictates of the Jewish tradition.

Exhibit, November the New Wine festival, and in December there is Paneolio, devoted to two other great local products, bread and olive oil. Between a winery and the next, do not miss the Sacred Art Museum at the lovely parish church of S. Pietro in Mercato.

Montalbano

Montalbano is a group of high hills that follows for a stretch the right-hand side of the Arno, downstream from Florence. Its slopes, especially suited to viticulture, give the newly created province of Prato a special reason for wine pride: prized Carmignano DOCG. Behind the success of this wine was the use (very seldom tried in Tuscany before) of Cabernet matched with the traditional Chianti blend of Sangiovese and Canaiolo.
Complementing this DOCG is the Barco Reale di Carmignano DOC, which includes a red (Barco Reale) and a rosé wine in a mixed-grape blend similar to that of top production, plus a Vin Santo and a Vin Santo Occhio di Pernice. Finally, we find Bianco dell'Empolese DOC, which keeps alive the tradition of the Trebbianos, so popular in Florence in the past.

THE MEDICI CARMIGNANO WINE ROUTE

This tour develops in the Carmignano territory and in part of Poggio al Caiano's; it is divided into three mini-excursions in an intersecting loop summarizing the area's oenological, scenic, and historical features. Participating in it are 22 wineries, 12 restaurants, 3 hotels, and 2 enoteche. The tourism office distributes a detailed leaflet on the route (Town Hall of Carmignano, Piazza Vittorio Emanuele II, 2). Following is also a suggested extension into the Empoli area, touching two Città del Vino (Wine Towns), Vinci and Cerreto Guidi, reached from Carmignano along the scenic Santa Cristina a Mezzana road.

CARMIGNANO. Local wine is an irresistible draw for the wine tourist. The route leads to wineries and ancient dwellings, including the superlative Medici Villa Artimino, designed by Bernardo Buontalenti in 1594 for Ferdinando I as a site "for hunting and grape harvesting", and the Tenuta di Capezzana in Seano, another huge Medici villa on a terrace overlooking the Arno, with annexed rural village. At Artimino you can also visit the Romanesque 12th-century church of S. Leonardo.

- **POGGIO A CAIANO.** This offers a chance to visit another celebrated Medici villa that opens on to the landscape with a portico-and-loggia and was frescoed to the glory of the reigning house by Pontorno and Andrea del Sarto.

- **VINCI.** On the southern slopes of Montalbano rises the castle once belonging to the Guidi counts. The Vinci Museum celebrates the genius of Leonardo da Vinci, child of the place; a pleasant foot path leads to Anchiano, where the artist was actually born.

- **CERRETO GUIDI.** High on a buttress, preceded by the scenic ramps designed by Buontalenti, is the famous Medici villa built in this lovely landscape for Grand Duke Cosimo I.

Wineries *pp. 417-441*
Bagno a Ripoli, Calenzano, Capraia e Limite, Carmignano, Castelfiorentino, Cerreto Guidi, Dicomano, Florence, Fucecchio, Gambassi Terme, Impruneta, Lastra a Signa, Montaione, Montelupo Fiorentino, Montemurlo, Montespertoli, Pelago, Poggio a Caiano, Pontassieve, San Casciano in Val di Pesa, Scandicci, Signa, Vaglia, Vinci.

The Northern Hills

In the Apennine foothills, from Pistoia to Massa, grapes grow whiter in a prelude to the vocation of Ligurian viticulture.

Tuscany's northernmost wine district, which covers the pre-Apennine hills in the provinces of Pistoia, Lucca, and Massa-Carrara, features a gradually increasing presence of white-grape vines of Ligurian ancestry. The reference is first and foremost to Vermentino, whose cultivation is first seen in the Pistoia area and becomes dominant, along with Albarola's, near the regional border.
For the rest, the grape panorama in the district follows the typically Tuscan standards, with traditional varieties growing alongside the imports from France – Cabernet Franc, Cabernet Sauvignon, and Merlot, which are giving truly impressive results.

From Chianti to Valdinievole

The Chianti production area in the Pistoia province has offshoots in the Montalbano hills, forming a specific sub-zone, and in the hills that embrace the provincial capital. Getting closer to the boundary with the province of Lucca, the vineyard changes in character, offering new opportunities. The Bianco della Valdinievole DOC covers a zone in which vine-growing is limited (about 175 acres) but gives excellent results. The local vignerons, with their centuries-old traditions, deserve praise for adding to the usual Trebbiano Toscano grapes both Malvasia and Canaiolo Bianco, and, more recently, Vermentino. DOC codes include the production of Vin Santo – dry, semi-sweet, and sweet – traditionally aged for three years in small casks.

To the Montalbano Wineries

This brief tour starting in Pistoia goes from the west side of Montalbano to the opposite side, facing Valdinievole.

Vine-lands in the Pistoia region

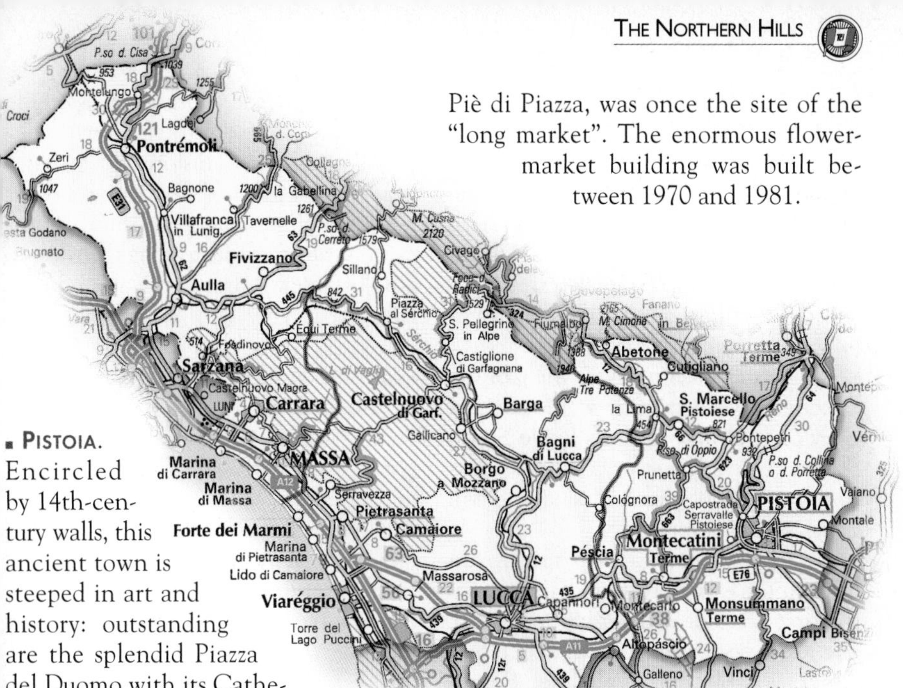

Piè di Piazza, was once the site of the "long market". The enormous flower-market building was built between 1970 and 1981.

▪ **PISTOIA.** Encircled by 14th-century walls, this ancient town is steeped in art and history: outstanding are the splendid Piazza del Duomo with its Cathedral, Baptistery, and Town Hall; the pulpit (1298-1301) by Giovanni Pisano in the church of S. Andrea; and another Pisan Romanesque church, S. Giovanni Fuorcivitas. On medieval buildings the green and white of the marble façades blends in harmoniously with the landscape.

▪ **MONTECATINI TERME.** At the center of this elegant spa resort are the gardens and hot-springs of Parco delle Terme, where an early 20th-century atmosphere still reigns. A scenic route leads to the picturesque town of Montecatini Alto.

▪ **MONSUMMANO TERME.** The spa resort lies on the plain, with the sanctuary of S. Maria di Fontenuova, while the medieval old village (Monsummano Alto) stands high on the rocky buttress, with a handful of ancient houses and a Romanesque church.

▪ **PESCIA.** An industrious town with a medieval layout: once a papermaking center, now a hub of the flower industry. Piazza Mazzini, flanked by the Palazzo dei Vicari and the oratory of the Madonna di

The Lucca Region and Montecarlo

The real star of the Lucca region viticulture is Montecarlo, a town renowned through the centuries for its Trebbiano wines, popular with pontiffs and royalty. The Montecarlo DOC covers the homonymous municipality together with Altopascio, Capannori, and Porcari. About 500 acres are planted with vines. The child of pebbly and gravelly soil, this white wine based on Trebbiano Toscano was made finer as early as the 19th century with the introduction of French improver varieties (Pinto Bianco, Roussanne, Sémillon, and Sauvignon). Recently, the Montecarlo DOC was allowed to include a red based on traditional Sangiovese, Canaiolo Nero, and other grapes, combined with Cabernet, Merlot, and Syrah. Lastly, there is the Colline Lucchesi DOC that includes: a red and a white wine obtained by traditional mixed-grape blends; specific labels for Merlot, Sangiovese, Sauvignon, and Vermentino; a Vin Santo and a Vin Santo Occhio di Pernice.

THE MONTECARLO AND COLLINE LUCCHESI WINE ROUTE

The route follows the Apennine foothills behind Lucca and is split in two by the national Abetone road that runs along the Serchio river valley bottom. The 35 participating wineries are described in a leaflet distributed by tourism offices (www.luccanet.it/stradadelvino).

• The western route covers the Colline Lucchesi DOC: starting at Monte San Quirico it climbs towards Pieve Santo Stefano and Castagnori, and then turns east towards Mutigliano, Arsina, and San Quirico di Moriano;

• across the Serchio, two routes run through the eastern section of the region: the first is an ideal continuation of the one just described and goes through San Pancrazio, Matraia, Valgiano, Segromigno in Monte, and Camigliano (still in the Colline Lucchesi zone); the second concerns the Montecarlo DOC zone and follows the Pesciatina road (national road no. 435) in the environs of the homonymous town.

▪ **LUCCA**. Girded by red walls, the city conserves the appearance of an ancient commune town and offers rare beauties; beginning with the Duomo (with the heart-touching tomb of Ilaria del Carretto) and the church of S. Michele in Foro, it is filled to the brim with medieval churches, mansions, houses, and towers, with picturesque spots and vistas – Piazza del Mercato, the Giunigi houses, and the promenade along the walls to cite just a few – that are an absolute delight.

▪ **MONTECARLO**. South of Pescia, on a hill overlooking Valdinievole, is this enchanting town hugging the 14th-century fortress of Cerruglio. The former name of the place was Viviana, from “Via Vinaria” (wine road), testifying to its ancient wine trade. Quite small, it features lovely buildings, a church with a 14th-century façade, the chapel of a former monastery, and a theater. The tidy countryside is dotted with farms and wineries.

▪ **ALTOPASCIO**. It is reached by passing through Capannori, a town of archeological interest (in the area of what was once Lake Sesto) and with noteworthy wineries. On the southern edges of the Montecarlo DOC zone, along the path of the old Via Francigena, Altopascio has an important historical center built around Piazza degli Ospitalieri: buildings (and remains of buildings) are

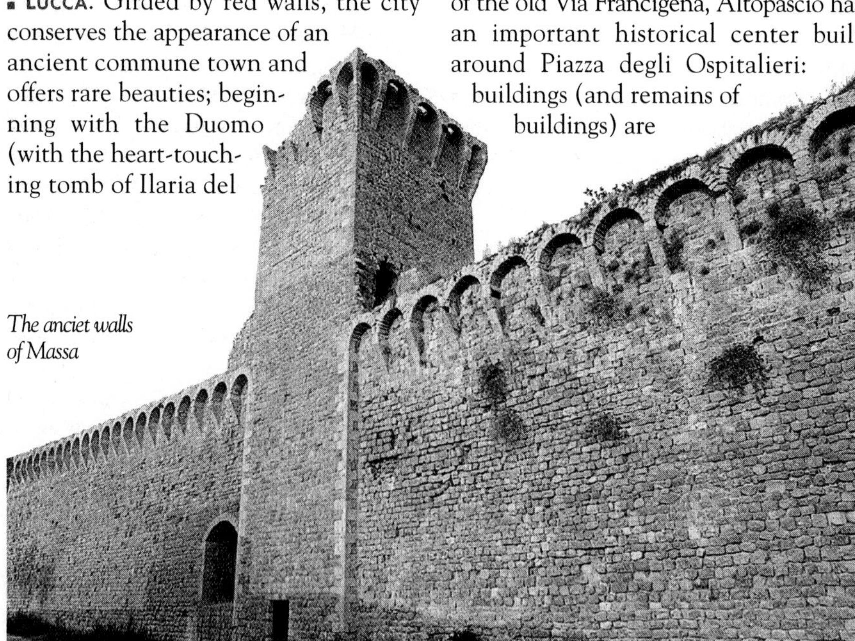

The anciet walls of Massa

reminders of the knightly order which had headquarters in them, running a hospice for pilgrims and a charity hospital.

The Colli Apuani and the Colli di Luni

On the northern limit to the Tuscan vine-lands you find the Candia dei Colli Apuani and the Colli di Luni DOCs, which give a foretaste of Liguria viticulture. Vineyards occupy steep slopes running towards the sea. This is laborious vine-growing, with low yield and high production costs, whose most famous product is to be found in nearby Cinque Terre, across the Liguria border.
Historically, the Candia dei Colli Apuani DOC is characterized by the production of a white wine, primarily from Vermentino grapes, mixed with Ligurian Albarola and possibly Trebbiano Toscano and Malvasia del Chianti. DOC codes provide for dry, semi-sweet or lightly sweet, and Vin Santo wines.
A denomination tipped even more towards Liguria is the Colli di Luni DOC: in fact, only 17.5 acres of vineyards are in Tuscany, yielding a white wine (from Vermentino and Trebbiano Toscano), a red wine (from Sangiovese, Canaiolo, Pollera, and Ciliegiolo), and a specific Vermentino label.

The Candia and Lunigiana Hills

This itinerary goes from Massa to Aulla following the recently instituted Colli di Candia e di Lunigiana wine route in the Magra valley up to Pontremoli.

▪ **MASSA.** The city's Medieval center is sheltered by the hill on which the scenic fortress of the Malaspinas stands; the 16th-century town, on the other hand, surrounds adjacent Piazza degli Aranci.

A wine estate plus farm holiday venue in Tuscany

Wineries *pp. 417-441*
Capannori, Carrara, Lucca, Massa, Montecarlo, Montignoso, Porcari, Pietrasanta.

▪ **CARRARA.** Encircled by olive groves and framed by the white-faced Apuan Alps, for two thousand years this has been the city of marble, and the best proof of that is its Romanesque Cathedral. A must is the climb to Colonnata, obviously to see the marble quarries but also to buy its famous lard, flavored by ageing in marble.

▪ **FOSDINOVO.** Crossing the Apuan Park on a winding, up-and-down road, you reach this town of ancient accents: from the castle you look out over the Colli di Luni DOC vineyards towards the sea that bathes La Spezia.

▪ **AULLA.** Lying at the crossroads of the Apennine-pass roads – Cisa, Lagastrello, and Cerreto – this is the gateway to the Lunigiana region, guarded by the Brunella fortress. The route ends on the other side of the Magra river, in Podenzana, the last Tuscan municipal district in the Colli di Luni DOC.

THE ETRUSCAN COAST

The Tuscan vine-land portion whose history is most linked to Etruscan culture stretches from Pisa to Livorno, with the very special appendix of the Elba Island.

The hills of Pisa and Livorno are the outermost flank of the Apennines in the stretch between the Arno and Cornia rivers. Gentle in slope, inland they border on the central Tuscan hills, while beyond Cecina they meet the Colline Metallifere. Proximity to the sea is quite favorable to viticulture. The prevalent grapes are the usual Sangiovese and Trebbiano, the only special note being the presence of Vermentino. Between the Arno and the Cecina rivers you find Chianti delle Colline Pisane and the local Bianco Pisano di San Torpé; between the Cecina and the Cornia rivers, first Montescudaio's wines and then, in the Livorno province, Bolgheri's ones.
Lastly, an independent vine-growing environment in terms of climate, geological structure, and grape varieties is the Elba Island, which the ancient Aleatico wine testify to.

The Colline Pisane

The Pisa province is composed primarily of the western spurs of Chianti, which here can vaunt the special geographical denomination of Colline Pisane.
Complementary to this DOCG is the Bianco Pisano San Torpé DOC, an appellation for white wines, especially from Trebbiano grapes. The Montescudaio DOC covers a zone close to the border with Livorno, in the Cecina valley, and is considered one of the up-and-coming areas in Tuscany. The hills of Montescudaio, Guardistallo, and the five other municipalities in the zone have a long wine history, almost certainly begun by the Etruscans. The red wine is quite similar to Chianti in its blend, but the seaside climate mellows its punch. A white from Trebbiano, Malvasia, and Vermentino, plus a Vin Santo, are the other types provided for, but the wineries have also been working at innovative wines.

View of San Miniato's Serra

THE COLLINE PISANE WINE ROUTE

This itinerary covers the broad band of hills in the province of Pisa to the left of the Arno, from its border with Florence to its border with Livorno (information can be had from Peccioli's Town Hall). The Route has 24 associates among vine-growers and wine-makers, farm holidays providers and wineries, and is divided into three connected itineraries: from San Miniato to Palaia, La Rotta, and Peccioli; from Laiatico to Terriciola and Lari; and from Cenaia to Crespina, Fauglia, Lorenzana, Casciana Terme, and Chianni.

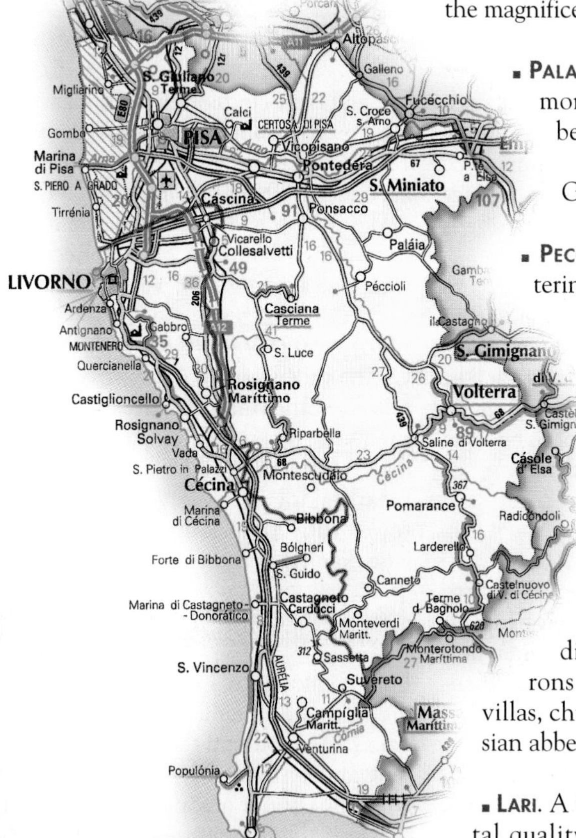

■ **PISA.** Campo dei Miracoli is a heavenly Romanesque scene created by the Duomo, the Baptistery, and the Leaning Tower (not to mention the annexed churchyard); this is the main, but not the only, attraction of this ancient city on the Arno river, rich in Gothic and Renaissance architecture and home to a prestigious university.

■ **SAN MINIATO.** The wine tour starts from this town, famed for its art, olive oil and truffles, overlooking the Arno from three charming knolls. Of the ancient fortress built by Frederick II on the highest point only the tower remains; two scenic squares connected by stairs open around the magnificent 13th-century Cathedral.

■ **PALAIA.** Art enthusiasts will be more then pleased by the beautiful S. Andrea parish church and the isolated Gothic church of S. Martino.

■ **PECCIOLI.** It is reached by entering the Era valley and climbing to the top of a lovely hill planted with vines. The town offers good wineries and Pisan architecture.

■ **TERRICCIOLA.** On the opposite slope of the Era valley, this is a town of Etruscan foundation and with a complex medieval history; in the environs you find lovely hamlets, villas, churches, and a Camaldolensian abbey.

■ **LARI.** A town of high environmental quality, set in a beautiful landscape, it features a huge Medici fortress with a double ring of walls and a church, dedicated to the Assunta, rich in works of art.

View of Castagneto Carducci

▪ **CRESPINA.** This little town is worth a visit to see an important painting by Bernardo Daddi in the church of S. Michele and the elegant 18th-century Belvedere oratory. It is also an important center for vine cloning.

▪ **CASCIANA TERME.** A popular spa resort in the 18th century but much older in origins, Casciana Terme rises on a hill amidst vineyards and olive trees. In panoramic Casciana Alta, the church of S. Niccolò has a Lippo Memmi's polyptych.

A QUICK TOUR OF THE MONTESCUDAIO DOC

Along the road from Casciana Terme to Lorenzana is the junction leading to Santa Luce and Castellina Marittima, municipalities belonging to the Montescudaio DOC zone.

▪ **CASTELLINA MARITTIMA.** High on a cliff, this village conserves traces of castle walls and a medieval fortress. Alabaster quarries are in the environs.

▪ **MONTESCUDAIO.** It stands on a hill from which you can see the Cecina plain, the sea, and the islands of Elba, Capraia, and Gorgona. Dating from before the year 1000 are the remains of a monastery around which the counts della Gherardesca built a village and castle dominating their lands. Good wineries continue the ancient local wine tradition.

▪ **MONTECATINI VAL DI CECINA.** Along the Cecina valley road that leads to Guardistallo (another municipality included in the DOC, together with Casale Marittimo) you find this resort commanding a breathtaking view of Volterra; a high tower with a black-and-white banded base dominates the older, medieval part.

The Livorno Coast

Driving along the Livorno coast, in addition to the aforementioned Montescudaio DOC, you find the small but excellent zone of Bolgheri, which now holds a place of honor among Tuscany's most dynamic wine zones. This is mainly thanks to the sub-zone of Sassicaia, where farsighted bets were placed on Cabernet Sauvignon, which is one of the prestigious reds whose introduction is

generating a positive trend in wine production harmonizing tradition and novelty. The Bolgheri DOC lies in the municipal territory of Castagneto Carducci; vineyards cover about 375 acres. DOC codes regulate: a white wine from Trebbiano, Vermentino, and Sauvignon; specific labels for Vermentino and Sauvignon; a red and a rosé wine made from Cabernet Sauvignon, Merlot, and Sangiovese; a Vin Santo Occhio di Pernice made from Sangiovese and Malvasia Nera; and the specific Sassicaia label, made from minimum 80% Cabernet Sauvignon.
Further south is the Val di Cornia, whose vineyards rise inland from the coast facing the Elba Island. Lying in the Val di Cornia DOC are the municipalities of Campiglia Marittima, Suvereto, San Vincenzo, and Piombino. This area is one of the finest representatives of the new trend in Tuscan viticulture, as its variety of labels demonstrates.

THE ETRUSCAN COAST WINE ROUTE

This itinerary begins in the initial part of the Maremma hinterland and includes a tour of the Elba vineyards. It is illustrated in detail in a leaflet distributed by local tourism offices and includes over 50 wineries, farm holiday providers, restaurants, and crafts shops.

- **CECINA**. The long beach bordered by pine groves is an attractive addition to a town of recent history reached from Livorno along the Aurelia road. From the hinterland come good fresh produce and a fair-sized harvest of truffles.

- **BOLGHERI**. About 6 miles further south, the S. Guido chapel and above all a famous cypress-lined avenue lead to a rustic village (a country ward of Castagneto Carducci) that has gained great fame for its wines.
Merit goes to Sassicaia, a Cabernet Sauvignon character-wine that stands for the new trend in Tuscan viticulture. In the environs is an extraordinary number of high-quality, internationally famous wineries.

- **CASTAGNETO CARDUCCI**. You get here from Bibbona and Bolgheri along the road that follows the first Maremma hills or along Via Aurelia, veering inland at Donoratico. Beyond the arch in the medieval walls you climb to the home of poet Giosuè Carducci (1835-1907), to whose memory is dedicated a Literature

The 16th-century fortifications of Portoferraio (Elba Island)

Park. The della Gherardesca Castle dominates the scene.

■ **SUVERETO.** The winding road climbing to Sassetta and beyond the watershed descends to Suvereto on the other side and into the land of the Val di Cornia DOC. The Town Hall and church of S. Giusto date from the time when the town was entirely walled and guarded by a fortress. Chiana valley beef and boar meat, along with wine – which can be tasted at excellent wineries – are the stars of local cuisine.

■ **CAMPIGLIA MARITTIMA.** Dominated by the ruins of a fortress, this town has a delightfully medieval flair, with its narrow lanes and stone houses, external flight of stairs and little loggias. Across the area, cooled by Tyrrhenian breezes, you can visit ancient Etruscan iron and copper foundries.

■ **SAN VINCENZO.** At this seaside resort, a 16th-century Pisan tower stays side by side with beach umbrellas and bathers crowding the sandy shore. For a taste of the old Maremma, you can visit the Rimigliano Park and the Folk Museum.

■ **PIOMBINO.** Largely modern in appearance, this town is the embarkation port for Elba and has long been a metal-working center – an industry which has been revived since the 20th century. Old buildings survive in the historical center and a broad vista of the sea opens from Piazza Bovio, at the end of the promontory, and from Viale del Popolo. Baratti is the site of the Etruscan ruins of Populonia. The vineyards of the hinterland contribute to Val di Cornia wine production.

Wineries *pp. 417-441*
Bibbona, Campiglia Marittima, Campo nell'Elba, Castagneto Carducci, Castellina Marittima, Cecina, Fauglia, Montecatini Val di Cecina, Montescudaio, Montopoli in Val d'Arno, Palaia, Peccioli, Piombino, Portoferraio, Riparbella, San Miniato, San Vincenzo, Suvereto, Terricciola.

The Elba Island

Vines are traditional to the sunny coasts of the Elba Island. However, their cultivation, documented as early as Roman times, requires heavy labor due to the steep terrain; nowadays the most inaccessible vineyards have been abandoned, but thanks to the hard work of a number of wineries viticulture is still alive.
Sangiovese and Trebbiano prevail over older varieties like Biancone, Moscato, and Aleatico, in any case well represented among the labels.
Special mention goes to Aleatico, the standard-bearer of local tradition: although the grapes are grown also elsewhere in Tuscany, in Latium, and in southern Italy, Elba's ancient sweet wine is truly unique.

DISCOVERING ELBA'S LAST WINERIES

■ **PORTOFERRAIO.** A seaside town, its heyday was in the 16th century when it was fortified under Cosimo I; Napoleon spent 10 months here and you can still visit his home-in-exile, with Empire-style furnishings and various intriguing memorabilia.

■ **MARCIANA MARINA.** A pretty coastal district in the western part of the island, whose main town has lovely winding lanes and is perched on the slopes of Mount Capanne, amidst unexpected chestnut woods.

▪ **CAMPO NELL'ELBA.** The tour of the island continues along its western coast, sunnier and sunnier, with beautiful Fetovaia and Cavoli beaches. Belonging to this scattered municipality are Marina di Campo, a lively resort built around a small harbor, and San Pietro, in the verdant interior.

▪ **PORTO AZZURRO.** This is one of the towns on the eastern coast. An interesting excursion can be made to Rio nell'Elba, the island's main mining center and today a tourist attraction, and to Capoliveri on Baia della Stella.

THE GROSSETO REGION

Only recently noticed by experts, this province promises to be the new frontier of Tuscan oenology.

In recent decades the province of Grosseto has shown considerable dynamism in the oenology field: the result is the splendid flowering of local traditions as well as of some innovative ideas that have put the district in the regional vanguard. Wine is produced in two different areas. Towards the border with Latium the hills of volcanic origin gently slope to the Orbetello lagoons; DOC production bears the names of Scansano, Pitigliano, Parrina, and Argentario. In addition to Sangiovese (locally called Morellino) and Trebbiano, the basis of many mixed-grape blends, the vineyards are planted with singular grapes: among the whites, Ansonica, of evident Sicilian origin, as well as Greco and Verdello, from Umbria; among the reds, Alicante, brought from Aragon in the 17th century and well known in Calabria and Sicily. To the north, on the other hand, you enter the Colline Metallifere district, where the Monteregio di Massa Marittima DOC has recently been created, with eight types of wine; even more recent is the institution of the Montecucco DOC, bordering on Montalcino and Brunello lands.

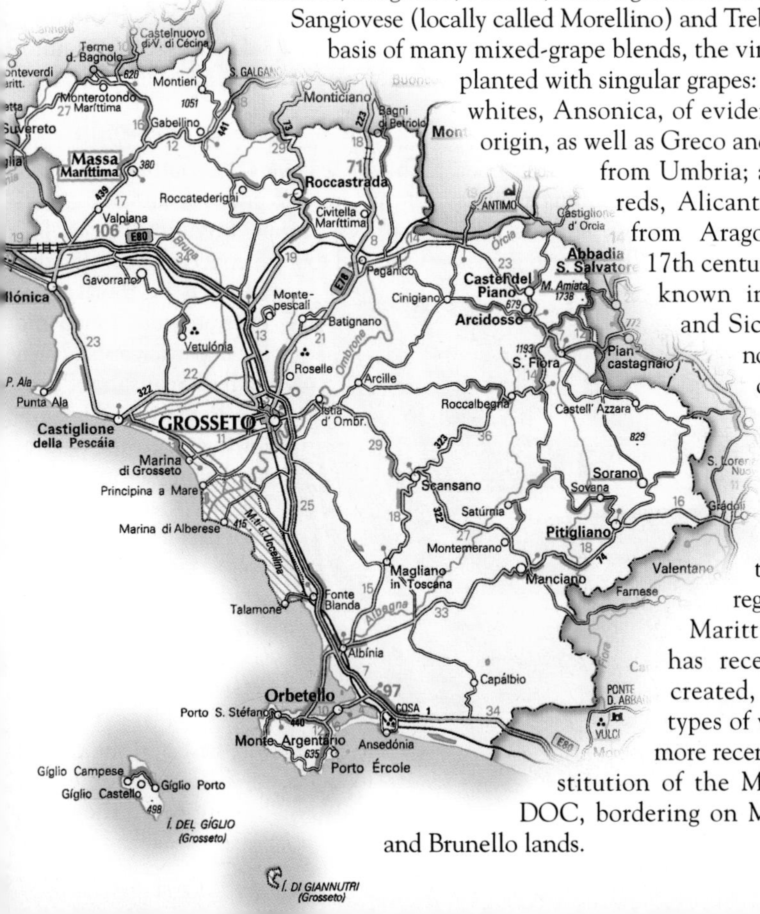

Maremma

The Ansonica Costa dell'Argentario DOC wines come from the municipalities of Capalbio, Manciano, Monte Argentario, and Orbetello, as well as from the Giglio island, where most of the vineyards are terraced. DOC codes account for a white wine made from a minimum of 85% Ansonica Bianco grapes. The Capalbio DOC, complementary to the former, covers the rest of the zone's wines: a Trebbiano-based white, a specific Vermentino, and a Vin Santo; a red and a rosé wine based on Sangiovese, and specifically labeled Cabernet Sauvignon and Sangiovese.
A special area is the Parrina DOC, whose name comes from a coastal village in the Orbetello territory and which has about 250 acres of excellently positioned vineyards. A white wine is produced from a mixed-grape blend of Trebbiano, Ansonica, and Chardonnay; red and rosé wines are based mainly on Sangiovese.
As far as the Bianco di Pitigliano DOC is concerned, in addition to the town of denomination, the area (covering about 2250 acres) includes the municipalities of Manciano, Scansano, and Sorano. The wine comes from Trebbiano grapes (50 to 80%) with traditional additions (Malvasia, Greco, Grechetto, Verdello) and innovative ones (Chardonnay, Sauvignon, Pinot Bianco, and Riesling Italico).
The Sovana DOC (*Sovana* is the name Etruscans gave to this land), a complement to the former, safeguard red wines in the same territory. Regulations refer to a red and a rosé wine based on Sangiovese and to a set of superior wines with varietal denomination (Aleatico, Cabernet Sauvignon, Merlot, Sangiovese).
Finally, the Morellino di Scansano DOC covers about 1250 acres of vineyards lying between the Ombrone and Albegna rivers in the municipalities of Scansano, Campagnatico, Grosseto, Manciano, Magliano in Toscana, Semproniano, and Roccalbegna. The famous local red wine is again produced from Sangiovese, in the variety locally known as Morellino, with possible additions of Canaiolo, Ciliegiolo, Alicante, and Malvasia Nera.

The Colli di Maremma Wine Route

This route covers the southernmost part of the Grosseto province and as many as five DOC zones, involving about 170 wine and tourism concerns. A leaflet distributed by tourism offices provides a map and list of participants (Town Hall of Scansano, Piazza del Pretorio). The following places are distributed along a sort of double loop that, leaving the provincial capital, goes east as far as Sorano and south as far as Mount Argentario.

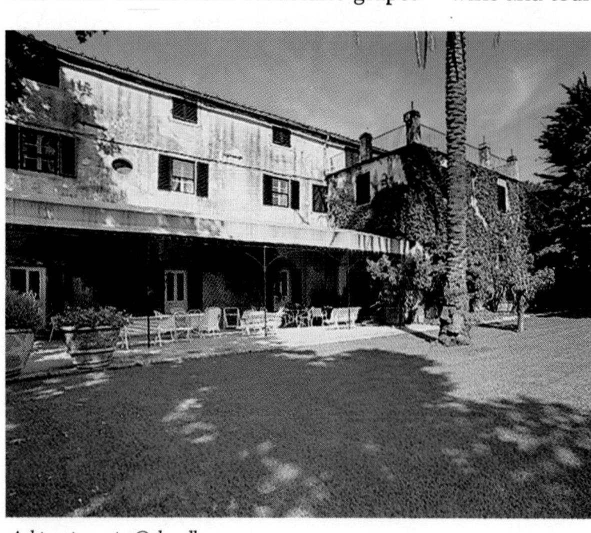
A big winery in Orbetello

▪ **Grosseto.** Within its hexagonal late-16th century bastions, the capital of Tuscany's Maremma has preserved the sights

A view of Feniglia sandbar, damming the Orbetello lagoon to the south

and atmosphere of past centuries. A market city of old history, it is still a hub for the province's produce.

▪ **SCANSANO**. This is the home of the Morellino DOC. Set in an elevated position, with a view of the sea and Mount Amiata, its historical center is full of medieval houses, often embellished with 14th and 15th-century portals. Among the attractions is a Vine and Wine Museum.

▪ **MAGLIANO IN TOSCANA**. High on the Albegna plain, on the site of Etruscan *Heba*, this little town still retains walls from the 15th century, the golden age of the Aldobrandeschi di Santa Fiora reign.

▪ **MANCIANO**. This little town of great atmosphere is perched on the top of an isolated knoll; from the 14th-century Sienese fortress you can look out to sea.

▪ **PITIGLIANO**. It stands on a cliff-like spur of tufa rock, softened here and there by underbrush and vineyards; the house façades blend in with the rock, so that the first glimpse visitors get of the village is absolutely breathtaking. A big mansion on the main square records the glories of the Orsini family. Many cellars are carved into the tufa rock.
Pitigliano, chief producer of the homonymous white wine, has for centuries been home to a Jewish community and a producer of kosher wine distributed nationwide.

▪ **SOVANA**. This isolated and quiet place in the Maremma countryside has stayed untouched since the Middle Ages: on one side stands the ruins of the Aldobrandeschi fortress, on the other the Romanesque Cathedral; in the middle the square and the original village with ancient buildings and brick pavements. You can visit Etruscan necropolises in the environs.

▪ **SORANO**. An Orsini fortress guards this village, hugging a sheer tufa crag and featuring steep lanes, underpasses, tunnels, and flights of steps.

■ **ROCCALBEGNA**. This farming town, particularly old in appearance, stands in a picturesque setting: a natural shelf between two jutting cliffs.

■ **CAMPAGNATICO**. On an olive-covered knoll that slopes down to the Ombrone valley, this village conserves examples of Romanesque architecture.

■ **ORBETELLO**. You are in the land of the Parrina and Ansonica Costa dell'Argentario DOCs and welcomed to this site of very ancient origins by the remains of Sienese (but also Etruscan) fortifications, on a spit of land jutting into the lagoon.

■ **MONTE ARGENTARIO**. The promontory – once an island – is covered with vineyards, olive groves, citrus fruit trees and other orchards, interspersed with underbrush. The towns, Porto Santo Stefano and Porto Ercole, share a common past as fishing villages and are now lovely seaside resorts.

■ **CAPALBIO**. Home to a DOC, the town is perched on a knoll, surrounded by the Maremma maquis; the medieval part is girded by walls.

The Colline Metallifere

The Monteregio di Massa Marittima DOC lies in the municipalities of Massa Marittima, Castiglione della Pescaia, Follonica, Gavorrano, Monterotondo Marittimo, Roccastrada, and Scarlino. Regulations envision a white from Trebbiano, Vermentino, Malvasia, and Ansonica, plus a specific label for Vermentino; a red (also new) and a rosé, made primarily from Sangiovese; a Vin Santo and a Vin Santo Occhio di Pernice.
The Montecucco DOC covers the band of hills running from Mount Amiata along the border with Siena and enters the municipalities of Cinigiano (with the neighboring village of Monte Cucco), Civitella Paganico, Campagnatico, Castel del Piano, Roccalbegna, Arcidosso, and Seggiano. Production includes a Trebbiano-based white and Vermentino varietal; a red based on Sangiovese and a specific label for Sangiovese only.

Massa Marittima's Duomo

Wineries *pp. 417-441*
Campagnatico, Cinigiano, Civitella Paganico, Gavorrano, Grosseto, Magliano in Toscana, Manciano, Massa Marittima, Monterotondo Marittimo, Orbetello, Pitigliano, Roccalbegna, Roccastrada, Scansano, Scarlino, Sorano.

THE MONTEREGIO DI MASSA MARITTIMA ROUTE

This route goes through the Colline Metallifere district, in the northern part of the Grosseto province. A leaflet distributed by the organizing committee describes the route and its three interconnected mini-itineraries, and lists its more than 40 participants (Town Hall of Massa Marittima, Via N. Parenti, 22, www.stradavino.it).

▪ **MASSA MARITTIMA**. A city of great monuments and history, headquarters of the Monteregio DOC. The lower, older city is deeply medieval in flavor and has great artistic worth (the crooked main square, overlooked by the Cathedral and the Town Hall, is outstanding). The "new" town, with a plain layout and set on a higher level, was an expansion designed in 1228.

▪ **SCARLINO**. A little town on a hill bordering the Follonica plain, with ruins of the castle that guarded it, ancient lanes, and a Romanesque church.

▪ **FOLLONICA**. Both an industrial town and a seaside resort, it shows its metal-working past in the singular church of S. Leopoldo, rich in wrought cast-iron decorations.

▪ **CASTIGLIONE DELLA PESCAIA**. The route finally reaches the sea and the Tombolo pine forest girding the sandy shore down to the picturesque canal harbor. Higher up is the medieval village, enclosed by a massive wall and featuring Pisan towers.

THE MONTECUCCO ROUTE

This recently instituted route takes in the municipalities of the homonymous DOC, covering a vast area in the foothills of Mount Amiata and centered in Cinigiano (Associazione Strada del Vino, Cinigiano, Piazza Bruchi, 13). Five mini-routes focus on individual municipal territories.

▪ **CINIGIANO**. A pretty farming town on the top of one of the hills that slope down from the western side of Mount Amiata to the Upper Maremma, between the Ombrone and Orcia rivers. This is a town of oil as well as of wine. The surrounding landscape is one of Tuscany's least known though it is among the most varied and worthwhile: solitary hills sometimes crowned by old villages, fields alternating with underbrush and woods, vineyards, pasturelands, and, higher up, chestnut woods.

▪ **ARCIDOSSO**. It features an historical center with winding lanes, dominated by the 15th-century fortress of the Aldobrandeschi family.
In addition to wine, you can enjoy excellent olive oil and Mount Amiata chestnuts.

▪ **SAGGIANO**. This is a wine and oil town, too, sitting on a steep knoll covered with olive trees and boasting a great view over the foothills of Mount Amiata. The church and Town Hall contain very old paintings. Wine cellars in the characteristic historical center are carved from living rock.

Specialties in Tuscany

A GOURMET TRIP through Tuscany doubtless begins in Florence. Trattorias and restaurants offer a complete menu of regional fare, from *ribollita* (hearty cabbage, bean and bread soup) to huge Florentine steaks, *pappa al pomodoro* (tomato-and-bread soup) and *fritto misto* (mixed fried seafood), *pappardelle* in wild hare sauce and grilled herbed chicken; but also dishes of great Florentine tradition such as meat pasty with truffles and *cibreo di rigaglie* (chicken giblets with egg, broth and lemon), or everyday meals like rice and beans and meat stew.

FANNING OUT FROM FLORENCE, along the road to the sea, you come to Prato, with its Medici villas and cuisine of Florentine imprint, and Pistoia, famous for its *brigidini* (crisp, thin wafers flavored with aniseed); Lucca, renowned for the olive oil from its hills, for Garfagnana spelt and for the seafood of the worldly Versilia resorts. Still on the Tyrrhenian coast, farther north, is Massa-Carrara, a province with a double gastronomic nature: by the sea the accents from Liguria are evident; in the hinterland, that is in Lunigiana, some dishes bear the influence of Emilia-Romagna. Taking Via Aurelia southwards, you go through the lovely Maremma landscape, with the Mediterranean maquis that alternates with pine groves and reclaimed lands. This leads to Pisa, Livorno, and Grosseto: the standard-bearers of a cuisine twixt sea and land are, respectively, *cacciucco* (a hearty mixed-seafood soup) and boar meat in its various preparations.
Inland, the area around Siena includes the southern portion of the Chianti hills, characterized by world renowned wine and olive oil, cold meats and *pecorino* cheese; in Valdichiana you get to the province of Arezzo, where huge white cattle give the finest *bistecche alla fiorentina* (T-bone steaks), and then pass to the mountains of Casentino, where meals feature mushrooms and game.

AS FOR WINE, make room for the reds, excellent with cold meat-based hors-d'oeuvres, flavorful first courses, and meat dishes in a rising scale of intensity that corresponds to the many expressions of Sangiovese grapes: young Chianti, Rosso di Montalcino, or Morellino di Scansano, for example, in a crescendo leading to Brunello, Vino Nobile di Montepulciano, and other great wines for important roasts and game dishes.
For seafood and vegetable preparations there is plenty of wines with a Trebbiano base, such as Montecarlo or Bianco Pisano di San Torpé. The intense Vernaccia di San Gimignano is for seasoned fish and seafood and also for white meats. As counterpoint to the "classics", there is a whole new generation made from international grapes: from the Cabernet Sauvignon of Bolgheri Sassicaia to the Pinot Bianco-Chardonnay of Pomino.
Also noteworthy is the range of rosés, accompanying seafood and medium-important meats. As an accompaniment to *pecorino* cheese, depending on its ageing, choose a full-bodied white like Ansonica dell'Elba or a red like Montescudaio. With dessert, Moscadello di Montalcino and ever-present Vin Santo.

Tenuta
IL POGGIONE

The history of Tenuta Il Poggione as we know it today begins in the late 19th century with the story of Lavinio Franceschi, who owned land in Scandicci (the hills around Florence). Franceschi was so fascinated by the stories of a shepherd who took his flock to summer pasture on the Maremma slopes of the hills between Montalcino and Sant' Angelo, that he organized an inspection of the area, unconcerned by the distance and dangers threatening travelers in those days. The visit proved to be so interesting, and the splendid scenery so bewitching that he bought the land. At the end of the 19th century the Franceschi family was registered in the records of the Tenuta, with the Tolomei and the Conti della Ciaia.

Franceschi's greatest virtue was to have sensed the winegrowing potential of this area and of the grape variety that has always been grown here.

The running of his winery marked the end of an almost Medieval-style farming tradition and the beginning of modern enterprise and methods. New Sangiovese clones were selected which were more suited to the production of quality wines, and new Sangiovese vineyards were planted in the most suitable areas, with the aim of producing really prestigious wines. The new cellar was built using more modern technology but without losing sight of traditions and typicality. More than a century later Lavinio Franceschi's work is still a fundamental benchmark for his heirs, who continue to develop the winery with the same commitment and unaltered passion, blending the old, expert winemaking traditions with the most innovative techniques. Today the vineyards of Tenuta Il Poggione, which are all south-facing and at an altitude of 200-400m above sea level, extend over 100 hectares, 60 of which are used for Brunello.

The constant work to protect typicality and improve quality continues alongside Il Poggione's research and selection with drastic reductions in production. Through bunch thinning and organic fertilizing, it is possible tò obtain an excellent product even in less favourable years. Harvesting is entirely carried out by hand at Il Poggione, and vinification takes place according to traditional methods, using more modern, avant garde technology. The winery now owns a surface area of about 590 hectares, divided between vineyards (100 hectares), olive groves (83 hectares), sowable land (110 hectares) woods, and other land (297 hectares). Tenuta Il Poggione's Brunello di Montalcino represents an admirable lesson in entrepreneurial far-sightedness and innovation, but also, as you drink it, tells a long story of will-power, courage and a passion for the land.

P.zza Castello, 14
53020 Sant'Angelo in Colle (SI)
Montalcino - ITALY
Tel. +39 0577 844029 - Fax +39 0577 844165
E-mail: ilpoggione@tin.it
www.tenutailpoggione.it

Azienda Agricola CAPANNA

di Cencioni Benito e Figli

Loc. Capanna, 333 - 53024 MONTALCINO (SI)
Tel. +39 0577/848298 - Fax +39 0577/848298

DIRECT SALES - OPEN EVERY DAY OF THE YEAR

The Capanna farm is owned and operated by the Cencioni family since 1957. It is located north of Montalcino in the area of Montosoli and has always been considered one of the best "crus" of the Brunello, outlasting all of the short-lived trends. The Capanna estate includes 12 hectares planted with vineyards and another 11 hectares planted with olive groves. The optimal exposure to the sun and the naturally gravely soil, together with the mild climate and gentle breezes, make a full-bodied and elegant Brunello, very well-suited to lengthy aging.
These favourable natural qualities are enhanced by an energetic pruning of the grapes, which ensures the superior quality of the product, even in years of less than optimal vintages. The winemakers at Capanna carefully select the fruit during harvesting, make the wine at strictly controlled temperatures, and monitor and select it during ageing. In fact, only a part of the final wine production will be aged for four years in Slavonia oak barrels to become DOCG Brunello while the other part will be aged for a year or two and bottled as Rosso di Montalcino DOC, or good quality red table wine. In the best vintages, the best barrels of Brunello are set aside to be labelled Reserve and are bottled after five years of ageing. This wine is left to further improve and mellow for a few months in the bottle. All of our wines are made from our own, estate-grown grapes.

BRUNELLO
DI MONTALCINO
DENOMINAZIONE DI ORIGINE CONTROLLATA E GARANTITA
CAPANNA
1999
imbottigliato all'origine dal viticultore
az. agr. Capanna di Cencioni Benito e figli
Montalcino - Italia - Prodotto in Italia
75cl e 14% vol

VITICOLA CASTELVECCHI

In our historic medieval wine cellar, we age our wines, produced with the right balance of modern technologies and respect for the ancient traditions of the estate. The hamlet offers a range of accommodation, including flats, rooms and a holiday farm to complete the farm hospitality. Guided tours of the wine cellars can be arranged with tasting of our products in addition to tasting courses held by the estate wine expert.

For information and reservations:
Viticola Castelvecchi, loc. Castelvecchi Radda in Chianti (SIENA)
Tel. +39 0577 738050 - Fax +39 0577 738608 - www.castelvecchi.com

Fattoria Montalbano

Loc. Montalbano, 112, I - 50060 Donnini - Reggello (Firenze)
Tel. 055 8652158 - Fax 055 8652285 - GSM 335 6678844
E-mail: info@montalbano.it - www.montalbano.it

The Fattoria Montalbano is located in the municipality of Reggello, just 27 km from Florence and convenient to the beautiful artistic cities of Tuscany and is open all the year round. Three great vineyards combine their resources to make the superb "Chianti D.O.C.G. Fattoria Montalbano" and "Il Buio": a great red, pure Sangiovese aged in barriques and produced only in the best vintages. The GRAPPA: full-bodied and silky, obtained by distilling our own fermented marc of Chianti grapes. The VIN SANTO: the quintessential sweet wine from the Tuscan countryside. The surrounding landscape is characterised by the "ledges" (ancient terraces, hand-carved into the land and sustained by stone walls) planted with olives groves, which give us our exquisite EXTRA VIRGIN OLIVE OIL. We can provide comfortable accommodation to our guests in apartments sleeping 2 to 6. Although recently renovated, our flats have maintained the charming feel of the old Tuscan country homes. All of our apartments have a kitchen, television, independent entrance, and terrace or garden furnished with a table, chairs, and chaise lounges for sunbathing. The flats each have an individual thermostat for winter comfort. Swimmingpool.
All of our guests at the Fattoria can take part in cooking courses in Tuscan and vegetarian cuisine, held in the spacious kitchen of the main house.

The Marches

A Region in Ferment

The viticulture of the Marches, once known only for its white wines, including its glorious Verdicchio, can now be well proud of red wines (from Sangiovese and Montepulciano grapes) of real stature as well.

A region with a classically hilly topography, the Marches are an homogeneous environment for the vine, with soils which are almost entirely clay-based, the sole exception being Mount Conero, calcareous in composition. The vineyards, once almost completely dominated by white grapes, are now more balanced: Sangiovese and Montepulciano for the reds, Trebbiano Toscano and the indigenous Verdicchio and Biancame for the whites, plus a myriad of minor varieties such as Vernaccia

Above, countryside of the Macerata area; left, San Leo fortress (top) and interior of a farmstead (bottom)

Nera and Lacrima, survivors of very old wine-making traditions. The region, nonetheless, shows substantial variations in its geography: to the north, Colli Pesaresi, in the sphere of influence of nearby Romagna; in the middle, the inland area of the provinces of Ancona and Macerata, Verdicchio territory; to the south, the border with Abruzzo and the Rosso Piceno zone.
The DOC production of the Marches' twelve zones is tenth among Italy's regions, and Verdicchio dei Castelli di Jesi is among the volume leaders of the country's single DOC areas. But significant changes are now under way: making the most of Verdicchio's eclectic character in the Riserva, Passito, and Spumante versions; giving maximum importance to Montepulciano and more attention to native white varietals compared to Trebbiano Toscano; showing an increasing interest in the question of how to obtain superior results with such international varieties as Merlot, Chardonnay, and Cabernet, though safeguarding the local wines traditional nature.

The Great Wines of the Marches

Verdicchio
Ensign of the Marches and Italy's viticulture worldwide, this wine's most traditional image is linked to the amphora bottle (still widely used) designed in 1954.
Verdicchio comes from a vine considered one of the best white-berry varieties in the world. The vine's origin is unknown, but its very ancient presence in the Marches makes it a native variety. The name derives both from the grapes color and from the green highlights of the wine. The grapes are vinified virtually pure under the denominations Verdicchio dei Castelli di Jesi and Verdicchio di Matelica. The resultant wine has deep aroma with a characteristic note of bitter almond; its outstanding acidity favors ageing, during which it develops a unique aromatic note.
The Riserva type (12.5% alcohol and 24 months of ageing) is great with fish, vegetables and white meats, even in the richest and most complex recipes. Also noteworthy is the character of Verdicchio made from late-harvest and dried grapes: amber color, deep aroma, velvety taste, 15% alcohol content, at least 12% developed. These passito wines are surprisingly good with desserts and sharp cheeses. Last but not least is Spumante, whose production is documented as early as the mid-19th century (a wine made "like real Champagne"). Today, Verdicchio dei Castelli di Jesi is produced using the traditional fermentation-in-bottle (or champenoise) method, and is a refined accompaniment throughout the meal.

Rosso Conero
The region's finest red comes from Montepulciano grapes. Rosso Conero is vinified pure or with limited additions of Sangiovese. It is ruby red in color, with vinous aroma and dry, fruity and medium tannic taste, it has good body and is suited to ageing; minimum alcohol content: 11.5%.
When young is goes well with hearty first courses like lasagne or roasted white meats. In the Riserva version (12.5% alcohol and two and a half years of obligatory ageing) it is excellent with meats of greater character, such as game, and longer-aged cheeses.

Rosso Piceno
This red wine comes from a blend of Montepulciano (35 to 70%) and Sangiovese (30 to 50%), which is the most widespread vine in the Marches. This combination creates a dry, full-bodied wine with balanced tannins, typical fruit aromas, and a final note of licorice. It goes well with highly seasoned dishes and white meats typical of the zone, such as rabbit, chicken, and pigeon. Rosso Piceno is also made in a Superiore version for important roasts and game. Finally, the Novello type (new wine, 11%) is a good accompaniment for cold meats and medium-aged cheeses.

Colli Pesaresi Bianco - Falerio Colli Ascolani
Most of the Marches' white wines are made from Trebbiano Toscano (Albanella) grapes. The Colli Pesaresi Bianco dry and delicate wine is obtained by almost pure vinification. In the Falerio dei Colli Ascolani wine, on the other hand, Trebbiano Toscano is blended with autochthonous Passerina and Pecorino grapes. Both are table wines when delicate fish dishes are on the menu.

The Marches' DOC zones

❶ **DOC Bianchello del Metauro**
❷ **DOC Colli Maceratini**
❸ **DOC Colli Pesaresi** *Bianco, Biancame, Roncaglia Bianco, Trebbiano ▪ Rosato ▪ Rosso, Focara Rosso, Focara Pinot Nero, Sangiovese*
❹ **DOC Esino** *Bianco - Rosso*
❺ **DOC Falerio dei Colli Ascolani**
❻ **DOC Lacrima di Morro d'Alba**
❼ **DOC Offida** *Passerina, Pecorino ▪ Rosso*
❽ **DOC Rosso Conero**
❾ **DOC Rosso Piceno** *Sangiovese*
❿ **DOC Verdicchio dei Castelli di Jesi**
⓫ **DOC Verdicchio di Matelica**
⓬ **DOC Vernaccia di Serrapetrona**

IGT- Typical Geographic Indication
Marches (Ancona - Ascoli Piceno - Macerata - Pesaro-Urbino)

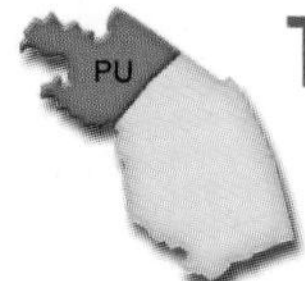

THE PESARO VINEYARDS

Bianchello del Metauro is the outstanding wine in a wine-making district that is still strongly influenced by neighboring Romagna.

The vine-growing area in the Pesaro-Urbino province, which from just inland from the coast extends to Sassocorvaro and Frontone, is composite in terms of the varieties grown: traditional grapes – like Sangiovese, of Romagnan ancestry, and Bianchello, native to the Metauro basin – coexist with French imports (specifically Pinot Nero, which also undergoes white vinification), representative of the latest vineyard evolution. The district's DOCs are Colli Pesaresi and Bianchello del Metauro.

Bianchello, Trebbiano, and More

The Colli Pesaresi DOC embraces many municipalities in the hilly range between Pesaro and Urbino, and specifically renowned among them are Colle San Bartolo, Monte Ardizio, Focara, and Fiorenzuola.
The Bianchello del Metauro DOC covers hillside vineyards with southern and southwestern exposures in the valley that opens into the Adriatic coast at Fano. There are eighteen municipalities in the cradle of Bianchello (also known as Biancame), a local ecotype of Trebbiano Toscano which produces a fresh, sparkling drink highly suited to accompanying local seafood dishes.

THE COLLI PESARESI AND THE METAURO VALLEY

This itinerary is a loop through the Foglia and Metauro valleys; main stops are at Pesaro, Urbino, Fossombrone, and Fano. A number of detours take you to minor towns.

- **PESARO**. The ancient town center embraces Piazza del Popolo, where the great Palazzo Ducale stands out. Close by, the Pinacoteca offers a masterpiece by Giovanni Bellini, The Coronation of Mary; then you can visit the Ceramics Museum, a historical review of exceptional local production. Pesaro was the birthplace, in 1792, of Gioacchino Rossini, and every August it is the site of the Rossini Opera Festival.

- **GRADARA**. Just inland from the coast, 14th-century walls encircle this town, whose fortress might have witnessed the tragic love story of Paolo and Francesca of Dante's Inferno. From the tower your eyes wander from the Romagna hills to those of Pesaro, evoking the pleasure of visiting wineries.

Wineries *pp. 441-446*
Fano, Mondavio, Pergola, Pesaro.

VISNER, THE SOUR CHERRY WINE

This drink was Federico da Montefeltro's favorite in ancient times – and it actually still has an old-fashioned flavor. The sour or marasca cherries were picked by country folk from wild plants at the end of June and macerated in wine to create a thirst-quenching drink. Equally homey is the recipe for making a true liqueur: to the wine-steeped cherries you add sugar and alcohol and let them ferment, then filter and wait for the liquid to clarify. The delectableness of Visner stems from the fruit's overlapping with the wine texture, from combining sweet, bitter, and tart tastes in a vigorous alcoholic drink. Visner is sipped chilled at the end of meals or in-between. With chocolate it makes an unforgettable match.

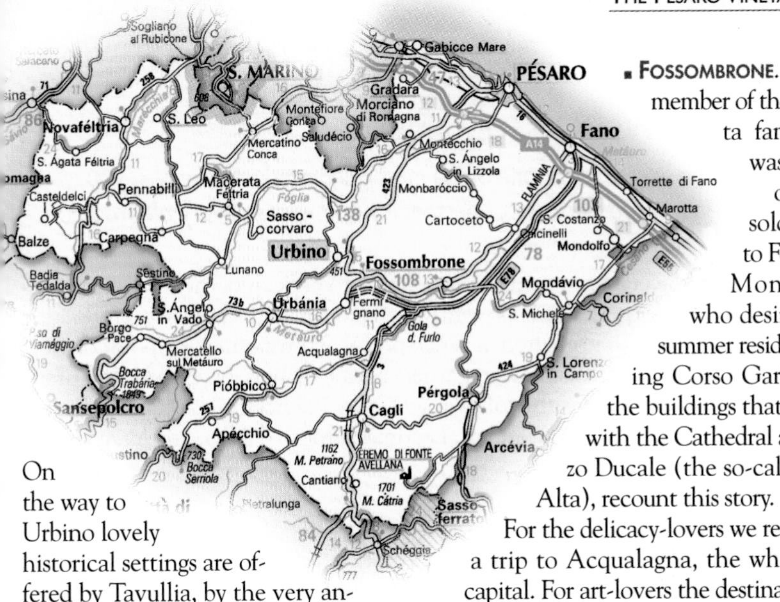

On the way to Urbino lovely historical settings are offered by Tavullia, by the very ancient turreted town of Colbordolo, and by Monteciccardo, in the hills that separate the Foglia and Metauro valleys.

■ **URBINO**. The city conserves clear reminiscences of the Montefeltros, the enlightened lords that transformed it into one of the most beautiful Renaissance courts, frequented by great artists and humanists. The symbol of the city's finest era is Palazzo Ducale, which combines the Laurana-style architecture with the splendors of its National Gallery. From Urbino you can extend the tour to Sassocorvaro, on the edge of the wine zone, where the Rocca Ubaldinesca stands out, "sentinel of Montefeltro".

■ **FOSSOMBRONE**. In 1444 a member of the Malatesta family, who was the lord of Pesaro, sold the site to Federico da Montefeltro, who desired it as a summer residence. Lining Corso Garibaldi are the buildings that, together with the Cathedral and Palazzo Ducale (the so-called Corte Alta), recount this story.

For the delicacy-lovers we recommend a trip to Acqualagna, the white truffle capital. For art-lovers the destination is instead Pergola, primarily known for one of the most thrilling archeological finds in recent decades (brought to light in Cartoceto): the so-called Gilt Bronzes, a spectacular sculpture group whose history remains a mystery and for which a special museum was "invented".

■ **FANO**. Before getting to Fano, two stops should be make on the opposite slopes of the valley: at Montemaggiore al Metauro (on the right-hand side of the river), with wide-open scenery, lovely churches, and Bianchello del Metauro on the table; and at Cartoceto, a picturesque town girded by walls with an ancient castle and prized olive oil from the surrounding countryside.

Remains of the Roman Fano, built where the Metauro river and Via Flaminia got at last to the Adriatic, are the Augustus Arch and the well-ordered layout of the town's old center. Fano's character is instead linked to the times of the Malatesta family, which reigned over the city from the late 13th century to 1463. The icon of their rule is the main square, with its Romanesque-Gothic Palazzo della Ragione and the family's Renaissance dwelling.

Urbino's Palazzo Ducale

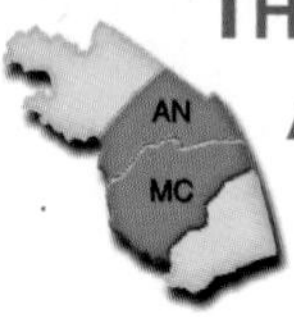

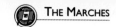

THE LANDS OF VERDICCHIO AND MOUNT CONERO

In the homeland of one of the most celebrated white wines, you discover reds with great personality and wines of very old tradition.

The Ancona and Macerata provinces are the land of Verdicchio, the most typical regional vine, which is experiencing presently a great re-launch thanks to production innovations. An area unto itself, from a geographical and wine-making point of view, is Mount Conero, at the doors of Ancona, where a wine route is supported by first-rank wineries. The district includes the following DOCs: Verdicchio dei Castelli di Jesi, Verdicchio di Matelica, Colli Maceratesi, Lacrima di Moro d'Alba, and Vernaccia di Serrapetrona.

The Ancona and Macerata regions

The Verdicchio dei Castelli di Jesi DOC embraces the hills in the central part of the Ancona hinterland, with a small extension beyond the Macerata border. The centers concerned are Cupramontana and Montecarotto.

The Verdicchio di Matelica DOC instead covers a valley parallel to the Apennine range, involving 8 municipalities, including Matelica, Castelraimondo, Camerino (in the province of Macerata), and Fabriano (in the province of Ancona). Where wines of other blends are concerned, the same area is covered by the Esino, Colli Maceratesi, Lacrima di Moro d'Alba, and Vernaccia di Serrapetrona DOCs. The Vernaccia di Serrapetrona DOC has a double special definition: for its vine, Vernaccia Nera; and for its territory, that is the municipality it is named from and part of the production centers of Belforte del Chienti and San Severino Marche, in the Macerata area. The wine is a peculiar red Spumante (Spumante Rosso), made through triple fermentation and suited to all the differ-

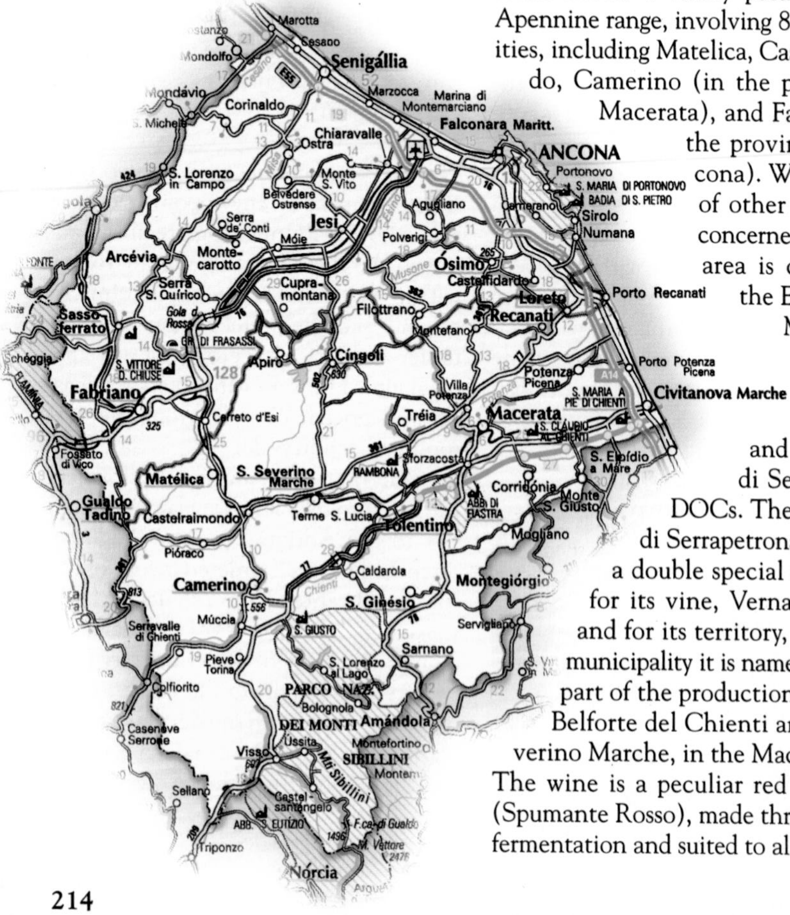

THE ENOTECA REGIONALE OF JESI

The 15th-century Palazzo Balleani, in the heart of Jesi (between Piazza Federico II and Palazzo della Signoria), houses the headquarters of the Enoteca Regionale run by Assivip, the Inter-provincial Association of Premium Wine Producers, representing the best of local oenology. The wine display, exhibited in underground rooms that are one with the castle walls, includes over 600 labels; sit-down tasting is assisted by professional sommeliers. The calendar includes various wine and food events and themed tastings.
Via Federico Conti 5
enoteca.jesi@libero.it

ent courses in a meal in its versions from dry to sweet. It is considered Italy's first and rarest red Spumante; its worrying decline in the late 19th century led to the institution of a DOC protected area of about 120 acres.

THE VERDICCHIO VINEYARDS

This is an ample itinerary involving the Ancona and Macerata provinces with main routes along the Apennine valleys and frequent connection detours. It can be divided in two and supplemented with the Rosso Conero Route, described further on, which takes in the Ancona environs.

▪ **SENIGALLIA.** The Misa river crosses this town forming a canal harbor, while a beautiful beach has made Senigallia a renowned seaside resort. Its fortress and 15th-century walls are reminders of a time in which the town drew great crowds to its annual Fiera Franca.
The Arcevia national road no. 360 leads you inland, suggesting detours: on one side to Corinaldo, a walled town with partly medieval and Renaissance architecture, and on the other to Ostra Vetere and the close-by ruins of Ostra, an important Roman municipium.
Wine-lovers can visit Morro d'Alba – a rare instance of castle-town entirely encircled by porticos set into the walls – and taste the Lacrima di Morro d'Alba DOC wine, an aromatic wine of marked character.

▪ **JESI.** Passing through Montecarotto and Castelpiano you leave the Misa valley and get to the Esino valley and to the Verdicchio region. If you are arriving

Verdicchio vineyards at Matelica

The countryside around Osimo

from the coast, on the other side, you follow the provincial road that leaving Falconara reaches Chiaravalle – with an important Gothic-Cistercian abbey – and finally get to Jesi, where the valley widens out.

The Old Town, surrounded by walls embellished with corbels and towers, has three squares with government buildings and the Pergolesi Theater – an important opera house. All around are some up-and-down quite little streets to explore in search of typical shops and restaurants. A historical building not far from Palazzo della Signoria is the Enoteca Regionale headquarters (see box).

▪ **CUPRAMONTANA.** The Verdicchio capital, set on the right bank of the Esino river, overlooks a peaceful scenery, which looks very much like the background in an ancient fresco. From the square where the Palazzo Comunale stands you can climb to the high part of the town, where the beautiful collegiate is located. Not to be missed, for collectors and common people alike, is the Label Museum. It is housed in 18th-century Palazzo Leoni and boasts an extraordinary collection of wine labels from early 19th-century on and from every part of the world. Not far away you reach Staffolo, a walled village featuring a Wine Museum; the parish church contains a lovely Lotto-school altarpiece.

▪ **MATELICA.** Following the national road through the Esino valley, you reach the turnoff for Matelica. This is a town of Roman origin, rich in monumental ruins, and presently the heart of the Verdicchio di Matelica Wine Route: this itinerary, running north to south, leads to Genga, a castled village surrounded by a regional park (Parco della Gola della Rossa e di Frasassi), to medieval Fabriano, famous for paper production and excellent salami, and finally to Camerino, rich in artistic and historic treasures from the Commune and Renaissance ages.

▪ **TOLENTINO.** The old flair of San Severino Marche and the aroma of famous Vernaccia di Serrapetrona (a characteristic Spumante Rosso) are an introduction to the visit to Tolentino.

The basilica of S. Nicola is one of Italy's most visited sanctuaries and conserves some majestic frescoes by Giotto. All around are the medieval streets and houses of the town, set among the hills of the Chienti valley.

On the road to Macerata stands the Cistercian abbey of Fiastra, located in a precious Natural Reserve.

▪ **MACERATA**. A round of walls embraces this town whose heyday was between the 16th and 19th centuries, as demonstrated by Renaissance Loggia dei Mercanti and Torre Maggiore that stand out among the noble 17th and 18th-century buildings at Piazza della Libertà.

▪ **RECANATI**. A graceful town of very ancient history, it is famous for being the birthplace of poet Giacomo Leopardi (1798-1837). The Civic Gallery contains paintings by Lorenzo Lotto.

The Conero Vineyards

The peculiarity of this wine district is the nature of its hills, belonging to a secondary Apennine spur that interrupts the continuity of the Adriatic sandy coast. The Conero promontory is a "heap" of calcareous materials that provide excellent habitats to the vine, specifically Montepulciano, which prevails over Sangiovese in giving body to Rosso Conero. This is a wine of ancient tradition with great current popularity, to be drunk young with fish casseroles or aged with more elaborate recipes.

Wineries *pp. 441-446*
Ancona, Apiro, Appignano, Barbara, Camerano, Castelplanio, Cingoli, Civitanova Marche, Cupra Montana, Fabriano, Jesi, Loreto, Macerata, Maiolati Spontini, Matelica, Montecarotto, Montefano, Morro d'Alba, Morrovalle, Numana, Offagna, Osimo, Ostra Vetere, Poggio San Marcello, Potenza Picena, Rosora, San Paolo di Jesi, Serra de' Conti, Serra San Quirico, Staffolo.

The Rosso Conero DOC embraces the seven municipalities surrounding this lovely promontory: Ancona, Camerano, Numana, Offagna, Sirolo, Castelfidardo, and Osimo. The planted area is small, and reduction in yield has changed this wine: once for local consumption, it is currently a drink for great wine connoisseurs.

THE ROSSO CONERO WINE ROUTE

From the outskirts of Ancona through much of the Mount Conero Nature Park winds one of the most recent and better

Sweeping view of Conero

organized of Italy's wine routes, illustrated in an exhaustive leaflet published by the Local Tourism Board.

■ **ANCONA**. A dynamic city, forming an amphitheater on the slopes of Mount Conero, with the old part looking westward and the modern districts stretching beyond the promontory to the eastern shore. For a first look at the city your reference point will have to be the Guasco Hill: on it stands the Cathedral of S. Ciriaco, one of the most interesting medieval churches in the Marches, and from there you can enjoy a charming panoramic view of the city and its port.

■ **NUMANA**. The itinerary can start in Portonuovo, a picturesque sea-side village at the foot of Mount Conero, and have a stop along the coast at Sirolo, which, in addition to vaunting a charming beach, is the starting point for excursions into the splendid natural beauties of the promontory.
Quickly reached Numana Alta lies on a slope of Mount Conero, immersed in greenery; the sea-side portion of the town, on the other hand, is an old maritime port, bordered by a beautiful beach.
Just inland you can visit the famous Virgin of Loreto sanctuary and then return to Ancona.

■ **CAMERANO**. Just inland from Ancona, you find this town full of history. Worth a visit are the church of San Francesco, with Gothic portal and annexed 14th-century cloister, and the Renaissance Italian-style gardens of Palazzo Mancinforte. But the real attraction is the maze of grottoes, with underground rooms cut into the tufa rock in the 17th and 18th centuries.

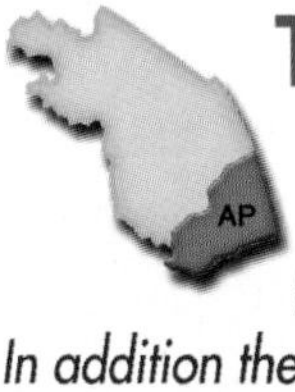

THE ROSSO PICENO VINEYARDS

In the Ascoli area, on the border with Abruzzo, Rosso Piceno finds its highest expression. In addition there is Falerio, a white wine from an interesting grape blend.

In the southern part of the province, on the border with Abruzzo, the Marches tour ends with a peak in quality for the Sangiovese-Montepulciano couple; on the white wine front, two old vines, Passerina and Pecorino, are the highlights. The Rosso Piceno, Falerio dei Colli Ascolani, and Offida DOCs cover the district.

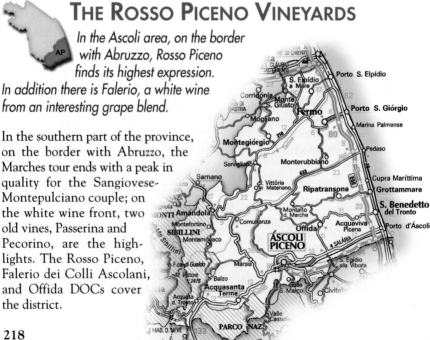

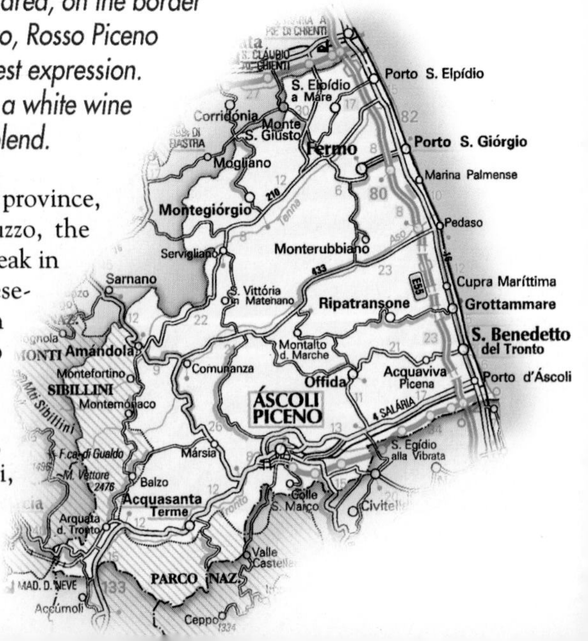

THE ENOTECA REGIONALE OF OFFIDA

Another public Marches enoteca is located in Offida, a town in the Tronto valley with an ancient wine-making history and involved today in the production of Rosso Piceno, Rosso Piceno Superiore, and Falerio dei Colli Ascolani DOC wines. It is housed in one of the loveliest sites in the Old Town, the former monastery of San Francesco. The activity is run by Vinea, the Piceno wine-producer association, which is also one of the main regional institution actively promoting typical wines. The exhibit includes hundreds of regional labels and gives the chance to taste and buy wines and other typical products: cold meats, cheeses, tender Ascoli's olives, extra virgin olive oil, and other delicacies.
Via G. Garibaldi 75
vinea@topnet.it

The Wines of the Southern Hills

The Rosso Piceno DOC is found in the region's most extensive wine zone, modeled by the range of hills that runs from Senigallia, in the Ancona province, to the regional border with Abruzzo. The leading wine comes from the traditional blend of Montepulciano and Sangiovese, with additions of international variety grapes or long tradition ones like Gaglioppa.
The Falerio dei Colli Ascolani DOC spreads over a good part of the Ascoli-Piceno province and complements Rosso Piceno with a white wine based on Trebbiano with characteristic additions of local grapes, Passerina and Pecorino.
The Offida DOC embraces the hillsides between the Aso and Tronto rivers; the most typical productions are varietal Pecorino and Passerina (also in the Spumante, Passito, and Vin Santo versions), due tribute to old local varieties.

THE ROSSO PICENO WINERIES

This route concerns the San Benedetto of Tronto-Fermo-Ascoli Piceno triangle, penetrating the Rosso Piceno Superiore area with a stop at Ripatransone and visits to the wineries in the surroundings.

▪ **SAN BENEDETTO DEL TRONTO.** Oleanders, pines, and palm trees line the miles-long beach that has made a successful sea resort of this town whose economy is traditionally dependent on fishing and dockyard activities.
A detour inland takes you to Acquaviva Picena, a town dominated by a fortress and the remains of castle walls, featuring old houses, medieval towers, and the church of S. Rocco with a Romanesque façade.

▪ **FERMO.** The tour continues along the coast towards Grottamare, a lovely medieval center with ruins of a 14th-century castle and a shoreline adorned with

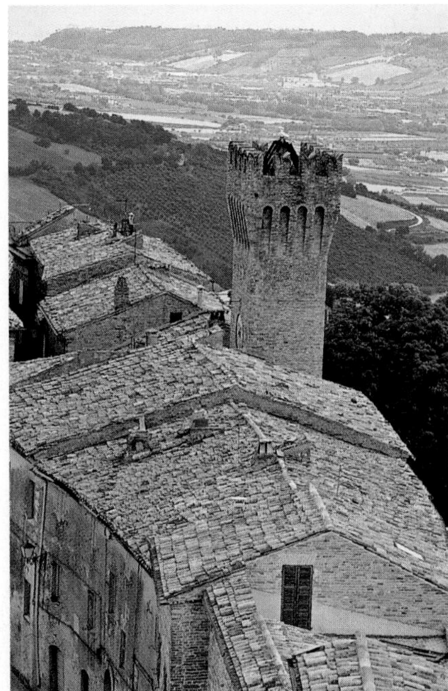

Ascoli Piceno's Moorish castle

palm trees and flowerbeds. You reach then Porto San Giorgio, originally Fermo's old seaport and presently an important resort and fishing center (host in mid-July to the Sea Festival with huge fish fries).
From there you follow a panoramic route to Fermo. On the hill top, former site of the Sforza fortress which was demolished by rioting citizens in 1446, stands the Duomo, set in the verdant frame of Girfalco. From the top descend various narrow medieval lanes, leading to some monumental squares, first and foremost the elongate Piazza del Popolo.

▪ **RIPATRANSONE.** You reach it via Monterubbiano, a scenic village in the Aso valley. Eloquently called "Piceno's Belvedere", Ripatransone rises on a hill and commands a sweeping view from Mount Conero to the Gargano and from the Gran Sasso Massif to the Sibillini mountains. The walled town has very old monuments, among them the Cathedral of Ss. Gregorio e Margherita.

▪ **OFFIDA**. Set on a isolated hilltop between the Tesino and Tronto valleys, it preserves images and traditions from the past – embroidery is the most outstanding. The wide panoramic square at the entrance to the Old Town holds the remains of a fortress; the main buildings, including the Palazzo Comunale with portico and 14th-century tower, overlook triangular Piazza Vittorio Emanuele II in the town center.

Wineries *pp. 441-446*
Ascoli Piceno, Castel di Lama, Cupra Marittima, Montegranaro, Offida, Pedaso, Ripatransone, Servigliano, Spinetoli.

▪ **ASCOLI PICENO**. Sheltered on three sides by the confluence of the Castellano into the Tronto river and on the fourth by the Annunziata Hill, the city retains inside its walls the Roman layout and medieval appearance, with worthy additions from later centuries. Around Piazza Arringo and Piazza del Popolo (the hubs of civic and religious power) most of the city's noteworthy monuments can be found. The Gothic church of San Francesco has particularly elegant lines, but the entire Old Town exudes austere nobility.

Rolling landscape in the Marches' interior

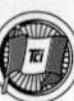

Specialties in the Marches

THE MOST CHARACTERISTIC image of the Marches is linked to its inland area: soft ups and downs that seem to rise from the Adriatic Sea into the yellow of wheat fields, the green of the rows of vines, and the silver of olive trees, slowly climbing and changing color towards the Apennines. The coastline is a ribbon of sand, hemmed with vegetable gardens and cut by the rocky jut of Mount Conero: Ancona, which lies at its foot, together with Pesaro and Porto San Giorgio, face a sea full of bluefish and other seafood, from clams to mullet. The region's mountains, which have their highest peaks in the Sibillini range, are home to livestock raising, with the big white steers of the Marches breed, and to dairy products made mostly from ewe's milk. At the region's heart are the hills, marked by parallel valleys and dotted with towns that welcome food-lovers.

THERE ARE FOUR provinces, aligned from north to south in a sequence that, in terms of food, is characterized by fine Emilia Romagna cuisine at one end and by the vigorous tastes of Abruzzo at the other. In the kitchens of Pesaro and Urbino, the two towns united in administrating the northernmost part, sea and land dishes coexist: fish soups in Rossini's hometown; meat and mushrooms in the old capital of Montefeltro, which is also prodigious with cheeses (*casciotta* and *pecorino di fossa*) and cold meats, such as Carpegna prosciutto. Do not overlook Acqualagna, the white truffle regional capital which makes the upper Metauro valley a primary gastronomic destination.
Then comes Ancona, with its fish broth and dried cod, prepared according to the typical Adriatic tradition, and the *vincisgrassi*, a hearty kind of lasagne of evident farmer origins. Inland you find two sanctuaries of Verdicchio – Jesi and Cupramontana – and one of the finest of Italy's cold meats, Fabriano salami.
The seesaw between land and sea continues in Macerata. Here the coastline is short but that does not prevent Porto Recanati and Civitanova from being famous for fish broths, fried fish dishes, and clams. Going up the Chienti valley, Tolentino is the first stop along the way to discover the inland flavors: Cingoli olive oil, Camerino cold meats, and one of the most popular regional dishes, *coniglio in porchetta* (stuffed rabbit seasoned with wild fennel).
Finally, Ascoli Piceno's gastronomic emblem is big stuffed olives. Local cuisine betrays the nearness of southern Italy: tastes get more vigorous, from cold meats to dishes that fire up with generous use of pepper and red chili.

AS FOR WINES, first in the list are the whites to accompany seafood: Verdicchio, in a crescendo of intensity that covers all needs, from the most delicate fare to robust fish soups. Then, going down the Adriatic coast, the various different blends of Trebbiano – from Bianco dei Colli Pesaresi to Falerio dei Colli Ascolani. With flavorful first courses, Rosso Conero and Rosso Piceno enter the scene, the youngest bottles accompanying the white meat typical of the region (rabbit and chicken) and medium-aged cheeses; vintage bottles instead go well with red meats, game, and sharper cheeses, such as *pecorino di fossa.*
At the end of the meal, choose two rare red wines – Lacrima di Morro d'Alba and Vernaccia di Serrapetrona – and the passito version of Verdicchio (to accompany cheeses streaked with green mold).

Umbria

Small Vineyard, Great Wines

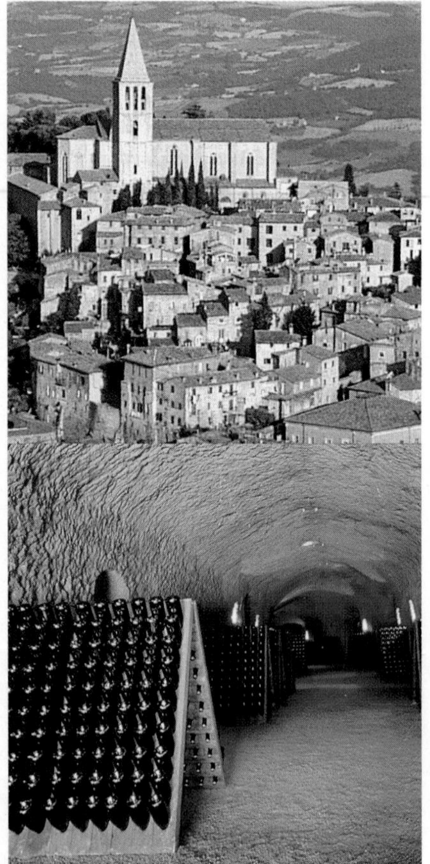

In the green heartland of central Italy, along the valley of the Tiber and the banks of Lake Trasimeno, extensive stretches of landscape are embellished by the geometry and colors of vineyards. A small production, but excellent in quality.

The first evidence of the cultivation of the vine in Umbria comes from Etruscan tombs and burial sites, which have yielded a variety of drinking and pouring utensils and the certitude of a quality production. Roman chronicles already speak of important wines, and the fame of Orvieto was already significant in the Middle Ages. Today's statistics show a region with small volumes of wine produced but of high level, an interesting and appreciated

Above, Umbria vineyards; left, view of Todi (top) and a pictoresque cellar in Orvieto (bottom)

group of DOC zones, and two areas of absolute excellence – Torgiano Rosso Riserva and Montefalco Sagrantino – rewarded with DOCG status.

Umbria, the sole Italian region in the Apennine area without a coastline, composed 70% by hillsides and the remaining 30% by mountainous areas, finds its central geographical feature in the valley of the Tiber. The hills which run along the river's course and those of its tributaries are a most favorable environment for the vine in soil and climate terms. Trasimeno (the forth largest Italian lake) is an area apart, a climatic island near the Tuscan border with a proven aptitude for high quality viticulture.

Gubbio's Palace of the Consuls

SAGRANTINO, AN OUTSTANDING UMBRIAN VARIETY

The region's vineyards feel the influence of bordering Tuscany: Trebbiano and Sangiovese by themselves account for three quarters of the total production and are the base of the blends of most Umbrian wines, even if their roles, compared to those they play in Tuscany, are somewhat reversed. Trebbiano is the more important of the two, a confirmation of the fact that Umbria is a region of white wines. Local varieties have, nonetheless, a significant role and make first rate wines, also thanks to appraisable experimentations. This is the case for Grechetto, which is part in the blends of the better white DOC wines, and this is even more true for Sagrantino, widely planted around Montefalco and used for the DOCG wine of the same name. The most common training system used to be *palmetta*, but it has been progressively substituted by cordon training as an evidence of a highly evolved viticulture.

2 DOCGS, 11 DOCS, AND 6 IGTS

Umbria ranks twelfth among Italy's region for DOC production with 6,472,000 gallons, a figure which represents 25% of the regional total. These are not impressive figures, particularly when one considers that Orvieto on its own represents two thirds of this total. In partial compensation, there are two DOCG zones, Montefalco Sagrantino and Torgiano Rosso Riserva, but it is nonetheless true that quality levels from the eleven regional DOC and 6 IGT zones have ample margins for improvement. But the situation is evolving, as evidenced since 1997 by the approval of the Assisi, Lago di Corbara, and Rosso Orvietano DOCs. The increase in quality is certainly encouraging; praises and prizes by connoisseurs have made a dozen firms known at international level and points of reference in excellence for local producers.

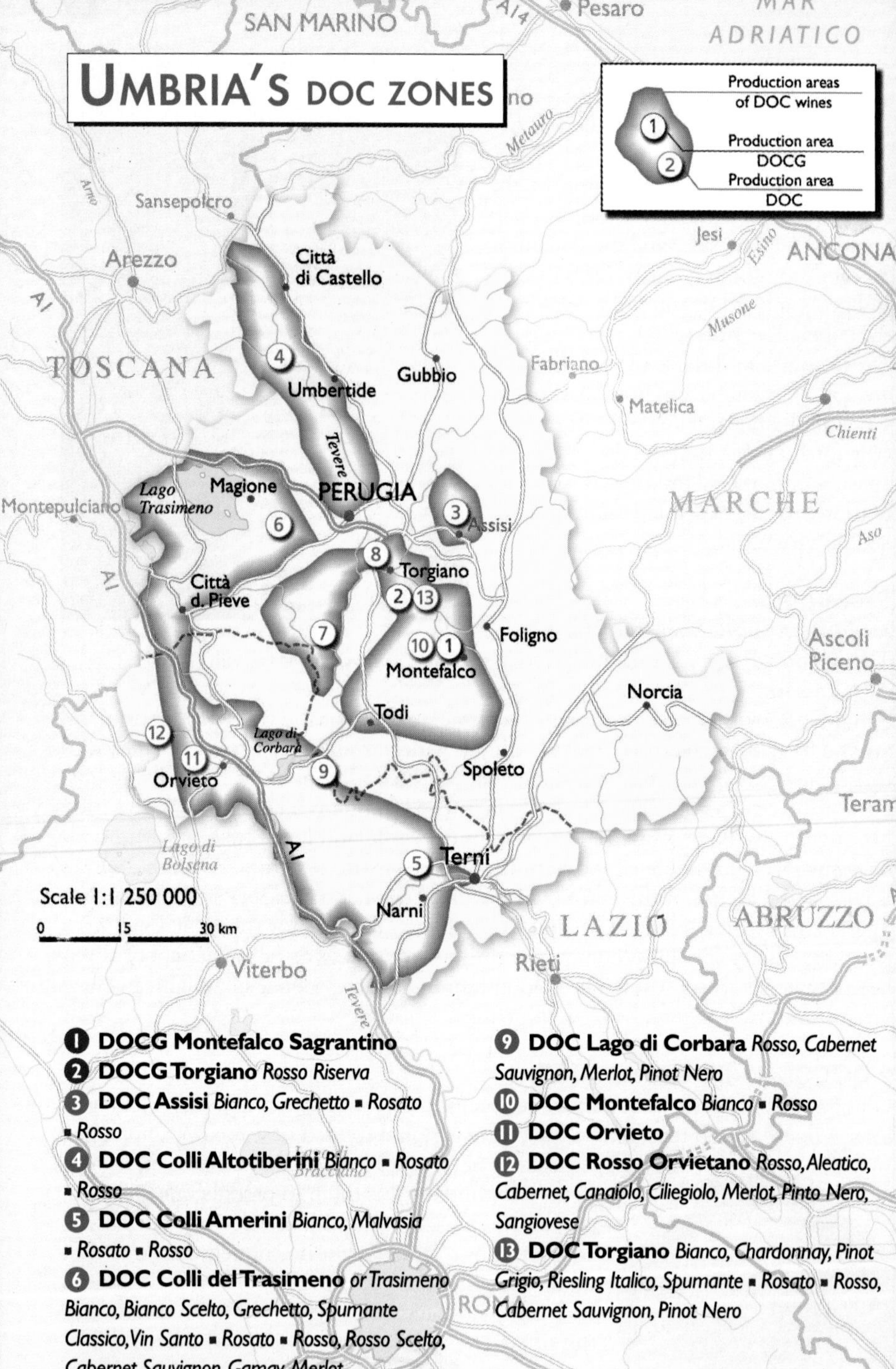

❶ DOCG Montefalco Sagrantino

❷ DOCG Torgiano *Rosso Riserva*

❸ DOC Assisi *Bianco, Grechetto ▪ Rosato ▪ Rosso*

❹ DOC Colli Altotiberini *Bianco ▪ Rosato ▪ Rosso*

❺ DOC Colli Amerini *Bianco, Malvasia ▪ Rosato ▪ Rosso*

❻ DOC Colli del Trasimeno *or Trasimeno Bianco, Bianco Scelto, Grechetto, Spumante Classico, Vin Santo ▪ Rosato ▪ Rosso, Rosso Scelto, Cabernet Sauvignon, Gamay, Merlot*

❼ DOC Colli Martani *Grechetto, Trebbiano ▪ Sangiovese*

❽ DOC Colli Perugini *Bianco ▪ Rosato ▪ Rosso*

❾ DOC Lago di Corbara *Rosso, Cabernet Sauvignon, Merlot, Pinot Nero*

❿ DOC Montefalco *Bianco ▪ Rosso*

⓫ DOC Orvieto

⓬ DOC Rosso Orvietano *Rosso, Aleatico, Cabernet, Canaiolo, Ciliegiolo, Merlot, Pinto Nero, Sangiovese*

⓭ DOC Torgiano *Bianco, Chardonnay, Pinot Grigio, Riesling Italico, Spumante ▪ Rosato ▪ Rosso, Cabernet Sauvignon, Pinot Nero*

IGT- Typical Geographic Indication

Allerona (Terni); Bettona (Perugia); Cannara (Perugia); Narni (Terni); Spello (Perugia); Umbria (Perugia-Terni)

The Great Wines of Umbria

Sagrantino di Montefalco DOCG
This red wine, exclusive to the homonymous locality in the province of Perugia, comes from a grape of unknown origin, although the name Sagrantino may suggest that it was brought from Greece in the Middle Ages by Byzantine monks. Vinified pure, this wine is deep ruby red in color, sometimes with purplish highlights, tending to garnet with ageing; it has a delicate aroma reminiscent of wild blackberries, and a dry, harmonious taste. Minimum alcohol: 13%. After obligatory ageing for 30 months in wooden casks, this red wine is at its best accompanying meats, from lamb to Chianina beef, and is traditionally served with wildfowl and dishes containing truffles. In the passito wine version the grape features are condensed: the minimum alcohol content is 14.5% and the color is deeper; the taste is characteristically semi-sweet. It is typically served with local desserts.

Torgiano Rosso Riserva DOCG
This wine, made in the homonymous locality in the province of Perugia, is representative of the Tuscan share of Umbrian vineyards: it is made with Sangiovese (50 to 75%), Canaiolo (15 to 30%), Trebbiano Toscano (max. 10%), and other red grapes including Ciliegiolo and Montepulciano (max. 10%). DOCG codes impose 3 years' obligatory ageing, at the end of which the wine has the following characteristics: the color is bright ruby red, the aroma is vinous and delicate; it has a harmonious taste and balanced body; minimum alcohol: 12.5%. Vintage bottles go well with one of the most typical local dishes, wild pigeon, as well as with other meats, especially if enriched with Norcia black truffles.

Orvieto DOC
This famous white is made from Trebbiano Toscano grapes, locally known as Procanico, in quantities of 40-60%, blended with Verdello (15 to 25%), Grechetto, and/or Canaiolo Bianco (Drupeggio), and/or Malvasia Bianca (15 to 45%). The wine is a fairly deep straw yellow color, with a delicate aroma and a dry taste with a slightly bitter aftertaste. It is excellent with fish dishes. Production from the most traditional zone qualifies as Classico, and as Superiore if it has 12% alcohol content and has undergone the obligatory 4-month fining.

Grechetto DOC
This wine has its name from a grape that is fairly common in the region and forms part of a variegated family that descends from or somewhat resembles to varieties imported from Greece long ago. This Grechetto, also called Todi, is part of the Orvieto mixed-grape blend and has varietal labels in the Assisi, Colli del Trasimeno, and Colli Martani DOCs.
The resulting wine is straw yellow in color with a delicate and distinctive pear aroma and a dry, slightly bitter taste. It is drunk typically with fish. It may be somewhat semi-sweet, and in this case it goes well with vegetable dishes, shellfish, and cheeses streaked with green mold, as well as with pastries.

A panoramic view of charming Amelia

THE PERUGIA REGION

In the heart of Umbria there are two DOCG productions – Montefalco Sagrantino and Torgiano Rosso Riserva – and a considerable number of DOC labels.

In the central portion of the Tiber basin, comprising Perugia and Todi along the course of the river and the Valle Umbra towns – Assisi, Foligno, Spoleto – bathed by its eastern tributaries, lies the richest and most interesting wine zone in the region. The variety of vineyard positions and exposures is matched by the considerable range of local grapes that flank Trebbiano-Sangiovese.

The first mention goes to Sagrantino di Montefalco, a vine of medieval origin and even earlier roots in Greece, used to make the homonymous red awarded DOCG certification. Then come Grechetto di Todi and Trebbiano di Spoleto, which are used in the blends of the zone's renowned whites.

Another important zone is around Lake Trasimeno, extending into the northwest of the province: climatically speaking, the lake creates particularly favorable conditions for vine-growing. Indeed, its shores and all the surrounding hills – which go as far as Città della Pieve to the southwest – are home to very old vineyards. Completing the province's wine geography, north of Perugia is the upper Tiber valley, where Tuscan influence is very strong.

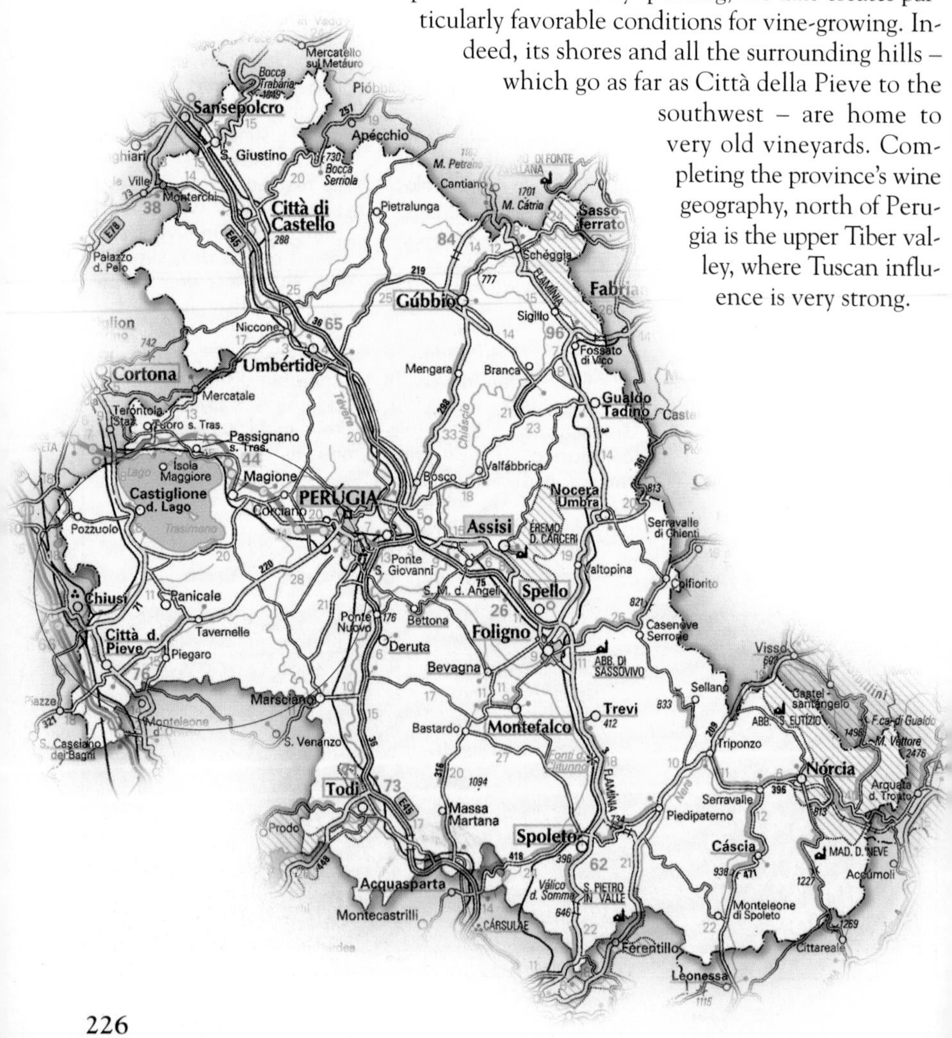

The Torgiano Wine Museum

This museum, one of the most important of its kind in the world and whose name is linked to the famous Lungarotti winery, is housed in the farm buildings of the monumental Palazzo Graziani-Baglioni, a 17th-century manor house. With its 19 rooms and more than 2800 items, the exhibition follows the dual theme of wine and of its role in history. The "shapes" of wine are one of the subjects treated, passing from archeology (pitchers from the Cyclades and Hittite vases; Greek, Etruscan, and Roman pottery; glassware and bronzes) to antiques (medieval, Renaissance, baroque ceramics) and then to contemporary art.
Also the technical-ethnographical aspect (tools for viticulture, vinification, and related crafts) and graphic representation (engravings and drawings dating from the 15th-20th centuries, old books, contemporary bookplates) are taken into account. The museum forms part of the extraordinary production and cultural organization linked to the Lungarotti wine estate.
In this sense, the exhibition has its ideal extension in the Olive and Oil Museum, set up in a nearby group of medieval houses, and its complements in the Osteria del Museo and in the guest facilities – a restaurant-hotel and a farm holiday accommodation.
Do not overlook the cultural events organized by the Lungarotti Foundation, which culminate in fall with the Italian Wine Tasting Fair that attracts the international press.

The Perugia-Todi-Spoleto Triangle

This is the heart of the Umbrian vinelands, lying between the Tiber to the west, with Perugia and Todi, and the Valle Umbra to the east, with Assisi and Spoleto. The zone is covered by two extensive DOCs, Colli Perugia and Colli Martani, and by denominations restricted to the towns of Assisi (DOC), Montefalco (DOCG and DOC), Torgiano (DOCG and DOC), Cannara (IGT), and Spello (IGT).

The *Cantico* Wine Route

The first part of this itinerary follows the Tiber, from Todi to Perugia; the second part goes into Valle Umbra, from Assisi to Spello. The exceptional nature of this tour stems principally from the beauty of the locations, although there will be plenty of opportunities to discover and enjoy extraordinary wines. As for good food, game, truffles, and cold meats are the stars of the wine season.

A pictoresque corner in the center of Montefalco

■ **TODI**. This town appears suddenly where the Tiber valley narrows, set high on a hill with its old bell-towers, stone buildings and roofs that change color with the daylight. This town with a distinctly medieval imprint, as splendidly exemplified in Piazza del Popolo, conserves one of the most significant monuments of the Umbrian Renaissance, the church of S. Maria della Consolazione. Events on the calendar in August and September include the National Handicrafts Fair and the Todi Festival, featuring theater, music, ballet, and cinema events.

■ **PERUGIA**. The regional capital can be reached from Todi along a route that passes through Marsciano (remains of the castle of the Bulgarelli counts and Colli Perugia and Colli Martani DOC vineyards), Torgiano (one of Umbria's oenological sanctuaries, in the homonymous DOCG, and site of the Wine Museum described in the box below), Bettona (a walled medieval town crowned with olive trees and local IGT vineyards), Cannara (a farming town whose Vernaccia and local red wine are IGT safeguarded), winding through Umbrian scenery, historical atmospheres, and good wines.
Perugia is spread along the crests of a hill in the Tiber valley, not far from Lake Trasimeno. It accumulated art treasures during its centuries of Papal government – from Fontana Maggiore to Palazzo dei Priori, from the frescoes by Perugino in the Collegio del Cambio to the masterpieces in the Umbria National Gallery. What is, however, most striking is the overall quality of the city and the indescribable flair of the Old Town. An outstanding event on the food and wine calendar is the Eurochocolate fair in October, devoted to one of the city's great gastronomical prides.

■ **SPELLO**. Perched on a spur of Mount Subasio, this town is rich in Roman, medieval, and Renaissance history and houses frescoes by Pinturicchio in the Baglioni chapel. The local wines come under the Spello Bianco, Rosso, and Rosato IGT, with varietal labels.

■ **ASSISI**. Founded by the Umbrians at the foot of Mount Subasio, was then ruled by the Etruscans and the Romans. It is most famous as the medieval town of St Francis and St Clare. The Basilica, with its sublime frescoes by Cimabue and Giotto, is only the start of a visit steeped in artistic and religious excitement. Last but not least are its gastronomy specialties and the wines of the recently instituted Assisi DOC; in pastry shops you will find marvelous *rocciata*, to be enjoyed with the region's great sweet wines.

Trim vine rows in Umbria's countryside

Not far away, in Bastia Umbra, more old-time atmospheres and excellent flavors await (the famed roast pork of Costano is the protagonist of a highly popular festival in late August).

THE SAGRANTINO ROUTE

This is a spiral itinerary that departs from Foligno and winds around the five municipalities involved in the production of Montefalco Sagrantino DOCG. The point of arrival is the main place of production.

■ **BEVAGNA.** Surrounded by walls, this is a solitary town at the foot of the green hills that enclose the Foligno plain to the west. The medieval setting of the main square is the point of departure for a visit full of attractions, from the Romanesque churches of S. Silvestro and S. Michele Arcangelo to the numerous Roman remains. In late June, Bevagna is the venue for the Mercato delle Gaite, a fascinating medieval re-enactment.

■ **GUALDO CATTANEO.** On a lovely road flanked by olive trees, you climb the 1460-foot hill on which this little town stands, surrounded by turreted walls. Prized works of art can be seen in the churches of S. Agostino (*Crucifixion*, 12th C.) and SS. Antonio e Antonino (crypt). The surrounding land is dotted with castles and fortresses – 11 in all. This is one of the principal production centers of the Colli Martani DOC.
Just south of it is Giano dell'Umbria, a scenic village of medieval appearance with lovely old churches, encircled by 14th century turreted walls.

■ **MONTEFALCO.** You pass through Castel Ritaldi, another medieval village within walls built around a 13th-century castle, to reach Montefalco. The vineyards of celebrated Sacrantino come right up to the medieval walls of this little town commanding a splendid view of the Topino valley and the Clitunno plain – Montefalco is deservedly called the "balcony of Umbria". Piazza del Comune has always been the hub of town life; the fulcrum of the visit is, on the other hand, the 14th-century church of San Francesco, which now houses a museum and where you can admire beautiful frescoes by Benozzo Gozzoli and Perugino. In honor of an ancient tradition of sweet wines, the Old Town is home to the Passito Wine Study Center.

Lake Trasimeno

The first production zone is the Colli di Trasimeno DOC and covers the band of hills overlooking the lake, reaching as far as Perugia and including ten municipalities. A second production area is the Colli Altotiberini DOC, in the hilly zone

Castiglione del Lago on Lake Trasimeno

crossed by the Tiber on the border with Tuscany and the Marches, with the great tourist attraction of Gubbio, which has a unique medieval atmosphere – outstanding even for Umbria!

THE COLLI DEL TRASIMENO WINE ROUTE

This route forms a large loop around the shores of the lake and is broken up into four themed itineraries: "Hannibal's Camps", from Tuoro to Passignano; "Following in the Footsteps of the Knights of Malta", from Magione to Corciano; "Perugino's Lands", from Città della Pieve to Piegaro and Panicale; and "The Marquisate of Ascanio Della Corgna", around Castiglione del Lago.

▪ **PASSIGNANO SUL TRASIMENO.** This is reached via Tuoro sul Trasimeno, where Hannibal of Carthage's army defeated Roman troops in a bloody battle in 217 BC.
Lying on a headland overlooking the lake, Passignano has an old center surrounded by walls, dark stone houses, and narrow lanes as well as a modern part spread along the lakeside. Boats to the pretty Isola Maggiore depart from here. Local events include in July the unusual Palio delle Barche, in which men run through the streets carrying boats on their backs.

▪ **MAGIONE.** This town rises on the eastern shore of Lake Trasimeno and has a beautiful castle of the Knights of Malta built around a Romanesque abbey. You can take a boat from San Feliciano (Fishing Museum) to Isola Polvese, the largest island in the lake and now a protected area.
Not far away, towards Perugia, is Corciano, within turreted walls and dominated by a 13th-century castle; the church of S. Maria contains a beautiful Nativity by Perugino.

▪ **CITTÀ DELLA PIEVE.** This town lying on a crest overlooking the Chiani valley was the birthplace to Pietro Vannucci, known as Perugino. His paintings can be seen inside the Cathedral, a baroque transformation of the ancient parish church around which the original settlement grew up. In the town, which is medieval in flavor and has unexpectedly scenic views, the end of August is the time of an historical procession and archery contest during the Palio dei Terzieri.

Heading towards Perugia through the Nestore valley, you come to Piegaro, a town of old glass-working traditions and with the Renaissance sanctuary of Madonna di Mongiovino. Also near Lake Trasimeno, you can stop at Panicale, set in a scenic position on the lake and with a picturesque medieval appearance. The church of S. Sebastiano conserves a Perugino's masterpieces, the *Martyrdom of St Sebastian*. In September Città della Pieve hosts a Grape Festival with floats, food tasting, and open-air concerts.

▪ **CASTIGLIONE DEL LAGO**. This town rises with turreted walls and a fortress on a headland covered with olive trees that juts out into the lake. It is primarily a summer resort, but the wine is an excellent incentive to explore the ring of hills on the horizon. Trasimeno fish, especially perch and tench, together with the wines and olive oil from the hills are the strong points of local dining.

Wineries *pp. 446-448*
Bevagna, Castiglione del Lago, Corciano, Foligno, Gualdo Cattaneo, Montefalco, Panicale, Spello, Torgiano, Umbertide.

THE ORVIETO REGION

On the border with Lazio, the province of Terni boasts a historical wine, Orvieto, now flanked by Colli Amerini and Lago di Corbara productions.

If judgment were based simply on the extension of vine-planted land and on DOC productions, the province of Terni would certainly be considered quite modest on the Umbrian wine scene. Instead, with its Orvieto wine, it plays a cameo role in bringing prestige to the region. This exceptionally fine wine, made from Trebbiano with the crucial addition of local grapes, is produced in the zone where the Paglia river joins the Tiber, straddling the border with Lazio. Terni's importance is also evident in normative terms, as it has a DOC all of its own and another two denominations – Rosso Orvietano and Lago di Corbara – which cover the reds produced in the same area.

In the east of the province, the Colli Amerini DOC safeguards the wine produced in the hills surrounding the provincial capital. Finally, two IGTs pay tribute to the interesting Allerona and Narni areas.

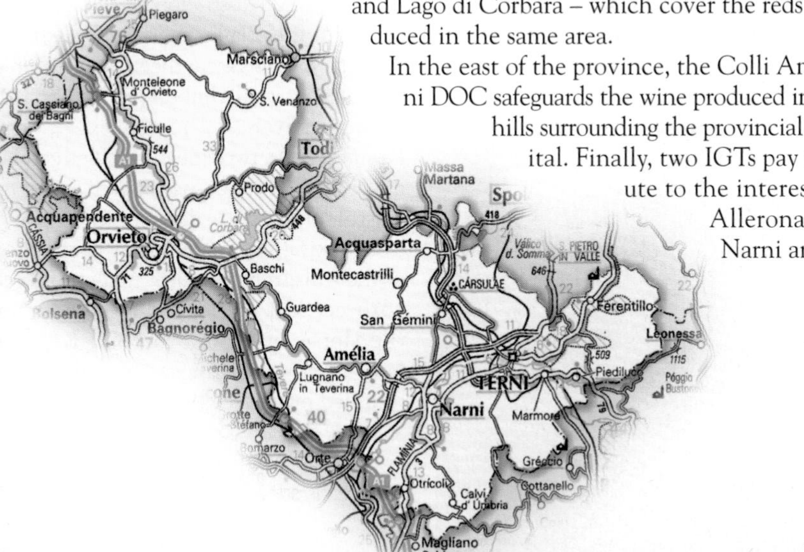

In the Kingdom of Orvieto

Attention is drawn to Orvieto wine for the excellence of local wineries and for the splendid natural and historical setting of its lands. The production zone slopes from Monteleone d'Orvieto towards Ficulle, Orvieto, and Alviano, bordering Lazio as far as Bagnoregio; following the Tiber, it even embraces the shores of Lake Corbara. The province's wine vocation also includes other wine varieties, which make an extended tour even more interesting.

Wineries *pp. 446-448*
Amelia, Baschi, Ficulle, Montecastrilli, Orvieto, Penna in Teverina, Stroncone.

THE ETRUSCAN-ROMAN WINE ROUTE

This itinerary starts in Terni and heads west, following the courses of the Nera and the Tiber rivers before eventually reaching Orvieto and Castel Viscardo. The route winds over hills and through valleys where Colli Amerini, Lago di Corbara, Orvieto, and Rosso Orvietano DOC wines are produced: these are lands of truly ancient wine-making traditions (the Etruscans were the first to make a sweet wine in the Orvieto area), but also of olive oil and white truffles, as well as of time-honored desserts.

▪ **NARNI**. The first stop on the tour is Narni, a medieval town hugging a hilltop between the Terni plain and the Nera valley. It is the home of the homonymous IGT, which covers many varieties of white, red, and rosé wines.

▪ **AMELIA**. A town with an age-old charm, set on a hill in the ridge that divides the Tiber and Nera valleys; its ancient origins are evident in the well-conserved polygonal walls that date from the 6th-4th centuries BC. Along the road to Orvieto is Baschi, a small wine-producing town already within the Orvieto Classico zone and also a point of reference for the Lago di Corbara DOC (as well as for Italian gastronomy, at Vissani's restaurant).

▪ **ORVIETO**. An isolated tufa cliff rises from the verdant valley of the Paglia river. The city perched on it is a treasure chest of art: the Duomo, sparkling like a Gothic triptych, is the first treasure on the list; you can then proceed with the visit, starting with the St Patrick's Well, a splendid example of Renaissance engineering. As a wine-town possessing a double DOC (Orvieto and Rosso Orvietano), it offers tasting at first-class wineries. The events calendar has a musical theme and features the international Umbria Jazz and Spazio Musica festivals.
From Orvieto, two fine excursions can be made along the scenic roads leading to Castel Viscardo, a quiet farming town overlooking the Paglia valley at the foot of the Volsini mountains, with an intact 15th-century castle, and to Ficulle, on the slopes of Mount Nibbio, another farming town with a castle, partly surrounded by medieval walls.

The Sala Castle in Ficulle

Specialties in Umbria

THE UMBRIAN LANDSCAPE, in the heart of the Apennines, is covered with hills that run along the valleys of the Tiber and its tributaries, opening up around Lake Trasimeno. This is countryside of age-old beauty, praised by travelers in every epoch, as lovely in its spontaneous vegetation as in its cultivated areas, where vineyards and olive groves are woven together. It is a land faithful to its past also in its cuisine, which uses traditional raw materials and recipes. With great simplicity, the table is set with country-style pastas and soups, cold meats and cheeses, meats grilled on the spit or oven-roasted, often enriched with black truffles, true glory of the region. The whole comes in the gilded frame of an excellent olive oil, and with the accompaniment of some of Italy's finest wines.

PERUGIA MARKS THE START of a journey through a world of timeless sights and tastes, such as the prosciutto of Norcia, a place which has become synonym for the most genuine cold meats. Castelluccio lentils and Spoleto spelt are the ingredients in hearty soups; worth mentioning are then the red onions of Cannara, the black celery of Trevi, and the red-skinned potatoes of Colfiorito. The meats are exceptional, with pork being the star. Its finest gastronomic expression is found in *porchetta al finocchio*, the fennel-seasoned roast pork that originated in Umbria; pork meat is also used to accompany *strangozzi* and other homemade pastas. Then there are the white Chianina bullocks, which provide wonderful grilled steaks, and the game: hare, stewed in white wine and seasoned with black olives; Norcia-style woodcock, stuffed with sausage and truffles and roasted on a spit; spit-roasted wild pigeons, continually basted with fat mixed with red wine and herbs. Last but not least are the fish, from the great carp of Lake Trasimeno, stuffed and roasted, to the trout from the Nera river, unusually combined with black truffles. Considering the small size of the territory, its olive oil production is extraordinary and based mainly on local varieties that give the product a unique fruity taste that can also be bitter and spicy.

AS REGARDS WINES, the whites are excellent with fish, which in Umbria come mostly from streams and lakes: Orvieto is considered one of the very best for these dishes; Grechetto, will delight travelers; and Torgiano Bianco is made from a grape bland which is a mixture of the two.
With cold meat hors-d'oeuvres and tasty first courses the simplest reds come into play – Torgiano Rosso or Montefalco Rosso – leaving their big brothers – Torgiano Rosso Riserva and Montefalco Sagrantino – to accompany red meats and game. In the cheese department, which comprises a wide range of flavor intensities, think of Rosso dell'Umbria, an umbrella for several "international" blends of grapes based on Merlot, Cabernet Sauvignon, and Pinot Nero.
At dessert time, there is a good assortment of classics – semi-sweet Orvieto and Montefalco Sagrantino passito wine – and a new generation of "musty" and "late-harvest" wines, both from local and imported grapes.

Latium

The Legendary Wines of the Castelli

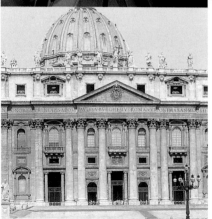

The Castelli Romani, whose praises have been sung by travelers of every epoch, even today represent one of the most powerful images in attracting wine-loving travelers to Italy. But they are also the point of reference of rapid evolving wine-growing.

Distributed with admirable balance among hillside, plain, and mountain slope, buttressed by a millenia-old tradition and a setting of art and landscape which are part of the common culture, Latium's wineries have all of the credentials to become widely popular as wine tourism destinations. They are, at this particular moment, slightly

Above, vineyards in the Castelli area; left, folk singer and good-wine lover (top) ande the façade of St. Peter in Rome (bottom)

behind in the development of the sector, but they are holding so many aces in their hands that a certain optimism is more than justified.

From the Castelli Romani to Etruscan Vineyards

Latium's viticulture is based principally upon two areas. The first is the Castelli Romani, located in the Colli Albani, the region's historic viticultural stronghold. The second is the province of Viterbo, also known under the ancient name of Tuscia, better suited to vine-growing in the lower Tiber valley. The province of Rieti shares a vineyard area with Rome (Colli della Sabina) along the River Tiber, just as Frosinone shares with Rome the production of Cesanese red wine. Latina, to conclude this rapid survey, is the new frontier of the region's oenology, with interesting wines from the zones of Aprilia and Circeo.

The Grand Vineyard of Malvasia and Trebbiano

Latium is white wine territory. Statistics are clear on this point: Malvasia del Lazio and Malvasia Bianca di Candia on their own account for over 55% of the total regional vineyard surface; if one adds Trebbiano Toscano and Trebbiano Giallo the total easily surpasses 70%. Good red wines are made from local vines, Nero Buono di Cori and the Cesanese varieties, while Sangiovese, Merlot, Montepulciano, and Cabernet are increasingly being introduced. In terms of vineyard training, the *spalliera* system is gaining ground against the *tendone* system (still in use in the 20% of vine-land). This is yet another demonstration of the concern for quality and of the notable effort invested in the improvement of the wines by producers in more recent years.

A Rapidly Evolving Viticulture

Latium's viticulture – 118,000 acres, 80% of which planted to white grapes – has received a legislative reorganization into 25 DOC zones and 5 IGT areas (Civitella d'Agliano, Colli Cimini, Frusinate, Lazio, and Nettuno). The aim is to improve wines by anchoring the public's awareness even more firmly to the precise areas which have most characterized them. Proof of this is given by the Atina DOC, of most recent institution, which has been the first to introduce varietal labels for Cabernet, Merlot, and Syrah. Overall production is close to 98 million US gallons, nineteen million of which – 20% of the total volume – are DOC wines. This is higher than the national average, but significantly lower than other regions with similar traditions of fine wine. Frascati, one of Italy's twenty most important DOC wines, is the region's pride and accounts on its own for 4.7 million US gallons, a fact which also demonstrates the rather limited quantities of the rest of quality outputs. Production is largely supported by wineries associations and consortia, while private wine firms are quite limited in number.

The town of Piglio and Cesanese vineyards

LATIUM'S DOC ZONES
Gubbio
Fabriano
Macer
Potenza
Montepulciano
Lago Trasimeno
Perugia
MARCHE
A1
Città d. Pieve
TOSCANA
Tevere
Foligno
UMBRIA
Orvieto
Spoleto
Nera
Pitigliano
Amatrice
Lago di Bolsena
Bolsena
Terni
Narni
Montefiascone
Lago di Campotosto
Marta
Fiora
Viterbo
Rieti
L'AQU
Lago di Vico
Tarquinia
Civita Castellana
Lago d. Salto
Mignone
Lago di Turano
Lago di Bracciano
Bracciano
Civitavecchia
A24
A25
Cerveteri
A12
Arrone
Avezz
Tivoli
Subiaco
G.R.A.
ROMA
Palestrina
Fiuggi
Frascati
L. di Albano
Lago di Nemi
Lido di Ostia
Sacco
Velletri
Frosinone
Pomezia
Aprilia
Ceccano
MAR
TIRRENO
Latina
Anzio
Sisto
Terracina
1
2
4
5
6
7
8
9
10
11
12
13
14
15
16
17
18
19
20
21
22
23
24
25
Scale 1:1 250 000
0
15
30 km

1 **DOC Aleatico di Gradoli**
2 **DOC Aprilia** *Trebbiano* ▪ *Merlot* ▪ *Sangiovese*
3 **DOC Atina** *Rosso, Cabernet Sauvignon, Pinot Nero* ▪ *Spumante*
4 **DOC Bianco Capena**
5 **DOC Castelli Romani** *Bianco* ▪ *Rosato* ▪ *Rosso*
6 **DOC Cerveteri** *Bianco* ▪ *Rosato* ▪ *Rosso*
7 **DOC Cesanese del Piglio or Piglio**
8 **DOC Cesanese di Affile or Affile**
9 **DOC Cesanese di Olevano Romano or Olevano Romano**
10 **DOC Circeo** *Bianco, Trebbiano* ▪ *Rosato* ▪ *Rosso, Sangiovese*
11 **DOC Colli Albani** *Bianco* ▪ *Rosso*
12 **DOC Colli della Sabina** *Bianco* ▪ *Rosato* ▪ *Rosso*
13 **DOC Colli Etruschi Viterbesi** *Bianco, Grechetto, Moscatello, Procanico, Rossetto* ▪ *Rosato, Sangiovese Rosato* ▪ *Rosso, Canaiolo, Grechetto, Merlot, Violone*
14 **DOC Colli Lanuvini**
15 **DOC Cori** *Bianco* ▪ *Rosso*
16 **DOC Est! Est!! Est!!! di Montefiascone**
17 **DOC Frascati**
18 **DOC Genazzano** *Bianco* ▪ *Rosso*
19 **DOC Marino**
20 **DOC Montecompatri-Colonna or Montecompatri or Colonna**
21 **DOC Orvieto** *see Umbria*
22 **DOC Tarquinia** *Bianco* ▪ *Rosato* ▪ *Rosso*
23 **DOC Velletri** *Bianco* ▪ *Rosato*
24 **DOC Vignanello** *Bianco, Greco* ▪ *Rosato* ▪ *Rosso*
25 **DOC Zagarolo**

IGT - Typical Geographic Indication
Civitella d'Agliano (Viterbo); Colli Cimini (Viterbo); Frusinate or del Frusinate (Frosinone); Lazio (Frosinone - Latina - Rieti - Rome - Viterbo); Nettuno (Rome)

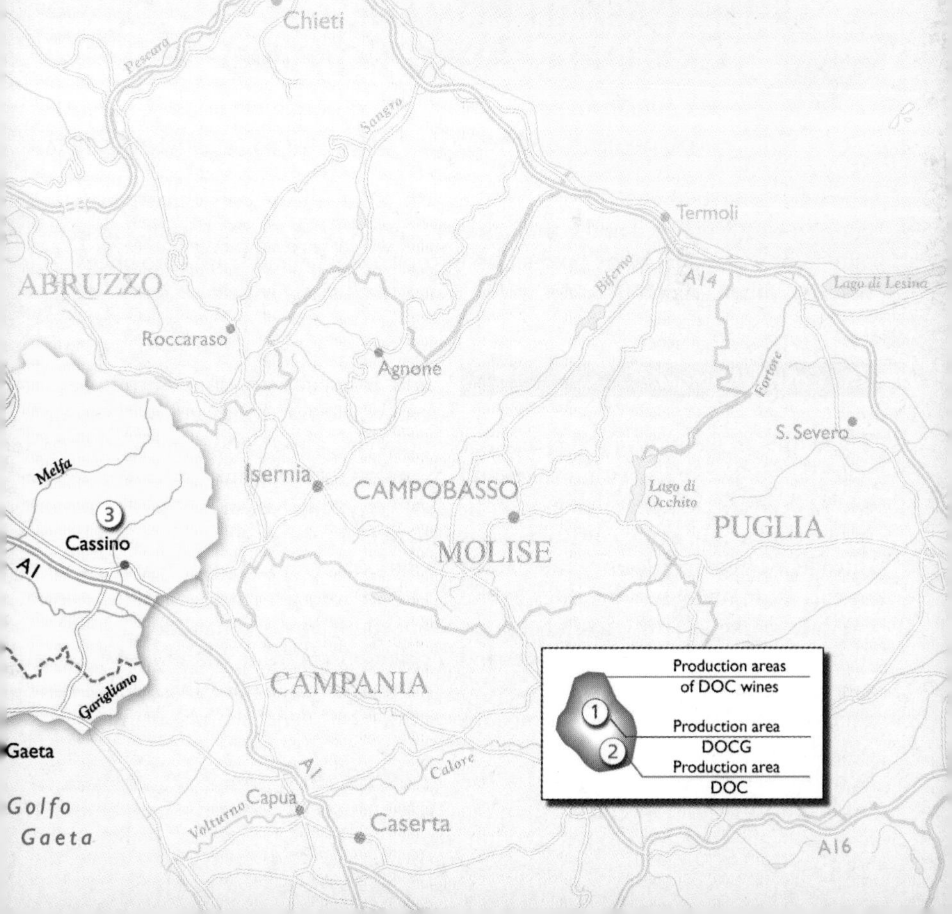

Production areas of DOC wines
1 Production area DOCG
2 Production area DOC

Chieti
Pescara
Sangro
Termoli
Biferno
A14
Lago di Lesina
ABRUZZO
Roccaraso
Agnone
Fortore
S. Severo
Melfa
3 Cassino
A1
Isernia
CAMPOBASSO
Lago di Occhito
PUGLIA
MOLISE
Garigliano
CAMPANIA
Gaeta
Golfo Gaeta
Calore
A1
Volturno
Capua
Caserta
A16

The Great Wines of Latium

Frascati DOC
The emblem of Latium oenology is this white wine made from Malvasia Bianca di Candia and Trebbiano Toscano grapes (70 to 100%). It is a fairly deep straw yellow in color, with a characteristic delicate vinous aroma, and a full, mellow, fine, and velvety taste; alcohol content is 11%. This wine is also produced in the Amabile, Cannellino, and Novello versions (10.5% alcohol) and as a spumante (11.5% alcohol). The most characteristic component of the blend is Malvasia, a grape very common to the Mediterranean area and found in this region in several varieties. The name probably refers to the ancient Greek city of Monemvasia, in the Peloponnese, known for its sweet and aromatic wine exported to Venice in the Middle Ages. Malvasia then became the name for the grapes producing wines with similar characteristics.

Est! Est!! Est!!! di Montefiascone
Trebbiano Toscano, locally known as Procanico, is the protagonist of this wine blend (65%), with additions of Malvasia Bianca Toscana and Rossetto (Trebbiano Giallo). The color is fairly deep straw yellow; the aroma is fine, characteristic, and slightly aromatic; taste is dry (but can also be semi-sweet), full, and persistent. Trebbiano Toscano, outstanding member of a big group of white-berry grapes, is quite flexible since it gives blends a basically neutral flavor component, which here combines well with Malvasia. Latium also features the Trebbiano Giallo variety, locally known as Greco or Rossetto.

THE CASTELLI ROMANI, CIOCIARIA, AGRO PONTINO

Just outside Rome lies the appealing world of the Castelli, amidst villas, gardens, and trattarias, home to wine since time immemorial.

The hills rising southeast of Rome, divided into Colli Albani and Colli Tuscolani but historically grouped under the name of Castelli Romani, are Latium's most important wine zone. Wine production in the Frosinone and Latina provinces is also localized around this area and so is described along with it.

The Castelli Romani

These hills are vestiges of a very ancient volcano whose craters became lakes and whose deposits created soil of extraordinary fertility. Grapevine cultivation was introduced here in ancient times, aided in part by immediate wine sales in the capital's markets. This is a land of great history, dotted with medieval villages and villas, vineyards and woodlands, and it is the traditional destination of excursions outside the city.
White-berry grapes predominate in the vineyards: first and foremost Malvasia and Trebbiano Toscano, both in several varieties, followed by Bellone, Bombino, Greco, and other native types. Among the red wines, prevalent are Cesanese, Sangiovese, and Montepulciano, flanked by some Merlot, Ciliegiolo, and Bombino Nero. The Castelli Romani DOC covers the entire area main output, but there are also outstanding local appellations: Frascati, Marino, Montecompatri Colonna, Colli Albani, Colli Lanuvini, Cori, Velletri, and Zagarolo.

TOURING THE CASTELLI FROM FRASCATI

This itinerary loops through the Colli

Romani zone north of Via Latina, with a side trip to Frusinate.

▪ **FRASCATI.** Set in the Colli Albani facing the capital, this amenable and much-visited part of the Castelli Romani is the site of ancient villas and century-old parks. Villa Aldobrandini (17th C.) is outstandingly ornate and dominates the environs with scenic terraces and play of water in fountains. Not far away are the ruins of *Tusculum*, a very ancient Latin city and later an imperial summer residence, whose destruction in 1191 paved the way for the rise of Frascati. Home to the homonymous DOC, Frascati has over 2500 acres of vineyards: Malvasia di Candia and Malvasia del Lazio, Trebbiano Toscano, and Greco grapes go into making the wine that has made the town known worldwide.

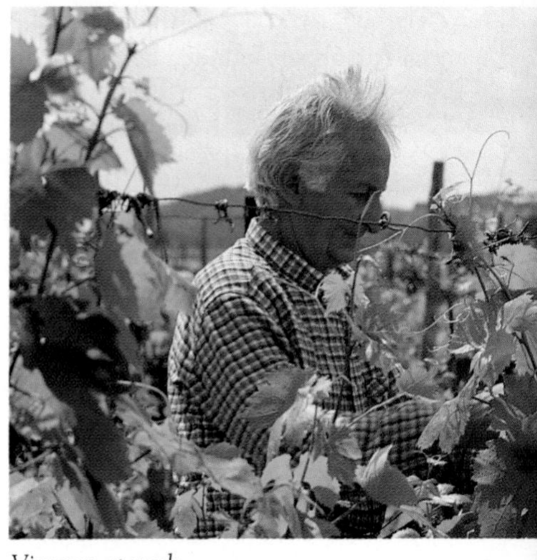

Vigneron at work

Not far to the east are Monte Porzio Catone, with 17th-century Palazzo Borghese incorporating the town gate and part of the walls; Colonna, a town built around the mansion of the powerful Colonna family, erected in the 15th century on the site of a former castle; Montecompatri, midst the vineyards in the heart of the Montecompatri Colonna DOC zone; Zagarolo, home to a DOC, which also spread around a mansion (first belonging to the Colonna family, then to the Pallavicinis) built from the 16th century on upon the ruins of a medieval castle; and Rocca Priora, the highest and most scenic of the Roman *castelli*, located in the Colli Tuscolani.

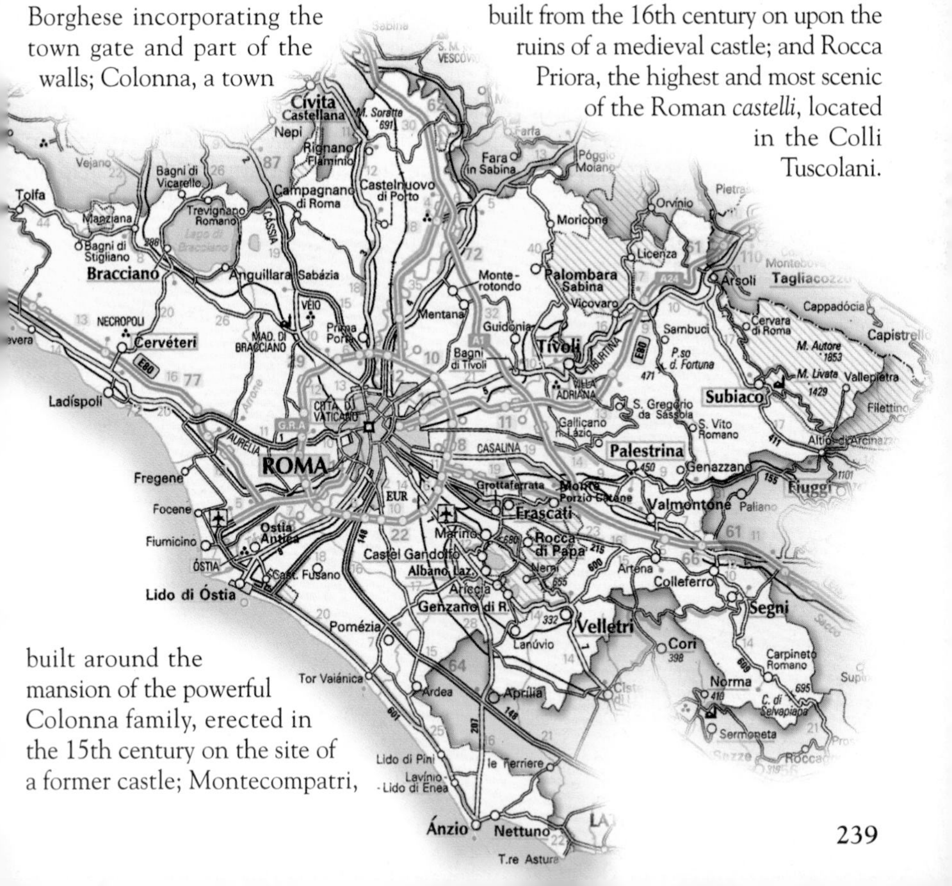

■ **GROTTAFERRATA.** This village grew up around an abbey, founded by St Nilo in 1004 on the ruins of a Roman villa, which in the late 15th century was given a moat and turreted walls.
The abbey, which still is the focal point of the Basilian Order in Italy, has a 13th-century bell tower and contains precious art treasures, including frescos by Domenichino (1610). In the surroundings is an early-Christian cemetery complex (3rd to 5th centuries AD), many of whose burial niches and original frescos are still intact.

■ **MARINO.** Renowned for its DOC white wines, it rises on a spur of peperino rock near Lake Albano. Piazza Matteotti was formerly the site of the ancient Frangipane Castle (three towers remain, incorporated into the present-day houses) and features the Mori fountain, beloved symbol of the city and ingeniously made to spout wine during the annual Grape Festival held in early October.
A scenic route takes you to Rocca di Papa, at 2230 feet of altitude on the flank of Mount Cavo, with its pretty church of the Assunta and its steep, very old Bavarian quarter.

■ **CASTEL GANDOLFO.** Popes had already chosen the Castelli Romani area as summer headquarters before 1625, when Pope Urban VIII commissioned Carlo Maderno his papal palace. The central square hosts the parish church of S. Tommaso, designed by Bernini, with beautiful paintings by Pietro da Cortona. Around it is the walled medieval town.

■ **ALBANO LAZIALE.** The hub of the Colli Albani DOC, this town offers many historical and architectural attractions, from the grandiose remains of the castra Albana gate to the S. Maria della Rotonda church (formerly the nymphaeum of a Roman villa) and the Cisternone, a huge underground cistern from Roman times. The architecture of nearby Ariccia is instead baroque and largely linked to Bernini, who designed its church of S. Maria dell'Assunzione and the mansion of Rome's powerful Chigi family.

■ **VELLETRI.** This town is reached via Genzano di Roma, a Colli Lanuvini DOC wine town (home to a DOP bread and to the famous Infiorata festival held in June), and medieval-looking Lanuvio,

Frascati's Villa Aldobrandini

Bird's eye view of Castel Gandolfo and Lake Albano

center of the same DOC, encircled by turreted walls.

Velletri, hub of the homonymous DOC, rises amidst vineyards on a spur of southern Colli Albani. The town has winding streets and three nerve centers: Piazza Cairoli, with the Romanesque Trivio Tower; Piazza del Comune, with the Town Hall and Archeological Museum; Piazza Umberto I, with the Cathedral and annexed Museo Capitolare (containing a Madonna and Child by Gentile da Fabriano and a prized gold-and-enamel reliquary cross).

Returning to Rome along the scenic Via dei Laghi (Road of the Lakes), you can visit Nemi, the smallest and best preserved of the Castelli Romani.

Towards Ciociaria, an Island of Red

Straddling the border between the provinces of Rome and Frosinone is a large area planted with Cesanese, an indigenous red-berry grape that produces dry and semi-sweet, sometimes fizzy, wines. In blends it teams up with Barbera, Montepulciano, and Sangiovese, with additions of Trebbiano Toscano and Bombino Bianco. The DOC areas combine the vine name with those of the principal production locations: Cesanese del Piglio, Cesanese di Affile, Cesanese di Olevano Romano. Other DOC wines produced in the district are: Genassano and Atina, the latter subdivided into Atina Cabernet (Sauvignon and Franc) and Atina Rosso (the result of an innovative blend based on Sauvignon and Franc Cabernets, Syrah, and Merlot).

In the Frosinone Vineyards

The first part of this itinerary winds on the mountain lower slopes delimiting the Ciociaria to the north, not far away from Subiaco and the places dear to St Benedict. Along the road to Atina, to the southeast and almost on the border with Molise, you can stop at Anagni, city of the popes and of the celebrated Abbey of Casamari, a perfectly conserved jewel of Gothic-Cistercian architecture.

▪ **Anagni.** Along the way you pass through Genazzano, a farming town built on a tufa spur at the foot of the Monti

Wine tasting in the shade in the Castelli Romani

Prenestini, with its scenic Colonna castle (now a museum of contemporary art) and the Gothic Apolloni House. Olevano Romano (a Cesanese DOC appellation) comes next, perched on Mount Celeste and featuring long stretches of surviving cyclopean walls and the close-by magnificent Serpentaria oak forest; then comes Piglio, home to another Cesanese DOC label, rich in medieval buildings (with Giotto-school frescos in the church of S. Rocco).
Remains of the period when Anagni was the "pontifical capital" are some austere medieval houses and palaces (including Pope Boniface VIII's) and the splendid Romanesque Cathedral, standing with its tall, separate bell tower on the top of a hill near the pre-Roman acropolis.

The Agro Pontino Lands

The province of Latina debuted fairly recently on the Latium wine scene: while lacking historical descent, it is currently one of Italy's most interesting and dynamic wine areas. Its enological history began in the 1930s, with the reclamation of the Pontine marshlands, practically virgin land for vines; it was soon "colonized" by Trebbiano, Merlot, and Sangiovese. Through time, despite a significant presence of white wines, the reds began to prevail and fly the banner of local production. The vine-lands are divided into the Aprilia, Circeo, and Cori DOCs.

IN THE LATINA VINEYARDS

This itinerary crosses the Agro Pontino, a wide plain lying between Monti Lepini, Colli Albani, and the Tyrrhenian shore, winding along the national road from Rome to Terracina and passing through the main sites of reclamation, new towns built on the farming land recently wrenched from the swamps.
Surviving wetlands of environmental interest are the Pontine lakes and the Circeo promontory, protected by the Circeo Regional Park.

■ **LATINA**. On the way to the provincial capital you can stop off in Aprilia, a rural town founded in 1936 (on April 25th, hence the name) and production center for the homonymous DOC in an area within the wider Castelli Romani DOC. Another place of interest is Cori, located on the slopes of Monti Lepini in the DOC zone bearing its name; it conserves the polygonal walls dating from the 5th century BC, medieval Via del Porticato, and the Temple of Hercules (1st C. BC), all located in Cori a Monte, on the top of a panoramic hill.
Littoria, one of the first cities built on the former Pontine swamps, changed its name to Latina in 1945 and is now Latium's second largest city in population and one of the region's busiest in commerce and industry. Piazza del Popolo, fulcrum of the city's concentric structure,

is surrounded by interesting examples of austere 1930's architecture.

■ **SABAUDIA.** This town lies within the boundaries of the Circeo National Park and along the sandy and dune-covered shoreline of the homonymous lake. Built in 1934 in the just-reclaimed lands of the Agro Pontino, it is one of Italy's most organic, interesting examples of rational city planning.
Close by is San Felice Circeo, an elegant resort on a scenic ledge of the Circeo promontory. It features many intriguing marine grottoes (one of which, according to Homeric legend, was inhabited by the sorceress Circe).

Wineries *pp. 448-449*
Acuto, Anagni, Cori, Frascati, Grottaferrata, Latina, Marino, Monte Porzio Catone, Rome, Serrone, Velletri

■ **TERRACINA.** On the southeastern edge of Agro Pontino, at the foot of the Monti Ausoni, this city has a wealth of monuments attesting to its millennia-old past: from the Temple of Jove Anxur (a very ancient Volscian sanctuary) to Roman ruins and the medieval core with the Duomo, an ancient Roman temple converted into a Christian church.

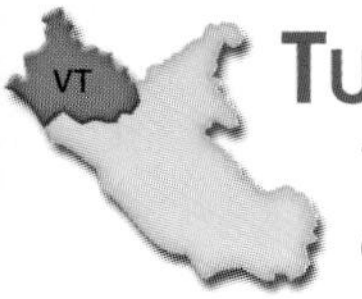

VT

TUSCIA AND THE COLLI DELLA SABINA

The northern part of the region, marked by the Tiber valley, offers wine-lovers great points of interest.

Administratively outdated, the term Tuscia effectively describes the vine district found in the province of Viterbo and the northwestern portion of Rome's. This territory is tied to Etruscan history and to very ancient viticulture, combining wine enjoyment with the pleasures of the natural and cultural beauties of one of the most interesting areas in central Italy.

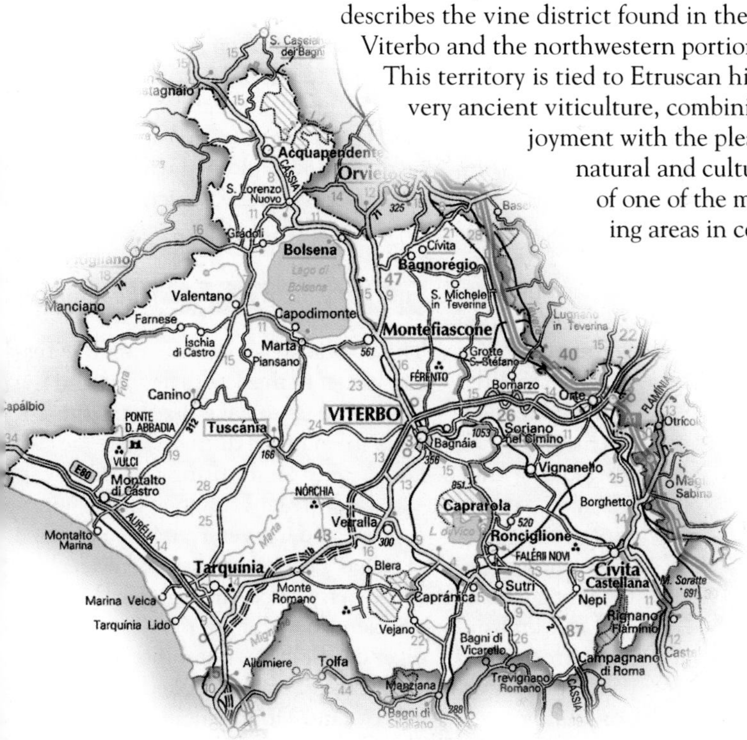

From Lake Bolsena, Est! Est!! Est!!!

The volcanic terrain surrounding Lake Bolsena offers a habitat quite favorable to the vine. There is a net predominance of white grapes with Trebbiano (Toscano and Giallo varieties), Malvasia di Candia, and Malvasia del Lazio. The result is the champion of Viterbo wines, Est! Est!! Est!!! di Montefiascone. Among the red wines Aleatico is worth a mention – in Gradoli production is covered by a specific DOC. Both zones are part of the broader Colli Etruschi Viterbesi DOC.

AMONG THE TIBER VALLEY HILLS

Leaving Viterbo, the route circles Lake Bolsena, runs along the regional border and takes in a good part of the Tiber valley.

▪ **VITERBO**. The historical capital of upper Latium (formerly Tuscia) is a city rich in atmosphere on the old pilgrimage route to Rome. Encircled by turreted walls, it offers memorable sights, especially the Cathedral of S. Lorenzo and the 13th-century Palazzo dei Papi, site of papal conclaves and other important events. The medieval quarter is splendid.

▪ **MONTEFIASCONE**. A must for wine tourists is the church of S. Flaviano containing the tomb of German baron Johann Defuk, who in the early 12th century coined the expression "Est, Est, Est" about the local wine, so good that he drank too much of it and it proved fatal to him. Anecdotes aside, the historic town overlooking Lake Bolsena is worth a visit for its beautiful architecture, including a domed Cathedral and a fortress with panoramic views. Continuing north

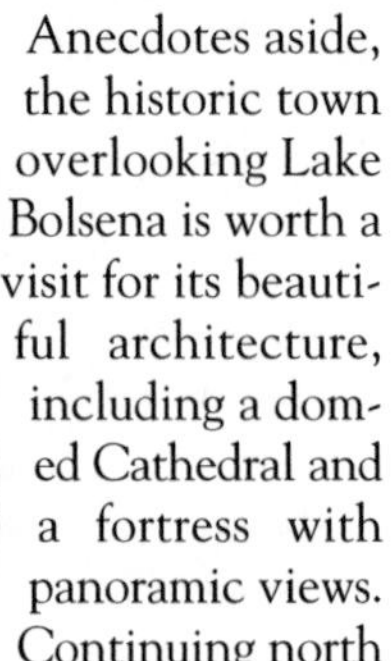

Viterbo's Barabbata

the route leads you first to Bagnoregio, on a tufa spur east of the lake, and to ancient Civita, an image of emblematic loveliness perched on an eroded rise. You then get to the lakeshore in Bolsena, with its pretty Romanesque church of S. Cristina. Finally, you reach Gradoli, a medieval town adorned with 16th-century Palazzo Farnese, which offers wine-lovers its Aleatico DOC.

From Tarquinia to the Colli Cimini

The coastal area (running from the Tuscan border to the Tiber's mouth) and the hinterland up to Lake Bracciano are Tuscia's second wine district. There are two DOC zones legitimizing the "Etruscan Vineyards" title: Tarquinia, in the Viterbo area, and Cerveteri, in the province of Rome. Here the undisputed leaders are white-berry grape Trebbiano and Malvasia, blended with minor varieties like indigenous Bellone, Bombino, Tocai, and Verdicchio. Among the red wines, Sangiovese and Montepulciano go hand in

hand with Canaiolo Nero and native Cesanese. Tarquinia and Cerveteri are the district's DOCs.

IN THE ETRUSCANS' VINEYARDS

This loop itinerary starts from Viterbo on Via del Tirreno, passes through Cerveteri, and re-enters the provincial capital past the Bracciano and Vico lakes.

■ **TUSCANIA.** A small town encircled by medieval walls, it lies in the isolated landscape of Valle del Marta, on the southern rim of the Monti Volsini. Just outside of it two gems of religious architecture shine: the splendid Romanesque churches of S. Pietro and S. Maria Maggiore. The necropolises and the Archeological Museum exhibits testify to the great Etruscan past of this land.

■ **TARQUINIA.** The present town, medieval in appearance and bristling with towers and old churches, is the heir to Etruscan Tarxuna, which once stood quite close by. Welcoming visitors is the 15th-century Palazzo Vitelleschi, a worthy home for the treasures unearthed by archeologists. S. Maria di Castello (13th century, with a splendid mosaic pavement) is in the oldest part of the town. Tarquinia gives its name to the DOC grape cultivations on the coast and in good part of the hinterland down to Rome.

■ **CERVETERI.** Past Civitavecchia and Renaissance Forte Michelangelo (designed by Bramante, Giuliano da Sangallo, and Michelangelo himself) you come to Cerveteri, extremely powerful in Etruscan times, when it owned three ports along the coast. Testifying to its importance are an extensive archeological area and the remains kept in the local museum, housed in the medieval fortress. The church of S. Maria and 16th-century Palazzo Ruspoli look onto the castle courtyard.

■ **BRACCIANO.** Rising on a cliff on the Monti Sabatini lower slopes and facing the lake, this town is dominated by the imposing 15th-century Orsini Odescalchi castle. The courtly scenes in its frescos and the view from the scenic sentinel's round will remain long in your memory after visiting this castle, one of Latium's most beautiful and well-preserved examples of military architecture.

Going back towards Viterbo you come to Sutri, a town full of history, starting with its Etruscan origins, and Ronciglione, charming medieval village on the outer slope of the volcanic crater of Lake Vico. In the environs, the Lake Vico Nature Reserve protects beautiful scenery and Caprarola, which is home to the late Renaissance splendors of Palazzo Farnese.

The Abbey of Vulci, home to the National Museum

Towords the Colli della Sabina

Along the Umbrian border, the Tiber flows past hills with a good wine tradition. In fact, the initial vineyards around Viterbo are an offshoot of Orvieto. The subsequent vineyards of the Colli Etruschi Viterbesi DOC, spread on both banks, are followed by the Vignanello and Colli della Sabina DOCs.

THE SABINE VINEYARDS ALONG THE TIBER

This itinerary follows the Tiber course from the Umbrian border down to the Monti Sabini, which run southwards on the left side of the river from Rieti to the Aniene.

▪ **CASTIGLIONE IN TEVERINA.** This village overlooks Val Tiberina in one of its most scenic points, not far from pleasant Lake Alviano. You can visit the 16th-century Rocca dei Monaldeschi (fortress) and the lovely church of Madonna della Neve. Close as it is to the Umbrian border, this is Orvieto land, and the wine produced is from dry to sweet in taste.

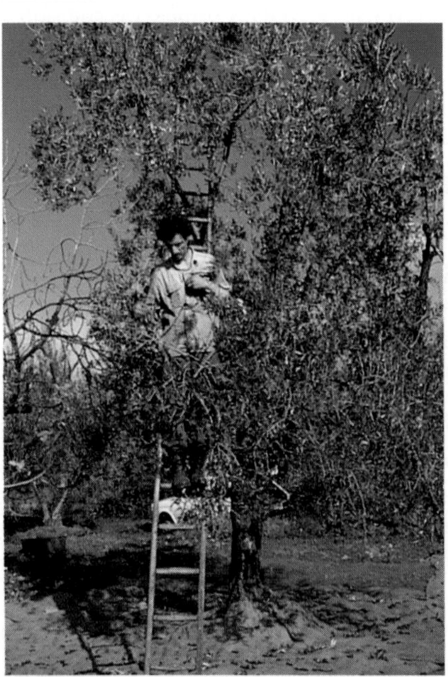

Olive picking in the Sabina area

Wineries *pp. 448-449*
Castiglione in Teverina, Cerveteri, Civitella d'Agliano, Montefiascone

Civitella d'Agliano, presently owning a specific IGT appellation, is a scenic wine town overlooking the spectacular Valle dei Calanchi.

▪ **BOMARZO.** Traveling down the Tiber valley you pass through Bomarzo, with its famous 16th-century Park of the Monsters (kids will have fun, too!), and Soriano nel Cimino, a town with a medieval atmosphere.
Just south is Vignanello, at the center of the homonymous DOC, a village with lovely views, characteristic little streets, and rural traditions. Further down the valley you enter the vineyards of the Colli della Sabina, the only DOC zone in the Rieti area.

▪ **CIVITA CASTELLANA.** It stands on a tufa ledge flanked by the gorges of two tributaries of the River Treia near the latter's confluence into the Tiber. The Cathedral's façade and bell tower date from 1210, the town's foundation year; its portico, the portal, and two internal pluteuses are precious cosmatesque works of art. The fortress, designed by Giuliano da Sangallo at the end of the 15th century and home to the Archeological Museum, surrounds a lovely courtyard with a frescoed portico.
The route continues towards Capena, hometown to the Bianco Capena DOC; it conserves a medieval nucleus and the remains of the Italic Lucus Feroniae settlement. Fara Sabina is a village lying on the top of a hill in a very panoramic position.
Just further on is the Farfa abbey, a major cultural and religious center in the Middle Ages and source of prized illuminated manuscripts.

Specialties in Latium

IN LATIUM, heterogeneous elements combine to paint a particularly lovely picture: a long coastline with seaside towns and resorts; a hinterland partly conserving typical Maremma vegetation or otherwise characterized by the tidy layout of reclaimed lands; further inland, the hills of volcanic origin, quite favorable to farming, especially on the shores of the lakes; finally, the Apennine mountains, with rushing waters and untouched scenery just 60 miles from Rome. Given this varied landscape, it is easy to imagine the variety of foodstuffs to choose from, particularly in Rome. From Rome's and Tuscia's farmlands come artichokes, broccoli, and produce of all types. From the Colli Albani, Ariccia *porchetta* (roast pork), Genzano homemade bread, and Nemi strawberries. From the Tyrrhenian Sea, but also from the lakes and the rivers, come the fish to stew and bake. From the mountains, lamb and beef meat, cold meats and *pecorino* cheese, mushrooms and truffles. The Sabina and Viterbo areas offer an excellent olive oil and Gaeta premium table olives.

HOWEVER HISTORY-LADEN and cosmopolitan it may be, Rome invites you to eat "alla romana", according to the local tradition. Trattorias continue to serve common-folk dishes like spaghetti seasoned with olive oil, garlic and red pepper, or even more simply with cheese and pepper, or offer richer fare like *bucatini alla carbonara*, made with bacon, cheese, and eggs to amalgamate the whole. The same earthy variety is found among entrées: baby lamb or *saltimbocca*, veal stew or oxtail ragout, salted cod or pike, artichokes or chicory sprouts.

However, the exuberance of the capital's cuisine should not keep you from exploring the rest of the region. Viterbo and Latina are on the coast and therefore devotees to seafood. The former is also influenced by the cuisine of Maremma (where boar is a specialty) and offers in the inland potion of its province Lake Bolsena fish and robust meat and game preparations from Monti Cimini. Latina, on the other hand, has a strong dairy tradition, and its buffalo mozzarella is a foretaste of Campania. Further inland are Rieti and Frosinone, with typical farmer and mountain cuisine; outstanding examples are to be found at Amatrice (in the heart of the Apennines), with its famous *bucatini all'amatriciana* (pasta with pork cheek, pecorino, and red pepper) and at Cassino, home to *maccheroni alla ciociara* but also to dishes of Neapolitan descent.

WINES OFFER A GREAT assortment of whites – from Frascati to Est! Est!! Est!!! di Montefiascone – to go with delicate hors-d'oeuvres, risottos and vegetables, baked fish, and fresh cheeses like *provola* and buffalo mozzarella. Red wines – from traditional Cesanese to Sangiovese and more recently introduced Merlot – accompany more important first courses, stewed fish and meat dishes typical of the region: baked spring lamb, chicken *alla cacciatora*, *saltimbocca alla romana* (rolled veal with prosciutto and sage). Aged Roman *pecorino* and red meat call for vintage wines, including the region's good Cabernets.
When dessert arrives, the surprise is Frascati Cannellino, sweet and fruity in taste, or rare Aleatico di Gradoli, a red of unusual aroma.

Abruzzo and Molise

The Grand Vineyard of Montepulciano

Encouraged by the enthusiastic worldwide reception accorded to its Montepulciano, Abruzzo is greatly investing in wine tourism. The Molise region appears a bit more isolated, though interesting from the wine offer point of view.

Abruzzo's Jump in Quality

Abruzzo was, until just a short time ago, considered a region whose vineyards were principally suited for producing blending wines. Over the past few years, instead, the percentage of bottled wine has significantly increased and its quality has also shown an important improvement. Production, 80% of which is in the hills

Above, Abruzzo countryside; left, the Bojano Gate of Saepinum *(top) and Molise country landscape (bottom); opposite, fields in the Teramo area*

along the coast, above all in the province of Chieti, has become more exacting, with rigorous choices of varieties and cultivation techniques most suited to each single estate, while cellar practices have evolved and taken into account the most innovative technology and methods for high quality wine.
Montepulciano is the single most important variety to be cultivated, to all extents and purposes 50% of the overall total. It is an eclectic grape, giving a wine to be drunk quite young in the Cerasuolo version, a red wine of great personality if aged for a couple of years in barrels, and a dessert wine in the passito version. It is the fifth DOC wine in Italy's production ranking. It is followed in the regional hit parade by Trebbiano Toscano and Trebbiano d'Abruzzo, used together for the second ranked regional DOC. A series of more recently planted grapes then follows: Chardonnay, Pinot Bianco, Pinot Grigio, Riesling Italico, Riesling Renano, Traminer, Cabernet, Merlot, and Pinot Nero. These are used for innovative wines, recently grouped together in the Controguerra DOC. There are also 9 IGT productions.

MOLISE, A TERRITORY TO DISCOVER

The viticulture of Molise, which goes all the way back to pre-Roman times, is not of primary importance in the regional economy. The nearby presence of the sea and the gentle hills immediately inland give an excellent olive oil, and the limited presence of the vine therefore must be a result of other historic and economic factors. It is, nonetheless, a fact that vineyards appear only in the lower valley of the Biferno river, in the vicinities of the Adriatic coast, and on the Apennine ridges, in the basins of the Trigno and Volturno rivers, where they are part of a mountain agriculture. The vineyards, although containing a great number of different traditional varieties, are dominated by red-grape Montepulciano, which on its own accounts for 64% of the total surface. If one adds Sangiovese and white-berried Trebbiano d'Abruzzo and Trebbiano Toscano the total rises to 85%, a demonstration of a massive influence from outside the region. In terms of the regulatory structure, Molise has three DOC zones – Molise, Biferno, and Pentro d'Isernia – and two IGT areas: Osco or Terre degli Osci and Rotae. This is also a sign that, even if total production is small, there is a notable commitment to improvement of the wines and of overall tourism.

Abruzzo's and Molise's DOC zones

ABRUZZO

❶ **DOCG Montepulciano d'Abruzzo Colline Teramane**

❷ **DOC Controguerra** *Bianco, Chardonnay, Malvasia, Moscato, Passerina, Riesling, Passito Bianco, Spumante ▪ Rosso, Cabernet, Ciliegiolo, Passito Rosso, Merlot, Pinot Nero*

❸ **DOC Montepulciano d'Abruzzo**

❹ **DOC Trebbiano d'Abruzzo**

IGT - Typical Geographic Indication

Alto Tirino (L'Aquila); Colli Aprutini (Teramo); Colli del Sangro (Chieti); Colline Frentane (Chieti); Colline Pescaresi (Pescara); Colline Teatine (Chieti); Del Vastese or Histonium (Chieti); Terre di Chieti (Chieti); Valle Peligna (L'Aquila)

MOLISE

❶ **DOC Biferno** *Bianco ▪ Rosato ▪ Rosso*

❷ **DOC Molise** *Chardonnay, Falanghina, Greco Bianco, Moscato, Pinot Bianco, Sauvignon, Trebbiano ▪ Rosso, Aglianico, Cabernet Sauvignon, Sangiovese, Tintilia*

❸ **DOC Pentro di Isernia** *Bianco ▪ Rosato ▪ Rosso*

IGT - Typical Geographic Indication

Osco or Terre degli Osci (Campobasso); Rotae (Isernia)

The Great Wines of Abruzzo

Montepulciano d'Abruzzo
Although it bears the same name as the Tuscan town of Montepulciano, the most representative wine of the region actually comes from grapes of unknown origin. Common in central Italy, this vine has its cradle in the regions of Abruzzo and Molise; in recent years it has significantly expanded southwards, the same as Sangiovese, Montepulciano's ideal blend complement. The two red-berried grape varieties are the base for the best regional production, the Montepulciano d'Abruzzo Colline Teramane DOCG (90 to 100% Montepulciano, 0 to 10% Sangiovese), a deep ruby red wine with light purple and orangey nuances, strong and characteristic aroma, dry, full and velvety taste; it goes very well with red meats and game. Montepulciano is also popular in a version called Cerasuolo, obtained by pink vinification.

Trebbiano d'Abruzzo
The main region's white wine is a blend of Trebbiano Toscano and Bombino Bianco, locally known as Trebbiano d'Abruzzo. The first and undisputed star of the central-southern oenology probably was *Tribulanum*, a wine which the roman author Pliny mentioned as a product of the Naples area – this would confirm the hypothesis of its eastern Mediterranean basin origin.
The resulting wine is straw yellow in color, with a light aroma, a fairly high alcoholic content, a neutral taste which acquires personality when blended with grapes of a stronger character such as Malvasia. This blend gives a wine that can be enjoyed throughout the meal, especially if based on fish.

THE TERAMO REGION

TE

A specific Montepulciano d'Abruzzo label and the innovative Controguerra DOC wines are the foundations of Teramo's oenology.

The northernmost of Abruzzo's provinces has two reasons for oenological distinction: the Colline Teramane sub-denomination, within the group of the DOC wines from the Montepulciano d'Abruzzo's region, and the exclusive Controguerra DOC wines, which come from the small area around the town bearing the same name and a few neighboring municipalities. The first reason highlights the great value of traditional production; the second one is the proof of the participation in new wine-making trends, according to which blends are varied through additions of imported grape types or of ancient local varieties (such as white Passerina, known since the Roman times). DOC production is implemented, in a wide hilly area, by the Colli Aprutini IGT, with generic or varietal labels.

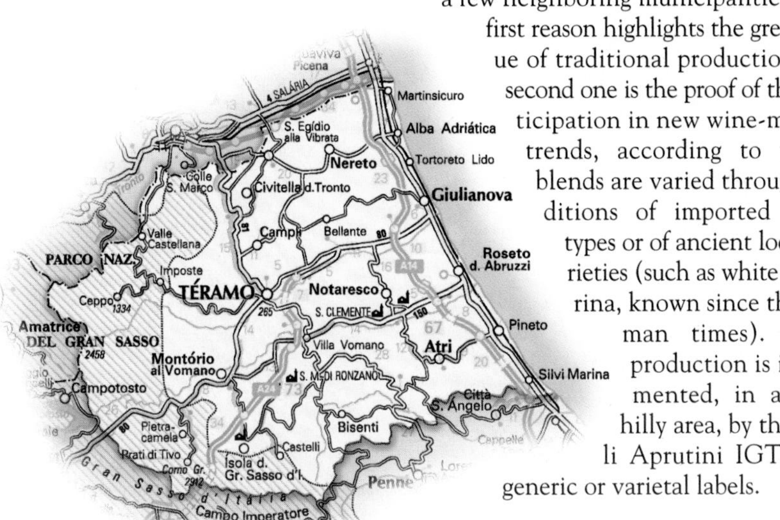

From Val Vibrata to the Vomano Valley

This area is covered by two regional DOCs: Montepulciano d'Abruzzo, which reaches excellence in the Colline Teramane IGT, and Trebbiano d'Abruzzo. The Controguerra DOC production is also of special interest and is limited to the municipality bearing the same name and to the centers of Torano Nuovo, Ancarano, Corropoli, and Colonnella.

The Controguerra and Colline del Ducato Route

This itinerary goes up from the Adriatic coast to the vine covered inner-land of Val Vibrata. From Torano Nuovo you proceed towards localities of historical and artistic interest such as Civitella del Tronto and Teramo, along the beautiful Aprutino-Picena road.
A second route is named after the Ducato d'Atri, which once ruled over the lands bathed by the Vomano river. These are places still dotted with medieval villages and solitary churches and are renowned for their wine and oil production.

■ **Alba Adriatica.** This lively seaside town at the mouth of the Vibrata stream invites visitors to getting to know the food and wine flavors of Abruzzo's northernmost wine district. Like the neighboring town of Martinsicuro, by the mouth of the Trigno river, it has been awarded a Blue Flag for unpolluted seawater.

■ **Colonnella.** Perched in a splendid position on a hilltop, the town has interesting monuments, testimonies of a 1300-year old history, which began when *Truentum*, a busy market center at the mouth of the Tronto river, famous for its purple fabrics, was destroyed. A characteristic flight of steps leads to the Old Town, dominated by a church and a clock tower.

■ **Controguerra.** The only tower left from the old Palazzo Ducale is a reminder of the tormented history of the town that gives its name to the latest of Abruzzo's DOCs. Controguerra wine is made either from Montepulciano, Cabernet Sauvignon, and Merlot – a blend which enhance smoothness – or, on the white wine side, from Trebbiano and Chardonnay grapes.
In mid-summer this town is host to a food festival featuring traditional pasta and grilled meat.

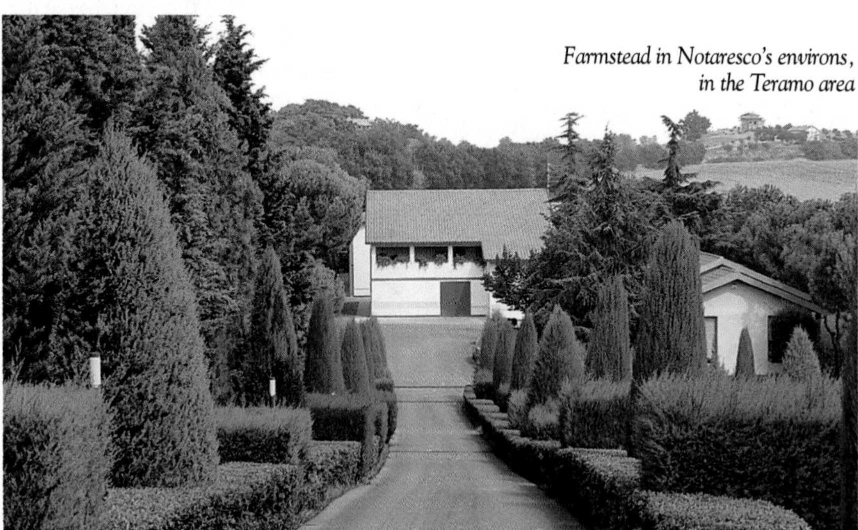

Farmstead in Notaresco's environs, in the Teramo area

Isola del Gran Sasso, on the lower slopes of Gran Sasso d'Italia

■ **CIVITELLA DEL TRONTO.** Passing through Corropoli (with its nice square adorned by a big fountain of 1837), Nereto, and Torano Nuovo (another Controguerra DOC center which is the venue to an August food festival) the route continues on to Civitella del Tronto.
This town sits on a hill in a magnificent position, commanding a view of both the mountains and the sea. Here you can admire a 16th-century fortress together with medieval and Renaissance buildings. On the way to Teramo a brief detour takes you to Campli, a town with several noble medieval buildings.

■ **TERAMO.** Then the route gets to the provincial capital, a mostly modern town though its old section is rich in historical atmosphere. Here wine is well matched with tasty country-style cuisine, which is somehow considered the base of Abruzzo's gastronomy.

■ **GIULIANOVA.** A well-known seaside resort and fishing port, it has a long beach stretching as far as the mouth of the Tordino river. In the upper part of town, lying on a low hill, you can visit the 15th-century Duomo.
Crossing the Tordino river you come to Notaresco, a farming town once host to a castle and now site of the famous church of S. Clemente al Vomano: the only remainders of the old Romanesque building (1108) are the portal and the altar with a prized ciborium.
The shoreline road to the left of the river quickly takes you to the lovely complex of S. Maria di Propezzano, with a church and a cloister painted with Romanesque-Gothic frescoes, and then to renowned Roseto degli Abruzzi, which has a pretty beach with pine groves and very clean seawater – the same can be said for Pineto, on the other side of the Vomano mouth.

■ **ATRI.** From Pineto, a detour along a scenic road brings you back through the hills to Atri, built around a superb Cathedral in Istria stone. This is one of the most impressive churches in Abruzzo, consecrated in 1223 and finished in 1305.

Wineries *pp. 450-452*
Castilenti, Colonnella, Controguerra, Notaresco, Roseto degli Abruzzi, Sant'Omero, Torano Nuovo.

THE PESCARA AND L'AQUILA REGIONS

The Pescara valley, crossed by Via Tiburtina, is the point of contact between two very different wine areas: the Adriatic hills and the Apennines.

The province of Pescara is not different from the others, in so far that the Montepulciano and Trebbiano d'Abruzzo DOC wines are the undisputed stars. As for the former, the valleys above Torre de Passeri are probably where the vine originated: a theory which seems to be born out by a production so exceptional that it deserved the specific Montepulciano Terre di Casauria denomination.
The province of L'Aquila is the furthest inland and the most mountainous; space for vineyards is limited but the quality of wines does not suffer from that at all. On the contrary, the mountainous part is particularly favorable to Montepulciano, especially in its Cerasuolo type, which gets elegant and delicate aromas from the temperate-to-cold climate.

From the Sea to the Mountains

The Montepulciano and Trebbiano d'Abruzzo DOCs cover most of the wine production of the region's central part. Traveling through it, however, the visitor's attention focuses on local wines that bring out native grapes. The Colline Pescaresi IGT, for example, devotes specific labels to the Cococciola, Maiolica, Mostosa, and Pecorino varieties. In L'Aquila's province the same can be said of the Alto Tirino IGT (23 varietal labels) and of the Valle Peligna IGT (9 varietal labels).

THE COLLINE APRUTINE AND THE UPPER PESCARA VALLEY WINE ROUTE

The first route proposed here is a circuit around the cities of Pescara, Penne, and Loreto Aprutino. The trip will take place along the Valle del Tavo and the Piceno Aprutina roads; those wishing to get closer to the Gran Sasso massif will take the Forca di Penne national road. Various detours lead to other places of historical, artistic, and scenic interest.
The second possible itinerary is across the upper Pescara valley, along Via Tiburtina, and L'Aquila's wine district, with a possible extension to the regional capital.

▪ **PESCARA.** This beautiful, vibrant, and modern city, which gave birth to the great poet D'Annunzio, is to be considered, from the wine and food point of

A view of Capestrano

view, as a springboard to the inland. Pleasant memories from the town's visit will be the colors of the fishing boats in the canal harbor, the lively promenades, the life testimonials preserved in the museum "Genti d'Abruzzo", and the green of the pine forest dedicated to D'Annunzio.

▪ **PENNE**. You can reach the town by turning inland at Montesilvano Marina, beyond Picciano. Penne is a lovely little town set on four hills between the Fino and Tavo valleys, rich of churches (there are seven of them in the historical center not counting the Cathedral), mansions, houses, towers, and loggias dating from the medieval and the baroque periods. The surrounding landscape is formed by small towns set on hilltops and by the far-away peaks of the Gran Sasso massif. Close by, instead, you find the Penne Lake Reserve, a noteworthy bird-watching site. From Penne a detour leads into the Apennines passing through the towns of Farindola, Montebello di Bertona, and Carpineto della Nora.

▪ **LORETO APRUTINO**. The next stop on this wine tour is at Loreto Aprutino, which is reached by descending from Penne through an open and hilly landscape of vineyards and olive groves. The town preserves some ancient buildings (such as the parish church and the monastic church of S. Maria in Piano, to the south) and a historical museum on Abruzzo's pottery.

▪ **PIANELLA**. This is a town of medieval origins, still enclosed by the walls against which some of the houses have been built. Just out of town you can visit the lovely church of S. Maria Maggiore, built in the 12th century. Through hills rich in olive groves and vineyards you can return to Pescara passing through the farming town of Spoltore or go on to Nocciano and Rosciano, with its well-preserved medieval castle.

▪ **TOCCO DA CASAURIA.** The town's name refers to the splendid nearby abbey church of S. Clemente a Casauria, built in the 12th century. In town you can visit the late-Renaissance church of Madonna delle Grazie and the castle. As for wine, noteworthy is Moscatello di Castiglione a Casauria, made from a local ecotype of Moscato and also produced in a passito wine version.
Continuing along Via Tiburtina, just before Popoli – at the edge of the Peligna valley and at the entrance to the Tremonti gorges, through which the Pescara river flows between the Gran Sasso and Maiella massifs – you come to the Abruzzo Apennine road that leads to the province's interior. You can go south to Sulmona, birthplace to the Latin poet Ovid, site of the Annunziata complex, and hometown to renowned *confetti* (almond sweet specialties); or you can go north towards L'Aquila, with a stop at Capestrano, one of the centers of L'Aquila's oenology, belonging to both the Montepulciano d'Abruzzo DOC and the Alto Tirino IGT.

▪ **L'AQUILA.** A city of mountain views and lovely monuments which has survived historical events and many earthquakes. Some monuments are part of the most classic iconography of the region, such as the churches of S. Maria di Collemaggio and S. Bernardino, the 99-Spout Fountain, and the castle.

Wineries *pp. 450-452*
Bolognano, Loreto Aprutino, Nocciano, Ofena, Popoli, Rosciano, Spoltore, Tocco da Casauria.

THE CHIETI REGION

CH

The Chieti region, Abruzzo's most dynamic wine district, is divided into a great number of sub-areas, homogeneous to one another in terms of historical, environmental, and viniculture features.

The province of Chieti accounts for 70% of the region's wine output in the Montepulciano and Trebbiano d'Abruzzo DOCs, as well as in several IGTs accounting for a wide array of wines made from traditional local varieties (Bombino, Cococciola, Passerina, Pecorino, Maiolica, Montonico), from national ones (Aglianico, Barbera, Sangiovese, etc.), and from imported types (Cabernet, Chardonnay, Pinot).

From Chieti to the Sangro Valley

The southern part of the region falls within the spheres of the Montepulciano and Trebbiano d'Abruzzo DOCs, but it has also interesting local wines with the following denominations: Colli del Sangro IGT (Fossacesia, Atessa), Colline Frentane IGT (San Vito Chietino, Lanciano, Roccaraso), Colline Teatine IGT

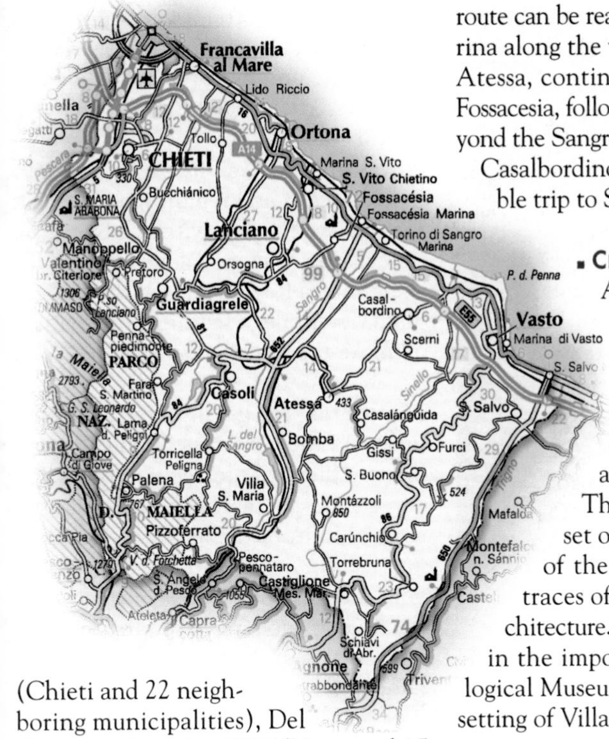

(Chieti and 22 neighboring municipalities), Del Vastese or Istonium IGT (Vasto and 15 neighboring municipalities).

THE COLLINE TEATINE AND THE TRATTURO DEL RE

The Colline Teatine wine route falls within the triangle delineated by Francavilla a Mare and Ortona on the coast and Guardiagrele inland: a wine district of such great interest that setting an itinerary might prove superfluous.
The Tratturo del Re is an ancient pathway to pasturelands going up the Sangro valley. The wine route suggests going from San Vito Chietino to Frisa, on to Lanciano and then to Atessa; the same route can be reached from Fossacesia Marina along the valley road to Piazzano di Atessa, continuing on to Bomba; from Fossacesia, following the coastline and beyond the Sangro river, you can also reach Casalbordino and Vasto, with a possible trip to Scerni in the interior.

▪ **CHIETI.** The road along the Alento valley leads to Chieti from Francavilla al Mare, a town with its historical center set on a hill and maritime district extending towards a lovely beach.
The capital of the province, set on scenic hills to the right of the Pescara river, preserves traces of classic and medieval architecture. Older relics can be found in the important National Archeological Museum immersed in the green setting of Villa Comunale.

▪ **GUARDIAGRELE.** Ripa Teatina, Villamagna, Vacri, and San Martino della Marrucina are possible stops along the way to Guardiagrele, among beautiful sweeping views of the sea or of the Maiella massif, artistic beauties, and a well-kept countryside which is a destination of choice for wine tourists and nature-lovers.
Guardiagrele is a town rich in stone buildings, with picturesque corners and great scenic views. In the museum which is part of the beautiful church of S. Maria Maggiore, of Romanesque origins (the bell tower was built in 1110-1202), you can admire the famous silver cross, a mas-

THE ENOTECA REGIONALE DELL'ABRUZZO

It is located in Ortona, in 17th-century Palazzo Corvo, close to the Aragonesi castle. Founded in 1995, it has 80 participating producers for a total of more than 200 labels selected each year by a special technical committee. On the ground floor are rooms for wine display and tasting, organized like a wine bar. Professional sommeliers welcome and guide visitors, who also have a chance to make good buys. On the upper floors there are a conference room and a classroom for guided tasting and oenology courses.

Blacksmith at work at Guardiagrele

terpiece by Nicola da Guardiagrele (1431), the highest exponent of the illustrious local goldsmith's school.

▪ **ORTONA.** Going back towards the coast you come to Orsogna, a wine town in the middle of the Moro valley; Canosa Sannita, a flourishing food and produce hub that provides quality wine, oil, and fruit; Crocchio, with its museum of artifacts of Abruzzo's Byzantine and medieval periods, housed in the rebuilt medieval castle; Tollo; and Miglianico, another outstanding wine town overlooking Val di Foro, between the mountains and the sea.

Ortona, heir to the ancient Frentani port, displays its curved beaches at the foot of the promontory guarded by the Aragonesi castle, on the edge of a lovely countryside full of vineyards and olive groves. In town you find the Cathedral, built in 1258 and rebuilt after the last war, Palazzo Farnese, with its library, the Cascella Art Gallery, Palazzo Corvo, with the Enoteca Regionale, and the Passeggiata Orientale, a seaside promenade – all make the visit worthwhile.

▪ **LANCIANO.** You get into town with the images of the *trabocchi* still lingering upon your mind (Abruzzo's typical fishing apparatuses are planted like stilts in the sea bed in front of San Vito Chietino) and a taste of the Moscato di Frisa in your mouth (this wine is made around the homonymous town from a local biotype of Moscato).
Lanciano is a lively town, with an older part set atop four hills full of medieval buildings and lovely views. Its industrial and mercantile traditions are very old. The most important monument is S. Maria Maggiore, a church dating from the 13th and 14th centuries, with a magnificent portal.
The Tratturo del Re road goes through the Sangro valley up to Bomba, a town with appealing stone buildings. An alternative road runs from Fossacesia to Vasto along the coast. Near Fossacesia you can visit Gothic-Cistercian S. Gio-

A sea of vineyards at Lanciano

vanni in Venere, one of Abruzzo's most important churches.

▪ **VASTO**. This lovely seaside resort can be reached along the coast past the rocky Penna Point or from inland, via the farming town of Scerni.
Vasto is one of the most interesting towns in the region for its cultural attractions, wine, and food. Worthy of notice are the museums of Palazzo D'Avalos and the castle. A walk along the beach will complement the enjoyment of the local fish soup.

Wineries *pp. 450-452*
Atessa, Francavilla al Mare, Ortona, San Martino sulla Marrucina, Tollo, Vacri, Villamagna.

MOLISE

The region's wine vocation is best revealed in the lower Biferno valley and in the wine districts of the Agnone area and the Volturno valley.

The lower valley of the Biferno river, which flows into the Adriatic Sea just a few miles south of Termoli, is the main wine zone of the Molise region. Its about 950 acres of registered DOC vineyards belong to the province of Campobasso. The best wine estates in this hilly environment gently sloping towards the coast are in the Larino and Guglionesi areas.
From the normative standpoint, the area is covered by the regional Molise DOC, by the Biferno DOC, and the provincial Osco or Terre degli Osci IGT.
The second Molise wine area is inland, in the province of Isernia, and is subdivided into a northern area, around Agnone, with its mountain vines, and a smaller area south-west of the provincial capital, towards the Campania region. Productions are protected by the regional Molise DOC and the provincial Pentro di Isernia or Pentro DOC and Rotae IGT.

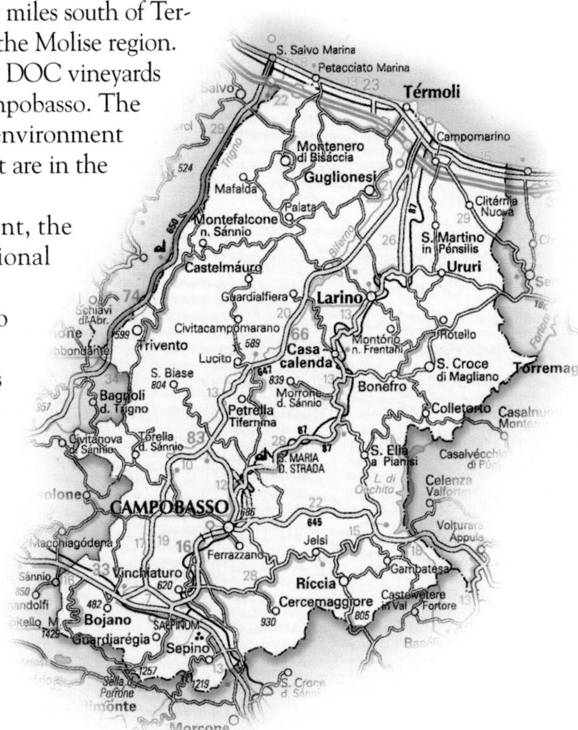

From the Adriatic Sea to the Apennines

Molise is a region yet to be discovered, a sort of virgin territory for tourism, especially as far as its interior is concerned. This also holds true for its wines, produced in a region which can base its future oenological expansion on environmental quality and precious ancient local vine varieties; the first-rate producers in Campomarino are proof to this potentials.

Wineries *pp. 452*
Campomarino.

BETWEEN THE BIFERNO AND TRIGNO VALLEYS

This is a circuit taking in both sides of the Biferno valley. The reference point is Termoli, in the center of Molise's short stretch of coastline; the itinerary can possibly be extended from Larino to Campobasso.
Agnone and the Sannio wine-producing centers can instead be reached by going up the Trigno Valley or down it from Isernia.

▪ **TERMOLI**. This picturesque old town, enclosed in an ellipse of walls and featuring a Romanesque Cathedral as well as a castle, rises on a promontory cutting into the sandy coast. To each side is the modern city, giving on to beaches, with an embarkation port for the Tremiti Islands. Close though far from the beach clamor is the church of S. Antonio – in the homonymous square, center of 19th century urban expansion –, housing a fine civic gallery of contemporary art.

▪ **CAMPOMARINO**. This town is set on a hill covered with vineyards and olive trees, with lovely views which space from the Biferno valley to the Tremiti Islands sea. The old town center, built on the ruins of the Roman Cliterna, retains its medieval structure. Campomarino, damaged by Saracen raids, by wars, and earthquakes, was repopulated in the 15th century by Albanians, whose heritage is evident in the local traditions and dialect. On the square stands the church of S. Maria a Mare with an old crypt adorned with lovely capitals. Campomarino is the standard-bearer of Molise's Biferno DOC.

▪ **LARINO**. Roman remains and medieval sights embellish this farming town, emerging from the green of a hill covered with olive trees on the right-hand side of the Biferno valley. Its pretty gothic Cathedral and Palazzo Ducale testify to its former high rank. Wine and oil are the stars on the tables and in the economy of this town.

▪ **CAMPOBASSO**. From Larino, a winding though very scenic road leads to Campobasso, the regional capital, whose older, medieval part with its steep flights of steps, old streets, and ancient churches rests on a hilltop; below lies the new city, founded in the 19th century.

▪ **AGNONE**. A very ancient town, set on a woody hill overlooking the valley of the Verrino river, a tributary of the Trigno. It has a worthy and still thriving handicrafts tradition and is famous for its bellmakers (visit the Pontificia Fonderia Marinelli, with annexed museum). From Agnone you quickly reach (along fairly winding roads) some small Sannio wine towns, from Belmonte del Sannio to Poggio Sannita to Castelverrino.

Specialties in Abruzzo and Molise

AMONG THE ADRIATIC REGIONS Abruzzo shows most the contrast between the coast and the Apennines, whith the peaks of the Gran Sasso and Maiella massifs. This has influenced administrative organization, with three of its four provinces (Chieti, Pescara, and Teramo) divided between maritime activity and farming, and the fourth, L'Aquila, outstandingly pastoral and mountainous. Connecting the two realities is a comb of parallel valleys covered with vineyards, olive groves, and fields of cereals. The same can be said for Molise, an historical southern appendage of Abruzzo, land of transit towards Apulia and Campania.

THE SAME LOGIC IS FOUND in the way wine and food resources are mapped. First mention goes to the sea, which offers bluefish but is also generous in soup ingredients such as mullet, scorpion fish, and monkfish. Immediately inland, in addition to wine, there is an important output of olive oil and durum wheat.
For the rest, most of the territory is grazing land, which provides fresh meat and is also the source of dairy and cured meats. These products are typically southern: among the cheeses, *caciocavallo*, *scamorza*, *mozzarella*, and *pecorino*; among the cold meats, *soppressata*, and *ventricina*, always spiced with hot red peppers. The Abruzzo and Molise cuisine gets its strength from the earth, its rural cooking consisting of pastas and soups, meats and vegetables, cold meats and cheeses, invariably with chili pepper.
In the seaside towns you find fish broth (also spicy) and fried fish, but no one would ever pass up a plate of *maccheroni alla chitarra*, the real regional celebrity, or lamb with cheese and eggs. Wherever you go, the prevailing wind is always onshore: *fettucine* with *pancetta* and *pecorino* cheese, pasta and beans with trotters and fatback, lentil soup... And then bullock stew, escallops with olives, turkey hen in black pepper seasoning, pork with bell peppers, rabbit *alla cacciatora*, baked trout. Not very well known outside the regions are truffles, especially Molise's, source of a surprising gourmet vein.

AS FOR WINE RECOMMENDATIONS, the first is for Trebbiano d'Abruzzo, to accompany delicate seafood dishes and preparations based on vegetables. Then comes Montepulciano d'Abruzzo Cerasuolo, a claret wine with an outstanding aroma that goes well with cold meats and medium-aged cheeses, fish broths, flavorful first courses, and poultry in delicate sauces. The same wine, vinified in red, covers all the entrées: when young it accompanies roast lamb; mature, roast wildfowl; in the Riserva version, savory meats and cheeses. To be discovered are the wines of ancient tradition, like white Passerina and Pecorino and others of recent introduction, especially Chardonnay and Cabernet Sauvignon. At dessert time, try the red passito wine from Montepulciano grapes and the white passito from Trebbiano. The spumante wines are also very good. Waiting to be tried are the Biferno DOC wines from Molise – white, rosé, and red – limited in quantity but quite well represented.

Campania and Basilicata

Lands of Ancient Wines

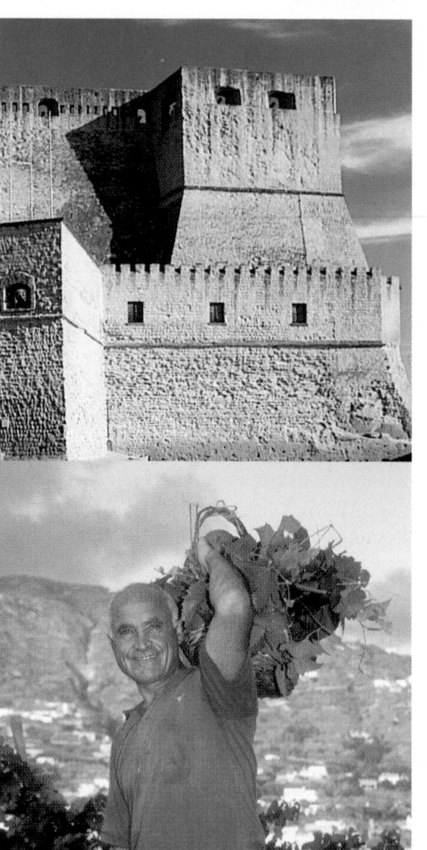

Along with the innumerable points of historic and artistic interest, Campania offers in addition wines whose praises were sung by the ancient Romans and which are an attraction for wine and food loving travelers. Who will also enjoy Basilicata's Aglianico del Vulture.

Campania and Its Great Traditional Patrimony

In all of Italy's regions, viticulture has an ancient history, but only a few places can boast, as Campania can, so enduringly close a link with its own origins. Literary citations are too many to count, and archeological evidence is no less significant. The ancient Romans, when de-

Above, Campania vineyards; left, Naples' Castel dell'Ovo (top) and grape harvest on the island of Ischia (bottom); opposite, Lagonegro's Old Town and castle, Basilicata

scribing what they called *Campania felix* (Happy Campania), were also referring to its refined wines. Among these Falerno excelled, and it has now found new life in the vineyards near the border with Latium, just as we find in present-day Aglianico traces of the ancient *Vitis hellenica* and in Fiano the celebrated *Vitis apiana*. Historically speaking, the most important zone of all is Naples', where the volcanic soils of Vesuvius, Campi Flegrei, and Ischia are in sharp contrast to the calcareous rock of the Sorrento peninsula and the island of Capri. In terms of production, however, first place goes to the inland provinces of Avellino and Benevento, with the fertile hills of Sannio and Irpinia. The viticulture of Caserta is concentrated at the northern end of the region, between the limestone heights of Mount Massico and the extinct volcano of Roccamonfina, while the vineyards at the opposite, southern end of the region, in the province of Salerno, stretch from the Costiera Amalfitana to Cilento. This is a most varied landscape scene, comprising the coastal terraces so much as the inland rolling countryside.

Wine-Making Renaissance on the Wake of Taurasi

The vineyards of Campania are almost entirely on hillsides (71%) or on mountain slopes (15%) and red grapes are of larger significance, with the trio of Aglianico, Sangiovese, and Barbera accounting for 40% of the total vineyard surface. The white Trebbiano Toscano, Malvasia Bianca di Candia, and Greco di Tufo are next in order of importance. There are also small percentages of indigenous grapes with local names: Piedirosso, Falanghina, Sciascinoso, Coda di Volpe Bianca, and Forastera, just to mention the best known. The current tendency is to work on improving the region's native grapes, in particular with a precise mapping of the soils to determine where they can give the most satisfying results. This has effectively worked to the detriment of imported varieties – Italian or foreign – planted in recent decades. In terms of training methods, the traditional *tendone* system, with 41%, is still of major importance, though some variations of the *spalliera* system are gaining in importance. There is still a presence, however, of the interesting ancient *alberata* system, with vine shoots trained high up between supports. A strong desire to re-launch their historical products animates the minds of producers and is reflected in the rapid increase in the number of DOC zones. The pride of the region is the Taurasi DOCG, the first southern Italy wine to win such recognition. It is joined by 18 other DOC areas and various IGT zones. The most striking aspect of this renewed activism are the 70 different types of wines produced, among them spumante, passito, and liquoroso wines. What is interesting is the desire to save from extinction certain wines with a very long history, linked to local grape varieties and old traditions. And in so do-

Vineyards and cultivated fields in the Potenza area; below, harvested Campania grapes

ing, the groundwork is being laid for a new type of wine tourism which deliberately seeks different emotions and looks for them off the beaten track.

BASILICATA: IN THE VULTURE VINEYARDS

A region renowned since ancient times for its green landscape and exceptional cured meats, Basilicata has carved out a place for itself in the field of viticulture as well. Not so much as far as quantity is concerned, considering the small planted surface, but for the tradition associated with Aglianico del Vulture red wine. Already praised by the Romans, Aglianico derives its name from *Hellenica* and, according to that, it should be a grape of Greek or at least Eastern origin. Recently this theory of the Aglianico vine being imported has been confuted by some – the question is now in the hands of paleobotany experts.

There is no doubt, though, that the finest area for the cultivation of Aglianico (the region's sole DOC) is concentrated around Mount Vulture, a mountain of volcanic origin rising at the border with Campania with quite favorable soil and slopes for wine-growing. In the group of regional varieties a couple stands out: Malvasia Nera di Basilicata (5.3%) and Aleatico (5%), which, in spite of their renown, have suffered from the fall in public favor towards sweet red wines. Next in order are grapes from neighboring Apulia and Campania plus more recently introduced grapes such as Chardonnay, Pinot Bianco, Pinot Grigio, Sauvignon, and Merlot, varieties which have enlivened the Basilicata and Grottino di Roccanova IGT productions.

The Great Wines of Campania and Basilicata

Taurasi DOCG – Aglianico del Vulture DOC
Taurasi, the emblem of Campania's oenology, is an exceptionally high-quality red wine made from Aglianico grapes (85 to 100%). It is deep ruby red in color, tending to garnet with possible orangey highlights when aged; it has a characteristic vinous aroma and dry taste, tannic when young, full and balanced with age, with a persistent aftertaste. Its high alcohol content (minimum 12%) and considerable acidity make it suitable for lengthy ageing. It goes well with hearty beef roasts, game, and aged cheeses.
The name of the vine indicates a Greek origin ("Hellenic", hence "Aglianico", term coined during Spanish domination), although recent genetic tests support the hypothesis of a local origin. It has found an ideal habitat in the volcanic soils of Irpinia and Sannio. This may be the grape the Romans used for famous Falerno wine. In Campania it has its own denominations – Taurasi DOCG, Aglianico del Taburno DOC – and a primary role in red-grape blends. Also worth mentioning is white vinification for spumante wines. In Basilicata first-rate production is in the Vulture area.

Fiano d'Avellino DOC
This white wine, already known in the Middle Ages, comes from Fiano grapes (85 to 100%). It is fairly deep straw yellow in color, with intense aroma bearing a note of toasted hazelnuts. Taste is dry and harmonious, alcohol content is 11.5%. This is one of the few Italian whites worthy of some ageing. It goes well with shellfish (even raw) and fish soups, besides being an excellent aperitif. The name of the vine is probably derived from ancient Apiana grapes, so called by the Romans because they were so sweet they attracted bees ("api", in Italian). Fiano is well suited to volcanic soil and is also widely cultivated in the Cilento and Sannio DOCs.

Greco di Tufo DOCG
This white wine from Irpinia (Avellino) comes from Greco di Tufo grapes (85 to 100%) and Coda di Volpe Bianca (0 to 15%). It is straw or golden yellow in color, with clear-cut aroma characterized by hints of peaches and bitter almonds; taste is dry, slight, and harmonious; minimum alcohol content is 11.5%. It is an ideal accompaniment to seafood – grilled fish, fish soup, mussels, and crustaceans – but also goes well with pizza. Greco di Tufo is a member of a large family of Greek vines imported in ancient times. Considering the frequency of occurrence of twinned grapes, it may correspond to the Aminea Gemella vine ("gemella" means "twin" in Italian) described in Latin georgics as growing on the slopes of Vesuvius. It is most widely grown in the province of Avellino, where it also produces a spumante wine. Important productions falls within the Sannio, Taburno, Sant'Agata de' Goti, and Capri DOCs.

CAMPANIA'S AND BASILICATA'S DOC ZONES

CAMPANIA

❶ **DOCG Taurasi**

❷ **DOCG Fiano d'Avellino**

❸ **DOCG Greco di Tufo**

❹ **DOC Aglianico del Taburno or Taburno** *Bianco, Coda di Volpe, Falanghina, Greco, Spumante* ▪ *Aglianico Rosato* ▪ *Rosso, Aglianico, Piedirosso*

❺ **DOC Asprinio di Aversa or Aversa** *Asprinio Spumante*

❻ **DOC Campi Flegrei** *Bianco, Falanghina* ▪ *Rosso, Piedirosso*

❼ **DOC Capri** *Bianco* ▪ *Rosso*

❽ **DOC Castel San Lorenzo** *Bianco, Moscato* ▪ *Rosso, Barbera*

❾ **DOC Cilento** *Bianco* ▪ *Rosato* ▪ *Rosso, Aglianico*

❿ **DOC Costa d'Amalfi** *Bianco* ▪ *Rosato* ▪ *Rosso*

⓫ **DOC Falerno del Massico** *Bianco* ▪ *Rosso, Primitivo*

⓬ **DOC Galluccio** *Bianco* ▪ *Rosato* ▪ *Rosso*

⓭ **DOC Guardia Sanframondi or Guardiolo** *Bianco* ▪ *Rosato* ▪ *Rosso, Aglianico*

⓮ **DOC Ischia** *Bianco, Biancolella, Forastera* ▪ *Rosso* ▪ *Piedirosso or Per'e Palummo*

⓯ **DOC Penisola Sorrentina** *Bianco* ▪ *Rosso*

⓰ **DOC Sannio** *Bianco, Coda di Volpe, Falanghina, Fiano, Greco, Moscato, Spumante Classico* ▪ *Rosato* ▪ *Rosso, Aglianico, Barbera, Piedirosso, Sciascinoso*

⓱ **DOC Sant'Agata de' Goti** *Bianco, Falanghina, Greco* ▪ *Rosato* ▪ *Rosso, Aglianico, Piedirosso*

⓲ **DOC Solopaca** *Bianco, Falanghina, Spumante* ▪ *Rosso, Aglianico*

⓳ **DOC Vesuvio** *Bianco* ▪ *Rosso*

IGT- Typical Geographic Indication

Beneventano (Benevento); Colli di Salerno (Salerno); Dugenta (Benevento); Epomeo (Naples); Irpinia (Avellino); Paestum (Salerno); Pompeiano (Naples); Roccamonfina (Caserta); Terre del Volturno (Caserta)

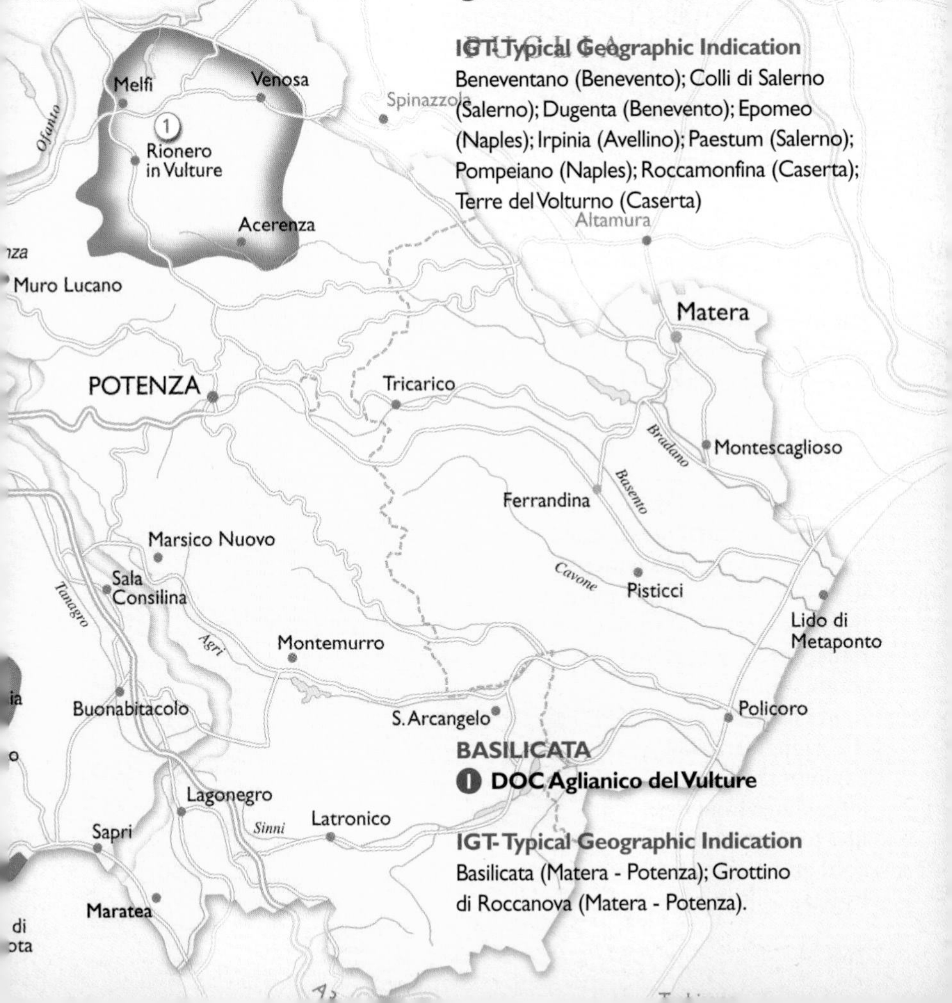

BASILICATA

❶ **DOC Aglianico del Vulture**

IGT- Typical Geographic Indication

Basilicata (Matera - Potenza); Grottino di Roccanova (Matera - Potenza).

NAPLES, THE ISLANDS, AND THE SORRENTO PENINSULA

From Vesuvius to Ischia and from Sorrento to Capri, the Bay of Naples is a wine-tourism scene truly unique in the world.

The Bay of Naples can be considered the birthplace to world viticulture. Were literary references not enough, tangible proof can be found in Pompeii's villas and in their wine cellars. This is a region that even today, despite the encroaching metropolis, plays a primary role in Campania's winemaking: limited in area but significant for the variety and traditional value of its output.

The Vineyards on Volcanic Soil

The focal point for Neapolitan wines is the Vesuvio DOC, covering the slopes of the volcano and protecting a long-famous wine, Lacryma Christi, today being significantly re-launched. Also benefiting from volcanic soil are the Campi Flegrei DOC, in the western part of the gulf, and the Ischia DOC, which together with the Epomeo IGT covers the region's largest island.
Paradoxically, Ischia has a mountain-type viticulture, a legacy from the time when, fearful of pirates, the inhabitants took to the hills and dug wine cellars in the tufa rock. The Pompeiano IGT is province-wide (Ischia excluded).

FROM NAPLES TO THE CAMPI FLEGREI AND ISCHIA

The Campania Wine Tourism Movement distributes a thick guide to the region's wineries, with six itineraries accompanied by the addresses of restaurants, hotels, and craft shops. One of the routes focuses on the capital, another explores the Campi Flegrei area from Posillipo to Pozzuoli and Bacoli, and a third takes you by ferry to Ischia.

■ **NAPLES.** The former capital of the Kingdom of Two Sicilies is universally known for its bay, for Vesuvius, for its architecture, and for the charm of its working-class quarters with their marketplaces and narrow streets – reminiscent of the Orient – emblematized in Spaccanapoli. It is a city full of history and art: the most important testimonies to the past are Castel Nuovo (or Maschio Angioino – Angevin Fortress), the oldest nucleus of the royal palace, commissioned by Charles of Anjou. Of major interest are the churches of Santa Chiara (with its cloister of the Poor Clair nuns) and San Lorenzo Maggiore, the Duomo, the treasures in the National Archeological Museum, the paintings and porcelain of the Capodimonte collections.

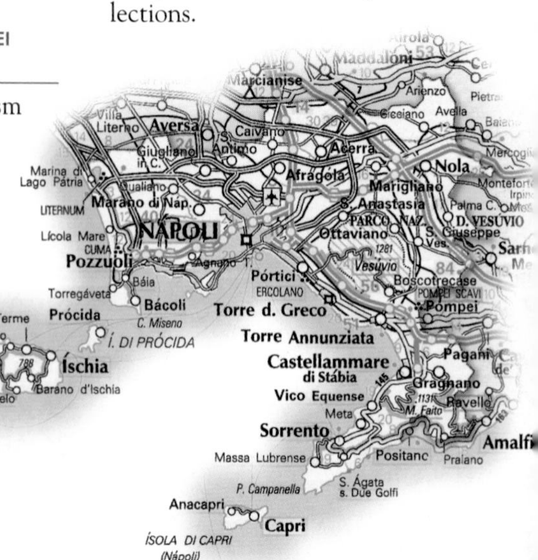

Vineyards around Quarto, in the Campi Flegrei region

Incredible but true, Naples still has various vineyards, some of great historical importance such as those of Posillipo or of the Certosa di San Martino – the charterhouse, built in 1400, and its splendid garden have recently been restored. Fairly close by is Pompeii, the world-famous city buried in ashes when Vesuvius erupted in 79 AC; it also features the Madonna del Rosario Sanctuary, destination of pilgrimages.

▪ **POZZUOLI**. This is the tourist hub of the Campi Flegrei area, a land characterized by amazing volcanic phenomena and old-time legends, where archeology and wine tourism are exciting attractions. Of Roman Puteolis remain a splendid amphitheater and the *macellum*, or city market, whose sea mollusk-embedded columns testify to the up-and-down seismic movement of the land.
Nearby is Bacoli, a famed seaside resort. In the environs, dotted with deep blue lakes and verdant hills, are important remnants of Imperial times, including the so-called Tomb of Agrippina, actually a patrician villa.

▪ **ISCHIA**. Main center of the homonymous island – reached by ferry from Naples and Pozzuoli –, this is a charming town, adorned with whitewashed and colored houses lining the crater lake, converted to a harbor by Bourbon king Ferdinand II, and with a dense pine forest stretching down to the beach. Outstanding among its many points of historical-artistic interest are the Aragonese Castle, the Cathedral of the Assunta, the parish church of S. Maria di Portosalvo, Palazzo del Seminario, and the collegiate of Spirito Santo.
Then you are off to explore the island,

Ancient millstones at Pompei

Sunrise on Vesuvius

along a wine route leading to Forio d'Ischia and Mount Epomeo. At the center of two headlands, between delightful beaches and luxuriant vineyards, the former village is the hub of Ischia's wine production and also an intact old settlement with alleyways, churches, and watchtowers.

Sorrento's Cliffside Terraced Vineyards

From gentle volcanic slopes to dolomite limestone walls: this is the contrasting Neapolitan landscape. The Sorrento Peninsula, an Apennine spur running down to the sea, is sculpted in rock, with villages hugging its ridges and terraces, laboriously cultivated with vines and citrus trees. This difficult terrain is home to three great traditional Campania wines: Lettere, Gragnano, and Sorrento, nowadays recognized as sub-zones of the Penisola Sorrentina DOC.
Capri is on the horizon, an island offshoot of the ridge; although farming has been abandoned, there are about 100 acres of vineyards left, protected by the homonymous DOC.

THE SORRENTO PENINSULA AND CAPRI

From Castellammare di Stabia to Sorrento and Punta Campanella (about 19 miles in all) – and, beyond, to enchanting Capri – you find yourself in one of the loveliest parts of the Italian coast, in a sequence of sights immortalized by artists and poets.

▪ **SORRENTO**. The historical center, lying on a ledge of the peninsula, is a jewelbox of scenic views and traditional arts and crafts. Its foodstuffs are famous: walnuts, tomatoes, citrus fruits, olive oil, wine, and cheeses, especially the so-called *provolone del monaco*. There are also many fine restaurants.

▪ **CAPRI**. Little tufa and limestone houses with terraced roofs, loggias, and arcades; winding narrow lanes lined with elegant shop windows: reached from Naples or Sorrento, Capri combines Mediterranean charm with a skillful touch of international refinement. The spirit of the place is condensed in its famous Piazzetta, with open air cafes and the bustle of tourists from all over the world. All around it, interesting history remnants and natural wonders.
Villa Jovis, the Faraglioni, the Blue Grotto... absolute musts in a "pilgrimage" around the island. Wine tourists will be delighted to taste the products of Mount Solaro vignerons.

Wineries *pp. 452-455*
Bacoli, Forio d'Ischia, Quarto, San Sebastiano al Vesuvio.

SANNIO AND IRPINIA

The hilly interior, truly surprising in its woodlands and varying scenery, is the region's biggest wine zone.

The hills farther inland, stretching between the Benevento and Avellino provinces, form the largest of Campania's vine-lands, accounting for nearly two-thirds of regional production. The most outstanding wine is Taurasi, first DOCG wine of southern Italy, but these verdant lands also have many pleasant surprises in store for the wine aficionado.

Benevento, Leader in Campania Wine

The Benevento's Sannio district is a dynamic and technologically in the vanguard wine-growing area, with vineyards in evolution and very well equipped cellars. This province is the engine for the whole region's wine sector, accounting for 40% of the output. A role reflected on the normative level, with total protection of the finer wine zones – two longstanding DOCs, Solopaca and Aglianico del Taburno; the more recent Guardiolo and Sant'Agata de' Goti DOCs; and the new province-wide Sannio DOC. There are two IGTs: Beneventano and Dugenta (in the municipality of the same name).

THE SANNIO VINEYARDS

The reference point of the route (described in detail in the *Il turismo del vino in Campania* guide) is Sannio. From there you go north along the Due Principati road (national route no. 88), leaving it a few miles later for the Telesina road no. 372, that follows the course of the Calore river. Possible detours lead to the most interesting and picturesque wine-producing centers: among others are Ponte, Paupisi, Torrecuso, Campoli del Monte Taburno, Solopaca (with its own DOC), Castelvenere, and Guardia Sanframondi.

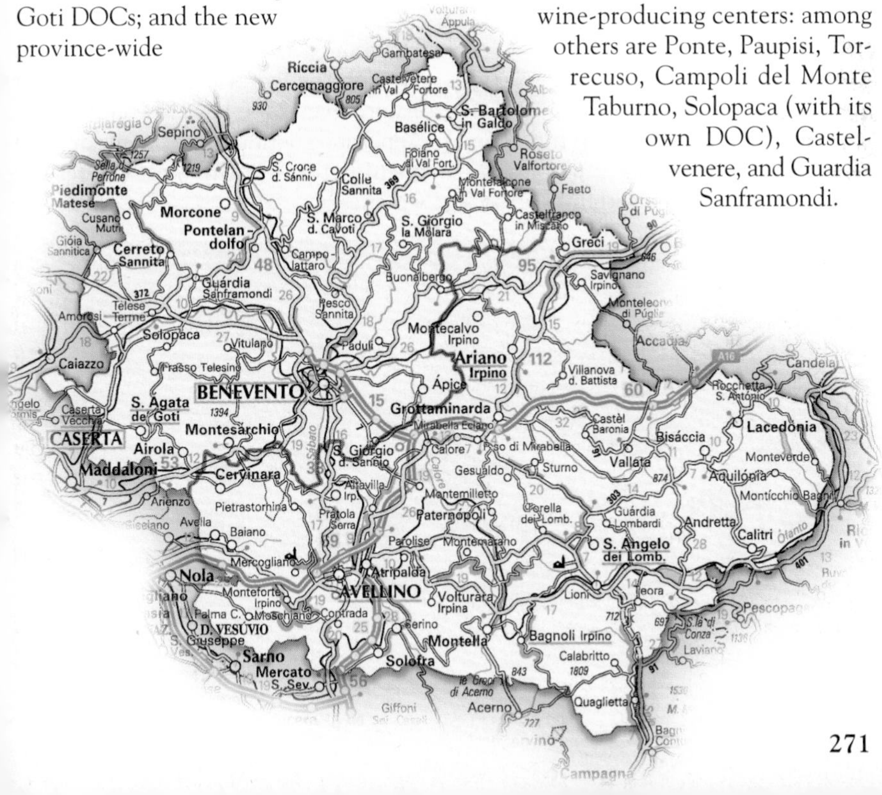

Benevento. A city of legendary origin on the banks of the Calore river, despite earthquakes and bombardments during WWII it still has important monuments and a noteworthy Archeological Museum housed in the cloister of Romanesque S. Sofia. Benevento is the focal point of Campania's most important vine-lands and home to the Enoteca Provinciale del Sannio: centrally located, this has two charming rooms where about 50 people can dine. The wine list has approximately 300 labels, with updated selections of Campania and national wines, besides a very long list of spirits (including famous Strega liqueur). The kitchen offers a good variety of typical dishes and products.

- **Sant'Agata de' Goti.** This ancient town merits a special mention for its DOC wine as well as for its history. The name comes from a colony of Goths who, defeated in the Battle of Vesuvius in 553, were allowed to remain here as Imperial subjects. A few miles away is Dugenta, a wine town with specific IGT production.

The Lush Lands of Taurasi

Irpinia, that is to say the Avellino province, is the roughest zone in Campania – two-thirds are covered with hills, the rest with mountains – with a quite cool climate (to be that south, that is) and vineyards framed by luxuriant woods.

Local viticulture accounts for a fifth of regional production and is excellent in quality, thanks to vines of longstanding tradition: Aglianico, which gives a DOCG-worthy red in the Taurasi zone, and two whites whose legal denominations link their names to the major production zones, Fiano di Avellino and Greco di Tufo. The Irpinia IGT is province-wide.

Wineries *pp. 452-455*
Atripalda, Castelvenere, Cesinali, Chianche, Foglianise, Guardia Sanframondi, Lapio, Manocalzati, Montefredane, Montefusco, Montemarano, Montemiletto, Ponte, Salza Irpina, Sant'Agata de' Goti, Serino, Sorbo Serpico, Taurasi, Torrecuso, Torre le Nocelle, Tufo.

Green Irpinia

The route begins in Avellino and winds through the valleys of the Sabato and Calore rivers. You leave the city on Via Appia and continue along it, making frequent detours to the most interesting wineries.

Benevento countryside

AVELLINO. Modern in look, it lies in a green basin of the Sabato valley, ringed by mountains. Fragments of the old Norman foundations can be seen between the Cathedral and the castle ruins.
From Avellino it is a quick drive to Atripalda, with first-rate wineries, and to Sorbo Serpico, a fortified town amidst hills covered with vines and olive trees, with an excellent roster of vignerons. Further north are Pratola Serra, a farming municipality within the Fiano d'Avellino DOC encompassing several villages (some with old buildings), and Altavilla Irpina, a wine town characterized by lovely buildings from the Campania Renaissance period.

TUFO. A small town whose reputed homonymous wine is celebrated in mid-September by the Greco di Tufo Wine Festival. From the fortress, the most evident remnant of the Lombard period, the view encompasses the Sabato valley vineyards. Also overlooking the valley and providing a spectacular view of the Partenio mountains, is Palazzo Di Marzo, headquarters of the homonymous winery. Not far away are Montefusco, noted for its embroidery handicraft and for the old castle, and Petruro Irpino, with lovely scenic views of woods and vineyards.

TAURASI. Set in the Calore valley, this is Aglianico's elective home – vinified pure, it produces the first, and up to now only, Campania DOCG wine. The town's old center retains the features of a fortified medieval settlement.

A grape composition on a float at Solopaca

LAPIO. The itinerary ends here, in the choicest land for both Fiano di Avellino and Taurasi. Featuring a baronial dwelling with a high square tower, the town is located on a hill surrounded by vineyards, olive groves, and orchards.

CASERTA AND THE TERRA DI LAVORO AREA

In ancient times the Romans were delighted by Falerno, which is presently the emblem of a new viticulture trend valorizing most genuine traditions.

Caserta's province contributes the least to regional output, yet it is hardly to be disregarded. Quite on the contrary. Nearly on Latium's doorstep, between the Massico limestone hills and the cone of the extinct Roccamonfina volcano, lies a wine zone of historical renown, joined by production on the Caserta plain.

The Terra del Lavoro Wines

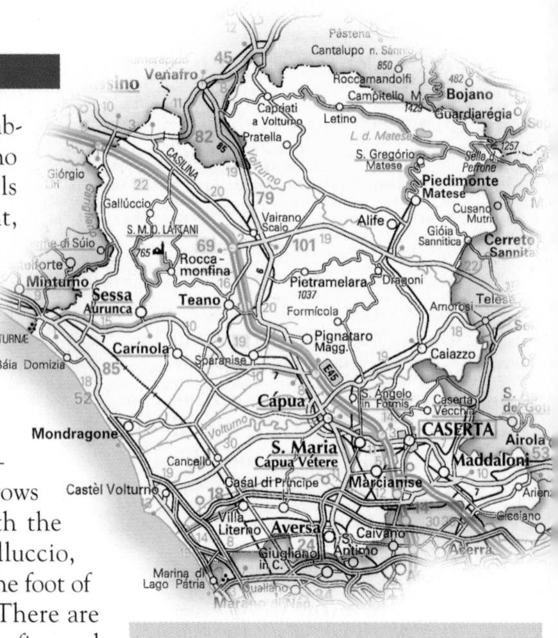

Ages before any DOC was established, the Romans kept Falerno in amphorae marked with seals of guarantee. Its descendent, Falerno del Massico DOC, combines the best Campania grapes with exceptionally suitable soil. Along with Falerno are two wines that DOC protection have saved from oblivion: Asprinio, an exceptionally dry white – whose grapes are grown amid rows of trees, shoots mingling with the branches of poplars – and Galluccio, whose vines are cultivated at the foot of the Roccamonfina volcano. There are two IGTs in the area: Roccamonfina and Terre del Volturno.

Wineries *pp. 452-455*
Aversa, Caiazzo, Castel Campagnano, Cellole, Galluccio, Mondragone, Sessa Aurunca, Teverola.

In the Falerno Vineyards

This route runs from the Caserta plain to the hills on the border with Latium, following the directions given in the *Il turismo del vino in Campania* guide, which describes the itinerary in detail.

▪ **Caserta.** One cannot miss a tour of the Reggia – the huge 18th-century marvelous royal palace that Vanvitelli designed for the Bourbons of Naples – and of the medieval Old Town (Caserta Vecchia). Nearby Capua and Santa Maria Capua Vetere are also highly recommended for their archeology value, baroque art treasures, very good wine and food.
Aversa is another attraction in the area, visited for its Norman Cathedral and the maze of lanes in its old center. A satellite town is Teverola, a rural center with very old wine traditions; it is a specific producer of Asprinio.

Caserta's countryside

▪ **Sessa Aurunca.** You can get to this town from Aversa along the coast via Mondragone, beyond the River Volturno mouth and at the core of old Agro Falerno (hence the wine's name), and then veering inland. This town features an old part with a medieval layout and various noteworthy monuments (especially the Romanesque Cathedral and the semi-interred portico from the 1st century BC). The last part of the route runs inland along the western slope of the extinct Roccamonfina volcano to Galluccio, at the center of its own DOC.

CILENTO AND THE COSTIERA AMALFITANA

The Salerno vine-lands, the largest in the region but least inclined to DOC production, have their emblem in the steep Amalfi vineyards.

The province of Salerno has the largest area planted with vines in the region (almost a third of the total) and, on the other hand, the smallest percentage of DOC wines (4.5%). This is due to its rough terrain, as much on the Amalfi coast (the famed Costiera Amalfitana) as in Cilento, which means patchwork vineyards and a lack of functional cultivation. Every cloud has a silver lining, though, and it is precisely because of its harshness that this territory has remained intact and its resources are just waiting to be valorized. Fine wineries are few, but their labels are the most pleasurable discovery of a journey through Campania.

Salerno's Grapes and Wines

The most characteristic image of Salerno viticulture is found in the Costa d'Amalfi DOC, where vines grow together with lemon trees on terraced cliffs dropping straight to the sea. The most common varieties are flanked by local ones, which give the final product unmistakable accents – peaks of excellence are to be found in the Furore, Ravello, and Tramonti sub-zones.

The Cilento DOC covers one of the loveliest landscapes in the region. Mountainous terrain hinders extensive cultivation, but important wineries are present. Most of the provincial output falls under the Castel San Lorenzo DOC, a hilly area sloping towards the Calore river, with clay soil quite good for quality grape-growing. In addition to local varieties, Barbera and Moscato can be found here and there. Colli di Salerno and Paestum are the names of the two IGTs.

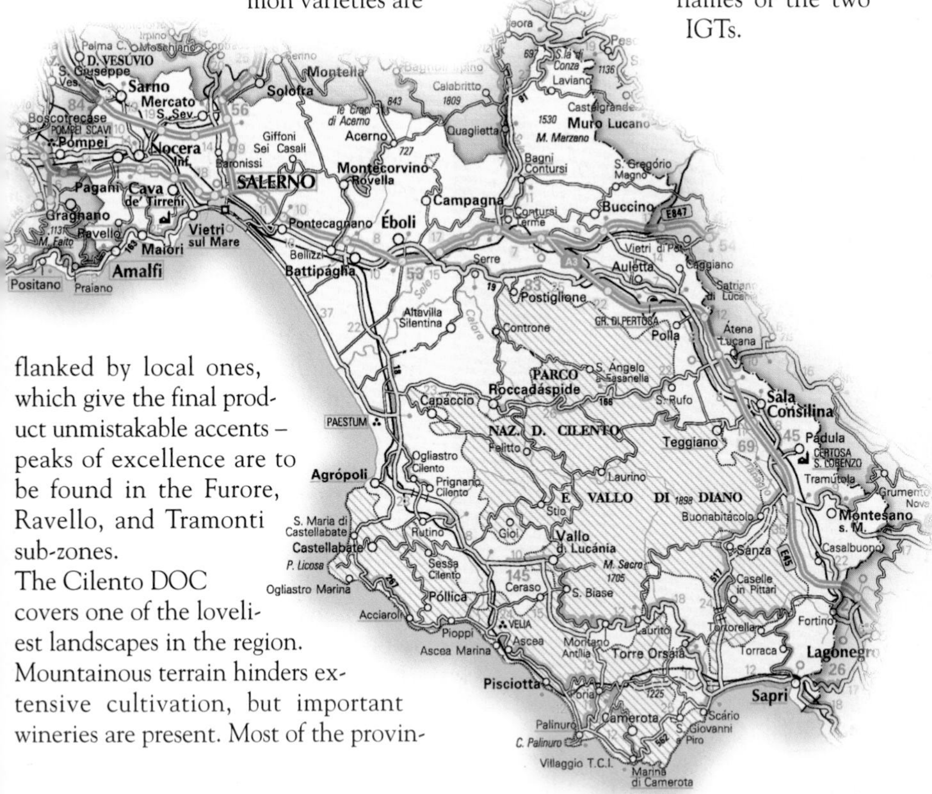

From Amalfi to the Cilento Park

The *Il turismo del vino in Campania* guide describes two wine and gastronomy routes departing from Salerno, which present the province's viticulture from different viewpoints. The first one explores the Costiera Amalfitana, while the second follows the shoreline south, beyond the Sele plain (the land of delicious buffalo-milk mozzarella), heading to Cilento.

▪ **Salerno**. The modern districts that first greet the visitors to Salerno soon make way for a lovely old center gradually leading up the slopes of the hill. After visiting the splendid Cathedral, which blends Arab and 18th-century motifs, and strolling along Via dei Mercanti, you prepare your palates for the delectable wine and food to taste in town and along the Costiera.

▪ **Amalfi**. The best route for the wine tourist coming from Salerno is a tightly-curved road that, passing through vineyards and olive groves, links the various rural municipalities of the Tramonti valley, famous for their wines and basket-weaving. The most traditional wine here is Tramonti Rosso Costa d'Amalfi DOC, whose grapes have been grown on terraces high above the sea since the time of the Maritime Republic. Going down you pass through Ravello, a romantic and rich-in-culture coastal resort, whose Arabian-style building recall the once-fervid trade with the Levant. Its ancient legacy is evident in the Duomo and villas (among which famous Villa Ruffolo), which peeking through umbrella pines and cypresses command the most beautiful scenic views in this part of the world. Every summer a Wagner Festival takes place here.

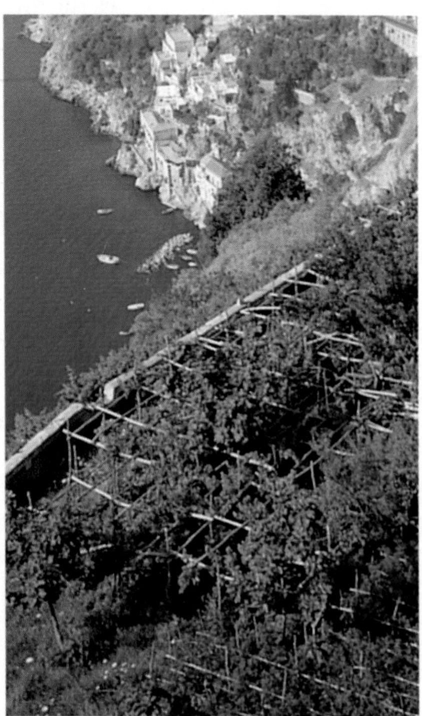

A view of the Costiera Amalfitana

Wineries *pp. 452-455*
Castellabate, Furore, Montecorvino Pugliano, Prignano Cilento, Rutino, San Cipriano Picentino.

Amalfi is so famous there is little to add: you stroll along its splendid promenade and visit the Cathedral, flanked by the famous Cloister of Paradise.
From here a scenic road climbs to the Agerola highland and descends to Furore, with gorgeous views of the sea and vineyards, then returns to the coast to reach Positano and its whitewashed houses and Sant'Agata sui Due Golfi, whose enchanting position is described by its name.

▪ **Paestum**. Going south from Salerno this is the first not-to-be-missed cultural stop, probably southern Italy's premier archeological center and one of the best of the all of Magna Grecia: its Doric temples are second only to the Theseion in Athens. The largest of them is dedicated to Poseidon and was built in 450 BC. The Archeological Museum is outstanding.

■ **AGROPOLI**. The ancient core of this town of probable Byzantine origin is intact, as are much of its walls with a 17th-century gate. Worthy of visiting are the Angevin-Aragonese castle, on the summit of the headland, and the coastal watchtower dedicated to St. Francis (16th C.), just west of the marina. From Agropoli you make a detour inland towards Prignano Cilento, site of first-class wineries. Then back to the coast to climb to Castellabbate, an old town in the National Cilento Park also renowned for its wineries. The itinerary ends in Marina di Camerota, a seaside resort on a stretch of coast rich in olive trees.

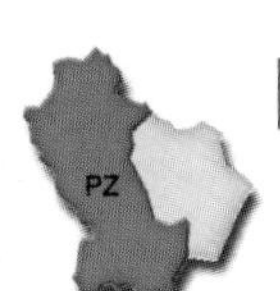

BASILICATA

Aglianico del Vulture is the emblem of a region whose tourism draws are uncontaminated nature and traditional tastes.

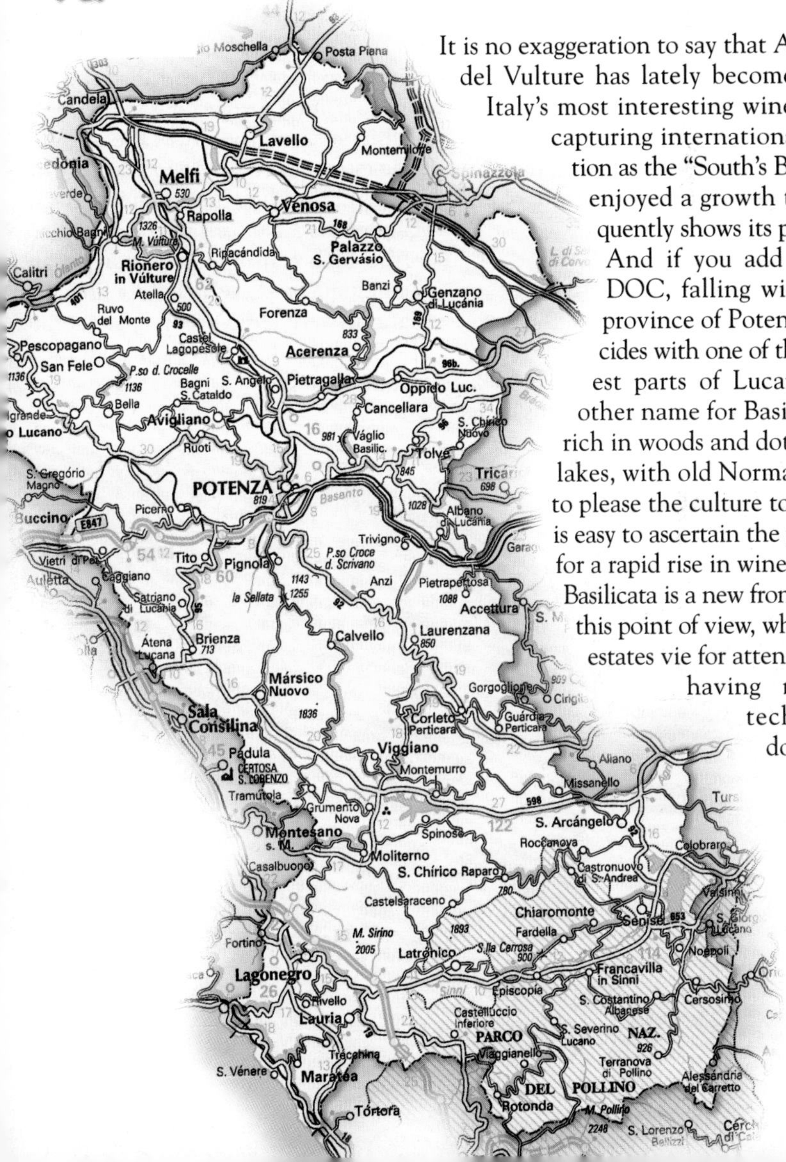

It is no exaggeration to say that Aglianico del Vulture has lately become one of Italy's most interesting wines. After capturing international attention as the "South's Barolo", it enjoyed a growth that eloquently shows its potential. And if you add that its DOC, falling within the province of Potenza, coincides with one of the loveliest parts of Lucania (the other name for Basilicata) – rich in woods and dotted with lakes, with old Norman towns to please the culture tourist – it is easy to ascertain the potential for a rapid rise in wine tourism. Basilicata is a new frontier from this point of view, where wine estates vie for attention and, having mastered technology, do so with quality wines.

From Vulture to the Pollino Massif

Aglianico del Vulture, Basilicata's only DOC wine, comes from the northern part of the Potenza province, the hub of production being Rionero in Vulture. A second wine zone in the southern area, at the foot of the Pollino Massif, is covered by the Grottino di Roccanova IGT and involves the municipalities of Roccanova, Castronuovo di Sant'Andrea, and Sant'Arcangelo. There is also a regional Basilicata IGT, with about thirty varietal wines.

IN THE LANDS OF AGLIANICO

This itinerary loops through the innermost part of the region. The route runs entirely within the province of Potenza but can also be followed coming from, or going to, Matera, a must on a tour of Lucania.

▪ **POTENZA.** It rises at an altitude of over 3000 ft on the crest of a hill in the upper Basento valley, dominating a wide mountain landscape. While modern in look, the city retains its old center in its higher part, with a Cathedral, several churches, and the provincial Archeological Museum, containing relics from prehistory to Roman times that are good documentation of Lucania's ancient past.
From here you take national Apulo-Lucana route no. 93, joined a bit further on by a scenic road leading to the Lagopesole castle (1242) and Atella. Further east is Acerenza, high on a cliff in the Bradano valley and visited for its French Romanesque-Gothic Cathedral built in 1080.
From the oenological point of view, however, the main targets of this tour are Rionero in Vulture, a time-weathered town between two hills (and departure point for excursions to the Monticchio lakes on the site of the old Vulture crater), and Barile, a renowned wine town still retaining the customs and language of the Albanians who settled there in the 15th century. Its best sights are the monumental 15th-century Steccato fountain and, close by, an agglomerate of original cellars carved in tufa rock, still in use today.

Matera's Sasso Barisano

Olive trees in the lands of Potenza

▪ **MELFI.** On the way is Rapolla, a spa resort spread on a hillside in a maze of little streets, with the church of S. Lucia (Norman-Byzantine in style) and the originally Romanesque Cathedral. Melfi stands on a volcanic hill at the foot of Vulture, with a big square castle and a Cathedral with 13th-century bell tower. This town was an important bishopric and a residence dear to Norman kings. The castle, home to Swabian king Frederick II, was the site of four papal councils and from here Urban II proclaimed the beginning of the First Crusade. It now hosts the National Archeological Museum, with material from the Melfi area dating from the 8th century BC on.

▪ **VENOSA.** On the way to Venosa from Melfi you can make a detour to Lavello, a farming town on a spur of the Tavolato delle Murge, overlooking the Olfanto river, with a well-conserved medieval nucleus.
Venosa descends from the Roman *Venusia*, a colony along Via Appia whose remains can be seen in the archeological park just outside of town. In addition to the park, worth visiting is the medieval abbey of SS. Trinità, one of the most unusual religious complexes in southern Italy: in the builder's plans the old church should have been incorporated by the new one, but the latter remained unfinished, consigning only its imagined beauty to posterity. You can also stroll along Corso Vittorio Emanuele from the castle to the Cathedral.

▪ **MATERA.** From the Potenza area the route enters the Matera province, reaching its capital city. This is known worldwide for its Sassi, a group of ancient dwellings carved into the cliff and in use until the 1960's. For an overall view of this interesting settlement – an extraordinary weave of caverns, terraces, little squares, walls, and stairs – you climb to Piazza del Duomo (Apulian Romanesque style), then descend along the road skirting the Old Town, once consider the "nation's shame" and now on UNESCO's World Heritage list.

Wineries *pp. 458-459*
Acerenza, Barile, Matera, Rionero in Vulture, Venosa.

Specialties in Campania and Basilicata

CAMPANIA'S WINE AND FOOD capital is Naples, whose main wealth is in local history and in the people's spontaneity, which is the civic virtue par excellence. Pizza is the city's gastronomic flag, born from a chemical and atmospheric combination that cannot be found elsewhere. For similar reasons pasta is another source of local pride, especially if seasoned with lengthily cooked ragout. Recipes are innumerable: Ischia offers *spaghetti alla puttanesca*, with olives, capers, and anchovies; in Sorrento tomatoes are used with melted *scamorza* cheese. Naples is clearly home to common-folk cooking: seafood, obviously, from peppery mussels to spaghetti with clam sauce, octopus stewed with tomato and olives, hearty fish soup, eel, and salted cod. It gets rural with chicory soup and meatloaf, chops *alla pizzaiola* and Ischia-style rabbit, stuffed bell peppers and eggplant *parmigiana*. Pastries are enjoyed at table and on the street: *pastiera*, *babà*, and *sfogliatelle ricce*.

Two provinces flank Naples on the Tyrrhenian coast. On the Latium border is Caserta, with its medieval Old Town and Bourbon palace; this is generous land, from the plain of Volturno (home to buffalo-milk mozzarella) to Massico (home to Falerno, wine dear to the Romans) and to the Matese area, with its meats and wild mountain produce.

Going south, down to the Calabria border, are the province of Salerno, with Amalfi and its coast, all terraced vineyards and citrus groves, and the Paestum plain, with its Magna Grecia temples and equally famous cheeses. Just waiting to be discovered is Cilento, with old-time country flavors and the seafood delights of Maratea.

Inland are Benevento and Avellino (namely Sannio and Irpinia), sharing excellent olive oil and wine and, in the Apennines, robust mountain flavors that are the unexpected surprise of Campania gastronomy.

AS FOR BASILICATA, with its mostly mountainous territory and farming-grazing economy, the most typical products are cheeses and sausages, which combines in sauces for homemade pasta. Lamb is the leader among meats, cooked with mushrooms or vegetables, but in any case spicy; and then there is Maratea's surprising fish soup, also flavored with chili pepper.

WHERE WINES ARE CONCERNED, first mention is for Aglianico, the common asset of Campania and Basilicata: it can be a whole-meal wine, suited to hearty inland tastes, although fine vintages of Taurasi best accompany the most important dishes, from meats to game and aged cheeses.

For seafood there is a wide assortment: Fiano di Avellino and Greco di Tufo rank first, while Falanghina (under the Taburno or Falerno del Massico Bianco labels) is a wine to be tried, as are Biancolella and Forastera from Ischia.

To accompany the fine cheeses of these regions, you can try one of the many reds acclaimed by connoisseurs: Falerno del Massico, Solopaca, Sannio, Cilento, and Ischia. With desserts, famous Lacryma Christi del Vesuvio Liquoroso is the most intriguing accompaniment.

APULIA

THE GREAT RED WINES OF THE SOUTH

The vineyards of Apulia, long known for their full-bodied reds, have the potential to become – with the assistance of the marvelous sea nearby – a top destination for wine-loving tourists in Italy.

The heir to a viticultural tradition which goes all the way back to the ancient Greeks, Apulia, until fairly recently, was known as "the cellar of Europe." And with good reason: the wines were excellent, full of character, highly regarded beyond the Alps and much sought out as blending wines to give force and color to wines produced in less fortunate climates.

Above: Apulia's red-berries vines; left, Alberobello's trulli *(top) and the Tavoliere landscape (bottom)*

From the Gargano to Santa Maria di Leuca

The region's vineyards, among the most productive in Europe, can be divided into three zones. To the north is Daunia, the province of Foggia, which includes the first Apennine hills, the Tavoliere high plateau, and the Gargano headland. This is the territory of Bianco di San Severo. On the other side of the Otranto river are the Terra di Bari vineyards, which give the famous Castel del Monte and other red wines of strong personality. The Murge, with its series of red-earth plateaus, is prime territory for vines and olive groves. The last zone, beyond the so-called Soglia Messapica between Taranto and Lecce, is the Salento peninsula. The landscape varies from the Tavoliere di Lecce expanse to the low hills of the Murge Tarantine and of the Serre; the white wines make gradually room for the most renowned reds and rosés.

A Territory With a Grand Tradition of Red Wines

Statistics about Apulia's wine output say that red wines are undoubtedly of major importance, and are, for the most part, made from native grapes such as Negro Amaro (22.5%) and Primitivo (11%), followed by Sangiovese (10%), brought to the region early in the 20th century in the wake of the destruction caused by the phylloxera. Other significant autochthonous varieties are Malvasia Nera di Brindisi, Uva di Troia, and Bombino Nero. Widely planted white grapes include – in addition to the indigenous Verdeca, Bianco d'Alessano, Bombino, and Pampanato – Trebbiano Toscano and Trebbiano dell'Abruzzo. As for training techniques, the *tendone* and the *alberello* systems dominate, with respectively 49% and 32% of the total, but more recently there has been a certain diffusion of the *spalliera* method. There is also an important production of table grapes such as Regina and Italia.

Current policy is to progressively substitute varieties from outside the region – though excellent results have been obtained from Cabernet and Chardonnay – with autochthonous grapes, rediscovered, improved, and once again appreciated for the quality they can give. A similar commitment to improvement also exists for cellar procedures. There are 25 DOC zones, but total DOC production is little more than 5 million US gallons, eleventh among Italy's regions and just ahead of Umbria. A disappointing figure, particularly when compared to Apulia's overall production, regularly between 200 and 270 million US gallons annually. Better results come from the six IGT zones, whose total production of close to 25 million US gallons gives a clearer pic-

Newly planted vines in Apulia

The Great Wines of Apulia

Primitivo di Manduria DOC
This celebrated wine from the Taranto province is vinified pure from the homonymous grapes, so named for their characteristic early ("primitive") ripening. The vine is presumed to have come from Dalmatia, a likelihood confirmed by its substantial similarity to Hungarian Zinfadel. Primitivo di Manduria wine is red, tending to purplish and orangey when aged; its aroma is light and characteristic and its taste is full, tending to velvety over the years; the alcohol content is high (14%). It goes well with flavorful first courses, lamb and pork meats, and aged cheeses like *pecorino* and *canestrato*. It is also made in natural sweet, natural sweet liquoroso, and dry liquoroso versions.

Gargano's olive groves

Cacc'e mmitte di Lucera
This red from the Foggia area comes from a blend of Uva di Troia (35 to 60%) with Malvasia Nera di Brindisi, Montepulciano or Sangiovese (25 to 30%), and white-grape varieties. Uva di Troia can be traced to three locations – Troia in the Foggia province, Cruja in Albania, and ancient Troy in Asia Minor – with no clearer indications of the vine's actual origins. Cacc'e mmitte di Lucera is ruby red in color (deepness varies), with characteristic aroma, full-bodied taste, and an unmistakable aftertaste. It goes well with cold meats (*soppressata*, sausages) and cheeses (*canestrato*, *caciocavallo*, *pecorino*).

Castel del Monte Rosato DOC
This wine from the Bari area, considered one of the region's finest, comes from a blend starring Bombino Nero grapes (cultivated since time immemorial but uncertain as to origin), along with Aglianico and Uva di Troia. The resultant wine is rose in color (deepness varies), it has vinous aroma with the fruity note typical of Bombino Nero and dry, harmonious taste. It goes well with flavorful seafood dishes (fish soups or shellfish), first courses seasoned with vegetables and cheese, white meats, cold meats, and cheeses.

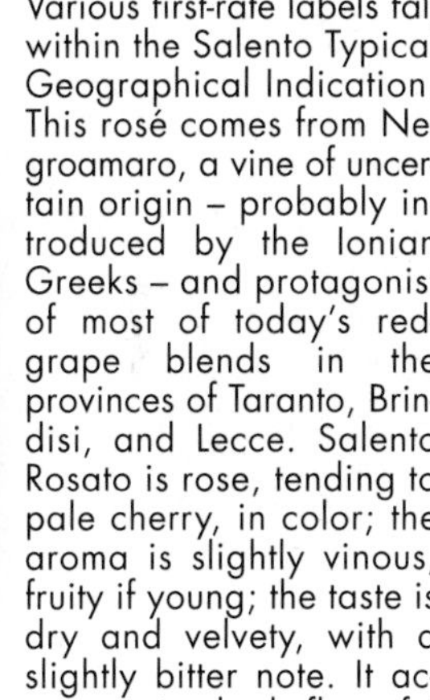

Salento Rosato IGT
Various first-rate labels fall within the Salento Typical Geographical Indication. This rosé comes from Negroamaro, a vine of uncertain origin – probably introduced by the Ionian Greeks – and protagonist of most of today's red-grape blends in the provinces of Taranto, Brindisi, and Lecce. Salento Rosato is rose, tending to pale cherry, in color; the aroma is slightly vinous, fruity if young; the taste is dry and velvety, with a slightly bitter note. It accompanies both flavorful fish and delicate meats.

Locorotondo
This high-quality white comes from Verdeca (50 to 60%) and Bianco d'Alessano (30 to 50%) grapes, uncertain in origin but common to the Taranto and neighboring areas. Verdeca provides a good, fairly neutral basis, suited to making wines with a high alcohol content, too; Bianco d'Alessano brings warmth and aroma. Locorotondo is greenish or pale straw yellow in color, with delicate, characteristic aroma and dry taste; it is also made in a spumante version. It goes well with grilled seafood, light vegetable-based dishes and fresh cheeses.

APULIA'S DOC ZONES

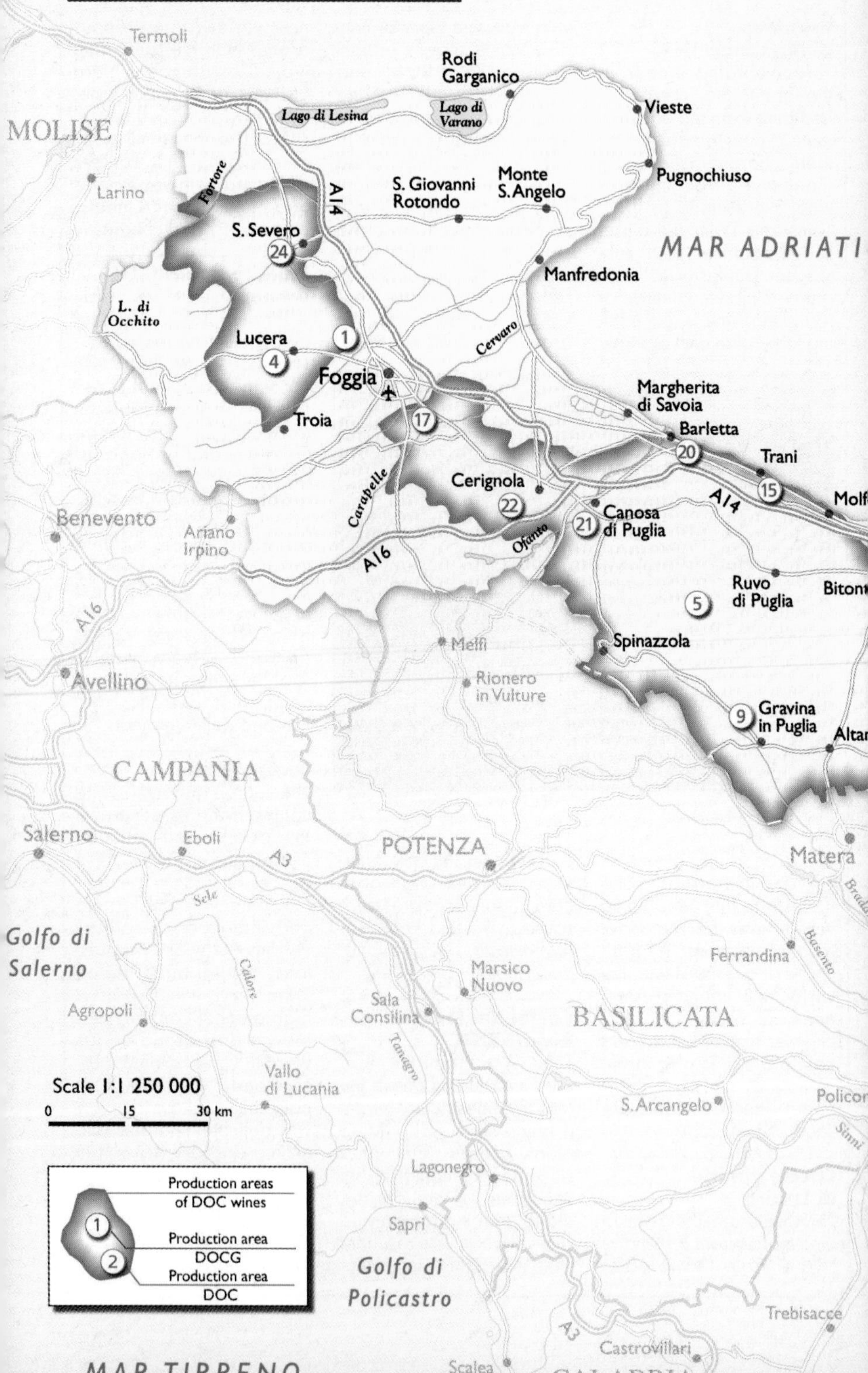

1 **DOC Aleatico di Puglia**
2 **DOC Alezio** *Rosato* ▪ *Rosso*
3 **DOC Brindisi** *Rosato* ▪ *Rosso*
4 **DOC Cacc'e mmitte di Lucera**
5 **DOC Castel del Monte** *Bianco, Bombino Bianco, Chardonnay, Pinot Bianco, Sauvignon* ▪ *Rosato, Aglianico Rosato, Bombino Nero* ▪ *Rosso, Aglianico, Cabernet, Pinot Nero, Uva di Troia*
6 **DOC Copertino** *Rosato* ▪ *Rosso*
7 **DOC Galatina** *Bianco, Chardonnay* ▪ *Rosato* ▪ *Rosso, Negro Amaro*
8 **DOC Gioia del Colle** *Bianco* ▪ *Rosato* ▪ *Rosso, Aleatico, Primitivo*
9 **DOC Gravina** *Bianco*
10 **DOC Leverano** *Bianco, Malvasia* ▪ *Rosato, Negro Amaro Rosato* ▪ *Rosso, Negro Amaro Rosso*
11 **DOC Lizzano** *Bianco* ▪ *Rosato, Negro Amaro Rosato* ▪ *Rosso, Malvasia Nera, Negro Amaro Rosso*
12 **DOC Locorotondo**
13 **DOC Martina or Martina Franca**
14 **DOC Matino** *Rosato* ▪ *Rosso*
15 **DOC Moscato di Trani**
16 **DOC Nardò** *Rosato* ▪ *Rosso*
17 **DOC Orta Nova** *Rosato* ▪ *Rosso*
18 **DOC Ostuni** *Bianco, Ottavianello*
19 **DOC Primitivo di Manduria**
20 **DOC Rosso Barletta**
21 **DOC Rosso Canosa or Canosium**
22 **DOC Rosso di Cerignola**
23 **DOC Salice Salentino** *Bianco, Pinot Bianco* ▪ *Rosato* ▪ *Rosso, Aleatico Dolce, Aleatico Liquoroso Dolce*
24 **DOC San Severo** *Bianco* ▪ *Rosso*
25 **DOC Squinzano** *Rosato* ▪ *Rosso*

IGT - Typical Geographic Indication
Daunia (Foggia); Murgia (Bari); Puglia (Bari - Brindisi - Foggia - Lecce - Taranto); Salento (Brindisi - Lecce - Taranto); Tarantino (Taranto); Valle d'Itria (Bari - Brindisi - Taranto)

IN THE DAUNIA VINELANDS

The vineyards of San Severo and Lucera, producing Foggia's most typical wines, stretch between the Apennine foothills and the Tavoliere plain.

The province of Foggia is Apulia's northernmost wine district. The provincial capital lies in the center of the Tavoliere, the major plain of peninsular Italy, which imperceptibly rises towards the Monti della Daunia – a hill chain, delimited by the Fortore and Carapelle rivers, which has a clayey soil landscape, divided by streams into various plateaus. For centuries the hub of Foggia viticulture has been renowned San Severo, home to a white DOC wine combining Bombino Bianco with Trebbiano Toscano. In addition, there is Lucera's production, historical stronghold of Uva di Troia grapes, from which red Cacc'e mmite is made. Finally, there are vineyards on the left side of the Ofanto river, with the Cerignola and Orta Nova wineries and the great Terra di Bari red wines.

From the Gargano to the Tavoliere

This area is characterized by white sea-cliffs, the Foresta Umbra ("shady forest") – heart of the Gargano Natural Park –, the wheat fields, vineyards, and olive groves of the Tavoliere, and finally the mountain pastures of Daunia. Foggia is a province of diversified scenery and surprising cuisine. As for wine, the DOC labels are Aleatico di Puglia, Cacc'e mmitte di Lucera, Orta Nova, Rosso di Carignola, and San Severo, plus the Daunia and Puglia IGTs.

AMIDST FOGGIA'S VINEYARDS

This itinerary begins in Foggia and crosses the Tavoliere and Monti della Daunia wine zones, with possible excursions (mainly for sightseeing) to the splendid Gargano coast. Foggia is also the arrival point for a wine route along the Barletta-Cerignola-Orta Nova axis that departs from the Terra di Bari zone described further on.

▪ **FOGGIA**. Its name, from the Latin *fovea*, grain silo, evokes the sunny fields of the Tavoliere plain surrounding the city. Its history is thousand-year old but its appearance, starting with the Cathedral, is modern.

▪ **SAN SEVERO**. The first wine stop is on the northern edge of the Tavoliere plain, at this town which boasts a long history of winemaking and presently owns its own DOC. The churches are baroque, but the left-hand side façade of S. Severino is Romanesque. The Civic Museum illustrates the history of the Daunia civilization from the early Paleolithic to Roman times.

From San Severo you can

Typical Apulia trulli

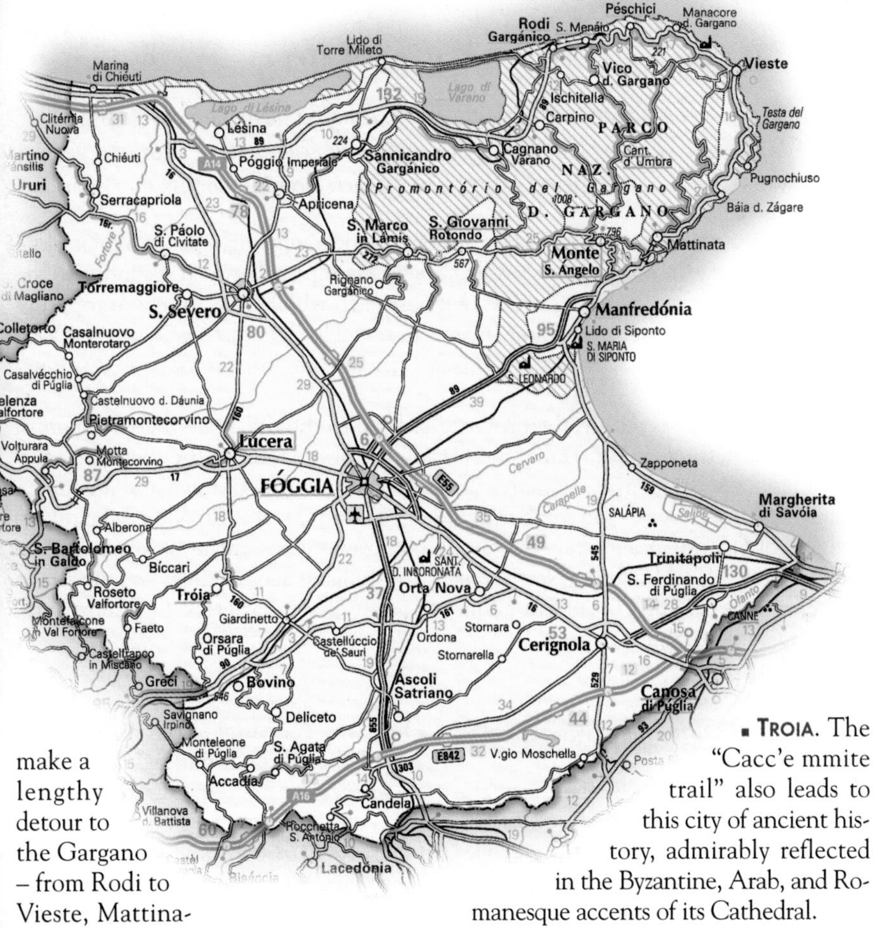

make a lengthy detour to the Gargano – from Rodi to Vieste, Mattinata, and Manfredonia – to enjoy seashores and natural beauties so much as good wine and food. Not far away, Monte Sant'Angelo and San Giovanni Rotondo are important destinations for religious pilgrimages.

■ **LUCERA**. Perched on a hill overlooking the western Tavoliere, it is steeped in Roman, Swabian, Saracen, and Angevin history. This can be traced by visiting the Cathedral, commissioned by Charles II of Anjou in the early 14th century (and partly built by French masons); the castle, built by the Swabians and later given two imposing towers; and the 1st-century amphitheater (restored in the 20th century). A visit to the Enoteca Regionale Permanente will give you the opportunity to taste local wines, starting with Cacc'e mmite.

■ **TROIA**. The "Cacc'e mmite trail" also leads to this city of ancient history, admirably reflected in the Byzantine, Arab, and Romanesque accents of its Cathedral.

■ **CERIGNOLA**. It lies in the southern part of the Tavoliere at the center of a formidable farming district that also produces full-bodied Rosso di Cerignola.
Just northwest is Orta Nova, within the territory of ancient *Herdonia*, whose excavation sites can be visited. The "new" town was founded in the 18th century, and a convent and three churches are reminders of that time; especially worth a stop are the excellent DOC red and gastronomy specialties, among which pasta and fresh produce stand out.

Wineries *pp. 456-458*
Cerignola, Orsara di Puglia, San Severo.

BARI AND THE MURGE HILLS

The province of Bari's territory, ranging from the coast to the Murge, with its red clay, limestone, green olive trees and vines, is associated to some of Apulia's greatest wines.

Apulia's second wine district covers the Murge, a moderately high, flat formation sloping from the Ofanto river to the so-called Soglia Messapica, between Taranto and the coast north of Brindisi. In its interior highest part, white limestone outcroppings emerge delineating the range frame; nearer to the coast, characteristic layers of clay gives the landscape a reddish color: this is Terra di Bari, known for its exceptional wine vocation.
Most of the Murge is within the province of Bari: to the north are the vineyards of the great Barletta, Canosa, Trani, and Castel del Monte reds; to the south, and further inland, are the Gravina wineries, around the homonymous town and Altamura. Finally, getting closer to the southern border, you find Gioia del Colle production, a foretaste of Salento viticulture. Among autochthonous vines, the most interesting are surely Primitivo and Bombino Nero, brought to Apulia in age-old times and the source of premium reds. Largely cultivated native white-grape varieties are Pampanuto, Palumbo, and Bombino Bianco.

From the Coast to the Murge

The Terra di Bari landscape, from the Adriatic coast to the first rise of the Murge – from farmlands to olive groves and to vineyards, so to speak – offers highly renowned reds and an itinerary of historical interest, starting from the enigmatic castle of Frederick II from which Castel del Monte DOC, the province's major production area, is named. Other DOCs are Moscato di Trani, Rosso Canosa, and Rosso di Barletta.

THE CASTEL DEL MONTE DOC ROUTE

This itinerary is divided into two circuits linking the areas involved in the Castel del Monte DOC production: Trani-Andria-Minervino-Corato and Ruvo di Puglia-Terlizzi-Bitonto-Palo del Colle-Toritto.
The first part of the route, between Barletta and Canosa di Puglia, makes you discover the ancient reds protected by these two towns' DOCs; at the end, instead, a visit to Bari is de rigueur.

▪ **BARLETTA.** A coastal town on the northern edge of Terra di Bari, whose historical attractions are reminders of the Crusades era: the church of Santo Sepolcro (12th to 13th century, with a Renaissance façade), the Romanesque-Gothic Cathedral, the castle founded by the Swabians, and also the Colossus, an enormous bronze statue from the classical period brought from Constantinople between the 13th and 14th centuries.

▪ **CANOSA DI PUGLIA.** This hill town overlooking the Ofanto valley and the Tavoliere is the site of important Norman monuments, first and foremost the Cathedral with the tomb of Beomondo, prince of Antioch, died in 1111. Traces of ancient Apulian (and perhaps Greek) Canosium can be seen in the Lagrasta underground burial chambers and the pottery conserved in the Civic Museum.

▪ **TRANI.** The superb rosy-white Cathedral, with its imposing bell tower, and the castle commissioned by Frederick II and

The impressive octagonal Castel del Monte

built in 1233-49 overlook the Old Town and the sea. Consecrated in 1186 and a masterpiece of Apulian Romanesque architecture, the Cathedral has a prized bronze portal sculpted by Barisano da Trani. Here Moscato di Trani (now a DOC production) has been made since time immemorial and it is a perfect accompaniment to marzipan, *carteddate*, and other local sweets.

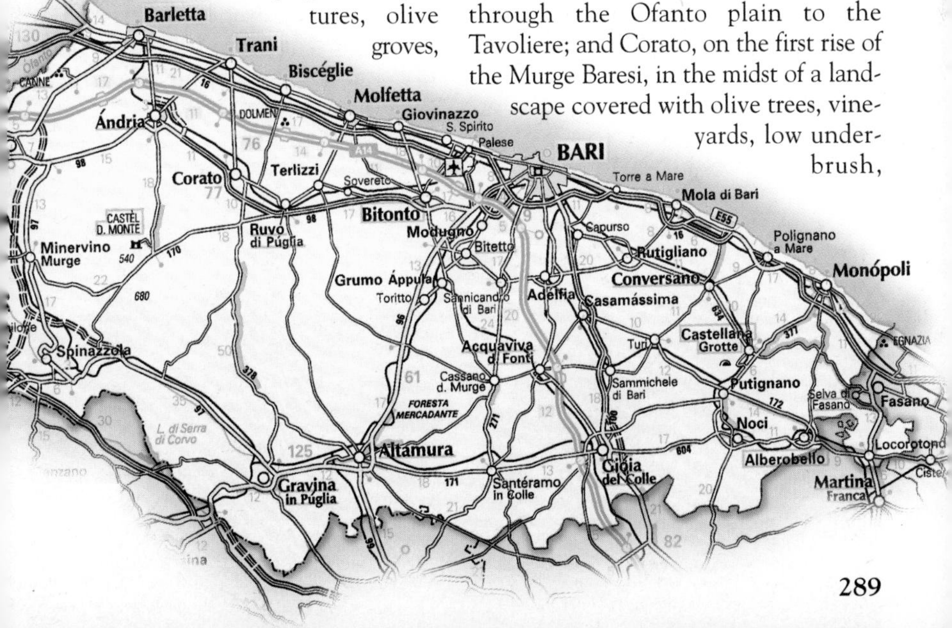

■ **CASTEL DEL MONTE.** The castle rises above the Murge commanding a sweeping view of pastures, olive groves, and vineyards. Frederick II had it built between 1229 and 1249 as a hunting lodge (some say) or as a symbolic imperial crown (according to others). Today, in addition to charming whoever sees it, it lends its name to one of Apulia's major wine zones. Not far away, Andria is first an olive oil and then a wine town, featuring monuments of note. Historical and scenic attractions can be found in two other Castel del Monte DOC centers: Minervino Murge, a picturesque town built at different levels around its Cathedral, Norman in foundation and with a great view through the Ofanto plain to the Tavoliere; and Corato, on the first rise of the Murge Baresi, in the midst of a landscape covered with olive trees, vineyards, low underbrush, copses, pebble-strewn and cultivated fields, and pretty old churches.

▪ **Ruvo di Puglia**. Again it is a cathedral, among the most emblematic of the region, to catch the visitor's eye: unusual for its cuspidate façade and steeply sloping roof, with a rose window and a rich central portal. The National Jatta Museum displays ancient Apulean pottery, which Ruvo was a major producer of. You then quickly come to Terlizzi, a produce and wine center with the lovely church of S. Rosario and interesting museums (Pinacoteca De Napoli and Folk Museum). A short detour takes you to Bisceglie and to yet another cathedral towering above olive trees and vineyards.

▪ **Bitonto**. In the heart of its medieval quarter (a maze of winding lanes) stands the great Romanesque Cathedral built in the 12th century with Bari's S. Nicola as a model; inside is an extraordinary pulpit from 1229, signed Nicolaus sacerdos et magister. The wine tour continues to Palo del Colle and Toritto, but just a few miles further Bari beckons to you.

▪ **Bari**. Worth at least brief mention is the thrilling sight of the Old Town, hugging winding streets and glorious in its history and Romanesque monuments, in particular the superb Cathedral of S. Nicola (consecrated in 1197) and the Cathedral built between the 12th and 13th centuries. Beyond are the evenly laid out 19th-century district and the 20th-century industry-and-commerce city.

From Murgia to the Valle dei Trulli

From the luxuriant Terra di Bari you pass through the rocky, karst scenery of the upper Murge on to the rows of archaic *trulli* in the Itria valley: landscapes of fascinating character, where white and rosé wines with deep territorial imprints are produced. The zone is covered by the Gioia del Colle, Gravina, and Locorotondo DOCs, and the Murgia and Valle d'Itria IGTs.

Amidst Vineyards, Gorges, Caves, and *Trulli*

The basic itinerary takes you through the most inland and high part of the Murge, in a landscape of olive trees and vineyards (on the lower ledges), pasture and farmlands, stony fields, caves, ravines, and gorges. The route crosses the region eastwards, from Spinazzola to Gavina in Puglia, Gioia del Colle, and Noci. It continues as far as Alberobello and Locorotondo, on the edges of the Itria valley, where the proximity with the provinces of Brindisi and Taranto is evident also from the wine point view.

Vine-planted landscape in Valle d'Itria

▪ **GRAVINA IN PUGLIA.** The name comes from the gorges (*gravine*) carved by water in the upper Murge limestone; the town, a tangle of medieval streets dominated by the imposing Cathedral of Norman origin, sits on the edge of one of these *gravine*. Other churches are worth visiting, but prevailing is the charm of the very special natural environment – as special is the homonymous DOC wine.

▪ **ALTAMURA.** It conserves the elliptic Old Town, re-founded by Frederick II after destruction by Saracens had led to abandonment of the site; it was the same king to commission the Romanesque Cathedral, with its splendid 15-spoke rose window. Nearby is the Altamura karst chasm, one of the region's largest.

▪ **GIOIA DEL COLLE.** Going through Cassano delle Murge and Aquaviva delle Fonti you get to Gioia del Colle, a DOC wine town located on a saddle of the Murge midway between Bari and Taranto. You are welcomed by the castle, again built by Frederick II, with its rusticated red façades.

▪ **CASTELLANA GROTTE.** The city is thousand-year old, as are its chasms: just outside town, the Castellana caves constitute the largest and most beautiful complex known in Italy so far. Discovered in 1938, they extend to over 1850 miles of tunnels suddenly opening into huge caves full of stalagmites and crystals.
Another cave – tall, karstic, and full of alabaster concretions – can be visited at Putignano, a nearby town with a well-preserved old center featuring baroque churches. Not far to the northwest are Turi and Conversano, while Noci stands to the south: these are three other Murge villages with old nucleuses worth visiting and surrounded by olive, almond, and cherry trees.

Wineries *pp. 456-458*
Andria, Corato, Gioia del Colle, Gravina di Puglia, Locorotondo.

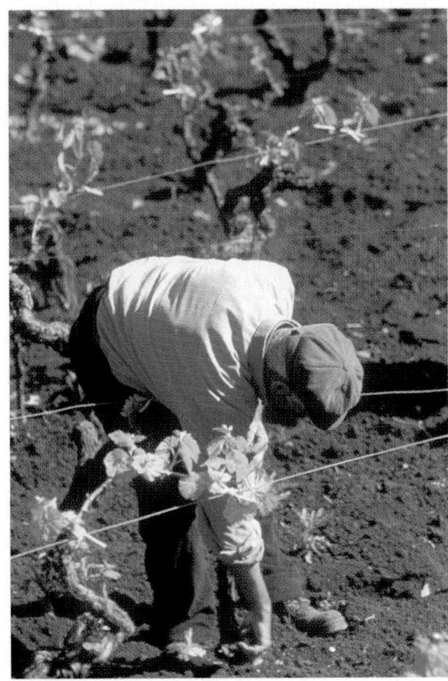

Valle d'Itria's vigneron at work

▪ **ALBEROBELLO.** The *trulli* giving their name to this section of the Murge – sloping in terraces towards the Gulf of Taranto and the Adriatic Sea between Mola di Bari and Ostuni – here make up a whole town. In the oldest part you can admire these archaic constructions with conical roofs; only one, the Trullo sovrano (sovereign trullo), is two-storied.

▪ **LOCOROTONDO.** This town, set almost on the border with Brindisi, offers from its hilltop enchanting views of the Itria valley dotted with *trulli*. Archeologists have found evidence of extremely ancient human inhabitation. You can visit the neoclassical Mother church and the Gothic church of S. Maria la Greca. In the environs over 1400 vignerons contribute to producing the highly renowned Locorotondo DOC wine.

THE SALENTO PENINSULA

A viniculture array of rare breadth and intensity characterizes production in the Salento peninsula, under the combined influence of the Adriatic and Ionian seas.

We are in the "heel" of Italy, the peninsula that separates the Adriatic from the Ionian Sea with cave-filled cliffs. These are the southern spurs of the Murge, which make way for the flatlands of the Tavoliere di Lecce and the Serre Salentine hills.
The vine-lands in the Brindisi, Taranto, and Lecce provinces are divided into two production areas. In fact, most common to the north are white wines, tied to the Martina Franca and Ostuni DOCs. The prevailing vines are traditional ones like Verdeca, Bianco d'Alessano, Bombino Bianco, and Fiano – to cite the best known – with an island of Impigno and Francavilla around Ostuni. To the south the reds and rosés are protagonists and the most important vine is Primitivo (so named for its early, "primitive", ripening and found mainly in the Taranto area). Alongside them is Negro Amaro, typical of the Salento zone but also found around Brindisi.

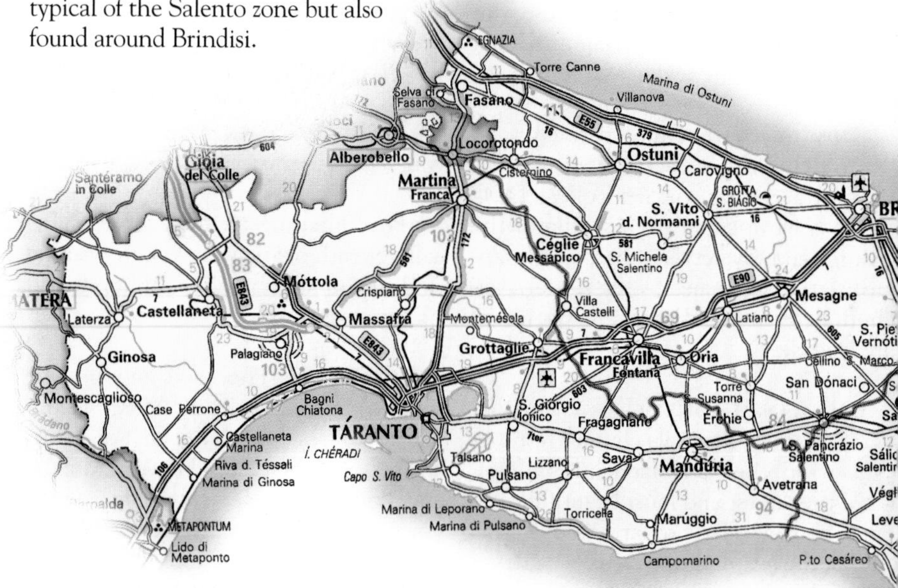

Between Brindisi and Taranto

At the root of the peninsula, between the Brindisi coast, the southern spurs of the Murgia dei Trulli, and the Murge Tarantine around the gulf, lies the Salento area. These are lands with lovely landscapes, where winemaking is an ancient tradition. There are many DOC labels: Brindisi, Lizzano, Martina Franca, Ostuni, and Primitivo di Manduria, along with the Salento and Tarantino IGTs.

ALONG THE PRIMITIVO TRAIL

A first itinerary takes you from Brindisi to Ostuni – from one DOC to another along the so-called "Via Appia of Wine" –, entering Taranto territory at Martina Franca.
Taranto's Mar Piccolo is the ideal point of departure for another fascinating route, running across the rolling Murge Tarantine to Manduria and ending with a stop at Oria, in the Brindisi province.

Interior of a farmstead at Ostuni

■ **BRINDISI.** A city of very ancient origin, standing on a tiny peninsula between two inlets forming a natural port (one of Adriatic's safest and source of the city's economic welfare since the age when traders following Via Appia took to sea from here to the East). Today the city features a modern look, but it has historical (especially medieval) remains: its pride is the Romanesque church of S. Giovanni al Sepolcro, built by the Knights Templars, with a lovely cloister.

■ **OSTUNI.** Going through Mesagne (with important relics of Messapi culture in the Ugo Granafei Archeological Museum), Latiano, and San Vito dei Normanni, you come to Ostuni, appellation of another DOC. The town covers the summits and saddles of seven hills: on the highest is Terra, a medieval nucleus of white houses amidst walls and towers, in which you can visit its 15th-century Cathedral. At the end of a straight stretch heading south is Ceglie Messapica, with a 15th-16th-century castle in the medieval district.

■ **MARTINA FRANCA.** The name of this lovely town (and its DOC appellation) comes from the S. Martino hills on which it stands and from the exemptions granted by Philip d'Anjou to whoever settled there. The walls embrace the baroque and Rococo buildings, including majestic Palazzo Ducale and the collegiate of S. Martino. At the old Montedoro farm you can visit the Trullo Culture Museum (while in the Itria valley

you can see *trulli* "live", amidst the green fields and vineyards).
Brief extensions take you to Cisternino, an ancient wine town with whitewashed, terraced Oriental-style houses, and to Fasano, ancient fief of the Knights of Malta set at the foot of the Murgia dei Trulli embankment, not far from the sea.

▪ **Taranto.** The city's illustrious Greek past is recounted in its very important National Archeological Museum; after visiting it, by crossing the canal separating the Mar Grande and Mar Piccolo waters, you can tour the Old Town, visiting the Aragonese castle and the Cathedral, founded in the 11th century and dedicated to S. Cataldo.
The route then lines up San Giorgio Jonico, Carosino, Faggiano, Pulsano, Lizzano, and Sava – all farming and wine towns, some with very old Albanian communities – between the coast and the Murge Tarantine, ending in Manduria.

▪ **Manduria.** This is the lovely capital of the Primitivo wine district, and takes its name from the ancient Messapian city: not far away you can visit its former site, with a triple circle of megalithic walls. Noteworthy in the town are the originally Romanesque Cathedral with Renaissance portals, the close-by old Jewish ghetto, and 18th-century Palazzo Imperiali in central Piazza Garibaldi.
Just a few miles north is Oria, on the low line of hills delimiting the Tavoliere di Lecce; the town retains its elliptic ancient part, packed with alleyways and whitewashed houses, and the castle built by Frederick II (1233) on the site of the old acropolis.

Wineries *pp. 456-458*
Alezio, Brindisi, Carosino, Cellino San Marco, Copertino, Galatina, Guagnano, Latiano, Lecce, Leverano, Manduria, Novoli, Salice Salentino, San Donaci, San Pietro Vernotico, Scorrano, Tuglie, Veglie.

Around Lecce

The last itinerary of this wine and gastronomy tour of Apulia, at the far end of the Salento peninsula, is perhaps the most exciting in terms of climate,

Olive trees characterize Brindisi's countryside – as well as the all of Apulia

scenery, and the relentless sequence of great wines. DOC wines in the zone take their names from the main wine towns: Alezio, Copertino, Galatina, Leverano, Matino, Nardò, Salice Salentino, and Squinzano.

THROUGH THE SALENTO VINEYARDS

Departing from the main city, this tour of Salerno's province embraces vast areas in the Tavoliere di Lecce – and the lands of the Salice Salentino, Leverano, Squinzano, and Copertino DOC wines – and then goes on to the Murge Salentine and the coast, from Gallipoli to Otranto, in search of new and equally pleasant oenological attractions.

▪ **LECCE**. The local stone, easy to work soon after quarrying, golden and almost pink in color when hardened, allowed the creation of extraordinary architecture and sculpture works of art. Inside Lecce's walls, winding streets and little squares are a baroque stage-set for churches and buildings of refined beauty. Do not miss S. Croce and Palazzo del Governo, the S. Nicolo and S. Cataldo churches, the Cathedral, and the Seminary.

From Lecce the wine route takes you – just north and west of the provincial capital – to Squinzano, San Pietro Vernotico (with a lovely 15th-century church and lively wine festivals in October and November), Cellino San Marco, and Salice Salentino.

Then you turn south through Leverano and Copertino to Galatina, in the middle of the Salento peninsula, famed for wine and for the Franciscan church of S. Caterina di Alessandria, built in the late 14th century and featuring frescoes reminiscent of Giotto.

▪ **NARDÒ**. A town not far from the Gulf of Taranto, with a noteworthy Cathedral (built in 1080, but with an 18th-century façade) and the baroque backdrop of Piazza Salandra encircling the spire of

Table grapes harvesting

the Immacolata. From Nardò you can head northwest to Porto Cesareo, fishing village and summer resort on the Gulf of Taranto coast, or southeast to Gallipoli.

▪ **GALLIPOLI**. It is located at the tip of a tiny peninsula, with a bridge connecting the modern checkerboard of the Borgo to the white houses of the Città, an "Oriental" maze of tiny streets. Here you can visit the castle, the 17th-century Cathedral, and the churches that dot the panoramic coastline.

From Gallipoli you cross the Salento peninsula from the Ionian to the Adriatic Sea, passing through Alezio, Matino (home to a DOC), and Maglie until you reach Otranto.

▪ **OTRANTO**. The last stop of this tour is at this town famous for the extraordinary mosaics paving its Apulian Romanesque Cathedral, built in memory of the "Otranto Martyrs", some 800 inhabitants killed by the Turkish army of Mohammed II in 1480. Marvelous scenic views open up from the top of the Aragonese castle.

Specialties in Apulia

SINCE THE TIME of Roman *Brundisium*, which was the final stop along Via Appia and an important port to the Levant, Apulia has developed great affinity with Greece. Many historical relics confirm this, but perhaps even more explicit is the matrix of a landscape shaped by the coast – high, white, and eroded –, with an interior of arid plateaus the color of karst rock and red clay, of olive trees and vines, of wheat and pasturelands.
Apulian wine and food are typically Mediterranean. From the region's wheat come many kinds of bread (Altamura is the most famous) and pasta, shaped into simple forms like orecchiette or strascinati, symbols of regional cooking. As for olive oil, the region is leader of Italian output, and from the Gargano to Terra d'Oltranto boasts several quality denominations. Extraordinary varieties of fruit and vegetables complete the picture: grapes and cherries, citrus fruits and figs, melons and watermelons; then broad beans and lentils, eggplant and bell peppers, artichokes and cardoons in an assortment culminating in *lampascioni*, tiny onions with a bitter taste. From livestock raising come cheeses like *canestrato* and *burrata*, cold meats like *soppressata* and *capocollo*. And from the sea come a host of ingredients for cooking, like the mollusks (especially oysters) which Taranto has been long famed for.

FOR ITS CENTRAL POSITION and extension, Bari is the reference point for Apulian cuisine. To the regional capital come all the products typical of the region, and seafood is as common as the products of the land. So you find fresh anchovy pie, stuffed mussels, spaghetti with mussel or cuttlefish sauce, fish in soups or grilled. Add to these *focaccia* and pizza, pasta with vegetables or meat (following the old Hellenic custom of all-in-one dishes, combining *orecchiette* with turnip greens or chops). Then come lamb, grilled or in casserole, and unique specialties like *gniummerieddi*, very delicate rolls of entrails. Two very different cuisines complete the scene: to the north, Foggia's (in the Gargano peninsula and in the Daunia area) and to the south Salento's (in the peninsula jutting out into the Adriatic and Ionian seas). While both are rich in foodstuffs, the first has mountain accents (with wide use of mushrooms) while the second specializes in seafood (especially shellfish) – all with excellent results.

AS FOR WINES, the region's real specialties are rosés. There are many excellent ones: Alezio, Castel del Monte, Leverano, Salento, Salice Salentino. They go well with many dishes, from hors-d'oeuvres of cold meats to the tastiest fish dishes, pasta with white meat sauces, and even cheeses like *pecorino* and *caciocavallo*.
For more delicate seafood, from shellfish to grilled fish, as well as for vegetarian dishes, there is a good variety of white wines: Locorotondo and San Severo – the best known –, but also some surprising Chardonnays.
For important meats and cheeses the recommendation is Primitivo di Manduria. And for desserts, you must try the famous Moscato di Trani or Aleatico, a red wine with a special aroma, which in Apulia has one of its shrines.

CALABRIA

VINEYARDS BETWEEN TWO SEAS

"The oldest wine in Europe" is the slogan that has been coined to draw attention to some of the most interesting wines of all of southern Italy, favored by the mild climate and a tradition which goes all the way back to the Magna Grecia time.

A very long coastline and an interior which is, for the most part, mountainous: these are the principal characteristics of a region whose viticultural traditions go all the way back to the world of Magna Grecia. The effects of the climate are easy to summarize: citron and bergamot trees bear fruit on the coast, where there is also a large-scale cultivation of jasmine – such a close contact between the sea and the mountains is, apparently, beneficial to plants that need very special climate conditions. As

Above, vineyards in the Savuto valley; left, Sangineto's castle, in the Cosenza, area (top) and an olive grove in Aspromonte (bottom)

far as the vine is concerned, its cultivation relates to three zones: the most northerly is the limestone Pollino massif, whose karst nature is responsible for the reduced presence of surface water. The other two are the Tyrrhennian and Ionian extensions of the Sila, green with woods, and of crystalline-rock Aspromonte, whose name ("harsh mountain") is self-descriptive.

The Cathedral of Santa Severina

THE VINEYARDS OF GAGLIOPPO AND GRECO BIANCO

Despite certain soil differences, the vineyards of Calabria are fairly homogeneous and with a prevalence of red-grape varieties. Among these, the most important is Gaglioppo, with 28% of the overall total; together with Nerello, Greco Nero, and a few others, these red varieties easily constitute a majority. As far as Gaglioppo is concerned, though it is to be found also along the lower Adriatic coast, it is considered indigenous of the Cosenza and Catanzaro provinces in Calabria. The resultant wine is a fine basis for full-bodied blends: together with red grapes it gives wines of great personality; with white grapes (a Calabrian traditional blend), it gives excellent table wines. Greco Bianco (11% of the overall total) is the major white grape; this is a variety which has had a fundamental role in the history of wine from ancient Greece to modern times. Today, grapes are vinified after being slightly dried and produce an amber-colored dessert wine. It is significant that 80% of Calabria's vines are *alberello* trained, evidence that production has always aimed at wines with a high alcohol content.

12 DOCs, 13 IGTs, 11 NEW WINE AND GASTRONOMY ROUTES

The future trend of Calabria's oenology is evident: after consolidating the quality improvement in wine growing and making, the aim is further gaining the national and international appreciation of the local production, also taking advantage of the region's extraordinary tourist attractions. From the normative standpoint, the presence of 25 DOC/IGT zones reflects an extremely varied panorama, where productions and wineries already appraised by connoisseurs (especially in the "historical" Greco di Bianco and Cirò areas) share the scene with traditional, though not as much well known, ones, which are increasingly drawing the attention of wine enthusiasts. That is to say that Calabria has to offer both consolidated high-quality wines and surprising ones to be discovered – with the added benefit of an excellent quality/price ratio. Furthermore, on the gastronomy side, Calabria boasts an unequalled variety of tastes, from cured meats to cheeses, from the swordfish of the Strait to Sila mushrooms, from Rossano licorice to Zibibbo grapes from Pizzo Calabro. In order to take advantage of these opportunities of fine dining, as many as 11 Wine and Gastronomy Routes have been designed and proposed to tourists, who can already explore them – although signs and services are not yet in place.

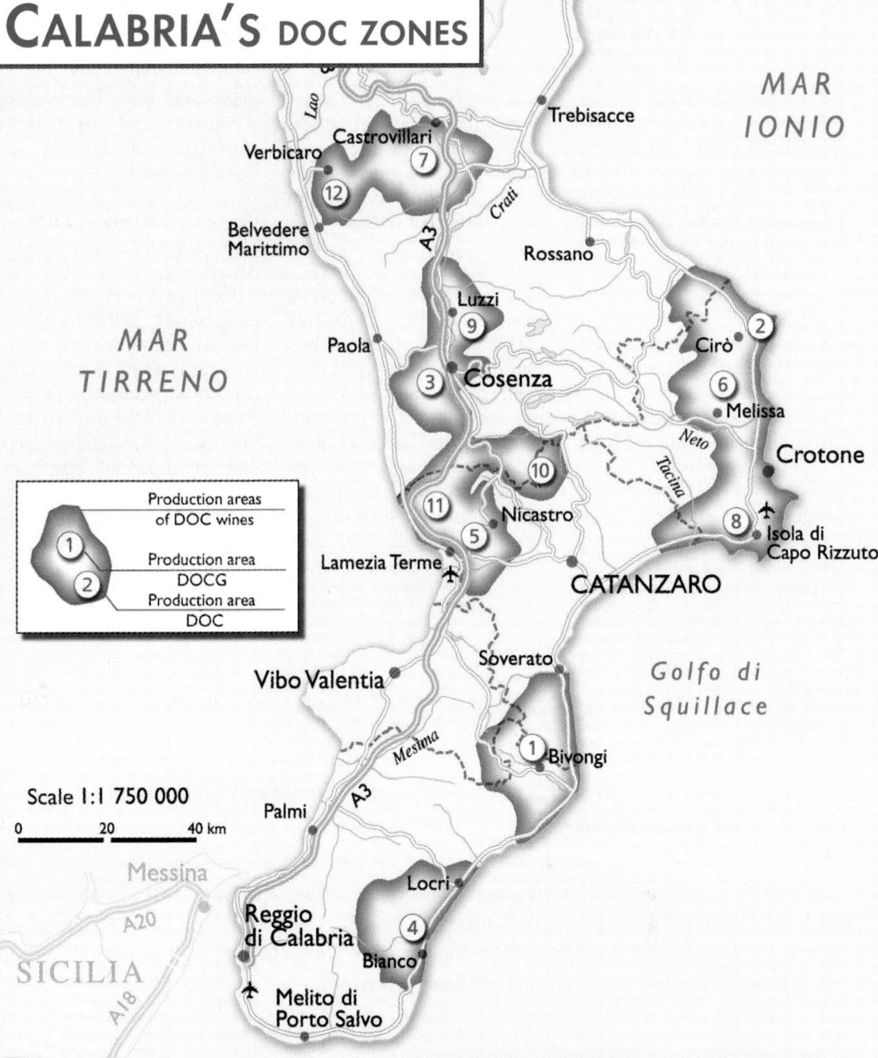

❶ **DOC Bivongi** *Bianco ▪ Rosato ▪ Rosso*
❷ **DOC Cirò** *Bianco ▪ Rosato ▪ Rosso*
❸ **DOC Donnici** *Bianco ▪ Rosato ▪ Rosso*
❹ **DOC Greco di Bianco**
❺ **DOC Lamezia** *Bianco, Greco ▪ Rosato ▪ Rosso*
❻ **DOC Melissa** *Bianco ▪ Rosso*
❼ **DOC Pollino**
❽ **DOC Sant'Anna di Isola Capo Rizzuto**
❾ **DOC San Vito di Luzzi** *Bianco ▪ Rosato ▪ Rosso*
❿ **DOC Savuto**
⓫ **DOC Scavigna** *Bianco ▪ Rosato ▪ Rosso*
⓬ **DOC Verbicaro** *Bianco ▪ Rosato ▪ Rosso*

IGT - Typical Geographic Indication

Arghillà (Reggio di Calabria); Calabria (Catanzaro - Cosenza - Crotone - Reggio di Calabria - Vibo Valenzia); Condoleo (Cosenza); Costa Viola (Reggio di Calabria); Esaro (Cosenza); Lipuda (Crotone); Locride (Reggio di Calabria); Palizzi (Reggio di Calabria); Pellaro (Reggio di Calabria); Scilla (Reggio di Calabria); Val di Neto (Crotone); Valle del Crati (Cosenza); Valdamato (Catanzaro)

The Great Wines of Calabria

Cirò Rosso DOC
The most representative of Calabria's reds comes from Gaglioppo grapes (95 to 100%). This vine, probably Greek in origin, is the most spread in the Cosenza and Catanzaro provinces. The wine resulting from pure vinification is ruby red in color (deepness varies, with a yellow tinge if aged; aroma is fresh and taste is vinous, full-bodied, and slightly tannic at times. Alcohol content is 12.5%, giving it a good aptitude to ageing. Production codes also permit Superiore (13.5%) and Riserva versions, with two years of obligatory ageing. It goes well with highly seasoned pasta dishes, stewed white meats, boiled and grilled red meats, and with *caciocavallo silano* cheese.

Cirò Bianco DOC
This dry white wine comes from Greco Bianco grapes (90 to 100%). The vine has Hellenic origins and has been grown since time immemorial in the Catanzaro and Reggio Calabria provinces. The wine is straw yellow in color (deepness varies) and it has vinous aroma; taste is dry, delicate, and characteristic; alcohol content is 11%. It goes well with light hors-d'oeuvres and fish dishes, starting with grilled or baked swordfish.

Greco di Bianco DOC
From slightly dried Greco Bianco grapes (95 to 100%) come sweet liquoroso wines, golden or amber in color, which with time acquire an outstanding aroma of orange blossoms. Taste is mellow and warm, with good persistence and hints of citrus fruit, figs, honey, and raisins. Minimum alcohol is 17%, at least 14% of which developed. This is a dessert and "meditation wine".

THE COSENZA REGION

The wines of the largest province in Calabria come from Sila, with its Crati and Savuto valleys, and from the Pollino massif and its Esaro valley.

With its two major mountain ranges – Pollino and Sila – and wide valleys with a strong wine-producing vocation, the province of Cosenza, the largest and most varied in the region, is a land with excellent potential for wine tourism. The main vine is Gaglioppo, whose grapes are used to make Pollino red wine.

On the Sila Slopes

The Sila area features two major wine-producing zones, whose merging point is at Cosenza: the valley of the Crati river, which flows in a large curve into the Ionian Sea, and the valley of the Savuto, which descends towards the Tyrrhenian Sea. The former valley boasts the Donnici and San Vito di Luzzi DOC denominations, as well as the Valle del Crati IGT; the latter has Savuto DOC, of which Rogliano is the epicenter of production. The Ionian side, almost on

A villa and its vineyards in the Cosenza's environs

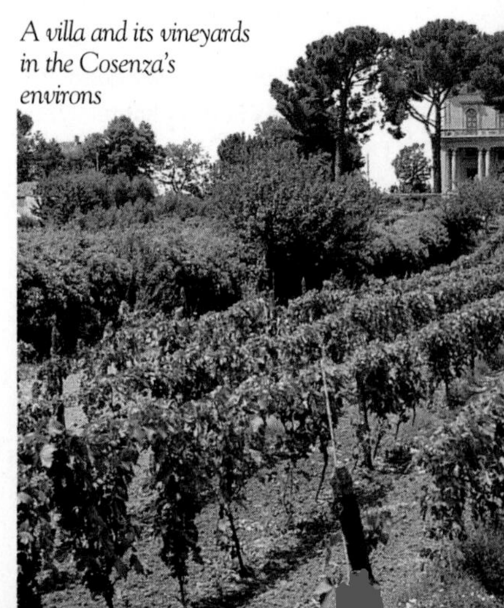

the border with Crotone, features Mandatoriccio, relating to the Condoleo IGT.

COSENZA AND THE CRATI AND SAVUTO VALLEYS

The province capital is the fulcrum of an itinerary that unfolds in opposite directions along the Crati and Savuto valleys. The recently approved Brutium Wine and Gastronomy Route passes through this zone, as do three other trails dedicated more generally to the province's renowned gastronomy.

■ **COSENZA.** Situated at the confluence of the Busento and the Crati rivers, the Old Town slopes down on one of the Pancrazio hill sides and was in its earliest times the stronghold of the Bruzii. Below it, the bustling modern city, which grew up at the end of the 19th century, is no less picturesque.
Its more recent development is bound to the futuristic University of Calabria, which renews a cultural tradition born nearly 500 years ago out of the Accademia Cosentina. The Old Town conserves a medieval atmosphere along Corso Telesio, which winds up to the Duomo. You must stop at the Gran Caffè Renzelli, in operation since two hundred years ago. The city is the center of gravity of the Donnici, San Vito di Luzzi and Savuto DOCs vine-lands, and therefore the ideal starting point from which to discover them.
From Cosenza, you travel south to Figline Vegliaturo, a local oenological point of reference that commands a sweeping view of the lively landscape of Casali Cosentini (the name of a group of villages scattered at various heights, for farming needs, on the slopes of the Crati valley).
From there, you cross the hills of the middle Savuto valley to Rogliano, with the Renaissance church of S. Giorgio and the Provitaro white wine oenological curiosity.

A view of Amantea

AMANTEA. You descend the main Silana road passing Grimaldi, Aiello, and (after reaching the Tyrrhenian Sea) Amantea, a farming and fishing village – and now also a seaside resort – with a ring of walls that goes all the way from the church of S. Bernardino to the port.
Going back towards the capital, you climb a winding road to the small medieval center of Dipignano. This is in the heart of the Donnici DOC production zone, also the home to a type of sponge cake that is named after the village.

MONTALTO UFFUGO. You set off from Cosenza to explore the middle Crati valley: first to Luzzi, with the nearby abbey of Sambucina, now reduced to a picturesque ruin framed by the Sila mountains, then, on the opposite side, halfway up the slope, to Montalto Uffugo. Stop and visit the Duomo, with its rococo design, and the church of S. Francesco, with Renaissance additions. You then go farther on, passing more villages in the Valle del Crati IGT – Rota Greca and Cerzeto – and San Marco Argentano, the outpost of the Valle dell'Esaro wine-producing district.

The Pollino Valleys

The Pollino massif, shared with Campania and Basilicata, provides vines with an extremely favorable limestone habitat. The most important DOC production, which is indeed Pollino DOC, comes from the Castrovillari area. Next to it are the Verbicaro DOC, named after the town on the Tyrrhenian coast, and the Esaro IGT, in the valley of the same name.

THE POLLINO MASSIF AND THE ESARO VALLEY

The northern portion of the Cosenza province is distinguished by the Pollino massif and forms a homogeneous oenological district with the Esaro valley be-

Traditional chili pepper drying

Wineries *pp. 459-460*
Montalto Uffugo, Saracena.

low. This itinerary, which Castrovillari is the point of reference of, follows the recently instituted Pollino-Castrovillari Wine and Gastronomy Route.

▪ **CASTROVILLARI**. Set in a large basin at the foot of Mount Pollino is Castrovillari, whose Old Town, the Civita, set on a spur, is partially crumbling and abandoned; the checkerboard of modern districts is instead on the plain. Local oenological features are a dessert wine called Lacrima di Castrovillari and the rare natural Moscato or Passito di Saracena.
A few miles away, in a hollow open to the Sibari plain, is Frascineto, a town of Albanian foundation (late 15th C.) and traditions. It is known for its Moscato wine – and for its cheeses and fruit, too. This is the point of departure for excursions into the Pollino National Park. Also nearby is Morano Calabro, full of beautiful art sights: from the Norman castle to the Collegiate and to the very structure of the town, with its houses neatly arranged on the sides of a perfectly conical hill against the harsh backdrop of Mount Pollino. The place offers remarkable gastronomic delights, starting with junket.

▪ **ALTOMONTE**. From Castrovillari, take the Tyrrhenian road and climb the Esaro valley, stopping at Altomonte, a small but lively art center dominated by the 14th-century church of S. Maria della Consolazione, which was inspired by French Gothic models. The gastronomic specialty is *lagane* (tagliatelle) with chickpeas. The local wine is Balbino di Altomonte, dry or passito.

▪ **VERBICARO**. After crossing the Scalone Pass, you descend to the Tyrrhenian Sea, passing Belvedere, a generous land of wines, figs, and citrus fruits, and Diamante, renowned for its fish dishes. You then prolong the trip into the hinterland and head to Verbicaro, a farming village with reminders in the medieval Bonifanti district. Its oenological interest stems from the DOC production, as much as from its famed Zibibbo Adduraca wine.

THE CROTONE REGION

The wine district of the hills on the Ionian side of the Sila is rooted in antiquity, when Kroton was an illustrious Magna Grecia city.

On the heights overlooking the Ionian Sea, from Punta Alice to Capo Rizzuto, you will pass the vineyards of the Cirò, Melissa, and Sant'Anna di Isola Capo Rizzuto DOCs and the Lipuda and Val di Neto IGTs. This is a homogeneous area bound to the vine-growing legacy of Magna Grecia.

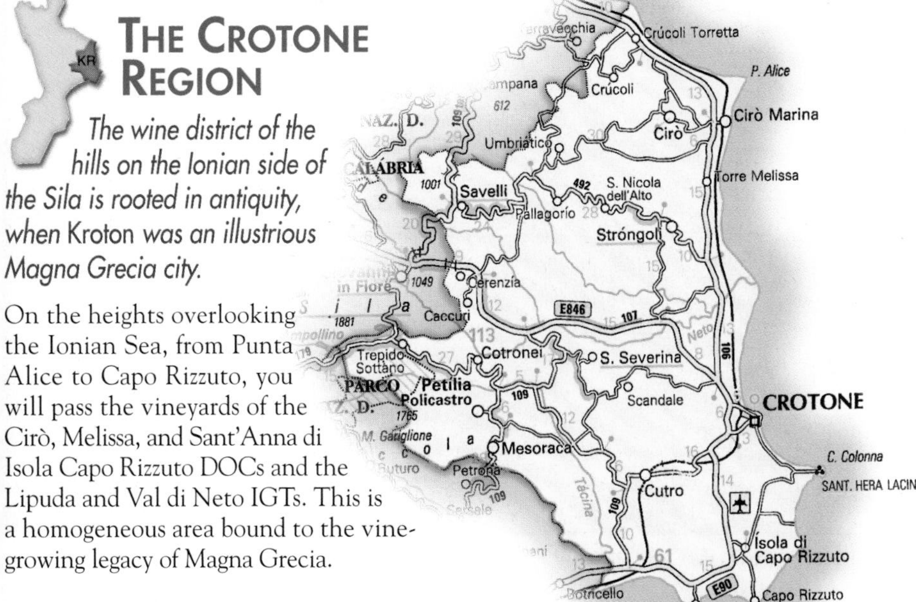

From Punta Alice to Capo Rizzuto

Production in this area relates to the Cirò, Melissa, and Sant'Anna di Isola Capo Rizzuto DOCs (with reference to the places of the same names), and the Lipuda and Val di Neto IGTs. The red-grape varieties still include Gaglioppo and Greco Nero with a foretaste, in the Sant'Anna zone, of Nerello, in the Cappuccio and Mascalese varieties, which is much more spread in Sicily. The most common white-grape vines include Trebbiano Toscano and Malvasia, but the true protagonist is Greco Bianco, which attains the maximum importance in the southern sector of the Ionian coast.

IN THE CIRÒ AND VAL DI NETO VINEYARDS

This itinerary sets off from Crotone and goes up the coast past Punta Alice in the Cirò DOC area. It returns inland describing a large curve across the Lipuda stream valley. A southern branch of the route develops along the coast, passing through the wine-producing district of Capo Rizzuto before heading north towards the Val di Neto area.

▪ **CROTONE.** The castle was built on the site of the acropolis of the powerful and outstanding Greek city that had twelve-mile long walls. The 16th-century ramparts surround the Old Town and its intricate weave of streets. The strictly Calabrian cuisine is excellent: gourmets will, for instance, look forward to the *quadaru*, a spicy fish soup that attains specialty status here.

▪ **STRONGOLI.** The heir of the ancient Petelia, first a Greek and later a Bruzii center, stands on a solitary rise. The Norman castle commands an exceptional view of the coast and the town's houses and churches. Local vine-growing features include the Chardonnay and Cabernet patches, which are responsible for some of the region's most innovatory wines.

▪ **CIRÒ MARINA.** Passing via Melissa, a town that is home to a DOC of the same name and is the main center in the Val di Neto IGT, you come to Cirò Marina. The remains of a Greek temple, at Punta Alice, conjure up the times of ancient *Cremisa*, the fame of which was partly

Rows of vines in the Crotone area

Crotone's castle bridge, built by the Spanish in the mid-16th century

bound to a proverbially fine wine. The same ancient vines, you could say, form today the Cirò DOC traditional zone. The importance of this producing area, one of the most important in the region, currently supplemented by the Lipuda IGT, is demonstrated by the concentration of wineries. In the neighborhood trattorias overlooking the sea, the dish to ask for is spaghetti with *sardella* (bluefish fry).

If you venture beyond the provincial border with Cosenza, you will reach Mandatoriccio and the wineries of the Condoleo IGT, concentrated in this municipality. Another stretch of road will take you to Rossano, a little town picturesquely arranged in a cascade on a hill overlooking the Ionian Sea. Here you will find vestiges of the Byzantine age as well as delicious food and wine bound to the Sila tradition.

As an alternative to the coastal road, you can return to Crotone with an exciting foray into the Lipuda stream valley, stopping off at Umbriatico, which offers local Sila culinary delights and beautiful views.

Wineries *pp. 459-460*
Cirò, Cirò Marina, Strongoli.

▪ **ISOLA DI CAPO RIZZUTO.** This is a large farming town known to most for the popular holiday villages that line the coast. Its best-known sight is Le Castella, with the Aragonese castle on the facing islet.

▪ **SANTA SEVERINA.** This village has a Byzantine and Norman feel and is immersed in citrus and olive groves slightly south of the course of the Neto river. Here you can visit the church of S. Filomena and the Baptistery, dating from Byzantine times. The Grecìa district, abandoned after the 1783 earthquake, bears witness to the age-old local history.

CATANZARO AND REGGIO DI CALABRIA

At Calabria's narrowest point, the hills that frame the Gulf of Sant'Eufemia are an area with a great oenological vocation. Greco di Bianco is, on the other hand, the pride of the whole Reggio di Calabria province, which lines up numerous other quality productions on a triple front.

The province of Catanzaro, overlooking the sea on two close sides, owes its enological pride to Tyrrhenian vines. Production covers mainly the Lamezia DOC, to which are to be added, in the circumscribed zone of Nocera Terinese at the end of the Savuto valley, the Scavigna DOC and Valdamato IGT.

The wine production of the Reggio di Calabria province, on the other hand, presents a highly varied picture, with two DOC productions and a good seven IGTs – an indication of a developing reality. There are three production centers, which roughly correspond to the geographic subdivision of the coast: the central part, which develops along the Strait of Messina, covers the Reggio neighborhood from north to south, with the Arghillà and Pellaro IGTs; the Tyrrhenian one, covered by the Costa Viola IGT, follows the arc traced between Scilla (which has its own IGT) and Palmi; and the Ionian one, which has the two Greco di Bianco and Bivongi DOCs and the large Locride IGT, with the southern appendix of Palizzi.

In the Reign of Greco Bianco

The area ampelographic review comprises an element of exceptional importance in Greco Bianco, which produces passito wines of age-old renown. The selection then includes the red-berry vines of Calabrian tradition, starting with Gaglioppo and going on with Sicilian vanguards such as Nero d'Avola; among the white-berry varieties Montonico grapes, also destined to be used after drying, are worthy of special note. International grapes have also been introduced, especially among IGT productions, with a view to modernizing the blends – Cabernet, Merlot, Chardonnay, Sauvignon, Incrocio Manzoni, and Traminer Aromatico.

FROM THE SANT'EUFEMIA GULF TO ASPROMONTE

The first itinerary starts from Catanzaro, in tribute to the wine and gastronomy high rank of the regional capital, and crosses the watershed to

A wine estate not far from Lamezia Terme

Lametino, the principal wine-producing district in the province.

A land of very contrasting landscapes, the province of Reggio di Calabria and its wine-producing centers are then explored principally along the coastal routes, with the option of venturing along the winding but fascinating roads that cross Aspromonte and offer vast sweeping views.

▪ **CATANZARO.** The city stands to the south of Sila Piccola, on a windy, scenic spur within sight of the Ionian Sea. The winding Corso Mazzini guides your visit past stately 19th-century mansions and monumental squares. Special features definitely include local taverns, the so-called *putiche*, where you can taste a few but memorable Calabrian specialties such as *morseddhu*, a spicy dish of pork tripe. The wines to look for include the renowned Malvasia di Catanzaro.

▪ **LAMEZIA TERME.** This municipality brings together three villages between mountain and sea: Byzantine Nicastro, the main center, which has a 17th-century Cathedral with a majestic façade; Sambiase, a first class wine-producing center; and Sant'Eufemia Lamezia, a modern center after which the gulf is named. Slightly farther north is Nocera Terinese, an important wine-producing center in the Scavigna DOC together with nearby Falerna, but also involved in the production of Savuto DOC. 17th-century churches can be visited here.

▪ **REGGIO DI CALABRIA.** The region capital, rich in culture and outstanding gastronomy, is also the center of gravity of the wine-producing zones on the Tyrrhenian Sea (Scilla, Costa delle Viole) and on the Strait of Messina (Arghillà, Pellaro). After paying tribute to the Riace Bronzes, masterpieces of classical Greek statue production and the pride of the National Museum, and enjoying a stroll along Lungomare Matteotti (seafront) to admire the view of the Strait, embellished with flowers and exotic trees, a gastronomical break will feature excellent fish dishes such as *piscicotto alla marinara* (stockfish), *nannata* (fish fry) and *fravagghia* (small anchovies and sardines fried).

Wine production features renowned reds and some liquoroso whites, too. North of the capital are the noteworthy productions of Arghillà, Sambatello, and Campo Calabro, south those of Pellaro and Motta San Giovanni.

Bagnara Calabra's beach

Wineries *pp. 459-460*
Casignana, Lamezia Terme, Nocera Terinese.

Immediately north of the Strait, the coast arches in the idyllic landscape of Costa Viola, with Bagnara Calabra, a true gem, famous for swordfish with *salmoriglio* sauce (oil, lemon, garlic, and parsley) and for Zibibbo grapes. The local wines come from the Costa Viola and Scilla IGTs, made from traditional grapes but also from some of recent introduction.

■ **LOCRI.** The heir of a famous Magna Grecia settlement, this farming and business town has recently added seaside tourism to its economy. As well as the Museum and archeological excavations, its main prides include the wines from the Locride IGT, which covers almost all the Reggio's Ionian coast and the immediate hinterland.
The provincial road to Gioia Tauro climbs into Aspromonte past beautiful scenery; a suggested stop immediately inland is at Gerace, a quiet village with an imposing Cathedral and flourishing fabric and pottery crafts.
Heading south, you enter the home to the ancient Greco wine, now a DOC, the main production center of which is Bianco. Farther south – past Bovalino, from which departs the road leading to the heart of the Aspromonte National Park – you will discover the wines of the Palizzi IGT, named after a delightful village-castle and comprising the centers of the so-called Costa dei Gelsomini around Capo Spartivento.

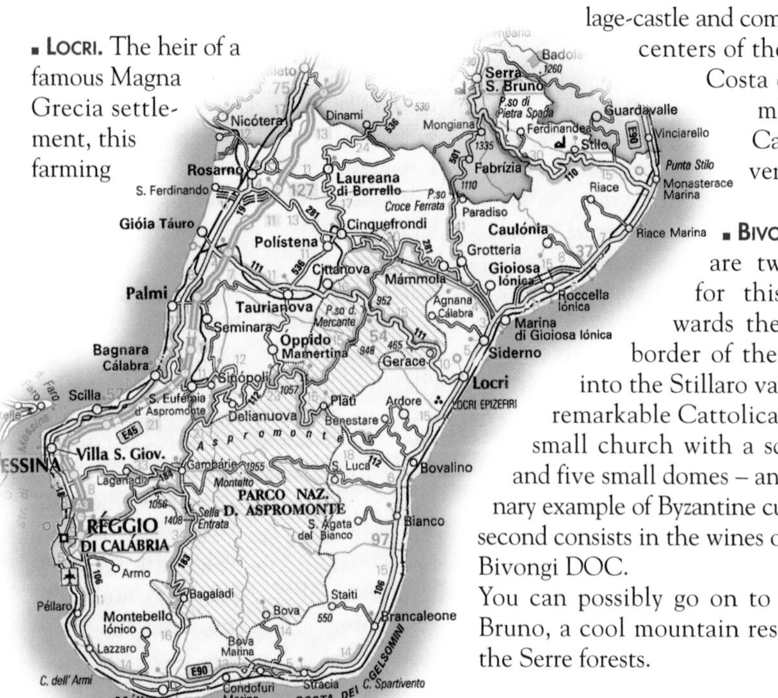

■ **BIVONGI.** There are two reasons for this trip towards the northern border of the province, into the Stillaro valley: one is remarkable Cattolica di Stilo, a small church with a square plan and five small domes – an extraordinary example of Byzantine culture – the second consists in the wines of the small Bivongi DOC.
You can possibly go on to Serra San Bruno, a cool mountain resort among the Serre forests.

▪ Specialties in Calabria ▪

CALABRIA'S LANDSCAPE features the contrasting environments of the coast (430 miles), on opposite though sometimes very close fronts, and of the mountains, which, instead of becoming lower as the Apennine ridge approaches its southern end, rises in the Pollino, Sila, and Aspromonte massifs. The effect of such contrasts is a unique alternation of exotic crops as citron, bergamot, and jasmine and high mountain vegetation, dominated by *Pinus leucodermis*, the pines that epitomize Calabria's natural beauty. A similar contrast is found at table, with Mediterranean flavors getting into contact with those of the mountains. Within sight of the sea are the olive groves that place the region, with its excellent productions, well near the top of the Italian ranking. Olive trees grow side by side with vines, the origins of which are rooted in Hellenic tradition. More Mediterranean flavors are those of the red onions of Tropea and the licorice of Rossano, the Zibibbo grapes of Pizzo and the torrone of Bagnara, the swordfish of the Strait of Messina and *rosamarina*, a fish preserve that is spread on bread. The market stalls also offer cheeses such as *caciocavallo silano* and *pecorino del Crotonese*, and cured meats hot with chili pepper (*soppressata* and sausages), or the *n'duja* of Spilingo, unique for it soft consistency and strong taste.

THE GENUINE CALABRIAN CUISINE, which lives on in village trattorias, simply exploits this wealth of flavors. Representatives of traditional gastronomy are *maccaruni*, especially when dressed alla pastora, with minced pork sauce and smoked ricotta; next comes kid goat, either simply cooked as a casserole with potatoes or accompanied by pasta with meat sauce, and deservingly eaten with eggplant or peppers, mere examples of the many country vegetable dishes. On the seaside, swordfish opens a completely different chapter with its various preparations, with *salmoriglio* sauce, *alla ghiotta*, as a roulade, etc. Last comes an old-fashioned dish, *pitta*, in which a bread base is combined with one of the options offered by tradition – one is *morseddu*, spicy sheep's offal cooked in red wine.

THE FIRST WINE RECOMMENDATION goes to the hearty reds made from Gaglioppo grapes; the labels to ask for are Cirò Rosso, Lamezia Rosso, Scavigna Rosso, and Savuto. Younger wines go well with cured meat hors-d'oeuvres, pastas dressed with strong sauces, first courses with meat, and with fresh *caciocavallo* cheese; the Riserva wines are for the great roasts, game, and matured cheeses.
Fish cuisine is well accompanied by dry white wines made from Greco grapes – Cirò Bianco, Lamezia Greco, Scavigna Bianco –; for heartier dishes, it is best to move on to a Cirò Rosato. Excellent results have been attained from international vines – Sauvignon and Cabernet, in particular. When the desserts arrive, the first request is for the famous Greco di Bianco, but with a little luck you can also taste rare wines such as Moscato di Saracena and Passito di Mantonico.

SICILY

THE FAR SOUTH: A NEW FRONTIER

In the last few years, Sicilian viticulture, long dedicated to the production of blending wines, has reaped the rewards of patient efforts at quality improvement in the vineyards and in the cellars, with truly interesting prospects for the future.

Sicily's vineyards, like the island itself, can be divided into three large areas: the western part, in the province of Trapani, with the celebrated Marsala wines; the northeastern sector around Mount Etna; the southern part, in the province of Ragusa. The entire island is a most felicitous setting for the vine: various soils combine with the warm and breezy climate to give excel-

Above, palm trees and vines on a farm in Sicily; left, Ragusa's countryside (top) and making ricotta at a local festival (bottom)

lent results with a minimum of human intervention. A naturalness which Sicily's growers and producers quite rightly present as one of the great virtues of their wines.

A view of Scopello's old tuna-fishing plant

SICILY, A LAND OF GREAT POTENTIAL

Given these benign natural conditions, it is easy to understand why Sicily, heir to traditions dating back to the Romans and the ancient Arabs, is traditionally Italy's most productive region, with present annual totals of almost 185 million US gallons. Less easy to accept are the reasons why, in the recent past, the region has been relegated to the role of blending-wine producer. It is a fact that, as recently as the 1950's, a large percentage of the island's wines was used to reinvigorate wines with a low level of alcohol. Then, in the space of two decades, a double revolution occurred. The first – from bulk wine to bottled wine, from quantity to quality – has come to a happy ending thanks to the combined action of improvements in the vineyards (that is the re-qualifying of stocks) and in the cellars, with the introduction of thermoconditioned vinification techniques. The second revolution is now under way, with an effort to express unfulfilled potential, as, for example, in the field of red wines. This is the new challenge for Sicilian viticulture, and the recent arrival of important producers from the North of Italy is an eloquent sign of its credibility.

TRADITION AND INNOVATION IN THE VINEYARDS

Traditional varieties dominate Sicily's ampelographic profile, in particular such white grapes as Catarratto Bianco Comune (35%) and Catarratto Bianco Lucido; along with Trebbiano Toscano, these varieties are easily in the majority. Nero d'Avola, also known as Calabrese, is the most important red grape, followed by Nerello Mascalese and Nerello Cappuccio. Less significant in percentage terms are white-berried Ansonica, Grecanico Dorato, Grillo, and Zibibbo, and red-berried Perricone and Frappato di Vittoria. *Alberello* is still the most widespread training system (38%) – reflecting a viticulture aimed at wines with a high alcohol content; *spalliera* and Guyot, with 35%, are now close behind and demonstrates a new search for quality. The *tendone* system, principally used for the cultivation of the Italia table grape, still account for 18%. An overall picture, therefore, strongly marked by tradition, but also so rapidly evoluting, as trend data show: native stocks are constantly improved through clone selection and they are more and more frequently supplemented by international varieties, mostly French.

Agrigento's countryside

Soon to Arrive: the Overall Sicily DOC

Change is even more evident in the cellars. One aspect is the increasing level of wines from indigenous grapes, producing varietal wines – pure Nero d'Avola is considered one of the world's best wines – or, alternatively, blended with international varieties which supplement and improve their features and bring them closer to current consumer taste. The other aspect is the more and more widespread usage of pure vinification for Chardonnay, Cabernet Sauvignon, Merlot, and Syrah, which draw special force from the Sicilian soil and climate. There are currently 19 DOC zones, including the very recent Monreale and Riesi. The future goal is the creation of a general Sicilia DOC, conceived as an umbrella appellation to give more precise identity on international markets to the whole island's production, a task presently assigned to the Sicilia IGT. In terms of future prospects, it should suffice to mention that, of the current 185 million US gallons produced, 3.3 million US gallons (only 2% of the regional total and 0.9% of the national total) are DOC wines. Lastly, it has to be said that a tourism-oriented region such is Sicily is also committed to the development of wine routes: the Istituto Regionale della Vite e del Vino (Regional Vine and Wine Institute) has designed as many as seven – the itineraries are described in detail in a brochure distributed free of charge and on the website www.vitevino.it.

Vineyards and dammusi *at Pantelleria, in the reign of Zibibbo grapes*

The Great Wines of Sicily

Marsala DOC
The oldest historical document referring to Marsala dates from 1773, when barrels of it were shipped from Trapani to England. Extra alcohol had been added to it so that it would better withstand the voyage, thus creating the strong wine esteemed through the centuries by connoisseurs worldwide. Current DOC regulations limit the zone of origin to the Trapani province plus the Alcamo area and the islands. Many white and red grape varieties go into its numerous versions: different types of Catarratto, Damaschino, Grillo, Inzolia; Nerello Mascalese, Nero d'Avola, Pignatello. The additional alcohol must come from wine or wine spirit and, if needed, from grape must concentrate.
The final product is divided into different categories, depending on sugar content (dry, semi-sweet, sweet), color (golden, amber, ruby), and ageing, from one to over ten years (Fine, Superiore, Superiore Riserva, Vergine and/or Soleras, Vergine and/or Soleras Stravecchio, Vergine and/or Soleras Riserva). It traditionally accompanies Sicilian pastries – *cannoli*, *cassata*, Martorana confections – and nowadays also cheeses streaked with green mold. Anyway, Marsala remains the "meditation wine" par excellence.

Florio's winery at Marsala

Bianco d'Alcamo DOC
This famous wine from Alcamo (a town on the Palermo-Trapani border) is made primarily from Cataratto grapes (min. 60%) grown in Sicily since time immemorial. Vinified pure, the grapes give a robust and harmonious wine, fairly pale straw yellow in color, with a Marsala-like aroma that intensifies with time; the taste is dry and full-bodied. The blend is completed with local grapes (Inzolia, Grillo, Grecanico) or more modern imports (Chardonnay, Müller Thurgau, Sauvignon). Bianco d'Alcamo, also made as spumante, goes well with seafood. In the late-harvest version it is a "meditation wine".

Nero d'Avola
Many labels carry the name of Sicily's most typical and exclusive red-berry grape. Its origins are unknown, and even its other name, Calabrese, could be misleading. Vinified pure, Nero d'Avola gives a wine with a characteristic cherry red color, fine in aroma and dry in taste, full-bodied and with a high alcohol content, which makes it suited to ageing. In blends with other Sicilian grapes such as Frappato or imports such as Cabernet Sauvignon, and it is found in all the island's DOC productions.
It goes with strongly flavored cheeses and robust meats, either used in pasta sauces or roasted or in sauce.

Moscato di Pantelleria DOC
This passito wine made on the homonymous island south of Sicily comes from Zibibbo grapes, a name of Arab origin meaning "dried grapes". One of its synonyms, Moscato d'Alessandria, indicates a probable Egyptian origin; the Romans, then, spread it through the Mediterranean Sea area. The wine is bright straw yellow with golden highlights in color, with a definite muscat aroma, dry taste, and a high alcohol content; drying the grapes accentuates these traits.

Malvasia delle Lipari
This famous dessert and "meditation wine" is the pride of the archipelago off the northeastern coast of Sicily. It is made from a variety of exclusive grapes, probably brought from Greek colonies in the 5th century BC, suitable for late-harvest and passito wines. Its aroma is fruity and its taste is sweet, with outstanding notes of honey.

SICILY'S DOC ZONES

❶ **DOC Alcamo** *Bianco, Ansonica (Inzolia), Cataratto, Chardonnay, Grecanico, Müller Thurgau, Sauvignon ▪ Rosato ▪ Rosso, Calabrese (Nero d'Avola), Cabernet Sauvignon, Syrah*

❷ **DOC Cerasuolo di Vittoria**

❸ **DOC Contea di Sclafani** *Bianco, Bianco Dolce, Ansonica (Insolia), Cataratto, Chardonnay, Grecanico, Grillo, Pinot Bianco, Sauvignon ▪ osato ▪ Rosso, Cabernet Sauvignon, Merlot, Nerello Mescalese Nero d'Avola, Pinot Nero, Perricone, Sangiovese, Syrah*

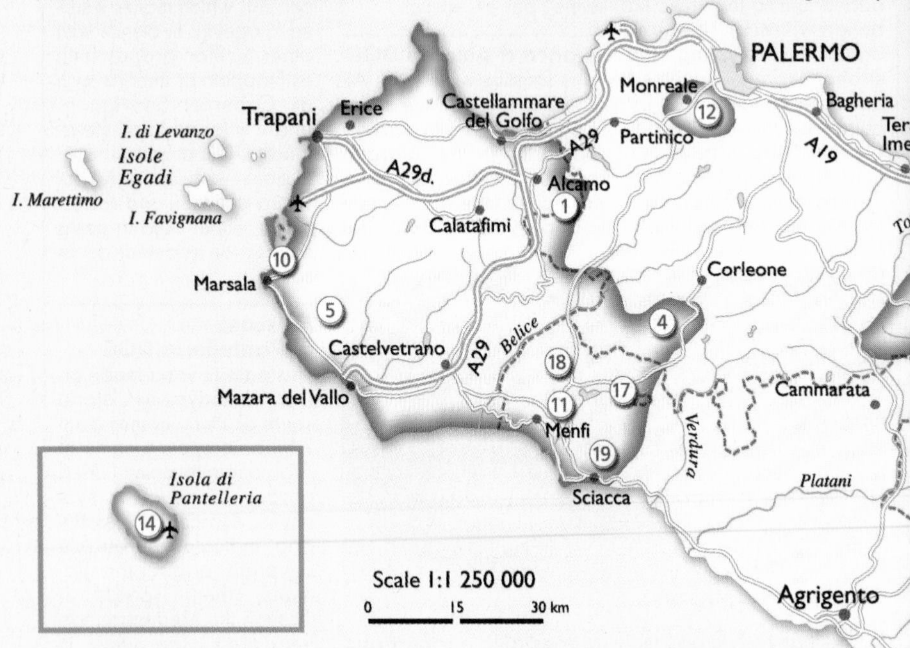

❹ **DOC Contessa Entellina** *Bianco, Ansonica, Chardonnay, Grecanico, Sauvignon ▪ Rosato ▪ Rosso, Cabernet Sauvignon, Merlot, Pinot Nero*

❺ **DOC Delia Nivolelli** *Bianco, Chardonnay, Damaschino, Grecanico, Grillo, Inzolia, Müller Thurgau, Sauvignon, Spumante ▪ Rosso ▪ Cabernet Sauvignon, Merlot, Nero d'Avola, Pignetello (Perricone), Sangiovese, Syrah*

❻ **DOC Eloro** *Rosato ▪ Rosso, Frappato, Nero d'Avola, Pachino, Pignatello*

❼ **DOC Etna** *Bianco ▪ Rosato ▪ Rosso*

❽ **DOC Faro**

❾ **DOC Malvasia delle Lipari**

❿ **DOC Marsala**

⓫ **DOC Menfi** *Bianco, Chardonnay, Feudo dei Fiori, Gracanico, Ansonica (Inzolia), Vendemmia Tardiva ▪ Rosso, Bonera, Cabernet Sauvignon, Merlot, Nero d'Avola, Sangiovese, Syrah*

⓬ **DOC Monreale** *Bianco, Ansonica (Inzolia), Cataratto, Chardonnay, Pinot Bianco ▪ Rosato ▪ Rosso ▪ Cabernet Sauvignon, Calabre (Nero d'Avola), Merlot, Perricone, Pinot Nero, Sangiovese, Syrah*

⓭ **DOC Moscato di Noto**

⓮ **DOC Moscato di Pantelleria or Moscato Passito di Pantelleria**

⓯ **DOC Moscato di Siracusa**

⓰ **DOC Riesi** *Bianco ▪ Rosato ▪ Rosso*

⓱ **DOC Sambuca di Sicilia** *Bianco, Chardonnay ▪ Rosato ▪ Rosso, Cabernet Sauvignon*

⓲ **DOC Santa Margherita di Belice** *Bianco, Ansonica, Cataratto, Grecanico ▪ Rosso, Nero d'Avola, Sangiovese*

⓳ **DOC Sciacca** *Bianco, Chardonnay, Grecanico, Riserva Rayana ▪ Rosato ▪ Rosso, Cabernet Sauvignon, Merlot, Nero d'Avola, Sangiovese*

IGT - Typical Geographic Indication

Camarro (Trapani); Colli Ericini (Trapani); Fontanarossa di Cerda (Palermo); Salemi (Trapani); Salina (Messina); Sicilia (Agrigento - Caltanisetta - Catania - Enna - Messina - Palermo - Ragusa - Siracusa - Trapani); Valle del Belice (Agrigento)

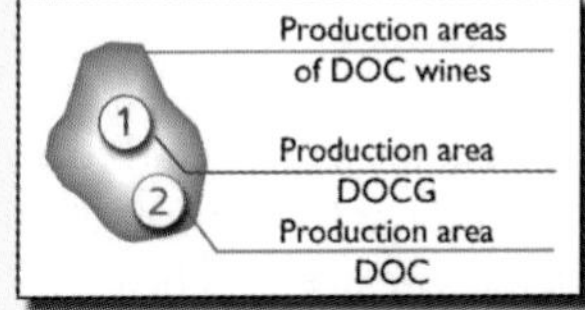

TRAPANI AND VAL DI MAZARA

This is Sicily's prime wine district for number of DOCs, solid traditions, and espousal of modern oenology principles.

The westernmost part of Sicily is its most important wine territory, featuring famous Marsala vines and Alcamo's, that give the well-known pleasant white. Soil has a high limestone content and the climate is dry and hot, although mitigated by sea breezes. The landscape is rural and covered with *alberello*-trained vines, mainly white-berry varieties. The island of Pantelleria is a world apart, where vines, seeking shelter from the wind in the tiniest valleys, create one of the loveliest wine landscapes in Italy. The prince of vines is Catarratto, of very ancient native origin and absolute first among Sicilian whites. Local grapes grown along with it include Grillo – the basis for the renowned Marsala vermouth – Ansonica or Inzolia, Damaschino, Grecanico, and a few more. Red-grape vines are Nero d'Avola and two varieties of Nerello. Pantelleria is instead the tiny realm of Zibibbo, from which moscato and passito wines are made.

The Vineyards of Western Sicily

Here DOC wines of longstanding history – Marsala, Alcamo, and Moscato di Pantelleria – go hand in hand with only recently recognized appellations such as Contessa Entellina, Delia Nivolelli, Sambuca di Sicilia, Contea di Sclafani, and Santa Margherita di Belice, as well as the Camarro and Colli Ericini IGTs. This confirms a trend to adding to traditional wines innovative products from French imported grapes.

FROM ALCAMO TO TRAPANI AND PANTELLERIA

This itinerary is partly in the Bianco d'Alcamo territory, from Alcamo to Segesta, and partly in Marsala land, from Trapani to Mazara; then, it heads towards the sea to reach Pantelleria, home to Zibibbo (which Moscato is made from). This is an exciting wine tour, steeped in history and splendid scenery.

▪ **ALCAMO**. Just inland from the Gulf of Castellammare, this town is Arab in name and origin. The oldest part retains its 14th-century orthogonal layout, featuring Corso VI Aprile together with a big central square and various churches with nice 16th-century works by the Gaginis. With its own DOC appellation, Alcamo is home to the experimental winery of the Istituto Regionale della Vite e del Vino (Regional Vine and Wine Institute), where you can taste a wide selection of Sicilian wines.

Vineyards, wine estates, and

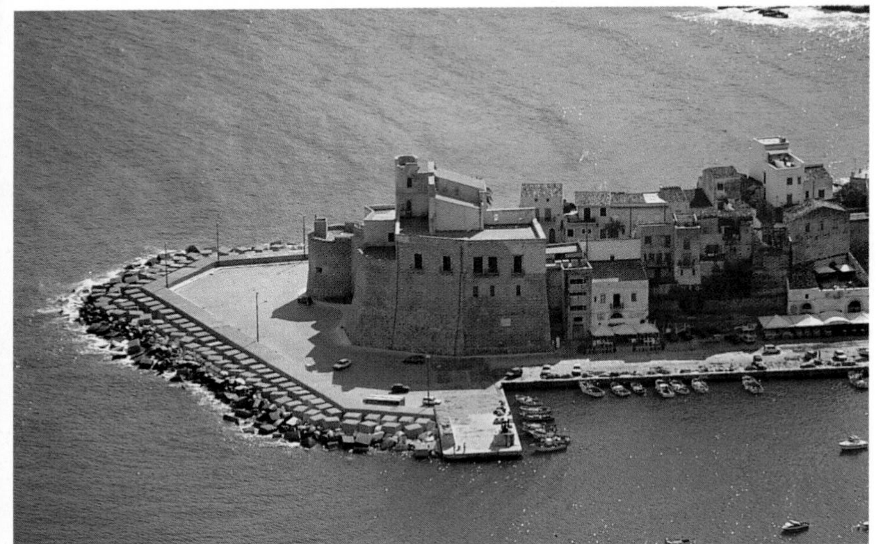

The castle standing on the Castellammare del Golfo promontory

cooperative wineries can also be seen in the countryside around nearby Partinico, along the road to Palermo.

▪ **CASTELLAMMARE DEL GOLFO**. In the center of a wide, sandy gulf, this town have its name from the Arab castle rising on a small headland near the inlet of the port. The town grew up later, in the 15th century. The long sandy beach is a safe place for bathing. Along the coast you quickly reach Scopello, a lovely town surrounding an old *baglio* (typical Sicilian farm) on a bay dominated by monolithic rocks and by the Zingaro Nature Reserve, where intact Mediterranean maquis plummets to the sea.

▪ **SEGESTA**. This is one of Sicily's "enchanted" places, with a huge Doric temple that appears out of nowhere, set in a timeless landscape. An amphitheater faces north from the summit of Mount Barbaro, with a panoramic view over the hills to the sea.

▪ **TRAPANI**. The sunny, windy provincial capital juts into the sea on a curving headland on Sicily's westernmost point. The old part is Arab in imprint. The Cathedral and ornate 18th-century buildings line Corso Vittorio Emanuele, and from the Regina Elena promenade you look out from the port to the salt pans and the Egadi Islands. Sculptures, paintings, pottery, jewelry, and precious coral items are on display at the Pepoli Regional Museum.

▪ **ERICE**. A very old town on the top of Mount San Giuliano, whose walls recount its history: with megalith foundations, dating from the time of the Elimi, they bear Roman features and Norman traits in the highest part and gates. The town conserves its medieval atmosphere, with narrow streets lined with stone houses. An exception is the Roman Via Regia, now Corso, rimmed with little baroque buildings and the Matrix church. A panoramic view of Trapani, the salt pans, and the Gulf of Bonagia opens out from the garden beneath the ancient acropolis.

▪ **MARSALA**. In the westernmost part of the island, the city was first a Phoenician trading center and then a Roman naval

A windmill in Trapani's salt-works

base. Its Roman name was *Lilibeus*, changed under centuries-long Arab occupation to *Marsa Allah* ("Allah's port"). Its latter-day fortunes came from its wine, a legacy of Roman tradition, refined by the Spaniards and introduced worldwide by the English in the late 18th century. The city has a wealth of monuments and museums (Tapestry Museum, Archeological Museum with the rare remains of a Punic ship) and from here you can visit Phoenician ruins on the Mozia islet in the Stagnone lagoon and the interesting pretty salt pans opposite. A first-rate wine town, Marsala has an exceptional concentration of wine companies and wineries.
An excursion inland takes you to Salemi with an imposing Frederick castle.

▪ **MAZARA DEL VALLO**. The center of spreading Arab conquests has its oldest part within the quadrangle overlooking the canal harbor on the Mazaro river; Piazza della Repubblica, with its Cathedral and other outstanding buildings, is the hub of city life, surrounded by the modern districts grown thanks to local fishing activities and wine. Among its specialties is couscous, reflecting its traditional contacts with North Africa.

▪ **PANTELLERIA**. Reached by sea from Trapani, this island has volcanic origins, accounting for its beautiful landscape and strange natural phenomena: Lake Venere, inside the old crater; the "stoves", steam-emitting caves; and the *favare*, crevices with boiling steam. In the heart of the Moscato DOC the vines are grown close to the ground, protected by dry walls from the strong winds that give Pantelleria the nickname of "Wind Island".

Wineries *pp.* 460-463
Alcamo, Marsala, Paceco, Pantelleria, Salaparuta, Trapani.

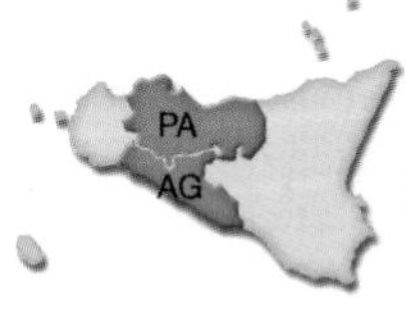

PALERMO AND AGRIGENTO

From coast to coast in the central-western part of the island is a big wine district differing both in scenery and in DOC production.

Palermo province is Sicily's largest and most heavily populated. To the west, its vineyards and olive groves touch on the Alcamo DOC zone, especially in the municipalities of Camporeale, Partinico, and San Cipirello. Eastward is the Madonie mountain group, with the centers of the Contea di Sclafani DOC. To the south it covers other wine areas and the Contessa Entellina DOC, on the borders with Agrigento. Agrigento has a number of localities known for table grapes and DOC wines (Sambuca di Sicilia, Menfi, Santa Margherita di Belice), and the entire province falls within the growing zone of Inzolia, the basis for many white wines. Another two DOC productions are in the heart of the island, Enna and Caltanisetta.

From Belice to the Madonie and the Ragusa Region

Agrigento, Palermo, and Piazza Armerina can be the tourist reference points of the diagonals crossing Sicily's central wine district. In some cases DOC labels in the zone come from famous places – Menfi, Monreale, Sciacca – and in others from lesser known ones – Contea di Sclafani, Contessa Entellina, Riesi, Sambuca di Sicilia, Santa Margherita di Belice –, but they all are of considerable caliber. The district is also covered by the Fontanarossa di Cerda and Valle del Belice IGTs.

ALONG THE INZOLIA AND NERO D'AVOLA ROUTES

The first itinerary, starting in Agrigento, covers a wide stretch of the southern coast and then crosses the interior along the Palermo-Sciacca road, ending at Monreale.

The second is the first part of the Nero d'Avola and Cerasuolo di Vittoria

Wheat fields and vineyards are the elements of the typical patchwork landscape in Sicily's inland

Route, a big wine tourism diagonal itinerary crossing the island from northwest to southeast, from the Palermo to the Ragusa province passing through Enna and Caltanisetta. This runs along the coast and then turns inland, climbing the Madonie slopes through woods and past little medieval hill towns.

▪ **AGRIGENTO.** Your attention is first caught by the great Doric temples standing high above the sea in fields of wheat and almond trees. Not far from the Valley of Temples you can visit the birth house (now converted into a museum) and tomb of great Italian playwright Luigi Pirandello (1867-1936), located in Caos. The tour of the city concludes with the regional Archeological Museum and a pleasant stroll through the beautiful Old Town.

▪ **SCIACCA.** Along the road from Agrigento, a Greek archeological site and a splendid beach call for a detour to Eraclea Minoa. Encircled by 16th-century walls, Sciacca's center is a maze of streets, courts, and lanes, with a square standing high above the sea. It is one of Sicily's most productive fishing ports and also a well frequented spa.

▪ **SELINUNTE.** Not far away, amidst rolling hills, lies Menfi, center of the homonymous DOC. A little further west another detour towards the coast leads to Selinunte, one of Sicily's finest archeological sites, with the ruins of ancient temples toppled by an earthquake. The area also features an acropolis high above the sea between the mouths of the Belice and Modione rivers.
The Belice valley is the gateway to the island's interior: Sambuca di Sicilia (with an Arab-style town imprint), Santa Margherita di Belice (center of the homimous DOC), Montevago, Poggioreale, Salaparuta (all partly rebuilt after the disastrous 1968 earthquake and with still visible ruins), Contessa Entellina, a DOC town and Albanian colony, San Cipirello, and finally Monreale.

▪ **MONREALE.** Perched on a hill overlooking the Conca d'Oro (the fertile plain surrounding Palermo), this town is famous

for its Norman Duomo, whose interior is entirely covered with a wealth of mosaics (12th-13th C.). Also of note are the cloister of the same period and the many baroque churches which dot the town.

▪ **PALERMO.** The "city of the Norman churches" – red domes rising from palm trees, mosaics gleaming in the shadows – is just one of Palermo's many profiles. In contrast are the stronger colors of the Vucciria, the old marketplace, and extremely diversified but always sumptuous wines and foods worthy of a capital city. Mondello, a little fishing village just outside the city, is Palermo's sea resort, with a crystal-clear water beach overlooked by Mount Pellegrino.
From Palermo you travel along the coast past the ruins of ancient Solunto heading for Casteldaccia, Cerda (known for its artichokes), and Sclafani Bagni, on the southern slopes of the Madonie mountain group, with its Contea di Sclafani DOC and a little spa.

▪ **CALTANISETTA.** Located in the heart of the island at the foot of Mount San Giuliano, it has its own heart is Piazza Garibaldi, with the Cathedral and church of S. Sebastiano, both built in the 16th century. It is famed for its sweets, especially its nougat and nut *torroncini*. From here the itinerary continues south, to Butera and the Gela plain, but well worth detours are Enna, with its scenic Castello di Lombardia, and Piazza Armerina, famous for the spectacular mosaics in the Casale Roman villa.

Sicilian cart at Agrigento

Wineries *pp. 460-463*
Butera, Camporeale, Castelbuono, Casteldaccia, Grotte, Menfi, Monreale, Palermo, Partinico, Piazza Armerina, Sambuca di Sicilia, San Cipirello, San Giuseppe Jato, Sclafani Bagni.

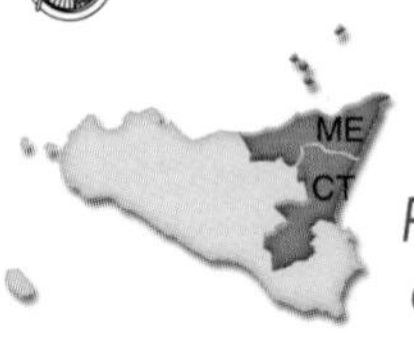

ETNA AND VAL DEMONE

Protagonists in northeastern Sicily are the Etna vineyards, along with the Peloritani's and Aeolian archipelago's ones.

The Catania area, dominated by Mount Etna, has its main viticulture zone on the volcano's fertile slopes. However, grapes are also grown in the province of Messina, in the lovely Alcantara valley and on the Peloritani hills, with Milazzo's production as much on the Strait side as on the Mediterranean Sea. Finally, vineyards are scattered over the volcanic rock territory of the Aeolian Islands.

Volcano Vineyards

The Etna DOC covers the outer slopes of the volcano from Randazzo to Adrano, at a height of 1650 ft.

Always favored by volcanic soil, vineyards show here a bend for red grapes, namely native Nerello in its Mascalese (first among the region's red-grape vines) and Cappuccio varieties. But white grapes are also grown here, such as ubiquitous Catarratto and the more characteristic Carricante (also called Catanese Bianco) and Minella Bianca. The Peloritani vineyards fall, instead, within the Faro DOC, where reds continue to prevail, enriched by

Nocera, once the basis for famous Milazzo strong blending wines.

As for the Aeolian Islands, the main center of production is verdant Salina, where Malvasia, laboriously cultivated on rugged terrain, has found its perfect habitat, to the point of being awarded a DOC. Aeolian production is also safeguarded by the Salina IGT.

THE ETNA WINES AND LIPARI MALVASIA ROUTE

This route goes from Catania to Taormina and beyond, with Mount Etna looming from above and landscapes changing from recent lava flows to centuries-old woods, Mediterranean maquis and vineyards hemmed with hedges of prickly-pear cactus. Next is a fascinating "voyage" to the Aeolian Islands, combining volcanic beaches with wineries.

▪ **CATANIA.** The emblem of Sicily's second-largest city is the Elephant Fountain, surmounted by an Egyptian obelisk and the insignia of Saint Agatha, city patroness. In addition to sumptuously baroque (and blackened by Etna's ashes) churches and mansions, you can visit the houses of novelist Giovanni Verga (1840-1922) and composer Vincenzo Bellini (1801-1835).

▪ **ACIREALE.** This town lies beyond Aci Castello and Aci Trezza, the three of them being legendary seafaring centers. Rising from the sea not far from the beach are the Faraglioni or Cyclops' Islands, basalt monoliths that Polyphemus is said to have hurled against fleeing Ulysses.

Of the nine "Aci" towns built in the 13th century from the ruins of earthquake-destroyed ancient *Akis*, this is the most important, with impressive baroque monuments and lovely citrus groves surrounding it. Going up the volcano's slopes you come to two wine towns, Viagrande and Trecastagni, on the edge of the Etna Nature Park: oak and pine forests, the crater's lunar landscapes, and endless scenic views from the hinterland to the sea are some of the attractions.

▪ **TAORMINA.** You continue on to Zafferana Etnea, with its baroque Mother church at the top of a scenic flight of stairs on the lava-flow rim, to Santa Venerina, Milo (a wine town), and 17th-century Sant'Alfio, famous for its millennium-old Hundred Horses Oak, considered Europe's oldest and biggest, until you finally reach Taormina.

This is a splendid, extremely elegant resort to be discovered by strolling along the Corso and through the square, steeped in

Vineyards and thick woods along the road up the Etna from Nicolosi

Aeolian Islands: the Strombolicchio seen from Stromboli

an enchanting scenery. The views from the Greek Theater are unforgettable, with Etna, the outline of Calabria, and the sea as backdrops.

■ **RANDAZZO.** Again at the foot of the volcano, passing through Piedimonte Etneo (with Carricante and Nerello Cappuccio vineyards climbing the slopes to a height of 2300 ft), you come to Linguaglossa, starting point of one of the easiest access roads to the Etna Park, going up to the crater (along the way you can taste cold meats and cheeses together with excellent local wines), and Castiglione di Sicilia, amidst vineyards and hazel groves. Finally, Randazzo is a medieval town built in volcanic stone, lying above Alcantara on the Etna northern slope within the Nebrodi Park. Three different ethnic communities settled here – Greek, Latin, and Lombard –, each gathering around their own church.

Fishers of Aci Trezza

Close by is the Maniace abbey, once owned by Admiral Nelson and now a sumptuous residence. Here pistachios are grown, on the furthest edge of the Etna DOC.

■ **MESSINA.** The "gateway to Sicily", lying between the Strait and the Peloritani mountains, is the main center of the Faro DOC production. It was rebuilt after the 1908 earthquake that destroyed almost all of it. In Piazza del Duomo are the 16th-century Orione Fountain and the Norman Cathedral, alongside the famous bell tower featuring a complex mechanical clock with automatons, inaugurated in 1933.

Along the Mediterranean coast, vineyards suddenly shift from the shore to the heights of the Peloritani mountains, yielding grapes of various types. A narrow, beach-lined peninsula juts out from nearby Milazzo, which features a castle on the headland facing the Aeolian Islands, an Old Town, and newer districts below it.

■ **LIPARI**. Archeological digs and sturdy architecture recount the history of the largest of the Aeolian Islands, colonized in ancient times and once a hub of Mediterranean culture (its castle contains the Aeolian Archeology Museum). Of volcanic origin, like the archipelago's other islands – Vulcano, Salina, Panarea, Stromboli, Filicudi, and Alicudi –, it has splendid white pumice beaches and a verdant interior.

Wineries *pp. 460-463*
Caltagirone, Castiglione di Sicilia, Catania, Messina, Santa Marina Salina, Santa Venerina, Viagrande.

■ **SANTA MARINA SALINA**. Green Salina, mountainous and rich in fresh water, is the archipelago's wine center. The island got its name from the old salt works built in the salty Lake Lingua, a wetland of environmental interest. It is also famous for its capers.

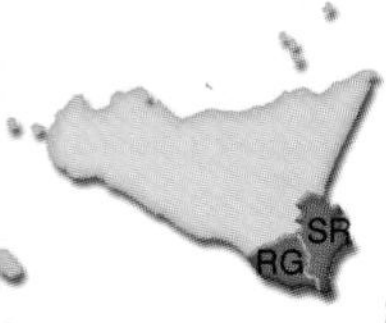

VAL DI NOTO

The southernmost part of the island, bordering on both the Ionian and the Sicilian seas, also marks the passage between two different wine zones.

The southernmost part of Sicily, with the Ibleo limestone plateau, has two interesting viticulture zones whose fame is based on traditional vines: overlooking the Ionian are the Moscato di Noto and Moscato di Siracusa DOC vineyards; facing south are the lands of renowned Cerasuolo di Vittoria.

The Southeastern Vineyards

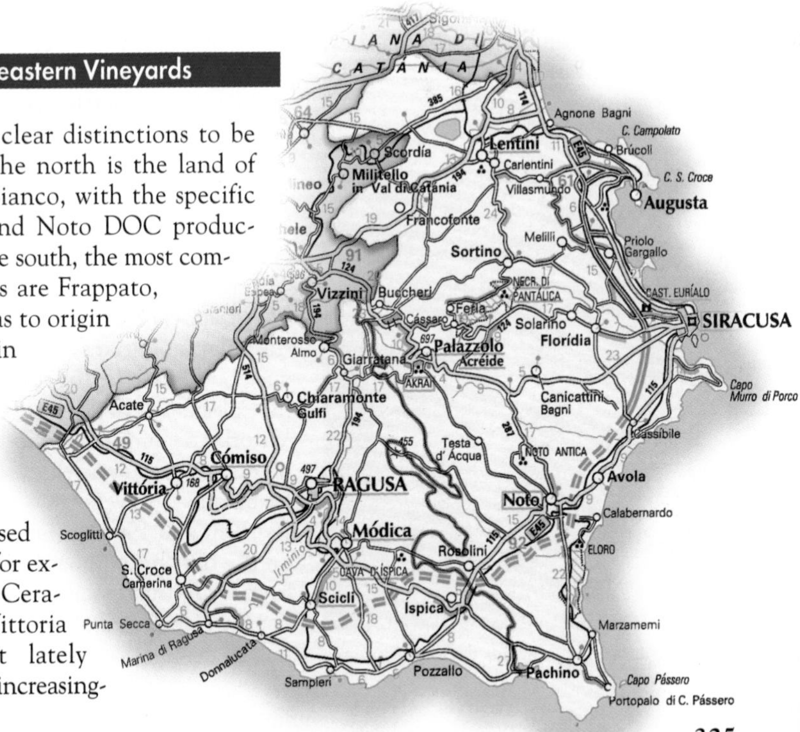

There are clear distinctions to be made: to the north is the land of Moscato Bianco, with the specific Siracusa and Noto DOC productions; to the south, the most common grapes are Frappato, unknown as to origin but grown in the Ragusa area since time immemorial. They are generally used in blends, for example in Cerasuolo di Vittoria DOC, but lately have been increasingly vinified pure. Alongside Frappato grows Nero d'Avola, also called Calabrese; while found all over the island, its best results are gotten here, by itself or in blends. Completing the picture is the Eloro DOC, instituted to valorize the reds in the southern part of the Siracusa province.

ALONG THE MOSCATO DI NOTO AND CERASUOLO DI VITTORIA ROUTES

Baroque extravagance and Moscato fame make Noto the focal point of a first brief wine tour starting from Siracusa.
The second part of this long "diagonal" itinerary from Palermo to Ragusa (also mentioned in the preceding pages) covers the Ragusa area.

▪ **SIRACUSA**. A city unique in charm, with the Ortigia Island condensing centuries of history and an Archeological Park perpetuating the history and legends of one of the most powerful Magna Grecia cities. The itinerary goes inland, stopping to visit the archeological sites of Pantalica and Palazzolo Acreide, and also to admire the beautiful Anapo river valley, now a Nature Reserve, that can also be visited on horse-drawn carts.

An estate at Pachino, towards the south-eastern tip of Sicily

Wineries *pp. 460-463*
Acate, Chiaramonte Gulfi, Comiso, Ispica, Siracusa, Vittoria.

▪ **NOTO**. A capital of baroque art and important wine town, it exemplifies the ideal wine tourism attraction. The Corso and square are splendid baroque backdrops, enriched with virtuoso sculptural detail. Its homogeneous architectural imprint stems from reconstruction after the 1693 earthquake. As for wines, the reds of the recent Eloro DOC rival famous Moscato.
Beautiful beaches and briny ponds can be seen around Capo Passero and Pachino, at the southern end of Sicily, amidst the Eloro DOC vineyards and hothouses for baby tomatoes and early produce.

▪ **RAGUSA**. A city of indigenous Siculi origin, it has a baroque imprint (typical of the southeastern part of the island) also stemming from reconstruction after the 1693 earthquake. Laid out like a checkerboard on the Ragusa Superiore plateau and picturesquely huddled on the mount of the primitive settlement (Ragusa Inferiore or Ibla), it is dotted with churches and dominated by the scenic Cathedral of S. Giorgio.
Nearby Modica, another jewel of Sicilian Baroque, is worth a side trip.

▪ **VITTORIA**. The town lies at the foot of the Iblei mountains, amidst early-produce hothouses. In 1607 countess Vittoria Colonna of Modica (hence the name Vittoria) commissioned the construction of the first urban nucleus to enhance her farmlands.
Its 18th- and 19th-century architecture on the old checkerboard layout derives from reconstruction after the earthquake of 1693. Nero d'Avola and Frappato are used to make Cerasuolo di Vittoria DOC.

Specialties in Sicily

IN THE HEART OF the Mediterranean, Sicily has been a cultural crossroads for many thousands of years. Never asserting itself, always dominated, but clever enough to absorb the special traits from the many different cultures: Greek and Phoenician, Roman and Byzantine, Arab and Norman, Spanish and French. From olives to oranges, from couscous to salted cod, Sicilians have inherited a little something from everyone. Even from the English, however short-lived their presence, who took Marsala to fame. To its complex history the island adds peerless natural resources: just think of Etna and how much its wines owe to its volcanic soil, or the tuna and swordfish that fill the sea, or even the humble caper plant, treasure of the smaller islands.

SICILY IS A WONDERFUL UNIVERSE, with which one is usually acquainted only superficially. Its fame is tied to its seaside resorts and the artistic heritage of just a few cities. Traveling through it, however, you become aware of the exceptional grazing and farming resources of its interior. Or visiting the Vucciria, Palermo's great market, steeped in aromas, images, and voices greeting the passer-by you get to know the region's most hidden nature. Here, on the street, you can begin to discover Sicilian cuisine: from rice *arancini* to batter-fried vegetables and *sfinciuni*, soft flatbread made expressly to hold tomato and anchovies, capers... Typical of Palermo is pasta with sardine sauce, which blends sea and land with its wild fennel seasoning. And then it is the turn of swordfish rolls, or tuna cooked in various ways: with tomatoes and olives, with white wine, even sweet-and-sour with onions; and *caponata*, the queen of side dishes. Fantastic are desserts, *cassata* and *cannoli*, combining the sweetness of ricotta with the aroma of pistachios, and Martorana "fruits", colorful almond paste confections. Another celebrity of Sicilian cooking is *pasta alla Norma*, a typical dish of Catania with a reference to Bellini, made with fried eggplant, tomato, and sharp pecorino. It lies midway between the two extremes of Sicilian cuisine, very simple on the one hand and very complicated on the other: from *pasta ca muddica*, with soft bread giving consistency to an oil and salted anchovy sauce, to *pasta ncasciata*, a sumptuous timbale enriched with everything you can imagine.

AS FOR WINES, it is hard to think of other regions as highly varied. White wines for seafood, like Alcamo or the new, surprising generations of Chardonnay, Pinot Bianco, and Sauvignon. Red wines for flavorsome cheeses and inland meats: Nero d'Avola, Rosso dell'Etna, Cerasuolo di Vittoria, or the international labels that have taken root on the island – Cabernet Sauvignon, Merlot, and Syrah.
There is an extraordinary variety of sweet and potently alcoholic wines, as if responding to the wealth of pastries: Malvasia di Lipari, Moscato di Noto, Passito di Pantelleria, ending with Marsala, under an exceptional assortment of labels. There is even a special sour cherry wine, among the few to measure up to the super-pure chocolate that is a great tradition of Modica.

SARDINIA

A HIGH-QUALITY ISLAND

A pristine natural environment and ancient traditions of high-quality wine-making are the strong points of new Sardinian viticulture which, beneath the banner of the Vermentino DOCG, is looking towards wine tourism as a stimulating factor in its growth.

The *Carta de Logu*, the act by which Eleonora, sovreign of the Giudicato di Arborea, ordered that vineyards be planted on uncultivated territory, dates back to 1392. Wine-making on the island already had a millennium-old history at that time, but it gained, by way of that initiative, an even larger place in the Sardinian economy and society, laying the base for its current fortunes.

Above, a winery in Alghero; left, sheep-raising in the Oristano area (top) and a view of Costa del Paradiso (bottom); opposite, Cala di Volpe on the Costa Smeralda

A Strong Tie With Tradition

Dry white wines of great character, a series of dessert wines which is virtually unique, rapidly improving red wines: this sums up, in a few words, the current Sardinian oenological picture. The vineyards, although they show the fairly homogeneous presence of certain varieties, can be divided into three areas. To the south is the ample zone of Cagliari, which includes not only the Campidano corridor but also the neighboring hills of Iglesias and Sarrabus. In the center are the plains of the upper Campidano and of Sinis, near Oristano, plus the hills of Arborea and Mandrolisai in the province of Nuoro. To the north are the territory of Nurra, near Alghero, the rolling countryside of Logudoro, south of Cagliari, and the harsh and rugged lands of Gallura, towards Olbia, swept and shaped by the sea winds.

Statistics show a region which, in terms of varieties, remains faithful to its traditions. Most of the cultivated vines are autochthonous, with pride of place going to the white Nuragus (22.1%) and the red Cannonau (20.8%) and Monica (17.8%). The total figure surpasses 88% if Pascale di Cagliari, Vermentino Bianco, and Carignano are added. Other grapes of a certain significance are the indigenous Malvasia di Sardegna, Vernaccia di Oristano, and Girò, with only Sangiovese and Trebbiano as major imported varieties. In terms of geographical distribution, many varieties are present well beyond their zones of origin. The most typical examples are Cannonau, Monica, and Moscato, but more recently Vermentino has advanced far beyond the boundaries of Gallura as well.

The Great Re-Launch of Wine-Making

Production trends are significant, with a drop from the over 66 million US gallons in the 1970's to the 20 million gallons of today. This can by explained by the financial incentives offered for vine uprooting, part of the European Economic Community program for reducing large wine surpluses, but also by the recurrent problems of drought, which drove many cultivators to give up wine-growing. This has led to a situation in which, despite an improved overall quality and a strong demand for its wines, Sardinia has found itself lacking in grapes. Over 90% of the region's wines are drunk on the island, but even this total can only satisfy 50-60% of local demand. To bring supply and demand into better balance, new vineyards are being planted both with indigenous and, at a lesser extent, imported varieties, the latter being looked at as a means to improve quality of the wines and offer a larger choice to consumers.

With one DOCG wine, Vermentino di Gallura, 19 DOC zones, and various IGTs, Sardinia demonstrates a notable attention to guaranteed quality. More than 10% of the island's wine is DOC labelled, a percentage significantly higher than other regions' in central and southern Italy. DOC codes have been shaped to encourage the production of varietal wines, while the category of table wines, more complex in their blends, offers producers space for more creativity. The standard-bearer of the viticulture of the future is Vermentino di Gallura, exported as a wine of the highest quality level.

SARDINIA'S DOC ZONES

Bocche di Bonifacio
I. Maddalena
I. Caprera
Santa Teresa Gallura
Palau
Liscia
I. Asinara
Golfo dell'Asinara
1
Olbia
Castelsardo
Tempio Pausania
Coghinas
Porto Torres
15
Sassari
Lago di Coghinas
R. Mannu
2
C. Caccia
Alghero
Ozieri
Siniscola
Capo Comino
14 18
5
Tirso
Cedrino
12
8
Nuoro
Bosa
Macomer
19
MAR DI SARDEGNA
5
Dorgali
Golfo di Orosei
Orgosolo
17
Abbasanta
Fonni
Lago Omodeo
Monti del Gennargentu
1834
10
Tirso
Oristano
Laconi
Arbatax
Lanusei
20
Arborea
3
18
Ierzu
5
Terralba
14
MAR TIRRENO
4
Mannu
Lago Mulargia
7 9 11
Guspini
Sanluri
16
Flumendosa
17
S. Andrea Frius
7
13
5
Muravera
Iglesias
9
Cixerri
11
Carbonia
Stagno di Cagliari
CAGLIARI
Villasimius
6
Isola di San Pietro
Golfo di Cagliari
Capo Carbonara
S. Antioco
Isola di Sant'Antioco
Teulada
Capo Teulada

Production areas of DOC wines
1 Production area DOCG
2 Production area DOC

Scale 1:1 500 000
0 15 30 km

1 **DOCG Vermentino di Gallura**
2 **DOC Alghero** *Bianco, Chardonnay, Sauvignon, Torbato, Vermentino ▪ Rosato ▪ Rosso, Cabernet, Cagnulari, Sangiovese*
3 **DOC Arborea** *Trebbiano ▪ Sangiovese*
4 **DOC Campidano di Terralba or Terralba**
5 **DOC Cannonau di Sardegna** *Rosato ▪ Rosso*
6 **DOC Carignano del Sulcis** *Rosato ▪ Rosso*
7 **DOC Girò di Cagliari**
8 **DOC Malvasia di Bosa**
9 **DOC Malvasia di Cagliari**
10 **DOC Mandrolisai** *Rosato ▪ Rosso*
11 **DOC Monica di Cagliari**
12 **DOC Monica di Sardegna**
13 **DOC Moscato di Cagliari**
14 **DOC Moscato di Sardegna**
15 **DOC Moscato di Sorso-Sennori**
16 **DOC Nasco di Cagliari**
17 **DOC Nuragus di Cagliari**
18 **DOC Sardegna Semidano**
19 **DOC Vermentino di Sardegna**
20 **DOC Vernaccia di Oristano**

IGT - Typical Geographic Indication

Barbagia (Nuoro); Colli del Limbara (Sassari - Nuoro); Isola dei Nuraghi (Cagliari - Nuoro - Oristano - Sassari); Marmilla (Cagliari - Oristano); Nurra (Sassari); Ogliastra (Nuoro - Cagliari); Parteolla (Cagliari); Planargia (Nuoro - Oristano); Provincia di Nuoro (Nuoro); Romangia (Sassari); Sibiola (Cagliari); Tharros (Oristano); Trexenta (Cagliari); Valle del Tirso (Oristano); Valli di Porto Pino (Cagliari).

The Great Wines of Sardinia

VERMENTINO DI GALLURA DOCG

The island's most prestigious wine, Vermentino di Gallura DOCG, has Spanish ancestry due to the Catalan settlement in Alghero and centuries of maritime contact with the Iberian Peninsula. The Vermentino production area involves 21 municipalities in the province of Sassari – including Santa Teresa, Gallura's main center, and Berchidda, the production hub – and two in the province of Nuoro.

Regulations dictate the use of at least 95% Vermentino grapes and codify the following organoleptic traits: straw yellow color with greenish higtlights; a subtle, deep, and delicate aroma, with apple and flower hints; alcoholic, mellow taste, full-bodied but elegant and with a slightly bitter aftertaste. Minimum alcohol content is 12%, rising to 13% for Superiore. It is finest with lobster, a Gallura specialty, but it also goes well with every kind of shellfish and fish, from hors-d'oeuvres to entrées.

A girl wearing the Sardinian costume

CANNONAU DI SARDEGNA DOC

Documented as early as 1612, the vine probably comes from a variety of Grenache brought to the island by the Spaniards. The wine from its grapes is ruby red (deepness varies), tending to orangey with age, with characteristic aroma and dry, bitterish taste; alcohol content is 12.5%. Regulations dictate production in the areas of Oliena, Nepente di Oliena, Capo Ferrato, and Jerzu, and provide for a Riserva version (13% alcohol content). Cannonau is also made in dry and naturally sweet liquoroso versions. It goes well with red meats and tasty cheeses; the Riserva is for game and ripe cheeses and the liquoroso type is ideal as dessert or "meditation" wine.

NURAGUS DI CAGLIARI DOC

This white wine comes from the Nuragus vine, probably brought here by the Phoenicians and now found mainly in the Cagliari and Oristano provinces. The wine is pale straw yellow, sometimes with greenish highlights, vinous in aroma with slightly tart, dry, or somewhat semi-sweet (Amabile) taste; it is also made in a fizzy (Frizzante) version. It accompanies fish and shellfish; the Frizzante and Amabile versions can be drunk throughout the meal.

VERNACCIA DI ORISTANO DOC

The homonymous vine, grown in the lower Tirso Valley, is thought by some to have been brought by Phoenicians from ancient Tharros, and by others to be a Spanish import. The wine is golden or amber in color, with a delicate, floral aroma and fine, warm taste with an almond aftertaste; alcohol content is 15% (15.5% for the Superiore type). It is good with all kinds of seafood. Regulations also provide for a liquoroso (16% alcohol) and a dry liquoroso (18%) version as "meditation" or, in the second case, as aperitif wines.

Vineyards near the Giants' Tombs at Arzachena

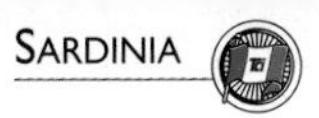

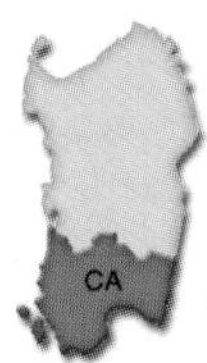

THE CAGLIARI REGION

The southern vineyards stretch from Campidano to Sulcis and Sant'Antioco on one side, and from Sarrabus to the Tyrrhenian coast on the other.

This is Sardinia's most important wine district, both for cultivated surface and production, since almost all of the region's DOCs are found here. The vines cover Campidano – the plain running from Cagliari to Oristano – and branch out onto the hills that sweep to the sea: Iglesias and Sulcis to the west, Trexenta and Sarrabus to the east. This is the stronghold of traditional wines, with exclusive productions and specific region-wide labels.

The best known among the dry white wines are Nuragus and Cannonau. The first is the leader in Sardinian viticulture and also considered to be the oldest vine, introduced by the Phoenicians or even native; it is also grown in the province of Oristano and in some municipalities in the Nuoro area. The second, thought to be of Iberian origin, is a relative of French Grenache and Aragon's Granaxa: around Cagliari there is geographical indication production in the eastern communities of Vallaputzu, Muravera, and Capo Ferrato.

On the opposite side, in Sulcis and especially in the Sant'Antioco zone, red Carignano stands out; also from Spain or the French Midi, it is a quite generous wine. Equally rich in color is Girò, delicately sweet and therefore best at the end of the meal. Next in the dessert wine selections is Monica, also from red grapes, while whites are Malvasia (thought to have been brought by the Byzantines) and Nasco, cultivated mainly in Campidano and one of Sardinia's oldest vines, probably autochthonous. Then come the IGTs: regional Isola dei Nuraghi; provincial Parteolla, Sibiola, Trexenta, and Valli di Porto Pino; Marmilla, on the border with Oristano; and Ogliastra, shared with Nuoro.

The Southern Vinelands

There are three wine districts around Cagliari. The first is Campidano, the inland plain, together with the Trexenta hills, that cover the northern part of the province; here regional wines are made, along with Monica, Nasco, Moscato, Malvasia, Girò, and Nuragus di Cagliari. The second is Sarrabus and the eastern coast, a part of Sardinia still unexplored, particularly interesting for the Cannonau di Sardegna produced in the Capo Ferrato area. Third are Sulcis and its islands, in the western part, home to Carignano, one of the up-and-coming reds of Sardinian viniculture, complemented by white Monica and Vermentino di Sardegna.

THE CAMPIDANO, TREXENTA, SARRABUS, AND SULCIS AREAS

The first part of this route is through the Cagliari inland and hills in the northern part of the province; here Monica, Nasco, Moscato, Malvasia, Girò, and Nuragus di Cagliari are produced in addition to regional wines.
It then moves to a part of Sardinia as yet to be discovered, Sarrabus, following a long inland diagonal and a scenic return to the coast. Here the wine interest is for Cannonau di Sardegna in its specific Capo Ferrato denomination.
Finally, Sulcis, from Iglesias to Santadi, with lovely land- and seascapes: this is the home to Carignano, one of the island's emerging wines together with Monica and Vermentino di Sardegna.

▪ **CAGLIARI**. Amidst salt pans and ponds home to flamingos, the region capital is a history-rich maritime city: it has Pisan towers and churches (starting with the Cathedral) and a Spanish-style castle, as well as 18th- and 19th-century districts of Ligurian and Piedmont influence. Many rooms of its Archeological Museum are devoted to Nuraghic culture, including splendid little votive bronzes.
As for other travel pleasures, there are quite a few, both in the city and around it. As soon as you start inland for Decimamannu, you can stop off at the WWF Oasis of Mount Arcosu, near Uta, part of the Sulcis massif and the last Sardinian deer sanctuary.

▪ **SENORBI**. From Monastir you take the scenic Centrale Sarda road to Senorbi,

The cork-oaks of the Giara di Gèsturi in the Cagliari area

Carloforte's salt pans on the San Pietro island

former capital of the region called Trexenta: this is a rolling land of hills and dales and great wine traditions, owner of a specific IGT. Senorbi radiates around its main square, site of the parish church of S. Barbara. Westward, on the border with Oristano, are the vineyards of the Marmilla IGT and the towns of Sanluri (with the 14th-century castle of Eleonora d'Arborea) and Sardara, a spa resort with a Romanesque-Gothic church and a Nuraghic temple.

▪ **DOLIANOVA**. Southwards again from Cagliari you come to this important wine town on the boundary between Sarrabus and Campidano, main center of the Parteolla IGT. You can visit the beautiful church of S. Pantaleo (12th and 13th C.), with fragments of ancient frescos in its interior. Close by is another small but significant wine town, Serdiana (Parteolla and Sibiola IGTs).

▪ **CASTIADAS**. This is a fundamental stop, "hinge-pin" of the southeastern tour to Sarrabus and the coast. Going past Cagliari's Poetto beach and Quartu Sant'Elena, you take the Orientale Sarda national road no. 125 that crosses the rugged Sette Fratelli mountain area, reaching the Tyrrhenian coast at San Priamo. Just a little north is Muravera, amidst vineyards, almond trees, and hedges of prickly-pear cactus, with the neighboring wine towns of San Vito and Villaputzu, on the southern rim of the Ogliastra IGT. Going south again, towards the lovely coast, you reach Castiadas, not far from Capo Ferrato (that lends its name to the local Cannonau di Sardegna). The town, in the center of reclamation lands, retains a 19th-century prison complex (which you can visit). The shoreline route returning to Cagliari starts from Villasimius, an enchanting resort on the southeastern tip of the island.

▪ **SANT'ANTIOCO**. This is reached from Iglesias – an old mining center with a beautiful Cathedral built in the 13th century – following the Sud-Occidentale Sarda road with possible scenic detours to Masua and Portoscuso, on the sea, or stops at the Nuraghic and Punic-Phoenician sites of Nuraxi Figus and Monte Sirai.
The road runs along the isthmus connecting Sardinia's main land with Sant'Antioco, and finally reaches the latter locality, on the site of Phoenician *Sulcis* (its current name comes from the Christian martyr, St Antioch, buried in the catacombs under the parish church). Worth visiting are the Archeological Museum and the Tophet di Sulcis (the remains of a Phoenician shrine with urns). You quickly get to the beautiful Calasetta beach, departure point for the ferries to Carloforte, the only village on mountainous San Pietro island which has old mines, salt works, tuna fisheries, and lovely sandy beaches on its eastern coast.

Wineries *pp. 463-465*
Dolianova, Santadi, Senorbì, Serdiana.

The parish church of S. Barlomeo is Ligurian in style; the remains of 18th-century walls and fortifications loom from above.

▪ **SANTADI.** Along the road heading inland you stop at Tratalìas to visit the Romanesque-Pisan church of S. Maria di Monserrato (1213) and continue among the Valli di Porto Pino IGT vineyards that cover the hilly zone arching towards Teulada. Santadi is an important farming town divided by the Mannu river into a lower and an older upper part, spread around the parish church of S. Nicolò. Just outside of town are the Phoenician-Punic Pani Loriga fortress and two caves of speleological and archeological interest. To return to Cagliari you can follow the Costa del Sud (Southern Coast) from Teulada to Pula and Sarroch, an extraordinary stretch of coast offering wonderful seascapes and archeological sites (beginning with the Nora excavations).

FROM ORISTANO TO NUORO

From the lower western coast to the Gennargentu mountain range, vines help designing the fascinating landscape of central Sardinia.

In the middle of the island, vineyards lie between the Campidano and Sinis plains, around Oristano, and the Arborea and Mandrolisai hills, at the foot of the Gennargentu range, but also in the two Tyrrhenian offshoots of the Ogliastra and Gulf of Orosei areas.
The zone typically combines traditional vines with those recently introduced, like Sangiovese and Trebbiano Toscano, grown in the Arborea DOC. Tradition standard-holders are Vernaccia di Oristano, autochthonous of the Tirso valley, and, among the whites, Malvasia di Bosa. Reds include the wines of the Campidano di Terralba and Mandrolisai DOCs. Bovale is the prevalent variety, probably Iberian in origin, grown in the Grande and Sardo types; alongside it are Cannonau and Monica. Localized cultivation of Cannonau can also be found in Oliena and Jerzu. IGTs in the district are: Barbagia, Ogliastra, Planargia; in the province of Nuoro, Tharros and Valle del Tirso.

The Central Sardinia Vineyards

The central part of the island has two quite different wine scenes. Around Oristano are the Sinis coastal area and the Campidano plain, rising from which are the Arborea and Mandrolisai hills. DOC labels: Vernaccia di Oristano, Arborea, Campidano di Terralba, Monica di Sardegna, Sardegna Semidano, Mandrolisai. In the province of Nuoro, instead, are Barbagia and Ogliastra, set against the rugged scenery of the Gennargentu range and Tyrrhenian coastline; by the sea there are specific productions of Cannonau and Vermentino.

FROM THE PLAIN AND THE ORISTANO HILLS TO BARBAGIA AND OGLIASTRA

The first itinerary crosses the hinterland of the Oristano province and the foothills of the Gennargentu range: various DOC wines are produced here: Vernaccia di Oristano, Arborea, Campidano

The natural environment of Gennargentu

di Terralba, Monica di Sardegna, Sardegna Semidano, and Mandrolisai. The second, from Nuoro, is a great nature route on the backdrop of the Gennargentu range and Tyrrhenian coastline; specific coastal productions of Cannonau and Vermentino.

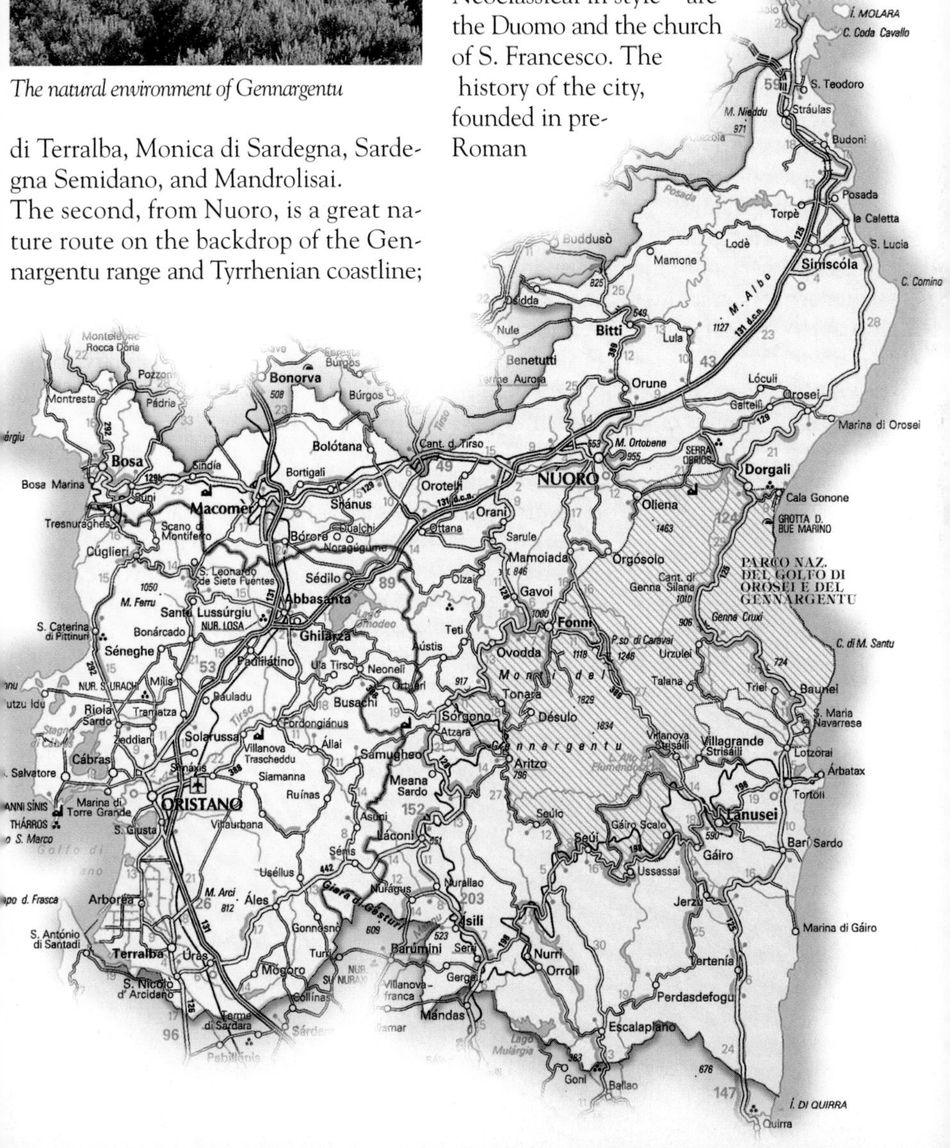

■ **ORISTANO**. The former capital of the old Giudicato di Arborea (one of the ancient Sardinia administrative districts), it conserves some medieval architecture remainders: the most noteworthy are the S. Cristoforo Tower and the Romanesque church of S. Giusta (1.8 miles to the southeast, near the homonymous pond). Of 13th-century origin – although respectively 18th-century and Neoclassical in style – are the Duomo and the church of S. Francesco. The history of the city, founded in pre-Roman times, is documented by fascinating remains in the Antiquarium Arborense. Just north is Cabras, on the edge of the pond where fishers still use archaic reed boats. The reed beds are inhabited by rare species of birds. From here you can proceed along the Sinis peninsula to the famous excavations of Tharros, an ancient Phoenician-Roman settlement.

▪ BARUMINI. The loop through the interior goes through Paulilatino, Abbasanta, Ghilarza and makes stops at Fondongianus – an isolated village on the left of the Tirso between the Campidano and Barbagia area, with ancient Roman spas lining the river – and at Sorgono, on the western buttresses of Gennargentu, nearly at the center of the island – this is a strategic point of departure for trips into the Barbagia lands.
You go south through Atzara, an old town lying amidst vineyards, and Laconi, atop a panoramic rise in the woody landscape of Sarcidano, to reach Barumini. This is a farming center in the verdant countryside at the foot of Giara di Gesturi (the remains of a volcanic plateau) and it is the base for visiting the *nuraghi* at Su Nuraxi, the most famous of Sardinia's prehistoric settlements. Also worthwhile is a nature tour of Giara di Gesturi, whose woods and underbrush are home to wild horses.
You turn back towards the sea at Arborea, site of large-scale land reclamation in 1919 and appellation of a DOC in the province of Oristano.

▪ NUORO. Near the sea but tied to the mountains, this city is the heart of the innermost part of the island. Sardinian novelist Grazia Deledda, Nobel prizewinner in 1926, was its greatest narrator; her house can be visited, as well as her tomb in the little church of Nostra Signora della Solitudine on the top of Mount Ortobene, destination for pleasant walks. You can also visit the Folk Museum.

▪ OLIENA. This typical Sardinian town is perched on the slope rising to the Corrasi massif, in Supramonte. The place name derives from olive cultivation, begun in the 17th century by the Jesuits, but the locality is also well known for a type of Cannonau that novelist and poet Gabriele D'Annunzio named Nepente – the drink that ancient Greeks believed to evoke dreams and visions. If you are in search of cultural and culinary attractions you can go on as far as Orgosolo, which has both.
On the way to Dorgali you quickly come to the spectacular karst spring Su Golognone and the Nuraghic village of Serra Orrios, with two temples and over 70 stone huts. Further on you come to Cala Gonone, on the gorgeous Gulf of Orosei coast, along which it is said that rare *Monachus monachus* seals still live.

Vineyards near Oliena with the Supramonte in the background

■ **LANUSEI**. It is reached by taking the Orientale Sarda national road no. 125 (winding in places though fascinating for its mountain scenery), with possible stops at Tortolì, in a splendid coastal area rich in prehistoric monuments and wines (like Cannonau and Vermentino di Sardegna DOC), and at Arbatax, a seaside resort amidst the Rocce Rosse (Red Rocks, porphyry reefs framing the harbor).
Lanusei is the historic capital of the Ogliastra area and it lies in a woody landscape within sight of the sea. The road then winds down to Bari Sardo, a village of ancient origin in a territory scattered with *nuraghi* and *domus de janas* (literally "fairy homes" but actually tombs). Further south, beyond Cardedu – a Cannonau DOC town with the exceptional Mediterranean natural environment around Mount Ferru and the Marina di Gairo shore –, you come to Jerzu, another old village high above the coast, set in a rugged though fertile territory, rich in vineyards and orchards, where Cannonau has been grown since the 18th century. Ending the tour is the long, lovely road crossing the Gennargentu range via Villanova Strisaili and Fonni.

Wineries *pp. 463-465*
Cabras, Cardedu, Dorgali, Jerzu, Mogoro, Nuoro, San Vero Milis.

THE SASSARI REGION

Amidst northern Sardinia's natural beauties shines the star of Vermentino di Gallura DOC, alongside the excellent wines of Alghero and its surroundings.

In the upper part of the island, vine-lands are homogeneously distributed: to the west, the Nurra district and reclaimed lands of Alghero; in the center is the hilly landscape of Anglona and Logudoro; to the east, the granite lands of Gallura.
The star of the Sassari province viticulture is Vermentino di Gallura, awarded a DOC in 1996. The vine originated in Iberia, but was probably imported from Liguria. Another vine worthy of mention is Moscato, which in the Sorso-Sennori zone has a DOC appellation. Westward, the main production zone is Alghero, with interesting mono-varietal wines from autochthonous grapes like Torbato and Cagnulari as well as from imported ones. On the border with Oristano you find Malvasia di Bosa. The district is also covered by the Colli del Limbara, Nurra, and Romangia IGTs.

The Northern Vineyards

The upper part of the island can be oenologically divided in two: to the west, Nurra and Logudoro, rich in scenery and history and home to the new and lively Alghero DOC along with the Malvasia di Bosa, Cannonau, and Vermentino di Sardegna traditional productions. To the east, Gallura and Anglona, where is produced the Vermentino di Gallura DOCG, an exceptional wine counterpart to the world-famous tourism paradise known as Costa Smeralda.

FROM NURRA TO THE LOGUDORO, GALLURA, AND ANGLONA AREAS

The first itinerary explores northwestern Sardinia in a circuit from Sassari, combining Romanesque basilicas, prehistoric monuments, and beautiful beaches as well as excellent wineries. The second, leaving from Olbia, takes in the main coastal resorts and the wine towns of the northeastern interior, in the wake of Vermentino di Gallura DOCG.

■ **SASSARI**. The itinerary starts from the provincial capital, on a limestone plateau sloping towards the Gulf of Asinara. Rich in traditions and culture, the city's history can be traced in the Sanna Museum and its old architecture seen along the Corso and around the Cathedral.

■ **ALGHERO**. This is reached after visiting the Monte d'Accoddi extraordinary prehistoric sanctuary and then passing through Porto Torres, with its Romanesque basilica of S. Gavino. Alghero is a beautiful town of Catalan imprint, with a Cathedral featuring a majolica-covered dome and a ring of walls overlooking the sea. Its wine pride lies in the DOC production that cleverly blends tradition with innovation. A must is a visit to the Sella & Mosca wine estates at I Piani: founded in 1899, this is Sardinia's premier winery, acclaimed as much for the impulse given to local vines as for its development of the international ones. An interesting corporate-cum-archeological museum is on the premises. An excursion to Capo Caccia offers sights of rare beauty, with high cliffs, caves, soaring falcons, and griffins.

■ **BOSA**. Heading south you enter Nuoro territory and reach the capital of the so-called Coral Riviera, home to the Malvasia di Bosa DOC. Bosa, full of tall houses sloping to the sea, is dominated by the panoramic Serravalle castle; close by, the beautiful church of S. Pietro extra Murus is worth a visit.
Further inland you find Bonorva and then Torralba, a Logudoro farming town at the entry to the famous Valley of the Nuraghi, with its spectacular Santu Antine complex begun in the 15th century BC and important Romanesque-Pisan churches scattered through the countryside. Outstanding among them are S. Pietro di Sorres, near Borutta, and, further north, SS. Trinità di Saccargia, unmistakable for its Tuscan-style banded façade and lovely bell

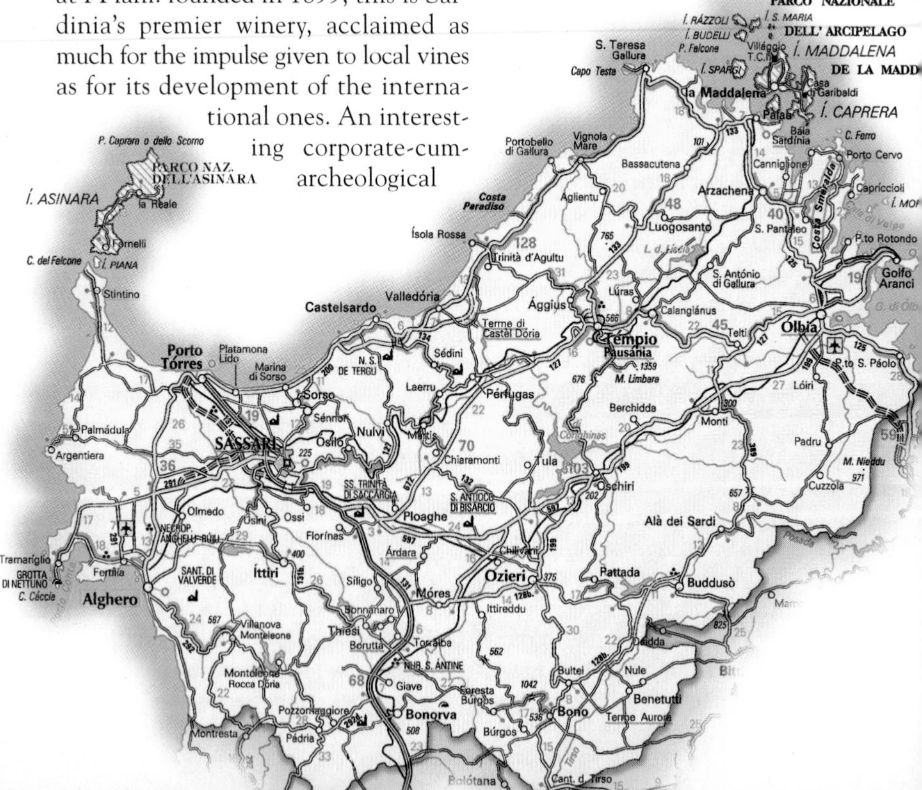

THE ENOTECA REGIONALE DELLA SARDEGNA AT BERCHIDDA

This wine museum is Italy's, and possibly the world's, only one to boast such a modern, purpose-designed architecture.
From its terraces your gaze runs from the roofs of the town to the mountains, glancing over the local experimental vineyard containing the best-known Sardinian vines, from Cannonau to Malvasia, but also the rarer ones, like Torbato and Cagnulari. Inside the building is a spacious display area, used for temporary exhibits (the subject of one of the most recent was "The origins of Sardinian viticulture") and presentations of ethnographic reports on the social and practical aspects of wine culture. It is supported by photos and audio-visuals as well as computer access to the Internet, so to be linked to other similar academic organizations worldwide. The visit to the museum ends in the cellars, which hold hundreds of Sardinian wines and serve as a regional enoteca. Here, too, the approach is innovative, with a sort of interactive sommelier who guides the aficionado to individual wines.
In the end, however, the virtual gives way to the real with actual traditional tasting.

tower with double and triple mullioned windows.

▪ **SENNORI.** Going back to Sassari can also include a loop detour to Mores – in an area full of *nuraghi*, "giants' tombs" and *domus de janas* –, Ozieri, with a rich Archeological Museum, and Ardara, with its Romanesque church of S. Maria del Regno. Along the way is the church of S. Antioco di Bisarcio, one of Sardinia's Romanesque masterpieces. Sennori, just further north, is a small but important wine town, with steep, granite-paved lanes rising to the parish church of S. Basilio. Just inland from the Gulf of Asinara are the vineyards of rare, prized Moscato di Sorso-Sennori; Vermentino and Cannonau di Sardegna are also grown here.

▪ **ARZACHENA.** Arriving from Olbia, the first Gallura town you meet gave its name to the long, deep inlet that faces Caprera Island. In the environs are the Capichera *nuraghi*, the Coddu Vecchiu and Li Lolghi "giants' tombs", and the Li Muri necropolis. The splendid coast is close by, as well as the Maddalena archipelago (now a National Park). Just further on is Santa Teresa di Gallura, a fishing village that has become a trendy tourist resort, founded by the House of Savoy and gateway to the windy Bonifacio Straits. Along Costa Paradiso you get to Castelsardo, an old bastion-ringed town overlooking the harbor and the Gulf of Asinara beach.

▪ **TEMPIO PAUSANIA.** Entering the inland Anglona area you find natural monuments (like the famous Elephant Rock, just east of Castelsardo), remains of the Nuraghic civilization, and Romanesque churches (S. Pietro di Simbranos). Beyond Perfugas you follow the Settentrionale Sarda road through landscapes dominated by the granite peaks of Mount Limbara. Tempio Pausania is a spa and tourist resort with austere buildings. Just north, around Luras, is one of Sardinia's largest concentrations of dolmens.
A nice excursion takes you from here to Berchidda, a noble old town with an economy based on wine, cheese, and cork productions, set on the southern Limbara slope. This is one of the shrines of Vermentino, with a wine museum that also serves as Enoteca Regionale (see box) – a name worth remembering.

Wineries *pp. 463-465*
Alghero, Arzachena, Berchidda, Florinas, Olbia, Sennori, Tempio Pausania, Usini.

Specialties in Sardinia

SARDINIA'S GREAT ALLURE lies in its archaic, mostly isolated, and intact nature; the rugged beauty of the island, made up of granite coasts and beaches, of expanses fragrant with Mediterranean maquis scents, of mountains where ancient pastoral society still survives, cannot but charm visitors. It is an island paradoxically bound more to its interior than to the sea, where tourism has brought fresh winds but has hardly touched the basic values, even on the gastronomy side, of millenniums-old traditions.
The matrix of typically Sardinian flavors in fact comes from sheep and goat rearing. Lamb and cheeses like Sardinian *pecorino* and Fiore make fundamental contributions to regional cuisine. But what comes from the Campidano plain should not be underestimated. Great expanses of wheat fields translate into *pane carasau*, wafer-thin bread also called *carta da musica* (music paper), and into varieties of pasta, *gnocchetti sardi* first of all. And then there is renowned produce, primarily artichokes and tomatoes, to be seasoned with the local olive oil, whose cardoon fragrance makes it unique.
Fishing is also an important sector of the region's economy, as proven by the many harbors; characteristic are the tuna fisheries in the Sulcis islands and the Oristano lagoons.

THE BEST-KNOWN DISHES of Sardinian cuisine derive from its farming-grazing traditions: *gnocchetti* seasoned with cheese and meat; ricotta-filled ravioli; spelt, broad-bean or cabbage soups; and then stewed or spit-roasted lamb or suckling pig, game and mushrooms, all seasoned with Mediterranean herbs like myrtle, bay leaf, and wild fennel. And of course the seafood, which can rely on tuna and on fish preserves, beginning with *bottarga*, dried mullet roe, an exceptional seasoning for spaghetti. Plus the North African influence, with couscous being a specialty of Carloforte, and the Spanish one, evident in Alghero's lobster *alla catalana*. As for desserts, you will be surprised by the variety of flavors, from sweet ricotta to the vigorous notes of honey, fragrant with Mediterranean scents.

STANDING OUT ON THE list are two wines that by themselves comply with any requirements: Vermentino, a great white for seafood and, in the spumante and semi-sweet versions, for desserts; and Cannonau, a versatile red fine with cheeses and meats of all types, which, as sweet or dry liquoroso, is also an excellent dessert or "meditation" wine. It would be a shame to end the list here, though, since Sardinia is a treasure-trove of typical wines: white Nuragus and Vernaccia di Oristano, not to mention the little-known Nasco, Torbato, and Semidano; among the reds, Carignano, Giro, Monica, and rare Cagnulari. And to assuage your doubts about how imported vines fare under the Sardinian sun, try the Chardonnay, Sauvignon, and Cabernet bearing the Alghero DOC labels.
Intentionally kept from the list are Malvasia and Moscato, with excellent production on the island and the inevitable choice at dessert time. As an after-dinner drink, try *mirto*, spirit made with myrtle berries and grappa so strong it is deservedly called *fil'e ferru* (iron wire).

TOWNS, WINERIES AND LABELS

EDITED BY SEMINARIO VERONELLI

Wineries of Italy

The following repertoire presents Italian wineries and their best wines, a great aid for those making purchases or about to set off on a trip. The addresses and wines listed are borne up by the authority and prestige of Seminario Veronelli.

This list of recommended producers and wines, divided by region and arranged in alphabetic order by municipality, represents the cream of Italian oenology. The principal reference – as seen and judged by Luigi Veronelli – is the quality of the wine, intended in the broadest sense that incorporates the enthusiasm and expertise of the viners, the historically precious structures, and the beautiful locations.

VALLE D'AOSTA

AOSTA/AOSTE

m 583

Wineries

Institut Agricole Regional ♟♟♟

Regione La Rochère 1/A, tel. 0165215811

r • Valle d'Aosta Gamay - Doc
r • Valle d'Aosta Petit Rouge - Doc
w • Valle d'Aosta Petite Arvine - Doc

ARNAD

Aosta/Aoste km 42 • m 340/2710

Wineries

Cooperativa La Kiuva ♟♟

Località Pied de Ville 42,
tel. 0125966351

r • Valle d'Aosta Arnad-Montjovet Superiore - Doc
w • Valle d'Aosta Chardonnay - Doc
w • Valle d'Aosta Petite Arvine - Doc

AYMAVILLES

Aosta/Aoste km 7 • m 640

Wineries

Cave des Onze Communes ♟♟

Località Urbains 14, tel. 0165902912

r • Valle d'Aosta Fumin - Doc
r • Valle d'Aosta Petit Rouge - Doc
r • Valle d'Aosta Torrette Superieur - Doc

Charrere Costantino ♟♟♟

Località Les Moulins 28, tel. 0165902135
www.lescretesvins.it

r • Valle d'Aosta Premetta - Doc
r • Valle d'Aosta Torrette - Doc
r • Vin de La Sabla - Vdt

Les Crêtes ♟♟♟♟♟

Località Villetos 50, tel. 0165902274
www.lescretes.it

r • Valle d'Aosta Fumin Vigne La Tour - Doc
r • Valle d'Aosta Pinot Nero Vigne La Tour - Doc
r • Valle d'Aosta Torrette Vigne Les Toules - Doc
w • Valle d'Aosta Chardonnay Frissonnière Cuvée Bois - Doc
w • Valle d'Aosta Petite Arvine Vigne Champorette - Doc

CHALLAND-SAINT-VICTOR

Aosta/Aoste km 43 • m 557/3016

Wineries

Minuzzo Gabriella ♟♟

Località Sizan 6, tel. 0125967365
gabriella.minuzzo@migrazioni.net

w • Valle d'Aosta Müller Thurgau - Doc

CHAMBAVE

Aosta/Aoste km 19 • m 480

Wineries

Soc. Cooperativa La Crotta di Vegneron ♟♟♟

Piazza Roncas 2,
tel. 016646670
www.lacrotta.it

r • Valle d'Aosta Chambave Rouge - Doc
r • Valle d'Aosta Fumin - Doc
r • Valle d'Aosta Gamay - Doc
s • Valle d'Aosta Chambave Muscat Passito - Doc
s • Valle d'Aosta Nus Malvoisie Fletri - Doc

Voyat Ezio ♟♟

Via Arberaz 31, tel. 016646139

r • Le Muraglie Rosso - Vdt
w • La Gazzella - Vdt
s • Le Muraglie Ambrato - Vdt

DONNAS

Aosta/Aoste km 49 • m 322

Legend

- ♟ Quality appraisal, from 1 to 5, attributed by Seminario Veronelli
- ★ TCI member discount
- *r* red wine
- *w* white wine
- *rs* rosé wine
- *s* sweet or dessert wine

Wineries

Caves Cooperatives de Donnas ♟♟
Via Roma 97, tel. 0125807096
www.donnasvini.com
r • Valle d'Aosta Donnas - Doc
r • Valle d'Aosta Donnas (Napoleone) - Doc
r • Valle d'Aosta Rosso Barmet - Doc

INTROD
Aosta/Aoste km 14 • m 678/2961

Wineries

Lo Triolet ♟♟
Località Junod 7, tel. 016595437
lotriolet@libero.it
r • Valle d'Aosta Gamay - Doc
r • Valle d'Aosta Nus Rouge - Doc
w • Valle d'Aosta Pinot Grigio - Doc

MORGEX
Aosta/Aoste km 26 • m 923

Wineries

Brunet Piero ♟
Via Valdigne 119, tel. 0165809120
ilaria134@virgilio.it
w • Valle d'Aosta Blanc de Morgex et de La Salle - Doc

Celegato Carlo ♟
Località Previllair 37, tel. 0165809461
w • Valle d'Aosta Blanc de Morgex et de La Salle - Doc

Pavese Ermes ♟♟
Località La Ruine, strada Pineta, tel. 0165800053
w • Valle d'Aosta Blanc de Morgex et de La Salle - Doc

Vevey Albert Maison ♟
Strada Villair 57, tel. 0165808930
w • Valle d'Aosta Blanc de Morgex et de La Salle - Doc

Vevey Marziano ♟
Località Villair 52, tel. 0165809836
w • Valle d'Aosta Blanc de Morgex et de La Salle - Doc

QUART
Aosta/Aoste km 8 • m 531/3205

Wineries

Fratelli Grosjean - Maison Vigneronne ♟♟♟♟
Località Ollignan 1, tel. 0165765283
r • Valle d'Aosta Fumin - Doc
r • Valle d'Aosta Torrette - Doc
w • Valle d'Aosta Petite Arvine - Doc

Vinirari ♟♟♟
Via Bas Villair 29, tel. 0165765673
www.vinirari.it
r • Valle d'Aosta Nus Rouge Vigne Cartesan - Doc
r • Valle d'Aosta Petit Rouge La Plantaz - Doc
r • Valle d'Aosta Pinot Noir Vigne Jacquemin - Doc

SARRE
Aosta/Aoste km 5 • m 591/3059

Wineries

Vallet - Rivelli ♟♟
Località Petit Cré 62, tel. 3383186683
w • Valle d'Aosta Chardonnay Sarre - Doc
w • Valle d'Aosta Müller Thurgau Sarre - Doc

VILLENEUVE
Aosta/Aoste km 10 • m 670

Wineries

Cave di Barrò ♟♟
Località Vevne 11,
tel. 016595260
www.mediavallee.it/ilvinaio/dibarro
r • Valle d'Aosta Torrette Superiore - Doc

Maison Anselmet ♟♟♟
Località La Crête 49, tel. 016595119
r • Valle d'Aosta Pinot Noir - Doc
r • Valle d'Aosta Torrette Superieur - Doc
w • Valle d'Aosta Chardonnay - Doc

PIEDMONT

ACQUI TERME
Alessandria km 34 • m 156

Wineries

Cantina Viticoltori dell'Acquese ♟♟
Via IV Novembre 14, tel. 0144322008
r • Barbera d'Asti Bricco - Doc
r • Dolcetto d'Acqui Statiellae - Doc
w • Piemonte Chardonnay Verdecielo - Doc
s • Moscato d'Asti Casarito - Docg
s • Moscato d'Asti Dolceoro - Docg

Il Cascinone ♟♟
Regione Boschi 2, tel. 014176319
r • Barbera d'Asti Superiore Rive - Doc
r • Monferrato Rosso Luce Monaca - Doc
w • Monferrato Bianco Camillona - Doc

AGLIANO TERME
Asti km 17 • m 263

Wineries

Dacapo ♟♟♟
Strada Asti-Mare 4, tel. 0141964921
info@dacapo.it
r • Barbera d'Asti Nizza Superiore Vigna Dacapo - Doc
r • Barbera d'Asti Sanbastiàn - Doc
r • Barbera d'Asti Vigna Dacapo - Doc

Ferraris Roberto ♟♟♟
Via Dogliani 33, tel. 0141954234
r • Barbera d'Asti Superiore La Cricca - Doc
r • Barbera d'Asti Vigneto Nobbio - Doc

La Luna del Rospo ♟♟♟
Località Salere 38, tel. 0141954222
r • Barbera d'Asti Solo per Laura - Doc
r • Grignolino d'Asti - Doc
r • Monferrato Rosso - Doc

Pavia Agostino e Figli ♟♟♟
Località Bologna 33, tel. 0141954125
mauro.pavia@crasti.it
r • Barbera d'Asti La Marescialla - Doc
r • Barbera d'Asti Moliss - Doc

Tenuta Garetto ♟♟♟♟
Via Asti-Mare 30, tel. 0141954068

r • Barbera d'Asti Superiore Favà - Doc
r • Barbera d'Asti Superiore In Pectore - Doc
r • Ruché di Castagnole Monferrato 'l Ciapin - Doc

Villa Terlina ♟♟♟
Regione Dani 82, tel. 0141964121
www.villaterlina.com
r • Barbera d'Asti Gradale - Doc
r • Barbera d'Asti Monsicuro - Doc

AGLIÈ

Turin km 34 • m 315

Wineries

Cieck ♟♟
Località San Grato, cascina Cieck, tel. 0124330522
www.cieck.it
r • Canavese Rosso Cieck - Doc
r • Canavese Rosso Neretto - Doc
w • Erbaluce di Caluso Calliope - Doc
w • Erbaluce di Caluso Misobolo - Doc
s • Caluso Passito Alladium - Doc

ALBA

Cuneo km 61 • m 172

Wineries

Boroli ♟♟♟
Località Madonna di Como 34, tel. 0173365477
www.borolivini.com
r • Barolo Bussia - Docg
r • Barolo Villero - Docg
r • Barbera d'Alba Bricco Fasano - Doc
r • Dolcetto d'Alba Madonna Como - Doc
s • Moscato d'Asti Aurem - Docg

Ceretto ♟♟♟♟♟
Località San Cassiano 34, tel. 0173282582
www.ceretto.com
r • Barbaresco Bricco Asili - Docg
r • Barbaresco Bricco Asili Bernardot - Docg
r • Barolo Bricco Rocche - Docg
r • Barolo Bricco Rocche Brunate - Docg
r • Barolo Bricco Rocche Prapò - Docg
r • Dolcetto d'Alba Rossana - Doc
r • Langhe Rosso Monsordo - Doc
r • Nebbiolo d'Alba Lantasco - Doc
w • Langhe Arneis Blangé - Doc

Fratelli Rivetti - Cairel ♟
Località Rivoli 27, tel. 017334181
r • Barolo - Docg
r • Dolcetto d'Alba Vigneto del Mandorlo - Doc

Lano Gianluigi ♟♟♟
Località San Rocco Seno d'Elvio 38, tel. 0173286958
r • Barbaresco - Doc
r • Barbera d'Alba Fondo Prà - Doc
r • Dolcetto d'Alba Ronchella - Doc

Penna Luigi e Figli ♟♟♟
Località San Rocco Seno d'Elvio 96,
tel. 0173286948
pennagiuliano@supereva.it
r • Barbera d'Alba N'giolina - Doc
r • Dolcetto d'Alba Superiore Galante - Doc
r • Nebbiolo d'Alba Vigioto - Doc

Piazzo Armando ♟♟♟
Località San Rocco Seno d'Elvio 31,
tel. 017335689
www.piazzo.it
r • Barbaresco Giaia - Docg
r • Barbaresco Sorì Fratin - Docg
r • Barolo - Docg
r • Barbera d'Alba Mugiot - Doc
r • Dolcetto d'Alba Scaletta - Doc

Pio Cesare ♟♟♟♟♟
Via Cesare Balbo 6, tel. 0173440386
r • Barbaresco Il Bricco - Docg
r • Barolo Ornato - Docg
r • Barbera d'Alba Fides - Doc
r • Langhe Rosso Il Nebbio - Doc
w • Langhe Arneis - Doc
w • Langhe Chardonnay Piodilei - Doc
w • Piemonte Chardonnay L'Altro - Doc

Poderi Colla ♟♟♟
Località San Rocco Seno d'Elvio 82,
tel. 0173290148
r • Barbaresco Tenuta Roncaglia - Docg
r • Barolo Bussia Dardi Le Rose - Docg
r • Barbera d'Alba Roncaglia - Doc
r • Dolcetto d'Alba Roncaglia - Doc
r • Langhe Rosso Bricco del Drago - Doc

Poderi Sinaglio ♟♟♟
Località San Rocco Cherasca 9/Bis,
tel. 0173612209
r • Barbera d'Alba Vigna Erta - Doc
r • Dolcetto di Diano d'Alba Bric Maiolica - Doc
r • Nebbiolo d'Alba Giachet - Doc
r • Langhe Rosso Sinaji - Doc
s • Moscato d'Asti La Mimosa - Docg

Prunotto ♟♟♟♟♟
Regione S. Cassiano 4/G, tel. 0173280017
www.prunotto.it
r • Barbaresco Bric Turot - Docg
r • Barolo Bussia - Docg
r • Barbera d'Alba Pian Romualdo - Doc
r • Barbera d'Asti Costamiole - Doc
r • Barbera d'Asti Fiulot - Doc
r • Nebbiolo d'Alba Occhetti - Doc
w • Roero Arneis - Doc

Rigo Secondo ♟♟
Località San Rocco Cherasca 15,
tel. 0173612103
s.rigoòlibero.it
r • Barbera d'Alba Superiore - Doc
r • Dolcetto di Diano d'Alba Vigneto Piadvenza - Doc
w • Roero Arneis - Doc

Sebaste Mauro ♟♟♟
Località Gallo, via Garibaldi 222, tel. 0173262148
r • Barolo Monvigliero - Docg
r • Barolo Prapò - Docg
r • Langhe Rosso Centobricchi - Doc
r • Nebbiolo d'Alba Paris - Doc
w • Roero Arneis - Doc

ALBUGNANO

Asti km 34 • m 549

Wineries

Pianfiorito ♟♟♟
Località Santo Stefano 6, tel. 0119920665
www.pianfiorito.com
r • Albugnano Superiore - Doc
r • Albugnano Vigna Carpinella - Doc
r • Barbera d'Asti La Giroira - Doc

ALFIANO NATTA

Alessandria km 44 • m 280

WINERIES

TENUTA CASTELLO DI RAZZANO ♟♟♟ ★10%
Località Razzano 2, tel. 0141922124
info@castellodirazzano.it
r • Barbera d'Asti Superiore Vigna del Beneficio - Doc
r • Barbera d'Asti Superiore Vigna Valentino Caligaris - Doc

ALICE BEL COLLE

Alessandria km 29 • m 418

WINERIES

CANTINA CA' BIANCA ♟♟
Regione Spagna 58, tel. 0144745420
www.giv.it
r • Barolo - Docg
r • Barbera d'Asti Superiore Chersì - Doc
s • Moscato d'Asti - Docg

ASTI

m 123

WINERIES

FRATELLI ROVERO ♟♟♟
Località San Marzanotto 218, tel. 0141592460
r • Barbera d'Asti Superiore Rouvè - Doc
r • Grignolino d'Asti Vigneto Casalina - Doc
r • Monferrato Rosso Rocca Schiavino - Doc
w • Monferrato Bianco Villa Guani - Doc

GIULIO COCCHI SPUMANTI ♟♟
Via Malta 17, tel. 0141907083
www.cocchi.com
rs • Giulio Cocchi Brut Rosé - Vdt
w • Giulio Cocchi Brut Millesimato - Vdt
s • Asti - Docg

BARBARESCO

Cuneo km 72 • m 274

WINERIES

CA' ROMÈ - ROMANO MARENGO ♟♟♟
Via Rabajà 36, tel. 0173635126
www.carome.com
r • Barbaresco Maria di Brun - Docg
r • Barbaresco Sori Rio Sordo - Docg
r • Barolo Rapet - Docg
r • Barolo Vigna Cerretta - Docg
r • Barbera d'Alba La Gamberaja - Doc

CANTINA DEL PINO ♟♟♟♟
Via Ovello 15, tel. 0173635147
r • Barbaresco Ovello - Docg

CASCINA LUISIN ♟♟♟♟
Via Rabajà 23, tel. 0173635154
r • Barbaresco Rabajà - Docg
r • Barbaresco Sorì Paolin - Docg
r • Barbera d'Alba Asili - Doc
r • Dolcetto d'Alba Bric Trifula - Doc
r • Langhe Nebbiolo - Doc

CASCINA MORASSINO ♟♟♟
Via Ovello 32, tel. 0173635149
r • Barbaresco Morassino - Docg
r • Barbaresco Ovello - Docg
r • Barbera d'Alba Vignot - Doc

COOPERATIVA PRODUTTORI DEL BARBARESCO ♟♟♟♟
Via Torino 52, tel. 0173635139
www.produttori-barbaresco.it
r • Barbaresco Riserva Montestefano - Docg
r • Barbaresco Riserva Ovello - Docg
r • Barbaresco Riserva Pajé - Docg
r • Barbaresco Riserva Pora - Docg
r • Barbaresco Riserva Rabajà - Docg

CORTESE GIUSEPPE ♟♟♟♟
Via Rabajà 35, tel. 0173635131
az-cortesegiuseppe@jumpy.it
r • Barbaresco Vigna in Rabajà - Docg
r • Barbera d'Alba Morassina - Doc
r • Dolcetto d'Alba Trifolera - Doc
r • Langhe Nebbiolo - Doc
w • Langhe Chardonnay Scapulin - Doc

GAJA ♟♟♟♟♟
Via Torino 36/A, tel. 0173635255
r • Barbaresco - Docg
r • Langhe Nebbiolo Costa Russi - Doc
r • Langhe Nebbiolo Sorì San Lorenzo - Doc
r • Langhe Nebbiolo Sorì Tildin - Doc
r • Langhe Nebbiolo Sperss - Doc
r • Langhe Rosso Darmagi - Doc
w • Langhe Chardonnay Gaia e Rey - Doc
w • Langhe Chardonnay Rossj-Bass - Doc
w • Langhe Sauvignon Alteni di Brassica - Doc

GIACOSA CARLO VITICOLTORE ♟♟♟
Via Ovello 8, tel. 0173635116
r • Barbaresco Montefico - Docg
r • Barbaresco Narin - Docg
r • Barbera d'Alba Lina - Doc

LA CA' NOVA ♟♟♟
Casa Nuova 1, tel. 0173635123
kocpiec1@tiscalinet.it
r • Barbaresco - Docg
r • Barbaresco Bric Mentina - Docg
r • Barbaresco Montestefano - Docg

LA SPINONA ♟♟♟
Via Secondine 22, tel. 0173635169
r • Barbaresco Faset - Docg
r • Barolo Sorì Gepin - Docg

MOCCAGATTA ♟♟♟♟♟
Via Rabajà 24, tel. 0173635152
moccagattaaz.agr@libero.it
r • Barbaresco Bric Balin - Docg
r • Barbaresco Basarin - Docg
r • Barbaresco Cole - Docg
r • Barbera d'Alba Basarin - Doc
w • Langhe Chardonnay Buschet - Doc

MONTARIBALDI ♟♟♟
Via Rio Sordo 30/A, tel. 0173638220
montaribaldi@tiscali.it
r • Barbaresco Sorì Montaribaldi - Docg
r • Barbera d'Alba Du Gir - Doc
r • Dolcetto d'Alba Niccolini - Doc
r • Langhe Nebbiolo - Doc
w • Roero Arneis - Doc

ROAGNA - I PAGLIERI ♟♟♟♟
Via Rabajà 8, tel. 0173635109
r • Barbaresco Crichet Pajé - Docg
r • Barolo La Rocca e La Pira - Docg
r • Barolo Riserva La Rocca e La Pira - Docg
r • Dolcetto d'Alba - Doc
r • Opera Prima XIV - Vdt

ROCCA ALBINO ♟♟♟♟♟
Via Rabajà 15, tel. 0173635145
roccaalbinoòglobwine.com
r • Barbaresco Vigneto Brich Ronchi - Docg
r • Barbaresco Vigneto Loreto - Docg
r • Barbera d'Alba Gèpin - Doc

r • Dolcetto d'Alba Vignalunga - Doc
w • Langhe Bianco La Rocca - Doc

Rocca Bruno - Rabajà ♟♟♟♟
Via Rabajà 29, tel. 0173635112
r • Barbaresco Coparossa - Docg
r • Barbaresco Rabajà - Docg
r • Barbera d'Alba - Doc
r • Dolcetto d'Alba Trifolè - Doc
w • Langhe Chardonnay Cadet - Doc

Ronchi ♟♟♟♟
Via Rabajà 14, tel. 0173635156
r • Barbaresco - Docg
r • Barbera d'Alba Terle - Doc
r • Dolcetto d'Alba Rosario - Doc

Tenute Cisa Asinari dei Marchesi di Gresy ♟♟♟♟♟ ★10%
Via Rabaja 43, tel. 0173635222
www.marchesidigresy.com
r • Barbaresco Martinenga Camp Gros - Docg
r • Barbaresco Martinenga Gaiun - Docg
r • Dolcetto d'Alba Monte Aribaldo - Doc
r • Langhe Rosso Virtus - Doc
w • Langhe Chardonnay Gresy - Doc
w • Langhe Sauvignon - Doc
s • Piemonte Moscato Passito L'Altro Moscato - Doc

Varaldo Rino ♟♟♟♟
Via Secondine 2, tel. 0173635160
varaldorino@hotmail.com
r • Barbaresco Bricco Libero - Docg
r • Barbaresco Sorì Loreto - Docg
r • Barolo Vigna di Aldo - Docg
r • Langhe Nebbiolo - Doc
r • Langhe Rosso Fantasia 4.20 - Doc

BAROLO

Cuneo km 51 • m 301

Wineries

Borgogno Giacomo e Figli ♟♟♟ ★10%
Via Gioberti 1, tel. 017356108
www.borgogno-wine.com
r • Barbaresco - Docg
r • Barolo Classico - Docg
r • Barolo Liste - Docg
r • Dolcetto d'Alba - Doc
r • Langhe Nebbiolo - Doc

Brezza Giacomo & Figli ♟♟♟
Via Lomondo 4, tel. 0173560921
www.brezza.it
r • Barolo Bricco Sarmassa - Docg
r • Barolo Cannubi - Docg
r • Barolo Castellero - Docg
r • Barbera d'Alba Cannubi Muscatel - Doc
r • Dolcetto d'Alba San Lorenzo - Doc

Cabutto - Tenuta La Volta ♟♟♟♟
Via S. Pietro 13, tel. 017356168
r • Barolo Riserva Vigna del Fondatore - Docg
r • Barolo Vigna La Volta - Docg
r • Barbera d'Alba Superiore Bricco delle Viole - Doc
r • Dolcetto d'Alba Vigna La Volta - Doc
r • Langhe Rosso Vendemmiaio - Doc

Cantina Mascarello Bartolo ♟♟♟♟
Via Roma 15, tel. 017356125
r • Barolo - Docg
r • Barbera d'Alba Vigna San Lorenzo - Doc
r • Dolcetto d'Alba - Doc

Cascina Adelaide ♟♟♟
Via Aie Sottane 14, tel. 0173560503
www.cascinaadelaide.com
r • Barolo Cannubi Preda - Docg
r • Barbera d'Alba Superiore D'Amabilin - Doc
r • Dolcetto d'Alba Bussia - Doc

Damilano ♟♟♟
Vicolo S. Sebastiano 2, tel. 017356265
www.damilanog.com
r • Barolo - Docg
r • Barolo Cannubi - Docg
r • Barolo Liste - Docg
r • Barbera d'Alba - Doc
r • Dolcetto d'Alba - Doc

Fratelli Barale ♟♟♟ ★10%
Via Roma 6, tel. 017356127
www.areacom.it/biz/cantine/barale
r • Barbaresco - Docg
r • Barolo Vigna Bussia - Docg
r • Barolo Vigna Castellero - Docg
r • Barbera d'Alba Vigna Preda - Doc
r • Dolcetto d'Alba Vigna Bussia - Doc

Grimaldi Giacomo ♟♟♟
Via L. Einaudi 8, tel. 017335256
r • Barolo Le Coste - Docg
r • Barbera d'Alba Fornaci - Doc
r • Dolcetto d'Alba - Doc

Marchesi di Barolo ♟♟♟♟
Via Alba 12, tel. 0173564400
r • Barolo Cannubi - Docg
r • Barolo Coste di Rose - Docg
r • Barolo Estate Vineyard - Docg
r • Barolo Sarmassa - Docg
r • Barbera d'Alba Paiagal - Doc
r • Dolcetto d'Alba Boschetti - Doc
r • Dolcetto d'Alba Madonna Como - Doc

Pira Enrico & Figli ♟♟♟
Via Vittorio Veneto 1, tel. 017356247
r • Barolo - Docg
r • Barolo Cannubi - Docg
r • Barbera d'Alba - Doc

Rinaldi Giuseppe ♟♟♟
Via Monforte 3, tel. 017356156
r • Barolo - Docg
r • Barolo Brunate - Le Coste - Docg
r • Barolo Cannubi - San Lorenzo - Ravera - Docg
r • Barbera d'Alba - Doc
r • Dolcetto d'Alba - Doc

Sandrone Luciano ♟♟♟♟♟
Via Alba 57, tel. 0173560023
www.sandroneluciano.com
r • Barolo Cannubi Boschis - Docg
r • Barolo Le Vigne - Docg
r • Barbera d'Alba - Doc
r • Nebbiolo d'Alba Valmaggiore - Doc
r • Langhe Rosso Pe Mol - Doc

Scarzello Giorgio & Figli ♟♟♟
Via Alba 29, tel. 017356170
cantina-scarzello@libero.it
r • Barolo - Docg
r • Barolo Vigna Merenda - Docg
r • Barbera d'Alba Superiore - Doc
r • Dolcetto d'Alba - Doc
r • Langhe Nebbiolo - Doc

SEBASTE - SYLLA SEBASTE ♟♟
Località San Pietro delle Viole,
tel. 017356266
www.syllasebaste.com
r • Barolo Bussia - Docg
r • Langhe Nebbiolo Passo delle Viole - Doc
r • Langhe Rosso Bricco Viole - Doc

TERRE DA VINO ♟♟
Via Bergesia 6, tel. 0173564611
www.terredavino.it
r • Barbaresco La Casa in Collina - Docg
r • Barolo Paesi Tuoi - Docg
r • Barolo Poderi Scarrone - Docg
r • Barbera d'Asti La Luna e i Falò - Doc
r • Dolcetto di Ovada Tenuta Magnona - Doc

VAJRA GIUSEPPE DOMENICO ♟♟♟♟
Via delle Viole 25,
tel. 017356257
r • Barolo Bricco delle Viole - Docg
r • Barolo Fossati - Docg
r • Barbera d'Alba Superiore - Doc
r • Dolcetto d'Alba Coste & Fossati - Doc
r • Langhe Freisa Kyé - Doc
w • Langhe Bianco - Doc

BASTIA MONDOVÌ
Cuneo km 36 • m 294

WINERIES

BRICCO DEL CUCÙ ♟♟
Località Bricco 21, tel. 017460153
briccocucu@libero.it
r • Dolcetto di Dogliani - Doc
r • Dolcetto di Dogliani Superiore Bricco San Bernardo - Doc
r • Langhe Dolcetto - Doc

BORGONE SUSA
Turin km 39 • m 394

WINERIES

CARLOTTA ♟♟
Via Condove 61, tel. 0119646150
rfrancesca@libero.it
r • Valsusa Rosso Costadoro - Doc
r • Valsusa Rosso Rocca del Lupo - Doc
r • Valsusa Rosso Vignacombe - Doc

BRA
Cuneo km 46 • m 290

WINERIES

ASCHERI ♟♟♟
Via Piumati 23, tel. 0172412394
www.ascherivini.it
r • Barolo Sorano di Serralunga d'Alba - Docg
r • Barbera d'Alba Fontanelle di La Morra - Doc
r • Dolcetto d'Alba San Rocco di Serralunga d'Alba - Doc
r • Nebbiolo d'Alba Bricco San Giacomo - Doc
r • Montalupa Rosso - Vdt

BRIGNANO-FRASCATA
Alessandria km 41 • m 264/694

WINERIES

POGGIO PAOLO ♟♟
Via Roma 67, tel. 0131784929
r • Colli Tortonesi Barbera Derio - Doc
w • Colli Tortonesi Bianco Timüraso - Doc

BRUSNENGO
Biella km 36 • m 295

WINERIES

BARNI GIUSEPPE FILIPPO ♟
Via Forte 63, tel. 015985977
r • Coste della Sesia Rosso Mesolone - Doc
r • Coste della Sesia Rosso Torrearsa - Doc

BUBBIO
Asti km 39 • m 224

WINERIES

LA DOGLIOLA ♟♟
Regione Infermiera 226, tel. 014483557
r • Barbera d'Asti - Doc
s • Brachetto d'Acqui - Docg
s • Moscato d'Asti - Docg

CALAMANDRANA
Asti km 29 • m 140/367

WINERIES

CHIARLO MICHELE ♟♟♟♟ ★10%
Strada Nizza-Canelli 99, tel. 0141769030
www.chiarlo.it
r • Barbaresco Asili - Docg
r • Barolo Cannubi - Docg
r • Barolo Cerequio - Docg
r • Barolo Riserva Triumvirato - Docg
r • Barbera d'Asti Superiore Cipressi della Court - Doc
r • Langhe Rosso Barilot - Doc
r • Monferrato Rosso Countacc! - Doc
w • Gavi del Comune di Gavi Rovereto - Docg
s • Moscato d'Asti Rocca dell'Uccellette - Docg

LA GIRIBALDINA ♟♟ ★10%
Regione S. Vito 39, tel. 0141718043
www.giribaldina.it
r • Barbera d'Asti Superiore Cala delle Mandrie - Doc
r • Barbera d'Asti Superiore Rossobaldo - Doc
s • Moscato d'Asti Apianae - Docg

CALLIANO
Asti km 14 • m 258

WINERIES

RABEZZANA RENATO ♟♟
Via Rabezzana 7, tel. 011543070
crabezz@tin.it
r • Barbera d'Asti Il Bricco Riserva Speciale - Doc
r • Grignolino d'Asti - Doc

CALOSSO
Asti km 23 • m 399

WINERIES

LA BADIA - BUSSI ALDO ♟♟
Via Castiglione 9, tel. 0141853319
az.labadia@libero.it
r • Barbera d'Asti Castello di Calosso - Doc
r • Barbera d'Asti Clotilde - Doc
s • Moscato d'Asti - Docg

SCAGLIOLA ♟♟♟
Località San Siro 42, tel. 0141853183
r • Barbera d'Asti Superiore San Si - Doc
r • Langhe Dolcetto Busiord - Doc
s • Moscato d'Asti Volo di Farfalle - Docg

TENUTA DEI FIORI ♟♟♟
Via Valcalosso 3, tel. 0141826938

info@tenutadeifiori.com
r • Barbera d'Asti Vigneto del Tulipano Nero - Doc
r • Monferrato Rosso - Doc

CAMINO

Alessandria km 46 • m 252

Wineries

Tenuta Gaiano
Via Trino 8, tel. 0142469440
tenutagaiano@tiscalinet.it
r • Barbera del Monferrato Gallianum - Doc
r • Barbera del Monferrato Vigna della Torretta - Doc
r • Grignolino del Monferrato Casalese - Doc

CANALE

Cuneo km 69 • m 193

Wineries

Cascina Ca' Rossa
Località Case Sparse 56, tel. 017398348
r • Barbera d'Alba Vigna Mulassa - Doc
r • Roero Vigna Audinaggio - Doc
w • Roero Arneis - Doc

Cascina Chicco
Via Valentino 144, tel. 0173979069
r • Barbera d'Alba Bric Loira - Doc
r • Nebbiolo d'Alba Monpissano - Doc
r • Roero Mulino della Costa - Doc
r • Roero Valmaggiore - Doc
s • Birbét Dolce - Vdt

Cornarea
Via Valentino 150, tel. 017365636
r • Roero Superiore - Doc
w • Roero Arneis - Doc
s • Tarasco Passito di Arneis - Vdt

Correggia
Via Santo Stefano Roero 124, tel. 0173978009
r • Barbera d'Alba Bric Marun - Doc
r • Nebbiolo d'Alba La Val dei Preti - Doc
r • Roero Rocche d'Ampsèy - Doc
w • Roero Arneis - Doc
s • Anthos - Vdt

Deltetto ★10%
Corso Alba 43, tel. 0173979383
www.deltetto.com
r • Barolo Bussia - Docg
r • Barbera d'Alba Rocca delle Marasche - Doc
r • Roero Braja - Doc
w • Roero Arneis San Michele - Doc
s • Bric du Liun Passito - Vdt

Enrico Serafino
Via Asti, tel. 0173967111
r • Barbera d'Alba Superiore Parduné - Doc
r • Roero Superiore Passiunà - Doc
w • Roero Arneis - Doc

Funtanin
Via Torino 191, tel. 0173979488
r • Barbera d'Alba Ciabot Pierin - Doc
r • Roero Bricco Barbida - Doc
w • Roero Arneis Pierin di Soc - Doc

Gallino Filippo
Località Valle del Pozzo 63, tel. 017398112
r • Barbera d'Alba Superiore - Doc
r • Roero Superiore - Doc
w • Roero Arneis - Doc

Giacomo Vico
Via Torino 80, tel. 0173979126
www.giacomovico.it
r • Barbera d'Alba Superiore - Doc
r • Nebbiolo d'Alba - Doc
r • Roero Superiore - Doc

Malabaila di Canale
Località Madonna dei Cavalli 19, cascina Pradvaj, tel. 017398381
www.malabaila.com
r • Barbera d'Alba Mezzavilla - Doc
r • Langhe Dolcetto - Doc
r • Nebbiolo d'Alba Bric Merli - Doc
r • Roero Superiore Bric Volta - Doc
w • Roero Arneis Pradvaj - Doc

Malvirà
Località Canova, via Santo Stefano Roero 144, tel. 0173978145
www.malvira.com
r • Barbera d'Alba Michele - Doc
r • Langhe Rosso San Guglielmo - Doc
r • Roero Superiore Montebeltramo - Doc
r • Roero Superiore Trinità - Doc
w • Roero Arneis Renesio - Doc
w • Roero Arneis Saglietto - Doc
w • Roero Arneis Trinità - Doc

Monchiero Carbone
Via Santo Stefano Roero 2, tel. 017395568
r • Barbera d'Alba Monbirone - Doc
r • Roero Printi - Doc
r • Roero Superiore Srü - Doc
w • Langhe Bianco Tamardi - Doc
w • Roero Arneis Recit - Doc

Porello Marco e Ettore
Corso Alba 71, tel. 0173979324
marcoporello@virgilio.it
r • Barbera d'Alba Bric Torretta - Doc
r • Roero Bric Torretta - Doc

CANELLI

Asti km 29 • m 157

Wineries

Cascina Barisel
Regione S. Giovanni 2, tel. 3394165913
barisel@inwind.it
r • Barbera d'Asti Superiore La Cappelletta - Doc
s • Moscato d'Asti Barisél - Docg

Contratto
Via G.B. Giuliani 56, tel. 0141823349
www.contratto.it
r • Barolo Cerequio - Docg
r • Barbera d'Asti Solus AD - Doc
w • Giuseppe Contratto Brut Riserva Millesimata - Vdt
s • Asti Spumante De Miranda - Docg
s • Moscato d'Asti Tenuta Gilardino - Docg

Coppo
Via Alba 68, tel. 0141823146
info@coppo.it
r • Barbera d'Asti Camp du Rouss - Doc
r • Barbera d'Asti Pomorosso - Doc
r • Langhe Rosso Mondaccione - Doc
w • Piemonte Chardonnay Costebianche - Doc
w • Piemonte Chardonnay Monteriolo - Doc
w • Riserva Coppo Brut - Vdt
s • Moscato d'Asti Moncalvina - Docg

GANCIA ♟
Corso Libertà 66, tel. 01418301
w • Carlo Gancia Metodo Classico Cuvée del Fondatore - Vdt

L'ARMANGIA ♟♟♟
Località San Giovanni 14/C, S.P. Bubbio Montegrosso, tel. 0141824947
armangia@inwind.it
r • Barbera d'Asti Castello di Calosso - Doc
r • Barbera d'Asti Superiore Titon - Doc
w • Monferrato Bianco Enne Enne - Doc
w • Piemonte Chardonnay Robi e Robi - Doc
s • Moscato d'Asti Il Giai - Docg

NERVI MAURIZIO E NEGRO EZIO ♟♟♟
Regione Serramasio 30, tel. 0141831152
r • Barbera d'Asti Marteleina - Doc
w • Valon - Vdt
s • Valentein - Vdt

SCAGLIOLA GIACOMO E FIGLIO ♟♟♟
Regione S. Libera 20, tel. 0141831146
www.scagliolagiacomo.it
r • Barbera d'Asti - Doc
r • Barbera d'Asti La Faia - Doc
r • Barbera d'Asti Vigna dei Mandorli - Doc
r • Monferrato Rosso La Virasa Veija - Doc
s • Moscato d'Asti - Docg

VILLA GIADA ♟♟♟
Regione Ceirole 4, tel. 0141831100
www.villagiadawine.it
r • Barbera d'Asti Superiore Ajan - Doc
r • Barbera d'Asti Superiore Riserva Bricco Dani - Doc
r • Barbera d'Asti Superiore Vigneto La Quercia - Doc
w • Piemonte Chardonnay Bricco Mané - Doc
s • Moscato d'Asti Ceirole - Docg

CAPRIATA D'ORBA
Alessandria km 25 • m 176

WINERIES

BERGAGLIO PIER CARLO ♟♟
Cascina Barcanello 15, tel. 014346292
r • Barbera del Monferrato Paradis - Doc
r • Dolcetto di Ovada Bric di Fra - Doc
w • Gavi Vigna del Parroco - Docg

CASORZO
Asti km 23 • m 275

WINERIES

FRATELLI BILETTA ♟♟
Via Roma 24, tel. 0141929303
r • Grignolino d'Asti Moncucchetto - Doc
r • Ruchetto - Vdt
s • Malvasia di Casorzo d'Asti Moncucchetto - Doc

CASSINASCO
Asti km 34 • m 447

WINERIES

CERUTTI ♟♟♟
Via Canelli 205, tel. 0141851286
livia.clara@tin.it
r • Barbera d'Asti Superiore Foie Russe - Doc
s • Moscato d'Asti Surì Sandrinet - Docg

HOHLER ♟♟♟
Bricco Bosetto 85, tel. 0141851209
remohohler@hotmail.com
r • Barbera d'Asti Pian Bosco - Doc
r • Barbera d'Asti Pian Bosco Etichetta Nera - Doc

CASTAGNOLE DELLE LANZE
Asti km 20 • m 271

WINERIES

RIVETTI GIUSEPPE ♟♟♟♟♟
Via Annunziata 33, tel. 0141877396
r • Barbaresco Vigneto Gallina - Docg
r • Barbaresco Starderi - Docg
r • Barbaresco Valeriano - Docg
r • Barbera d'Alba Gallina - Doc
r • Barbera d'Asti Cà di Pian - Doc
r • Barbera d'Asti Superiore - Doc
r • Monferrato Rosso Pin - Doc
s • Moscato d'Asti Bricco Quaglia - Docg
s • Moscato d'Asti Passito Oro - Docg

CASTAGNOLE MONFERRATO
Asti km 14 • m 232

WINERIES

BORGOGNONE FRANCESCO ♟♟
Piazza Statuto 2, tel. 0141292249
r • Barbera d'Asti - Doc
r • Ruché di Castagnole Monferrato Vigna del Parroco - Doc

TENUTA DEI RE ♟
Regione Cascina Nuova 1, tel. 0141292147
www.tenutadeire.it
r • Grignolino d'Asti - Doc
r • Ruchè di Castagnole Monferrato - Doc

CASTEL BOGLIONE
Asti km 35 • m 260

WINERIES

CASCINA GARITINA ♟♟
Via Gianola 20, tel. 0141762162
www.cascinagaritina.it
r • Monferrato Rosso Amis - Doc

CASTELLINALDO
Cuneo km 70 • m 285

WINERIES

GILI RAFFAELE ♟♟
Regione Pautasso 7, tel. 0173639011
r • Barbera d'Alba Castellinaldo - Doc
r • Nebbiolo d'Alba Sansivé - Doc
r • Roero Bric Angelino - Doc

MARSAGLIA ♟♟ ★10%
Via Mussone 2, tel. 0173213048
r • Barbera d'Alba Castellinaldo - Doc
r • Nebbiolo d'Alba San Pietro - Doc
r • Roero Superiore Brich d'America - Doc
w • Roero Arneis San Servasio - Doc
w • Roero Arneis Serramiana - Doc

PINSOGLIO FABRIZIO ♟♟♟
Località Madonna dei Cavalli 8, tel. 0173213078
r • Barbera d'Alba Bric La Rondolina - Doc
r • Roero - Doc
w • Roero Arneis Vigneto Malinot - Doc

SELEZIONE TEO COSTA ♟♟♟
Via S. Salvario 1, tel. 0173213066
www.teocosta.it
r • Barbaresco Lancaia - Docg

r • Barbera d'Alba Castellinaldo - Doc
r • Roero Superiore Vigna Bataiòt - Doc
w • Roero Arneis Serramiana - Doc

Tenuta Ca' du Russ ♟♟♟
Via S. Pellico 7, tel. 0173213069
r • Barbera d'Alba Castellinaldo - Doc
r • Nebbiolo d'Alba San Pietro - Doc
r • Roero Superiore Francesca Marsaglia - Doc
w • Roero Arneis Costa delle Rose - Doc

Vielmin ♟♟♟
Via S. Damiano 16, tel. 0173213298
ivan.gili@tin.it
r • Barbera d'Alba Castellinaldo - Doc
r • Barbera d'Alba Srei - Doc
r • Roero La Rocca - Doc

CASTELLO DI ANNONE

Asti km 10 • m 109

Wineries

Villa Fiorita ♟♟♟
Via Case Sparse 2, tel. 0141401231
www.villafiorita-wines.com
r • Barbera d'Asti Superiore Il Giorgione - Doc
r • Barbera d'Asti Superiore Villa Fiorita - Doc
r • Grignolino d'Asti Pian delle Querce - Doc
r • Monferrato Rosso Maniero - Doc
r • Monferrato Rosso Nero di Villa - Doc

CASTELNUOVO BELBO

Asti km 34 • m 122

Wineries

Cossetti Clemente e Figli ♟♟♟
Via Vittorio Emanuele 19, tel. 0141799803
www.cossetti.it
r • Barbera d'Asti La Vigna Vecchia - Doc
r • Barbera d'Asti Superiore Cereda - Doc
r • Barbera d'Asti Venti di Marzo - Doc
w • Gavi del Comune di Gavi - Docg
s • Moscato d'Asti La Vita - Docg

CASTELNUOVO DON BOSCO

Asti km 31 • m 245

Wineries

Cantina Sociale del Freisa ♟
Via S. Giovanni 6, tel. 0119876117
csf@castelnuovodonbosco.it
r • Barbera d'Asti - Doc
r • Freisa d'Asti Vezzolano - Doc
s • Malvasia di Castelnuovo Don Bosco - Doc

Cascina Gilli ♟♟
Via Nevissano 36, tel. 0119876984
www.cascinagilli.it
r • Barbera d'Asti Vigna delle More - Doc
r • Freisa d'Asti Vigna del Forno - Doc
s • Malvasia di Castelnuovo Don Bosco - Doc

Graglia Renaldo ♟♟♟
Località Barbella 67, tel. 0119874708
www.castelnuovodonbosco.it:graglia
r • Barbera d'Asti Bric d'la Buta - Doc
r • Barbera d'Asti Superiore - Doc
r • Freisa d'Asti Parlapà - Doc
r • Grignolino d'Asti - Doc
s • Malvasia di Castelnuovo Don Bosco - Doc

CASTEL ROCCHERO

Asti km 36 • m 414

Wineries

Viticoltori Associati
La Torre di Castel Rocchero ♟♟
Strada Acqui 7, tel. 0141760139
www.immagine.com/latorre
r • Barbera d'Asti La Sernia - Doc
r • Barbera d'Asti Superiore - Doc
r • Dolcetto d'Asti - Doc

CASTIGLIONE FALLETTO

Cuneo km 54 • m 350

Wineries

Azelia ♟♟♟♟
Via Alba-Barolo 27, tel. 017362859
r • Barolo - Docg
r • Barolo Bricco Fiasco - Docg
r • Barolo San Rocco - Docg
r • Barbera d'Alba Vigneto Punta - Doc
r • Dolcetto d'Alba Bricco dell'Oriolo - Doc

Bongiovanni ♟♟♟♟
Via Alba-Barolo 4, tel. 0173262184
r • Barolo - Docg
r • Barolo Pernanno - Docg
r • Barbera d'Alba - Doc
r • Dolcetto di Diano d'Alba - Doc
r • Langhe Rosso Faletto - Doc

Brovia ♟♟♟♟♟
Via Alba-Barolo 54, tel. 017362852
www.brovia.net
r • Barbaresco Rio Sordo - Docg
r • Barolo Cà Mia - Docg
r • Barolo Rocche dei Brovia - Docg
r • Barolo Villero - Docg
r • Barbera d'Alba Brea - Doc
r • Dolcetto d'Alba Vignavillej - Doc
r • Dolcetto d'Alba Solatio Brovia - Doc

Cantina Gigi Rosso ♟♟♟
Via Alba-Barolo 20, tel. 0173262369
www.gigirosso.com
r • Barbaresco Vigneto Viglino - Docg
r • Barolo Castelletto - Docg
r • Barolo Arione - Docg
r • Barbera d'Alba Vino del Buon Ricordo - Doc
r • Dolcetto di Diano d'Alba Vigna Vecchia del Pinnacolo - Doc

Cantina Terre del Barolo ♟
Via Alba-Barolo 5, tel. 0173262053
www.terredelbarolo.com
r • Barolo Castiglione Falletto - Docg
r • Barbera d'Alba Sorì della Roncaglia - Doc
r • Diano d'Alba Sorì del Montagrillo - Doc

Cantina Vietti ♟♟♟♟♟
Piazza Vittorio Veneto 5, tel. 017362825
r • Barbaresco Masseria - Docg
r • Barolo Brunate - Docg
r • Barolo Lazzarito - Docg
r • Barolo Riserva Villero - Docg
r • Barolo Rocche - Docg
r • Barbera d'Alba Scarrone Vigna Vecchia - Doc
r • Barbera d'Asti La Crena - Doc
r • Dolcetto d'Alba Sant'Anna - Doc
r • Nebbiolo d'Alba San Michele - Doc

Fontana Ettore - Livia Fontana ♟♟♟
Via Pugnane 12, tel. 017362844
www.liviafontana.com

r • Barolo Villero - Docg
r • Barbera d'Alba - Doc
r • Dolcetto d'Alba - Doc
r • Langhe Rosso Insieme - Doc
w • Roero Arneis - Doc

FRATELLI MONCHIERO ♟♟♟
Via Alba Monforte 58, tel. 017362820
r • Barolo Le Rocche - Docg
r • Barolo Montanello - Docg
r • Barolo Roere - Docg
r • Barbera d'Alba - Doc
r • Dolcetto d'Alba - Doc

LA BRUNELLA - SILVANO ED ELENA BOROLI ♟♟♟
Via Pugnane 2, tel. 0173365477
www.borolivini.com
r • Barolo - Docg
r • Barolo Villero - Docg
r • Barbera d'Alba Bricco Fasano - Doc

MASCARELLO GIUSEPPE E FIGLIO ♟♟♟♟
Strada del Grosso 1, tel. 0173792126
www.mascarello1881.com
r • Barolo Monprivato - Docg
r • Barolo Riserva Monprivato Cà d'Morissio - Docg
r • Barolo Santo Stefano di Perno - Docg
r • Barbera d'Alba Santo Stefano - Doc
r • Dolcetto d'Alba Santo Stefano - Doc
r • Langhe Rosso Status - Doc
r • Nebbiolo d'Alba San Rocco - Doc

SCAVINO PAOLO ♟♟♟♟♟
Via Alba-Barolo 59, tel. 017362850
e.scavino@libero.it
r • Barolo Bric del Fiasc - Docg
r • Barolo Cannubi - Docg
r • Barolo Carobric - Docg
r • Barolo Riserva Rocche dell'Annunziata - Docg
r • Barbera d'Alba Carati - Doc

TENUTA CAVALLOTTO - BRICCO BOSCHIS ♟♟♟♟
Località Bricco Boschis, tel. 017362814
r • Barolo Bricco Boschis - Docg
r • Barolo Riserva Bricco Boschis Vigna San Giuseppe - Docg
r • Barolo Riserva Vigna Punta Vignolo - Docg
r • Dolcetto d'Alba Vigna Melera - Doc
r • Dolcetto d'Alba Vigna Scot - Doc

CASTIGLIONE TINELLA

Cuneo km 86 • m 408

WINERIES

CAUDRINA ♟♟♟♟
Strada Brosia 20, tel. 0141855126
www.caudrina.it
r • Barbera d'Asti Superiore Montevenere - Doc
w • Piemonte Chardonnay Mej - Doc
s • Asti La Selvatica - Docg
s • Moscato d'Asti La Caudrina - Docg
s • Moscato d'Asti La Galeisa - Docg

ICARDI ♟♟♟
Via Balbi 30, tel. 0141855159
r • Barolo Parej - Docg
r • Barbera d'Alba Surì di Mù - Doc
r • Langhe Rosso Pafoj - Doc
w • Monferrato Bianco Pafoj - Doc
s • Moscato d'Asti La Rosa Selvatica - Docg

LA MORANDINA ♟♟♟
Strada Morandini 11, tel. 0141855261
lamorandina@tin.it
r • Barbera d'Asti Zucchetto - Doc
r • Varmat - Vdt
s • Moscato d'Asti - Docg

PERRONE ELIO ♟♟
Via S. Martino 3 bis, tel. 0141855803
r • Barbera d'Asti Grivò - Doc
s • Moscato d'Asti Clarté - Docg
s • Moscato d'Asti Sourgal - Docg

SARACCO ♟♟♟♟
Via Circonvallazione 6, tel. 0141855113
w • Bianch del Luv - Vdt
w • Prasuè - Vdt
s • Moscato d'Asti - Docg
s • Moscato d'Asti d'Autunno - Docg

CERRO TANARO

Asti km 14 • m 109

WINERIES

CARNEVALE GIORGIO ♟♟
Via Trombetta 157, tel. 0141409115
r • Barbera d'Asti de la Rocchetta - Doc
r • Barbera d'Asti Il Crottino - Doc
s • Brachetto d'Acqui - Docg
s • Moscato d'Asti - Docg
s • Moscato d'Asti Sorì - Docg

CLAVESANA

Cuneo km 34 • m 300

WINERIES

CANTINA CLAVESANA ♟♟
Località Madonna della Neve 13, tel. 0173790451
r • Barbera d'Alba Superiore Armonie - Doc
r • Dolcetto di Dogliani - Doc
r • Dolcetto di Dogliani Superiore Pensieri - Doc

TENUTA COSTA PRA ♟♟
Località Costa Prà, tel. 0173790467
www.costapra.com
r • Dolcetto di Dogliani Superiore L'Re d'ij Piasì - Doc
r • Dolcetto di Dogliani Superiore Vigna Isabella - Doc

COCCONATO

Asti km 31 • m 491

WINERIES

BAVA ♟♟♟ ★10%
Strada Monferrato 2, tel. 0141907083
www.bava.com
r • Barbera d'Asti Superiore Piano Alto - Doc
r • Barbera d'Asti Superiore Stradivario - Doc
w • Monferrato Bianco Alteserre - Doc
s • Moscato d'Asti Bass Tuba - Docg
s • Malvaxia - Doc

FRATELLI DEZZANI ♟♟♟
Via Pinin Giachino 140, tel. 0141907236
www.dezzani.it
r • Barbaresco - Docg
r • Barolo - Docg
r • Barbera d'Asti Gli Scaglioni - Doc
r • Monferrato Rosso La Guardia - Doc
r • Ruché di Castagnole Monferrato - Doc
w • Roero Arneis Il Monfrigio - Doc
s • Moscato d'Asti I Morelli - Docg

CORNELIANO D'ALBA
Cuneo km 60 • m 204

Wineries

Valdinera ♟♟♟
Via Cavour 1, tel. 0173619881
www.valdinera.it
- *r* • Barbera d'Alba Superiore Ca' Rusa Brume di Luna - Doc
- *r* • Nebbiolo d'Alba Sontuoso - Doc
- *r* • Roero Superiore San Carlo - Doc
- *w* • Roero Arneis Vigna Cumigiano - Doc

CORSIONE
Asti km 15 • m 287

Wineries

L'Columbè ♟♟
Cascina Colombaro 1, tel. 3355336177
columbe@inwind.it
- *r* • Barbera d'Asti Superiore Bricco Colombaro - Doc
- *r* • Ruché di Castagnole Monferrato Rouet - Doc

COSSOMBRATO
Asti km 14 • m 275

Wineries

Quarello Carlo ♟♟
Via Marconi 3, tel. 0141905204
- *r* • Grignolino del Monferrato Casalese Cré Marcaleone - Doc
- *r* • Monferrato Rosso Crebarné - Doc

COSTA VESCOVATO
Alessandria km 31 • m 305

Wineries

Boveri ♟♟
Via XX Settembre 6, tel. 0131838165
boveriluigimichele@virgilio.it
- *r* • Colli Tortonesi Barbera Vignalunga - Doc
- *w* • Colli Tortonesi Cortese - Doc
- *w* • Colli Tortonesi Timorasso Filari - Doc

COSTIGLIOLE D'ASTI
Asti km 15 • m 242

Wineries

Beccaris Renzo ♟♟
Località Madonnina 26, tel. 0141966592
- *r* • Barbera d'Asti Superiore Bric d'Alì - Doc
- *r* • Barbera d'Asti Superiore San Lorenzo - Doc
- *r* • Monferrato Bricco della Ghiandaia - Doc

Benotto Carlo ♟♟♟
Via S. Carlo 52, tel. 0141966406
- *r* • Barbera d'Asti Superiore Rupestris - Doc
- *r* • Monferrato Dolcetto Plissé - Doc
- *r* • Monferrato Rosso Gamba di Pernice - Doc

Boeri Alfonso ♟♟
Via Bionzo 2, tel. 0141968171
www.boerivini.it
- *r* • Barbera d'Asti Superiore Parlapà - Doc
- *w* • Piemonte Chardonnay Beviòn - Doc
- *s* • Moscato d'Asti Ribota - Docg

Casa Constantin ♟
Strada Chiappino 8, tel. 0141968642
casaconstantin@web.de
- *r* • Barbera d'Asti Casa Constantin - Doc

Cascina Castlet ♟♟♟
Strada Castelletto 6, tel. 0141966651
- *r* • Barbera d'Asti Superiore Litina - Doc
- *r* • Barbera d'Asti Superiore Passum - Doc
- *r* • Monferrato Rosso Policalpo - Doc
- *s* • Moscato d'Asti - Docg
- *s* • Piemonte Moscato Passito Aviè - Doc

Cascina Ferro ♟♟♟
Strada Nosserio, tel. 0141966693
- *r* • Barbera d'Asti Superiore Bric - Doc
- *r* • Barbera d'Asti Superiore Vanet - Doc
- *r* • Monferrato Rosso Cin - Doc

Cascina Roera ♟♟
Località Bionzo 32, tel. 0141968437
- *r* • Barbera d'Asti Superiore Cardin - Doc
- *r* • Barbera d'Asti Superiore San Martino - Doc
- *w* • Piemonte Chardonnay Selezione Le Aie - Doc

Gozzelino Sergio ♟♟♟
Strada Bricco Lu 7, tel. 0141966134
gozzelino@tin.it
- *r* • Barbera d'Asti Superiore Ciabot d'La Mandorla - Doc
- *r* • Barbera d'Asti Superiore Selezione Lorenzo Gozzelino - Doc
- *r* • Grignolino d'Asti Bric d'la Riva - Doc
- *r* • Monferrato Dolcetto - Doc
- *s* • Moscato d'Asti Bric da Lu - Docg

Nebiolo Luigi ♟♟
Via Aie 17, tel. 0141966030
- *r* • Barbera d'Asti - Doc
- *r* • Barbera d'Asti Superiore San Martino - Doc
- *w* • Piemonte Chardonnay Selezione - Doc

Negri Marco ♟♟
Località Piazzo 14, tel. 0141968596
- *s* • Moscato d'Asti - Docg

Poderi Bertelli ♟♟♟♟
Località San Carlo 38, tel. 0141966137
- *r* • Barbera d'Asti Giarone - Doc
- *r* • Barbera d'Asti Montetusa - Doc
- *r* • Barbera d'Asti San Antonio Vielles Vignes - Doc
- *r* • Monferrato Rosso I Fossaretti - Doc
- *w* • Monferrato Bianco I Fossaretti - Doc
- *w* • Piemonte Chardonnay Giarone - Doc

Sciorio ♟♟♟
Via Asti-Nizza 87, tel. 0141966610
- *r* • Barbera d'Asti Reginal - Doc
- *r* • Barbera d'Asti Sciorio - Doc
- *r* • Barbera d'Asti Superiore Vigna Beneficio - Doc
- *r* • Monferrato Rosso Antico Vitigno - Doc
- *w* • Piemonte Chardonnay Vigna Levi - Doc

Scovero Andrea ♟♟♟
tel. 0141968212
ascover@tin.it
- *r* • Barbera d'Asti Superiore - Doc
- *r* • Monferrato Dolcetto - Doc

Valfieri ♟♟
Strada Loreto 5, tel. 0141966881
ncler@tin.it
- *r* • Barbera d'Asti Superiore Filari Lunghi - Doc
- *r* • Monferrato Rosso Matot - Doc
- *w* • Langhe Chardonnay - Doc

CREVOLADOSSOLA
Verbano-Cusio-Ossola km 97 • m 337

Wineries

Garrone ♟
Via Chavez 12, tel. 0324242990
garronevini@tin.it

r • Cà d'Matè - Vdt
r • Prunent - Vdt
r • Tarlap - Vdt

CUCCARO MONFERRATO

Alessandria km 18 • m 232

WINERIES

LIEDHOLM ♟♟♟
Villa Boemia 4, tel. 0131771916
r • Barbera d'Asti Tonneau - Doc
r • Rosso della Boemia - Vdt
w • Bianco della Boemia - Vdt

DIANO D'ALBA

Cuneo km 63 • m 496

WINERIES

ABRIGO GIOVANNI ♟♟
Via S. Croce 9, tel. 017369129
www.abrigo.it
r • Barbera d'Alba Marminela - Doc
r • Dolcetto di Diano d'Alba Garabei - Doc
r • Dolcetto di Diano d'Alba Söri Crava - Doc
r • Nebbiolo d'Alba - Doc

ALARIO ♟♟♟
Via S. Croce 23, tel. 0173231808
r • Barolo Riva - Docg
r • Barbera d'Alba Valletta - Doc
r • Dolcetto di Diano d'Alba Vigneto Costa Fiore - Doc
r • Nebbiolo d'Alba Vigneto Cascinotto - Doc
r • Pelaverga - Vdt

BRICCO MAIOLICA ♟♟♟♟♟
Via Bolangino 7, tel. 0173612049
www.briccomaiolica.it
r • Barbera d'Alba Vigna Vigia - Doc
r • Dolcetto di Diano d'Alba Sorì Bricco Maiolica - Doc
r • Langhe Rosso Loriè - Doc
w • Langhe Bianco Rolando - Doc
s • Moscato d'Asti Valdavì - Docg

CASAVECCHIA ♟
Via Roma 2, tel. 017369321
r • Barolo Piantà - Docg
r • Barbera d'Alba San Quirico - Doc
r • Dolcetto di Diano d'Alba Sorì Bruni - Doc

CASCINA FLINO ♟♟
Via Abelloni 7, tel. 017369231
r • Barbera d'Alba Flin - Doc
r • Dolcetto di Diano d'Alba Vigna Vecchia - Doc

COLLA ANGELO ♟♟
Via Provinciale 30, tel. 017369422
r • Dolcetto di Diano d'Alba Sorì du Rabin - Doc

FRATELLI ABRIGO ♟♟♟
Via Moglia Gerlotto 2, tel. 017369104
r • Barbera d'Alba La Galupa - Doc
r • Dolcetto di Diano d'Alba Sorì dei Berfi - Doc
r • Dolcetto di Diano d'Alba Vigna Bric Tulmìn - Doc
r • Dolcetto di Diano d'Alba Vigna Pietrin - Doc
r • Nebbiolo d'Alba Tardiss - Doc

FRATELLI BOFFA ♟♟
Località Ricca, via Cortemilia 142, tel. 0173612055
r • Barbera d'Alba - Doc
r • Dolcetto di Diano d'Alba Sorì Parisio - Doc
r • Nebbiolo d'Alba - Doc

ODDERO MASSIMO ♟♟♟
Via S. Sebastiano 1, tel. 017369169
massimo.oddero@inline.it
r • Barbera d'Alba Carbea - Doc
r • Dolcetto di Diano d'Alba Sorba - Doc
r • Nebbiolo d'Alba Rapalin - Doc
r • Rosso del Notaio - Vdt
w • Langhe Chardonnay Remondà - Doc

PRANDI GIOVANNI ♟
Regione Colombè, via Farinetti 5, tel. 017369414
r • Dolcetto di Diano d'Alba Sorì Colombè - Doc
r • Dolcetto di Diano d'Alba Sorì Cristina - Doc

PRODUTTORI DIANESI ♟
Via S. Croce 1/bis, tel. 017369221
www.produttoridianesi.com
r • Dolcetto di Diano d'Alba Sorì La Rocca - Doc
r • Dolcetto di Diano d'Alba Sorì Santa Lucia - Doc
r • Barilat - Vdt

SAVIGLIANO FRATELLI ♟♟
Via Cane Guido 20, tel. 0173231758
r • Dolcetto di Diano d'Alba Sorì Autin Grand - Doc
r • Dolcetto di Diano d'Alba Sorì Autin Gross - Doc
r • Dolcetto di Diano d'Alba Sorì del Sot - Doc

DOGLIANI

Cuneo km 40 • m 295

WINERIES

ABBONA CELSO ♟♟
Località Santa Lucia 36, tel. 017370668
caneuva@libero.it
r • Dolcetto di Dogliani Ca' Neuva - Doc
r • Dolcetto di Dogliani L'Sambu - Doc

ABBONA MARZIANO E ENRICO ♟♟♟♟
Via Torino 242, tel. 0173721317
r • Barolo Pressenda - Docg
r • Barolo Terlo Ravera - Docg
r • Barbera d'Alba Rinaldi - Doc
r • Dolcetto di Dogliani Papà Celso - Doc
r • Langhe Rosso I Due Ricu - Doc

BARBERIS OSVALDO ♟♟
Via Valdibà 113, tel. 017370054
brekos@jumpu.it
r • Dolcetto di Dogliani Puncin - Doc
r • Dolcetto di Dogliani San Lorenzo - Doc

BOSCHIS FRANCESCO ♟♟♟
Località San Martino di Pianezzo 57, tel. 017370574
r • Barbera d'Alba Le Masserie - Doc
r • Dolcetto di Dogliani Pianezzo - Doc
r • Barbera d'Alba San Cristoforo - Doc
r • Dolcetto di Dogliani Vigna Sorì San Martino - Doc
r • Dolcetto di Dogliani Vigna dei Prey - Doc

CHIONETTI QUINTO ♟♟♟♟
Località San Luigi 44, tel. 017371179
www.chionettiquinto.com
r • Dolcetto di Dogliani Briccolero - Doc
r • Dolcetto di Dogliani San Luigi - Doc

DEL TUFO ANTONIO ♟♟♟ ★10%
Via Madonna delle Grazie 33, tel. 017370692
r • Dolcetto di Dogliani - Doc
r • Dolcetto di Dogliani Vigna Spina - Doc

LA FUSINA ♟♟♟
Cascina Peracchio S. Lucia, tel. 017370488
lafusina@libero.it
r • Barbera d'Alba La Fusina - Doc

r • Barbera d'Alba Vigna Scarrone - Doc
r • Dolcetto di Dogliani Vigna Gombe - Doc

MARENCO ALDO ♟♟♟
Località Pamparato Pironi 25, tel. 0173720903
www.marencoaldo.it
r • Dolcetto di Dogliani Bric - Doc
r • Dolcetto di Dogliani Superiore Parlapà - Doc
r • Dolcetto di Dogliani Surì - Doc

PECCHENINO ♟♟♟♟♟
Via Valdiberti 59, tel. 017370686
www.pecchenino.com
r • Dolcetto di Dogliani San Luigi - Doc
r • Dolcetto di Dogliani Superiore Bricco Botti - Doc
r • Dolcetto di Dogliani Sirì d'Yermu - Doc
r • Langhe Rosso La Castella - Doc

PODERI EINAUDI LUIGI ♟♟♟♟
Cascina Tecc, borgata Gombe 31, tel. 017370191
r • Barolo Cannubi - Docg
r • Barolo Costa Grimaldi - Docg
r • Dolcetto di Dogliani I Filari - Doc
r • Dolcetto di Dogliani Vigna Tecc - Doc
r • Langhe Nebbiolo - Doc
r • Langhe Rosso Luigi Einaudi - Doc
w • Langhe Bianco Vigna Meira - Doc

PODERI LA COLLINA ♟♟♟ ★10%
Via D. Alighieri 42, tel. 017370155
r • Barbera d'Alba Superiore - Doc
r • Dolcetto di Dogliani Bricco Castiglia - Doc
r • Dolcetto di Dogliani San Luigi - Doc
r • Dolcetto di Dogliani Superiore Bricco Castiglia - Doc
r • Langhe Rosso Primo Assolo - Doc

RIBOTE - PORRO BRUNO E FIGLIO ♟♟
Via Valdiberti 24, tel. 017370371
r • Dolcetto di Dogliani Monetti - Doc
r • Dolcetto di Dogliani Ribote - Doc
r • Langhe Rosso Il Porro - Doc

ROMANA CARLO ♟♟♟♟ ★10%
Località Gombe 16, tel. 017376315
www.viniromana.it
r • Dolcetto di Dogliani Rumanot - Doc
r • Dolcetto di Dogliani Vigna Bric dij Nor - Doc
r • Dolcetto di Dogliani Vigna Suri Vinsant - Doc
r • Piemonte Barbera Rumanota - Doc

SAN FEREOLO ♟♟♟♟
Borgata Valdibà 58/59, tel. 0173742075
www.sanfereolo.com
r • Dolcetto di Dogliani "1593" - Doc
r • Dolcetto di Dogliani Superiore San Fereolo - Doc
r • Dolcetto di Dogliani Valdibà - Doc
r • Langhe Rosso Brumaio - Doc

SAN ROMANO ♟♟♟
Borgata Giachelli 8, tel. 017376289
r • Dolcetto di Dogliani - Doc
r • Dolcetto di Dogliani Vigna del Pilone - Doc
r • Dolcetto di Dogliani Superiore Dolianum - Doc
r • Langhe Pinot Nero Martin Sec - Doc

FARA NOVARESE

Novara km 19 • m 210

WINERIES

DESSILANI LUIGI & FIGLIO ♟♟♟♟
Via C. Battisti 21, tel. 0321829252
dessilani@onw.net
r • Ghemme Riserva - Docg
r • Colline Novaresi Nebbiolo - Doc
r • Fara Riserva Caramino - Doc
r • Fara Riserva Lochera - Doc
r • Sizzano Riserva - Doc

FARIGLIANO

Cuneo km 36 • m 263

WINERIES

ABBONA ANNA MARIA ♟♟♟
Località Moncucco 21, tel. 0173797228
r • Dolcetto di Dogliani Maioli - Doc
r • Dolcetto di Dogliani Sorì dij But - Doc
r • Dolcetto di Dogliani Superiore Maioli - Doc

GILLARDI ♟♟♟
Cascina Corsaletto, tel. 017376306
r • Dolcetto di Dogliani Vigneto Cursalet - Doc
r • Dolcetto di Dogliani Vigneto Maestra - Doc
r • Harys - Vdt

REVELLI ERALDO ♟
Località Pianbosco 29, tel. 0173797154
eraldorevelli@tin.it
r • Dolcetto di Dogliani Autin Lungh - Doc
r • Langhe Dolcetto Otto Filari - Doc

FRASSINELLO MONFERRATO

Alessandria km 27 • m 261

WINERIES

CASTELLO DI LIGNANO ♟♟
Regione Lignano, tel. 0142334511
r • Barbera d'Asti Vigna Stramba - Doc
r • Grignolino del Monferrato Casalese Vigna Tufara - Doc
r • Monferrato Rosso Lhennius - Doc

GALLIATE

Novara km 8 • m 153

WINERIES

FERRARI ANTONIO ♟♟♟♟
Via Monte Nero 19, tel. 0321861600
www.viniferrari.it
r • Salice Salentino La Canestra - Doc
s • Solaria Jonica - Vdt

GATTINARA

Vercelli km 34 • m 263

WINERIES

ANTONIOLO ♟♟
Corso Valsesia 277, tel. 0163833612
r • Gattinara Vigneto Castelle - Docg
r • Gattinara Vigneto Osso San Grato - Docg
r • Gattinara Vigneto San Francesco - Docg

GATTINARA SERGIO ♟♟♟
Piazza Monsignore Francese, tel. 0163832704
r • Gattinara - Docg
r • Gattinara Alice - Docg
r • Coste della Sesia Rosso Mercurino - Doc

NERVI ♟
Corso Vercelli 117, tel. 0163833228
r • Gattinara Vigneto Molsino - Docg
r • Amore - Vdt

TRAVAGLINI GIANCARLO ♟♟♟
Strada delle Vigne 36, tel. 0163833588
www.travaglinigattinara.it
r • Gattinara Riserva - Docg

r • Gattinara Selezione - Docg
r • Gattinara Tre Vigne - Docg

GAVI

Alessandria km 33 • m 233

WINERIES

BERGAGLIO NICOLA ♟♟
Località Rovereto, tel. 0143682195
w • Gavi del Comune di Gavi - Docg
w • Gavi del Comune di Gavi Minaia - Docg

BROGLIA GIAN PIERO ♟♟♟
Località Lomellina 14, tel. 0143642998
www.immagine.com/broglia
r • Monferrato Rosso Bruno Broglia - Doc
r • Monferrato Rosso Le Pernici - Doc
w • Gavi di Gavi Bruno Broglia - Docg
w • Gavi di Gavi La Meirana - Docg
w • Gavi di Gavi Villa Broglia - Docg

CANTINA PRODUTTORI DEL GAVI ♟
Via Cavalieri di Vittorio Veneto 45, tel. 0143642786
cantina.prodgavi@libero.it
w • Gavi del Comune di Gavi Cascine dell'Aureliana - Docg
w • Gavi del Comune di Gavi La Maddalena - Docg
w • Piemonte Cortese DiVino - Doc

CASTELLARI BERGAGLIO ♟♟♟
Località Rovereto 136, tel. 0143644000
www.castellaribergagli.it
w • Gavi di Gavi Rolona - Docg
w • Gavi di Gavi Rovereto Vigna Vecchia - Docg
w • Gavi Fornaci - Docg
w • Pilin - Vdt

LA CHIARA ♟♟♟
Località Vallegge 24, tel. 0143642293
w • Gavi del Comune di Gavi - Docg
w • Gavi del Comune di Gavi Vigneto Groppella - Docg

LA SCOLCA ♟♟♟ ★10%
Località Rovereto, tel. 0143682176
w • Gavi del Comune di Gavi Bianco Secco La Scolca - Docg
w • Gavi del Comune di Gavi Bianco Secco Villa Scolca - Docg
w • Gavi Spumante Brut Soldati La Scolca - Doc
w • Gavi Spumante Pas Dosé Soldati La Scolca - Doc
w • Spumante Brut Soldati La Scolca - Vdt

MORGASSI SUPERIORE ♟♟
Case sparse Sermoria 7, tel. 0143642007
www.morgassisuperiore.it
w • Gavi del Comune di Gavi Etichetta Oro - Docg
w • Piemonte Chardonnay Fiordiligi - Doc
w • Cherubino - Vdt

PICOLLO ERNESTO ♟♟
Località Rovereto, via Chiesa 60, tel. 0143682175
w • Gavi del Comune di Gavi Rovereto - Docg
w • Gavi del Comune di Gavi Rughè - Docg

SAN BARTOLOMEO ♟♟
Cascina S. Bartolomeo 26, tel. 0143643180
w • Gavi del Comune di Gavi Cappello del Diavolo - Docg
w • Gavi del Comune di Gavi Pelöia - Docg
w • Cortese dell'Alto Monferrato - Doc

TENUTA LA GIUSTINIANA ♟♟♟ ★10%
Località Rovereto 5, tel. 0143682132
lagiustiniana@libarnanet.it
r • Monferrato Rosso Just - Doc
w • Gavi del Comune di Gavi Lugarara - Docg
w • Gavi del Comune di Gavi Montessora - Docg
w • Just - Vdt

TENUTA NUOVA CA' DA MEO ♟♟
Via Pratolungo 163, tel. 0143667923
tncadameo@iol.it
w • Gavi del Comune di Gavi Cà da Meo - Docg

VILLA SPARINA ♟♟♟
Località Monterotondo 56, tel. 0143633835
r • Dolcetto d'Acqui d'Giusep - Doc
r • Monferrato Rosso Rivalta - Doc
r • Monferrato Rosso Sanpo - Doc
w • Gavi del Comune di Gavi La Villa - Docg
w • Gavi del Comune di Gavi Monterotondo - Docg

GHEMME

Novara km 25 • m 241

WINERIES

ANTICHI VIGNETI DI CANTALUPO ♟♟♟♟
Via Michelangelo Buonarroti 5, tel. 0163840041
www.cantalupo.net
r • Ghemme Collis Breclemae - Docg
r • Ghemme Collis Carellae - Docg
r • Ghemme Signore di Bayard - Docg
r • Colline Novaresi Rosso Agamium - Doc
rs • Colline Novaresi Nebbiolo Il Mimo - Doc

LA TORRACCIA DEL PIANTAVIGNA ♟♟
Corso Romagnano 69/A, tel. 0163840040
www.francoli.it
r • Gattinara Podere Jerbiön - Docg
r • Ghemme Podere Punciön - Doc

ROVELLOTTI ♟♟
Via Privata Tamiotti 3, tel. 0163840478
info@rovellotti.it
r • Ghemme - Docg
r • Ghemme Riserva - Docg

GOVONE

Cuneo km 76 • m 301

WINERIES

CANTAMESSA MARIA ♟
Via S. Pietro 22/A, tel. 017358551
www.casacantamessa.it
r • Barbera d'Alba Rossodelcolle - Doc
r • Collerosso - Vdt
w • Roero Arneis - Doc

GRINZANE CAVOUR

Cuneo km 58 • m 183/310

WINERIES

CANTINA LE GINESTRE ♟♟
Via Grinzane 15, tel. 0173262910
r • Barolo - Docg
r • Barbera d'Alba Pian Romualdo - Doc
r • Dolcetto d'Alba Madonna Como - Doc
r • Langhe Rosso Bricco Tampirì - Doc
w • Langhe Chardonnay Traisorì - Doc

INCISA SCAPACCINO

Asti km 30 • m 131

WINERIES

BREMA CASCINA CROCE ♟♟♟♟♟
Via Pozzo Magna 9, tel. 014174019
vinibrema@inwind.it

r • Barbera d'Asti Bricconizza - Doc
r • Barbera d'Asti Bricco della Volpettona - Doc
r • Barbera d'Asti Cascina Croce - Doc
r • Barbera d'Asti Superiore Le Cascine - Doc
r • Dolcetto d'Asti Vigna Impagnato - Doc

Tenuta Olim Bauda 🍷🍷🍷
Via Prata 50, tel. 014174266
www.tenutaolimbauda.it
r • Barbera d'Asti Superiore - Doc
s • Piemonte Moscato Passito - Doc

ISOLA D'ASTI

Asti km 9 • m 125/276

Wineries

Tartaglino Alessandro 🍷
Via Repergo 35, tel. 0141958271
r • Barbera d'Asti Brichet d'Oro - Doc

Vigneti Brichet 🍷 ★10%
Località Repergo, via Castellazzo 53,
tel. 0141958684
www.vignetibrichet.it
r • Barbera d'Asti Vigneto La Dama - Doc
r • Grignolino d'Asti Non Ti Scordar di Me - Doc
r • Il Cavaliere - Vdt

IVREA

Turin km 50 • m 253

Wineries

Ferrando 🍷🍷🍷
Via Torino 599/A, tel. 0125641176
www.ferrandovini.it
r • Carema - Doc
r • Carema Riserva Etichetta Nera - Doc
w • Erbaluce di Caluso Vigneto Cariola - Doc
s • Caluso Passito - Doc
s • Solativo - Vdt

LA MORRA

Cuneo km 50 • m 513

Wineries

Alessandria Crissante 🍷🍷🍷
Borgata Roggeri di S. Maria 43, tel. 017350834
r • Barolo Otin Capalot - Docg
r • Barolo Vigna dei Roggeri - Docg
r • Monferrato Rosso Rugé - Doc

Altare Elio 🍷🍷🍷🍷🍷
Località Annunziata 51, tel. 017350835
r • Barolo Arborina - Docg
r • Barolo Brunate - Docg
r • Dolcetto d'Alba - Doc
r • Langhe Arborina - Doc
r • Langhe Larigi - Doc
r • Langhe La Villa - Doc
r • L'Insieme - Vdt

Batasiolo 🍷🍷🍷
Località Annunziata 87, tel. 017350130
www.batasiolo.com
r • Barbaresco - Docg
r • Barolo Vigneto Briccolina - Docg
r • Barolo Vigneto Cerequio - Docg
r • Barbera d'Alba Sovrana - Doc
r • Dolcetto d'Alba Bricco Vergne - Doc

Bocchino Eugenio 🍷🍷🍷
Località Santa Maria, borgata Serra,
tel. 0173364226
laperucca@libero.it
r • Barbera d'Alba - Doc
r • Barbera d'Asti Alteville - Doc
r • Langhe Rosso Bricco del Gufo - Doc
r • Langhe Rosso Suo di Giacomo - Doc
r • Nebbiolo d'Alba La Perucca - Doc

Boglietti Enzo 🍷🍷🍷🍷
Via Roma 37, tel. 017350330
r • Barolo Brunate - Docg
r • Barolo Fossati - Docg
r • Barolo Vigna Case Nere - Docg
r • Barbera d'Alba Roscaleto - Doc
r • Barbera d'Alba Vigna dei Romani - Doc
r • Dolcetto d'Alba Tiglineri - Doc
r • Langhe Rosso Buio - Doc

Bovio 🍷🍷🍷
Borgata Ciotto 63, tel. 017350190
r • Barolo Rocchettevino - Docg
r • Barolo Vigna Arborina - Docg
r • Barolo Vigna Gattera - Docg
r • Barbera d'Alba Vigneto Regia Veja - Doc
r • Dolcetto d'Alba Vigneto Dabbene dell'Annunziata - Doc

Cantina Ciabot Berton 🍷🍷🍷
Località Santa Maria 1, tel. 017350217
r • Barolo - Docg
r • Barolo Roggeri - Docg
r • Barbera d'Alba - Doc
r • Barbera d'Alba Bricco San Biagio - Doc
r • Dolcetto d'Alba - Doc

Cantina Voerzio Gianni 🍷🍷🍷🍷
Strada Loreto 1, tel. 0173509194
r • Barolo La Serra - Docg
r • Barbera d'Alba Ciabot della Luna - Doc
r • Dolcetto d'Alba Rochettevino - Doc
r • Langhe Nebbiolo Ciabot della Luna - Doc
r • Langhe Rosso Serrapiù - Doc

Cascina Ballarin 🍷🍷🍷
Località Annunziata 115, tel. 017350365
www.cascinaballarin.it
r • Barolo Bricco Rocca - Docg
r • Barolo Bussia - Docg
r • Barbera d'Alba Giuli - Doc
r • Dolcetto d'Alba Bussia - Doc
r • Langhe Rosso Ballarin - Doc

Cascina del Monastero 🍷🍷
Località Annunziata 112/A, tel. 0173509245
cascinadelmonastero@libero.it
r • Barolo - Docg
r • Barolo Bricco Luciani - Docg

Corino Giovanni 🍷🍷🍷🍷🍷
Località Annunziata 24, tel. 017350219
r • Barolo Arborina - Docg
r • Barolo Giachini - Docg
r • Barolo Rocche dell'Annunziata - Docg
r • Barolo Vecchie Vigne - Docg
r • Barbera d'Alba Pozzo - Doc
r • Dolcetto d'Alba - Doc
r • L'Insieme - Vdt

Dosio Vigneti 🍷🍷🍷
Località Serradenari 6, tel. 017350677
cantine.dosio@tin.it
r • Barolo Vigna Fossati - Docg
r • Barbera d'Alba Superiore - Doc
r • Dolcetto d'Alba Vigna Nassone - Doc
r • Langhe Rosso Eventi - Doc
r • Langhe Rosso Momenti - Doc

ERBALUNA ♟♟
Località Annunziata 43, tel. 017350800
r • Barolo - Docg
r • Barolo Vigna Rocche - Docg
r • Barbera d'Alba La Rosina - Doc
r • Dolcetto d'Alba Le Ghiaie - Doc
r • Dolcetto d'Alba Le Liste - Doc

FRATELLI REVELLO ♟♟♟
Località Annunziata 103, tel. 017350276
www.revellofratelli.com
r • Barolo Conca - Docg
r • Barolo Giachini - Docg
r • Barolo Rocche dell'Annunziata - Docg
r • Barbera d'Alba Ciabot du Re - Doc
r • Dolcetto d'Alba - Doc

GAGLIARDO GIANNI ♟♟♟
Località Santa Maria, borgata Serra dei Turchi 88, tel. 017350829
www.gagliardo.it
r • Barolo Preve - Docg
r • Barbera d'Alba La Matta - Doc
r • Dolcetto d'Alba Paulin - Doc
r • Langhe Favorita Neirole - Doc
r • Langhe Rosso Batié - Doc

GRASSO SILVIO ♟♟♟♟
Cascina Luciani 112, tel. 017350322
r • Barolo Bricco Luciani - Docg
r • Barolo Ciabot Manzoni - Docg
r • Barbera d'Alba Vigna Fontanile - Doc
r • Langhe Nebbiolo Peirass - Doc
r • L'Insieme - Vdt

GROMIS ♟♟♟♟♟
Via del Laghetto 1, tel. 0173635158
r • Barolo - Docg

MARENGO MARIO ♟♟♟
Via XX Settembre 32, tel. 017350127
r • Barolo Brunate - Docg
r • Dolcetto d'Alba - Doc
r • Nebbiolo d'Alba Valmaggiore - Doc

MARRONE GIAN PIERO ♟♟♟
Località Annunciata 13, tel. 0173509288
www.agricolamarrone.com
r • Barolo Pichemej - Docg
r • Barbera d'Alba Superiore La Pantalera - Doc
s • Moscato d'Asti Sole d'Oro - Docg

MOLINO FRANCO ♟♟♟
Località Annunziata 117, tel. 017350380
www.cascinarocca.com
r • Barolo Rocche dell'Annunziata - Docg
r • Barolo Zuncai - Docg

MOLINO MAURO ♟♟♟♟
Località Annunziata 111, tel. 017350814
r • Barolo Gancia - Docg
r • Barolo Vigna Conca - Docg
r • Barbera d'Alba Gattere - Doc
r • Dolcetto d'Alba - Doc
r • Langhe Rosso Acanzio - Doc

MONFALLETTO ♟♟♟♟♟
Località Annunziata 67, tel. 017350344
www.corderodimontezemolo.com
r • Barolo Bricco Gattera - Docg
r • Barolo Monfalletto - Docg
r • Barolo Vigna Enrico VI di Castiglione Falletto - Docg
r • Barbera d'Alba Superiore Funtanì - Doc
r • Dolcetto d'Alba Monfalletto - Doc
r • Langhe Rosso - Doc
w • Langhe Chardonnay Elioro - Doc

OBERTO ANDREA ♟♟♟♟♟
Via G. Marconi 25, tel. 0173509262
r • Barolo Rocche - Docg
r • Barolo Vigneto Albarella - Docg
r • Barbera d'Alba Giada - Doc
r • Dolcetto d'Alba Vantrino Albarella - Doc
r • Langhe Rosso Fabio - Doc

PODERI E CANTINE FRATELLI ODDERO ♟♟♟♟♟
Località Santa Maria 28, tel. 017350618
r • Barolo Mondoca di Bussia - Docg
r • Barolo Rocche di Castiglione - Docg
r • Barolo Vigna Rionda - Docg
r • Dolcetto d'Alba - Doc
w • Langhe Chardonnay Collaretto - Doc

PODERI MARCARINI ♟♟♟
Piazza Martiri 2, tel. 017350222
www.marcarini.it
r • Barolo Brunate - Docg
r • Barolo La Serra - Docg
r • Barbera d'Alba Ciabot Camerano - Doc
r • Dolcetto d'Alba Boschi di Berri - Doc
r • Langhe Nebbiolo Lasarin - Doc

RENATO RATTI - ANTICHE CANTINE DELL'ABBAZIA DELL'ANNUNZIATA ♟♟♟
Località Annunziata 7, tel. 017350185
r • Barolo Conca di Marcenasco - Docg
r • Barolo Rocche di Marcenasco - Docg
r • Barbera d'Alba Torriglione - Doc
r • Dolcetto d'Alba Colombè - Doc
r • Nebbiolo d'Alba Ochetti di Monteu - Doc

ROCCHE COSTAMAGNA ♟♟♟
Via Vittorio Emanuele 8, tel. 0173509225
barolo@rocchecostamagna.it
r • Barolo Bricco Francesco - Docg
r • Barolo Rocche dell'Annunziata - Docg
r • Barbera d'Alba Annunziata - Doc
r • Dolcetto d'Alba Rubis - Doc
r • Langhe Nebbiolo Roccardo - Doc

SETTIMO AURELIO ♟♟♟
Località Annunziata 30, tel. 017350803
www.winecompany.net
r • Barolo - Docg
r • Barolo Riserva Rocche - Docg
r • Barolo Vigneti Rocche - Docg
r • Dolcetto d'Alba - Doc
r • Langhe Nebbiolo - Doc

STROPPIANA ORESTE ♟♟♟
Località Rivalta, via S. Giacomo 6, tel. 0173509419
stroppiana.vini@libero.it
r • Barolo Vigna San Giacomo - Docg
r • Dolcetto d'Alba - Doc

VEGLIO MAURO ♟♟♟♟
Località Annunziata 50, tel. 0173509212
r • Barolo Castelletto - Docg
r • Barolo Vigneto Arborina - Docg
r • Barolo Vigneto Gattera - Docg
r • Barbera d'Alba Cascina Nuova - Doc
r • Dolcetto d'Alba - Doc

VIBERTI ERALDO ♟♟♟
Località Santa Maria, borgata Tetti 53, tel. 017350308
r • Barolo - Docg

r • Barbera d'Alba Vigna Clara - Doc
r • Dolcetto d'Alba - Doc

Viberti Osvaldo ♟♟♟
Località Santa Maria, borgata Serra dei Turchi 95, tel. 017350374
r • Barolo Serra dei Turchi - Docg
r • Barbera d'Alba Mancine - Doc

Voerzio Roberto ♟♟♟♟♟
Località Cerreto 1, tel. 0173509196
r • Barolo Brunate - Docg
r • Barolo Cerequio - Docg
r • Barolo La Serra - Docg
r • Barolo Riserva Capalot e Brunate - Docg
r • Barolo Sarmassa - Docg
r • Barbera d'Alba Vigna Pozzo - Doc
r • Dolcetto d'Alba Priavino - Doc

LERMA
Alessandria km 39 • m 293

Wineries

La Casanella ♟♟
Cascina Casanella 13, tel. 0143877249
lacasanella@tiscalinet.it
r • Dolcetto di Ovada Riserva Torre Vallescura - Doc
r • Dolcetto di Ovada Superiore Bricco Casanella - Doc
r • Dolcetto di Ovada Vigna Rivarotta - Doc
r • Dolcetto di Ovada Vigna Sorito - Doc
w • Monferrato Bianco Soasì - Doc

LESSONA
Biella km 37 • m 360

Wineries

Sella ♟♟♟
Via IV Novembre 110, tel. 01599455
r • Bramaterra - Doc
r • Lessona Il Chioso - Doc
r • Lessona San Sebastiano allo Zoppo - Doc

LOAZZOLO
Asti km 40 • m 430

Wineries

Forteto della Luja ♟♟♟♟♟
Regione Bricco, borgata Rosso, tel. 0141831596
fortetodellaluj@inwind.it
r • Monferrato Rosso Le Grive - Doc
s • Moscato d'Asti Piasa San Maurizio - Docg
s • Loazzolo Vendemmia Tardiva Forteto della Luja Piasa Rischei - Doc
s • Piemonte Brachetto Forteto Pian dei Sogni - Doc

MANGO
Cuneo km 78 • m 521

Wineries

Cascina Fonda ♟♟♟♟
Località Cascina Fonda 45, tel. 0173677156
www.cascinafonda.com
r • Barbera d'Alba Bruseisa - Doc
s • Asti Spumante - Docg
s • Moscato d'Asti - Docg
s • Driveri Moscato Spumante - Igt
s • Cascina Fonda Vendemmia Tardiva - Vdt

Cascina Pian d'Or ♟♟♟
Località Bosi 15, tel. 014189440
s • Asti Spumante Acini - Docg
s • Moscato d'Asti Bricco Riella - Docg
s • Piemonte Brachetto Grappoli Rossi - Doc

Cascina Tinnirello ♟♟
Località Flori-Boschi 55, tel. 014189416
www.cascinatinnirello.com
w • Langhe Chardonnay Le Perle - Doc
s • Moscato d'Asti Flori - Docg

Terrabianca ♟♟
Regione Terrabianca 41, tel. 014189434
giorgioalpiste@tin.it
r • Dolcetto d'Alba Brichet - Doc
w • Langhe Chardonnay - Doc
s • Moscato d'Asti - Docg

MOASCA
Asti km 23 • m 260

Wineries

Barbero Pietro - Cascina La Ghersa ♟♟♟
Via S. Giuseppe 19, tel. 0141856012
r • Barbera d'Asti Superiore Bricco Verlenga - Doc
r • Barbera d'Asti Superiore La Vignassa - Doc
r • Monferrato Rosso La Ghersa - Doc

MOMBARUZZO
Asti km 37 • m 275

Wineries

Cascina Monreale ♟♟♟
Via Cordara 70, tel. 014177326
www.cascinamonreale.it
r • Barbera d'Asti Superiore Valentina - Doc
r • Dolcetto d'Asti - Doc
r • Monferrato Rosso Giorgio I - Doc

Malgrà ♟♟♟
Via Nizza 8, tel. 0141725055
www.malgra.it
r • Barbera d'Asti Superiore Gaiana - Doc
r • Barbera d'Asti Superiore Mora di Sassi - Doc
w • Gavi del comune di Gavi Poggio Basco - Docg

Tenute Neirano ♟♟
Località Casalotto, via S. Michele 39, tel. 0141739382
tenuteneirano@libero.it
r • Barbera d'Asti Superiore Tirteo - Doc
r • Barbera d'Asti Superiore Vigna Le Croci - Doc
r • Monferrato Rosso Tindaro - Doc

Tre Roveri ♟♟
Via Cordara 61, tel. 0141774522
vitaliano@picomaccario.it
r • Barbera d'Asti Lavignone - Doc
r • Barbera d'Asti Superiore Tre Roveri - Doc
r • Monferrato Rosso Cantamerli - Doc

MOMBERCELLI
Asti km 20 • m 233

Wineries

Castino Luigi ♟♟♟
Regione Moncucco 17, tel. 0141959608
www.castino.it
r • Barbera d'Asti - Doc
r • Barbera d'Asti Superiore - Doc

MONCALVO
Asti km 19 • m 305

Wineries

Cascina Orsolina ♟♟♟
Via Caminata 28, tel. 0141917277

www.orsolina.com
r • Barbera d'Asti Superiore Bricco dei Cappuccini - Doc
r • Monferrato Rosso Sole - Doc
w • Piemonte Chardonnay Rosanna - Doc

MONFORTE D'ALBA

Cuneo km 48 • m 480

WINERIES

ALESSANDRIA GIANFRANCO ♟♟♟♟♟
Località Manzoni 12, tel. 017378576
r • Barolo - Docg
r • Barolo San Giovanni - Docg
r • Barbera d'Alba Vittoria - Doc
r • Dolcetto d'Alba - Doc
r • L'Insieme - Doc

BOLMIDA SILVANO ♟♟
Località Bussia 30, tel. 0173789877
www.silvanobolmida.com
r • Barbera d'Alba Conca del Grillo - Doc
r • Dolcetto d'Alba Manescott - Doc

BUSSIA SOPRANA ♟♟♟♟
Località Bussia 81, tel. 039305182
r • Barolo Bussia - Docg
r • Barolo Mosconi - Docg
r • Barolo Vigna Colonnello - Docg
r • Barbera d'Alba Vin del Ross - Doc
r • Dolcetto d'Alba - Doc

CLERICO DOMENICO ♟♟♟♟♟
Località Manzoni-Cucchi 67, tel. 017378171
r • Barolo Ciabot Mentin Ginestra - Docg
r • Barolo Pajana - Docg
r • Barolo Per Cristina - Docg
r • Barbera d'Alba Trevigne - Doc
r • Langhe Rosso Arte - Doc

CONTERNO FANTINO ♟♟♟♟
Località Bricco Bastia, via Ginestra 1, tel. 017378204
r • Barolo Sorì Ginestra - Docg
r • Barolo Vigna Parussi - Docg
r • Barbera d'Alba Vignota - Doc
r • Langhe Rosso Monprà - Doc
w • Langhe Chardonnay Bastia - Doc

CONTERNO GIACOMO ♟♟♟♟♟
Località Ornati 2, tel. 017378221
r • Barolo Cascina Francia di Serralunga - Docg
r • Barolo Riserva Monfortino - Docg
r • Barbera d'Alba Cascina Francia - Doc

CONTERNO PAOLO ♟♟♟
Via Ginestra 34, tel. 017378415
www.paoloconterno.com
r • Barolo Ginestra - Docg
r • Barolo Ginestra Riserva - Docg
r • Barbera d'Alba Ginestra - Doc
r • Dolcetto d'Alba Ginestra - Doc
r • Langhe Nebbiolo Bric Ginestra - Doc

FAMIGLIA ANSELMA ♟♟♟
Località San Giuseppe 38, tel. 0173787217
www.anselma.it
r • Barolo Anselma - Docg
r • Barolo Riserva Adasi - Docg

FANTINO ALESSANDRO E GIAN NATALE ♟♟♟
Via G. Silvano 18, tel. 017378253
r • Barolo Vigna dei Dardi - Docg
r • Barbera d'Alba Superiore Vigna dei Dardi - Doc
r • Dolcetto d'Alba - Doc

FENOCCHIO GIACOMO ♟♟♟
Località Bussia 72, tel. 017378675
c.fenocchio@areacom.it
r • Barolo Bussia Sottana - Docg
r • Barolo Cannubi - Docg
r • Barolo Villero - Docg
r • Barbera d'Alba Superiore Bussia Sottana - Doc
r • Dolcetto d'Alba Bussia Sottana - Doc

FRATELLI DE NICOLA ♟
Rione Settevie 30, tel. 017378170
r • Barbaresco Montesommo - Docg
r • Barbaresco Riserva Feyles - Docg
r • Barolo Riserva Feyles - Docg

GHISOLFI ATTILIO ♟♟♟♟
Località Bussia 27, tel. 017378345
r • Barolo Bricco Visette - Docg
r • Barbera d'Alba - Doc
r • Barbera d'Alba Vigna Lisi - Doc
r • Langhe Rosso Carlin - Doc
r • Langhe Rosso Pinay - Doc

GRASSO ELIO ♟♟♟♟♟
Località Ginestra 40, tel. 017378491
r • Barolo Gavarini Vigna Chiniera - Docg
r • Barolo Ginestra Vigna Casa Matè - Docg
r • Barolo Runcot - Docg
r • Barbera d'Alba Vigna Martina - Doc
w • Langhe Chardonnay Educato - Doc

MANZONE ♟♟♟ ★10%
Località Manzoni 33, tel. 017378110
manzone@tiscalinet.it
r • Barolo Vigna Fraschin - Docg
r • Barbera d'Alba Vigna Barilot - Doc
r • Dolcetto d'Alba Vigna Castlè - Doc

MANZONE GIOVANNI - CIABOT DEL PREVE ♟♟♟♟
Via Castelletto 9, tel. 017378114
r • Barolo Le Gramolere - Docg
r • Barolo Le Gramolere Vigna Bricat - Docg
r • Barolo Santo Stefano di Perno - Docg
r • Barbera d'Alba La Serra - Doc
r • Dolcetto d'Alba La Serra - Doc

MONTI ♟♟♟
Località San Sebastiano 39, tel. 017378391
www.paolomonti.com
r • Barbera d'Alba - Doc
r • Langhe Rosso Dossi Rossi - Doc
w • Langhe Bianco L'Aura - Doc

PARUSSO ARMANDO ♟♟♟♟♟
Località Bussia 55, tel. 017378257
r • Barolo Bussia Vigna Fiorin - Docg
r • Barolo Bussia Vigna Munie - Docg
r • Barolo Bussia Vigna Rocche - Docg
r • Barolo Mariondino - Docg
r • Barbera d'Alba Superiore - Doc
r • Dolcetto d'Alba Piani Noce - Doc
w • Langhe Bianco Bricco Rovella - Doc

PIRA ♟♟♟♟♟
Località San Sebastiano 59, tel. 017378538
vini.pira@onw.net
r • Barbera d'Alba Vigna Fornaci - Doc
r • Dolcetto d'Alba Vigna Fornaci - Doc
r • Dolcetto di Dogliani Vigna Bricco dei Botti - Doc
r • Dolcetto di Dogliani Vigna Landes - Doc
r • Langhe Rosso Camerlot - Doc

PIRA GIORGIO ♟♟♟
Località Perno, via Cavour 35, tel. 017378413
r • Barolo - Docg

r • Barbera d'Alba - Doc
r • Dolcetto d'Alba - Doc

Podere Rocche dei Manzoni
Località Manzoni Soprani 3, tel. 017378421
r • Barolo Cappella di Santo Stefano - Docg
r • Barolo Pianpolvere Soprano Bussia - Docg
r • Barolo Vigna Big - Docg
r • Barolo Vigna d'la Roul - Docg
r • Dolcetto d'Alba Vigna Matinera - Doc

Podere Ruggeri Corsini
Località Bussia Corsini 106, tel. 017378625
podereruggericorsini@libero.it
r • Barolo Corsini - Docg
r • Barbera d'Alba - Doc
r • Barbera d'Alba Superiore Armujan - Doc

Poderi Conterno Aldo
Località Bussia 48, tel. 017378150
www.poderialdoconterno.com
r • Barolo Bricco Bussia Vigna Cicala - Docg
r • Barolo Bricco Bussia Vigna Colonnello - Docg
r • Barolo Bussia Soprana - Docg
r • Barolo Granbussia Riserva - Docg
r • Barbera d'Alba Conca Tre Pile - Doc
r • Langhe Nebbiolo Il Favot - Doc
w • Langhe Bianco Bussiador - Doc

Principiano Ferdinando
Via Alba 19, tel. 0173787158
ferdi.principiano@libero.it
r • Barolo Boscareto - Docg
r • Barolo Le Coste - Docg
r • Barbera d'Alba La Romualda - Doc

Roddolo Flavio
Località Sant'Anna 5, tel. 017378535
r • Barolo Ravera - Docg
r • Barbera d'Alba Superiore - Doc
r • Nebbiolo d'Alba - Doc

Seghesio Aldo e Riccardo
Località Castelletto 19, tel. 017378108
r • Barolo Vigneto La Villa - Docg
r • Barbera d'Alba Vigneto della Chiesa - Doc
r • Dolcetto d'Alba Vigneto della Chiesa - Doc

Tenuta Arnulfo - Costa di Bussia
Località Bussia 26, tel. 017377017
r • Barolo Campo dei Buoi - Docg
r • Barolo Riserva 1874 Luigi Arnulfo - Docg
r • Barbera d'Alba Campo del Gatto - Doc

Tenuta Rocca
Località Ornati 19, tel. 017378412
www.tenutarocca.com
r • Barolo Tenuta Rocca - Docg
r • Barbera d'Alba Vigna Ròca Neira - Doc
r • Dolcetto d'Alba Vigna Sorì Rocca - Doc
r • Langhe Rosso Ornati - Doc
r • Nebbiolo d'Alba Vigna Sorì Ornati - Doc

MONGARDINO
Asti km 10 • m 292

Wineries

I Vigneti di Dante
Via S. Antonio 4, tel. 0141291251
r • Barbera d'Asti - Doc
r • Barbera d'Asti Bricco Zoccola - Doc

MONLEALE
Alessandria km 32 • m 320

Wineries

Vigneti Massa
Piazza Capsoni 10, tel. 013180302
r • Colli Tortonesi Barbera Monleale - Doc
r • Colli Tortonesi Rosso Bigolla - Doc
r • Colli Tortonesi Rosso Pertichetta - Doc
w • Colli Tortonesi Bianco Casareggio - Doc
w • Colli Tortonesi Bianco Costa del Vento - Doc

MONTÀ
Cuneo km 73 • m 316

Wineries

Almondo Giovanni
Via S. Rocco 26, tel. 0173975256
r • Barbera d'Alba Valbianchera - Doc
r • Roero Superiore Bric Valdiana - Doc
r • Roero Superiore Giovanni Almondo - Doc
w • Roero Arneis Bricco delle Ciliegie - Doc
w • Roero Arneis Vigne Sparse - Doc

Taliano Michele
Corso Manzoni 24, tel. 0173976512
taliano@libero.it
r • Barbaresco Ad Altiora - Docg
r • Barbera d'Alba La Boriosa - Doc
r • Roero Ròche dra Bossora - Doc

MONTEGROSSO D'ASTI
Asti km 15 • m 244

Wineries

Bianco Pasquale
Via Gorra 3, tel. 0141956163
bianco_red@tin.it
r • Barbera d'Asti Superiore Vigna del Casot - Doc
r • Barbera d'Asti Vigna La Saretta - Doc

Tenuta La Meridiana
Località Tana Bassa 5, tel. 0141956172
www.viniternet.com/propduttori:meridiana
r • Barbera d'Asti Le Gagie - Doc
r • Barbera d'Asti Superiore Tra la Terra e il Cielo - Doc
r • Monferrato Rosso Rivaia - Doc

MONTELUPO ALBESE
Cuneo km 65 • m 564

Wineries

Ca' Viola
Via Langa 17, tel. 0173617570
r • Dolcetto d'Alba Barturot - Doc
r • Dolcetto d'Alba Vilot - Doc
r • Bric du Luv - Vdt
r • Rangone - Vdt

Destefanis
Via Mortizzo 8, tel. 0173617189
marcodestefanis@marcodestefanis.com
r • Barbera d'Alba - Doc
r • Dolcetto d'Alba Vigna Monia Bassa - Doc
r • Nebbiolo d'Alba rosso - Doc

MONTEU ROERO
Cuneo km 64 • m 395

Wineries

Cascina Pellerino
Località Sant'Anna, tel. 0173979083
r • Barbera d'Alba Superiore Gran Madre - Doc
r • Roero Vicot - Doc
w • Roero Arneis Boneur - Doc

NEGRO ANGELO & FIGLI ♟♟♟
Località Sant'Anna 1, cascina Riveri, tel. 017390252
www.negroangelo.it
r • Barbera d'Alba Bric Bertu - Doc
r • Roero Prachiosso - Doc
r • Roero Superiore Sodisfà - Doc
w • Roero Arneis Perdaudin - Doc
s • Perdaudin Passito - Vdt

MORBELLO
Alessandria km 44 • m 240/720
WINERIES
CAMPAZZO ♟
Località Costa 36, tel. 0144768975
campazzovini@libero.it
r • Barbera d'Asti La Pellegrina - Doc
r • Freisa d'Asti La Pateca - Doc
s • Brachetto d'Acqui Macramè - Docg

MORSASCO
Alessandria km 33 • m 328
WINERIES
LA GUARDIA ♟♟
Villa Delfini, tel. 014473076
r • Barbera del Monferrato La Vigna di Dante - Doc
r • Dolcetto di Ovada Bricco Lencina - Doc
r • Dolcetto di Ovada Superiore Bricco Riccardo - Doc

MURISENGO
Alessandria km 52 • m 338
WINERIES
ISABELLA ♟♟
Località Corteranzo, via Gianoli 64, tel. 0141693000
calvo@isabellavini.com
r • Barbera d'Asti Truccone - Doc
r • Grignolino del Monferrato Casalese Montecastello - Doc
w • Piemonte Chardonnay - Doc

NEIVE
Cuneo km 73 • m 308
WINERIES
ANTICHI PODERI DEI GALLINA - FRANCONE ♟♟ ★10%
Via Tanaro 45, tel. 017367068
www.franconevini.com
r • Barbaresco Gallina Vigneto Il Ciaciaret - Docg
r • Dolcetto d'Alba Gallina Vigneto Menturin - Doc
s • Moscato d'Asti Gallina Vigna del Rovere - Docg
BUSSO PIERO ♟♟♟
Località Albesani 8, tel. 017367156
r • Barbaresco Bricco Mondino - Docg
r • Barbaresco Gallina - Docg
r • Barbaresco Vigna Borgese - Docg
r • Barbera d'Alba Vigna Majano - Doc
r • Dolcetto d'Alba Vigna Majano - Doc
CANTINA DEL BRICCHETTO ♟♟♟
Regione Crocetta 4, tel. 0173677307
r • Barbaresco Albesani Vigna Ronco - Docg
r • Barbera d'Alba Bricco Sterpone - Doc
CANTINA DEL GLICINE ♟♟♟ ★10%
Via Giulio Cesare 1, tel. 017367215
caninaglicine@tiscalinet.it
r • Barbaresco Marcorino - Docg
r • Barbaresco Vigneto Curà - Docg
r • Barbera d'Alba Nebbiolata Marcorino La Sconsolata - Doc
r • Dolcetto d'Alba Olmiolo - Doc
CANTINA NEGRO GIUSEPPE ♟♟♟
Via Gallina 22, tel. 0173677468
www.negrogiuseppe.com
r • Barbaresco Pian Cavallo - Docg
r • Langhe Nebbiolo Monsù - Doc
w • Roero Arneis - Doc
CASCINA VANO ♟♟♟
Via Rivetti 9, tel. 0173677705
cascina.vano@tiscalinet.it
r • Barbaresco Canova - Docg
r • Barbera d'Alba Carulot - Doc
r • Langhe Rosso Duetto - Doc
CASTELLO DI NEIVE ♟♟♟
Via Castelborgo 1, tel. 017367171
neive.castello@tin.it
r • Barbaresco La Rocca di Santo Stefano - Docg
r • Barbaresco Santo Stefano - Docg
r • Barbera d'Alba Mattarello - Doc
r • Dolcetto d'Alba Messoirano - Doc
r • Langhe Rosso I Cortini - Doc
FATTORIA SAN GIULIANO ♟♟
Via Circonvallazione 14, tel. 017367364
r • Barbaresco - Docg
s • Piemonte Moscato Passito Quattordicesimo Anno - Doc
FONTANABIANCA ♟♟♟♟♟
Via Bordini 15, tel. 017367195
fontanabianca@libero.it
r • Barbaresco Sory Burdin - Docg
r • Barbera d'Alba Brunet - Doc
r • Dolcetto d'Alba Vigneto Bordini - Doc
r • Langhe Nebbiolo - Doc
w • Langhe Arneis - Doc
FRATELLI CIGLIUTI ♟♟♟
Via Serraboella 17, tel. 0173677185
cigliutirenato@libero.it
r • Barbaresco Serraboella - Docg
r • Barbera d'Alba Campass - Doc
r • Barbera d'Alba Serraboella - Doc
r • Dolcetto d'Alba Serraboella - Doc
r • Langhe Rosso Briccoserra - Doc
FRATELLI GIACOSA ♟♟♟
Via XX Settembre 64, tel. 017367013
www.giacosa.it
r • Barbaresco Rio Sordo - Docg
r • Barolo Bussia - Docg
r • Barbera d'Alba Maria Gioana - Doc
r • Dolcetto d'Alba Madonna Como - Doc
w • Langhe Chardonnay Cà Lunga - Doc
GASTALDI ♟♟♟
Borgata Albesani 20, tel. 0173677400
r • Barbaresco - Doc
r • Dolcetto d'Alba Moriolo - Doc
r • Langhe Rosso Castlè - Doc
r • Rosso Gastaldi - Vdt
w • Bianco Gastaldi - Vdt
GIACOSA BRUNO ♟♟♟♟♟
Via XX Settembre 52, tel. 017367027
www.brunogiacosa.it
r • Barbaresco Asili - Docg
r • Barbaresco Gallina di Neive - Docg
r • Barbaresco Rabajà - Docg
r • Barbaresco Santo Stefano di Neive - Docg

r • Barolo Collina Rionda di Serralunga - Docg
r • Barolo Falletto di Serralunga - Docg
r • Barolo Rocche di Falletto - Docg
r • Barolo Villero di Castiglione Falletto - Docg
w • Roero Arneis - Doc

La Contea ♟♟♟♟
Vicolo Asilo 13,
tel. 0173677585
r • Barbaresco Ripa Sorita 1998 - Docg
r • Barbera d'Alba Vigna Caplin - Doc
r • Nebbiolo d'Alba Castelvecchio - Doc
w • Langhe Chardonnay Mary - Doc

Paitin ♟♟♟♟
Via Serra Boella 20, tel. 017367343
www.paitin.com
r • Barbaresco Sorì Paitin Vecchie Vigne - Docg
r • Barbera d'Alba Campolive - Doc
r • Dolcetto d'Alba Sorì Paitin - Doc
r • Langhe Rosso Paitin - Doc
w • Roero Arneis Vigna Elisa - Doc

Prinsi ♟♟♟
Via Gaia 5, tel. 017367192
r • Barbaresco Prinsi - Docg
r • Dolcetto d'Alba San Cristoforo - Doc
w • Langhe Chardonnay - Doc

Punset ♟♟♟
Località Moretta 42, tel. 017367072
www.punset.com
r • Barbaresco Campo Quadro - Docg
r • Dolcetto d'Alba - Doc
r • Langhe Rosso Dualis - Doc

Rivetti Dante ♟♟♟
Località Bricco di Neive 12, tel. 017367125
r • Barbaresco Bricco de Neveis - Docg
r • Barbera d'Alba Alabarda - Doc
s • Moscato d'Asti Riveto - Docg

Serragrilli ♟♟♟
Via Serragrilli 30, tel. 0173677010
www.serragrilli.it
r • Barbaresco Serragrilli - Docg
r • Barbera d'Alba Collina Serragrilli - Doc
r • Langhe Rosso Grillo Rosso - Doc

Sottimano ♟♟♟♟
Località Cottà 21, tel. 0173635186
r • Barbaresco Cottà - Docg
r • Barbaresco Currà - Docg
r • Barbaresco Fansoni - Docg
r • Barbera d'Alba Pairolero - Doc
r • Dolcetto d'Alba Cottà - Doc

Voghera Luigi ♟♟♟
Via Tetti 6, tel. 0173677144
r • Barbaresco - Docg
r • Barbera d'Alba Vigneto Basarin - Doc
r • Dolcetto d'Alba Vigneto Basarin - Doc

NEVIGLIE

Cuneo km 74 • m 461

Wineries

Bera Fratelli ♟♟♟♟
Cascina Palazzo, via Castellero 12,
tel. 0173630194
r • Barbera d'Alba Superiore - Doc
r • Langhe Nebbiolo - Doc
r • Langhe Rosso Sassisto - Doc
s • Asti Spumante Cascina Palazzo - Docg
s • Moscato d'Asti Su Reimond - Docg

NIZZA MONFERRATO

Asti km 27 • m 138

Wineries

Antica Casa Vinicola Scarpa ♟♟
Via Montegrappa 6, tel. 0141721331
www.il-vino.com/scarpa
r • Barbera d'Asti La Bogliona - Doc
r • Monferrato Freisa La Selva di Moirano - Doc

Bersano e Riccadonna ♟♟♟
Piazza Dante 21, tel. 0141720211
r • Barolo Badarina - Docg
r • Barbera d'Asti Cremosina - Doc
r • Barbera d'Asti Generala - Doc
r • Monferrato Rosso Pomona - Doc
s • Moscato d'Asti San Michele - Docg

Bonfante Marco ♟♟
Strada Vaglio Serra 72, tel. 0141725012
marco.bonfante@libero.it
r • Barolo Poggio al Fante - Docg
r • Barbera d'Asti Superiore Menego - Doc
w • Gavi del Comune di Gavi Cà del Rosso - Docg

Guasti Clemente & Figli ♟♟
Corso IV Novembre 80, tel. 0141721350
r • Barbera d'Asti Superiore Barcarato - Doc
r • Nebbiolo d'Alba - Doc
s • Moscato d'Asti - Docg

La Barbatella ♟♟♟♟
Strada Annunziata 55, tel. 0141701434
r • Barbera d'Asti La Barbatella - Doc
r • Barbera d'Asti Superiore Vigna dell'Angelo - Doc
r • Monferrato Rosso Mystère - Doc
r • Monferrato Rosso Sonvico - Doc
w • Monferrato Bianco Noè - Doc

La Gironda ♟♟♟
Strada Bricco 12, tel. 0141823069
www.lagironda.com
r • Barbera d'Asti La Gena - Doc
r • Barbera d'Asti Superiore Le Nicchie - Doc

Scrimaglio Franco & Mario ♟♟♟♟
Via Alessandria 67, tel. 0141721385
www.scrimaglio.it
r • Barbera d'Asti Crutin - Doc
r • Barbera d'Asti Superiore Acsé - Doc
r • Monferrato Rosso Tantra - Doc
r • Piemonte Barbera Crowncap - Doc
w • Monferrato Bianco Bricco Sant'Ippolito - Doc

NOVELLO

Cuneo km 48 • m 471

Wineries

Cogno Elvio ♟♟♟
Località Ravera 2, tel. 0173744006
www.elviocogno.com
r • Barolo Ravera - Docg
r • Barolo Vigna Elena - Docg
r • Barbera d'Alba Bricco del Merlo - Doc
r • Dolcetto d'Alba Vigna del Mandorlo - Doc
w • Nascetta - Vdt

Le Strette ♟♟
Via Le Strette 2, tel. 0173744002
lestrette@lestrette.com
r • Barolo Bergeisa - Docg
r • Barbera d'Alba Vigneto Pezzole - Doc
w • Nas-Cetta - Vdt

NOVI LIGURE
Alessandria km 23 • m 197

WINERIES

CASCINA DEGLI ULIVI
Strada Mazzola 14, tel. 0143744598
- r • Monferrato Dolcetto Nibiò - Doc
- r • Piemonte Barbera Mounbè - Doc
- w • Gavi del Comune di Gavi Filagnotti di Tassarolo - Docg

OTTIGLIO
Alessandria km 31 • m 264

WINERIES

CAVE DI MOLETO
Regione Moleto 4, tel. 0142921468
www.moleto.it
- r • Barbera del Monferrato Bricco alla Prera - Doc
- r • Monferrato Rosso Mulej - Doc
- w • Piemonte Chardonnay - Doc

OVADA
Alessandria km 34 • m 186

WINERIES

ROSSI CONTINI ANNALYSA
Strada S. Lorenzo 20, tel. 0143822530
www.rossicontini.it
- r • Dolcetto di Ovada San Lorenzo - Doc
- r • Dolcetto di Ovada Superiore Vigneto Ninan - Doc
- r • Cras Tibi - Vdt

OZZANO MONFERRATO
Alessandria km 33 • m 246

WINERIES

VALPANE
Cascina Valpane 10/1, tel. 0142486713
www.cantinevalpane.com
- r • Barbera del Monferrato - Doc
- r • Barbera del Monferrato Valpane - Doc

PIOBESI D'ALBA
Cuneo km 61 • m 194

WINERIES

BUGANZA RENATO
Cascina Carbianotto 4, tel. 0173619370
rbuganz@tin.it
- r • Barbera d'Alba Gerbole - Doc
- r • Nebbiolo d'Alba Bric Paradis - Doc
- r • Roero Bric Paradis - Doc

TENUTA CARRETTA
Località Carretta 2, tel. 0173619119
- r • Barbaresco Cascina Bordino - Docg
- r • Barolo Cannubi - Docg
- r • Dolcetto d'Alba Vigna Tavoleto - Doc
- r • Roero Superiore Bric Paradiso - Doc
- w • Roero Arneis Vigna Canorei - Doc

PORTACOMARO
Asti km 10 • m 232

WINERIES

CALDERA FABRIZIA
Località Stazione 53/B, tel. 0141296154
www.vinicaldera.it
- r • Barbera d'Asti Balmèt - Doc
- r • Dolcetto di Dogliani - Doc
- r • Ruchè di Castagnole Monferrato - Doc

CASTELLO DEL POGGIO
Località Poggio, tel. 0141202543
info@poggio.it
- r • Barbera d'Asti Masaréj - Doc
- r • Piemonte Barbera Bunéis - Doc
- s • Moscato d'Asti - Docg

PRASCO
Alessandria km 37 • m 245

WINERIES

CAVELLI GIANPIETRO
Via Provinciale 77, tel. 0144375706
cavellivini@libero.it
- r • Dolcetto di Ovada Selezione Le Zerbe - Doc

PRIOCCA
Cuneo km 75 • m 253

WINERIES

CASCINA VAL DEL PRETE
Strada Santuario 2, tel. 0173616534
- r • Barbera d'Alba Carolina - Doc
- r • Nebbiolo d'Alba Vigna di Lino - Doc
- r • Roero - Doc

HILBERG - PASQUERO
Via Bricco Gatti 16, tel. 0173616197
- r • Barbera d'Alba Superiore - Doc
- r • Langhe Rosso Pedrocha - Doc
- r • Nebbiolo d'Alba - Doc

QUARGNENTO
Alessandria km 11 • m 121

WINERIES

COLLE MANORA
Via Bozzole 4, tel. 0131219252
info@collemanora.it
- r • Barbera del Monferrato Manora - Doc
- r • Monferrato Rosso Paloalto - Doc
- r • Manora Collezione - Vdt
- w • Monferrato Bianco Mimosa Collezione - Doc
- w • Mila Collezione - Vdt

RICALDONE
Alessandria km 27 • m 285

WINERIES

RINALDI VINI
Via Roma 31, tel. 014474144
rinaldi-vini@libero.it
- r • Barbera d'Asti Superiore Sisula - Doc
- r • Barbera d'Asti Vigneto Rioglio - Doc
- s • Moscato d'Asti Bricco Cardogno - Docg

ROCCA GRIMALDA
Alessandria km 30 • m 273

WINERIES

CASCINA LA MADDALENA
Località Piani del Padrone 258, tel. 0143876074
www.cascina-maddalena.com
- r • Monferrato Rosso Bricco della Maddalena - Doc

RATTO GIUSEPPE - CASCINA SCARSI
Località San Lorenzo, tel. 0143831888
- r • Dolcetto di Ovada Bricco Trionzo - Doc
- r • Dolcetto di Ovada Gli Scarsi - Doc
- r • Dolcetto di Ovada Le Olive - Doc

ROCCHETTA TANARO
Asti km 15 • m 107

Wineries

Braida di Bologna Giacomo ★10%
Via Roma 94, tel. 0141644113
www.braida.it
- r • Barbera d'Asti Ai Suma - Doc
- r • Barbera d'Asti Bricco della Bigotta - Doc
- r • Barbera d'Asti Bricco dell'Uccellone - Doc
- r • Barbera d'Asti Montebruna - Doc
- r • Barbera del Monferrato Vivace La Monella - Doc
- r • Monferrato Rosso Il Bacialé - Doc
- s • Moscato d'Asti Vigna Senza Nome - Docg

Hastae
Piazza Italia 1/bis, tel. 0141644113
- r • Barbera d'Asti Quorum - Doc

'l Post dal Vin - Terre del Barbera
Via Salie 19, tel. 0141644143
terredelbarbera@vignaioli.it
- r • Barbera d'Asti Superiore Bricco Fiore - Doc
- r • Barbera d'Asti Superiore Castagnassa - Doc

Marchesi Incisa della Rocchetta
Via Roma 66, tel. 0141644647
www.lacortechiusa.it
- r • Barbera d'Asti Superiore Sant'Emiliano - Doc
- r • Grignolino d'Asti - Doc
- r • Piemonte Grignolino Sansoero - Doc

RODDINO
Cuneo km 51 • m 610

Wineries

Le Vigne di Ca' Nova
Cascina Canova, tel. 0173794247
www.vignedicanova.com
- r • Barbera d'Alba I Filari de I Maschi - Doc
- r • Dolcetto d'Alba Superiore - Doc
- w • Langhe Chardonnay Varenne - Doc

RODELLO
Cuneo km 65 • m 537

Wineries

Fratelli Mossio
Cascina Caramelli, via Montà 12, tel. 0173617149
www.mossio.com
- r • Dolcetto d'Alba Bricco Caramelli - Doc
- r • Dolcetto d'Alba Piano delli Perdoni - Doc
- r • Langhe Rosso - Doc

Giribaldi Mario
Cascina Massolino, via Rittano 6, tel. 0173617000
- r • Barbera d'Alba Superiore - Doc
- r • Langhe Rosso - Doc
- r • Nebbiolo d'Alba Dame & Fuet - Doc

ROSIGNANO MONFERRATO
Alessandria km 34 • m 280

Wineries

Visconti Cassinis Ravizza
Cascina Madonna delle Grazie 5, tel. 0142488054
www.vicara.it
- r • Barbera del Monferrato Superiore - Doc
- r • Barbera del Monferrato Superiore Cantico della Crosia - Doc
- r • Grignolino del Monferrato Casalese - Doc
- r • Monferrato Rosso Rubello - Doc
- w • Monferrato Bianco Airales - Doc

SAN GIORGIO CANAVESE
Turin km 34 • m 300

Wineries

Orsolani
Via Michele Chiesa 12, tel. 012432386
- w • Erbaluce di Caluso La Rustìa - Doc
- w • Erbaluce di Caluso Vignot Sant'Antonio - Doc
- s • Caluso Passito Sulè - Doc

SAN MARTINO ALFIERI
Asti km 14 • m 257

Wineries

Marchesi Alfieri
Castello Alfieri, tel. 0141976015
www.wines.com/alfieri
- r • Barbera d'Asti La Tota - Doc
- r • Barbera d'Asti Superiore Alfiera - Doc
- r • Monferrato Rosso San Germano - Doc

SAN MARZANO OLIVETO
Asti km 24 • m 301

Wineries

Berta
Regione Saline 53, tel. 0141856193
- r • Barbera d'Asti - Doc
- r • Barbera d'Asti Canto di Luna - Doc

Boffa Alfiero - Vigne Uniche
Regione Leiso 50, tel. 0141856115
www.alfieroboffa.com
- r • Barbera d'Asti Superiore Vigna Collina della Vedova - Doc
- r • Barbera d'Asti Superiore Vigna Cua Longa - Doc
- r • Barbera d'Asti Superiore Vigna La Riva - Doc

Carussin
Regione Mariano 22, tel. 0141831358
www.carussin.com
- r • Barbera d'Asti Lia Vì - Doc
- r • Barbera d'Asti Superiore Ferro Carlo - Doc
- s • Moscato d'Asti Filari Corti - Docg

Cascina L'Arbiola ★10%
Regione Saline 67, tel. 0141856194
www.arbiola.it
- r • Barbera d'Asti Superiore Romilda - Doc
- r • Monferrato Rosso Arbiola - Doc
- w • Monferrato Sauvignon Clelie VI - Doc

Francomondo
Regione Mariano 33, tel. 0141834096
francomondo@inwind.it
- r • Barbera d'Asti Superiore Vigna delle Rose - Doc
- r • Barbera d'Asti Vigna del Salice - Doc

SANTA VITTORIA D'ALBA
Cuneo km 53 • m 179/346

Wineries

Fratelli Rabino
Via Rolfi 5, tel. 0172478045
az.rabino@libero.it
- r • Nebbiolo d'Alba - Doc
- r • Roero - Doc
- w • Roero Arneis - Doc

SANTO STEFANO BELBO
Cuneo km 81 • m 170

Wineries

Amerio Agostino - Cascina Carbonere ♟♟
Località Bauda 4, tel. 0141840416
s • Moscato d'Asti Bricco Carbonere - Docg
s • Moscato d'Asti La Casa in Collina - Docg

Ca' d'Gal ♟♟♟
Località Valdivilla, via Strada Vecchia 108, tel. 0141847103
r • Langhe Rosso Pian del Gaje - Doc
w • Langhe Chardonnay - Doc
s • Moscato d'Asti Vigna Vecchia - Docg

Cascina Galletto ♟
Località Valdivilla 69, tel. 0141847123
s • Moscato d'Asti Cascina Galletto - Docg

Fratelli Santero ♟♟
Via Cesare Pavese 28, tel. 0141841212
s • Asti Spumante - Docg
s • Brachetto d'Acqui - Docg

Gallina Pierino ♟♟
Località San Maurizio 7, tel. 0141844855
s • Moscato d'Asti - Docg

Gatti Piero ♟
Località Moncucco 28, tel. 0141840918
s • Piemonte Moscato Vigneto Moncucco - Doc

Grimaldi Sergio ♟
Località San Grato 7, tel. 0141840341
s • Moscato d'Asti Cà du Sindic - Docg

I Vignaioli di Santo Stefano ♟♟♟
Località Marini 26, tel. 0141840419
www.ceretto.com
s • Asti Spumante - Docg
s • Moscato d'Asti - Docg
s • Piemonte Moscato Passito "Il" - Doc

Marino Beppe ♟♟♟
Via della Stazione 23, tel. 0141840677
r • Barbera d'Asti Vigna delle Pietre - Doc
r • Langhe Rosso Taldin - Doc
s • Moscato d'Asti Bricco Allegro - Docg
s • Moscato d'Asti Muray - Docg
s • Piemonte Moscato Passito Albarosa - Doc

Tenuta Il Falchetto ♟♟♟♟
Località Ciombi, via Valletinella 16, tel. 0141840344
www.ilfalchetto.com
r • Barbera d'Asti Superiore Bricco Paradiso - Doc
r • Barbera d'Asti Superiore La Rossa - Doc
r • Dolcetto d'Alba Soulì Braida - Doc
r • Nebbiolo d'Alba Barbarossa - Doc
s • Moscato d'Asti Tenuta del Fant - Docg

SAREZZANO

Alessandria km 27 • m 300

Wineries

Mutti ♟♟♟
Località San Ruffino 49, tel. 0131884119
r • Colli Tortonesi Rosso Rivadestra - Doc
r • Colli Tortonesi Rosso San Ruffino - Doc
w • Colli Tortonesi Bianco Castagnoli - Doc

SCURZOLENGO

Asti km 14 • m 253

Wineries

Sant'Agata ♟♟
Regione Mezzena 19, tel. 0141203186
r • Barbera d'Asti Superiore Cavalè - Doc
r • Barbera d'Asti Superiore Piatin - Doc
w • Piemonte Chardonnay Eliseo - Doc

SERRALUNGA D'ALBA

Cuneo km 58 • m 414

Wineries

Baudana Luigi ♟♟♟
Località Baudana 43, tel. 0173613354
r • Barolo Cerretta Piani - Docg
r • Barolo Per Cristina - Docg
r • Dolcetto d'Alba Sorì Baudana - Doc
r • Langhe Rosso Lorenzo - Doc
w • Langhe Bianco - Doc

Boasso Franco ♟♟♟
Borgata Gabutti 3/A, tel. 0173613165
gabutt.boasso@libero.it
r • Barolo Gabutti - Docg
r • Barolo Serralunga - Docg
r • Dolcetto d'Alba Meriane - Doc

Eredi di Ferrero Virginia ♟♟
Località San Rocco 71, tel. 0173613283
r • Barolo San Rocco - Docg
r • Dolcetto d'Alba Ciabot - Doc

Fontanafredda ♟♟♟♟♟
Via Alba 15, tel. 0173613161
www.fontanafredda.it
r • Barbaresco Coste Rubin - Docg
r • Barolo Vigna La Rosa - Docg
r • Barolo Vigna Lazzarito - Docg
r • Barolo Vigna La Villa - Docg
r • Barolo Vigna La Delizia - Docg
r • Barbera d'Alba Superiore Papagena - Doc
r • Diano d'Alba La Lepre - Doc
w • Langhe Chardonnay Ampelio - Doc
s • Moscato d'Asti Le Fronde - Docg

Gemma ♟♟♟♟
Via Mazzini 19, tel. 0173613502
r • Barolo Giblin - Docg
r • Barbera d'Alba Bricco Angelini - Doc
r • Dolcetto d'Alba Madonna della Neve - Doc

Germano Ettore ♟♟♟♟
Località Cerreta 1, tel. 0173613528
www.germanoettore.com
r • Barolo Cerretta - Docg
r • Barolo Prapò - Docg
r • Barbera d'Alba Vigna della Madre - Doc
r • Dolcetto d'Alba Pra di Po - Doc
r • Langhe Rosso Balau - Doc

Palladino ♟♟♟
Piazza Cappellano 9, tel. 0173613108
r • Barolo Serralunga - Docg
r • Barolo Vigna Broglio - Docg
r • Barolo Vigna San Bernardo - Docg
r • Barbera d'Alba Superiore Bricco delle Olive - Doc
r • Dolcetto d'Alba Vigna San Bernardo - Doc

Pira Luigi ♟♟♟♟♟
Via XX Settembre 9, tel. 0173613106
r • Barolo - Docg
r • Barolo Marenca - Docg
r • Barolo Margheria - Docg
r • Barolo Vigna Rionda - Docg
r • Dolcetto d'Alba - Doc

Porro Guido ♟♟♟
Via Alba 1, tel. 0173613306
www.guidoporro.com
r • Barolo Vigna Lazzairasco - Docg
r • Barolo Vigna Santa Caterina - Docg
r • Barbera d'Alba Vigna Santa Caterina - Doc

r • Dolcetto d'Alba Vigna L'Pari - Doc
r • Langhe Rosso Paesan - Doc

Rosso Giovanni
Via Foglio 18, tel. 0173613142
www.giovannirosso.com
r • Barolo Cerretta - Docg
r • Barbera d'Alba Donna Margherita - Doc
r • Dolcetto d'Alba Le 4 Vigne - Doc

Schiavenza
Via Mazzini 4, tel. 0173613115
r • Barolo Prapò - Docg
r • Barbera d'Alba - Doc
r • Dolcetto d'Alba Vughera - Doc

Vigna Rionda
Piazza Cappellano 8, tel. 0173613138
www.il-vino.com
r • Barolo Margherìa - Docg
r • Barolo Parafada - Docg
r • Barolo Riserva Vigna Rionda - Docg
r • Barbera d'Alba Gisep - Doc
r • Dolcetto d'Alba Vigneto Barilot - Doc

SERRALUNGA DI CREA
Alessandria km 40 • m 240

Wineries

Tenuta La Tenaglia ★10%
Via Santuario di Crea 6, tel. 0142940252
www.latenaglia.com
r • Barbera d'Asti Emozioni - Doc
r • Barbera d'Asti Giorgio Tenaglia - Doc
r • Grignolino del Monferrato Casalese - Doc
r • Paradiso - Vdt
w • Piemonte Chardonnay Oltre - Doc

STREVI
Alessandria km 28 • m 150

Wineries

Banfi Strevi
Via Vittorio Veneto 22, tel. 0144363485
s • Asti Spumante - Docg
s • Brachetto d'Acqui Vigneto della Rosa - Docg
s • Moscato d'Asti - Docg

Contero
Regione Contero 22, tel. 0143682132
r • Dolcetto d'Acqui - Doc
s • Brachetto d'Acqui - Docg
s • Moscato d'Asti di Strevi - Docg

Marenco
Piazza Vittorio Emanuele 10, tel. 0144363133
r • Barbera d'Asti Ciresa - Doc
r • Dolcetto d'Acqui Marchesa - Doc
w • Piemonte Chardonnay Galet - Doc
s • Brachetto d'Acqui Pineto - Docg
s • Moscato d'Asti Scrapona - Docg

SUNO
Novara km 24 • m 251

Wineries

Brigatti
Via Olmi 29, tel. 032285037
brigatti@libero.it
r • Colline Novaresi Rosso Möt Ziflon - Doc

TAGLIOLO MONFERRATO
Alessandria km 35 • m 315

Wineries

Castello di Tagliolo ★10%
Via Castello 1, tel. 014389195
r • Dolcetto di Ovada - Doc
r • Dolcetto di Ovada La Castagnola - Doc
r • Dolcetto di Ovada Superiore - Doc

TASSAROLO
Alessandria km 28 • m 250

Wineries

Castello di Tassarolo
Località Alborina 1, tel. 0143342248
r • Monferrato Rosso - Doc
w • Gavi Castello di Tassarolo - Docg
w • Gavi Castello di Tassarolo Vigneto Alborina - Docg

Ferraro Bruno - Tenuta San Pietro
Località San Pietro 2, tel. 0143342125
r • Barbera d'Asti Superiore I Ronchi del Conte - Doc
r • Barbera d'Asti U Tenent - Doc
w • Gavi San Pietro - Docg

TURIN
m 239

Wineries

Martinetti Franco M.
Via S. Francesco da Paola 18, tel. 0118395937
gmartinetti@ciaoweb.it
r • Barolo Marasco - Docg
r • Barbera d'Asti Superiore Montruc - Doc
r • Monferrato Rosso Sulbric - Doc
w • Gavi Minaia - Docg
w • Colli Tortonesi Bianco Martin - Doc

TORTONA
Alessandria km 21 • m 122

Wineries

La Colombera
Strada comunale per Vho 7, tel. 0131867795
la.semina@libero.it
r • Colli Tortonesi Rosso Vegia Rampana - Doc
w • Colli Tortonesi Bianco Brillo - Doc
w • Colli Tortonesi Timorasso Derthona - Doc

Mariotto Claudio
Strada per Sarazzano 29, tel. 0131868500
claudiomariotto@libero.it
r • Piemonte Barbera Territorio - Doc
w • Colli Tortonesi Bianco Profilo - Doc
w • Colli Tortonesi Timorasso Derthona - Doc

Terralba
Località Inselmina 13, tel. 0131866791
r • Colli Tortonesi Rosso Monleale - Doc
r • Colli Tortonesi Rosso Sito di Inselmina - Doc
r • Colli Tortonesi Rosso Stra Loja - Doc
w • Colli Tortonesi Bianco La Vetta - Doc
w • Colli Tortonesi Timorasso Stato - Doc

TREISO
Cuneo km 69 • m 410

Wineries

Abrigo Orlando
Località Cappelletto, tel. 0173630232
r • Barbaresco Pajoré - Docg
r • Barbaresco Vigna Montersino - Docg
r • Barbaresco Vigna Rongallo - Docg

r • Barbera d'Alba Vigna Campo della Fontana - Doc
w • Dolcetto d'Alba Vigna dell'Erto - Doc

CA' DEL BAIO ♟♟♟
Via Ferrere 33, tel. 0173638219
www.cadelbaio.com
r • Barbaresco Asili - Docg
r • Barbaresco Valgrande - Docg
r • Dolcetto d'Alba Lodoli - Doc
w • Langhe Chardonnay Sermine - Doc

CANTINA VIGNAIOLI PERTINACE ELVIO ♟♟♟
Località Pertinace 2, tel. 0173442238
r • Barbaresco Vigneto Castellizzano - Docg
r • Barbaresco Vigneto Marcarini - Docg
r • Barbaresco Vigneto Nervo - Docg
r • Dolcetto d'Alba Vigneto Castellizzano - Doc
r • Dolcetto d'Alba Vigneto Nervo - Doc

FRATELLI GRASSO ♟♟♟
Località Valgrande, via Giacosa 1/B, tel. 0173638194
i.grasso@areacom.it
r • Barbaresco Bricco Spessa - Docg
r • Barbaresco Sorì Valgrande - Docg
r • Barbera d'Alba - Doc
s • Moscato d'Asti - Docg

MOLINO FRATELLI ♟♟♟
Via Ausario 5, tel. 0173638384
r • Barbaresco Ausario - Docg
r • Barbaresco Teorema - Docg
r • Barbera d'Alba Ausario - Doc
r • Dolcetto d'Alba Ausario - Doc

NADA ADA ♟♟♟
Località Rombone, via Ausario 12/B, tel. 0173638127
www.barbaresco.com
r • Barbaresco Valeirano - Docg
r • Barbaresco Vigneto Cichin - Docg
r • Barbera d'Alba Salgà - Doc
r • Dolcetto d'Alba Autinot - Doc
r • Langhe Rosso La Bisbetica - Doc

NADA FIORENZO ♟♟♟♟
Località Rombone, tel. 0173638254
www.nada.it
r • Barbaresco - Docg
r • Barbaresco Rombone - Docg
r • Barbera d'Alba - Doc
r • Dolcetto d'Alba - Doc
r • Langhe Rosso Seifile - Doc

PELISSERO ♟♟♟♟
Via Ferrere 10, tel. 0173638430
www.pelissero.com
r • Barbaresco Vanotu - Docg
r • Barbera d'Alba Piani - Doc
r • Dolcetto d'Alba Augenta - Doc
r • Langhe Nebbiolo - Doc
r • Langhe Rosso Long Now - Doc

RIZZI ♟♟
Via Rizzi 15, tel. 0173638161
www.cantinarizzi.it
r • Barbaresco Fondetta - Docg

VILLA ILE ♟♟♟
Via Rizzi 18, tel. 0173362333
www.villaile.it
r • Barbaresco - Docg
r • Barbera d'Alba Garassino - Doc
r • Dolcetto d'Alba Tre Colonne - Doc

TREVILLE
Alessandria km 35 • m 300

WINERIES

PAVESE LIVIO ♟♟
Regione Bettola, tel. 0142487215
r • Barbera d'Asti Superiore Podere Sant'Antonio - Doc
r • Barbera del Monferrato Vivace Morabella - Doc
r • Monferrato Rosso Montarucco - Doc

TREZZO TINELLA
Cuneo km 75 • m 341

WINERIES

SERRA DEI FIORI ♟♟♟♟
Via dei Fiori, tel. 0141644113
r • Dolcetto d'Alba Serra dei Fiori - Doc
w • Langhe Bianco Il Fiore di Serra dei Fiori - Doc
w • Langhe Chardonnay Asso di Fiori - Doc

VERDUNO
Cuneo km 54 • m 381

WINERIES

BEL COLLE ♟♟♟
Borgata Castagni 56, tel. 0172470196
belcolle@tin.it
r • Barbaresco Roncaglie - Docg
r • Barolo Monvigliero - Docg
r • Barbera d'Alba Le Masche - Doc
r • Nebbiolo d'Alba Bricco Reala - Doc

CASTELLO DI VERDUNO ♟♟♟
Via Umberto I nr. 9, tel. 0172470284
r • Barbaresco Rabajà - Docg
r • Barolo Massara - Docg
r • Verduno Pelaverga Massara - Doc

COMMENDATOR BURLOTTO G.B. ♟♟♟
Via Vittorio Emanuele 28, tel. 0172470122
r • Barolo Cannubi - Docg
r • Barolo Monvigliero - Docg
r • Barbera d'Alba Aves - Doc
r • Dolcetto d'Alba Neirane - Doc
r • Verduno Pelaverga - Doc

FRATELLI ALESSANDRIA ♟♟♟
Via Valfrè 59, tel. 0172470113
r • Barolo Monvigliero - Docg
r • Barolo San Lorenzo - Docg
r • Barbera d'Alba - Doc
r • Dolcetto d'Alba - Doc
r • Verduno Pelaverga - Doc

VESIME
Asti km 40 • m 225

WINERIES

CAVALLERO GIACOMO ♟
Regione Cavallero 102, tel. 014489054
cavallerovini@libero.it
s • Moscato d'Asti - Docg

VEZZA D'ALBA
Cuneo km 66 • m 353

WINERIES

DEMARIE GIOVANNI & FIGLI ♟♟
Via Salerio 26, tel. 017365454
www.demarie.com
r • Barbera d'Alba d'Valentin - Doc
r • Barbera d'Alba Superiore - Doc
r • Nebbiolo d'Alba Varasca - Doc

r • Roero - Doc
w • Roero Arneis Torion del'Castlé - Doc

Fratelli Casetta ♟♟♟
Via Castellero 5, tel. 017365010
r • Barbaresco Vigna Magallo - Docg
r • Barolo Case Nere - Docg
r • Barbera d'Alba Vigna Surì - Doc
r • Roero Superiore Vigna Pioiero - Doc

Pasquero Bruno ♟
Via IV Novembre 61, tel. 017365458
pasquerovini@libero.it
r • Barbera d'Alba - Doc
r • Nebbiolo d'Alba Vignadogna - Doc
w • Roero Arneis - Doc

VIGNALE MONFERRATO

Alessandria km 24 • m 308

Wineries

Accornero Ca' Cima ♟♟♟♟
Ca' Cima 1, tel. 0142933317
www.accornerovini.it
r • Barbera del Monferrato Giulin - Doc
r • Barbera del Monferrato Superiore Bricco Battista - Doc
r • Barbera del Monferrato Superiore Riserva Cima - Doc
r • Monferrato Rosso Centenario - Doc
s • Malvasia di Casorzo d'Asti Passito Pico Conte Giovanni Pastore - Doc

Bricco Mondalino ♟♟♟
Località Bricco Mondalino, tel. 0142933204
r • Barbera d'Asti Il Bergantino - Doc
r • Barbera del Monferrato Superiore Selezione Amilcare Gaudio - Doc
r • Barbera del Monferrato Zerolegno - Doc
r • Grignolino del Monferrato Casalese Bricco Mondalino - Doc
r • Gaudium Magnum - Vdt

Canato Marco ♟♟♟
Località Ca' Baldea 18/2, tel. 0142933653
www.canatovini.it
r • Barbera del Monferrato La Baldea - Doc
r • Barbera del Monferrato Rapet - Doc
w • Piemonte Chardonnay Piasì - Doc

Colonna ♟♟♟ ★10%
Località San Lorenzo, Ca' Accattino 1, tel. 0142933239
www.vinicolonna.it
r • Barbera del Monferrato Superiore Alessandra - Doc
r • Grignolino del Monferrato Casalese - Doc
r • Monferrato Rosso Amani - Doc

Il Mongetto di Santopietro Carlo ♟♟♟♟
Via Piave 2, tel. 0142933442
www.mongetto.it
r • Barbera d'Asti Vigneto Guera - Doc
r • Grignolino del Monferrato Casalese Vigneto Rudifrà - Doc
w • Piemonte Chardonnay Vigneto Palareto - Doc

Nuova Cappelletta ♟♟
Ca' Cappelletta 9, tel. 0142933135
r • Barbera del Monferrato - Doc
r • Barbera del Monferrato Vigneto Minola - Doc
r • Grignolino del Monferrato Casalese - Doc

VINCHIO

Asti km 22 • m 269

Wineries

Cantina Sociale di Vinchio e Vaglio Serra ♟♟♟
S.P. 40, regione S. Pancrazio 1, tel. 0141950903
www.vinchio.com
r • Barbera d'Asti Superiore - Doc
r • Barbera d'Asti Superiore Vigne Vecchie - Doc
r • Monferrato Freisa - Doc

Costa Olmo ♟♟
Via S. Michele 18, tel. 0141950423
r • Barbera d'Asti La Madrina - Doc
r • Barbera d'Asti Superiore Costa Olmo - Doc
w • Monferrato Bianco A Paola - Doc

Due Pini ♟♟♟
Bricco Due Pini, via Laioli 14, tel. 0141950146
r • Barbera d'Asti Superiore Truchet - Doc
r • Grignolino d'Asti - Doc
r • Vigna di Mezzo Nebbiolo - Vdt

LOMBARDY

ADRO

Brescia km 25 • m 271

Wineries

Cola Battista ♟♟♟
Via Sant'Anna 22, tel. 0307356195
r • Terre di Franciacorta Rosso Tamino - Doc
w • Franciacorta Brut - Docg
w • Franciacorta Extra Brut - Docg
w • Terre di Franciacorta Bianco Tinazza - Doc

Contadi Castaldi ♟♟♟ ★10%
Località Fornace Biasca, via Colzano 32, tel. 0307450126
www.contadicastaldi.it
r • Terre di Franciacorta Rosso - Doc
w • Franciacorta Brut Magno - Docg
w • Franciacorta Brut Satèn - Docg
w • Franciacorta Brut Zero - Docg
w • Terre di Franciacorta Bianco Mancapane - Doc

Cornaleto ♟♟♟ ★15%
Via Cornaletto 2, tel. 0307450565
www.cornaleto.it
r • Terre di Franciacorta Rosso Selezione Poligono - Doc
w • Franciacorta Brut Millesimato - Docg
w • Franciacorta Pas Dosé - Docg
w • Franciacorta Satèn - Docg
w • Terre di Franciacorta Bianco Vigna Saline - Doc

Ronco Calino ♟♟♟♟
Località 4 Camini, via Fenice, tel. 0307451073
www.roncocalino.com
r • Terre di Franciacorta Rosso - Doc
r • L'Arturo Sebino Pinot Nero - Igt
w • Franciacorta Brut Millesimato - Docg
w • Terre di Franciacorta Bianco - Doc
w • Terre di Franciacorta Bianco Sottobosco - Doc

BEDIZZOLE
Brescia km 17 • m 135/208
WINERIES
CANTRINA ♟♟♟
Via Colombera 7, tel. 0306871052
r • Garda Merlot Nepomuceno - Doc
s • Sole di Dario - Vdt

BORGO PRIOLO
Pavia km 28 • m 144
WINERIES
PERCIVALLE ♟♟
Località Torchi 15, tel. 0383871175
r • Oltrepò Pavese Barbera Dea Demetra - Doc
r • Oltrepò Pavese Bonarda Amanti - Doc
w • Oltrepò Pavese Chardonnay Prima Luce - Doc

BRONI
Pavia km 19 • m 88
WINERIES
BARBACARLO ♟
Via Mazzini 50, tel. 038551212
r • Oltrepò Pavese Rosso Barbacarlo - Doc
r • Oltrepò Pavese Rosso Montebuono - Doc

CALVAGESE DELLA RIVIERA
Brescia km 21 • m 225
WINERIES
LA TORRE ♟♟ ★10%
Località Mocasina, via Torre 1/3, tel. 030601034
www.pasini-latorre.com
r • Garda Classico Groppello - Doc
r • Garda Classico Superiore - Doc
r • Garda Classico Superiore Il Torrione - Doc
REDAELLI DE ZINIS ♟ ★10%
Via Ugo De Zinis 1, tel. 030601001
r • Garda Classico Groppello Mocasina - Doc
r • Garda Classico Rosso Superiore Calvagese - Doc
r • Garda Classico Rosso Superiore Rosse Emozioni - Doc
r • Garda Classico Rosso Superiore Vigna La Bolina - Doc
w • Garda Classico Bianco Poggio Belvedere - Doc

CANEVINO
Pavia km 37 • m 300/645
WINERIES
CASEO ♟
Località Caseo 9, tel. 038599937
r • Oltrepò Pavese Rosso Canabium - Doc
r • Oltrepò Pavese Rosso Riserva Canabium - Doc
w • Oltrepò Pavese Riesling Renano Le Segrete - Doc

CANNETO PAVESE
Pavia km 23 • m 233
WINERIES
FRATELLI GIORGI ♟♟
Località Camponoce 39/A, tel. 0385262151
fgiorgi@tin.it
r • Oltrepò Pavese Buttafuoco Casa del Corno - Doc
r • Oltrepò Pavese Sangue di Giuda La Badalucca - Doc
QUAQUARINI FRANCESCO ♟♟
Località Monteveneroso, via Zambianchi 26, tel. 038560152
r • Oltrepò Pavese Buttafuoco Vigna Pregana - Doc
r • Oltrepò Pavese Rosso Magister - Doc
r • Oltrepò Pavese Sangue di Giuda - Doc
VERDI BRUNO ♟♟
Via Vergomberra 5, tel. 038588023
www.verdibruno.it
r • Oltrepò Pavese Barbera Campo del Marrone - Doc
r • Oltrepò Pavese Rosso Riserva Cavariola - Doc
s • Oltrepò Pavese Moscato di Volpara - Doc

CAPRIOLO
Brescia km 28 • m 216
WINERIES
FRATELLI MURATORI - TENUTA VILLA CRESPIA ♟♟♟
Via Palazzolo 168, tel. 0307461599
www.fratellimuratori.com
w • Franciacorta Dosaggio Zero Villa Crespia - Docg
w • Franciacorta Dosaggio Zero Villa Crespia Cisiolo - Docg
LANTIERI DE PARATICO ♟♟♟
Via S. Paratico 50, tel. 030736151
w • Franciacorta Brut - Docg
w • Franciacorta Brut Millesimato Arcadia - Docg
w • Terre di Franciacorta Bianco Colzano - Doc
RICCI CURBASTRO ♟♟♟
Via Adro 37, tel. 030736094
www.riccicurbastro.it
r • Terre di Franciacorta Rosso Vigna Santella del Grom - Doc
r • Pinot Nero Sebino - Igt
w • Franciacorta Brut - Docg
w • Franciacorta Extra Brut Millesimato - Docg
w • Franciacorta Satèn Brut - Docg
w • Terre di Franciacorta Bianco Vigna Bosco Alto - Doc

CAROBBIO DEGLI ANGELI
Bergamo km 13 • m 232
WINERIES
CASTELLO DEGLI ANGELI ♟♟♟
Via agli Angeli 2, tel. 035953667
r • Valcalepio Rosso Amedeo - Doc
r • Valcalepio Rosso Barbariccia - Doc
w • Estereta Chardonnay della Bergamasca - Igt

CASTEGGIO
Pavia km 21 • m 90
WINERIES
ALBANI RICCARDO ♟♟
Strada S. Biagio 46, tel. 038383622
www.vinialbani.it
r • Oltrepò Pavese Bonarda - Doc
r • Oltrepò Pavese Pinot Nero - Doc
r • Oltrepò Pavese Rosso Costa del Morone - Doc
r • Oltrepò Pavese Rosso Riserva Vigna della Casona - Doc
w • Oltrepò Pavese Riesling Italico - Doc
BELLARIA ♟♟
Via Castel del Lupo 28, tel. 038383203
r • Oltrepò Pavese Barbera Olmetto - Doc
r • La Macchia Provincia di Pavia Rosso - Igt
w • Oltrepò Pavese Chardonnay Costa Soprana - Doc

Le Fracce ♟♟♟
Via Castel del Lupo 5, tel. 038382526
info@le-fracce.it
r • Oltrepò Pavese Bonarda La Rubiosa - Doc
r • Oltrepò Pavese Rosso Bohemi - Doc
r • Oltrepò Pavese Rosso Cirgà - Doc
w • Oltrepò Pavese Pinot Grigio Levriere - Doc
w • Oltrepò Pavese Riesling Renano Landò - Doc

Ruiz de Cardenas ♟♟♟ ★10%
Strada alle Mollie 35, tel. 0383823011
www.ruizdecardenas.it
r • Oltrepò Pavese Pinot Nero Vigna Brumano - Doc
r • Oltrepò Pavese Pinot Nero Vigna Miraggi - Doc
w • Ruiz De Cardenas Blanc de Blanc Brut Nature - Vdt
w • Ruiz de Cardenas Galanta Brut - Vdt

Tenuta Frecciarossa ♟♟♟♟
Via Vigorelli 141, tel. 0383804465
www.frecciarossa.com
r • Oltrepò Pavese Pinot Nero - Doc
r • Oltrepò Pavese Rosso Le Praielle - Doc
r • Oltrepò Pavese Rosso Riserva Villa Odero - Doc
r • Uva Rara della Provincia di Pavia - Igt
w • Oltrepò Pavese Riesling Italico - Doc

Travaglino ♟
Località Calvignano, tel. 0383872222
r • Oltrepò Pavese Pinot Nero Poggio della Buttinera - Doc
r • Oltrepò Pavese Rosso Marc'Antonio - Doc
rs • Oltrepò Pavese Riesling Italico V.T. Pajarolo - Doc
w • Oltrepò Pavese Riesling Italico La Fojada - Doc
w • Oltrepò Pavese Spumante Brut Classese Millesimato - Doc

CAZZAGO SAN MARTINO
Brescia km 17 • m 200

Wineries

Bettoni Cazzago Vincenzo ♟♟
Via Marconi 6, tel. 0307750875
r • Terre di Franciacorta Rosso - Doc
w • Franciacorta Brut Selezione Tetellus - Docg
w • Terre di Franciacorta Bianco Selezione Tetellus - Doc

Castel Faglia ♟♟♟♟
Località Boschi 3, tel. 0307751042
r • Terre di Franciacorta Rosso - Doc
w • Franciacorta Brut Millesimato Monogram - Docg
w • Franciacorta Brut Monogram Cuvée Giunone - Docg
w • Terre di Franciacorta Bianco - Doc
w • Terre di Franciacorta Bianco Campo Marte - Doc

Monte Rossa ♟♟♟♟♟
Località Bornato, via Luca Marenzio 14, tel. 030725066
www.monterossa.com
w • Franciacorta Brut - Docg
w • Franciacorta Brut Millesimato Cabochon - Docg
w • Franciacorta Brut Satèn - Docg
w • Franciacorta Extra Brut Millesimato - Docg

CELLATICA
Brescia km 7 • m 170

Wineries

Gatta ♟♟
Via Stella 27/A, tel. 0302772950
r • Cellatica Superiore Negus - Doc
w • Terrer di Franciacorta Bianco - Doc
w • Terre di Franciacorta Bianco Febo - Doc

CENATE SOTTO
Bergamo km 12 • m 267

Wineries

Caminella ♟♟
Via Dante Alighieri 13, tel. 035941828
www.caminella.it
r • Valcalepio Rosso Ripa di Luna - Doc
r • Luna Nera - Vdt
r • Luna Rossa - Vdt

CHIURO
Sondrio km 10 • m 390

Wineries

Negri Nino ♟♟♟♟♟
Via Ghibellini 3, tel. 0342482521
www.giv.it
r • Valtellina Superiore Grumello Vigna Sassorosso - Docg
r • Valtellina Superiore Inferno Mazér - Docg
r • Valtellina Superiore Sassella Le Tense - Docg
r • Valtellina Superiore Vigneto Fracia - Docg
r • Valtellina Sfursat 5 Stelle - Doc

Nera Pietro ♟♟♟
Via IV Novembre 43, tel. 0342482631
www.neravini.com
r • Valtellina Superiore Grumello Riserva - Docg
r • Valtellina Superiore Inferno Riserva - Docg
r • Valtellina Superiore Riserva Signorie - Docg
r • Valtellina Sforzato - Doc

Rainoldi Aldo ♟♟♟♟
Via Stelvio 128, tel. 0342482225
www.rainoldi.com
r • Valtellina Superiore Grumello - Docg
r • Valtellina Superiore Il Crespino - Docg
r • Valtellina Superiore Inferno - Docg
r • Valtellina Superiore Inferno Riserva Barrique - Docg
r • Valtellina Superiore Sassella Riserva - Docg
r • Valtellina Sfursat Fruttaio Cà Rizzieri - Doc

Valtellinese ♟♟♟
Via Ghibellini 3, tel. 0342483103
r • Valtellina Superiore Riserva Antica Rhaetia - Docg
r • Valtellina Superiore Riserva Castel Grumello - Docg
r • Valtellina Superiore Vigna Paradiso - Docg

COCCAGLIO
Brescia km 20 • m 162

Wineries

Tenuta Castellino ♟♟♟
Via S. Pietro 46, tel. 0307721015
r • Terre di Franciacorta Rosso Capineto - Doc
w • Franciacorta Brut - Docg
w • Franciacorta Brut Millesimato - Docg
w • Franciacorta Satèn - Docg
w • Terre di Franciacorta Bianco Solicano - Doc

COLOGNE
Brescia km 24 • m 187
WINERIES
LA BOSCAIOLA ♟♟♟ ★10%
Via Madonna della Pace 18, tel. 0307156386
www.laboscaiola.com
r • Terre di Franciacorta Rosso Giuliana C. - Doc
w • Franciacorta Brut - Docg
w • Franciacorta Brut Millesimato - Docg
w • Terre di Franciacorta Bianco Giuliana C. - Doc
w • Terre di Franciacorta Bianco Primo Essere - Doc

CORTE FRANCA
Brescia km 23 • m 185/651
WINERIES
BARBOGLIO DE GAIONCELLI ♟♟
Località Colombaro, via Nazario Sauro, tel. 0309826831
r • Terre di Franciacorta Rosso Vigna Breda - Doc
w • Franciacorta Brut - Docg
w • Terre di Franciacorta Bianco - Doc
BARONE PIZZINI ♟♟♟♟ ★10%
Località Timoline, via Brescia 3/A, tel. 030984136
www.baronepizzini.it
r • Pinot Nero Sebino - Igt
w • Franciacorta Brut - Docg
w • Franciacorta Brut Bagnadore I - Docg
w • Terre di Franciacorta Bianco - Doc
w • Terre di Franciacorta Bianco Polzina - Doc
BERLUCCHI GUIDO & C. ♟♟
Località Borgonato, piazza Duranti 4, tel. 030984381
www.berlucchi.com
rs • Cuvée Imperiale Spumante Max Rosé - Vdt
w • Terre di Franciacorta Bianco Le Arzelle - Doc
w • Cellarius Brut Riserva Speciale - Vdt
w • Cuvée Imperiale Spumante Brut - Vdt
w • Extreme Brut - Vdt
FRATELLI BERLUCCHI ♟♟
Località Borgonato, via Broletto 2, tel. 030984451
r • Terre di Franciacorta Rosso Dossi delle Querce - Doc
rs • Franciacorta Brut Rosé Millesimato - Docg
w • Franciacorta Brut Millesimato - Docg
w • Franciacorta Brut Satèn Millesimato - Docg
w • Terre di Franciacorta Bianco Dossi delle Querce - Doc
MONZIO COMPAGNONI ♟♟♟
Località Nigoline, contrada della Corte 2, tel. 0309884157
www.monziocompagnoni.com
r • Terre di Franciacorta Rosso Ronco della Seta - Doc
w • Franciacorta Brut Monzio Compagnoni - Docg
w • Franciacorta Extra Brut Monzio Compagnoni - Docg
w • Franciacorta Satèn Monzio Compagnoni - Docg
w • Terre di Franciacorta Bianco Ronco della Seta - Doc

CORVINO SAN QUIRICO
Pavia km 23 • m 80/263
WINERIES
TENUTA MAZZOLINO ♟♟♟♟
Via Mazzolino 26, tel. 0383876122
www.tenuta-mazzolino.com
r • Oltrepò Pavese Bonarda - Doc
r • Oltrepò Pavese Cabernet Sauvignon Corvino - Doc
r • Oltrepò Pavese Pinot Nero Noir - Doc
w • Oltrepò Pavese Chardonnay Blanc - Doc
w • Oltrepò Pavese Riesling Italico Camarà - Doc

DESENZANO DEL GARDA
Brescia km 28 • m 67
WINERIES
CANTINE DEL GARDA VISCONTI - PODERE S. ONORATA ♟♟
Via C. Battisti 139, tel. 0309120681
www.luganavisconti.it
w • Lugana Etichetta Nera - Doc
w • Lugana Sant'Onorata - Doc
w • Lugana Superiore - Doc
PROVENZA ♟♟
Via Colli Storici, tel. 0309910006
r • Garda Classico Chiaretto Cà Maiöl - Doc
r • Garda Classico Rosso Selezione Fabio Contato - Doc
r • Garda Classico Rosso Negresco - Doc
w • Lugana Selezione Fabio Contato - Doc
w • Lugana Superiore Cà Molin - Doc

ERBUSCO
Brescia km 22 • m 236
WINERIES
BELLAVISTA ♟♟♟♟♟
Via Bellavista 5, tel. 0307762000
r • Casotte Sebino - Vdt
r • Solesine Rosso del Sebino - Vdt
rs • Franciacorta Gran Cuvée Brut Rosé - Docg
w • Franciacorta Gran Cuvée Brut - Docg
w • Franciacorta Gran Cuvée Extra-Brut Pas Operé - Docg
w • Franciacorta Gran Cuvée Satèn - Docg
w • Terre di Franciacorta Bianco Convento dell'Annunciata - Doc
w • Terre di Franciacorta Bianco Uccellanda - Doc
CA' DEL BOSCO ♟♟♟♟♟
Via Case Sparse 20, tel. 0307766111
cadelbosco@cadelbosco.com
r • Carmenero Sebino Rosso - Igt
r • Maurizio Zanella Rosso del Sebino - Igt
r • Pinero Sebino Pinot Nero - Igt
rs • Franciacorta Rosé Brut Millesimato - Docg
w • Franciacorta Brut Millesimato - Docg
w • Franciacorta Cuvée Brut Annamaria Clementi - Docg
w • Franciacorta Extra Brut Dosage Zéro - Docg
w • Franciacorta Satèn Millesimato - Docg
w • Terre di Franciacorta Chardonnay - Doc
CAVALLERI GIAN PAOLO E GIOVANNI ♟♟♟♟♟
Via Provinciale 96, tel. 0307760217
www.cavalleri.it
r • Terre di Franciacorta Rosso Vigna Tajardino - Doc
w • Franciacorta Brut Collezione - Docg
w • Franciacorta Brut Blanc de Blancs - Docg

w • Franciacorta Extra Brut Pas Dosé Blanc de Blancs - Docg
w • Franciacorta Satèn Blanc de Blancs - Docg
w • Terre di Franciacorta Bianco Rampaneto - Doc
w • Terre di Franciacorta Bianco Seradina - Doc

Ferghettina ♟♟♟♟
Via Case Sparse 4, tel. 0307760120
r • Baladello Rosso Sebino - Igt
w • Franciacorta Extra Brut - Docg
w • Franciacorta Brut - Docg
w • Franciacorta Satèn - Docg
w • Terre di Franciacorta Bianco - Doc

Gatti Enrico ♟♟♟♟
Via Metelli 9, tel. 0307267999
r • Terre di Franciacorta Rosso - Doc
r • Gatti Rosso Sebino - Igt
w • Franciacorta Brut - Docg
w • Franciacorta Satèn - Docg
w • Terre di Franciacorta Gatti Bianco - Doc

Principe Banfi - Podere Pio IX ♟♟
Località Villa, via Iseo 25, tel. 0307750387
r • Terre di Franciacorta Rosso Principe Banfi - Doc
w • Franciacorta Brut Satèn Principe Banfi - Docg
w • Franciacorta Brut Principe Banfi - Docg
w • Franciacorta Extra Brut Principe Banfi - Docg
w • Terre di Franciacorta Bianco Principe Banfi - Doc

San Cristoforo ♟♟♟
Via Villanuova 2, tel. 0307760482
r • Terre di Franciacorta Rosso - Doc
r • Terre di Franciacorta Rosso San Cristoforo Uno - Doc
r • San Cristoforo Uno - Vdt
w • Franciacorta Brut - Docg
w • Terre di Franciacorta Bianco - Doc

Uberti ♟♟♟♟♟
Via Fermi 2, tel. 0307267476
r • Rosso dei Frati Priori - Vdt
rs • Franciacorta Brut Rosé - Docg
w • Franciacorta Brut Francesco I - Docg
w • Franciacorta Extra Brut Comari del Salem - Docg
w • Franciacorta Magnificentia - Docg
w • Franciacorta Satén - Docg
w • Terre di Franciacorta Bianco Maria Medici - Doc

Vezzoli Giuseppe ♟♟♟
Via Costa di Sopra 22, tel. 0307267601
niteovezzoli@libero.it
r • Terre di Franciacorta Rosso - Doc
r • Nitéo Rosso - Vdt
w • Franciacorta Brut Millesimato - Docg
w • Franciacorta Brut Satèn Millesimato - Docg
w • Terre di Franciacorta Bianco - Doc

FORESTO SPARSO
Bergamo km 29 • m 245/730

Wineries

Podere della Cavaga ♟♟
Via Gafforelli 1, tel. 035930939
www.vinicavaga.it
r • Valcalepio Rosso Foresto - Doc
w • Valcalepio Bianco Adamante Vigneto del Colletto - Doc

GANDOSSO
Bergamo km 23 • m 488

Wineries

Il Fontanile di Tallarini ♟♟ ★10%
Via Fontanile 7/9, tel. 035834003
r • Valcalepio Rosso Libero - Doc
r • Valcalepio Rosso Riserva San Giovannino - Doc
r • Satiro Cabernet Sauvignon della Bergamasca - Igt
w • Valcalepio Bianco Libero - Doc
s • Valcalepio Moscato Passito di Scanzo - Doc

GODIASCO
Pavia km 36 • m 196

Wineries

Fattoria Cabanon ♟♟
Località Cabanon 1, tel. 0383940912
info@cabanon.it
r • Oltrepò Pavese Barbera Piccolo Principe - Doc
r • Oltrepò Pavese Barbera Prunello - Doc
r • Oltrepò Pavese Rosso Cuore di Vino - Doc

GRUMELLO DEL MONTE
Bergamo km 18 • m 208

Wineries

Carlozadra ♟♟♟
Via Gandossi 13, tel. 035832066
r • Don Lodovico - Vdt
w • Carlozadra Brut - Vdt
w • Carlozadra Extra Dry Tradizione - Vdt
w • Carlozadra Non Dosato - Vdt
w • Donna Nunzia - Vdt

Corne ♟ ★10%
Località Corne 4, via S. Pantaleone, tel. 035830215
www.lecorne.it
r • Valcalepio Rosso Riserva Messernero - Doc
w • Valcalepio Bianco Gonzaghesco - Doc

Tenuta Castello di Grumello ♟♟♟
Via Fosse 11, tel. 0354420817
www.castellodigrumello.it
r • Valcalepio Rosso - Doc
r • Valcalepio Rosso Colle del Calvario - Doc
w • Valcalepio Bianco - Doc
w • Aurito Chardonnay della Bergamasca - Igt
s • Valcalepio Moscato Passito di Grumello - Doc

LONATO
Brescia km 23 • m 188

Wineries

Cascina Spia d'Italia ♟
Via Marziale Cerutti 61, tel. 0309130233
r • Garda Bresciano Rosso Superiore - Doc
w • San Martino della Battaglia Affinato - Doc
w • Millesimato Brut - Vdt

MANERBA DEL GARDA
Brescia km 32 • m 65/216

Wineries

Avanzi Cantine e Frantoio olive ♟
Via Risorgimento 32, tel. 03042059
www.avanzi.net
r • Garda Cabernet Sauvignon Vigna Bragagna - Doc
r • Garda Classico Rosso Superiore - Doc

rs • Garda Classico Chiaretto Vino di Una Notte - Doc
w • Lugana Vigna Antica Bragagna - Doc

MARIANA MANTOVANA
Mantua km 35 • m 36
WINERIES
SPEZIA STEFANO ♟♟
Via Matteotti 90, tel. 0376735012
r • Ancellotta della Provincia di Mantova - Igt
r • Lambrusco della Provincia di Mantova Frizzante - Igt
r • Morenot - Vdt

MAZZANO
Brescia km 12 • m 134/500
WINERIES
BERARDI ♟♟
Via Brescia 83, tel. 0302620152
www.viniberardi.it
r • Terre di Franciacorta Rosso Brugai - Doc
w • Lugana Le Brede - Doc
w • Terre di Franciacorta Bianco Le Poffe - Doc

MESE
Sondrio km 60 • m 274
WINERIES
PREVOSTINI MAMETE ♟♟♟
Via Lucchinetti 65, tel. 034341003
info@mameteprevostini.com
r • Valtellina Superiore Corte di Cama - Docg
r • Valtellina Superiore Sassella Sommarovina - Docg
r • Valtellina Sforzato Albareda - Doc

MONIGA DEL GARDA
Brescia km 29 • m 125
WINERIES
COSTARIPA ♟♟
Via Cialdini 12, tel. 0365502010
r • Pradamonte - Vdt
rs • Garda Classico Chiaretto - Doc
rs • Garda Classico Chiaretto Rosamara - Doc
MONTE CICOGNA ♟
Via delle Vigne 15, tel. 0365502007
www.montecicogna.it
r • Garda Classico Rosso Superiore Don Lisander - Doc
rs • Garda Classico Chiaretto di Moniga Siclì - Doc
w • Lugana Il Torrione - Doc

MONTALTO PAVESE
Pavia km 31 • m 380
WINERIES
DORIA ♟
Casa Tacconi 3, tel. 0383870143
r • A.D. Provincia di Pavia - Igt
w • Oltrepò Pavese Pinot Nero Querciolo (in bianco) - Doc
w • Oltrepò Pavese Riesling Renano Roncobianco - Doc

MONTEBELLO DELLA BATTAGLIA
Pavia km 23 • m 110
WINERIES
TENUTA LA COSTAIOLA ♟♟ ★10%
Località Costaiola 11, tel. 038383169
r • Oltrepò Pavese Barbera Due Draghi - Doc
r • Oltrepò Pavese Bonarda Giada - Doc
r • Oltrepò Pavese Pinot Nero Bellarmino - Doc
r • Oltrepò Pavese Rosso Aiole - Doc
r • Oltrepò Pavese Rosso Riserva La Vigna Bricca - Doc

MONTECALVO VERSIGGIA
Pavia km 32 • m 164/477
WINERIES
CASA RÈ ♟♟♟ ★20%
Località Casa Rè, tel. 038599986
casare@laselezione.com
r • Oltrepò Pavese Bonarda Riserva Casa Re - Doc
r • Oltrepò Pavese Cabernet Sauvignon Riserva - Doc
r • Oltrepò Pavese Pinot Nero - Doc
w • Oltrepò Pavese Chardonnay - Doc
w • Oltrepò Pavese Riesling Italico Vigna Il Fossone - Doc
TENIMENTI CASTELROTTO ♟♟
Località Castelrotto 6, tel. 0385951000
www.tortiwinepinotnero.com
r • Oltrepò Pavese Barbera - Doc
r • Oltrepò Pavese Pinot Nero - Doc

MONTICELLI BRUSATI
Brescia km 18 • m 205/712
WINERIES
ANTICA CANTINA FRATTA ♟♟
Via Fontana 11, tel. 030652661
www.anticafratta.it
w • Franciacorta Brut - Docg
w • Franciacorta Brut Millesimato - Docg
w • Franciacorta Brut Satèn - Docg
w • Terre di Franciacorta Bianco Curtefranca - Doc
w • Terre di Franciacorta Bianco Curtefranca La Tinaia - Doc
CASA CATERINA ♟
Via Foina, 32, tel. 0306852466
r • Terre di Franciacorta Rosso - Doc
w • Franciacorta Brut - Docg
CASTELVEDER ♟♟♟
Via Belvedere 4, tel. 030652308
castelveder@libero.it
r • Curtefranca Terre di Franciacorta Rosso - Doc
w • Franciacorta Brut Castelveder - Docg
w • Franciacorta Brut Millesimato Castelveder - Docg
w • Curtefranca Terre di Franciacorta Bianco - Doc
IL PENDIO DI GIANLUIGI BALESTRA ♟♟♟
Via Panoramica 50, tel. 0306852570
r • Terre di Franciacorta Rosso - Doc
w • Franciacorta Brut Brusato - Docg
w • Terre di Franciacorta Bianco Etichetta Nera - Doc
LO SPARVIERE ♟♟♟
Via Costa 2, tel. 030652382
www.losparviere.it
r • Terre di Franciacorta Rosso Il Cacciatore - Doc
w • Franciacorta Brut - Docg
w • Terre di Franciacorta Bianco Barricato - Doc

Tenuta La Montina ♟♟♟
Via Baiana 17, tel. 030653278
www.lamontina.it
- *r* • Terre di Franciacorta Rosso Dossi - Doc
- *w* • Franciacorta Brut - Docg
- *w* • Franciacorta Brut Millesimato - Docg
- *w* • Franciacorta Satèn - Docg
- *w* • Terre di Franciacorta Bianco Palanca - Doc

Villa ♟♟♟♟
Via Villa 12, tel. 030652329
www.villa-franciacorta.it
- *r* • Terre di Franciacorta Rosso Gradoni - Doc
- *w* • Franciacorta Brut Millesimato - Docg
- *w* • Franciacorta Brut Satèn Millesimato - Docg
- *w* • Franciacorta Cuvette Extra Dry Millesimato - Docg
- *w* • Franciacorta Extra Brut Millesimato - Docg
- *w* • Terre di Franciacorta Bianco Marengo - Doc
- *w* • Terre di Franciacorta Bianco Pian della Villa - Doc

MONTÙ BECCARIA
Pavia km 28 • m 277

Wineries

Piccolo Bacco dei Quaroni ♟♟
Località Costa Montefedele, tel. 038560521
- *r* • Oltrepò Pavese Bonarda Il Fornacione - Doc
- *r* • Oltrepò Pavese Buttafuoco Cà dei Padroni - Doc
- *r* • Oltrepò Pavese Pinot Nero La Fiocca - Doc
- *w* • Oltrepò Pavese Malvasia Vigna Il Campasso - Doc
- *w* • Oltrepò Pavese Riesling Italico Vigna del Pozzo - Doc

Vercesi del Castellazzo ♟♟
Via Aureliano 36, tel. 038560067
- *r* • Oltrepò Pavese Barbera Clà - Doc
- *r* • Oltrepò Pavese Bonarda Fatila - Doc
- *r* • Oltrepò Pavese Pinot Nero Luogo dei Monti - Doc
- *r* • Oltrepò Pavese Rosso Orto di San Giacomo - Doc
- *r* • Castellazzo Provincia di Pavia Rosso - Igt

MONZAMBANO
Mantua km 34 • m 88

Wineries

La Prendina ♟♟♟♟
Strada S. Pietro 86, tel. 0376809450
www.prendina.com
- *r* • Garda Cabernet Sauvignon Vigneto del Falcone - Doc
- *r* • Garda Merlot Faial Vigneto La Prendina - Doc
- *rs* • Garda Chiaretto - Doc
- *w* • Garda Garganega Paroni - Doc
- *w* • Garda Sauvignon Valbruna - Doc

MORNICO LOSANA
Pavia km 27 • m 284

Wineries

Ca' di Frara ♟♟♟
Casa Ferrari 1, tel. 0383892299
www.cadifrara.com
- *r* • Oltrepò Pavese Pinot Nero Il Raro - Doc
- *r* • Oltrepò Pavese Rosso Riserva Il Frater - Doc
- *r* • Io Provincia di Pavia Rosso - Igt
- *w* • Oltrepò Pavese Pinot Grigio Raccolta Tardiva - Doc
- *w* • Oltrepò Pavese Riesling Italico Apogeo - Doc

OME
Brescia km 17 • m 231

Wineries

Majolini ♟♟♟
Località Valle, via Manzoni, tel. 0306527378
www.majolini.it
- *r* • Terre di Franciacorta Rosso Dordaro - Doc
- *w* • Franciacorta Brut - Docg
- *w* • Franciacorta Brut Millesimato Electo - Docg
- *w* • Franciacorta Satèn Millesimato Ante Omnia - Docg
- *w* • Terre di Franciacorta Bianco Ronchello - Doc

PASSIRANO
Brescia km 16 • m 210

Wineries

Il Mosnel ♟♟♟
Località Camignone, via Barboglio 14, tel. 030653117
www.ilmosnel.com
- *r* • Terre di Franciacorta Rosso Fontecolo - Doc
- *w* • Franciacorta Brut Millesimato - Docg
- *w* • Franciacorta Extra Brut - Docg
- *w* • Franciacorta Saten Millesimato - Docg
- *w* • Terre di Franciacorta Bianco Campolarga - Doc
- *w* • Terre di Franciacorta Bianco Sulif - Doc
- *s* • Passito Sebino - Igt

Marchesi Fassati di Balzola ♟♟
Via Castello 2, tel. 0306850753
www.fassatidibalzola.com
- *w* • Franciacorta Brut - Docg

PIETRA DE' GIORGI
Pavia km 27 • m 311

Wineries

Conte Giorgi Carlo di Vistarino ♟
Località Scorzoletta 82/84, tel. 038585117
- *r* • Oltrepò Pavese Pinot Nero Pernice - Doc
- *w* • Oltrepò Pavese Chardonnay Elaisa - Doc
- *w* • Oltrepò Pavese Chardonnay Ginestre - Doc

POLPENAZZE DEL GARDA
Brescia km 28 • m 207

Wineries

Cascina La Pertica ♟♟♟♟
Località Picedo 24, tel. 0365651471
asalvetti@cascinalapertica.it
- *r* • Garda Cabernet Le Zalte - Doc
- *r* • Garda Classico Rosso Le Sincette - Doc
- *rs* • Garda Classico Chiaretto Le Sincette - Doc
- *w* • Garda Chardonnay Brut Le Sincette - Doc
- *w* • Garda Chardonnay Le Sincette - Doc

POZZOLENGO
Brescia km 40 • m 135

Wineries

Cantina Marangona ♟♟ ★10%
Via Antica Corte Ialidy, tel. 030919379
- *r* • Garda Classico Rosso Superiore Antica Corte Ialidy - Doc

rs • Garda Classico Chiaretto Antica Corte Ialidy - Doc
w • Lugana Superiore Il Rintocco - Doc

TENUTA ROVEGLIA ♟

Località Roveglia 1, tel. 030918663
tenuta.roveglia@gsnet.it
w • Lugana Superiore Filo di Arianna - Doc
w • Lugana Superiore Vigna di Catullo - Doc

PROVAGLIO D'ISEO

Brescia km 18 • m 185/674

WINERIES

BERSI SERLINI ♟♟♟

Via Cerreto 7, tel. 0309823338
r • Terre di Franciacorta Rosso - Doc
w • Franciacorta Brut Millesimato - Docg
w • Franciacorta Extra Brut - Docg
w • Franciacorta Satèn - Docg
w • Terre di Franciacorta Bianco - Doc

PUEGNAGO DEL GARDA

Brescia km 30 • m 130/367

WINERIES

COMINCIOLI ♟♟♟

Via Roma 10, tel. 0365651141
www.comincioli.it
r • Riviera del Garda Bresciano Groppello Gropel - Doc
r • Riviera del Garda Bresciano Groppello Sulèr - Doc
rs • Riviera del Garda Bresciano Chiaretto - Doc

FATTORIA CA' GRANDA ♟

Località Raffa, via S. Vincenzo 30, tel. 0365651023
www.fattoriacagranda.it
r • Garda Classico Groppello - Doc
r • Garda Classico Rosso Superiore - Doc

MASSERINO ♟

Via Masserino 2, tel. 0365651757
masserino@libero.it
r • Garda Classico Rosso - Doc
r • Garda Marzemino - Doc

PASINI PRODUTTORI ♟♟ ★10%

Località Raffa, via Videlle 2, tel. 0365651419
www.produttoripasini.it
r • Garda Cabernet Sauvignon Vigneto Montezalto - Doc
r • Garda Classico Groppello Riserva Vigneto Arzane - Doc
r • Garda Classico Rosso Superiore Cap del Priù Il Riviera - Doc
rs • Garda Classico Chiaretto Il Vino di Una Notte - Doc
w • Lugana - Doc

RETORBIDO

Pavia km 30 • m 169

WINERIES

LITUBIUM ♟♟

Via Rocca Susella 13, tel. 0383374485
www.litubium.com
r • Oltrepò Pavese Bonarda - Doc
r • Oltrepò Pavese Pinot Nero Tre Campane - Doc
r • Oltrepò Pavese Rosso Senior - Doc
s • Oltrepò Pavese Moscato - Doc
s • Oltrepò Pavese Moscato Passito - Doc

ROCCA DE' GIORGI

Pavia km 32 • m 213/523

WINERIES

ANTEO ♟♟

Località Chiesa, tel. 038548583
r • Coste del Roccolo - Vdt
w • Oltrepò Pavese Spumante Brut Blanc de Noirs - Doc
w • Oltrepò Pavese Spumante Brut Selezione del Gourmet - Doc

RODENGO SAIANO

Brescia km 13 • m 176

WINERIES

MIRABELLA ♟♟♟

Via Cantarana 2, tel. 030611197
www.mirabellavini.it
r • Terre di Franciacorta Rosso Vigna Maniero - Doc
w • Franciacorta Brut - Docg
w • Franciacorta Extra Brut Pas Dosé Millesimato - Docg
w • Franciacorta Satèn - Docg
w • Terre di Franciacorta Bianco Vigna Palazzina - Doc

ROVATO

Brescia km 18 • m 192

WINERIES

CONTI TERZI ♟ ★10%

Via Sopramura 8, tel. 0307721037
www.letuecantine.it
r • Terre di Franciacorta Rosso - Doc
w • Franciacorta Brut - Docg

ROVESCALA

Pavia km 34 • m 250

WINERIES

CASTELLO DI LUZZANO ♟♟

Località Luzzano 5, tel. 0523863277
www.castelloluzzano.it
r • Colli Piacentini Cabernet Sauvignon Caplass - Doc
r • Colli Piacentini Gutturnio Riserva Romeo - Doc
r • Oltrepò Pavese Bonarda Carlino - Doc
r • Oltrepò Pavese Rosso Riserva Luzzano 270 - Doc

FRATELLI AGNES ♟♟

Via Campo del Monte 1, tel. 038575206
info@fratelliagnes.it
r • Oltrepò Pavese Bonarda Campo del Monte - Doc
r • Oltrepò Pavese Bonarda Millenium - Doc
r • Oltrepò Pavese Bonarda Vignazzo - Doc

MARTILDE ♟♟♟ ★10%

Località Croce 4, tel. 0385756280
www.martilde.it
r • Oltrepò Pavese Barbera Diluvio - Doc
r • Oltrepò Pavese Barbera La Strega, La Gazza e Il Pioppo - Doc
r • Oltrepò Pavese Bonarda Ghiro Rosso d'Inverno - Doc
r • Oltrepò Pavese Pinot Nero Martuffo del Glicine - Doc
r • Oltrepò Pavese Rosso Riserva Pindaro - Doc

SAN COLOMBANO AL LAMBRO
Milan km 42 • m 80

Wineries

Panigada Antonio - Vino Banino ♟♟
Via Vittoria 13, tel. 037189103
vinobanino@hotmail.com
r • San Colombano Rosso Banino Giovane - Doc
r • San Colombano Rosso Riserva Banino Vigna La Merla - Doc

Pietrasanta Carlo ♟♟ ★10%
Via Sforza 55/57, tel. 0371897540
r • San Colombano Riserva - Doc
r • Rosso della Costa Collina del Milanese - Igt
w • Bianco della Costa Collina del Milanese - Igt

Riccardi Enrico - Nettare dei Santi ♟♟
Via Capra 17, tel. 0371897381
viniriccardi@libero.it
r • San Colombano Rosso Nettare dei Santi - Doc
r • San Colombano Rosso Roverone - Doc

SAN DAMIANO AL COLLE
Pavia km 33 • m 216

Wineries

Bisi ♟♟♟
Cascina S. Michele, tel. 038575037
r • Oltrepò Pavese Barbera Roncolongo - Doc
r • Oltrepò Pavese Bonarda - Doc
r • Oltrepò Pavese Cabernet Sauvignon - Doc
w • Oltrepò Pavese Riesling - Doc
s • Villa Marone Passito - Vdt

SAN FELICE DEL BENACO
Brescia km 35 • m 109

Wineries

Le Chiusure ♟
Via Boschette 2, tel. 0365626243
info@lechiusure.net
r • Mal Borghetto Benaco Bresciano Rosso - Igt

SANTA GIULETTA
Pavia km 22 • m 78

Wineries

Isimbarda ♟♟ ★10%
Località Castello, tel. 0383899256
www.tenutaisimbarda.com
r • Oltrepò Pavese Bonarda - Doc
r • Oltrepò Pavese Pinot Nero Vigne del Cardinale - Doc
r • Oltrepò Pavese Rosso Riserva Montezavo - Doc

Podere San Giorgio ♟♟ ★10%
Località Castello 1, tel. 0383899168
www.poderesangiorgio.it
r • Oltrepò Pavese Barbera Becco Giallo - Doc
r • Oltrepò Pavese Pinot Nero Renero - Doc
w • Oltrepò Pavese Pinot Grigio - Doc
s • Doré - Vdt

SANTA MARIA DELLA VERSA
Pavia km 32 • m 199

Wineries

Cantina Sociale La Versa ♟♟
Via F. Crispi 13, tel. 0385278229
r • Oltrepò Pavese Barbera - Doc
r • Oltrepò Pavese Bonarda Cabella - Doc
r • Oltrepò Pavese Rosso Donelasco - Doc
w • Oltrepò Pavese Pinot Nero Brut - Doc
w • Oltrepò Pavese Spumante Extra Brut Millesimato - Doc

SCANZOROSCIATE
Bergamo km 6 • m 279

Wineries

La Brugherata ♟♟♟
Via Medolago 47, tel. 035655202
www.labrugherata.it
r • Valcalepio Rosso Riserva Doglio - Doc
w • Valcalepio Bianco Vescovado - Doc
s • Valcalepio Moscato di Scanzo Passito Doge - Doc

Monzio Compagnoni ♟♟♟
Località Donnecco, via Seradesca, tel. 0309884157
www.monziocompagnoni.com
r • Valcalepio Rosso di Luna - Doc
w • Valcalepio Bianco Colle della Luna - Doc
s • Valcalepio Moscato Passito di Cenate Sotto Don Quijote - Doc

SIRMIONE
Brescia km 37 • m 66

Wineries

Ca' dei Frati ♟♟♟
Via Frati 22, tel. 030919468
www.cadeifrati.it/com
w • Lugana Brolettino - Doc
w • Lugana Brolettino Grande Annata - Doc
w • Lugana I Frati - Doc
w • Pratto Benaco Bresciano - Igt
s • Tre Filer - Vdt

Podere Corte Tosini ♟♟
Località Lugana, via Chiodi 34, tel. 0309906612
www.digilander/iol/cortetosini
w • Lugana Superiore Il Gruccione - Doc
w • Lugana Superiore Pigno D'Oro - Doc

SONDRIO
m 307

Wineries

Pelizzatti Perego Arturo - AR.PE.PE. ♟♟♟ ★10%
Via Buon Consiglio 4, tel. 0342214120
www.arpepe.com
r • Valtellina Superiore Grumello Rocca de Piro - Docg
r • Valtellina Superiore Inferno Fiamme Antiche - Docg
r • Valtellina Superiore Sassella Stella Retica - Docg

SORISOLE
Bergamo km 7 • m 415

Wineries

Bonaldi - Cascina del Bosco ♟ ★10%
Località Petosino, via Gasparotto 96, tel. 035571701
www.winereport.com/bonaldi
r • Valcalepio Rosso Riserva Cantoalto - Doc
w • Valcalepio Bianco Cascina del Bosco - Doc
w • Cantoalto Bianco - Vdt

TEGLIO
Sondrio km 18 • m 851

WINERIES

CAVEN CAMUNA ♟♟♟
Via Caven 1, tel. 0342482631
- *r* • Valtellina Superiore Giupa - Docg
- *r* • Valtellina Superiore Inferno Al Carmine - Docg
- *r* • Valtellina Superiore Sassella La Priora - Docg
- *r* • Valtellina Sforzato Messere - Doc

FAY SANDRO ♟♟♟♟♟
Località San Giacomo, via Pila Caselli 1, tel. 0342786071
elefay@tin.it
- *r* • Valtellina Superiore Sassella Il Glicine - Docg
- *r* • Valtellina Superiore Valgella Ca' Morei - Docg
- *r* • Valgella Superiore Valgella Carteria - Docg
- *r* • Valtellina Sforzato Ronco del Picchio - Doc

FRATELLI BETTINI ♟♟♟
Località San Giacomo, via Nazionale 68, tel. 0342786068
bettvini@tin.it
- *r* • Valtellina Superiore Inferno Prodigio - Docg
- *r* • Valtellina Superiore Valgella Vigna La Cornella - Docg
- *r* • Valtellina Sforzato Vigneti di Spina - Doc

TIRANO

Sondrio km 28 • m 441

WINERIES

CONTI SERTOLI SALIS ♟♟♟♟♟ ★10%
Piazza Salis 3, tel. 0342710404
www.sertolisalis.com
- *r* • Valtellina Superiore Capo di Terra - Docg
- *r* • Valtellina Superiore Corte della Meridiana - Docg
- *r* • Valtellina Superiore Sassella - Docg
- *r* • Valtellina Sforzato Canua - Doc
- *w* • Torre della Sirena Terrazze Retiche di Sondrio - Vdt

TORRE DE' ROVERI

Bergamo km 9 • m 271

WINERIES

LA TORDELA ♟♟
Via Torricella 1, tel. 035580172
- *r* • Valcalepio Rosso Riserva - Doc
- *s* • Valcalepio Moscato Passito di Torre de' Roveri - Doc
- *s* • Brumaio Moscato Giallo Passito della Bergamasca - Igt

TORRICELLA VERZATE

Pavia km 25 • m 78/235

WINERIES

MONSUPELLO ♟♟♟
Via S. Lazzaro 5, tel. 0383896043
- *r* • Oltrepò Pavese Pinot Nero 3309 - Doc
- *r* • Oltrepò Pavese Rosso Podere La Borla - Doc
- *r* • Oltrepò Pavese Rosso Riserva Mosaico - Doc
- *w* • Oltrepò Pavese Chardonnay Senso - Doc
- *w* • Oltrepò Pavese Pinot Nero Spumante Monsupello Brut Classese - Doc

TRESCORE BALNEARIO

Bergamo km 14 • m 271

WINERIES

MEDOLAGO ALBANI ♟♟
Via Redona 12, tel. 035942022
- *r* • Valcalepio Rosso - Doc
- *r* • Valcalepio Rosso Riserva - Doc

VILLA DI TIRANO

Sondrio km 23 • m 400

WINERIES

TRIACCA ♟♟♟♟♟
Via Nazionale 121, tel. 0342701352
www.triacca.com
- *r* • Valtellina Superiore Prestigio - Docg
- *r* • Valtellina Superiore Riserva Triacca - Docg
- *r* • Valtellina Superiore Sassella - Docg
- *r* • Valtellina Sforzato - Doc
- *w* • Del Frate Terrazze Retiche di Sondrio Bianco - Igt

ZENEVREDO

Pavia km 25 • m 204

WINERIES

TENUTA IL BOSCO ♟♟
tel. 0385245326
- *r* • Oltrepò Pavese Rosso Teodote - Doc
- *r* • Oltrepò Pavese Rosso Teodote Collezione Aristos - Doc
- *w* • Oltrepò Pavese Brut Collezi

TRENTINO-ALTO ADIGE

ALA

Trento km 40 • m 180

WINERIES

LA CADALORA ♟♟♟
Località Santa Margherita, via Trento 44, tel. 0464696443
lacadalora@vivacity.it
- *r* • Majere Rosso della Vallagarina - Igt
- *r* • Vignalet Pinot Nero della Vallagarina - Igt
- *w* • Cadalora Chardonnay della Vallagarina - Igt
- *w* • Sauvignon della Vallagarina - Igt
- *w* • Traminer Aromatico della Vallagarina - Igt

SECCHI ALESSANDRO ♟♟♟
Località Coleri, tel. 0464696647
www.secchivini.it
- *r* • Trentino Marzemino - Doc
- *r* • Trentino Cabernet Sauvignon - Doc
- *r* • Trentino Merlot - Doc

ALDENO

Trento km 12 • m 209

WINERIES

SPAGNOLLI ♟♟♟
Via Stretta 1, tel. 0461842578
- *w* • Spagnolli Brut - Vdt
- *w* • Spagnolli Brut Millesimato - Vdt

ANDRIANO/ANDRIAN

Bolzano km 13 • m 274

Wineries

Cantina Produttori Andriano 🍷🍷🍷
Via della Chiesa 2, tel. 0471510137
www.andrianer-kellerei.it
r • Alto Adige Cabernet Tor di Lupo - Doc
r • Alto Adige Lagrein Dunkel Tor di Lupo - Doc
r • Alto Adige Merlot Tor di Lupo Siebeneich - Doc
w • Alto Adige Chardonnay Tor di Lupo - Doc
w • Alto Adige Terlano Pinot Bianco Classico Sonnengut - Doc

APPIANO SULLA STRADA DEL VINO /EPPAN AN DER WEINSTRASSE

Bolzano km 10 • m 239/1866

Wineries

Cantina Brigl Josef 🍷🍷🍷
Località Cornaiano, via S. Floriano 8, tel. 0471662419
brigl@brigl.com
r • Alto Adige Cabernet Briglhof - Doc
r • Alto Adige Lagrein Dunkel Briglhof - Doc
r • Alto Adige Pinot Nero Briglhof - Doc
w • Alto Adige Gewürztraminer Windegg - Doc
w • Alto Adige Sauvignon - Doc

Cantina Kössler 🍷🍷🍷
Località San Paolo 15, tel. 0471662182
ebner@koessler.it
r • Alto Adige Lagrein Dunkel Koessler - Doc
w • Alto Adige Gewürztraminer Johannisbrunnen - Doc
w • Alto Adige Pinot Nero Riserva Herr von Zobel - Doc
w • Alto Adige Spumante Riserva Praeclarus Noblesse - Doc
w • Alto Adige Spumante Praeclarus Brut - Doc

Cantina Martini & Sohn 🍷🍷🍷
Località Cornaiano, via Lamm 28, tel. 0471663156
www.weinkellerei-martini.it
r • Alto Adige Lago di Caldaro Classico Felton - Doc
r • Alto Adige Lagrein Dunkel Maturum - Doc
w • Alto Adige Chardonnay Palladium - Doc
w • Alto Adige Gewürztraminer - Doc
w • Alto Adige Pinot Bianco Lamm - Doc
w • Alto Adige Sauvignon Palladium - Doc
s • Alto Adige Moscato Rosa - Doc

Cantina Produttori Colterenzio 🍷🍷🍷🍷🍷
Località Cornaiano, strada del Vino 8, tel. 0471664246
www.colterenzio.com
r • Alto Adige Cabernet Sauvignon Lafoa - Doc
r • Alto Adige Lagrein Dunkel Cornell - Doc
r • Alto Adige Pinot Nero Schwarzhaus - Doc
w • Alto Adige Chardonnay Cornell - Doc
w • Alto Adige Gewürztraminer Cornell - Doc
w • Alto Adige Pinot Grigio Cornell - Doc
w • Alto Adige Sauvignon Lafoa - Doc

Cantina Produttori Cornaiano 🍷🍷🍷
Località Cornaiano, via S. Martino 24, tel. 0471662403
www.girlan.it
r • Alto Adige Cabernet Sauvignon Riserva Selectart Flora - Doc
r • Alto Adige Lagrein Riserva Selectart Flora - Doc
r • Alto Adige Pinot Nero Trattmannhof Selectart Flora - Doc
w • Alto Adige Chardonnay Selectart - Doc
w • Alto Adige Gewürztraminer Selectart Flora - Doc
w • Alto Adige Pinot Bianco Plattenriegel Premium - Doc
w • Alto Adige Sauvignon Selectart Flora - Doc

Cantina Produttori San Michele Appiano 🍷🍷🍷🍷🍷
Via Circonvallazione 17/19, tel. 0471664466
www.stmichael.it
r • Alto Adige Cabernet Sanct Valentin - Doc
r • Alto Adige Lagrein Sanct Valentin - Doc
w • Alto Adige Chardonnay Sanct Valentin - Doc
w • Alto Adige Gewürztraminer Sanct Valentin - Doc
w • Alto Adige Pinot Grigio Sanct Valentin - Doc
w • Alto Adige Sauvignon Sanct Valentin - Doc
s • Alto Adige Bianco Passito Comtess Sanct Valentin - Doc

Cantina Spumanti Martini Lorenz 🍷🍷
Via Pranzoll 2/D, tel. 0471664136
w • Alto Adige Spumante Brut Riserva Comitissa - Doc

Cantina Weger Josef 🍷🍷
Località Cornaiano, via Casa di Gesù 17, tel. 0471662416
www.wegerhof.it
r • Alto Adige Lagrein Dunkel Ansitz Girlaner Wegerhof - Doc
r • Alto Adige Schiava Ansitz Girlaner Wegerhof - Doc
w • Alto Adige Chardonnay - Doc
w • Alto Adige Gewürztraminer - Doc

Niedermayr Josef 🍷🍷🍷🍷🍷
Località Cornaiano, via Casa di Gesù 15, tel. 0471662451
r • Alto Adige Lagrein Dunkel Aus Gries Riserva - Doc
r • Alto Adige Pinot Nero Riserva - Doc
r • Euforius Vigneti delle Dolomiti Rosso - Igt
w • Alto Adige Gewürztraminer Lage Doss - Doc
w • Alto Adige Sauvignon Allure - Doc
s • Aureus Vigneti delle Dolomiti Bianco Passito - Igt

Niedrist Ignaz 🍷🍷🍷
Località Cornaiano, via Ronco 5, tel. 0471664494
r • Alto Adige Lagrein Gries Riserva Berger-Gei - Doc
r • Alto Adige Merlot Mühlweg - Doc
r • Alto Adige Pinot Nero - Doc
w • Alto Adige Riesling Renano - Doc
w • Alto Adige Terlano Sauvignon - Doc

San Paolo 🍷🍷🍷
Località San Paolo, via Castel Guardia 21, tel. 0471662183
r • Alto Adige Lagrein Dunkel Riserva DiVinus - Doc
r • Alto Adige Merlot DiVinus - Doc
r • Alto Adige Pinot Nero DiVinus - Doc
w • Alto Adige Terlano Pinot Bianco Exclusiv Plötzner - Doc
w • Alto Adige Sauvignon Gfill Hof Exclusiv - Doc

TENUTA STROBLHOF
Via Pigano 23, tel. 0471662250
www.stroblhof.it
r • Alto Adige Pinot Nero Pigeno - Doc
r • Alto Adige Pinot Nero Riserva - Doc
w • Alto Adige Chardonnay Schwarzhaus - Doc
w • Alto Adige Gewürztraminer Pigeno - Doc
w • Alto Adige Pinot Bianco Strahler - Doc

AVIO

Trento km 47 • m 131

WINERIES

MASO ROVERI
Località Maso Roveri, tel. 0464684395
r • Trentino Cabernet - Doc
r • Trentino Lagrein - Doc
r • Trentino Pinot Nero - Doc
r • Valdadige Enantio Terra dei Forti Riserva - Doc
w • Trentino Pinot Bianco - Doc

TENUTA SAN LEONARDO
Località Borghetto, tel. 0464689004
r • Merlot di San Leonardo - Igt
r • San Leonardo Vallagarina Rosso - Igt

VALLAROM
Località Masi, tel. 0464684297
www.vallarom.com
r • Trentino Cabernet Sauvignon - Doc
r • Trentino Pinot Nero - Doc
w • Trentino Chardonnay Riserva Vigna di Brioni - Doc

BOLZANO/BOZEN

m 262

WINERIES

CANTINA CONVENTO MURI - GRIES
Piazza Gries 21, tel. 0471282287
r • Alto Adige Cabernet Riserva - Doc
r • Alto Adige Lagrein Dunkel Gries - Doc
r • Alto Adige Lagrein Dunkel Riserva Abtei - Doc
s • Alto Adige Moscato Rosa Abtei - Doc

CANTINA PRODUTTORI GRIES
Località Gries, piazza Gries 2, tel. 0471270909
r • Alto Adige Lagrein Dunkel Riserva Prestige - Doc
r • Alto Adige Lagrein-Merlot Mauritius - Doc
r • Alto Adige Merlot Riserva Siebeneich Prestige - Doc
r • Alto Adige Santa Maddalena Collection Tröglerhof - Doc
s • Alto Adige Moscato Giallo Passito Vinalia - Doc

CANTINA PRODUTTORI SANTA MADDALENA
Via Brennero 15, tel. 0471972944
r • Alto Adige Cabernet Riserva Mumelterhof - Doc
r • Alto Adige Lagrein Dunkel Riserva Taberhof - Doc
r • Alto Adige Santa Maddalena Classico - Doc
r • Alto Adige Santa Maddalena Classico Huck am Bach - Doc
w • Alto Adige Gewürztraminer Kleinstein - Doc

CANTINA R. MALOJER
Via Weggenstein 36, tel. 0471972885
www.malojer.it
r • Alto Adige Cabernet Riserva - Doc
r • Alto Adige Lagrein-Cabernet Riserva Cuvée Bautzanum - Doc
r • Alto Adige Lagrein Dunkel Riserva - Doc
r • Alto Adige Merlot Riserva - Doc
w • Alto Adige Sauvignon Gur zu Sand - Doc

CANTINA ROTTENSTEINER HANS
Via Sarentino 1/A, tel. 0471282015
r • Alto Adige Cabernet Riserva Select - Doc
r • Alto Adige Lagrein Dunkel Grieser Riserva Select - Doc
r • Alto Adige Pinot Nero Riserva Mazon Select - Doc
r • Alto Adige Santa Maddalena Classico Premstallerhof - Doc
w • Alto Adige Gewürztraminer Cancenai - Doc
w • Alto Adige Pinot Grigio - Doc
s • Alto Adige Gewürztraminer Passito Cresta - Doc

GOJER FRANZ
Località Santa Maddalena, via Rivellone 1, tel. 0471978775
r • Alto Adige Lagrein Dunkel - Doc
r • Alto Adige Lagrein Dunkel Riserva Glögglhof - Doc
r • Alto Adige Merlot Spitz - Doc
r • Alto Adige Santa Maddalena Classico - Doc
r • Alto Adige Santa Maddalena Classico Rondell - Doc

MAYR HEINRICH NUSSERHOF
Via Mayr Nusser 72, tel. 0471978388
r • Alto Adige Lagrein Dunkel Riserva - Doc

MAYR THOMAS & SÖHNE
Via Mendola 56, tel. 0471281030
www.mayr.cjb.net
r • Alto Adige Lagrein Dunkel - Doc
r • Alto Adige Lagrein Dunkel Selezione - Doc
r • Alto Adige Santa Maddalena Classico Rumpler Hof - Doc
w • Alto Adige Chardonnay - Doc

MUMELTER GEORG GRIESBAUERHOF
Via Rencio 66, tel. 0471973090
mumelter.g@rolmail.net
r • Alto Adige Lagrein Dunkel - Doc
r • Alto Adige Lagrein Dunkel Riserva - Doc
r • Alto Adige Santa Maddalena Classico Griesbauerhof - Doc
r • Isarcus Vigneti delle Dolomiti Rosso - Igt
w • Alto Adige Pinot Grigio - Doc

OBERMOSER - ROTTENSTEINER HEINRICH & THOMAS
Via S. Maddalena 35, tel. 0471973549
r • Alto Adige Cabernet Merlot Riserva Putz - Doc
r • Alto Adige Lagrein Riserva Grafenleiten - Doc
w • Alto Adige Sauvignon - Doc

PFANNENSTIELHOF - PFEIFER JOHANNES
Via Pfannenstiel 9, tel. 0471970884
info@pfannenstielhof.it
r • Alto Adige Lagrein Dunkel Pfannenstielhof - Doc
r • Alto Adige Lagrein Dunkel Riserva Pfannenstielhof - Doc
r • Alto Adige Pinot Nero Pfannenstielhof - Doc
r • Alto Adige Santa Maddalena Classico Pfannenstielhof - Doc

PLATTNER WALDGRIES
Località Santa Giustina 2, tel. 0471973245
r • Alto Adige Cabernet Sauvignon Waldgries - Doc

r • Alto Adige Lagrein Dunkel Riserva Mirell Waldgries - Doc
r • Alto Adige Lagrein Dunkel Riserva Waldgries - Doc
w • Alto Adige Terlano Pinot Bianco Riol Waldgries - Doc
w • Alto Adige Pinot Grigio Rivelaun Waldgries - Doc
s • Alto Adige Bianco Passito Peperum Waldgries - Doc
s • Alto Adige Moscato Rosa Passito Waldgries - Doc

Ramoser Georg Untermoserhof
Località Santa Maddalena 36, tel. 0471975481
r • Alto Adige Lagrein Riserva Untermoserhof - Doc
r • Alto Adige Merlot Untermoserhof - Doc
r • Alto Adige Santa Maddalena Classico Untermoserhof - Doc

Ramoser Stephan - Fliederhof
Località Santa Maddalena di Sotto 33, tel. 0471979048
fliederhof@dnet.it
r • Alto Adige Lagrein Riserva - Doc
r • Alto Adige Santa Maddalena Classico - Doc

Tenuta Egger Ramer
Via Guncina 5, tel. 0471280541
r • Alto Adige Lagrein Dunkel Kristan - Doc
r • Alto Adige Lagrein Dunkel Riserva Kristan - Doc
r • Alto Adige Santa Maddalena Classico - Doc

Tenuta Loacker Schwarhof
Località Santa Giustina 3, tel. 0471365125
www.loacker.net
r • Alto Adige Cabernet Kastlet Riserva - Doc
r • Alto Adige Lagrein Dunkel Riserva Piz Thurii - Doc
r • Jus Osculi Cuvée - Vdt
w • Alto Adige Chardonnay Ateyon - Doc
w • Alto Adige Sauvignon Blanc Tasnim - Doc

Thurnhof
Via Castel Flavon 7, tel. 0471288460
www.thurnhof.com
r • Alto Adige Cabernet Sauvignon Riserva - Doc
r • Alto Adige Lagrein Dunkel - Doc
s • Alto Adige Moscato Giallo - Doc
s • Passaurum - Vdt

Weingut Eberlehof Zisser
Località Santa Maddalena 26, tel. 0471978607
r • Alto Adige Cabernet - Doc
r • Alto Adige Lagrein-Cabernet Cuvée Mabon - Doc
r • Alto Adige Lagrein Riserva - Doc
r • Alto Adige Santa Maddalena Classico - Doc

Weinkellerei Schmid Anton Oberrautner
Via M. Pacher 3, tel. 0471281440
r • Alto Adige Lagrein Dunkel - Doc
r • Alto Adige Lagrein Grieser Riserva - Doc

BRESSANONE/BRIXEN

Bolzano km 40 • m 559

Wineries

Hoandlhof Nössing Manfred
Via Weinberg 66, tel. 0472832672
w • Alto Adige Valle Isarco Gewürztraminer - Doc
w • Alto Adige Valle Isarco Müller Thurgau - Doc
w • Alto Adige Valle Isarco Sylvaner - Doc
w • Alto Adige Valle Isarco Kerner - Doc

Kuenhof - Peter Pliger
Località Mara 110, tel. 0472850546
w • Alto Adige Valle Isarco Gewürztraminer - Doc
w • Alto Adige Valle Isarco Sylvaner - Doc
w • Alto Adige Valle Isarco Veltliner - Doc
w • Kaiton - Vdt

Vonklausner Karl
Via Castellano 30/A, tel. 0472833700
info@vonklausner.it
w • Alto Adige Valle Isarco Gewurztraminer - Doc
w • Alto Adige Valle Isarco Kerner - Doc
w • Alto Adige Valle Isarco Müller Thurgau - Doc
w • Alto Adige Valle Isarco Sylvaner - Doc

Wachtler Peter Taschlerhof
Località Mara 107, tel. 0473851091
wachtler.peter@taschlerhof.com
w • Alto Adige Valle Isarco Gewürztraminer - Doc
w • Alto Adige Valle Isarco Sylvaner - Doc

CALAVINO

Trento km 17 • m 409

Wineries

Cantina di Toblino
Località Sarche, via Ponte Oliveti 1, tel. 0461564168
r • Trentino Lagrein Dunkel - Doc
w • Trentino Pinot Grigio - Doc
s • Trentino Vino Santo - Doc

CALDARO SULLA STRADA DEL VINO /KALTERN AN DER WEINSTRASSE

Bolzano km 15 • m 425

Wineries

Caldaro
Via delle Cantine 12, tel. 0471963149
www.kellereikaltern.com
r • Alto Adige Cabernet Sauvignon Riserva Campaner - Doc
r • Alto Adige Merlot Lason - Doc
r • Alto Adige Pinot Nero Riserva - Doc
w • Alto Adige Gewürztraminer Campaner - Doc
s • Alto Adige Moscato Giallo Passito Serenade - Doc

Cantina Sociale Erste & Neue - Prima & Nuova
Via delle Cantine 5/10, tel. 0471963122
r • Alto Adige Cabernet Puntay - Doc
r • Alto Adige Lago di Caldaro Scelto Puntay - Doc
r • Alto Adige Lagrein Puntay - Doc
r • Alto Adige Merlot Puntay - Doc
w • Alto Adige Chardonnay Puntay - Doc
w • Alto Adige Gewürztraminer Puntay - Doc
w • Alto Adige Pinot Bianco Puntay - Doc

Castel Sallegg
Vicolo di Sotto 15, tel. 0471963132
www.castelsallegg.it
r • Alto Adige Cabernet Riserva - Doc
r • Alto Adige Merlot Riserva - Doc
w • Alto Adige Chardonnay - Doc
w • Alto Adige Gewürztraminer Selectart Flora - Doc
s • Alto Adige Moscato Rosa - Doc

Kettmeir
Via delle Cantine 4, tel. 0471963135
kettmeir@kettmeir.com

r • Alto Adige Cavernet Sauvignon Maso Castello - Doc
w • Alto Adige Pinot Grigio Maso Reiner - Doc
w • Alto Adige Spumante Brut - Doc

KLOSTERHOF
Via Clavenz 40, tel. 0471961046
r • Alto Adige Pinot Nero Panigl - Doc
w • Alto Adige Gewürztraminer Trifall - Doc
w • Alto Adige Pinot Bianco Trifall - Doc
s • Alto Adige Moscato Giallo Passito Oscar - Doc

SÖLVA JOSEF - NIKLASERHOF
Via Brunnen 31, tel. 0471963432
www.niklaserhof.it
r • Alto Adige Lagrein-Cabernet Riserva Klaser - Doc
w • Alto Adige Bianco Mondevinum - Doc
w • Alto Adige Pinot Bianco Klaser - Doc
w • Alto Adige Sauvignon - Doc
w • Justinus Kerner - Igt

TENUTA MANINCOR GRAF ENZENBERG
Via Giuseppe al Lago 4, tel. 0471960043
r • Alto Adige Lago di Caldaro Scelto Classico - Doc
r • Alto Adige Pinot Nero Mason - Doc
w • Alto Adige Chardonnay Cuvée Sophie - Doc
w • Alto Adige Terlano Pinot Bianco - Doc
s • Alto Adige Moscato Giallo - Doc

TENUTA RITTERHOF
Strada del Vino 1, tel. 0471963298
www.ritterhof.it
r • Alto Adige Cabernet Merlot Crescendo - Doc
r • Alto Adige Lagrein Dunkel Riserva Crescendo - Doc
r • Alto Adige Merlot Riserva Crecendo - Doc
r • Perlhof Crescendo Vigneti delle Dolomiti Rosso - Igt
w • Alto Adige Gewürztraminer - Doc

TENUTA SÖLVA PETER E FIGLI
Via dell'Oro 33, tel. 0471964650
www.soelva.com
r • Alto Adige Lagrein Dunkel Desilvas - Doc
r • Alto Adige Lagrein-Merlot - Doc
r • Amistar Rosso - Vdt
w • Alto Adige Terlano Bianco Desilvas - Doc
w • Amistar Bianco - Vdt

CALLIANO
Trento km 15 • m 187

WINERIES

VALLIS AGRI
Via Valentini 37, tel. 0464834113
r • Trentino Marzemino Vigna Fornas - Doc
r • Trentino Merlot Borgo Sacco - Doc

CASTELBELLO CIARDES /KASTELBELL TSCHARS
Bolzano km 51 • m 556/2912

WINERIES

KÖFELGUT - POHL
Rione ai Tre Canti 12, tel. 0473624142
info@koefelgut.com
r • Alto Adige Val Venosta Pinot Nero Fleck - Doc
w • Alto Adige Val Venosta Gewürztraminer - Doc
w • Alto Adige Val Venosta Pinot Grigio - Doc
w • Alto Adige Val Venosta Riesling - Doc

TENUTA UNTERORTL
Località Juval 1b, tel. 0473667580
familie.aurich@dnet.it
r • Alto Adige Valle Venosta Pinot Nero Castel Juval - Doc
w • Alto Adige Valle Venosta Pinot Bianco Castel Juval - Doc
w • Alto Adige Valle Venosta Riesling Castel Juval - Doc

CERMES/TSCHERMS
Bolzano km 27 • m 292

WINERIES

TENUTA KRÄNZL GRAF PFEIL
Via Palade 1, tel. 0473564549
r • Alto Adige Cabernet-Merlot Sagittarius - Doc
r • Alto Adige Pinot Nero - Doc
w • Alto Adige Pinot Bianco Helios - Doc
w • Alto Adige Sauvignon - Doc
s • Alto Adige Gewürztraminer Passito - Doc

CHIUSA/KLAUSEN
Bolzano km 28 • m 523

WINERIES

CANTINA PRODUTTORI VALLE ISARCO
Località Coste 50, tel. 0472847553
www.cantinavalleisarco.it
w • Alto Adige Valle Isarco Gewürztraminer Aristos - Doc
w • Alto Adige Valle Isarco Kerner - Doc
w • Alto Adige Valle Isarco Müller Thurgau Aristos - Doc
w • Alto Adige Valle Isarco Sylvaner Aristos - Doc
w • Alto Adige Valle Isarco Veltliner - Doc

CIVEZZANO
Trento km 7 • m 469

WINERIES

MASO CANTANGHEL
Via Madonnina 33, tel. 0461859050
r • Trentino Cabernet Sauvignon Rosso di Pila - Doc
r • Trentino Merlot Tajapreda - Doc
r • Trentino Pinot Nero Piero Zabini - Doc
w • Trentino Chardonnay Vigna Piccola - Doc
w • Trentino Sauvignon Solitaire - Doc

CORNEDO ALL'ISARCO/KARNEID
Bolzano km 3 • m 283/1680

WINERIES

ERBHOF UNTERGANZNER MAYR JOSEPHUS
Località Cardano, via Campiglio 15, tel. 0471365582
mayr.unterganzner@dnet.it
r • Alto Adige Cabernet Sauvignon - Doc
r • Alto Adige Lagrein Dunkel - Doc
r • Alto Adige Lagrein Dunkel Riserva - Doc
r • Alto Adige Santa Maddalena Classico - Doc
r • Composition Reif - Vdt

PLATTNER JOHANNES EBNERHOF
Località Laste Basse 21, tel. 0471365120
r • Alto Adige Pinot Nero - Doc
r • Alto Adige Santa Maddalena - Doc
w • Alto Adige Sauvignon - Doc

CORTACCIA SULLA STRADA DEL VINO/ KURTATSCH AN DER WEINSTRASSE

Bolzano km 28 • m 333

Wineries

Baron Widmann ♟♟♟♟♟

Via Im Feld 1, tel. 0471880092

- r • Alto Adige Cabernet-Merlot Auhof - Doc
- r • Alto Adige Schiava - Doc
- w • Alto Adige Bianco - Doc
- w • Alto Adige Gewürztraminer - Doc
- w • Alto Adige Sauvignon - Doc

Cantina Produttori Cortaccia ♟♟♟♟♟

Via Strada del Vino 23, tel. 0471880115
www.kellerei-kurtatsch.it

- r • Alto Adige Cabernet Freienfeld - Doc
- r • Alto Adige Cabernet-Merlot Soma - Doc
- r • Alto Adige Lagrein Forhof - Doc
- r • Alto Adige Merlot Brenntal - Doc
- r • Alto Adige Pinot Nero Vorhof - Doc
- w • Alto Adige Chardonnay Eberle Hof - Doc
- w • Alto Adige Gewürztraminer Brenntal - Doc

Cantina Tiefenbrunner - Castello Turmhof ♟♟♟

Località Niclara, via Castello 4, tel. 0471880122
www.tiefenbrunner.com

- r • Alto Adige Cabernet Sauvignon Linticlarus - Doc
- r • Alto Adige Lagrein Riserva Linticlarus - Doc
- r • Alto Adige Pinot Nero Riserva Linticlarus - Doc
- w • Alto Adige Chardonnay Linticlarus - Doc
- w • Alto Adige Gewürztraminer Castel Turmhof - Doc
- w • Feldmarschall von Fenner - Vdt

CORTINA SULLA STRADA DEL VINO /KURTINIG AN DER WEINSTRASSE

Bolzano km 31 • m 212

Wineries

Cantina Kupelwieser ♟♟

Strada del Vino 24, tel. 0471817143
p.zemmer@zemmer.com

- r • Alto Adige Lagrein Dunkel Intenditore - Doc
- w • Alto Adige Chardonnay - Doc
- w • Alto Adige Müller Thurgau Intenditore - Doc
- w • Alto Adige Pinot Bianco - Doc
- w • Alto Adige Pinot Grigio - Doc

Cantina Spumanti Maffei Giorgio ♟♟

Via del Doss 7, tel. 0471817707
www.maffei.altoadige.net

- w • Alto Adige Brut Maffei - Doc

Cantina Zemmer Peter ♟♟♟

Strada del Vino 24, tel. 0471817143
www.zemmer.com

- r • Alto Adige Lagrein-Cabernet Riserva - Doc
- w • Alto Adige Chardonnay - Doc
- w • Alto Adige Pinot Bianco - Doc
- w • Alto Adige Pinot Grigio - Doc
- w • Alto Adige Sauvignon - Doc

EGNA/NEUMARKT

Bolzano km 24 • m 214

Wineries

Cantina H. Lun ♟♟

Via Villa 22-24, tel. 0471813256

- r • Alto Adige Cabernet Sauvignon Riserva Albertus - Doc
- r • Alto Adige Lagrein Dunkel Riserva Albertus - Doc
- w • Alto Adige Bianco Sandbichler - Doc
- w • Alto Adige Gewürztraminer Albertus - Doc
- w • Alto Adige Sauvignon Albertus - Doc

Dipoli Peter ♟♟♟♟

Via Villa 5, tel. 0471954227

- r • Alto Adige Merlot-Cabernet Sauvignon Iugum - Doc
- w • Alto Adige Sauvignon Voglar - Doc

Gottardi ♟♟♟♟

Via degli Alpini 17, tel. 0471812773

- r • Alto Adige Pinot Nero Mazzon - Doc

FAEDO

Trento km 20 • m 591

Wineries

Fontana Graziano ♟♟♟

Via Case Sparse 9, tel. 0461650400

- r • Trentino Lagrein - Doc
- r • Trentino Pinot Nero - Doc
- w • Trentino Chardonnay - Doc
- w • Trentino Sauvignon - Doc
- w • Trentino Traminer - Doc

Pojer & Sandri ♟♟♟♟♟

Località Molini 4-6, tel. 0461650342
www.pojeresandri.it

- r • Pinot Nero Selezione Vigneti delle Dolomiti - Igt
- r • Rosso Faye Vigneti delle Dolomiti - Igt
- w • Bianco Faye Vigneti delle Dolomiti - Igt
- w • Chardonnay Vigneti delle Dolomiti - Igt
- w • Palai Müller Thurgau Vigneti delle Dolomiti - Igt
- w • Sauvignon Vigneti delle Dolomiti - Igt
- s • Essenzia V.T. Vigneti delle Dolomiti Bianco - Igt

FIÈ ALLO SCILIAR/VÖLS AM SCHLERN

Bolzano km 16 • m 880

Wineries

Prackwieser Markus Gumphof ♟♟

Località Novale di Presule 8, tel. 0471601190

- w • Alto Adige Pinot Bianco Praesulis Gumphof - Doc
- w • Alto Adige Sauvignon Praesulis Gumphof - Doc

ISERA

Trento km 27 • m 243

Wineries

De Tarczal ♟♟♟

Località Marano, via G.B. Miori 4, tel. 0464409134

- r • Trentino Cabernet Sauvignon Piani Longhi - Doc
- r • Trentino Marzemino di Isera Husar - Doc
- r • Trentino Merlot di Isera Campiano - Doc
- r • Pragiara Vallagarina Rosso - Igt
- w • Trentino Chardonnay - Doc

La Vigne ♟♟♟

Località La Vigne 1, tel. 0464433182

- r • Fiore di Ciliegio - Vdt

Spagnolli Enrico ♟♟♟

Via G.B. Rosina 4/A, tel. 0464409054

- r • Trentino Marzemino - Doc
- r • Trentino Pinot Nero - Doc
- r • Trentino Rosso Tebro - Doc

w • Trentino Müller Thurgau - Doc
w • Trentino Nosiola - Doc

LASINO

Trento km 20 • m 463

WINERIES

PISONI DI MARCO E STEFANO ♟♟
Località Pergolese-Sarche, via S. Siro 7/B, tel. 0461563216
www.pisoniepisoni.it
w • Trentino Nosiola - Doc
w • Trento Extra Brut - Doc
w • Trento Brut Riserva - Doc

PRAVIS ♟♟♟♟
Via Lagolo 26, tel. 0461564305
www.pravis.it
r • Madruzzo Pinot Nero Vigneti delle Dolomiti - Igt
r • Niergal Vigneti delle Dolomiti Rosso - Igt
w • San Thomà Müller Thurgau Vigneti delle Dolomiti - Igt

LAVIS

Trento km 8 • m 232

WINERIES

BOLOGNANI ♟♟
Via Stazione 19, tel. 0461246354
dibolog@tin.it
r • Armilo Teroldego Vigneti delle Dolomiti - Igt
w • Trentino Moscato Giallo - Doc
w • Trentino Müller Thurgau - Doc
w • Trentino Nosiola - Doc
w • Trentino Sauvignon - Doc

CANTINA LA VIS ♟♟♟♟
Via del Carmine 7, tel. 0461246325
www.la-vis.com
r • Trentino Cabernet Sauvignon Ritratti - Doc
r • Trentino Merlot Ritratti - Doc
r • Trentino Pinot Nero Ritratti - Doc
r • Ritratto Rosso Vigneti delle Dolomiti - Igt
w • Trentino Chardonnay Ritratti - Doc
w • Trentino Pinot Grigio Ritratti - Doc
w • Ritratto Bianco Vigneti delle Dolomiti - Igt

CASATA MONFORT ♟♟♟ ★10%
Via Carlo Sette 21, tel. 0461241484
www.casatamonfort.it
r • Teroldego Rotaliano - Doc
w • Trentino Traminer Aromatico - Doc

CESCONI PAOLO ♟♟♟♟
Via G. Marconi 39, tel. 0461240355
r • Trentino Merlot - Doc
r • Pivier Vigneti delle Dolomiti Rosso - Igt
w • Trentino Chardonnay - Doc
w • Trentino Sauvignon - Doc
w • Trentino Traminer Aromatico - Doc

FANTI GIUSEPPE ♟♟
Località Pressano, piazza Croce 3, tel. 0461240809
alessandro.fanti@katamail.com
r • Portico Rosso - Vdt
w • Trentino Chardonnay - Doc
w • Trentino Chardonnay Robur - Doc

MASO FURLI ♟♟♟
Località Furli, tel. 0461240667
masofurli@libero.it
r • Maso Furli Vigneti delle Dolomiti Rosso - Igt
w • Trentino Traminer - Doc
w • Trentino Sauvignon - Doc

MAGRÈ SULLA STRADA DEL VINO/MARGREID AN DER WEINSTRASSE

Bolzano km 31 • m 241

WINERIES

CASON HIRSCHPRUNN ♟♟♟♟♟
Piazza S. Geltrude 5, tel. 0471809590
www.lageder.com
r • Casòn Hirschprunn Mitterberg - Igt
r • Corolle Hirschprunn Mitterberg - Igt
w • Contest Hirschprunn Mitterberg - Igt
w • Etelle Hirschprunn Mitterberg - Igt

LAGEDER ALOIS - TENUTA LÖWENGANG ♟♟♟♟♟
Via dei Conti 9, tel. 0471809500
www.lageder.com
r • Alto Adige Cabernet Löwengang - Doc
r • Alto Adige Cabernet Sauvignon Cor Römigberg - Doc
r • Alto Adige Lagrein Lindenburg - Doc
r • Alto Adige Pinot Nero Krafuss - Doc
w • Alto Adige Chardonnay Löwengang - Doc
w • Alto Adige Gewürztraminer Am Sand - Doc
w • Alto Adige Pinot Bianco Haberlerhof - Doc
w • Alto Adige Sauvignon - Doc
w • Alto Adige Terlano Sauvignon Lehenhof - Doc

MARLENGO/MARLING

Bolzano km 29 • m 363

WINERIES

CANTINA PRODUTTORI BURGGRÄFLER ♟♟♟
Via Palade 64, tel. 0473447137
www.burggraefler.it
r • Alto Adige Cabernet-Merlot Jubilaeum - Doc
r • Alto Adige Lagrein - Doc
r • Alto Adige Merlot - Doc
w • Alto Adige Gewürztraminer Tiefenthaler - Doc
w • Alto Adige Pinot Bianco Ansitz Guggenberg - Doc
w • Alto Adige Pinot Nero MerVin Tiefenthaler - Doc
s • Alto Adige Pinot Bianco MerVin Vendemmia Tardiva - Doc

MENZ ANDREAS - MASO POPP ♟♟
Via Terzo di Mezzo 5, tel. 0473447180
r • Alto Adige Cabernet - Doc
r • Alto Adige Merlot - Doc
rs • Alto Adige Lagrein Kretzer Popphof - Doc
w • Alto Adige Chardonnay Unterberger - Doc
w • Alto Adige Riesling Unterberg - Doc

MELTINA/MÖLTEN

Bolzano km 22 • m 1142

WINERIES

CANTINA VIVALDI - ARUNDA ♟♟♟
Via Civica 53, tel. 0471668033
arunda@dnet.it
w • Alto Adige Spumante Brut Vivaldi - Doc
w • Alto Adige Spumante Extra Brut Blanc des Blancs Vivaldi - Doc
w • Alto Adige Spumante Extra Brut Cuvée Marianne - Doc
w • Alto Adige Spumante Extra Brut Riserva Vivaldi - Doc

MERANO/MERAN

Bolzano km 28 • m 325

Wineries

Cantina Produttori Merano 🍷🍷🍷🍷

Via S. Marco 11, tel. 0473235544
www.cantinamerano.it

- *r* • Alto Adige Cabernet-Merlot Graf Von Meran - Doc
- *r* • Alto Adige Cabernet Riserva Graf Von Meran - Doc
- *w* • Alto Adige Gewürztraminer Graf Von Meran - Doc
- *w* • Alto Adige Sauvignon Graf Von Meran - Doc
- *s* • Alto Adige Moscato Giallo Sissi Graf Von Meran - Doc

Castello Rametz 🍷🍷

Via Labers 4, tel. 0473211011
info@rametz.com

- *r* • Alto Adige Pinot Nero - Doc
- *w* • Césuret Vigneti delle DOlomiti Chardonnay - Igt

MEZZOCORONA

Trento km 18 • m 219

Wineries

Donati Marco 🍷🍷

Via C. Battisti 41, tel. 0461604141

- *r* • Teroldego Rotaliano Bagolari - Doc
- *r* • Teroldego Rotaliano Dangue del Drago - Doc

Fratelli Dorigati 🍷🍷🍷🍷

Via Dante 5, tel. 0461605313
www.dorigati.it

- *r* • Teroldego Rotaliano Diedri - Doc
- *r* • Trentino Cabernet Sauvignon Grener - Doc
- *w* • Trento Brut Riserva Methius - Doc

MEZZOLOMBARDO

Trento km 19 • m 227

Wineries

Barone De Cles 🍷🍷🍷

Via Mazzini 18, tel. 0461602673
baronedecles@tin.it

- *r* • Teroldego Rotaliano Maso Scari - Doc
- *r* • Trentino Lagrein Scuro - Doc
- *w* • Trentino Chardonnay - Doc

Cantina Rotaliana 🍷🍷

Corso del Popolo 6, tel. 0461601010
info@cantinarotaliana.it

- *r* • Teroldego Rotaliano Canevarie - Doc
- *r* • Teroldego Rotaliano Clesurae - Doc

Fedrizzi Cipriano 🍷🍷🍷

Via IV Novembre 1, tel. 0461602328

- *r* • Teroldego Rotaliano - Doc
- *r* • Teroldego Rotaliano Due Vigneti - Doc
- *r* • Trentino Lagrein - Doc

Foradori 🍷🍷🍷🍷🍷

Via D. Chiesa 1, tel. 0461601046
www.elisabettaforadori.com

- *r* • Teroldego Rotaliano - Doc
- *r* • Ailanpa Vigneti delle Dolomiti Rosso - Igt
- *r* • Granato Vigneti delle Dolomiti Rosso - Igt
- *r* • Karanar Vigneti delle Dolomiti Rosso - Igt
- *w* • Myrto Vigneti delle Dolomiti - Igt

MONTAGNA/MONTAN

Bolzano km 24 • m 497

Wineries

Haas Franz 🍷🍷🍷🍷🍷

Via Villa 5-6, tel. 0471812280
www.franz-haas.it

- *r* • Alto Adige Lagrein Dunkel - Doc
- *r* • Alto Adige Merlot Schweizer - Doc
- *r* • Alto Adige Pinot Nero Schweizer - Doc
- *r* • Istante Vigneti delle Dolomiti - Igt
- *w* • Alto Adige Bianco Manna - Doc
- *w* • Alto Adige Gewürztraminer - Doc
- *s* • Alto Adige Moscato Rosa Schweizer - Doc

Weingut Pfitscherhof 🍷🍷🍷

Via Gleno 9, tel. 0471819773
www.weingutpfitscherhof.it

- *r* • Alto Adige Pinot Nero Fuchsleiten - Doc
- *r* • Alto Adige Pinot Nero Matan - Doc
- *r* • Alto Adige Pinot Nero Riserva - Doc

NALLES/NALS

Bolzano km 16 • m 321

Wineries

Cantina Produttori Nalles & Magrè Niclara 🍷🍷🍷

Via Heiligenberg 2, tel. 0471678626
www.kellerei.it

- *r* • Alto Adige Merlot Levad - Doc
- *w* • Alto Adige Chardonnay Baron Salvadori - Doc
- *w* • Alto Adige Gewürztraminer Baron Salvadori - Doc
- *w* • Alto Adige Terlano Pinot Bianco Sirmian - Doc
- *w* • Alto Adige Terlano Sauvignon Mantele - Doc

Castel Schwanburg 🍷🍷

Via Schwanburg 16, tel. 0471678622
www.schwanburg.com

- *r* • Alto Adige Cabernet Sauvignon Castel Schwanburg - Doc
- *r* • Alto Adige Lagrein Dunkel Riserva - Doc
- *r* • Alto Adige Pinot Nero Riserva - Doc
- *w* • Alto Adige Bianco Pallas - Doc
- *w* • Alto Adige Terlano Sauvignon Castel Schwanburg - Doc

NATURNO/NATURNS

Bolzano km 42 • m 528

Wineries

Falkenstein 🍷🍷🍷🍷

Via Castello 15, tel. 0473666054

- *w* • Alto Adige Valle Venosta Pinot Bianco - Doc
- *w* • Alto Adige Valle Venosta Riesling - Doc
- *w* • Alto Adige Valle Venosta Sauvignon - Doc
- *s* • Alto Adige Valle Venosta Gewürztraminer Vendemmia Tardiva - Doc

NOGAREDO

Trento km 24 • m 216

Wineries

Castel Noarna 🍷🍷🍷

Località Noarna, via Castelnuovo 19, tel. 0464413295
www.castelnoarna.com

- *r* • Mercuria Vigneti delle Dolomiti Rosso - Igt
- *r* • Romeo Vigneti delle Dolomiti Rosso - Igt
- *w* • Bianco di Castelnuovo Vigneti delle Dolomiti Bianco - Igt

w • Campogrande Vigneti delle Dolomiti Chardonnay - Igt
w • Sauvignon Vigneti delle Dolomiti - Igt

NOMI
Trento km 18 • m 179
WINERIES
BATTISTOTTI RICCARDO ♟♟
Via 3 Novembre 31, tel. 0464834145
mail@battistotti.com
r • Trentino Marzemino Verdini - Doc
s • Trentino Moscato Rosa - Doc
CANTINA DI NOMI ♟♟
Via Roma 1, tel. 0464834195
www.trentinodoc.it/cantinanomi
r • Trentino Merlot Le Campagne Antichi Portali - Doc
w • Trentino Bianco Resorso Le Comete - Doc
w • Trentino Chardonnay Collezione I Fiori del Trentino - Doc
w • Trentino Müller Thurgau Nambiol Antichi Portali - Doc
w • Trentino Pinot Bianco Valbone Antichi Portali - Doc
GRIGOLETTI BRUNO VINCENZO ♟♟
Via Garibaldi, tel. 0464834215
grigolettivini@tin.it
r • Trentino Cabernet - Doc
r • Trentino Merlot Antica Vigna di Nomi - Doc
w • Trentino Chardonnay L'Opera - Doc

ORA/AUER
Bolzano km 20 • m 242
WINERIES
ISTITUTO TECNICO AGRARIO DI ORA - MASO HAPPACHER ♟♟
Via del Monte 20, tel. 0471810538 www.dfl-auer.it
r • Alto Adige Cabernet-Merlot Happacherhof - Doc
r • Alto Adige Lagrein Dunkel Happacherhof - Doc
w • Alto Adige Chardonnay Happacherhof - Doc
PODERE PROVINCIALE LAIMBURG ♟♟♟♟♟
Località Vadena, via Laimburg 6, tel. 0471969700
www.laimburg.it
r • Alto Adige Cabernet Riserva - Doc
r • Alto Adige Lagrein Dunkel Riserva - Doc
r • Alto Adige Pinot Nero - Doc
w • Alto Adige Chardonnay Doa - Doc
w • Alto Adige Gewürztraminer - Doc
w • Alto Adige Riesling - Doc
s • Alto Adige Moscato Rosa - Doc
WALDTHALER CLEMENS ♟♟
Via del Rio 4, tel. 0471810182
r • Alto Adige Cabernet - Doc
r • Alto Adige Lagrein - Doc
r • Alto Adige Merlot - Doc
r • Alto Adige Pinot Nero - Doc

PARCINES/PARTSCHINS
Bolzano km 35 • m 626
WINERIES
CANTINA CASTELLO STACHLBURG ♟♟
Via Peter Mitterhofer 2, tel. 0473968014
r • Alto Adige Valle Venosta Pinot Nero - Doc
w • Alto Adige Valle Venosta Chardonnay - Doc
w • Alto Adige Valle Venosta Gewürztraminer - Doc

ROVERÈ DELLA LUNA
Trento km 24 • m 251
WINERIES
GAIERHOF ♟♟♟
Via 4 Novembre 51, tel. 0461658514
www.gaierhof.com
r • Teroldego Rotaliano Superiore - Doc
r • Trentino Lagrein - Doc
w • Trentino Müller Thurgau dei 700 - Doc
s • Trentino Moscato Giallo - Doc
s • Trentino Moscato Rosa - Doc
MASO POLI ♟♟♟
Località Pressano, tel. 0461658514
www.hgblu.com/masopoli
r • Trentino Pinot Nero Maso Poli - Doc
w • Sorni Bianco Maso Poli - Doc
w • Trentino Chardonnay Costa Erta - Doc

ROVERETO
Trento km 24 • m 204
WINERIES
BALTER ♟♟♟
Via Vallunga II 24, tel. 0464430101
w • Sauvignon Blanc Vallagarina - Igt
w • Traminer Aromatico Vallagarina - Igt
w • Balter Brut - Vdt
CONTI BOSSI FEDRIGOTTI ♟♟♟
Via Unione 43, tel. 0464439250
www.fedrigotti.com
r • Trentino Marzemino - Doc
r • Trentino Merlot - Doc
r • Conte Federico Rosso Vallagarina - Igt
w • Trentino Chardonnay - Doc
w • Trentino Traminer Aromatico - Doc
LETRARI ♟♟♟
Via Monte Baldo 13/15, tel. 0464480200
www.letrari.com
r • Trentino Lagrein Vigneto Cuna - Doc
r • Trentino Marzemino Selezione Letrari - Doc
r • Trentino Rosso Maso Lodron - Doc
r • Valdadige Enantio Terra dei Forti - Doc
w • Trentino Chardonnay - Doc
w • Trentino Sauvignon Blanc - Doc
w • Trento Brut Riserva - Doc
LONGARIVA ♟♟♟
Località Borgo Sacco, via Zandonai 6, tel. 0464437200
www.acg.it/bacchus/longariv/longariva.html
r • Trentino Marzemino - Doc
r • Trentino Merlot Riserva Tovi - Doc
r • Trentino Pinot Nero Zinzèle - Doc
r • Trentino Rosso Riserva Tre Cesure Selezione Marco Manica - Doc
w • Trentino Chardonnay Praistèl - Doc
SIMONCELLI ♟♟
Località Navesel 7, tel. 0464432373
r • Trentino Marzemino - Doc
r • Trentino Rosso Navesel - Doc

SALORNO/SALURN
Bolzano km 34 • m 224
WINERIES
HADERBURG - ALOIS OCHSENREITER ♟♟♟
Località Pochi 31, tel. 0471889097
r • Alto Adige Pinot Nero Hausmannhof - Doc
w • Alto Adige Chardonny Hausmannhof - Doc

w • Alto Adige Gewürztraminer Blaspichl - Doc
w • Alto Adige Sauvignon Hausmannhof - Doc
w • Alto Adige Spumante Brut Haderburg - Doc
w • Alto Adige Spumante Brut Riserva Hausmannhof - Doc
w • Alto Adige Spumante Pas Dosé Millesimato Haderburg - Doc

Tenuta Steinhauserhof - Ochsenreiter Anton 🍷🍷
Località Pochi 37, tel. 0471889031
www.oxenreiter.net
r • Alto Adige Pinot Nero Steinhauserhof Oxenreiter - Doc
w • Alto Adige Chardonnay Steinhauserhof Oxenreiter - Doc
w • Alto Adige Gewürztraminer Steinhauserhof Oxenreiter - Doc
w • Alto Adige Sauvignon Steinhauserhof Oxenreiter - Doc

SAN MICHELE ALL'ADIGE
Trento km 15 • m 228

Wineries

Endrizzi 🍷🍷🍷 ★10%
Località Masetto, tel. 0461650129
www.endrizzi.it
r • Teroldego Rotaliano Superiore Riserva Maso Camorz - Doc
r • Trentino Cabernet Sauvignon Tradizione - Doc
r • Trentino Pinot Nero Riserva Pian del Castello - Doc
r • Masetto Nero Vigneti delle Dolomiti - Igt
w • Trentino Chardonnay Collezione - Doc

Istituto Agrario di San Michele all'Adige 🍷🍷🍷
Via Edmondo Mach 1, tel. 0461615111
r • Trentino Pinot Nero - Doc
r • Trentino Rosso Castel San Michele - Doc
w • Trentino Bianco Castel San Michele - Doc
w • Trentino Müller Thurgau - Doc
w • Trentino Nosiola - Doc

Zeni Roberto 🍷🍷🍷 ★10%
Località Grumo, via Stretta 2, tel. 0461650456
www.zenir.it
r • Teroldego Rotaliano Pini - Doc
r • Trentino Pinot Nero Spiazol - Doc
w • Trentino Pinot Bianco Sortì - Doc
w • Trentino Sauvignon Maso Nero - Doc
s • Trentino Moscato Rosa - Doc

SILANDRO/SCHLANDERS
Bolzano km 62 • m 721

Wineries

Schuster Oswald Befehlhof 🍷🍷
Località Vezzano 14, tel. 0473742197
w • Alto Adige Valle Venosta Müller Thurgau - Doc
w • Alto Adige Valle Venosta Riesling - Doc

TERLANO/TERLAN
Bolzano km 10 • m 248

Wineries

Cantina Braunbach 🍷🍷
Località Settequerce, via Bolzano 23, tel. 0471910184
r • Alto Adige Cabernet Lagrein Calldiv Prestige - Doc
w • Alto Adige Chardonnay - Doc

Cantina Produttori Terlano 🍷🍷🍷🍷🍷
Via Silberleiten 7, tel. 0471257135
www.cantinaterlano.com
r • Alto Adige Lagrein Riserva Porphyr - Doc
r • Alto Adige Merlot Riserva Siebeneich - Doc
w • Alto Adige Gewürztraminer Lunare - Doc
w • Alto Adige Terlano Classico Nova Domus - Doc
w • Alto Adige Terlano Pinot Bianco Vorberg - Doc
w • Alto Adige Terlano Sauvignon Quarz - Doc
w • Alto Adige Terlano Sauvignon Winkl - Doc

TERMENO SULLA STRADA DEL VINO /TRAMIN AN DER WEINSTRASSE
Bolzano km 24 • m 276

Wineries

Cantina Produttori Termeno 🍷🍷🍷🍷
Strada del Vino 144, tel. 0471860126
www.tramin-wine.it
r • Alto Adige Lagrein Urbanhof Terminum - Doc
r • Alto Adige Pinot Nero Schiesstandhof - Doc
w • Alto Adige Chardonnay Glassien - Doc
w • Alto Adige Gewürztraminer Nussbaumerhof - Doc
w • Alto Adige Pinot Bianco Tauris - Doc
s • Alto Adige Gewürztraminer Passito Terminum - Doc
s • Alto Adige Moscato Rosa Terminum - Doc

Elena Walch - Castel Ringberg e Kastelaz 🍷🍷🍷
Via A. Hofer 1, tel. 0471860172
www.elenawalch.com
r • Alto Adige Cabernet Istrice - Doc
r • Alto Adige Lagrein Dunkel Riserva Castel Ringberg - Doc
w • Alto Adige Gewürztraminer Kastelaz - Doc
w • Alto Adige Sauvignon Castel Ringberg - Doc
s • Alto Adige Bianco Passito Cashmere - Doc

Hofstätter 🍷🍷🍷🍷
Piazza Municipio 5, tel. 0471860161
www.hofstatter.com
r • Alto Adige Lagrein Steinraffler - Doc
r • Alto Adige Pinot Nero Riserva - Doc
r • Alto Adige Pinot Nero Riserva Barthenau Vigna Sant'Urbano - Doc
r • Yngram Rosso - Vdt
w • Alto Adige Bianco Barthenau Vigna San Michele - Doc
w • Alto Adige Gewürztraminer Kolbenhof Soll - Doc
w • Alto Adige Pinot Bianco Barthenau Vigna San Michele - Doc

TESIMO/TISENS
Bolzano km 20 • m 635

Wineries

Castel Katzenzungen 🍷🍷
Località Prissiano, via Prissiano 11, tel. 0473927018
r • Alto Adige Cabernet-Merlot - Doc
r • Alto Adige Lagrein Dunkel Riserva - Doc

TRENTO
m 194

Wineries

CaVit 🍷🍷🍷
Località Ravina, via del Ponte 31, tel. 0461381711
www.cavit.it

r • Trentino Cabernet Sauvignon Bottega dei Vinai - Doc
r • Trentino Pinot Nero Maso San Valentino - Doc
r • Trentino Rosso Quattro Vicariati - Doc
w • Trentino Chardonnay Maso Toresella - Doc
w • Trento Brut Riserva Speciale Graal - Doc

FERRARI - FRATELLI LUNELLI ♟♟♟♟
Via Ponte di Ravina 15, tel. 0461972311
www.cantineferrari.it
rs • Trento Rosé Perlé Ferrari - Doc
w • Trento Brut Ferrari - Doc
w • Trento Brut Giulio Ferrari Riserva del Fondatore - Doc
w • Trento Brut Perlé Millesimato Ferrari - Doc
w • Trento Maximum Brut Ferrari - Doc

LUNELLI ♟♟♟
Via Ponte di Ravina 15, tel. 0461972311
www.cantineferrari.it
r • Trentino Pinot Nero Maso Montalto - Doc
r • Trentino Rosso Maso Le Viane - Doc
w • Trentino Bianco Villa Margon - Doc
w • Trentino Chardonnay Villa Gentilotti - Doc
w • Trentino Sauvignon Villa San Nicolò - Doc

MASO BERGAMINI ♟♟♟
Località Cognola, tel. 0461983079
www.masobergamini.com
r • Trentino Lagrein Dunkel Maso Bergamini - Doc
r • Trentino Pinot Nero Maso Bergamini - Doc
r • Maderno Vigneti delle Dolomiti Rosso - Igt
w • Trentino Chardonnay Maso Bergamini - Doc
s • Trentino Moscato Rosa Maso Bergamini - Doc

MASO MARTIS ♟♟♟
Località Martignano, via dell'Albera 52, tel. 0461821057
www.masomartis.it
r • Trentino Cabernet Sauvignon - Doc
r • Trentino Pinot Nero - Doc
w • Trentino Chardonnay L'Incanto - Doc
w • Trento Brut Maso Martis - Doc
s • Sole d'Autunno Chardonnay Passito Vigneti delle Dolomiti - Igt

VIGNETI DELLE MERIDIANE ♟♟
Località Casteller 9, tel. 0464419343
r • Trentino Merlot Ravina - Doc
r • Cernidor Teroldego Atesino - Igt
w • Trentino Chardonnay Ravina - Doc

VARNA/VAHRN

Bolzano km 43 • m 671

WINERIES

CANTINA DELL'ABBAZIA DI NOVACELLA ♟♟♟
Via Abbazia 1, tel. 0472836189
www.kloster-neustift.it
r • Alto Adige Pinot Nero Riserva Praepositus - Doc
w • Alto Adige Valle Isarco Gewurztraminer Praepositus - Doc
w • Alto Adige Valle Isarco Bressanone Sauvignon - Doc
w • Alto Adige Valle Isarco Kerner Praepositus - Doc
w • Alto Adige Valle Isarco Müller Thurgau - Doc
w • Alto Adige Valle Isarco Sylvaner Praepositus - Doc
w • Praepositus Mitterberg Bianco - Igt

KOFERERHOF ♟♟
Strada Val Pusteria-Novacella 3, tel. 0472836649
w • Alto Adige Valle Isarco Gewürztraminer - Doc
w • Alto Adige Valle Isarco Kerner - Doc
w • Alto Adige Valle Isarco Müller Thurgau - Doc
w • Alto Adige Valle Isarco Pinot Grigio - Doc
w • Alto Adige Valle Isarco Sylvaner - Doc

VEZZANO

Trento km 13 • m 385

WINERIES

POLI GIOVANNI ♟♟
Località Santa Massenza 37, tel. 0461864119
r • Trentino Cabernet Fuggè - Doc
w • Trentino Nosiola Goccia d'Oro - Doc
s • Trentino Vino Santo - Doc

VILLANDRO/VILLANDERS

Bolzano km 30 • m 880

WINERIES

RÖCK - KONRAD AUGSCHÖLL ♟♟
Via S. Valentino 9, tel. 0472847130
w • Alto Adige Valle Isarco Müller Thurgau - Doc
w • Alto Adige Valle Isarco Sylvaner - Doc
w • Caruess - Vdt

VOLANO

Trento km 19 • m 189

WINERIES

CONCILIO VINI ♟♟
Via Nazionale 24, tel. 0464411000
r • Trentino Rosso Mori Vecio - Doc
w • Trentino Chardonnay - Doc
w • Trentino Traminer Aromatico - Doc

MASO BASTIE ♟♟♟
Via 4 Novembre 51, tel. 0464412747
masobastie@tin.it
r • Trentino Rosso Bastie Alte - Doc
w • Trentino Traminer Aromatico - Doc
s • Trentino Moscato Rosa - Doc

ROSI EUGENIO ♟♟♟
Via Tavernelle 3, tel. 0464461375
tamaramar@virgilio.it
r • Trentino Marzemino Poiema - Doc
r • Trentino Rosso Esegesi - Doc
one Aristos - Doc

VENETO

ANNONE VENETO

Venice km 64 • m 9

WINERIES

BOSCO DEL MERLO ♟♟
Via Postumia 14,
tel. 0422768167 www.paladin.it
r • Lison Pramaggiore Refosco dal Peduncolo Rosso Roggio dei Roveri - Doc
r • Vineargenti Rosso delle Venezie - Igt
w • Priné Bianco delle Venezie - Igt

Paladin & Paladin ♟♟ ★10%
Via Postumia 12, tel. 0422768167
www.paladin.it
r • Lison-Pramaggiore Refosco dal Peduncolo Rosso - Doc
r • Vigna degli Aceri Malbech del Veneto - Igt
w • Incorcio Manzoni 6.0.13 del Veneto - Igt

Tenuta Sant'Anna ♟♟ ★10%
Località Loncon, via P.L. Zovatto 71, tel. 042286451 I
tntsanna@genagricola.it
w • Lison Pramaggiore Chardonnay - Doc
s • Colli Orientali del Friuli Verduzzo Friulano Ronco del Miele - Doc

ARQUÀ PETRARCA
Padua km 22 • m 80

Wineries

Vignalta ♟♟♟
Via Marlunghe 7, tel. 0429777225
www.vignalta.it
r • Colli Euganei Rosso Gemola - Doc
r • Agno Tinto Veneto Rosso - Igt
s • Colli Euganei Fior d'Arancio Alpianae - Doc

BAGNOLI DI SOPRA
Padua km 27 • m 5

Wineries

Dominio di Bagnoli ♟♟ ★10%
Piazza Marconi 63, tel. 0495380008
www.ildominiodibagnoli.it
r • Bagnoli Classico Cabernet - Doc
r • Bagnoli Classico Friularo - Doc
s • Bagnoli Classico Friularo V.T. - Doc

BARDOLINO
Verona km 28 • m 65

Wineries

Cantina Fratelli Zeni ♟♟♟
Via Costabella 9, tel. 0457210022
www.zeni.it
r • Amarone della Valpolicella Classico Vigne Alte - Doc
r • Bardolino Classico Superiore Vigne Alte - Doc
r • Valpolicella Classico Superiore Vigne Alte - Doc
w • Soave Classico Vigne Alte - Doc
s • Recioto della Valpolicella Vigne Alte - Doc

Conti Guerrieri Rizzardi ♟♟♟
Via Verdi 4, tel. 0457210028
www.guerrieririzzardi.com
r • Amarone della Valpolicella Classico Calcarole - Doc
r • Bardolino Classico Fontis Vinae Munus - Doc
r • Bardolino Classico Tacchetto - Doc
r • Valpolicella Classico Superiore Vigneto Pojega - Doc
w • Soave Classico Costeggiola - Doc

Lenotti ♟♟
Via S. Cristina 1, tel. 0457210484
r • Amarone della Valpolicella Classico Selezione Carlo Lenotti - Doc
r • Bardolino Classico Vigna Le Giare - Doc
r • Valpolicella Classico Superiore Le Crosare - Doc
r • Massimo Veneto Rosso - Igt
w • Soave Classico Capocolle - Doc

Tenuta Valleselle ♟♟♟
Località Valleselle 1, tel. 0456211128
www.tenutavalleselle.com
r • Amarone della Valpolicella Rovertondo - Doc
r • Bardolino Classico Superiore Pieve San Vito - Doc

Valetti Luigi ♟
Località Calmasino, via Pragrande 5, tel. 0457235075
www.valetti.it
r • Bardolino Classico - Doc
r • Bardolino Classico Superiore - Doc

BASSANO DEL GRAPPA
Vicenza km 35 • m 129

Wineries

Due Santi ♟♟
Viale Asiago 174, tel. 0424502074
info@duesanti.it
r • Breganze Cabernet Vigneto Due Santi - Doc
w • Breganze Sauvignon Vigneto Due Santi - Doc

BREGANZE
Vicenza km 20 • m 110

Wineries

Maculan ♟♟♟♟♟
Via Castelletto 3, tel. 0445873733
www.maculan.net
r • Breganze Cabernet Palazzotto - Doc
r • Breganze Merlot Crosara - Doc
r • Fratta Rosso del Veneto - Igt
w • Breganze Chardonnay Ferrata - Doc
s • Breganze Torcolato - Doc
s • Acininobili Veneto Bianco - Igt
s • Dindarello Moscato del Veneto - Igt

CASTELNUOVO DEL GARDA
Verona km 18 • m 130

Wineries

Corte Sant'Arcadio ♟
Via Ca' Brusa 12, tel. 0457575331
r • Bardolino Classico - Doc
r • Cortigiano Cabernet Sauvignon del Veneto - Igt
rs • Bardolino Chiaretto Classico - Doc

CAVAION VERONESE
Verona km 23 • m 190

Wineries

Le Fraghe ♟♟
Via La Colombara, tel. 0457236832
www.fraghe.it
r • Bardolino Classico Le Fraghe - Doc
rs • Bardolino Chiaretto Le Fraghe - Doc
w • Valdadige Chardonnay Montalto - Doc

Tinazzi Eugenio & Figli ♟♟
Località Policchia 3, tel. 0457235394
info@tinazzi.it
r • Amarone della Valpolicella Classico La Bastia Cà dé Rocchi - Doc
r • Valpolicella Classico Cà dé Rocchi - Doc
r • Dugal Cà dé Rocchi Rosso del Veneto - Igt

CINTO EUGANEO
Padua km 30 • m 10/575

Wineries

Ca' Lustra
Via S. Pietro 50, tel. 042994128
info@calustra.it
r • Colli Euganei Cabernet Vigna Girapoggio - Doc
r • Colli Euganei Merlot Vigna Sasso Nero - Doc
w • Colli Euganei Chardonnay Passo Roverello - Doc

COLOGNOLA AI COLLI

Verona km 17 • m 23/226

Wineries

Fasoli Gino
Località San Zeno, via C. Battisti 47, tel. 0457650741
www.fasoligino.com
r • Orgno Rosso Veronese - Igt
w • Soave Superiore Pieve Vecchia - Doc
s • Recioto di Soave San Zeno - Docg

Tenuta Sant'Antonio ★10%
Località San Zeno, via Ceriani 23, tel. 0457650383
www.tenutasantantonio.it
r • Amarone della Valpolicella Campo dei Gigli - Doc
r • Valpolicella Superiore La Bandina - Doc
w • Soave Superiore Monte Ceriani - Doc
s • Recioto della Valpolicella Argille Bianche - Doc
s • Colori d'Autunno Passito Veneto - Igt

CONEGLIANO

Treviso km 28 • m 72

Wineries

Carpenè Malvolti
Via Carpené 1, tel. 04383646l l
w • Prosecco di Conegliano Brut Cuvée - Doc
w • Prosecco di Conegliano Dry Cuvée Oro - Doc
w • Spumante Metodo Classico Millesimato - Vdt

San Giovanni
Via Manzana 4, tel. 043831598
www.vinisangiovanni.com
r • Piave Cabernet San Giovanni - Doc
w • Prosecco di Valdobbiadene Extra Dry San Giovanni - Doc

Tenuta di Collalbrigo
Via Marsiglion 77, tel. 0438455229
r • Rosso di Collalbrigo - Igt
w • Prosecco di Conegliano Spumante Brut - Doc

Zardetto Spumanti
Località Ogliano, via Marcorà 15/A, tel. 0438208909
w • Prosecco di Conegliano Spumante Brut - Doc
w • Prosecco di Conegliano Dry Zeroventi - Doc
w • Prosecco di Valdobbiadene Superiore di Cartizze Dry - Doc

CORNEDO VICENTINO

Vicenza km 27 • m 200

Wineries

Frigo dal 1876 - Le Pignole
Via Marconi 14, tel. 0445951334
www.lepignole.com
r • Colli Berici Cabernet Sauvignon Corte dei Roda - Doc
r • Colli Berici Cabernet Rosso del Buielo - Doc
r • Roan Cabernet Malbech del Veneto - Igt

CROCETTA DEL MONTELLO

Treviso km 26 • m 146

Wineries

Villa Sandi
Via Erizzo 11/B, tel. 0423665033
www.villasandi.it
r • Piave Cabernet Sauvignon - Doc
w • Prosecco di Valdobbiadene Superiore di Cartizze - Doc
w • Opere Trevigiane Brut Millesimato - Vdt

FOSSALTA DI PIAVE

Venice km 35 • m 5

Wineries

Botter Carlo
Via Cadorna 17, tel. 042167194
www.botter.it
r • Piave Merlot - Doc
w • Piave Chardonnay - Doc

Santo Stefano
Via Cadorna 92, tel. 042167502
w • Piave Chardonnay Terre Nobili Le Ronche - Doc
w • Olmera Veneto Bianco - Igt

FOSSALTA DI PORTOGRUARO

Venice km 72 • m 8

Wineries

Santa Margherita
Via Ita Marzotto 8, tel. 0421246111
www.santamargherita.com
r • Laudato Malbech del Veneto Orientale - Igt
w • Alto Adige Chardonnay Cà d'Archi - Doc
w • Prosecco di Valdobbiadene Sumante Extra Dry - Doc
w • Prosecco di Valdobbiadene Spumante Superiore di Cartizze Extra Dry - Doc
w • Luna dei Feldi Vigneti delle Dolomiti Bianco - Igt

FUMANE

Verona km 17 • m 198

Wineries

Allegrini
Corte Giara 9/11, tel. 0456832011
r • Amarone della Valpolicella Classico - Doc
r • La Grola Rosso Veronese - Igt
r • La Poja Corvina Veronese - Igt
r • Palazzo della Torre Rosso del Veronese - Igt
s • Recioto della Valpolicella Classico Giovanni Allegrini - Doc

Corteforte
Via Osan 45, tel. 0458344304
www.valpolicella.it
r • Amarone della Valpolicella Classico Bertarole - Doc
r • Amarone della Valpolicella Classico Vigneti di Osan - Doc
r • Valpolicella Classico Superiore Podere Bertarole - Doc

Le Bertarole
Via Bertarole 8/A, tel. 0456839220
az.bertarole@tiscali.net
r • Amarone della Valpolicella Classico Le Marognole - Doc
r • Valpolicella Classico - Doc

r • Valpolicella Classico Superiore Le Portarine - Doc

Le Salette ♟♟♟
Via Pio Brugnoli 11/C, tel. 0457701027
vinosal@tin.it
r • Amarone della Valpolicella Classico Pergole Vece - Doc
r • Valpolicella Classico Superiore I Progni - Doc
s • Recioto della Valpolicella Classico Pergole Vece - Doc

Scriani ♟♟♟
Via Ponte Scrivan, tel. 0456839093
r • Amarone della Valpolicella Classico - Doc
r • Recioto della Valpolicella Classico - Doc
r • Valpolicella Classico Superiore - Doc

GAMBELLARA
Vicenza km 22 • m 70

Wineries

La Biancara ♟♟
Contrada Biancara 8, tel. 0444444244
w • Gambellara Superiore La Sassaia - Doc
w • Pico dei Laorenti - Vdt
s • Recioto di Gambellara - Doc

Zonin ♟♟
Via Borgolecco 9, tel. 0444640111
www.zonin.it
r • Berengario Venezia Giulia - Igt

GORGO AL MONTICANO
Treviso km 32 • m 10

Wineries

Villa Brunesca ♟♟
Via Serenissima 12, tel. 0422800026
villabrunesca@villabrunesca.it
r • Malbech del Veneto - Igt
r • Vigna Olinda Veneto Refosco dal Peduncolo Rosso - Igt

ILLASI
Verona km 18 • m 157

Wineries

Dal Forno Romano ♟♟♟♟♟
Località Lodoletta 1, tel. 0457834923
az.dalforno@tiscalinet.it
r • Amarone della Valpolicella Vigneto di Monte Lodoletta - Doc
r • Valpolicella Superiore Monte Lodoletta - Doc
s • Recioto della Valpolicella Vigneto di Monte Lodoletta - Doc

Santi ♟♟
Via Ungheria 33, tel. 0456520077
www.giv.it
r • Amarone della Valpolicella Proemio - Doc
r • Valpolicella Classico Superiore Solane - Doc
w • Soave Classico Sanfederici - Doc

Trabucchi ♟♟♟♟
Località Monte Tenda 4, tel. 0457833233
raffaella.trabucchi@tin.it
r • Amarone della Valpolicella - Doc
r • Valpolicella Superiore Terre del Cereolo - Doc
s • Recioto della Valpolicella - Doc

LAZISE
Verona km 23 • m 76

Wineries

Lamberti ♟
Via Gardesana, tel. 0457580034
www.giv.it
r • Bardolino Classico Santepietre - Doc
r • Bardolino Chiaretto Classico Santepietre - Doc
w • Bianco di Custoza Orchidea Platino - Doc

Le Tende ♟♟♟
Località Le Tende 6, tel. 0457590748
www.letende.it
r • Bardolino Classico Superiore - Doc
w • Bianco di Custoza Oro - Doc
s • Amoroso Passito Bianco del Veneto - Igt

LONGARE
Vicenza km 10 • m 29

Wineries

Costozza - Conti A. & G. da Schio ♟♟ ★10%
Località Costozza, piazza Giovanni da Schio 4, tel. 0444555032
giuliodaschio@libero.it
r • Colli Berici Cabernet Franc - Doc
r • Costozza Rosso del Veneto - Igt

MANSUÈ
Treviso km 32 • m 13

Wineries

Tenuta Setten ♟♟
Località Basalghelle, piazza Aganoor 2, tel. 0422755288
r • Piave Cabernet Sauvignon Vigneto Baite - Doc
r • Setten Rosso Veneto - Igt
w • Vitha Marca Trevigiana - Igt

MARANO DI VALPOLICELLA
Verona km 19 • m 350

Wineries

Ca' La Bionda ♟♟
Località Bionda 4, tel. 0456801198
casbionda@tin.it
r • Amarone della Valpolicella Classico Vigneti di Ravazzol - Doc
r • Valpolicella Classico Superiore Campo Casal Vegri - Doc
s • Recioto della Valpolicella Classico Vigneto Le Tordare - Doc

Campagnola Giuseppe ♟♟♟
Località Valgatara, via Agnella 9, tel. 0457703900
r • Amarone della Valpolicella Classico Caterina Zardini - Doc
r • Valpolicella Classico Superiore Le Bine Vigneti di Purano - Doc
s • Recioto della Valpolicella Classico Casotto del Merlo - Doc

Castellani Michele e Figli ♟♟♟♟
Località Valgatara, via Grande 1, tel. 0457701253
www.castellanimichele.it
r • Amarone della Valpolicella Classico Cà del Pipa Le Vigne - Doc
r • Valpolicella Classico Superiore Ripasso I Castei - Doc
s • Recioto della Valpolicella Classico I Castei Campo Casalin - Doc

Corte Campagnola ♟♟♟
Località Valgatara, via Paverno 21, tel. 0457701237

r • Amarone della Valpolicella Classico Gli Archi - Doc
r • Valpolicella Classico Superiore Gli Archi - Doc
s • Recioto della Valpolicella Classico Gli Archi - Doc

CORTE RUGOLIN 🍷🍷🍷
Località Rugolin 1, tel. 0457702153
www.corterugolin.it
r • Amarone della Valpolicella Classico Monte Danieli - Doc
r • Valpolicella Classico Superiore Ripasso - Doc
s • Recioto della Valpolicella Classico - Doc

FRATELLI BONAZZI 🍷🍷🍷
Via Badin 10, tel. 0457701454
r • Valpolicella Classico Superiore - Doc

FRATELLI DEGANI 🍷🍷 ★10%
Località Valgatara, via Tobele 3/A, tel. 0457701850
aldo.degani@tin.it
r • Amarone della Valpolicella Classico La Rosta - Doc
r • Valpolicella Classico Superiore - Doc
r • Valpolicella Classico Superiore Cicilio - Doc

LONARDI GIUSEPPE 🍷🍷
Via delle Poste 2, tel. 0457755154
www.lonardivini.it
r • Amarone della Valpolicella Classico - Doc
r • Valpolicella Classico Superiore Ripasso - Doc
s • Recioto della Valpolicella Classico Le Arele - Doc

NOVAIA 🍷🍷
Località Novaia 3, tel. 0457755129
www.novaia.it
r • Amarone della Valpolicella Classico - Doc
r • Valpolicella Classico Superiore - Doc
s • Recioto della Valpolicella Classico - Doc

SAN RUSTICO 🍷
Località Valgatara, via Pozzo 2, tel. 0457703348
www.sanrustico.it
r • Amarone della Valpolicella Classico - Doc
r • Amarone della Valpolicella Classico Vigneti del Gaso - Doc
r • Valpolicella Classico Superiore Vigneti del Gaso - Doc

MASER

Treviso km 28 • m 147

WINERIES

VILLA DI MASER 🍷🍷
Via Cornuda 1, tel. 0423923003
r • Montello e Colli Asolani Cabernet Sauvignon - Doc
r • Montello e Colli Asolani Merlot - Doc
r • Pinot Nero Colli Trevigiani - Igt

MEZZANE DI SOTTO

Verona km 19 • m 122

WINERIES

CORTE SANT'ALDA 🍷🍷🍷
Località Fioi, tel. 0458880006
www.cortesantalda.it
r • Amarone della Valpolicella - Doc
r • Valpolicella Superiore Mithas - Doc
s • Recioto della Valpolicella - Doc

ROCCOLO GRASSI 🍷🍷🍷
Via S. Giovanni di Dio 19, tel. 0458880089
roccolograssi@libero.it
r • Amarone della Valpolicella Roccolo Grassi - Doc
r • Valpolicella Superiore Roccolo Grassi - Doc
s • Recioto di Soave La Broia - Docg

VILLA ERBICE 🍷🍷
Via Villa 22, tel. 0458880086
r • Amarone della Valpolicella Tremenel - Doc
r • Valpolicella Superiore Montetombole - Doc
s • Recioto della Valpolicella Torrazzine - Doc

MONSELICE

Padua km 22 • m 9

WINERIES

BORIN VINI & VIGNE 🍷🍷🍷
Via dei Colli 5, tel. 042974384
www.viniborin.it
r • Colli Euganei Cabernet Sauvignon Riserva Mons Silicis - Doc
w • Colli Euganei Chardonnay Vigna Bianca - Doc
s • Colli Euganei Moscato Fior d'Arancio Passito - Doc

MONTEBELLO VICENTINO

Vicenza km 17 • m 53

WINERIES

CAVAZZA 🍷🍷
Via Selva 22, tel. 0444649166
r • Colli Berici Cabernet Cicogna - Doc
w • Gambellara Classico Monte La Bocara - Doc
s • Recioto di Gambellara Capitel Santa Libera - Doc

DAL MASO LUIGINO 🍷🍷
Via Selva 62, tel. 0444649104
dalmasovini@infinito.it
w • Gambellara Classico Vigneti Cà Cischele - Doc
w • Gambellara Recioto Classico Vigneto Riva dei Perari - Doc
w • Terra dei Rovi Bianco del Veneto - Igt

MONTECCHIA DI CROSARA

Verona km 33 • m 87

WINERIES

POSENATO STEFANO 🍷🍷
Via Pergola 69, tel. 0456175131
w • Soave Classico Superiore Vigna dello Stefano - Doc

MONTEFORTE D'ALPONE

Verona km 25 • m 38

WINERIES

ANSELMI ROBERTO 🍷🍷🍷🍷🍷
Via S. Carlo 46, tel. 0457611488
capitelfoscarino@libero.it
r • Realda Cabernet Sauvignon Veneto - Igt
w • Capitel Croce Bianco Veneto - Igt
w • Capitel Foscarino Bianco Veneto - Igt
w • San Vincenzo Bianco Veneto - Igt
s • I Capitelli Passito Veneto - Igt

CA' RUGATE 🍷🍷🍷
Via Mezzavilla 12, tel. 0456175082
www.carugate.it
w • Soave Classico Superiore Monte Alto - Doc
s • Recioto di Soave La Perlara - Docg
s • Corte Durlo Veneto Bianco Passito - Igt

DAL BOSCO GIOVANNI BATTISTA 🍷🍷
Via Fontananuova, tel. 0456175083
w • Soave Classico Superiore Le Mandolare - Doc

Fattori & Graney ♟♟♟
Via Zoppega 14, tel. 0457460041
w • Soave Classico Superiore - Doc
w • Soave Classico Superiore Motto Piane - Doc
s • Recioto di Soave Motto Piane - Docg

Gini ♟♟♟♟
Via G. Matteotti 42, tel. 0457611908
azagricolagini@tiscalinet.it
r • Campo alle More Pinot Nero del Veneto - Igt
w • Soave Classico Superiore Contrada Salvarenza Vecchie Vigne - Doc
w • Soave Classico Superiore La Froscà - Doc
w • Maciete Fumé Sauvignon del Veneto - Igt
s • Recioto di Soave Renobilis - Docg

La Cappuccina ♟♟♟
Località Costalunga, via S. Brizio 125, tel. 0456175840
www.lacappuccina.it
w • Soave Superiore Fontégo - Doc
w • Soave Superiore San Brizio - Doc
s • Arzimo Passito Veneto - Igt

Portinari Umberto ♟♟
Via Santo Stefano 2, tel. 0456175087
w • Soave Classico Superiore Ronchetto - Doc
w • Soave Superiore Santo Stefano - Doc
s • Recioto di Soave Oro - Docg

Pra Graziano e Sergio ♟♟
Via della Fontana 31, tel. 0457612125
w • Soave Classico Colle Sant'Antonio - Doc
w • Soave Classico Superiore - Doc
w • Soave Classico Vigneto Monte Grande - Doc

NEGRAR

Verona km 14 • m 190

Wineries

Bertani Cav. G.B. ♟♟♟♟
Località Arbizzano, tel. 0456011211
www.bertani.net
r • Amarone della Valpolicella Classico - Doc
r • Valpolicella Classico Superiore Ognissanti - Doc
w • Soave Classico Superiore Sereole - Doc

Bussola Tommaso ♟♟♟♟♟
Via Molino Turri 30, tel. 0457501740
r • Amarone della Valpolicella Classico TB - Doc
r • Amarone della Valpolicella Classico TB Vigneto Alto - Doc
r • Valpolicella Classico Superiore TB - Doc
s • Recioto della Valpolicella Classico TB - Doc
s • Recioto della Valpolicella Classico BG - Doc

Ca' del Monte ♟♟
Via Ca' del Monte, tel. 0457500230
r • Amarone della Valpolicella Classico - Doc
r • Valpolicella Classico Superiore - Doc
r • Valpolicella Classico Superiore Vigneto Scaiso - Doc

Cantina Sociale Valpolicella ♟♟♟
Ca' Salgari 2, tel. 0456014300
www.cantinanegrar.it
r • Amarone della Valpolicella Classico Domini Veneti - Doc
r • Amarone della Valpolicella Classico Vigneti di Jago Domini Veneti - Doc
r • Valpolicella Classico Superiore Vigneti di Jago - Doc
s • Recioto della Valpolicella Classico Domini Veneti - Doc
s • Recioto della Valpolicella Vigneti di Moron Domini Veneti - Doc

Le Ragose ♟♟♟♟
Località Arbizzano, tel. 0457513241
www.leragose.com
r • Amarone della Valpolicella Marta Galli - Doc
r • Amarone della Valpolicella Raghos - Doc
r • Valpolicella Classico Superiore Le Sassine - Doc
r • Valpolicella Classico Superiore Marta Galli - Doc
s • Recioto della Valpolicella Classico - Doc

Mazzi Roberto e Figli ♟♟♟
Località Sanperetto, via Crosetta 8, tel. 0457502072
r • Amarone della Valpolicella Classico Punta di Villa - Doc
r • Valpolicella Classico Superiore Vigneto Poiega - Doc
r • Libero Rosso Veronese - Igt
s • Recioto della Valpolicella Classico Vigneto Le Calcarole - Doc
s • San Francesco Passito Bianco del Veneto - Igt

Quintarelli Giuseppe ♟♟♟♟♟
Via Cerè 1, tel. 0457500016
r • Amarone della Valpolicella Monte Cà Paletta - Doc
r • Amarone della Valpolicella Riserva Monte Cà Paletta - Doc
r • Valpolicella Classico Superiore Monte Cà Paletta - Doc
s • Recioto della Valpolicella Classico Riserva Monte Cà Paletta - Doc
s • Amabile del Ceré Passito Bianco del Veneto - Igt

Sartori ♟♟♟
Via Casette 2, tel. 045602801
www.sartorinet.com
r • Amarone della Valpolicella Classico - Doc
r • Amarone della Valpolicella Classico Corte Brà - Doc
r • Valpolicella Classico Superiore Vigneti di Montegradella - Doc
r • Cent'anni Rosso Veronese - Igt
w • Soave Classico Superiore Vigneti di Sella - Doc

Villa Spinosa ♟♟♟
Località Jago, tel. 0457500093
r • Amarone della Valpolicella Classico - Doc
r • Valpolicella Classico Superiore Vigneto Jago - Doc
s • Recioto della Valpolicella Classico Francesca Finato Spinosa - Doc

Viviani ♟♟♟
Località Mazzano, via Mazzano 8, tel. 0457500286
r • Amarone della Valpolicella Classico Ammandorlato - Doc
r • Valpolicella Classico Superiore - Doc
s • Recioto della Valpolicella Classico La Mandrella - Doc

NERVESA DELLA BATTAGLIA

Treviso km 20 • m 78

Wineries

Serafini e Vidotto ♟♟♟
Via Arditi 1, tel. 0422773281

r • Colli Trevigiani Pinot Nero - Doc
r • Il Rosso dell'Abazia Rosso del Veneto - Igt
r • Phigaia After the Red delle Venezie - Igt

PESCHIERA DEL GARDA

Verona km 24 • m 68

WINERIES

SANTA CRISTINA ♟♟

Località San Benedetto di Lugana, via Massoni 2, tel. 0457550300
www.zenato.it
r • Cabernet Sauvignon del Veneto Santa Cristina Barrique - Igt
w • Lugana Santa Cristina Vigneto Massoni - Doc
s • Rigoletto Bianco Dolce - Vdt

ZENATO ♟♟♟

Via S. Benedetto 8, tel. 0457550369
www.zenato.it
r • Amarone della Valpolicella Classico Riserva Sergio Zenato - Doc
r • Valpolicella Classico Superiore Ripassa - Doc
w • Lugana Riserva Sergio Zenato - Doc

PIEVE DI SOLIGO

Treviso km 31 • m 132

WINERIES

COL SANDAGO - CASE BIANCHE ♟♟♟

Via Chisini 79, tel. 0438841608
www.martinozanetti.it
r • Col Sandago Camoi Rosso delle Venezie - Igt
r • Col Sandago Wildbacher Colli Trevigiani - Igt
w • Prosecco di Conegliano Spumante Extra Dry Case Bianche - Doc
w • Prosecco di Conegliano Valdobbiadene Brut Vigna del Cuc - Doc
s • Col Sandago Passito del Veneto - Igt

REFRONTOLO

Treviso km 34 • m 216

WINERIES

TOFFOLI VINCENZO ♟ ★10%

Via Liberazione 26, tel. 0438894240
www.paginegialle.it/vincenzotoffoli
w • Prosecco di Conegliano Extra Dry - Doc
w • Prosecco dei Colli Trevigiani - Vdt
s • Colli di Conegliano Marzemino Passito di Refrontolo Passito - Doc

RONCADE

Treviso km 13 • m 8

WINERIES

CASTELLO DI RONCADE ♟ ★10%

Via Roma 141, tel. 0422708736
r • Piave Cabernet - Doc
r • Piave Merlot - Doc
w • Piave Tocai Italico - Doc

SALGAREDA

Treviso km 22 • m 3/13

WINERIES

MOLON ORNELLA ♟♟♟ ★10%

Località Campodipietra, via Risorgimento 40, tel. 0422804807
www.molon.it
r • Piave Cabernet Ornella Molon - Doc
r • Piave Merlot Ornella Molon - Doc
r • Piave Raboso Ornella Molon - Doc
w • Piave Chardonnay Ornella Molon - Doc
w • Ornella Molon Sauvignon Blanc Veneto - Igt

SAN BONIFACIO

Verona km 22 • m 31

WINERIES

INAMA ♟♟♟

Via IV Novembre 1, tel. 0456104343
www.inamaaziendaagricola.it
r • Bradisismo Rosso del Veneto - Igt
w • Soave Classico Superiore Vigneti di Foscarino - Doc
w • Soave Classico Superiore Vin Soave Cuvée Speciale - Doc
w • Vulcaia Fumé Sauvignon Blanc del Veneto - Igt
s • Vulcaia Aprés - Vdt

SAN FIOR

Treviso km 34 • m 57

WINERIES

MASOTTINA ♟

Località Castello Roganzuolo, via Brandolini 54, tel. 0438400775
www.masottina.it
r • Piave Merlot Riserva Vigneto Ai Palazzi - Doc
w • Colli di Conegliano Bianco - Doc
w • Piave Pinot Grigio Vigneto Ai Palazzi - Doc

SAN GERMANO DEI BERICI

Vicenza km 28 • m 90

WINERIES

VILLA DAL FERRO - LAZZARINI ♟♟♟

Località Villa dal Ferro, via Chiesa 23, tel. 0444868025
r • Colli Berici Cabernet Riserva Le Rive Rosse - Doc
r • Colli Berici Merlot Campo del Lago - Doc
r • Rosso del Rocolo - Vdt

SAN MARTINO BUON ALBERGO

Verona km 8 • m 45

WINERIES

CORTE SOTTORIVA ♟♟

Località Marcellise, via Cao di Sopra 35, tel. 0458740039
r • Valpolicella Superiore - Doc
s • Passito Bianco del Veneto - Igt

MARION ♟♟

Località Marcellise, via Borgo 1, tel. 0458740021
campedelli@inwind.it
r • Valpolicella Superiore Marion - Doc
r • Marion Cabernet Sauvignon del Veneto - Igt
s • Marion Bianco Passito del Veneto - Igt

MUSELLA ♟♟♟

Località Monte del Drago 1, tel. 045973385
www.musella.it
r • Amarone della Valpolicella - Doc
r • Valpolicella Superiore - Doc
s • Recioto della Valpolicella - Doc

SAN PIETRO IN CARIANO

Verona km 14 • m 151

WINERIES

ACCORDINI IGINO ♟♟♟

Località Pedemonte, via A. Bolla 7, tel. 0456020604

r • Amarone della Valpolicella Classico Superiore Le Viole - Doc
r • Recioto della Valpolicella Classico Superiore Le Viole - Doc
r • Valpolicella Classico Superiore Le Bessole - Doc

Accordini Stefano ♟♟♟♟
Località Pedemonte, via A. Bolla 9, tel. 0457701733
www.accordini.stefano.it
r • Amarone della Valpolicella Classico Acinatico - Doc
r • Valpolicella Classico Superiore Acinatico - Doc
s • Recioto della Valpolicella Classico Acinatico - Doc

Begali Lorenzo ♟♟♟
Località Negarine, via Cengia 10, tel. 0457725148
www.begaliwine.it
r • Amarone della Valpolicella Classico Monte Cà Bianca - Doc
r • Valpolicella Classico Superiore La Cengia - Doc
s • Recioto della Valpolicella Classico - Doc

Bonazzi Dario e Fabio ♟♟
Via Valpolicella 24, tel. 0457702469
r • Amarone della Valpolicella Classico Vigneto dei Comparsi - Doc
r • Valpolicella Classico Superiore Monte Gradela - Doc
s • Recioto della Valpolicella Classico Monte Gradela - Doc

Brigaldara ♟♟
Località San Floriano Valpolicella, via Brigaldara 20, tel. 0457701055
r • Amarone della Valpolicella Classico - Doc
r • Valpolicella Classico - Doc
s • Recioto della Valpolicella Classico - Doc

Brunelli ♟♟♟
Via Cariano 10, tel. 0457701118
www.brunelliwine.com
r • Amarone della Valpolicella Classico Campo degli Inferi - Doc
r • Amarone della Valpolicella Classico Campo del Titari - Doc
r • Valpolicella Classico Superiore Pariondo - Doc
w • Carianum Garganega del Veneto - Igt
s • Recioto della Valpolicella Classico Il Mestiere del Papà - Doc

Ca' Pitti ♟♟
Località Bure Alto, via Villa Girardi 40, tel. 0457701461
r • Amarone della Valpolicella Classico Cà Pitti - Doc
r • Valpolicella Classico Superiore Corte Quaranta - Doc

Cesari Gerardo ♟♟
Località San Floriano, via Don Cesare Biasi 13/A, tel. 0456801210
r • Amarone della Valpolicella Il Bosco - Doc
r • Valpolicella Classico Superiore Ripasso Mara - Doc
r • Mitico Merlot delle Venezie - Igt
w • Mitico Chardonnay delle Venezie - Igt
s • Recioto della Valpolicella Classico - Doc

Corte Lenguin ♟♟
Località San Floriano, via Ca' dell'Ebreo 5, tel. 0457701406
r • Amarone della Valpolicella Classico La Masua - Doc
r • Valpolicella Classico Superiore - Doc
s • Recioto della Valpolicella Classico - Doc

Fornaser ♟♟
Via Bure Alto 1, tel. 0457701651
www.montefaustino.com - www.fornaser.com
r • Amarone della Valpolicella Classico Monte Faustino - Doc
r • Valpolicella Classico Superiore Monte Faustino La Traversagna - Doc
s • Recioto della Valpolicella Classico Monte Faustino - Doc

Fratelli Farina ♟♟♟
Località Pedemonte, via Fontana 8, tel. 0457701349
www.farinawines.com
r • Amarone della Valpolicella Classico Remo Farina - Doc
r • Valpolicella Classico Superiore Ripasso Remo Farina - Doc
r • Valpolicella Classico Superiore Ripasso Vigna Montecorna - Doc

Fratelli Speri ♟♟♟ ★10%
Località Pedemonte, via Fontana 14, tel. 0457701154
www.speri.com
r • Amarone della Valpolicella Classico Vigneto Monte Sant'Urbano - Doc
r • Valpolicella Classico Superiore Monte Sant'Urbano - Doc
s • Recioto della Valpolicella Classico I Comunai - Doc

Fratelli Tedeschi ♟♟♟♟
Località Pedemonte, via Verdi 4, tel. 0457701487
www.tedeschiwines.com
r • Amarone della Valpolicella Classico Capitel Monte Olmi - Doc
r • Amarone della Valpolicella La Fabriseria - Doc
r • Valpolicella Classico Superiore Capitel dei Nicalò - Doc
r • Rosso La Fabriseria Rosso del Veronese - Igt
s • Recioto della Valpolicella Classico Capitel Monte Fontana - Doc

Il Sestante ♟♟
Località Pedemonte, via Masua 11, tel. 0457701266
www.tommasiwine.it
r • Amarone della Valpolicella Classico Vigneto Monte Masua - Doc
r • Valpolicella Classico Superiore I Pianeti - Doc

Manara ♟
Località San Floriano, via Don Cesare Biasi 53, tel. 0457701086
www.manaravini.it
r • Amarone della Valpolicella Classico Postera - Doc
s • Recioto della Valpolicella Classico El Rocolo - Doc

Marchesi Fumanelli ♟
Località Squarano, tel. 0457704875
r • Valpolicella Classico Superiore - Doc
w • Terso Bianco del Veneto - Igt

Mizzon Giuseppe ♟
Località Pedemonte, via Quar 23, tel. 0457725705
r • Amarone della Valpolicella Classico - Doc
r • Valpolicella Classico Superiore - Doc

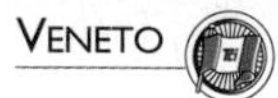

NICOLIS ANGELO E FIGLI
Via Villa Girardi 29, tel. 0457701261
www.vininicolis.com
- *r* • Amarone della Valpolicella Classico Ambrosan - Doc
- *r* • Valpolicella Classico Superiore Seccal - Doc
- *r* • Testal Rosso del Veronese - Igt
- *s* • Recioto della Valpolicella Classico - Doc
- *s* • Cà Girardi Passito Bianco - Igt

SANTA SOFIA
Località Pedemonte, via Ca' Dedé 61, tel. 0457701074
www.santasofia.com
- *r* • Amarone della Valpolicella Classico Gioè - Doc
- *r* • Bardolino Chiaretto Classico - Doc
- *r* • Valpolicella Classico Superiore Montegradella - Doc
- *w* • Soave Classico Superiore Costalta - Doc
- *s* • Recioto della Valpolicella Classico - Doc

TENUTA VILLA GIRARDI
Via Villa Girardi 1, tel. 0456801977
www.villagirardi.it
- *r* • Amarone della Valpolicella Classico - Doc
- *r* • Valpolicella Classico Superiore Bure Alto Ripasso - Doc

TOMMASI VITICOLTORI
Località Pedemonte, via Ronchetto 2, tel. 0457701266
www.tommasiwine.it
- *r* • Amarone della Valpolicella Classico - Doc
- *r* • Amarone della Valpolicella Classico Campo Cà Florian - Doc
- *r* • Valpolicella Classico Superiore Ripasso - Doc
- *r* • La Pieve della Conca d'Oro Rosso del Veronese - Igt
- *s* • Recioto della Valpolicella Classico Campo Fiorato - Doc

VANTINI LUIGI E FIGLI
Località San Floriano, via Ca' dell'Ebreo 7, tel. 0457701374
- *r* • Valpolicella Classico Superiore Ripasso - Doc

VENTURINI MASSIMINO
Località San Floriano Valpolicella, via Semonte 20, tel. 0457703320
azagrventurinimassimino@tin.it
- *r* • Amarone della Valpolicella Classico - Doc
- *r* • Valpolicella Classico Superiore Semonte Alto - Doc
- *s* • Recioto della Valpolicella Classico Le Brugnine - Doc

VILLA BELLINI
Località Castelrotto, via dei Froccaroli 6, tel. 0457725630
www.villabellini.com
- *r* • Valpolicella Classico Superiore Taso - Doc
- *s* • Recioto della Valpolicella Classico Amandorlato - Doc

SANT'AMBROGIO DI VALPOLICELLA
Verona km 19 • m 174

WINERIES

ALDEGHERI
Via A. Volta 9, tel. 0456861356
www.cantinealdegheri.it
- *r* • Amarone della Valpolicella Classico - Doc
- *r* • Amarone della Valpolicella Classico Riserva - Doc
- *r* • Recioto della Valpolicella Classico - Doc

FERRARI ALEARDO
Località Gargagnago, via Giare 15, tel. 0457701379
- *r* • Amarone della Valpolicella Classico - Doc
- *r* • Valpolicella Classico Superiore Corte Aleardi - Doc
- *r* • Valpolicella Classico Superiore Ripasso Bure Alto - Doc
- *s* • Recioto della Valpolicella Classico - Doc

MASI AGRICOLA
Località Gargagnago, via Monteleone, tel. 0456832511
www.masi.it
- *r* • Amarone della Valpolicella Classico Campolongo di Torbe - Doc
- *r* • Amarone della Valpolicella Classico Mazzano - Doc
- *r* • Recioto della Valpolicella Classico Amandorlato Mezzanella - Doc
- *r* • Valpolicella Classico Superiore - Doc
- *r* • Brolo di Campofiorin Rosso del Veronese - Igt
- *r* • Osar Rosso del Veronese - Igt
- *r* • Toar Rosso del Veronese - Igt

MERONI
Via Roma 16/A, tel. 0456861783
agricolameroni@tin.it
- *r* • Amarone della Valpolicella Classico Il Velluto - Doc
- *r* • Valpolicella Classico Superiore Il Velluto - Doc

SEREGO ALIGHIERI
Località Gargagnago, via Stazione, tel. 0457703622
www.seregoalighieri.it
- *r* • Amarone della Valpolicella Vajo Armaron - Doc
- *r* • Valpolicella Classico Superiore Possessioni Rosso Serègo Alighieri - Doc
- *s* • Recioto della Valpolicella Classico Casal dei Ronchi - Doc

VILLA MONTELEONE ★10%
Località Gargagnago, via Monteleone 12, tel. 0456800533
www.villamonteleone.com
- *r* • Amarone della Valpolicella Classico Campo San Paolo - Doc
- *r* • Valpolicella Classico Superiore Campo Santa Lena - Doc
- *r* • Valpolicella Classico Superiore Campo San Vito - Doc
- *s* • Recioto della Valpolicella Classico Palsun - Doc
- *s* • Raimondi Passito Bianco Veronese - Igt

SANTO STINO DI LIVENZA
Venice km 55 • m 6

WINERIES

TENUTA MOSOLE
Via Annone Veneto 60, tel. 0421310404
www.mosole.com
- *r* • Lison Pramaggiore Cabernet Hora Sexta - Doc
- *w* • Hora Sexta Bianco del Veneto Orientale - Igt

SELVAZZANO DENTRO
Padua km 9 • m 18

WINERIES

CONTE GIORDANO EMO CAPODILISTA
Via Montecchia 18, tel. 049637294
www.classica.it

r • Colli Euganei Cabernet Sauvignon Irenèo - Doc

La Montecchia ♟♟ ★10%
Via Montecchia 16, tel. 049637294
www.lamontecchia.it
r • Colli Euganei Merlot Bandiera - Doc
r • Colli Euganei Rosso Villa Capodilista - Doc
w • Colli Euganei Chardonnay - Doc

SOAVE

Verona km 21 • m 40

Wineries

Bisson ♟
Via Bisson 17, tel. 0457680775
vinibisson@tin.it
w • Soave Bissoncello - Doc
w • Soave Classico - Doc

Cantina del Castello ♟♟♟
Corte Pittora 5, tel. 0457680093
www.cantinacastello.it
w • Soave Classico Superiore Acini Soavi V.T. - Doc
s • Recioto di Soave Classico Cortepittora - Doc
s • Acini Dolci Veneto Bianco Passito - Igt

Coffele ♟♟
Via Roma 5, tel. 0457680007
www.coffele.it
w • Soave Classico Superiore Alzari - Doc
w • Soave Classico Superiore Cà Visco - Doc
s • Recioto di Soave Classico Le Sponde - Docg

Monte Tondo ♟
Via S. Lorenzo 89, tel. 0457680347
www.montetondo.it
w • Soave Classico Superiore Casette Foscarin - Doc

Pieropan ♟♟♟♟♟
Via Giulio Camuzzoni 3,
tel. 0456190171
www.pieropan.it
w • Soave Classico Superiore - Doc
w • Soave Classico Superiore Calvarino - Doc
w • Soave Classico Superiore La Rocca - Doc
s • Recioto di Soave Le Colombare - Docg
s • La Rocca Passito Bianco del Veneto - Igt

Suavia ♟♟♟
Località Fittà, via Centro 14, tel. 0457675089
www.suavia.it
w • Soave Classico Superiore Le Rive - Doc
w • Soave Classico Superiore Monte Carbonare - Doc
s • Recioto di Soave Acinatium - Doc

Tamellini ♟♟♟
Località Costeggiola, via Tamellini 4,
tel. 0457675328
w • Soave Classico Anguane - Doc
w • Soave Classico Le Bine - Doc
s • Recioto di Soave - Docg

SOMMACAMPAGNA

Verona km 13 • m 121

Wineries

Cavalchina ♟♟♟
Località Custoza, tel. 045516002
www.cavalchina.com
r • Bardolino Superiore Santa Lucia - Doc
rs • Bardolino Chiaretto - Doc
w • Bianco di Custoza Amadeo - Doc
s • La Rosa Veneto Bianco Passito - Igt
s • Le Pergole del Sole Müller Thurgau Dolce del Veneto - Igt

Gorgo ♟♟
Località Custoza, tel. 045516063
www.cantinagorgo.com
r • Bardolino Superiore Podere Montemaggiore - Doc
r • Il Rabitto Veneto Rosso - Igt
w • Bianco di Custoza Superiore Podere San Michelin - Doc

Le Vigne di San Pietro ♟♟♟
Via S. Pietro 23, tel. 045510016
r • I Balconi Rossi Rosso del Veneto - Igt
r • Refolà Cabernet Sauvignon del Veneto - Igt
rs • Bardolino Chiaretto - Doc
w • Bianco di Custoza San Pietro - Doc
s • Due Cuori - Vdt

SONA

Verona km 13 • m 169

Wineries

Fratelli Fabiano ♟♟
Via Verona 6, tel. 0456081111
www.fabiano.it
r • Amarone della Valpolicella Classico I Fondatori - Doc
r • Vajo Rosso Veronese - Igt
s • Recioto della Valpolicella Classico Rugola - Doc

Zamuner Daniele ♟♟
Via Valecchia 40, tel. 0458342168
www.zamuner.it
r • Valecchia Rosso Cabernet Sauvignon-Merlot del Veneto - Igt
w • Zamuner Brut - Vdt
w • Zamuner Brut Riserva - Vdt
w • Zamuner Extra Brut - Vdt
s • Passito Bianco Zamuner - Vdt

SPRESIANO

Treviso km 14 • m 56

Wineries

Tenconi ♟
Località Visnadello, via Papa Giovanni XXIII 19,
tel. 042292639
vinitenconi@libero.it
r • Friuli Aquileia Cabernet Sauvignon - Doc
w • Friuli Aquileia Bianco Natissa - Doc

SUSEGANA

Treviso km 22 • m 76

Wineries

Conte Collalto ♟
Via 24 maggio 1, tel. 0438738241
www.collalto.it
r • Wildbacher Colli Trevigiani - Igt
w • Prosecco di Conegliano Brut Castello di San Salvatore - Doc
w • Prosecco di Conegliano Extra Dry - Doc

VALDOBBIADENE

Treviso km 36 • m 253

Wineries

Bisol Desiderio e Figli ♟♟♟ ★10%
Località Santo Stefano, via Fol 33, tel. 0423900138
www.bisol.it

w • Prosecco di Valdobbiadene Spumante Dry Garnei - Doc
w • Prosecco di Valdobbiadene Spumante Extra Dry Vigneti del Fol - Doc
w • Prosecco di Valdobbiadene Spumante Superiore di Cartizze Dry - Doc
w • Spumante Eliseo Bisol Cuvée del Fondatore - Vdt
w • Spumante Pas Dosé Extra Brut Millesimato - Vdt

Bortolomiol ♟
Via Garibaldi 142, tel. 0423975794
info@bortolomiol.com
w • Prosecco di Valdobbiadene Dry - Doc
w • Prosecco di Valdobbiadene Extra Dry Selezione Banda Rossa - Doc

Canevel ♟♟♟
Via Roccat e Ferrari 17, tel. 0423975940
www.canevel.it
w • Prosecco di Valdobbiadene Spumante Brut - Doc
w • Prosecco di Valdobbiadene Spumante Extra Dry - Doc
w • Prosecco di Valdobbiadene Spumante Extra Dry Il Millesimato - Doc
w • Prosecco di Valdobbiadene Spumante Extra Dry Vigneto del Faé - Doc
w • Prosecco di Valdobbiadene Spumante Superiore di Cartizze Dry - Doc

Col Vetoraz ♟♟ ★10%
Località Santo Stefano, via Tresiese 1,
tel. 0423975291
colvetoraz@libero.it
w • Prosecco di Valdobbiadene Dry Millesimanto - Doc
w • Prosecco di Valdobbiadene Extra Dry - Doc
w • Prosecco di Valdobbiadene Superiore di Cartizze - Doc

Franco Nino Spumanti ♟♟♟♟
Via Garibaldi 147, tel. 0423972051
info@ninofranco.it
w • Prosecco di Valdobbiadene Brut Nino Franco - Doc
w • Prosecco di Valdobbiadene Secco Sassi Bianchi - Doc
w • Prosecco di Valdobbiadene Spumante Brut Rive di San Floriano - Doc
w • Prosecco di Valdobbiadene Spumante Primo Franco - Doc
w • Prosecco di Valdobbiadene Spumante Superiore di Cartizze - Doc

Le Colture ♟
Località Santo Stefano, via Follo 5,
tel. 0423900192
www.lecolture.it
w • Prosecco di Valdobbiadene Spumante Brut - Doc

Ruggeri & C. ♟♟♟♟
Via Prà Fontana, tel. 04239092
www.ruggeri.it
w • Prosecco di Valdobbiadene Spumante Brut - Doc
w • Prosecco di Valdobbiadene Spumante Dry Santo Stefano - Doc
w • Prosecco di Valdobbiadene Spumante Extra Dry Selezione Giustino B. - Doc
w • Prosecco di Valdobbiadene Spumante Superiore di Cartizze Dry - Doc
w • Prosecco di Valdobbiadene Tranquillo La Bastia Bianco del Tabellionato - Doc

Ruggeri Angelo - Le Bellerive ♟♟
Località Santo Stefano, via Follo 5, tel. 0423900235
info@lebellerive.it
w • Prosecco di Valdobbiadene Dry Funer - Doc
w • Prosecco di Valdobbiadene Extra Dry - Doc
w • Prosecco di Valdobbiadene Extra Superiore di Cartizze - Doc

Sant'Eurosia ♟♟
Località San Pietro di Barbozza, via della Cima 8,
tel. 0423973236
w • Prosecco di Valdobbiadene Brut - Doc
w • Prosecco di Valdobbiadene Dry Millesimanto - Doc
w • Prosecco di Valdobbiadene Extra Dry - Doc

VALEGGIO SUL MINCIO

Verona km 25 • m 88

Wineries

Corte Gardoni ♟♟♟
Località Gardoni, tel. 0457950382
www.cortegardoni.it
r • Bardolino Superiore - Doc
r • Garda Merlot Vallidium - Doc
r • Bardolino Chiaretto - Doc
w • Bianco di Custoza - Doc

VERONA

m 59

Wineries

Baltieri ♟♟♟
Località Mizzole, via Villa Piatti 5, tel. 045557616
r • Amarone della Valpolicella Sortilegio - Doc
r • Valpolicella Superiore Monte Paradiso - Doc
s • Recioto della Valpolicella Dolce della Regina - Doc

Beretta Cecilia ♟♟♟
Località San Felice Extra, via Belvedere 135,
tel. 0458402021
www.pasqua.it
r • Amarone della Valpolicella Classico Terre di Cariano - Doc
r • Valpolicella Classico Superiore Terre di Cariano - Doc
w • Soave Classico Brognoligo - Doc

Cantina Sociale Valpantena ♟♟♟
Località Quinto di Valpantena, via Orfani di Guerra 5/B, tel. 045550032
www.cantinavalpantena.it
r • Amarone della Valpolicella Falasco - Doc
r • Valpolicella Valpantena Ritocco - Doc
s • Recioto della Valpolicella Valpantena - Doc

Fratelli Bolla ♟♟
Piazza Cittadella 3, tel. 0458670911
www.bolla.it
r • Amarone della Valpolicella Classico Le Origini - Doc
r • Valpolicella Classico Superiore Le Poiane - Doc
w • Soave Classico Tufaie - Doc

Montresor Giacomo ♟♟♟
Via Ca' di Cozzi 16, tel. 045913399
www.vinimontresor.com

r • Amarone della Valpolicella Classico Capitel della Crosara - Doc
r • Valpolicella Classico Capitel della Crosara - Doc
w • Soave Classico Capitel Alto - Doc
s • Recioto della Valpolicella Re Teodorico - Doc
s • Terranatia Passito Bianco del Veneto - Igt

Poggio Toccalta ♟
Località Quinzano, via Arezovo 19/C, tel. 0458345559
www.poggiotoccalta.it
r • Valpolicella Superiore - Doc

Tezza Viticoltori in Valpantena ♟♟♟
Località Poiano, via Maioli 4, tel. 045550267
www.tezzawines.it
r • Amarone della Valpolicella Valpantena Monte delle Fontane - Doc
r • Amarone della Valpolicella Valpantena Brolo delle Giare - Doc
r • Valpolicella Valpantena Superiore Brolo delle Giare - Doc
s • Recioto della Valpolicella Valpantena - Doc
s • Brolo delle Giare Bianco Passito del Veneto - Igt

Vigneti e Cantine Pasqua ♟♟♟
Via Belviglieri 30, tel. 0458402111
www.pasqua.it
r • Amarone della Valpolicella Classico Villa Borghetti - Doc
r • Valpolicella Classico Superiore Vigneti Casterna - Doc
r • Fhior Veronese - Igt
r • Korae Rosso Veronese - Igt
w • Soave Classico Vigneti di Montegrande - Doc

VIDOR

Treviso km 30 • m 152

Wineries

Adami ♟♟♟♟ ★10%
Via Rovede 21, tel. 0423982110
www.adamispumanti.it
w • Prosecco di Valdobbiadene Giardino - Doc
w • Prosecco di Valdobbiadene Spumante Brut Bosco di Gica - Doc
w • Prosecco di Valdobbiadene Spumante Dry Vigneto Giardino - Doc
w • Prosecco di Valdobbiadene Spumante Extra Dry Dei Casel - Doc
w • Prosecco di Valdobbiadene Superiore di Cartizze Dry - Doc

De Faveri ♟♟
Località Bosco, via Sartori 21, tel. 0423987673
www.defaverispumanti.it
w • Prosecco di Valdobbiadene Brut Selezione - Doc
w • Prosecco di Valdobbiadene Dry Selezione - Doc

Sorelle Bronca ♟♟♟
Località Colbertaldo, via Martiri 20, tel. 0423987201
sorellebronca@wappi.com
r • Colli di Conegliano Rosso Ser Bele - Doc
w • Prosecco di Valdobbiadene Brut - Doc
w • Prosecco di Valdobbiadene Extra Dry - Doc

VILLAGA

Vicenza km 23 • m 45

Wineries

Piovene Porto Godi Alessandro ♟♟
Località Toara, via Villa 14, tel. 0444885142
tpiovene@protec.it
r • Colli Berici Cabernet Vigneto Pozzare - Doc
r • Colli Berici Merlot Fra i Broli - Doc

VITTORIO VENETO

Treviso km 40 • m 138

Wineries

Bellenda ♟♟ ★10%
Via Giardino 90, tel. 0438920025
www.bellenda.it
r • Colli di Conegliano Rosso Contrada di Concenigo - Doc
w • Prosecco di Conegliano Valdobbiadene Extra Dry - Doc
w • Prosecco di Conegliano Valdobbiadene Superiore di Cartizze Dry - Doc

VOLPAGO DEL MONTELLO

Treviso km 18 • m 94

Wineries

Conte Loredan Gasparini ♟♟♟
Località Venegazzù, via Martignago Alto 23, tel. 0423870024 www.venegazzu.com
r • Montello e Colli Asolani Cabernet Sauvignon - Doc
r • Loredan Gasparini Capo di Stato Colli Trevigiani - Igt
r • Venegazzù della Casa Colli Trevigiani Rosso - Igt

FRIULI-VENEZIA GIULIA

BAGNARIA ARSA

Udine km 23 • m 3/22

Wineries

Tenuta Beltrame ♟
Località Antonini 4, tel. 0432923670
tenutabeltrame@libero.it
r • Friuli Aquileia Cabernet Sauvignon Riserva - Doc
w • Friuli Aquileia Chardonnay Pribus - Doc
w • Friuli Aquileia Tocai Friulano - Doc

BERTIOLO

Udine km 22 • m 33

Wineries

Cabert - Cantina del Friuli ♟♟
Via Madonna 27, tel. 0432917434
r • Friuli Grave Merlot Riserva - Doc
w • Friuli Grave Chardonnay - Doc
w • Friuli Grave Sauvignon - Doc

BUTTRIO
Udine km 11 • m 79

WINERIES

BUIATTI LIVIO E CLAUDIO ♟♟
Via Lippe 25, tel. 0432674317
www.buiattivini.it
r • Colli Orientali del Friuli Merlot - Doc
w • Colli Orientali del Friuli Pinot Bianco - Doc
w • Colli Orientali del Friuli Sauvignon - Doc

CASTELLO DI BUTTRIO ♟♟♟
Via Morpurgo 9, tel. 0432673015
www.marcofelluga.it
r • Castello di Buttrio Rosso Marburg Venezia Giulia - Igt
w • Castello di Buttrio Bianco Ovestein Venezia Giulia - Igt

CONTE D'ATTIMIS MANIAGO - TENUTA SOTTOMONTE ♟♟♟
Via Sottomonte 21, tel. 0432674027
info@contedattimismaniago.it
r • Colli Orientali del Friuli Cabernet - Doc
r • Colli Orientali del Friuli Merlot - Doc
r • Colli Orientali del Friuli Refosco dal Peduncolo Rosso - Doc
r • Colli Orientali del Friuli Rosso Vignaricco - Doc
r • Colli Orientali del Friuli Tazzelenghe - Doc

DORIGO GIROLAMO ♟♟♟♟♟
Via del Pozzo 5, tel. 0432674268
girdorig@tin.it
r • Colli Orientali del Friuli Pignolo di Buttrio Vigneto Ronc di Juri - Doc
r • Colli Orientali del Friuli Refosco dal Peduncolo Rosso Vigneto Montsclapade - Doc
r • Colli Orientali del Friuli Rosso Montsclapade - Doc
r • Colli Orientali del Friuli Tazzelenghe di Buttrio Vigneto Ronc di Juri - Doc
w • Colli Orientali del Friuli Chardonnay Vigneto Ronc di Jury - Doc
w • Colli Orientali del Friuli Sauvignon Vigneto Ronc di Juri - Doc
s • Picolit Vigneto Montsclapade Venezia Giulia - Igt

MEROI DAVINO ♟♟♟♟♟
Via Stretta del Parco 7, tel. 0432674025
r • Colli Orientali del Friuli Rosso Ros di Buri - Doc
r • Dominin - Vdt
w • Colli Orientali del Friuli Bianco Blanc di Buri - Doc
w • Colli Orientali del Friuli Chardonnay - Doc
w • Colli Orientali del Friuli Sauvignon - Doc
w • Colli Orientali del Friuli Tocai Friulano - Doc
s • Colli Orientali del Friuli Picolit - Doc

MIANI ♟♟♟♟♟
Località Vicinale, via Peruzzi 10, tel. 0432674327
r • Colli Orientali del Friuli Merlot - Doc
r • Miani Rosso - Vdt
r • Refosco dal Peduncolo Rosso Vigna Calvari - Vdt
w • Colli Orientali del Friuli Chardonnay - Doc
w • Colli Orientali del Friuli Sauvignon - Doc
w • Colli Orientali del Friuli Tocai - Doc
w • Miani Bianco - Vdt

PETRUCCO ♟ ★10%
Via Morpurgo 12, tel. 0432674387
www.petrucco.com
w • Colli Orientali del Friuli Chardonnay - Doc
s • Colli Orientali del Friuli Picolit - Doc

VALLE ♟♟ ★10%
Via Nazionale 3, tel. 0432674289
www.valle.it
r • Colli Orientali del Friuli Cabernet Riserva Collezione Gigi Valle - Doc
r • Colli Orientali del Friuli Merlot Riserva Collezione Gigi Valle - Doc
w • Colli Orientali del Friuli Chardonnay Selezione Sans Blas barrique - Doc
w • Colli Orientali del Friuli Ribolla Gialla Selezione Sans Blas barrique - Doc
w • Colli Orientali del Friuli Riesling Selezione Araldica - Doc
w • Colli Orientali del Friuli Tocai Friulano Selezione Sans Blas - Doc
s • L'Ambrosie Selezione Sans Blas - Vdt

CAPRIVA DEL FRIULI
Gorizia km 10 • m 49

WINERIES

CASTELLO DI SPESSA ♟♟
Via Spessa 1, tel. 0481639914
www.castellospessa.com
r • Collio Merlot Torriani - Doc
r • Collio Rosso Conte di Spessa - Doc
w • Collio Pinot Bianco di Santarosa - Doc
w • Collio Ribolla Gialla - Doc
w • Collio Sauvignon Segré - Doc

FRATELLI PIGHIN ♟♟♟
Via S. Antonio 3, tel. 0432675444
azpighin@tin.it
w • Collio Chardonnay - Doc
w • Collio Pinot Bianco - Doc
w • Collio Pinot Grigio - Doc
w • Collio Sauvignon - Doc
w • Soreli Bianco - Igt

RONCUS ♟♟♟
Via Mazzini 26, tel. 0481809349
r • Merlot - Vdt
r • Val di Miez - Vdt
w • Pinot Bianco - Vdt
w • Sauvignon - Vdt
w • Tocai - Vdt

RUSSIZ SUPERIORE ♟♟♟♟
Via Russiz 7, tel. 048180328
www.marcofelluga.it
r • Collio Rosso Riserva degli Orzoni - Doc
w • Collio Bianco Russiz Disore - Doc
w • Collio Pinot Bianco - Doc
w • Collio Pinot Grigio - Doc
w • Collio Sauvignon - Doc
w • Collio Tocai Friulano - Doc
s • Verduzzo Venezia Giulia - Igt

SCHIOPETTO MARIO ♟♟♟♟♟
Via Palazzo vescovile 1, tel. 048180332
www.schiopetto.it
r • Rivarossa Rosso Venezia Giulia - Igt
w • Collio Pinot Bianco - Doc
w • Collio Pinot Grigio - Doc
w • Collio Ribolla Gialla - Doc
w • Collio Sauvignon - Doc
w • Collio Tocai Friulano - Doc
w • Blanc des Rosis Bianco Venezia Giulia - Igt

Vidussi - Gestioni Agricole - Podere di Spessa ♟♟
Via Spessa 18, tel. 048180072
r • Collio Rosso Are di Miùte - Doc
w • Collio Malvasia - Doc
w • Collio Ribolla Gialla - Doc
w • Collio Tocai Friulano Croce Alta - Doc
s • Colli Orientali del Friuli Picolit Soreli a Mont - Doc

Villa Russiz ♟♟♟♟♟
Via Russiz 6, tel. 048180047
www.villarussiz.it
r • Collio Merlot Graf de La Tour - Doc
w • Collio Chardonnay Gräfin de La Tour - Doc
w • Collio Malvasia - Doc
w • Collio Pinot Bianco - Doc
w • Collio Pinot Grigio - Doc
w • Collio Sauvignon de La Tour - Doc
w • Collio Tocai Friulano - Doc

CERVIGNANO DEL FRIULI

Udine km 30 • m 2

Wineries

Tenuta Ca' Bolani ♟
Via Ca' Bolani 1, tel. 043132670
info@cabolani.it
r • Friuli Aquileia Cabernet Franc - Doc
r • Friuli Aquileia Merlot - Doc

CIVIDALE DEL FRIULI

Udine km 17 • m 135

Wineries

Centa Sant'Anna ♟
Località Spessa, via Sant'Anna 5, tel. 0432716289
centasantanna@libero.it
r • Colli Orientali del Friuli Rosso Gastàlt - Doc

Dal Fari ♟♟ ★10%
Località Gagliano, via Darnazzacco 20, tel. 0432731219
www.vinodelfriuli.com
r • Colli Orientali del Friuli Rosso d'Orsone - Doc
w • Colli Orientali del Friuli Bianco delle Grazie - Doc
w • Colli Orientali del Friuli Chardonnay - Doc
w • Colli Orientali del Friuli Sauvignon - Doc
w • Colli Orientali del Friuli Tocai Friulano - Doc

Il Roncal ♟♟
Località Montebello, via Fornalis 100, tel. 0432716156
ilroncal@tin.it
r • Colli Orientali del Friuli Schioppettino - Doc
w • Colli Orientali del Friuli Bianco Ploe di Stelis - Doc

Moschioni Davide ♟♟♟♟
Località Gagliano, via Doria 30, tel. 0432730210
r • Colli Orientali del Friuli Pignolo - Doc
r • Colli Orientali del Friuli Refosco dal Peduncolo Rosso - Doc
r • Colli Orientali del Friuli Rosso Reàl - Doc
r • Colli Orientali del Friuli Schioppettino - Doc
s • Colli Orientali del Friuli Picolit - Doc

Rodaro Paolo ♟♟
Via Cormons 60, tel. 0432716066
paolorodaro@yahoo.it
r • Colli Orientali del Friuli Merlot Romain - Doc
r • Colli Orientali del Friuli Refosco dal Peduncolo Rosso - Doc
w • Colli Orientali del Friuli Sauvignon - Doc
w • Ronc Venezia Giulia Bianco - Igt
s • Colli Orientali del Friuli Verduzzo Friulano - Doc

CORMONS

Gorizia km 13 • m 56

Wineries

Borgo del Tiglio ♟♟♟♟♟
Località Brazzano, via S. Giorgio 71, tel. 048162166
r • Collio Rosso della Centa - Doc
w • Collio Bianco Studio di Bianco - Doc
w • Collio Chardonnay Selezione Cà delle Vallade - Doc
w • Collio Malvasia Selezione - Doc
w • Collio Tocai Ronco della Chiesa - Doc

Borgo San Daniele ♟♟♟♟
Via S. Daniele 16, tel. 048160552
borgosandaniele@tin.it
r • Arbis Rosso Venezia Giulia - Igt
r • Gortmarin Rosso Venezia Giulia - Igt
w • Isonzo Bianco Arbis - Doc
w • Isonzo Pinot Grigio - Doc
w • Isonzo Tocai Friulano - Doc

Branko - Igor Erzetic ♟♟
Località Zegla 20, tel. 0481639826
w • Collio Pinot Grigio - Doc
w • Collio Sauvignon - Doc
w • Collio Tocai Friulano - Doc

Caccese Paolo ♟♟
Località Pradis 6, tel. 048161062
w • Collio Pinot Bianco - Doc
w • Collio Pinot Grigio - Doc
w • Collio Tocai Friulano - Doc

Cantina Produttori di Cormons ♟ ★20%
Via Vino della Pace 31, tel. 048161798
www.cormons.com
w • Collio Bianco Collio e Collio - Doc
w • Collio Ribolla Gialla - Doc
w • Friuli Isonzo Bianco Pietraverde - Doc

Colle Duga ♟♟
Località Zegla, tel. 048161177
r • Collio Merlot - Doc
w • Collio Bianco - Doc
w • Collio Chardonnay - Doc
w • Collio Pinot Grigio - Doc
w • Collio Tocai Friulano - Doc

Drius ♟♟
Via Filanda 100, tel. 048160998
r • Friuli Isonzo Merlot - Doc
w • Collio Sauvignon - Doc
w • Collio Tocai Friulano - Doc
w • Friuli Isonzo Pinot Bianco - Doc
w • Friuli Isonzo Pinot Grigio - Doc

Fain Luigi ♟♟
Via Zorutti 8, tel. 048160038
www.fainluigi.com
w • Isonzo Pinot Bianco - Doc
w • Isonzo Pinot Grigio - Doc
w • Isonzo Tocai - Doc

Felluga Livio ♟♟♟♟♟
Località Brazzano, via Risorgimento 1, tel. 048160203
www.liviofelluga.it

r • Colli Orientali del Friuli Merlot Riserva Sossò - Doc
r • Colli Orientali del Friuli Refosco dal Peduncolo Rosso - Doc
w • Colli Orientali del Friuli Bianco Illivio - Doc
w • Colli Orientali del Friuli Pinot Grigio - Doc
w • Colli Orientali del Friuli Sauvignon - Doc
w • Colli Orientali del Friuli Tocai - Doc
s • Colli Orientali del Friuli Rosazzo Picolit Riserva - Doc

KEBER RENATO ♟♟♟
Località Zegla 15, tel. 048161196
r • Collio Merlot Grici - Doc
w • Collio Bianco Beli Grici - Doc
w • Collio Chardonnay Grici - Doc
w • Collio Pinot Bianco Zegla - Doc
w • Collio Pinot Grigio - Doc
w • Collio Sauvignon Grici - Doc
w • Collio Tocai Grici - Doc

LA BOATINA ♟
Via Corona 62, tel. 048160445
www.boatina.com
r • Collio Rosso Riserva Picol Maggiore - Doc
w • Collio Bianco Pertè - Doc
s • Perlé Venezia Giulia Bianco - Igt

PICECH ♟♟
Località Pradis 11, tel. 048160347
picech@libero.it
w • Collio Bianco Jelka - Doc
w • Collio Malvasia - Doc
w • Collio Pinot Bianco - Doc

POLENCIC ALDO ♟♟♟
Località Pessiva 13, tel. 048161027
r • Collio Merlot degli Ulivi - Doc
w • Collio Pinot Bianco degli Ulivi - Doc
w • Collio Pinot Grigio - Doc
w • Collio Sauvignon - Doc
w • Collio Tocai Friulano - Doc

PRINCIC ALESSANDRO ♟♟♟
Località Pradis 5, tel. 048160723
prcarl@libero.it
r • Collio Merlot - Doc
w • Collio Malvasia - Doc
w • Collio Pinot Bianco - Doc

PRINCIC MAURIZIO - RONCO DI ZEGLA ♟♟
Località Zegla 12, tel. 048161155
w • Collio Pinot Grigio - Doc
w • Collio Sauvignon - Doc
w • Collio Tocai - Doc

RACCARO DARIO ♟♟
Località Rolat, via S. Giovanni 87, tel. 048161425
w • Collio Bianco - Doc
w • Collio Malvasia - Doc
w • Collio Tocai Friulano - Doc

RONCO DEI TASSI ♟♟
Località Monte 38, tel. 048160155
www.roncodeitassi.it
r • Collio Rosso Cjarandon - Doc
w • Collio Sauvignon - Doc
w • Collio Tocai Friulano - Doc

RONCO DEL GELSO ♟♟♟
Via Isonzo 117, tel. 048161310
r • Isonzo Cabernet Franc - Doc
w • Isonzo Pinot Bianco - Doc
w • Isonzo Pinot Grigio Sot Lis Rivis - Doc
w • Isonzo Sauvignon - Doc
w • Isonzo Tocai Friulano - Doc

STURM OSCAR ♟
Località Zegla 1, tel. 048160720
sturm@sturm.it
r • Collio Merlot - Doc
w • Collio Pinot Grigio - Doc

SUBIDA DI MONTE ♟♟
Località Monte 9, tel. 048161011
subida@liberto.it
r • Collio Merlot Cristian Antonutti - Doc
r • Collio Rosso Poncaia - Doc
w • Collio Chardonnay Cristian Antonutti - Doc

TENUTA DI ANGORIS ♟
Località Angoris 7, tel. 048160923
www.angoris.it
r • Collio Merlot Podere Ronco Antico - Doc
w • Colli Orientali del Friuli Bianco Spìule - Doc

TIARE - ROBERTO SNIDG ♟♟♟
Via Monte 58, tel. 048160064
www.tiaredoc.com
w • Collio Bianco Cuvée Bianco - Doc
w • Collio Chardonnay - Doc
w • Collio Pinot Bianco - Doc
w • Collio Ribolla Gialla Tiare - Doc
w • Collio Sauvignon Tiare - Doc

TOROS FRANCO ♟♟
Via Novali 12, tel. 048161327
r • Collio Merlot Selezione - Doc
w • Collio Pinot Bianco - Doc
w • Collio Pinot Grigio - Doc
w • Collio Sauvignon - Doc
w • Collio Tocai Friulano - Doc

VILLA MARTINA ♟♟
Località Ca' delle Vallate, tel. 048160733
www.villamartina.it
r • Villa Martina Cabernet Franc Venezia Giulia - Igt
w • Collio Sauvignon - Doc
w • Collio Tocai Friulano - Doc

CORNO DI ROSAZZO

Udine km 23 • m 88

WINERIES

BUTUSSI VALENTINO ♟♟
Via Pra di Corte 1, tel. 0432759194
www.butussi.it
r • Colli Orientali del Friuli Cabernet Sauvignon Vigna Prà di Corte - Doc
w • Colli Orientali del Friuli Chardonnay Vigna Prà di Corte - Doc
w • Colli Orientali del Friuli Sauvignon Vigna Prà di Corte - Doc
w • Colli Orientali del Friuli Tocai Friulano - Doc
s • Colli Orientali del Friuli Picolit - Doc

CA' DI BON ♟
Via Casali Gallo 1, tel. 0432759316
cadibon55@tin.it
w • Colli Orientali del Friuli Ribolla Gialla - Doc
w • Colli Orientali del Friuli Tocai Friulano - Doc
w • Friuli Grave Sauvignon - Doc

GIGANTE ♟♟
Via Rocca Bernarda 3, tel. 0432755835
w • Colli Orientali del Friuli Chardonnay - Doc
w • Colli Orientali del Friuli Pinot Grigio - Doc
w • Colli Orientali del Friuli Tocai Friulano Storico - Doc

Perusini ♟♟
Località Gramogliano, via Torrione 13,
tel. 0432675018
info@perusini.com
r • Colli Orientali del Friuli Rosso del Postiglione - Doc
w • Colli Orientali del Friuli Pinot Grigio - Doc
s • Colli Orientali del Friuli Picolit - Doc

Specogna
Località Rocca Bernarda 4, tel. 0432755840
r • Colli Orientali del Friuli Merlot - Doc
w • Colli Orientali del Friuli Sauvignon - Doc
w • Colli Orientali del Friuli Tocai - Doc
s • Colli Orientali del Friuli Picolit - Doc
s • Colli Orientali del Friuli Verduzzo - Doc

Visintini Andrea ♟♟♟
Via Gramogliano 27, tel. 0432755813
info@vinivisintini.com
w • Colli Orientali del Friuli Bianco - Doc
w • Colli Orienali del Friuli Pinot Bianco - Doc
w • Colli Orientali del Friuli Pinot Grigio - Doc
w • Colli Orientali del Friuli Ribolla Gialla - Doc
w • Collio Tocai Friulano - Doc

Zof ♟♟♟
Via Giovanni XXIII nr. 32/A, tel. 0432759673
info@zof.it
r • Va Pensiero - Vdt
w • Colli Orientali del Friuli Bianco Sonata - Doc
w • Colli Orientali del Friuli Sauvignon - Doc
w • Colli Orientali del Friuli Tocai Friulano - Doc
s • Colli Orientali del Friuli Picolit - Doc

DOLEGNA DEL COLLIO

Gorizia km 24 • m 90

Wineries

Ca' Ronesca ♟♟♟
Località Lonzano 27, tel. 048160034
www.caronesca.it
r • Collio Cabernet Franc Podere San Giacomo - Doc
w • Collio Bianco Marnà - Doc
w • Collio Bianco Sermar - Doc
w • Collio Ribolla Gialla - Doc
w • Colli Orientali del Friuli Pinot Grigio del Podere di Ipplis - Doc
w • Colli Orientali del Friuli Sauvignon del Podere di Ipplis - Doc
s • Colli Orientali del Friuli Picolit - Doc

La Rajade ♟♟
Località Restocina 12, tel. 0481639897
r • Collio Cabernet Sauvignon Stratin - Doc
r • Collio Merlot Riserva - Doc

Venica & Venica ♟♟♟♟
Località Cerò, via Mernico 42, tel. 048161264
r • Collio Merlot Perilla - Doc
r • Bottaz Refosco dal Peduncolo Rosso Venezia Giulia - Igt
w • Collio Bianco Tre Vignis - Doc
w • Collio Chardonnay Ronco Bernizza - Doc
w • Collio Rosso Rosso delle Cime - Doc
w • Collio Sauvignon Ronco delle Mele - Doc
w • Collio Tocai Friulano Ronco delle Cime - Doc

DUINO-AURISINA

Trieste km 16 • m 343

Wineries

Kante ♟♟♟♟
Località Prepotto 1/A, tel. 040200255
r • Carso Terrano - Doc
w • Carso Chardonnay - Doc
w • Carso Malvasia - Doc
w • Carso Sauvignon - Doc
w • Carso Vitovska - Doc

Zidarich ♟♟♟♟
Località Prepotto 23, tel. 040201223
www.zidarich.com
r • Carso Terrano - Doc
w • Carso Malvasia - Doc
w • Carso Vitovska - Doc
w • Prulke - Vdt

FARRA D'ISONZO

Gorizia km 10 • m 46

Wineries

Jermann ♟♟♟
Località Villanova, via Monte Fortino 21,
tel. 0481888080
w • Capo Martino in Ruttaris - Vdt
w • Chardonnay - Vdt
w • Müller Thurgau - Vdt
w • Sauvignon - Vdt
w • Vinnae - Vdt
w • Vintage Tunina - Vdt
w • Where the Dreams now it is just wine - Vdt

Tenuta Villanova ♟♟
Via Contessa Beretta 29, tel. 0481888013
r • Collio Cabernet Sauvignon Monte Cucco - Doc
w • Collio Chardonnay Monte Cucco - Doc
w • Collio Tocai - Doc
w • Isonzo del Friuli Malvasia - Doc
w • Isonzo del Friuli Sauvignon Vigna Sassoline - Doc

GONARS

Udine km 20 • m 21

Wineries

Di Lenardo ♟♟
Località Ontagnano, via Cesare Battisti 1,
tel. 0432928633
www.dilenardo.it
r • Ronco Nolé - Vdt
w • Friuli Grave Chardonnay Woody - Doc
w • Friuli Grave Pinot Bianco Vigne dai Vieris - Doc
w • Friuli Grave Sauvignon Vigne dai Vieris - Doc
w • Father's Eye Venezia Giulia Bianco - Igt

GORIZIA

m 84

Wineries

Conti Attems ♟♟♟
Località Lucinico, via Giulio Cesare 36/A,
tel. 0481393619
virginia.attems@attems.it
w • Collio Pinot Grigio Attems - Doc
w • Collio Ribolla Gialla - Doc
w • Collio Sauvignon Attems - Doc

Damijan ♟♟♟♟
Via Brigata Pavia 61, tel. 048178217
r • Collio Rosso - Doc
w • Collio Bianco - Doc
w • Collio Ribolla Gialla - Doc

Fiegl ♟♟♟
Località Oslavia, tel. 048131072
www.fieglvini.com
r • Collio Merlot - Doc
r • Leopold Cuvée Rouge Venezia Giulia - Igt
w • Collio Pinot Bianco - Doc
w • Collio Pinot Grigio - Doc
w • Collio Ribolla Gialla - Doc
w • Collio Sauvignon - Doc
w • Collio Tocai Friulano - Doc

Gravner Francesco ♟♟♟♟♟
Via Lenzuolo Bianco 9, tel. 048130882
www.remedia.it/gravner
r • Rosso Gravner - Igt
w • Collio Bianco Breg - Doc
w • Collio Ribolla - Doc

Il Carpino ♟♟♟♟
Via Sovenza 14/A, tel. 0481884097
www.ilcarpino.com
r • Rosso Carpino - Vdt
w • Collio Ribolla Gialla - Doc
w • Collio Sauvignon - Doc
w • Collio Sauvignon Vigna Runc - Doc
w • Bianco Carpino - Vdt

La Castellada ♟♟♟♟
Località Oslavia 1, tel. 048133670
r • Collio Rosso della Castellada - Doc
w • Collio Chardonnay - Doc
w • Collio Bianco della Castellada - Doc
w • Collio Ribolla Gialla - Doc
s • Colli Orientali del Friuli Picolit Monastrium Rosarium - Doc

Primosic ♟♟♟
Località Madonnina di Oslavia 3, tel. 0481535153
www.primosic.com
r • Collio Merlot Riserva - Doc
w • Collio Chardonnay Gmajne - Doc
w • Collio Pinot Grigio Gmajne - Doc
w • Collio Ribolla Gialla Gmajne - Doc
w • Collio Sauvignon Gmajne - Doc

Radikon ♟♟♟♟
Località Oslavia, tel. 048132804
w • Collio Bianco Oslavje - Doc
w • Collio Ribolla Gialla - Doc

GRADISCA D'ISONZO

Gorizia km 12 • m 32

Wineries

Felluga Marco ♟♟♟
Via Gorizia 121, tel. 048199164
www.marcofelluga.it
r • Carantan Venezia Giulia Rosso - Igt
w • Collio Bianco Molamatta - Doc
w • Collio Pinot Grigio - Doc
w • Collio Ribolla Gialla Bellanotte - Doc
w • Collio Sauvignon - Doc
w • Collio Tocai Friulano - Doc
s • Moscato Rosa Venezia Giulia - Igt

MANZANO

Udine km 16 • m 71

Wineries

Cencig Nicola e Mauro ♟♟
Via Sottomonte 171, tel. 0432740789
www.cencig.com
r • Colli Orientali del Friuli Merlot - Doc
r • Colli Orientali del Friuli Refosco dal Peduncolo Rosso - Doc
w • Colli Orientali del Friuli Sauvignon Vigna Dolina - Doc

Colutta Gianpaolo ♟♟
Via Orsaria 32, tel. 0432510654
www.coluttagianpaolo.com
r • Colli Orientali del Friuli Schioppettino - Doc
r • Colli Orientali del Friuli Tazzelenghe - Doc
w • Colli Orientali del Friuli Pinot Bianco - Doc

Colutta Giorgio ♟♟
Via Orsaria 32, tel. 0432740315
www.colutta.it
w • Colli Orientali del Friuli Ribolla Gialla - Doc
w • Colli Orientali del Friuli Sauvignon - Doc
w • Colli Orientali del Friuli Tocai Friulano - Doc

Filiputti Walter ♟♟♟♟
Località Rosazzo, piazza dell'Abbazia 15, tel. 0432759429
r • Colli Orientali del Friuli Pignolo - Doc
r • Colli Orientali del Friuli Rosso Ronco dei Domenicani - Doc
w • Colli Orientali del Friuli Bianco Poiesis - Doc
w • Colli Orientali del Friuli Bianco Ronco degli Agostiniani - Doc
w • Colli Orientali del Friuli Ribolla Gialla - Doc
w • Colli Orientali del Friuli Sauvignon Suvignis - Doc
s • Colli Orientali del Friuli Picolit Riserva Abbazia di Rosazzo - Doc

Le Vigne di Zamò ♟♟♟♟♟
Località Rosazzo, via Abate Corrado 4, tel. 0432759693
www.levignedizamo.com
r • Colli Orientali del Friuli Merlot Vigne Cinquant'anni - Doc
r • Colli Orientali del Friuli Refosco dal Peduncolo Rosso - Doc
r • Colli Orientali del Friuli Rosso Ronco dei Roseti - Doc
w • Colli Orientali del Friuli Bianco Ronco delle Acacie - Doc
w • Colli Orientali del Friuli Pinot Bianco Tullio Zamò - Doc
w • Colli Orientali del Friuli Sauvignon - Doc
w • Colli Orientali del Friuli Friulano Tocai Vigne Cinquant'anni - Doc

Midolini ♟♟♟
Via Udine 40, tel. 0432754555
www.midolini.com
r • Colli Orientali del Friuli Refosco dal Peduncolo Rosso - Doc
r • Colli Orientali del Friuli Rosso Soresta'nt Ròs - Doc
w • Colli Orientali del Friuli Pinot Grigio - Doc
w • Colli Orientali del Friuli Sauvignon - Doc
w • Colli Orientali del Friuli Tocai Friulano - Doc

Ronchi di Manzano ♟♟♟
Via Orsaria 42, tel. 0432740718
www.ronchidimanzano.it
r • Colli Orientali del Friuli Merlot Ronc di Subule - Doc
r • Colli Orientali del Friuli Refosco dal Peduncolo Rosso - Doc
r • Colli Orientali del Friuli Rosazzo Rosso - Doc
r • Le Zuccule Rosso Venezia Giulia - Igt

w • Colli Orientali del Friuli Chardonnay - Doc
w • Colli Orientali del Friuli Sauvignon - Doc
s • Colli Orientali del Friuli Rosazzo Picolit Ronc di Rosazzo - Doc

Ronco delle Betulle ♟♟♟
Via Colonna 24,
tel. 0432740547
www.roncodellebetulle.it
r • Colli Orientali del Friuli Rosazzo Rosso Nso - Doc
w • Colli Orientali del Friuli Rosazzo Bianco Nso - Doc
w • Colli Orientali del Friuli Rosazzo Ribolla Gialla - Doc
w • Colli Orientali del Friuli Sauvignon - Doc
w • Colli Orientali del Friuli Tocai Friulano - Doc

Rosa Bosco ♟♟♟♟
Località Rosazzo, via Abate Colonna 20,
tel. 0432751522
r • Colli Orientali del Friuli Rosso Boscorosso - Doc
w • Colli Orientali del Friuli Sauvignon Blanc - Doc

Torre Rosazza ♟♟
Località Poggiobello, tel. 0432750180
r • Colli Orientali del Friuli Merlot L'Altromerlot - Doc
r • Colli Orientali del Friuli Refosco dal Peduncolo Rosso - Doc
w • Colli Orientali del Friuli Chardonnay - Doc
w • Colli Orientali del Friuli Pinot Bianco Ronco delle Magnolie - Doc
w • Colli Orientali del Friuli Sauvignon Silterra - Doc

MARIANO DEL FRIULI

Gorizia km 14 • m 32

Wineries

Luisa Eddi ♟
Località Corona, via Cormons 19,
tel. 048169680
www.viniluisa.com
r • Isonzo del Friuli Merlot I Ferretti Terre Rosse di Corona - Doc
r • Isonzo del Friuli Refosco dal Peduncolo Rosso I Ferretti - Doc
w • Isonzo del Friuli Chardonnay I Ferretti Terre Rosse di Corona - Doc

Masut da Rive ♟♟♟♟
Via Manzoni 82, tel. 048169200
masutdarive@libero.it
r • Isonzo Merlot - Doc
w • Isonzo Chardonnay Maurus - Doc
w • Isonzo Pinot Bianco - Doc
w • Isonzo Pinot Grigio Maurus - Doc
w • Isonzo Sauvignon - Doc

Vie di Romans ♟♟♟♟♟
Località Vie di Romans 1, tel. 048169600
viediromans@tiscalinet.it
r • Isonzo Rosso Voos dai Ciamps - Doc
w • Isonzo Bianco Flors di Uis - Doc
w • Isonzo Chardonnay Vie di Romans - Doc
w • Isonzo Sauvignon Pière - Doc
w • Isonzo Sauvignon Vieris - Doc

MOSSA

Gorizia km 6 • m 59

Wineries

Vazzoler Redi ♟♟
Località Blanchis, tel. 0432505807
w • Collio Chardonnay - Doc
w • Collio Pinot Bianco - Doc
w • Collio Pinot Grigio - Doc
w • Collio Sauvignon - Doc
w • Ronco Blanchis - Vdt

NIMIS

Udine km 17 • m 207

Wineries

Coos Dario ♟♟♟
Località Ramandolo, via Pescia 1,
tel. 0432790320
darioccos@libero.it
w • Colli Orientali del Friuli Ramandolo Il Longhino - Doc
s • Colli Orientali del Friuli Picolit Romandus - Doc

Dri Giovanni - Il Roncat ♟♟♟
Località Ramandolo, via Pescia 7, tel. 0432790260
www.drironcat.com
w • Colli Orientali del Friuli Refosco dal Peduncolo Rosso - Doc
w • Colli Orientali del Friuli Sauvignon V.T. Il Roncat - Doc
s • Colli Orientali del Friuli Picolit - Doc
s • Colli Orientali del Friuli Ramandolo Il Roncat - Doc
s • Colli Orientali del Friuli Ramandolo Uve Decembrine - Doc

La Roncaia - Zuvin ♟♟
Località Cergneu, via Verdi 26, tel. 0432790280
www.laroncaia.com
r • Colli Orientali del Friuli Rosso Gheppio - Doc
r • Il Fusco Rosso delle Venezie - Igt
s • Colli Orientali del Friuli Ramandolo - Doc

PALAZZOLO DELLO STELLA

Udine km 34 • m 5

Wineries

Isola Augusta ♟
Casali Isola Augusta 4, tel. 043158046
www.isolaugusta.com
r • Augusteo - Vdt
w • Friuli Latisana Sauvignon - Doc

PAVIA DI UDINE

Udine km 10 • m 45/77

Wineries

Fratelli Pighin ♟♟
Località Risano, viale Grado 1, tel. 0432675444
azpighin@tin.it
r • Friuli Grave Rosso Risano - Doc
r • Baredo Rosso Venezia Giulia - Igt
w • Friuli Grave Sauvignon Vigna Casette - Doc

Le Fredis - Scarbolo ♟♟
Località Lauzacco, viale Grado 4,
tel. 0432675612
r • Friuli Grave Merlot Campo del Viotto - Doc
r • Friuli Grave Refosco dal Peduncolo Rosso Campo del Viotto - Doc
w • Friuli Grave Sauvignon - Doc

PORCIA

Pordenone km 4 • m 29

WINERIES

PRINCIPI DI PORCIA - CASTELLO DI PORCIA ♟
Via Castello 1, tel. 0434921408
www.porcia.com
w • Friuli Grave Chardonnay Cà Bembo - Doc
w • Friuli Grave Pinot Grigio Cà Bembo - Doc

SAN SIMONE ♟ ★10%
Via Prata 30, tel. 0434578633
www.sansimone.it
r • Friuli Grave Cabernet Sauvignon Vigneti Sant'Helena - Doc

PRAVISDOMINI
Pordenone km 23 • m 11

WINERIES

PODERE DEL GER ♟♟
Strada della Meduna 13, tel. 0434644452
info@poderedelger.it
r • Lison Pramaggiore Merlot - Doc
r • El Masut Rosso delle Venezie - Igt
w • Limine Verduzzo delle Venezie - Igt

PREMARIACCO
Udine km 13 • m 112

WINERIES

BASTIANICH ♟♟♟
Casali Ottelio 7, tel. 0432675612
bastianich@aol.it
r • Calabrone Rosso - Vdt
w • Colli Orientali del Friuli Tocai Friulano Plus - Doc
w • Vespa Bianco - Vdt

ERMACORA ♟
Località Ipplis, via Solzaredo 9, tel. 0432716250
www.ermacora.com
w • Colli Orientali del Friuli Tocai Friulano - Doc

FIORE DEI LIBERI ♟♟♟
Località Rocca Bernarda, via Case Sparse 21, tel. 0432716501
fioredeiliberi@tin.it
r • Colli Orientali del Friuli Merlot Camillo - Doc
r • Colli Orientali del Friuli Rosso Cassiopea - Doc
w • Colli Orientali del Friuli Chardonnay Flysch - Doc
w • Colli Orientali del Friuli Pinot Bianco - Doc
w • Colli Orientali del Friuli Ribolla Gialla - Doc

LA TUNELLA ♟
Località Ipplis, via del Collio 14, tel. 0432716030
www.latunella.it
r • Colli Orientali del Friuli Rosso L'one - Doc

ROCCA BERNARDA ♟♟♟
Località Ipplis, via Rocca Bernarda 27, tel. 0432716273
www.roccabernarda.com
r • Colli Orientali del Friuli Merlot Centis - Doc
w • Colli Orientali del Friuli Chardonnay - Doc
w • Colli Orientali del Friuli Sauvignon - Doc
w • Colli Orientali del Friuli Tocai Friulano - Doc
s • Colli Orientali del Friuli Picolit - Doc

SCUBLA ROBERTO ♟♟♟ ★10%
Località Ipplis, via Rocca Bernarda 22, tel. 0432716258
www.scubla.com
r • Colli Orientali del Friuli Rosso Scuro - Doc
w • Colli Orientali del Friuli Bianco Pomédes - Doc
w • Colli Orientali del Friuli Pinot Bianco - Doc
w • Colli Orientali del Friuli Sauvignon - Doc
w • Colli Orientali del Friuli Tocai Friulano - Doc

VIGNE FANTIN NODA'R ♟♟
Via Casali Otellio 4, tel. 043428735
vignefantin@libero.it
r • Colli Orientali del Friuli Cabernet - Doc
r • Colli Orientali del Friuli Rosso Carato - Doc
w • Colli Orientali del Friuli Bianco Carato - Doc

PREPOTTO
Udine km 21 • m 105

WINERIES

GRILLO IOLE ♟
Via Albana 60, tel. 0432713201
www.vinigrillo.it
r • Colli Orientali del Friuli Schioppettino - Doc

LA VIARTE ♟♟♟
Via Novacuzzo 50, tel. 0432759458
www.laviarte.it
r • Colli Orientali del Friuli Refosco dal Peduncolo Rosso - Doc
r • Colli Orientali del Friuli Rosso Rol - Doc
w • Colli Orientali del Friuli Bianco Liende - Doc
w • Colli Orientali del Friuli Tocai Friulano - Doc
s • Siùm - Vdt

LE DUE TERRE ♟♟♟♟♟
Via Roma 68/B, tel. 0432713189
r • Colli Orientali del Friuli Merlot - Doc
r • Colli Orientali del Friuli Pinot Nero - Doc
r • Colli Orientali del Friuli Rosso Sacrisassi - Doc
w • Colli Orientali del Friuli Bianco Sacrisassi - Doc

MARINIG ♟♟
Via Brolo 41, tel. 0432713012
www.marinig.it
r • Biel Cur - Vdt

PETRUSSA ♟♟♟
Via Albana 49, tel. 0432713192
www.petrussa.it
r • Colli Orientali del Friuli Rosso Petrussa Rosso - Doc
r • Colli Orientali del Friuli Schioppettino - Doc
w • Colli Orientali del Friuli Bianco Petrussa - Doc

PIZZULIN GIORDANO ♟♟
Via Albana 27, tel. 0432713073
www.pizzulin.com
r • Colli Orientali del Friuli Schioppettino - Doc
w • Colli Orientali del Friuli Tocai Friulano - Doc

RONCHI DI CIALLA ♟♟♟
Località Cialla 47, tel. 0432731679
www.ronchidicialla.com
r • Colli Orientali del Friuli Cialla Refosco dal Peduncolo Rosso - Doc
r • Colli Orientali del Friuli Schioppettino - Doc
w • Colli Orietali del Friuli Cialla Bianco Ciallabianco - Doc
s • Colli Orientali del Friuli Cialla Picolit - Doc
s • Colli Orientali del Friuli Cialla Verduzzo - Doc

RONCO DEI PINI ♟♟
Via Ronchi 93, tel. 0432713239
www.roncodeipini.com
r • Colli Orientali del Friuli Cabernet - Doc
r • Limes - Vdt
w • Leucòs - Vdt

RONCO SEVERO ♟♟
Via Ronchi 93, tel. 043374017
w • Colli Orientali del Friuli Chardonnay - Doc

w • Colli Orientali del Friuli Pinot Grigio - Doc
w • Colli Orientali del Friuli Tocai Friulano - Doc

Tenuta di Novacuzzo ♟♟
Via Novacuzzo 42, tel. 0432713005
w • Colli Orientali del Friuli Pinot Grigio - Doc

Vigna Petrussa ♟
Via Albana 47, tel. 0432713021
www.vignapetrussa.it
s • Colli Orientali del Friuli Picolit - Doc

Vigna Traverso ♟♟♟
Via Ronchi 73, tel. 0432713072
r • Colli Orientali del Friuli Merlot Riserva Sottocastello - Doc
r • Colli Orientali del Friuli Refosco dal Peduncolo Rosso - Doc
w • Colli Orientali del Friuli Chardonnay - Doc
w • Colli Orientali del Friuli Pinot Grigio - Doc
w • Colli Orientali del Friuli Sauvignon - Doc

RONCHI DEI LEGIONARI
Gorizia km 21 • m 11

Wineries

Do Ville ♟
Via Mitraglieri 2, tel. 0481775561
info@doville.it
w • Friuli Isonzo Chardonnay Barrique Do Ville - Doc
w • Friuli Isonzo Pinot Grigio Do Ville - Doc
w • Friuli Isonzo Sauvignon Ars Vivendi - Doc

SACILE
Pordenone km 12 • m 25

Wineries

Vistorta ♟♟
Località Vistorta, tel. 043471135
www.vistorta.it
r • Friuli Grave Merlot Vistorta - Doc

SAGRADO
Gorizia km 15 • m 32

Wineries

Castelvecchio ♟♟♟
Via Castelnuovo 2, tel. 048199742
www.castelvecchio.com
r • Carso Refosco dal Peduncolo Rosso - Doc
r • Sagrado Rosso Cuvée Privata Giovanni Bignucolo Venezia Giulia - Igt
w • Carso Malvasia Istriana - Doc
w • Carso Sauvignon - Doc
w • Sagrado Bianco Cuvée Privata Giovanni Bignucolo Venezia Giulia - Igt

SAN CANZIAN D'ISONZO
Gorizia km 27 • m 1/13

Wineries

Lorenzon - I Feudi di Romans ♟ ★10%
Località Pieris, via Ca' del Bosco 6, tel. 048176445
www.ifeudi.it
r • Isonzo del Friuli Cabernet Franc I Feudi di Romans - Doc
w • Isonzo del Friuli Pinot Bianco I Feudi di Romans - Doc
w • Ribolla Gialla Venezia Giulia I Feudi di Romans - Igt

SAN FLORIANO DEL COLLIO
Gorizia km 7 • m 276

Wineries

Ascevi Luwa ♟♟
Via Uclanzi 24, tel. 0481884140
r • Le Vigne Venezia Giulia Rosso - Igt
w • Collio Sauvignon Ronco dei Sassi - Doc
w • Col Martin Selezione Luwa Venezia Giulia Bianco - Igt

Conti Formentini ♟♟
Via Oslavia 5, tel. 0481884131
www.giv.it
r • Collio Merlot Tajut - Doc
w • Collio Bianco Rylint - Doc
w • Collio Chardonnay Torre di Tramontana - Doc
w • Collio Pinot Bianco Vigneto Orto - Doc
w • Collio Tocai Vigneto Orto - Doc

Draga ♟♟
Località Scedina 8, tel. 0481884182
vinidraga@hotmail.com
r • Collio Cabernet Sauvignon Miklus - Doc
w • Collio Bianco Draga - Doc
w • Collio Ribolla Gialla Draga - Doc
w • Collio Sauvignon Draga - Doc
s • Collio Picolit Miklus - Doc

Graunar Giovanni e Francesco ♟
Località Scedina 26, tel. 0481884116
w • Collio Sauvignon - Doc

Komjanc Alessio ♟♟
Via Giasbana 35, tel. 0481391228
komjanc@libero.it
w • Collio Sauvignon - Doc
w • Collio Tocai Friulano - Doc

Tercic Matjaz ♟♟♟
Località Bucuie 9, tel. 0481884193
tercic@tiscalinet.it
w • Collio Bianco Planta - Doc
w • Collio Chardonnay - Doc
w • Collio Pinot Grigio - Doc
w • Collio Ribolla Gialla - Doc
w • Collio Sauvignon - Doc

Terpin Franco ♟♟♟
Località Valerisce 6/A, tel. 0481884215
r • Collio Rosso - Doc
w • Collio Bianco - Doc
w • Collio Ribolla Gialla - Doc

SAN GIORGIO DELLA RICHINVELDA
Pordenone km 25 • m 86

Wineries

Furlan Gianfranco ♟♟♟
Località Cosa, via Palazzo 1, tel. 042796134
r • Castelcosa Cabernet Venezia Giulia - Igt
w • Collio Tocai Friulano Pra di Pradis - Doc
w • Castelcosa Chardonnay Venezia Giulia - Igt
w • Castelcosa Sauvignon Venezia Giulia - Igt
s • Collio Picolit Castelcosa - Doc

SAN GIOVANNI AL NATISONE
Udine km 18 • m 66

Wineries

Cantarutti Alfieri ♟♟♟
Via Ronchi 9, tel. 0432756317
alficant@tin.it
r • Colli Orientali del Friuli Cabernet Sauvignon - Doc

r • Colli Orientali del Friuli Merlot - Doc
w • Colli Orientali del Friuli Pinot Grigio - Doc
w • Colli Orientali del Friuli Sauvignon - Doc
w • Colli Orientali del Friuli Tocai Friulano - Doc

LIVON ♟♟♟♟
Località Dolegnano, via Montarezza 33, tel. 0432757173
r • Collio Merlot Tiaremate - Doc
r • Colli Orientali del Friuli Refosco dal Peduncolo Rosso Riul - Doc
r • Colli Orientali del Friuli Schioppettino Picotis - Doc
w • Collio Chardonnay Braide Mate - Doc
w • Collio Pinot Grigio Braide Grande - Doc
w • Collio Sauvignon Valbuins - Doc

RONCO DEL GNEMIZ ♟♟♟♟
Via Ronchi 5, tel. 0432756238
r • Colli Orientali del Friuli Merlot - Doc
r • Colli Orientali del Friuli Rosso del Gnemiz - Doc
r • Colli Orientali del Friuli Schioppettino - Doc
w • Colli Orientali del Friuli Chardonnay - Doc
w • Colli Orientali del Friuli Pinot Grigio - Doc
w • Colli Orientali del Friuli Sauvignon Riserva - Doc
w • Colli Orientali del Friuli Tocai Friulano - Doc

TENUTA RONCALTO ♟♟
Località Dolegnano, via Montarezza 33, tel. 0432757173
r • Collio Cabernet Sauvignon Roncalto - Doc
w • Collio Ribolla Gialla Roncalto - Doc

SAN LORENZO ISONTINO

Gorizia km 8 • m 54

WINERIES

LIS NERIS ♟♟♟♟♟
Via Gavinana 5, tel. 048180105
www.lisneris.it
w • Isonzo Chardonnay St. Jurosa - Doc
w • Isonzo Pinot Grigio Gris - Doc
w • Isonzo Sauvignon Picol - Doc
w • Confini Venezia Giulia Bianco - Igt
w • Lis Venezia Giulia Bianco - Igt
s • Colli Orientali del Friuli Picolit Monastrium Rosarium - Doc
s • Tal Lùc Verduzzo Passito - Vdt

PECORARI PIERPAOLO ♟♟♟♟
Via Tommaseo 36/C, tel. 0481808775
www.pierpaolopecorari.it
r • Panta Rei Refosco dal Peduncolo Rosso Venezia Giulia - Igt
w • Isonzo Pinot Grigio Altis - Doc
w • Isonzo Sauvignon Altis - Doc
w • Kolaus Sauvignon Venezia Giulia - Igt
w • Olivers Pinot Grigio Venezia Giulia - Igt

SCOLARIS ♟♟
Via Boschetto 4, tel. 0481809920
r • Ocelot - Vdt
w • Collio Bianco Campo dei Fiori Selezione Marco Scolaris - Doc

SAN MARTINO AL TAGLIAMENTO

Pordenone km 23 • m 71

WINERIES

TENUTA PINNI ♟
Via Sant'Osvaldo 1, tel. 0434899464
www.tenutapinni.it
r • Friuli Grave Cabernet Franc - Doc
r • Friuli Grave Refosco dal Peduncolo Rosso - Doc
w • Friuli Grave Chardonnay Superiore - Doc

SAN QUIRINO

Pordenone km 10 • m 116

WINERIES

RUSSOLO ♟♟
Via S. Rocco 58/A, tel. 043491 9577
www.russolo.it
r • I Legni Merlot Venezia Giulia - Igt
r • I Legni Refosco dal Peduncolo Rosso Venezia Giulia - Igt
r • Ronco Calaj Refosco dal Peduncolo Rosso Venezia Giulia - Igt
w • I Legni Chardonnay Venezia Giulia - Igt
w • I Legni Sauvignon Venezia Giulia - Igt

SPILIMBERGO

Pordenone km 33 • m 132

WINERIES

FANTINEL ♟♟
Località Tauriano, via Tesis 8, tel. 0427591520
www.fantinel.com
r • Barone Rosso Platinum Rosso delle Venezie - Igt
w • Collio Bianco Trilogy - Doc

TALMASSONS

Udine km 18 • m 30

WINERIES

MANGILLI ♟♟ ★10%
Località Flumignano, via Tre Avieri 12, tel. 0432766248
www.mangilli.com
w • Collio Pinot Bianco - Doc
w • Collio Pinot Grigio - Doc
w • Collio Sauvignon - Doc
w • Collio Tocai Friulano - Doc
w • Colli Orientali del Friuli Ramandolo - Doc

TORREANO

Udine km 22 • m 189

WINERIES

JACÙSS ♟♟
Località Montina, viale Kennedy 35/A, tel. 0432715147
www.jacus.com
r • Colli Orientali del Friuli Refosco dal Peduncolo Rosso - Doc
r • Colli Orientali del Friuli Rosso Lindi Uà - Doc
r • Colli Orientali del Friuli Schioppettino - Doc
w • Colli Orientali del Friuli Bianco Lindi Uà - Doc
w • Colli Orientali del Friuli Tocai Friulano - Doc

VOLPE PASINI ♟♟♟ ★10%
Località Togliano, via Cividale 16, tel. 0432715151
www.volpepasini.net
r • Colli Orientali del Friuli Cabernet Zuc di Volpe - Doc
r • Colli Orientali del Friuli Merlot Focus Zuc di Volpe - Doc
w • Colli Orientali del Friuli Bianco Le Roverelle Zuc di Volpe - Doc

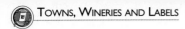

w • Colli Orientali del Friuli Chardonnay Zuc di Volpe - Doc
w • Colli Orientali del Friuli Pinot Grigio Zuc di Volpe - Doc

VILLA VICENTINA
Udine km 34 • m 9

Wineries

Valpanera ♟
Via Trieste 5/A, tel. 0431970395
www.valpanera.it
r • Friuli Aquileia Rosso Alma - Doc
r • Friuli Aquileia Refosco dal Peduncolo Rosso Riserva - Doc

LIGURIA

ALBENGA
Savona km 44 • m 5

Wineries

Anfossi ♟♟
Località Bastia, via Paccini 39, tel. 018220024
anfossi@aziendaaagrariaanfossi.it
r • Riviera Ligure di Ponente Rossese - Doc

Calleri ♟♟
Regione Fratti 2, tel. 018220085
w • Riviera Ligure di Ponente Pigato Saleasco - Doc
w • Riviera Ligure di Ponente Vermentino I Murazzi - Doc

Cascina Feipu dei Massaretti ♟♟♟
Località Bastia, tel. 018220131
r • Riviera Ligure di Ponente Rossese di Albenga - Vdt
r • Russu du Fèipu - Vdt
w • Riviera Ligure di Ponente Pigato Cascina Fèipu - Doc

Sartori Luigi - Torre Pernice ♟♟
Località Leca, regione Torre Pernice 3, tel. 018220042
sartoripigato@libero.it
w • Riviera Ligure di Ponente Pigato Torre Pernice Selezione Bianca Maria Dulbecco - Doc
w • Riviera Ligure di Ponente Vementino Torre Pernice - Doc
s • Oro di Aleramo Passito - Vdt

CAMPOROSSO
Imperia km 44 • m 25

Wineries

Foresti ♟♟
Località Camporosso Mare, via Braie 223, tel. 0184292377
www.forestiwine.it
r • Rossese di Dolceacqua Vigneto Luvaira di Bertù - Doc
w • Riviera Ligure di Ponente Pigato I Soli - Doc
w • Riviera Ligure di Ponente Vermentino Vigneto Selvadolce - Doc

Tenuta Giuncheo ♟♟♟
Località Giuncheo, tel. 0184288639
info@tenutagiuncheo.it
r • Rossese di Dolceacqua Vigneto Pian del Vescovo - Doc
w • Riviera Ligure di Ponente Vermentino - Doc
w • Riviera Ligure di Ponente Vermentino Le Palme - Doc

CASTELNUOVO MAGRA
La Spezia km 25 • m 181

Wineries

Il Torchio ♟♟
Via Provinciale 202, tel. 0187674075
r • Colli di Luni Rosso Il Torchio - Doc
w • Colli di Luni Vermentino - Doc

La Colombiera ♟♟
Via Montecchio 92, tel. 0187674265
www.lacolombiera.it
r • Colli di Luni Rosso Riserva Terrizzo - Doc
w • Colli di Luni Vermentino Albachiara - Doc
w • Colli di Luni Vermentino Celsus - Doc

CHIAVARI
Genoa km 43 • m 5

Wineries

Bisson ♟♟♟
Corso Gianelli 28, tel. 0185314462
r • Golfo del Tigullio Rosso Il Musaico - Doc
r • Musaico Novantanove Rosso - Igt
w • Golfo del Tigullio Bianchetta Genovese U Pastine - Doc
w • Golfo del Tigullio Vermentino Vigna Erta - Doc
s • Golfo del Tigullio Passito Acinirari - Doc

CHIUSANICO
Imperia km 16 • m 360

Wineries

La Rocca di San Nicolao ♟♟♟
Località Gazzelli, via Dante 10, tel. 018352850
www.roccasannicolao.it
w • Riviera Ligure di Ponente Pigato Riviera dei Fiori Vigna dei Proxi - Doc
w • Riviera Ligure di Ponente Vermentino Riviera dei Fiori Vigna dei Proxi - Doc
w • Riviera Ligure di Ponente Vermentino Vigna dei Proxi Barrique - Doc

CHIUSAVECCHIA
Imperia km 12 • m 140

Wineries

Ramoino ♟♟♟
Località Sarola, via XX Settembre, tel. 018352645
w • Riviera Ligure di Ponente Pigato - Doc
w • Riviera Ligure di Ponente Pigato Anchisa - Doc
w • Riviera Ligure di Ponente Vermentino - Doc

DIANO CASTELLO
Imperia km 8 • m 135

Wineries

Bianchi Maria Donata ♟♟
Via delle Torri 16, tel. 0183498233
w • Riviera Ligure di Ponente Pigato - Doc
w • Riviera Ligure di Ponente Vermentino - Doc

w • Riviera Ligure di Ponente Vermentino Diana - Doc

DOLCEACQUA
Imperia km 48 • m 51

WINERIES

CANE GIOVAN BATTISTA ♟♟
Via Roma 21, tel. 0184206120
r • Rossese di Dolceacqua Superiore Vigneto Arcagna - Doc
r • Rossese di Dolceacqua Superiore Vigneto Morghe - Doc

TERRE BIANCHE ♟♟♟
Località Arcagna, tel. 018431426
www.terrebianche.com
r • Rossese di Dolceacqua Bricco Arcagna - Doc
r • Arcagna Rosso - Vdt
w • Riviera Ligure di Ponente Pigato - Doc
w • Riviera Ligure di Ponente Vermentino - Doc
w • Arcagna Bianco - Vdt

FINALE LIGURE
Savona km 24 • m 10

WINERIES

TERRE ROSSE ♟♟♟
Via Manie 3, tel. 019698782
w • Riviera Ligure di Ponente Pigato - Doc
w • Riviera Ligure di Ponente Pigato Apogèo - Doc
w • Riviera Ligure di Ponente Vermentino - Doc

IMPERIA
m 10

WINERIES

TENUTA COLLE DEI BARDELLINI ♟♟♟
Località Bardellini, via Fontanarosa 12, tel. 0183291370
r • Riviera Ligure di Ponente Rossese - Doc
w • Riviera Ligure di Ponente Pigato Vigna La Torretta - Doc
w • Riviera Ligure di Ponente Vermentino Vigna U Munte - Doc

ISOLABONA
Imperia km 52 • m 106

WINERIES

CANTINE DEL ROSSESE - FRATELLI GAJAUDO ♟♟
Via Provinciale 7, tel. 0184208095
www.cantinagajaudo.com
r • Rossese di Dolceacqua Superiore - Doc
w • Riviera Ligure di Ponente Pigato di Albenga - Doc
w • Riviera Ligure di Ponente Vermentino - Doc

ORTONOVO
La Spezia km 29 • m 2/698

WINERIES

LA PIETRA DEL FOCOLARE ♟♟
Via Dogana 209, tel. 0187662129
lapietradelfocolare@libero.it
r • Colli di Luni Rosso Re Carlo - Doc
w • Colli di Luni Vermentino Santo Paterno - Doc
w • Colli di Luni Vermentino Solarancio - Doc

LUNAE BOSONI ♟♟♟
Località Luni, via Bozzi 63, tel. 0187669222
www.cantinelunae.com
r • Colli di Luni Rosso Niccolò V da Sarzana - Doc
w • Colli di Luni Bianco Onda di Luna - Doc
w • Colli di Luni Vermentino Cavagino - Doc
w • Colli di Luni Vermentino Etichetta Grigia - Doc
w • Colli di Luni Vermentino Etichetta Nera - Doc

ORTOVERO
Savona km 56 • m 63

WINERIES

DURIN ♟♟♟
Via Roma 92, tel. 0182547007
aa_durin@libero.it
r • Riviera Ligure di Ponente Ormeasco - Doc
r • Riviera Ligure di Ponente Rossese - Doc
r • Granaccia Colline Savonesi - Igt
w • Riviera Ligure di Ponente Pigato - Doc
w • Riviera Ligure di Ponente Vermentino - Doc

PIEVE DI TECO
Imperia km 24 • m 240

WINERIES

LUPI ♟♟♟
Via Mazzini 9, tel. 0183276090
www.lupi.it
r • Riviera Ligure di Ponente Ormeasco Superiore Le Braje - Doc
w • Riviera Ligure di Ponente Pigato Le Petraie - Doc
w • Riviera Ligure di Ponente Vermentino Le Serre - Doc
w • Vignamare Colline Savonesi Bianco - Igt

PONTEDASSIO
Imperia km 8 • m 80

WINERIES

ASCHERO ♟♟
Piazza Vittorio Emanuele 7, tel. 0183293515
w • Riviera Ligure di Ponente Pigato - Doc
w • Riviera Ligure di Ponente Vermentino - Doc

QUILIANO
Savona km 8 • m 32

WINERIES

TURCO INNOCENZO ♟♟
Via Bertone 7/A, tel. 019887120
granacciaturco@libero.it
r • Dei Cappuccini Colline Savonesi Granaccia - Igt
r • Vigneto Cappuccini Riserva Colline Savonesi Granaccia - Igt

RANZO
Imperia km 31 • m 118/920

WINERIES

ALESSANDRI MASSIMO ♟
Località Costa Parrocchia, tel. 018253458
w • Riviera Ligure di Ponente Pigato Costa de Vigne - Doc

BRUNA ♟♟
Via Umberto I nr. 81, tel. 0183318082
aziendaagricolabruna@libero.it
w • Riviera Ligure di Ponente Pigato Le Russeghine - Doc
w • Riviera Ligure di Ponente Pigato Villa Torrachetta - Doc

RIOMAGGIORE
La Spezia km 13 • m 35

Wineries

Cooperativa Agricoltura di Riomaggiore ♟♟♟
Località Groppo,
tel. 0187920435
www.cantinacinqueterre.com
- *w* • Cinque Terre Costa de Campu di Manarola - Doc
- *w* • Cinque Terre Costa de Sèra di Riomaggiore - Doc
- *w* • Cinque Terre Costa de'posa di Volastra - Doc
- *s* • Cinque Terre Sciacchetrà - Doc
- *s* • Cinque Terre Sciacchetrà Riserva - Doc

De Battè ♟♟
Via Pecunia 168,
tel. 0187920127
- *w* • Cinque Terre - Doc
- *w* • Cinque Terre Sciacchetrà - Doc
- *w* • Cinque Terre Sciacchetrà Riserva - Doc

Forlini e Cappellini ♟♟
Località Manarola, piazza Duomo 6,
tel. 0187920496
- *w* • Cinque Terre - Doc

SARZANA
La Spezia km 16 • m 21

Wineries

Fattoria Picedi Benettini ♟♟
Via Mazzini 57, tel. 0187625147
- *r* • Colli di Luni Rosso Gran Baccano - Doc
- *r* • Val di Magra Merlot Fattoria di Cesarano - Igt
- *w* • Colli di Luni Vermentino Il Chioso - Doc

Il Monticello ♟♟
Via Grappolo 7, tel. 0187621432
sub@libero.it
- *r* • Colli di Luni Rosso Poggio dei Magni - Doc

SOLDANO
Imperia km 45 • m 80

Wineries

Guglielmi Enzo - Poggio Pini ♟
Corso Verbone 143, tel. 0184289042
- *r* • Rossese di Dolceacqua Superiore - Doc

VENDONE
Savona km 57 • m 140/1092

Wineries

Vio Claudio ♟♟
Località Crosa 16, tel. 018276338
- *w* • Riviera Ligure di Ponente Pigato dell'Albenganese - Doc
- *w* • Riviera Ligure di Ponente Vermentino dell'Albenganese - Doc

EMILIA-ROMAGNA

BAGNACAVALLO
Ravenna km 19 • m 11

Wineries

Ercolani Roberto ♟♟
Via Albergone 24, tel. 054562381
- *r* • Burson Rosso Ravenna - Igt
- *s* • Armonia Passito Bianco Ravenna - Igt

Longanesi Daniele ♟♟
Via Boncellino 114, tel. 054560289
- *r* • Burson di Burson Rosso Ravenna Etichetta Blu - Igt
- *r* • Burson di Burson Rosso Ravenna Etichetta Nera - Igt

BERTINORO
Forlì-Cesena km 15 • m 254

Wineries

Celli ♟♟♟
Viale Carducci 5, tel. 0543445183
www.celli-vini.com
- *r* • Sangiovese di Romagna Superiore Riserva Le Grillaie - Doc
- *r* • Bron e Ruseval Sangiovese Cabernet di Forlì - Igt
- *w* • Albana di Romagna Secco I Croppi - Docg
- *w* • Bron e Ruseval Chardonnay di Forlì - Igt
- *s* • Albana di Romagna Passito Solara - Docg

Fattoria Ca' Rossa ♟♟ ★10%
Via Cellaimo 735, tel. 0543445130
www.fattoriacarossa.it
- *r* • Sangiovese di Romagna Superiore Riserva Ripagrande - Doc
- *r* • Cesubeo Forlì Rosso - Igt
- *s* • Albana di Romagna Passito Stilloro - Docg

Fattoria Paradiso ♟♟
Via Palmeggiana 285, tel. 0543445044
www.fattoriaparadiso.com
- *r* • Sangiovese di Romagna Superiore Riserva Castello Ugarte Vigna delle Lepri - Doc
- *r* • Barbarossa Il Dosso Forlì Rosso - Igt
- *r* • Mito Forlì Rosso - Igt
- *w* • Jacopo Bianco Forlì - Igt
- *s* • Albana di Romagna Dolce Contessina Ugarte Vigna del Viale - Docg

Madonia Giovanna ♟♟♟♟
Via Cappuccini 130, tel. 0543444361
giovanna.madonia@libero.it
- *r* • Sangiovese di Romagna Superiore Fermavento - Doc
- *r* • Sangiovese di Romagna Superiore Riserva Ombroso - Doc
- *r* • Sterpigno Merlot Forlì - Igt
- *w* • Albana di Romagna Secco Neblina - Docg
- *s* • Albana di Romagna Passito Remoto - Docg

BOMPORTO
Modena km 14 • m 25

Wineries

Cantina Bellei Francesco & C. ♟♟
Via per Modena 80, tel. 059818002
- *r* • Lambrusco di Sorbara fermentazione naturale - Doc
- *w* • Spumante Brut Millesimato Spéciale Cuvée - Vdt
- *w* • Spumante Brut Riserva Millenium - Vdt

BORGONOVO VAL TIDONE
Piacenza km 22 • m 114

WINERIES

BORGO DI RIVALTA - DIVISIONE VINI VALTIDONE ♟♟
Via Moretta 58, tel. 0523862168
borgorivalta@libero.it
- r • Colli Piacentini Cabernet Sauvignon Borgo di Rivalta Mabilia - Doc
- r • Colli Piacentini Gutturnio Riserva Borgo di Rivalta Giannone - Doc

BRISIGHELLA

Ravenna km 43 • m 115
WINERIES

LA BERTA ♟♟♟
Via Pideura 48, tel. 054684998
- r • Colli di Faenza Rosso Ca' di Berta - Doc
- r • Sangiovese di Romagna Superiore Riserva Olmatello - Doc
- r • Sangiovese di Romagna Superiore Solano - Doc
- r • Almante - Igt
- s • Infavato - Vdt

CASALECCHIO DI RENO

Bologna km 8 • m 61
WINERIES

TIZZANO ♟♟
Via Marescalchi 13, tel. 051571208
- r • Colli Bolognesi Cabernet Sauvignon - Doc
- r • Colli Bolognesi Cabernet Sauvignon Riserva - Doc

CASTEL BOLOGNESE

Ravenna km 39 • m 42
WINERIES

FATTORIA CAMERONE ♟♟♟ ★10%
Via Biancanigo 1485, tel. 054650434
www.fattoriacamerone.it
- r • Sangiovese di Romagna Superiore - Doc
- r • Sangiovese di Romagna Superiore Riserva Millennium - Doc
- r • Sangiovese di Romagna Superiore Riserva Rosso del Camerone - Doc

FERRUCCI STEFANO ♟♟
Via Casolana 3045/2, tel. 0546651068
www.stefanoferrucci.it
- r • Sangiovese di Romagna Riserva Domus Caia - Doc
- r • Sangiovese di Romanga Superiore Centurione - Doc
- s • Albana di Romagna Passito Domus Aurea - Docg

CASTELLO DI SERRAVALLE

Bologna km 38 • m 147/480
WINERIES

BEGHELLI GIUSEPPE ♟♟
Via Castello 2257, tel. 0516704786
beghelli@collibolognesi.com
- r • Colli Bolognesi Cabernet Sauvignon - Doc
- w • Colli Bolognesi Pignoletto Classico - Doc

FATTORIE VALLONA ♟♟♟
Località Fagnano, tel. 0516703058
- r • Colli Bolognesi Cabernet Sauvignon - Doc
- w • Colli Bolognesi Chardonnay Selezione - Doc
- w • Colli Bolognesi Pignoletto - Doc

SANDONI VIRGILIO ♟
Via Valle del Samoggia 780, tel. 0516703188
virgiliosandoni@libero.it
- r • Colli Bolognesi Barbera - Doc

CASTEL SAN PIETRO TERME

Bologna km 22 • m 75
WINERIES

CESARI UMBERTO ♟♟
Via Stanzano 1120, tel. 051941896
www.umbertocesari.it
- r • Sangiovese di Romagna Riserva - Doc
- r • Liano Sangiovese Cabernet Sauvignon Rubicone - Igt
- r • Tauleto Sangiovese Rubicone - Igt

CASTELVETRO DI MODENA

Modena km 21 • m 152
WINERIES

CORTE MANZINI ♟♟
Località Ca' di Sola, via Modena 131/3, tel. 059702658
- r • Lambrusco Grasparossa di Castelvetro L'Acino - Doc
- r • Lambrusco Grasparossa di Castelvetro Secco - Doc

TENUTA PEDERZANA ♟♟♟
Via Palona 12/A, tel. 059799677
francesco.gibellini@tin.it
- r • Lambrusco Grasparossa di Castelvetro Semisecco - Doc
- r • Puntamora Rosso Amabile - Vdt
- r • Ronchigliano - Vdt

CIVITELLA DI ROMAGNA

Forlì-Cesena km 30 • m 219
WINERIES

PODERI DAL NESPOLI ♟♟♟
Località Nespoli, villa Rossi 50, tel. 0543989637
www.poderidalnespoli.com
- r • Borgo dei Guidi Forlì Rosso - Igt
- r • Il Nespoli Forlì Sangiovese - Igt
- s • Albana di Romagna Passito Bradamante - Docg

COLLECCHIO

Parma km 11 • m 112
WINERIES

MONTE DELLE VIGNE ♟♟
Località Ozzano Taro, via Costa 25/27, tel. 0521809105
montevigne@libero.it
- r • Monte delle Vigne Rosso - Vdt
- r • Nabucco - Vdt
- w • Callas - Vdt

CORIANO

Rimini km 59 • m 102
WINERIES

COOPERATIVA SOCIALE SAN PATRIGNANO ♟♟♟♟♟
Via S. Patrignano 53, tel. 0541362362
www.sanpatrignano.org
- r • Sangiovese di Romagna Riserva Avi - Doc
- r • Sangiovese di Romagna Superiore Aulente - Doc
- r • Montepirolo Rubicone Rosso - Igt
- r • Zarricante Rubicone Rosso - Igt
- w • Vintàn Rubicone Bianco - Igt

Podere Vecciano
Località Ospedaletto, via Vecciano 23/X, tel. 0541658388
www.poderevecciano.it
- *r* • Collli di Rimini Rosso Vignalavolta - Doc
- *r* • Sangiovese di Romagna Superiore Vignalmonte - Doc
- *w* • Colli di Rimini Rebola Vignalaginestra - Doc

FAENZA
Ravenna km 31 • m 35

Wineries

Fattoria Zerbina
Località Marzeno, via Vicchio 11, tel. 054640022
www.zerbina.com
- *r* • Sangiovese di Romagna Riserva Pietramora - Doc
- *r* • Sangiovese di Romagna Superiore Torre di Ceparano - Doc
- *r* • Marzieno Ravenna Rosso - Igt
- *s* • Albana di Romagna Passito Arrocco - Docg
- *s* • Albana di Romagna Passito Scacco Matto - Docg

Fratelli Conti
Località Santa Lucia, via Pozzo 1, tel. 0546642149
- *r* • Sangiovese di Romagna Superiore Riserva - Doc
- *w* • Albana di Romagna Vignapozzo - Docg
- *s* • Albana di Romagna Passito Non Ti Scordar di Me - Docg

Istituto Professionale di Stato per l'Agricoltura e l'Ambiente - Persolino
Via Firenze 194, tel. 054622932
www.racine.ravenna.it/ipapersolino
- *r* • Varrone Ravenna Rosso - Igt
- *s* • Albana di Romagna Passito Ultimo Giorno di Scuola - Doc
- *s* • Poesia d'Inverno Passito Bianco - Vdt

Morini Alessandro
Via Firenze 493, tel. 0546634257
www.cantinamorini.com
- *r* • Sangiovese di Romagna Superiore Riserva Nonno Rico - Doc

Spinetta
Via Pozzo 26, tel. 0546642037
- *r* • Sangiovese di Romagna Riserva Bacchicus - Doc
- *r* • Sangiovese di Romagna Superiore Sanguis Jovis - Doc
- *s* • Albana di Romagna Passito Luxuria - Docg

Trerè
Località Monti Coralli, via Casale 19, tel. 054647034
www.trere.com
- *r* • Colli di Faenza Rosso Riserva Montecorallo - Doc
- *r* • Colli di Faenza Sangiovese Renero - Doc
- *r* • Sangiovese di Romagna Riserva Amarcord d'un Ross - Doc
- *r* • Sangiovese di Romagna Superiore Vigna dello Sperone - Doc
- *s* • Albana di Romagna Passito Tre Rè - Docg

FORLÌ
m 34

Wineries

Berti Stefano
Località Ravaldino in Monte, via La Scagna 18, tel. 0543488074
renbante@tin.it
- *r* • Sangiovese di Romagna Superiore Calisto - Doc
- *r* • Sangiovese di Romagna Superiore Ravaldo - Doc

Calonga
Via Castel Leone 8, tel. 0543753044
- *r* • Sangiovese di Romagna Superiore Il Bruno - Doc
- *r* • Sangiovese di Romagna Superiore Riserva Michelangiolo - Doc
- *r* • Castellione Cabernet Sauvignon Forlì - Igt

Drei Donà - Tenuta La Palazza
Località Massa di Vecchiazzano, via del Tesoro 23, tel. 0543769371
dreidona@tin.it
- *r* • Sangiovese di Romagna Superiore Riserva Pruno - Doc
- *r* • Graf Noir Forlì Rosso - Igt
- *r* • Magnificat Forlì - Igt
- *r* • Notturno in Fa Maggiore Forlì - Igt
- *w* • Il Tornese Forlì - Igt

GAZZOLA
Piacenza km 21 • m 139

Wineries

Luretta
Castello di Momeliano, tel. 0523976500
www.luretta-vini.com
- *r* • Colli Piacentini Pinot Nero Achab - Doc
- *w* • Colli Piacentini Chardonnay Selin d'Armari - Doc
- *w* • Colli Piacentini Malvasia Bocca di Rosa - Doc
- *w* • Colli Piacentini Malvasia Le Rane - Doc
- *w* • Colli Piacentini Sauvignon I Nani e Le Ballerine - Doc

IMOLA
Bologna km 33 • m 47

Wineries

Fattoria Pasolini dall'Onda
Via Montericco 9, tel. 054240054
- *r* • Sangiovese di Romagna Superiore Montericco - Doc
- *r* • Sangiovese di Romagna Superiore Riserva Montericco Alto - Doc

Tre Monti ★10%
Via Lola 3, tel. 0542657116
www.tremonti.it
- *r* • Colli di Imola Rosso Boldo - Doc
- *r* • Sangiovese di Romagna Superiore Thea - Doc
- *w* • Albana di Romagna Secco Vigna della Rocca - Docg
- *w* • Trebbiano di Romagna Vigna del Rio - Doc
- *s* • Albana di Romagna Passito - Docg

LANGHIRANO
Parma km 23 • m 265

Wineries

Lamoretti
Località Casatico, via della Nave 6, tel. 0521863590
www.lamoretti.com
- *r* • Vigna Lunga '71 - Vdt

LUGO
Ravenna km 25 • m 12

Wineries

Cantina Ronchi 🍷
tel. 054523041
www.ronchivini.it
r • Sangiovese di Romagna Superiore Riserva Borsignolo - Doc

MELDOLA
Forlì-Cesena km 12 • m 58

Wineries

Le Calbane 🍷🍷🍷
Località Ricò, via Possaduro 9, tel. 0543494486
r • Sangiovese di Romagna Superiore Baricò - Doc
r • Sangiovese di Romagna Superiore Le Calbane - Doc
r • Calbanesco - Vdt

MODIGLIANA
Forlì-Cesena km 34 • m 185

Wineries

Castelluccio 🍷🍷🍷🍷
Via Tramonto 15, tel. 0546942486
www.ronchidicastelluccio.it
r • Sangiovese di Romagna Le More - Doc
r • Ronco dei Ciliegi Forlì Rosso - Igt
r • Ronco delle Ginestre Forlì Rosso - Igt
w • Lunaria Forlì Bianco - Igt
w • Ronco del Re Forlì Bianco - Igt

Il Pratello 🍷🍷
Via Morano 14, tel. 0546942038
pratello@libero.it
r • Colli di Faenza Rosso Calenzone - Doc
r • Colli di Faenza Sangiovese Mantignano - Doc
r • Badia Raustignolo - Vdt

MONTE SAN PIETRO
Bologna km 15 • m 60/776

Wineries

Santarosa 🍷🍷🍷🍷
Via S. Martino 82, tel. 051969203
info@santarosavini.it
r • Colli Bolognesi Cabernet Giòrosso - Doc
r • Colli Bolognesi Merlot Giòtondo - Doc
r • Santarosa Emilia Rosso - Igt
w • Colli Bolognesi Chardonnay Giocoliere - Doc
w • Colli Bolognesi Pignoletto Classico - Doc

Tenuta Bonzara 🍷🍷🍷
Via S. Chierlo 37/A, tel. 0516768324
www.bonzara.it
r • Colli Bolognesi Cabernet Sauvignon Bonzarone - Doc
r • Colli Bolognesi Merlot Rocca di Bonacciara - Doc
w • Colli Bolognesi Pignoletto Classico Vigna Antica - Doc
w • Colli Bolognesi Pinot Bianco Borgo di Qua - Doc
w • Colli Bolognesi Sauvignon Superiore Le Carrate - Doc

MONTEVEGLIO
Bologna km 26 • m 114

Wineries

Bonfiglio 🍷🍷
Via Cassola 21, tel. 051830758
www.paginegialle.it/bonfivini
r • Colli Bolognesi Cabernet Sauvignon Pio Vannozzi - Doc
w • Colli Bolognesi Pignoletto Superiore - Doc
w • Colli Bolognesi Pignoletto Superiore Prova d'Autore - Doc
s • Colli Bolognesi Colline di Oliveto Pignoletto Passito - Doc

Ognibene Luigi e Figli - Gradizzolo 🍷🍷
Via Invernata 2, tel. 051830265
vinicolaognibene@libero.it
r • Colli Bolognesi Barbera Riserva - Doc
r • Colli Bolognesi Merlot Calastrino - Doc
w • Colli Bolognesi Pinot Bianco - Doc

San Vito 🍷🍷
Località Oliveto, via Monte Rodano 6, tel. 051964521
r • Colli Bolognesi Cabernet Sauvignon - Doc
w • Colli Bolognesi Chardonnay - Doc
w • Colli Bolognesi Pignoletto Superiore - Doc

NIBBIANO
Piacenza km 40 • m 284

Wineries

Tenuta La Torretta 🍷🍷
Località La Torretta, tel. 0523997008
www.lavaltidone.it
r • Colli Piacentini Cabernet Sauvignon - Doc
r • Colli Piacentini Gutturnio Vigna della Villa - Doc
r • Colli Piacentini Pinot Nero Dioniso - Doc

PIACENZA
m 61

Wineries

Castelli del Duca 🍷🍷
Via S. Franca 60, tel. 0522942135
castelli@medici.it
r • Colli Piacentini Gutturnio Riserva Sigillum - Doc
r • Colli Piacentini Gutturnio Superiore - Doc
s • Colli Piacentini Malvasia Passito Soleste - Doc

PONTE DELL'OLIO
Piacenza km 22 • m 216

Wineries

Perinelli 🍷🍷
Località I Perinelli, tel. 0523571610
stefano-mastrivignai@libero.it
r • Vigna Vecchia - Vdt
w • Colli Piacentini Malvasia - Doc

PREDAPPIO
Forlì-Cesena km 15 • m 133

Wineries

Fattoria Casetto dei Mandorli - Nicolucci 🍷🍷
Località Predappio Alta, via Umberto I nr. 21, tel. 0543922361
www.italiadoc.it
r • Sangiovese di Romagna Predappio di Predappio Riserva Vigna del Generale - Doc
r • Sangiovese di Romagna Superiore Tre Rocche - Doc
r • Sangiovese di Romagna Vigna dei Mandorli - Doc

Pandolfa 🍷🍷
Località Fiumana, via Pandolfa 35, tel. 0543940073
www.pandolfa.it

r • Sangiovese di Romagna Superiore Riserva Godenza - Doc
r • Pezzolo Cabernet Sauvignon di Forlì - Igt
r • Rosso Le Forche Forlì - Igt

RIVERGARO
Piacenza km 18 • m 140
Wineries
La Stoppa ♟♟♟
Località Ancarano, tel. 0523958159
www.lastoppa.it
r • Colli Piacentini Barbera della Stoppa - Doc
r • Colli Piacentini Cabernet Sauvignon Stoppa - Doc
r • Colli Piacentini Gutturnio Fermo - Doc
r • Macchiona Emilia Rosso - Igt
s • Colli Piacentini Malvasia Passita Vigna del Volta - Doc

RUSSI
Ravenna km 15 • m 13
Wineries
Tenuta Uccellina ♟♟
Via Garibaldi 51, tel. 0544580144
r • Sangiovese di Romagna Superiore Riserva - Doc
r • Burson Rosso Ravenna - Igt
r • Rucchetto dell'Uccellina - Vdt
s • Albana di Romagna Dolce - Docg
s • Albana di Romagna Passito - Docg

SANT'ILARIO D'ENZA
Reggio nell'Emilia km 16 • m 59
Wineries
Moro - Rinaldini ♟♟♟
Località Calerno, via Andrea Rivasi 27, tel. 0522679190
www.rinaldinivini.it
r • Colli di Scandiano e di Canossa Cabernet Sauvignon Riserva - Doc
r • Colli di Scandiano e di Canossa Lambrusco Grasparossa Frizzante Vecchio Moro - Doc
r • Vigna del Picchio Rosso dell'Emilia - Igt
r • Lambrusco Spumante Morone - Vdt
r • Lambrusco Spumante Pjcol Ross - Vdt

SASSO MARCONI
Bologna km 17 • m 128
Wineries
Cinti Floriano ♟♟
Località San Lorenzo, via Gamberi 48, tel. 0516751646
cinti@collibolognesi.com
r • Colli Bolognesi Cabernet Sauvignon Selezione - Doc
r • Colli Bolognesi Merlot Selezione - Doc

SAVIGNANO SUL RUBICONE
Forlì-Cesena km 33 • m 32
Wineries
Colonna Giovanni - Spalletti Vini ♟♟
Via Matteotti 62, tel. 0541945111
luisamontemar@jumpy.it
r • Sangiovese di Romagna Superiore Rocca di Ribano - Doc
w • Albana di Romagna Secco - Docg
s • Albana di Romagna Passito Maolù - Docg

TRAVO
Piacenza km 30 • m 176
Wineries
Il Poggiarello ♟♟♟
Località Il Poggiarello, tel. 0523957241
poggiarello@iol.it
r • Colli Piacentini Cabernet Sauvignon Perticato del Novarei - Doc
r • Colli Piacentini Gutturnio Riserva La Barbona - Doc
r • Colli Piacentini Pinot Nero Perticato Le Giastre - Doc
w • Colli Piacentini Chardonnay Perticato La Piana - Doc
w • Colli Piacentini Malvasia Perticato Beatrice Quadri - Doc

VIGOLZONE
Piacenza km 15 • m 165
Wineries
Conte Otto Barattieri di San Pietro ♟♟
Località Albarola, tel. 0523875111
r • Colli Piacentini Cabernet Sauvignon Il Pergolo - Doc
r • Colli Piacentini Gutturnio - Doc
s • Colli Piacentini Vin Santo Albarola - Doc
La Tosa ♟♟♟
Località La Tosa, tel. 0523870727
r • Colli Piacentini Cabernet Sauvignon Luna Selvatica - Doc
r • Colli Piacentini Gutturnio La Tosa - Doc
r • Colli Piacentini Gutturnio Vignamorello - Doc
w • Colli Piacentini Sauvignon La Tosa - Doc
s • Colli Piacentini Malvasia Sorriso di Cielo - Doc

ZIANO PIACENTINO
Piacenza km 27 • m 220
Wineries
Lusenti ♟♟
Località Casepiccioni di Vicobarone, tel. 0523868479
ludovica.lusenti@tin.it
r • Colli Piacentini Cabernet Sauvignon Villante - Doc
r • Colli Piacentini Gutturnio Superiore Cresta al Sole - Doc
Mossi ♟♟
Località Albareto, tel. 0523860201
r • Colli Piacentini Gutturnio Classico Riserva - Doc
r • Colli Piacentini Gutturnio Riserva Vigna Riva del Sole - Doc
r • Infernotto - Vdt
Torre Fornello ♟♟♟
Località Fornello, tel. 0523861001
www.torrefornello.it
r • Colli Piacentini Gutturnio Classico Riserva Diacono Gerardo 1028 - Doc
r • Colli Piacentini Gutturnio Superiore Sinsal - Doc
w • Colli Piacentini Malvasia Donna Luigia - Doc
w • Colli Piacentini Sauvignon Cà del Rio - Doc
w • Vigna Pratobianco - Vdt

ZOLA PREDOSA
Bologna km 14 • m 74

WINERIES
VIGNETO BAGAZZANA ♙♙ ★10%
Via Raibolini 55, tel. 051753489
r • Colli Bolognesi Cabernet Sauvignon - Doc
r • Colli Bolognesi Merlot Vigneto Bagazzana - Doc
VIGNETO DELLE TERRE ROSSE ♙♙♙
Via Predosa 83, tel. 051755845
r • Colli Bolognesi Cabernet Sauvignon Il Rosso di Enrico Vallania - Doc
w • Colli Bolognesi Chardonnay Cuvée Giovanni Vallania - Doc
w • Adriana Vallania Malvasia Aromatica di Candia Emilia - Igt

TUSCANY

AREZZO
m 296
WINERIES
FATTORIA DI GRATENA ♙♙
Località Pieve a Maiano, tel. 0575368664
www.gratena.it
r • Chianti Gratena - Docg
r • Rapozzo da Maiano Rosso Toscana - Igt
r • Siro Toscana Rosso - Igt
VILLA CILNIA ♙♙♙ ★10%
Località Bagnoro, tel. 0575365017
www.villacilnia.com
r • Chianti Colli Aretini - Docg
r • Chianti Colli Aretini Riserva - Docg
r • Cign'Oro Colli della Toscana Centrale - Igt

BAGNO A RIPOLI
Florence km 7 • m 75
WINERIES
CASTEL RUGGERO ♙♙
Località Antella, via di Castel Ruggero 33, tel. 0556499423
castelruggero@tiscalinet.it
r • Chianti Classico - Docg
r • Chianti Classico Riserva - Docg
FATTORIA LE SORGENTI ♙♙♙
Via Docciola 8, tel. 055696004
www.fattoria-lesorgenti.com
r • Chianti Colli Fiorentini - Docg
r • Scirus Toscana - Igt
w • Sghiràs Toscana - Igt
FATTORIA LILLIANO ♙♙♙
Località Antella, via Lilliano 82, tel. 055642602
www.mega.it\fattoria.lilliano
r • Chianti Colli Fiorentini - Docg
r • Bruzzico Toscana Rosso - Igt

BARBERINO VAL D'ELSA
Florence km 32 • m 373
WINERIES
CASA EMMA ♙♙♙
Località Cortine, tel. 0558072859
r • Chianti Classico - Docg
r • Chianti Classico Riserva - Docg
r • Soloio - Igt
CASA SOLA ♙♙♙
Via Cortine 5, tel. 0558075028
www.chianticlassico.com/casasola
r • Chianti Classico Casa Sola - Docg
r • Chianti Classico Riserva Casa Sola - Docg
r • Montarsiccio Rosso Toscana - Igt
CASTELLO DELLA PANERETTA ♙♙♙
Strada della Paneretta 35, tel. 0558059003
stefano.paneretta@tin.it
r • Chianti Classico Riserva - Docg
r • Chianti Classico Riserva Vigneto Torre a Destra - Docg
r • Quattrocentenario Rosso di Toscana - Igt
r • Terrine Rosso di Toscana - Igt
s • Vinsanto del Chianti Classico - Doc
CASTELLO DI MONSANTO ♙♙♙♙
Via Monsanto 8, tel. 0558059000
r • Chianti Classico Riserva il Poggio - Docg
r • Fabrizio Bianchi - Vdt
r • Nemo - Vdt
r • Tinscvil - Vdt
w • Fabrizio Bianchi Chardonnay - Vdt
CASTELLO DI TAVOLESE ♙♙
Località Marcialla, via Tavolese 71, tel. 0571660110
r • Rubicondo Toscana - Igt
FATTORIA ISOLE E OLENA ♙♙♙♙♙
Località Isole 1, tel. 0558072763
isolena@tin.it
r • Chianti Classico - Docg
r • Cabernet Sauvignon Collezione De Marchi Toscana - Igt
r • Cepparello Toscana - Igt
w • Chardonnay Collezione De Marchi Toscana - Igt
s • Vin Santo del Chianti Classico - Doc
FATTORIA LE FILIGARE ♙♙♙
Località San Donato in Poggio, via Sicella 37, tel. 0558072796
r • Chianti Classico - Docg
r • Chianti Classico Riserva - Docg
r • Podere Le Rocce - Vdt
FATTORIA PASOLINI DALL'ONDA ♙♙♙ ★10%
Piazza Mazzini 10, tel. 0558075019
r • Chianti Classico Badia a Sicelle - Docg
r • Chianti Riserva Montoli - Docg
r • Sanzanobi Rosso Toscana - Igt
w • Le Macchie Chardonnay di Toscana - Igt
w • Montepetri Chardonnay-Pinot Grigio Toscana - Igt
I BALZINI ♙♙♙♙
Località Pastine 19, tel. 0558075503
segreteria@disantoassociati.com
r • I Balzini Colli della Toscana Centrale Rosso - Igt
r • I Balzini Etichetta Nera Colli della Toscana Centrale Rosso - Igt
MARCHESE TORRIGIANI - TORRE ♙♙♙
Località Torrigiani, vico d'Elsa 8, tel. 0558073001
r • Guidaccio Toscana - Igt
r • Torre di Ciardo Toscana - Igt

BIBBONA
Livorno km 46 • m 80

Wineries
Villa Caprareccia ♟♟♟
Via Bolgherese, tel. 0586677483
r • Maestremilio Toscana Rosso - Igt
w • Alighino Toscana Bianco - Igt
w • Argileto Toscana Bianco - Igt

BUCINE
Arezzo km 30 • m 249
Wineries
Fattoria D'Ambra ♟♟
Via Trieste 97, tel. 055996806
r • Chianti Riserva La Bigattiera - Docg
r • Casamurli - Igt
r • Gavignano - Igt
Fattoria Villa La Selva ♟♟♟
Località Montebenichi, tel. 055998203
r • Felciaia Colli della Toscana Centrale Rosso - Igt
r • Selvamaggio Colli della Toscana Centrale - Igt
s • Vinsanto del Chianti Vigna del Papa - Doc

CALENZANO
Florence km 15 • m 68
Wineries
Tenuta di San Donato - Marchesi Pancrazi ♟♟♟
Viale dei Cipressi 8, tel. 0558879457
r • Casaglia Rosso Toscano - Igt
r • San Donato Rosso - Igt

CAMPAGNATICO
Grosseto km 22 • m 275
Wineries
Valle - Podere Ex E.M. 348 ♟♟
Località Lle, tel. 0564998142
r • Morellino di Scansano Llle - Doc
r • Morellino di Scansano Valle - Doc

CAMPIGLIA MARITTIMA
Livorno km 72 • m 231
Wineries
Banti Jacopo ♟♟♟♟
Località Citerna 24, tel. 0565838802
www.jacopobanti.it
r • Val di Cornia Ciliegiolo - Doc
r • Val di Cornia Rosso Aleatico - Doc
r • Val di Cornia Rosso Di Campalto - Doc
r • Val di Cornia Rosso Il Peccato - Doc
w • Val di Cornia Bianco Poggio Angelica - Doc
Graziani Giovanni ♟♟♟
Località Casalappi 62, tel. 0565843043
r • Val di Cornia Rosso Diciocco - Doc
w • Val di Cornia Bianco Corniello - Doc
w • Diciocco Vermentino Toscana - Igt
Le Volpaiole ♟♟
Via Fonte Corboli 13, tel. 0565843194
r • Val di Cornia Rosso Volpaiole - Doc
Rigoli ♟♟♟
Via degli Ulivi 8, tel. 0565843079
r • Val di Cornia Rosso Montepitti - Doc
r • Val di Cornia Rosso Testalto - Doc

CAMPO NELL'ELBA
Livorno km 99 • m 905
Wineries
Cecilia ♟
Località La Pila, tel. 0565977322
vini.cecilia@virgilio.it
r • Elba Rosso Riserva - Doc
w • Elba Ansonica - Doc
s • Elba Moscato - Doc

CAPANNORI
Lucca km 6 • m 15
Wineries
Colle di Bordocheo ♟
Località Segromigno in Monte,
via Piaggiori Basso 123, tel. 0583929821
r • Colline Lucchesi Rosso Picchio - Doc
Fattoria Colle Verde ♟♟♟
Località Castello, tel. 0583402262
r • Colline Lucchesi Rosso Brania delle Ghiandaie - Doc
r • Nero della Spinosa Toscana - Igt
w • Brania del Cancello Bianco Toscana - Igt
Fattoria di Fubbiano ♟♟♟
Località San Gennaro, via per Fubbiano 6,
tel. 058397801 I
www.fattoriadifubbiano.it
r • Colline Lucchesi Rosso San Gennaro - Doc
r • I Pampini Toscana Rosso - Igt
w • Colline Lucchesi Vermentino - Doc
La Badiola ♟♟♟
Località Marlia, via del Parco, tel. 0583309633
r • Colline Lucchesi Merlot - Doc
r • Colline Lucchesi Rosso - Doc
w • Stoppielle - Igt
La Vigna di Gragnano ♟♟♟
Località Gragnano, via della Chiesa 44,
tel. 0583974037
r • Colline Lucchesi Merlot - Doc
r • Colline Lucchesi Merlot Poggio dei Paoli - Doc
Maionchi ♟♟
Località Tofori, via di Tofori 81, tel. 0583978197
r • Collegrosso Toscana Rosso - Igt
r • Rubino di Selvata Toscana Rosso - Igt
Tenuta di Valgiano ♟♟♟
Località Valgiano, via di Valgiano 7, tel. 0583402271
r • Colline Lucchesi Scasso dei Cesari - Doc
r • Palistorti Toscana Rosso - Igt
w • Colline Lucchesi Giallo dei Muri - Doc

CAPRAIA E LIMITE
Florence km 30 • m 24/410
Wineries
Matroneo ♟♟♟
Località Capraia, via Valicarda 35, tel. 0571910078
www.enricopierazzuoli.com
r • Chianti Classico Matroneo - Docg
Tenuta Cantagallo ♟♟♟
Via Valicarda 35, tel. 0571910078
www.enricopierazzuoli.com
r • Chianti Montalbano - Docg
r • Chianti Montalbano Riserva - Docg
r • Gioveto Colli della Toscana Centrale Rosso - Igt

CARMIGNANO
Prato km 13 • m 189
Wineries
Fattoria Ambra ♟♟♟
Via Lombarda 85, tel. 055486488
r • Carmignano Riserva Elzana - Docg

r • Carmignano Riserva Le Vigne Alte Montalbiolo - Docg
r • Carmignano Santa Cristina in Pilli - Docg

Pratesi ♟♟♟
Località Seano, via Rizzelli 10, tel. 0558953531
lolocco@libero.it
r • Carmignano - Docg

Tenuta di Capezzana ♟♟♟♟♟
Località Seano, via di Capezzana 100,
tel. 0558706005
www.capezzana.it
r • Carmignano Villa di Capezzana - Docg
r • Carmignano Trefiano - Docg
r • Ghiaie della Furba Toscana Rosso - Igt
w • Capezzana Chardonnay di Toscana - Igt
s • Carmignano Vin Santo Riserva - Doc

Tenuta Le Farnete ♟♟♟
Località Corneana, via Macia 144, tel. 0571910078
www.enricopierazzuoli.com
r • Carmignano - Docg
r • Carmignano Riserva - Docg
r • Unico - Igt

CARRARA

Massa-Carrara km 7 • m 100

Wineries

VIN.CA. ♟♟♟
Località Avenza, via Candia Bassa 27 bis,
tel. 0585834217
r • Gialosguardo Merlot - Igt
w • Candia dei Colli Apuani Terrafranca - Doc
w • Candia dei Colli Apuani Vermentino Ultramarina - Doc

CASTAGNETO CARDUCCI

Livorno km 58 • m 194

Wineries

Caccia al Piano 1868 ♟♟♟
Località Caccia al Piano, via Bolgherese 279,
tel. 3356250887
r • Bolgheri Ruit Hora - Doc
r • Levia Gravia Toscana - Igt

Ceralti ♟♟♟
Piazza del Popolo 13, tel. 0565763989
www.ceralti.com
r • Bolgheri Rosso Alfeo - Doc
w • Bolgheri Bianco Ceralti - Doc
w • Il Sogno di Cleofe Toscana - Igt

Chiappini Giovanni ♟♟♟
Località Le Preselle, podere Felciaino 189,
tel. 0565749665
chiappini.giovanni@tiscalinet.it
r • Felciaino Toscana Rosso - Igt
r • Guado De' Gemoli Toscana Rosso - Igt

Cipriana ♟♟♟
Podere Campastrello, tel. 0565775568
www.terra-toscana.com\lacipriana
r • Bolgheri Rosso Superiore S. Martino - Doc

Collemassari ♟♟♟♟♟
Località Grattamacco, tel. 0564990496
r • Bolgheri Rosso Superiore Grattamacco - Doc
w • Bolgheri Bianco Grattamacco - Doc

Greppi Cupi - Gasser Bagnoli ♟♟♟
Località Greppi Cupi 212, tel. 0565775272
r • Bolgheri Rosso Rubino dei Greppi - Doc
w • Bolgheri Bianco Greppi Cupi - Doc

Le Macchiole ♟♟♟♟♟
Via Bolgherese 189/A, tel. 0565766092
r • Bolgheri Rosso Superiore Paléo - Doc
r • Macchiole Rosso Toscana - Igt
r • Messorio Rosso Toscana - Igt
r • Scrio Rosso Toscana - Igt
w • Paléo Bianco Toscana - Igt

Santini Enrico ♟♟♟♟
Località Campo alla Casa 74, tel. 0565774375
r • Bolgheri Rosso Montepergoli - Doc
r • Bolgheri Rosso Poggio al Moro - Doc
w • Bolgheri Bianco Campo alla Casa - Doc

Satta Michele ♟♟♟♟ ★10%
Località Vigna al Cavaliere 61, tel. 0565773041
satta@infol.it
r • Bolgheri Rosso Piastraia - Doc
r • Cavaliere Rosso di Toscana - Igt
r • Diambra Rosso di Toscana - Igt
w • Costa di Giulia Bianco di Toscana - Igt
w • Giovin Re Bianco di Toscana - Igt

Tenuta dell'Ornellaia ♟♟♟♟♟
Via Bolgherese 191, tel. 0565762140
r • Bolgheri Rosso Le Serre Nuove - Doc
r • Bolgheri Rosso Superiore Ornellaia - Doc
r • Masseto - Vdt

Tenuta Guado al Tasso ♟♟♟♟♟
Località Belvedere - Bolgheri, tel. 0565749735
www.antinori.it
r • Bolgheri Rosso Superiore Guado al Tasso - Doc
r • Bolgheri Rosato Scalabrone - Doc
w • Bolgheri Vermentino - Doc

Tenuta San Guido ♟♟♟♟♟
Località Capanne 27, tel. 0565762003
r • Bolgheri Sassicaia - Doc
r • Guidalberto Toscana Rosso - Igt

CASTELFIORENTINO

Florence km 39 • m 50

Wineries

Castello di Oliveto ♟♟
Via di Monte Olivo 6, tel. 057164322
www.castellooliveto.it
r • Chianti Castello di Oliveto - Docg
r • Leone X Toscana Rosso - Igt
s • Vin Santo del Chianti - Doc

CASTELLINA IN CHIANTI

Siena km 21 • m 578

Wineries

Buondonno - Casavecchia alla Piazza ♟♟♟
Località Casavecchia alla Piazza 37, tel. 0577749754
buondonno@chianticlassico.com
r • Chianti Classico - Docg
r • Chianti Classico Riserva - Docg
r • Campo ai Ciliegi Syrah di Toscana - Igt

Casina di Cornia ♟♟♟
Località Casina di Cornia, tel. 0577743052
www.casinadicornia.com
r • Chianti Classico - Docg
r • Chianti Classico Riserva Vigna La Casina - Docg
r • L'Amaranto Toscana Cabernet Sauvignon - Igt

Castellare di Castellina ♟♟♟♟
Località Castellare, tel. 0577740490
www.castellare.it
r • Chianti Classico - Docg

r • Chianti Classico Riserva Vigna Poggiale - Docg
r • Coniale di Castellare Toscana Rosso - Igt
r • I Sodi di San Niccolò Toscana - Igt
r • Poggio ai Merli di Castellare Toscana - Igt

Castello di Fonterutoli ♟♟♟♟♟
Località Fonterutoli, tel. 057773571
www.fonterutoli.it
r • Chianti Classico Fonterutoli - Docg
r • Chianti Classico Castello di Fonterutoli - Docg
r • Siepi Toscana - Igt

Castello La Leccia ♟♟♟
Località La Leccia, tel. 0577743148
r • Chianti Classico - Docg
r • Chianti Classico Riserva - Docg
r • Bruciagna - Igt

Cecchi ♟♟♟
Località Casina dei Ponti 56, tel. 0577743024
www.cecchi.net
r • Chianti Classico - Docg
r • Chianti Classico Messer Pietro di Teuzzo - Docg
r • La Gavina Cabernet Sauvignon di Toscana - Igt
r • Spargolo Sangiovese di Toscana - Igt
w • Sagrato di San Lorenzo a Montauto Chardonnay di Toscana - Igt

Concadoro ♟♟♟
Località Concadoro 67, tel. 0577741285
concadoro@chiantinet.it
r • Chianti Classico Concadoro - Docg
r • Chianti Classico Vigna di Gaversa - Docg

Fattoria Campoperi - Casale dello Sparviero ♟♟♟
Località Casale 93, tel. 0577743062
fattoriacampoperi@libero.it
r • Chianti Classico Casale dello Sparviero - Docg
r • Chianti Classico Riserva Casale dello Sparviero - Docg

Fattoria Nittardi ♟♟♟
Località Nittardi, tel. 0577740269
r • Chianti Classico Casanuova di Nittardi - Docg
r • Chianti Classico Riserva Nittardi - Docg
w • Biondo di Nittardi - Igt

Fattoria San Leonino ♟♟
Località I Cipressi, tel. 0577743108
r • Chianti Classico San Leonino - Docg
r • Chianti Classico Selezione Monsenese - Docg

Gagliole ♟♟♟
Località Gagliole 42, tel. 0577740369
www.gagliole.com
r • Gagliole Rosso Colli della Toscana Centrale - Igt
r • Pecchia Rosso Colli della Toscana Centrale - Igt

Podere Collelungo ♟♟♟♟
Località Collelungo, tel. 0577740489
r • Chianti Classico - Docg
r • Chianti Classico Roveto - Docg

Poggio Amorelli ♟♟
Località Poggio Amorelli, tel. 0571668733
r • Chianti Classico Poggio Amorelli - Docg
r • Chianti Classico Riserva Poggio Amorelli - Docg

Querceto di Castellina ♟♟
Via Chiantigiana, tel. 0577733590
www.querceto.com
r • Chianti Classico L'Aura - Docg
r • Podalirio Toscana Rosso - Igt

Rocca delle Macìe ♟♟♟
Località Le Macie, tel. 05777321
r • Chianti Classico Riserva di Fizzano - Docg
r • Chianti Classico Tenuta Sant'Alfonso - Docg
r • Roccato Toscana - Igt

Rodano ♟♟♟
Località Rodano 84, tel. 0577743107
rodano@chianticlassico.com
r • Chianti Classico Riserva Viacosta - Docg
r • Lazzicante Merlot di Toscana - Igt
r • Monna Claudia - Vdt

San Fabiano Calcinaia ♟♟♟♟
Località Cellole, tel. 0577979232
www.chianticlassico.com
r • Chianti Classico - Docg
r • Cerviolo Rosso - Igt
w • Cerviolo Bianco - Igt

Tenuta di Bibbiano ♟♟♟ ★10%
Via Bibbiano 76, tel. 0577743065
www.tenutadibibbiano.com
r • Chianti Classico Montornello - Docg
r • Chianti Classico Riserva Vigna del Capannino - Docg

Tenuta di Lilliano ♟♟♟
Località Lilliano, tel. 0577743070
www.lilliano.com
r • Chianti Classico - Docg
r • Anagallis Colli della Toscana Centrale - Igt
r • Vignacatena Colli della Toscana Centrale - Igt

Villa Cerna ♟♟♟
Località Cerna, tel. 0577743024
www.villacerna.it
r • Chianti Classico - Docg
w • Chianti Classico Riserva - Docg

CASTELLINA MARITTIMA

Pisa km 49 • m 375

Wineries

Castello del Terriccio ♟♟♟♟♟
Via Bagnoli 20, tel. 050699709
www.terriccio.it
r • Lupicaia - Igt
r • Tassinaia - Igt
w • Con Vento - Igt
w • Rondinaia - Igt
w • Saluccio - Igt

CASTELNUOVO BERARDENGA

Siena km 20 • m 351

Wineries

Antico Podere Colle ai Lecci ♟
Località San Gusmè, S.S. 484 Nord, tel. 0577359084
www.colleailecci.com
r • Chianti Classico Riserva San Cosma Girasole - Docg

Canonica a Cerreto ♟♟
Località Canonica, tel. 0577363261
www.canonicacerreto.it
r • Chianti Classico Canonica a Cerreto - Docg

Castell'in Villa ♟♟♟
Località Castell'in Villa, tel. 0577359074
www.castellinvilla.com
r • Chianti Classico Riserva Poggio delle Rose - Docg
r • Santacroce Toscana - Igt
s • Vin Santo del Chianti Classico - Doc

CASTELLO DI BOSSI ♟♟♟♟
Località Bossi in Chianti, tel. 0577359330
www.castellodibossi.it
r • Chianti Classico - Docg
r • Chianti Classico Riserva Berardo - Docg
r • Corbaia Toscana Rosso - Igt
r • Girolamo Toscana Rosso - Igt

CASTELLO DI MONASTERO ♟♟♟
Località Monastero d'Ombrone 19,
tel. 0577355789
r • Chianti Classico - Docg
r • Chianti Superiore Montetondo - Docg
r • Infinito Rosso di Toscana - Igt
r • Sangiovese di Toscana - Igt
s • Vin Santo del Chianti Lunanuova - Doc

CASTELLO DI SELVOLE ♟♟♟
Località Selvole, tel. 0577322662
www.selvole.com
r • Chianti Classico - Docg
r • Chianti Classico Riserva - Docg
r • Barullo Toscana Rosso - Igt

FATTORIA CARPINETO FONTALPINA ♟♟♟
Località Carpineto Montaperti, tel. 0577283228
r • Chianti Colli Senesi Gioia - Doc
r • Do ut Des - Vdt

FATTORIA DELLA AIOLA ♟♟
Località Vagliagli, tel. 0577322615
www.aiola.net
r • Chianti Classico Aiola - Docg
r • Chianti Classico Riserva Aiola - Docg
r • Chianti Classico Riserva Cancello Rosso - Docg
r • Logaiolo Colli della Toscana Centrale Rosso - Igt
r • Rosso del Senatore Colli della Toscana Centrale Rosso - Igt

FATTORIA DI FELSINA ♟♟♟♟♟
Strada Chiantigiana 484, tel. 0577355117
felsina@dodo.it
r • Chianti Classico Berardenga - Docg
r • Chianti Classico Riserva Rancia Berardenga - Docg
r • Vin Santo del Chianti Classico - Doc
r • Fontalloro Sangiovese di Toscana - Igt
r • Maestro Raro Toscana - Igt

FATTORIA DI PETROIO ♟♟♟
Località Quercegrossa, via Mocenni 7,
tel. 0577328045
www.chianticlassico.com
r • Chianti Classico - Docg
r • Chianti Classico Poggio al Mandorlo - Docg
r • Chianti Classico Riserva - Docg

FATTORIA DIEVOLE ♟♟♟
Località Vagliagli, tel. 0577322613
www.dievole.it
r • Chianti Classico - Docg
r • Chianti Classico Duemila Dievole - Docg
r • Chianti Classico Riserva Novecento - Docg
r • Broccato Toscana - Igt
r • Rinascimento Toscana - Igt

FATTORIE CHIGI SARACINI - AGRICOLA POGGIO BONELLI ♟♟♟
Via dell'Arbia 2, tel. 0577355113
e.fattoriechigi@mps.it
r • Chianti - Docg
r • Chianti Superiore - Docg
r • Il Poggiassai Rosso Toscano - Igt

LA CASACCIA ♟♟
Località San Gusmè, tel. 0577222436
www.casaccia.com
r • Chianti Classico - Docg
r • Chianti Classico Riserva - Docg

PODERE LE BONCIE ♟♟
tel. 0577359383
r • Chianti Classico Le Trame - Docg

POGGIO BONELLI ♟♟♟
Località Poggio Bonelli, tel. 0577355382
www.poggiobonelli.it
r • Chianti Classico - Docg
r • Chianti Classico Riserva - Docg
r • Tramonto d'Oca Toscana Rosso - Igt

QUERCIAVALLE - LOSI ♟♟♟
Località Pontignano, tel. 0577356842
az.agricolalosi@libero.it
r • Chianti Classico Pontignanello - Docg
r • Chianti Classico Riserva Millennium - Docg
r • Chianti Classico Riserva Pontignanello - Docg
r • Chianti Classico Riserva Querciavalle - Docg
r • Armonia Colli della Toscana Centrale Rosso - Igt

CASTIGLIONE D'ORCIA
Siena km 51 • m 540

WINERIES

CASTELLO DI RIPA D'ORCIA ♟♟♟
Località Ripa d'Orcia, tel. 0577897376
www.castellodiripadorcia.com
r • Orcia Rosso - Doc

CECINA
Livorno km 36 • m 15

WINERIES

ELISABETTA ♟♟♟♟
Località San Pietro in Palazzi, via Tronto 10/14,
tel. 0586661096
www.agrihotel-elisabetta.com
r • Brunetti Toscana Rosso - Igt
r • Le Marze Rosso Toscana - Igt
w • Le Marze Bianco Toscana - Igt

FERRARI IRIS E FIGLI ♟♟
Via Pasubio 87, tel. 0586677543
r • Montescudaio Rosso Fattoria Santa Perpetua - Doc
r • Argine Rosso Toscana - Igt
r • Penso Rosso Toscana - Igt

CERRETO GUIDI
Florence km 40 • m 123

WINERIES

PETRIOLO ♟♟♟ ★15%
Via di Petriolo 7, tel. 0571509491
www.villapetriolo.com
r • Chianti Villa Petriolo - Docg
r • Golpaja Toscana Rosso - Igt
s • Vinsanto del Chianti Villa Petriolo - Doc

CETONA
Siena km 88 • m 385

WINERIES

CANTINA GENTILI CARLO ♟♟
Località Piazze, via del Tamburino 96,
tel. 0578244321
www.gentiliwine.com

r • La Favorita Toscana Rosso - Igt

Duca di Saragnano 🍷🍷

Località Piazze, via del Palazzone 4, tel. 0578244174

www.enogest.com

r • Vino Nobile di Montepulciano Duca di Saragnano - Docg

r • Duca di Saragnano Sangiovese di Toscana - Igt

CHIANCIANO TERME

Siena km 77 • m 475

Wineries

Gavioli 🍷🍷🍷 ★10%

Località Maglianella, S.S. 146, tel. 057863995

r • Chianti Superiore Brandesco - Docg

r • Vino Nobile di Montepulciano - Docg

r • Vino Nobile di Montepulciano Riserva - Docg

r • Rosso di Montepulciano - Doc

r • Sergavio Toscana Rosso - Igt

CHIUSI

Siena km 77 • m 398

Wineries

Colle Santa Mustiola 🍷🍷🍷🍷

Via delle Torri 86/A, tel. 057863462

r • Poggio ai Chiari - Vdt

CINIGIANO

Grosseto km 36 • m 324

Wineries

Montecucco 🍷🍷🍷

Località Monte Cucco, tel. 0564999029

www.amiatacommerce.it\montecucco

r • Montecucco Rosso Passonaia - Doc

r • Montecucco Sangiovese Le Coste - Doc

w • Montecucco Vermentino - Doc

CIVITELLA PAGANICO

Grosseto km 32 • m 44/596

Wineries

Fattoria Capannacce 🍷🍷🍷🍷

Località Pari, tel. 0564908848

r • Poggio Crocino Rosso della Maremma Toscana - Igt

r • Rosso della Maremma Toscana - Igt

COLLE DI VAL D'ELSA

Siena km 24 • m 141

Wineries

Podere San Luigi 🍷🍷

Località Mugnano 59, tel. 0577959724

sanluigi21@hotmail.com

r • Aprelis Toscana Rosso - Igt

r • San Luigi Toscana Rosso - Igt

r • Vigna Casanova - Vdt

CORTONA

Arezzo km 28 • m 494

Wineries

Tenimenti Luigi d'Alessandro 🍷🍷🍷🍷🍷

Località Camucia, via Manzano 15, tel. 0575618667

tenimenti.dalessandro@flashnet.it

r • Cortona Syrah Il Bosco - Doc

w • Cortona Chardonnay Fontarca - Doc

s • Vin Santo - Vdt

DICOMANO

Florence km 35 • m 162

Wineries

Frascole 🍷🍷🍷

Località Frascole, tel. 0558386340

www.frascole.it

r • Chianti Rufina Frascole - Docg

r • Chianti Rufina Riserva Il Santo - Docg

s • Vin Santo del Chianti Rufina - Doc

FAUGLIA

Pisa km 22 • m 91

Wineries

Fattoria Uccelliera 🍷🍷🍷

Via Pontita 26, tel. 050662747

www.uccelliera.com

r • Chianti - Docg

r • Castellaccio Toscana Rosso - Igt

w • Castellaccio Toscana Bianco - Igt

I Giusti & Zanza Vigneti 🍷🍷🍷🍷

Via dei Puntoni 9, tel. 058544354

www.igiustiezanza.it

r • Belcore - Igt

r • Dulcamara - Igt

FLORENCE

m 50

Wineries

Compagnia del Vino 🍷🍷🍷

Borgo degli Albizi 14, tel. 055243101

www.compagniadelvino.it

r • Morellino di Scansano Il Grillesino - Doc

r • Ceccante Il Grillesino Toscana - Vdt

w • Prosecco di Valdobbiadene Brut Col de' Salici - Doc

w • Prosecco di Valdobbiadene Extra Dry Col de' Salici - Doc

w • Prosecco di Valdobbiadene Superiore di Cartizze Dry Col de' Salici - Doc

Marchesi Antinori 🍷🍷🍷🍷🍷

Piazza degli Antinori 3, tel. 05523595

www.antinori.it

r • Chianti Classico Pèppoli - Docg

r • Chianti Classico Riserva Badia a Passignano - Docg

r • Chianti Classico Riserva Tenute Marchese Antinori - Docg

r • Santa Cristina Rosso Toscana - Igt

r • Solaia Rosso Toscana - Igt

r • Tignanello Rosso Toscana - Igt

s • Fattoria Aldobrandesca Aleatico di Toscana - Igt

Marchesi de' Frescobaldi 🍷🍷🍷🍷

Via Santo Spirito 11, tel. 05527141

r • Chianti Rufina Montesodi - Docg

r • Chianti Rufina Riserva Nipozzano - Docg

r • Pomino Rosso Castello di Pomino - Doc

r • Mormoreto Toscana Rosso - Igt

w • Pomino Bianco Il Benefizio - Doc

Tenuta Conti Spalletti 🍷🍷

Via di S. Maria, tel. 0552385901

r • Chianti Rufina Riserva Poggio Reale - Docg

FOIANO DELLA CHIANA

Arezzo km 28 • m 318

WINERIES

FATTORIA SANTA VITTORIA ♟♟
Località Pozzo, via Piana 43, tel. 057566807
www.fattoriasantavittoria.com
r • Valdichiana Rosso Poggio al Tempio - Doc
w • Le Gaggiole Toscana Bianco - Igt
s • Vinsanto Santa Vittoria - Vdt

FUCECCHIO

Florence km 44 • m 25

WINERIES

FATTORIA MONTELLORI ♟♟♟
Via Pistoiese 5, tel. 0571260641
montellori@tin.it
r • Chianti - Docg
r • Castelrapiti Rosso Toscana - Igt
r • Salamartano Rosso Toscana - Igt
r • Vigne del Moro Rosso Toscano - Igt
s • Bianco dell'Empolese Vin Santo - Doc

GAIOLE IN CHIANTI

Siena km 28 • m 360

WINERIES

AGRICOLTORI DEL CHIANTI GEOGRAFICO ♟♟♟
Via Mulinaccio 10, tel. 0577749489
www.chiantigeografico.it
r • Chianti Classico - Docg
r • Chianti Classico Contessa di Radda - Docg
r • Chianti Colline Senesi - Docg
r • Ferraiolo Toscana - Igt
r • Pulleraia Toscana - Igt

BADIA A COLTIBUONO ♟♟♟♟
Località Badia a Coltibuono, tel. 057774481
www.coltibuono.com
r • Chianti Cetamura - Docg
r • Chianti Classico Badia a Coltibuono - Docg
r • Chianti Classico RS - Docg
r • Sangioveto Toscana Rosso - Igt
s • Vin Santo del Chianti Classico - Doc

BARONE RICASOLI - CASTELLO DI BROLIO ♟♟♟♟♟
Località Cantine del Castello di Brolio, tel. 05777301
www.ricasoli.it
r • Chianti Classico Castello di Brolio - Docg
r • Chianti Classico Riserva Rocca Guicciarda - Docg
r • Casalferro Toscana - Igt
w • Torricella Toscana Chardonnay - Igt
s • Vin Santo del Chianti Classico Brolio - Doc

CAPANNELLE ♟♟♟♟♟
Località Capannelle, tel. 0577749691
www.capannelle.com
r • Chianti Classico Riserva - Docg
r • Capannelle - Vdt
r • Solare - Vdt
r • 50 & 50 - Vdt
w • Capannelle Chardonnay - Igt

CASTELLO DI AMA ♟♟♟♟♟
Località Lecchi in Chianti, tel. 0577746031
www.castellodiama.com
r • Chianti Classico Castello di Ama Vigneto Bellavista - Docg
r • Chianti Classico Castello di Ama Vigneto La Casuccia - Docg
r • Castello di Ama Il Chiuso - Igt
r • Castello di Ama L'Apparita - Igt
w • Castello di Ama Al Poggio - Igt

CASTELLO DI CACCHIANO ♟♟♟
Località Cacchiano, tel. 0577747018
www.chianticlassico.com/cacchiano
r • Chianti Classico Millennio - Docg
r • R.F. Castello di Cacchiano Toscana - Igt
s • Vin Santo del Chianti Classico - Doc

CASTELLO DI LUCIGNANO ♟♟♟♟
Località Lucignano 1, tel. 0577747810
r • Chianti Classico - Docg
r • Chianti Classico Riserva - Docg
r • Il Solissimo Toscana - Igt

CASTELLO DI MELETO ♟♟♟♟
Località Meleto, tel. 0577749217
www.castellomeleto.it
r • Chianti Classico Castello di Meleto - Docg
r • Chianti Classico Pieve di Spaltenna - Docg
r • Fiore di Meleto Sangiovese Toscana - Igt
r • Rainero Toscana Rosso - Igt
s • Vin Santo del Chianti Classico - Doc

COLOMBAIO DI CENCIO ♟♟♟♟
Località Cornia, tel. 0577747178
colombaiodicencio@tin.it
r • Chianti Classico I Massi del Colombaio - Docg
r • Chianti Classico Riserva I Massi del Colombaio - Docg
r • Il Futuro Toscana Rosso - Igt

FATTORIA SAN GIUSTO A RENTENNANO ♟♟♟♟♟
Località San Giusto 20, tel. 0577747121
www.italywines.com
r • Chianti Classico - Docg
r • Chianti Classico Riserva - Docg
r • La Ricolma Rosso Toscana - Vdt
r • Percarlo Rosso Toscana - Vdt
s • San Giusto Vin Santo Toscano - Vdt

FATTORIA VALTELLINA ♟♟♟♟
Località Rietine, tel. 0577731005
r • Chianti Classico - Docg
r • Convivio Rosso Toscana - Igt
r • Il Duca di Montechioccioli Rosso Toscana - Igt

MONTIVERDI ♟♟♟
Località Montiverdi, tel. 0577749305
r • Chianti Classico - Docg
r • Chianti Classico Vigneto Carpinaia - Docg
r • Vigneto Le Borranine - Vdt

PODERE IL PALAZZINO ♟♟♟♟
Località Monti, tel. 0577747008
www.chianticlassico.com
r • Chianti Classico Argenina - Docg
r • Chianti Classico La Pieve - Docg
r • Chianti Classico Riserva Grosso Sanese - Docg

RIECINE ♟♟♟♟♟
Località Riecine, tel. 0577749098
www.riecine.com
r • Chianti Classico - Docg
r • Chianti Classico Riserva - Docg
r • La Gioia di Riecine Rosso Toscana - Igt

RIETINE ♟♟♟
Località Rietine 27, tel. 0577738482
r • Chianti Classico - Docg
r • Chianti Classico Riserva - Docg
r • Tiziano - Igt

ROCCA DI CASTAGNOLI ♟♟♟♟ ★10%
Località Castagnoli, tel. 0577731004
www.roccadicastagnoli.com
r • Chianti Classico - Docg

r • Chianti Classico Riserva Capraia - Docg
r • Chianti Classico Riserva Poggio a'Frati - Docg
r • Stielle Toscana Toscana Rosso - Igt
s • Vin Santo del Chianti Classico - Doc

Rocca di Montegrossi ♟♟♟♟
Località Monti in Chianti,
tel. 0577747977
r • Chianti Classico Riserva San Marcellino - Docg
r • Geremia Toscana Rosso - Vdt
s • Vin Santo del Chianti Classico Rocca di Montegrossi - Doc

San Vincenti ♟♟♟
Località San Vincenti, podere di Stignano,
tel. 0577734047
svincent@chiantinet.it
r • Chianti Classico - Docg
r • Chianti Classico Riserva Podere Stignano - Docg
r • Stignano Rosso Toscana - Igt

Tenimenti Pile e Lamole e Vistarenni ♟♟♟
Località Vistarenni,
tel. 0577738186
a.ali@vistarenni.com
r • Chianti Classico Lamole di Lamole - Docg
r • Chianti Classico Lamole di Lamole Etichetta Blu - Docg
r • Chianti Classico Lamole di Lamole Riserva Vigneto di Campolungo - Docg
r • Chianti Classico Villa Vistarenni - Docg
r • Codirosso Rosso Toscana - Igt

GAMBASSI TERME
Florence km 47 • m 332

Wineries

Villa Pillo ♟♟♟
Via Volterrana 24, tel. 0571680212
www.villapillo.com
r • Sant'Adele Toscana Merlot - Igt
r • Villa Pillo Toscana Syrah - Igt
r • Vivaldaia Toscana Cabernet Franc - Igt

GAVORRANO
Grosseto km 38 • m 273

Wineries

Fattoria Poggio Valpazza ♟♟
Località Poggio Ventoso, tel. 056681819
gianni.dormi@libero.it
r • Monteregio di Massa Marittima Rosso - Doc

Montebelli ♟♟♟
Località Caldana, tel. 0566887100
www.montebelli.com
r • Monteregio di Massa Marittima Rosso Fabula - Doc
r • Monteregio di Massa Marittima Rosso Fabula Riserva - Doc

GREVE IN CHIANTI
Florence km 30 • m 236

Wineries

Carobbio ♟♟♟
Località Panzano, via S. Martino in Cecione 26,
tel. 0558560133
info@carobbiowine.com
r • Chianti Classico - Docg
r • Leone del Carobbio - Igt
r • Pietraforte del Carobbio - Igt

Carpineto ♟♟♟♟
Località Dudda 17/B, tel. 0558549062
www.carpineto.com
r • Chianti Classico - Docg
r • Vino Nobile di Montepulciano Riserva - Docg
r • Rosso di Montepulciano - Doc
r • Dogajolo Rosso Toscano - Igt
r • Farnito Toscana Cabernet Sauvignon - Igt

Castello di Querceto ♟♟♟
Località Dudda 61, tel. 05585921
r • Chianti Classico Castello di Querceto - Docg
r • Chianti Classico Riserva Il Picchio - Docg
r • Il Querciolaia - Igt

Castello Vicchiomaggio ♟♟♟
Via Vicchiomaggio 4, tel. 055854079
www.vicchiomaggio.it
r • Chianti Classico Riserva Petri - Docg
r • Chianti Classico Riserva La Prima - Docg
r • Chianti Classico San Jacopo - Docg
r • Ripa delle Mandorle - Igt
r • Ripa delle More - Igt

Cennatoio ♟♟♟♟
Località Panzano, via S. Leolino 35, tel. 0558963230
r • Chianti Classico Cennatoio - Docg
r • Chianti Classico Riserva O'Leandro - Docg
r • baldo Rosso Toscana - Igt
r • Etrusco Sangiovese di Toscana - Igt
s • Vin Santo del Chianti Classico Occhio di Pernice - Doc

Fattoria Casaloste ♟♟♟
Località Panzano, via Montagliari 32,
tel. 055852725
www.casaloste.it
r • Chianti Classico - Docg
r • Chianti Classico Riserva - Docg
r • Chianti Classico Riserva Don Vincenzo - Docg

Fattoria Castello di Verrazzano ♟♟♟ ★10%
Località Castello di Verrazzano, tel. 055854243
r • Chianti Classico - Docg
r • Sassello - Vdt
s • Vin Santo del Chianti Classico - Doc

Fattoria Le Bocce ♟♟♟
Località Panzano, via Case Sparse 77,
tel. 055852153
r • Chianti Classico - Docg
r • Chianti Classico Riserva - Docg
r • Vigna del Paladino - Igt

Fattoria Le Fonti ♟♟♟
Località Panzano, via Le Fonti, tel. 055852194
www.fattorialefonti.it
r • Chianti Classico Riserva - Docg
r • Fontissimo Alta Valle della Greve - Igt

Fattoria Villa Cafaggio ♟♟♟♟♟
Località Panzano, via S. Martino in Cecione 5,
tel. 0558549094
r • Chianti Classico - Docg
r • Cortaccio Toscana Rosso - Igt
r • San Martino Toscana Rosso - Igt

Fattoria Viticcio ♟♟♟♟
Via S. Cresci 12/A, tel. 055854210
www.fattoriaviticcio.com
r • Chianti Classico Riserva Viticcio - Docg
r • Chianti Classico Riserva Beatrice - Docg
r • Chianti Classico Viticcio - Docg
r • Monile Rosso Toscana - Igt
r • Prunaio Rosso Toscana - Igt

Fontodi ♟♟♟♟♟
Località Panzano, via S. Leolino 89, tel. 055852005
r • Chianti Classico - Docg
r • Chianti Classico Riserva Vigna del Sorbo - Docg
r • Flaccianello della Pieve Colli della Toscana Centrale - Igt
r • Pinot Nero Case Via Colli della Toscana Centrale - Igt
r • Syrah Case Via Colli della Toscana Centrale - Igt

La Madonnina - Triacca ♟♟♟
Località Strada in Chianti, via Palaia 39, tel. 055858003
r • Chianti Classico Bello Stento - Docg
r • Chianti Classico La Madonnina La Palaia - Docg
r • Chianti Classico Riserva La Madonnina - Docg
r • Vino Nobile di Montepulciano Santa Venere - Docg
r • Il Mandorlo Rosso Toscana - Igt

La Massa ♟♟♟♟
Località Panzano, via Case Sparse 9, tel. 055852722
r • Chianti Classico - Docg
r • Chianti Classico Riserva Giorgio Primo - Docg

La Torraccia di Presura ♟♟♟
Via della Montagnola 130, tel. 0558588656
www.torracciaadipresura.it
r • Chianti Classico Il Tarrocco - Docg
r • Chianti Classico Torraccia di Presura - Docg
r • Lucciolaio Rosso Toscano - Igt

Le Cinciole ♟♟♟
Località Panzano, via Case Sparse 83, tel. 055852636
cinciole@chianticlassico.com
r • Chianti Classico Le Cinciole - Docg
r • Chianti Classico Riserva Petresco - Docg

Le Masse di San Leolino ♟♟♟
Località Panzano, tel. 055852144
r • Chianti Classico - Docg
r • Chianti Classico Riserva - Docg

Monte Bernardi ♟♟♟
Località Panzano, via Chiantigiana, tel. 055852400
r • Chianti Classico - Docg
r • Sa'etta - Vdt
r • Tzingana - Vdt

Panzanello ♟♟♟ ★10%
Località Panzano, via Case Sparse 86, tel. 055852470
www.panzanello.it
r • Chianti Classico - Docg
r • Chianti Classico Riserva - Docg
r • Il Mastio Rosso Toscana - Igt

Poggio Scalette ♟♟♟♟♟
Località Ruffoli, via di Barbiano 7, tel. 0558546108
j.fiore@tiscalinet.it
r • Il Carbonaione Alta Valle della Greve - Igt
r • Piantonaia Alta Valle della Greve - Igt

Querciabella ♟♟♟♟♟
Località Ruffoli, via di Barbiano 17, tel. 0272002256
www.querciabella.com
r • Chianti Classico Querciabella - Docg
r • Chianti Classico Riserva Querciabella - Docg
r • Camartina Toscana - Igt
r • Palafreno Toscana - Igt
w • Batàr Toscana - Igt

S. Lucia in Faulle - Castello dei Rampolla ♟♟♟♟
Località Panzano, via S. Lucia in Faulle, tel. 055852001
r • Chianti Classico - Docg
r • La Vigna di Alceo - Igt
r • Sammarco - Igt
w • Tre Bianco Vendemmia Tardiva Toscana - Igt
s • Tre Bianco Vendemmia Tardiva Toscana - Igt

San Cresci ♟♟♟
Via S. Cresci 1, tel. 055853255
r • Chianti Classico San Cresci - Docg
r • San Cresci Alta Valle della Greve - Igt

Savignola Paolina ♟♟
Via Petriolo 58, tel. 055853139
savignola@libero.it
r • Chianti Classico - Docg
r • Chianti Classico Riserva - Docg
r • Il Sasso - Vdt

Tenuta di Nozzole ♟♟♟♟♟
Via Nozzole 12, tel. 055859811
r • Chianti Classico Nozzole - Docg
r • Chianti Classico Riserva La Forra - Docg
r • Il Pareto Rosso Toscana - Igt

Tenuta di Riseccoli ♟♟♟♟
Via Convertoie 9, tel. 055853598
www.riseccoli.com
r • Chianti Classico Tenuta di Riseccoli - Docg
r • Saeculum di Riseccoli Toscana - Igt
s • Vin Santo del Chianti Classico - Doc

Tenuta di Vignole ♟♟♟
Località Panzano, via Case Sparse 12, tel. 0574592025
r • Chianti Classico - Docg
r • Chianti Classico Riserva - Docg

Tenuta La Novella ♟♟♟
Località San Polo, via Musignana 11, tel. 0558337749
lanovella@iol.it
r • Chianti Classico - Docg
r • Chianti Classico Riserva - Docg

Tenuta Montecalvi ♟♟♟♟
Via Citille 85, tel. 0558544665
bollij@tin.it
r • Montecalvi Rosso Alta Valle della Greve - Igt

Tenute del Cabreo ♟♟♟♟
Località S. Cresci, via di Zano 14, tel. 0552385901
r • Cabreo Il Borgo Rosso Toscana - Igt
w • Cabreo La Pietra Bianco Toscana - Igt

Vecchie Terre di Montefili ♟♟♟♟
Via S. Cresci 45, tel. 055853739
r • Chianti Classico Vecchie Terre di Montefili - Docg
r • Anfiteatro Colli della Toscana Centrale - Igt
r • Bruno di Rocca Colli della Toscana Centrale - Igt

Villa Calcinaia ♟♟♟
Via di Citille 84, tel. 055854008
www.villacalcinaia.it
r • Chianti Classico Riserva Villa Calcinaia - Docg
r • Chianti Classico Villa Calcinaia - Docg
r • Casarsa Villa Calcinaia Rosso Toscana - Igt

Villa Vignamaggio ♟♟♟♟ ★10%
Via Petriolo 5, tel. 055854661
www.vignamaggio.com

r • Chianti Classico Riserva Castello di Monna Lisa - Docg
r • Chianti Classico Terre di Prenzano - Docg
r • Chianti Classico Vignamaggio - Docg
r • Wine Obsession Toscana - Igt
s • Vinsanto del Chianti Classico - Doc

GROSSETO

m 10

Wineries

Belguardo ♟♟♟
Località Montebottigli, VIII Zona, tel. 057773571
www.fonterutoli.it
r • Tenuta Belguardo Maremma Rosso - Igt

Fattoria Le Pupille ♟♟♟♟♟
Località Istia d'Ombrone, piagge del Maiano 92/A, tel. 0564409517
www.elisabettageppetti.it
r • Morellino di Scansano - Doc
r • Morellino di Scansano Poggio Valente - Doc
r • Morellino di Scansano Riserva - Doc
r • Saffredi - Igt
w • Solalto - Igt

Poggio Argentiera ♟♟♟
Località Banditella di Alberese, tel. 0564405099
www.poggioargentiera.com
r • Morellino di Scansano Bellamarsilia - Doc
r • Morellino di Scansano Capatosta - Doc

Poggiolungo ♟♟♟
Località Grancia, VIII Zona, tel. 0564409268
r • Morellino di Scansano - Doc
r • Morellino di Scansano Riserva - Doc

Val delle Rose ♟♟
Località Poggio la Mozza, tel. 0564409062

Fax: +39 (577) 743057
www.valdellerose.it
r • Morellino di Scansano Riserva Val delle Rose - Doc
r • Morellino di Scansano Val delle Rose - Doc

IMPRUNETA

Florence km 15 • m 275

Wineries

Fattoria di Bagnolo ♟♟♟ ★10%
Via Imprunetana per Tavarnuzze 48, tel. 0552313403
www.bartolinibaldelli.it
r • Chianti dei Colli Fiorentini - Docg
r • Chianti dei Colli Fiorentini Riserva - Docg
r • Capro Rosso Colli della Toscana Centrale - Igt

Fattoria Montanine ♟
Via Volterrana 45, tel. 0552373055
lemontanine@libero.it
r • Chianti - Docg

La Querce ♟♟♟♟
Via Imprunetana per Tavarnuzze 41, tel. 0552011380
www.laquerce.com
r • Chianti dei Colli Fiorentini La Torretta - Docg
r • Chianti Sorrettole - Docg
r • La Querce Toscana - Igt

Lanciola ♟♟♟ ★10%
Via Impruneta per Pozzolatico 210, tel. 055208324
r • Chianti Classico Le Masse di Greve - Docg
r • Chianti dei Colli Fiorentini - Docg
r • Riccineri Toscana - Igt
r • Terricci Rosso Toscana - Igt
s • Vin Santo del Chianti Classico - Doc

LASTRA A SIGNA

Florence km 13 • m 36

Wineries

I Mori ♟
Via Maremmana 22, tel. 0558784452
www.i-mori.it
r • Moresco Toscana Rosso - Igt

LUCCA

m 19

Wineries

Eredi Bini Dora ♟♟
Località Mulerna, tel. 058340521
info@mennucci.it
r • Solgirato - Vdt
w • Mulerna Chardonnay di Toscana - Igt

Fondin ♟♟
Località San Marco, via delle Tagliate 124, tel. 0583490420
r • Colline Lucchesi Sangiovese Il Camiliano - Doc
w • Colline Lucchesi Bianco Camiliano - Doc
w • Camiliano Vermentino Toscano - Igt

Tenuta di Forci ♟♟
Via per Pieve S. Stefano 7165, tel. 0583349007
www.tenutadiforci.com
r • Cardinal Buonvisi Rosso Toscano - Igt
r • Forciano Rosso Toscano - Igt
w • Colline Lucchesi Bianco Panterino - Doc

Terre del Sillabo ♟♟♟
Località Cappella, via per Camaiore, traversa V, tel. 0583394487
mail@terredelsillabo.it
r • Niffo Toscana Rosso - Igt
w • Colline Lucchesi Sauvignon - Doc
w • Chardonnay Toscana - Igt
w • Gana Toscana - Igt
w • Spante Toscana - Igt

Valle del Sole ♟♟
Località Monte San Quirico, via delle Querce 325, tel. 0583395093
azagricolavalledelsole@virgilio.it
r • Ebrius Toscana Rosso - Igt

MAGLIANO IN TOSCANA

Grosseto km 28 • m 128

Wineries

Boschetto di Montiano ♟♟♟
Località Montiano, tel. 0564589621
www.boschettodimontiano.com
r • Morellino di Scansano Roviccio - Doc
r • Verriolo Toscana Rosso - Igt

Fattoria Mantellassi ♟♟♟
Località Banditaccia 26, tel. 0564592037
www.fatt-mantellassi.it
r • Morellino di Scansano Riserva - Doc
r • Morellino di Scansano Riserva Le Sentinelle - Doc
r • Morellino di Scansano San Giuseppe - Doc
r • Querciolaia Toscana Rosso - Igt
w • Lucumone Vermentino di Toscana - Igt

LOHSA ♟♟♟
Località La Carla 75, tel. 0578738171
www.carlettipoliziano.com
r • Morellino di Scansano - Doc

MALFATTI COSTANZA ♟♟♟
Località Sant'Andrea, tel. 0564862636
r • Morellino di Scansano Costanza Malfatti - Doc

MANCIANO

Grosseto km 56 • m 444

WINERIES

LA STELLATA ♟♟
Via Fornacina 18, tel. 0564620190
r • Lunaia Rosso - Vdt
w • Bianco di Pitigliano Lunaia - Doc

TENUTA MARSILIANA ♟♟♟♟
Località Marsialiana, tel. 055829301
info@principecorsini.com
r • Marsiliana Maremma Toscana Rosso - Igt

MASSA

m 65

WINERIES

CIMA ♟♟♟♟
Località Romagnano, via del Fagiano 1, tel. 0585830835
www.aziendagricolacima.it
r • Anchigi Sangiovese Toscana - Igt
r • Massaretta Toscana Rosso - Igt
r • Montervo Toscana - Igt
r • Romalbo Toscana - Igt
r • Vermentino Nero Toscana - Igt
w • Candia dei Colli Apuani Vigneto Candia Alto - Doc
w • Vermentino Toscana - Igt

PODERE SCURTAROLA ♟♟ ★10%
Via dell'Uva 3, tel. 0585833523
www.scurtarola.com
r • Scurtarola Vermentino Nero Toscana - Igt
w • Scurtarola Vermentino Toscana - Igt

MASSA MARITTIMA

Grosseto km 50 • m 380

WINERIES

FATTORIA COLIBERTO ♟♟
Località Coliberto, tel. 0566919039
r • Monteregio di Massa Marittima Rosso - Doc
r • Monteregio di Massa Marittima Rosso Thesan - Doc
w • Monteregio di Massa Marittima Bianco Aurora - Doc

MASSA VECCHIA ♟♟♟
Zona Rocche, podere Fornace 11, tel. 0566904144
r • Il Matto delle Giuncaie Maremma Toscana - Igt
r • La Fonte di Pietrarsa Maremma Toscana - Igt
r • Terziere Alicante della Maremma Toscana - Igt
w • Ariento Maremma Toscana - Igt
w • Patrizia Bartolini Maremma Toscana - Igt

MORIS FARMS ♟♟♟♟
Località Curanuova, tel. 0566919135
www.morisfarms.it
r • Morellino di Scansano Riserva - Doc
r • Avvoltore Maremma Toscana - Vdt
w • Monteregio di Massa Marittima Bianco Santa Chiara - Doc

MONTAIONE

Florence km 49 • m 342

WINERIES

TOGNETTI - PODERE IL SAPITO ♟
Via Poggio alla Terra 20, tel. 0571698381
www.poderitogneti.it
r • Il Brigante Toscana Rosso - Igt

MONTALCINO

Siena km 41 • m 567

WINERIES

ALTESINO ♟♟♟♟♟ ★10%
Località Altesino, tel. 0577806208
altesino@iol.it
r • Brunello di Montalcino - Docg
r • Brunello di Montalcino Montosoli - Docg
r • Rosso di Montalcino - Doc
r • Alte d'Altesi Toscana Rosso - Igt
s • Val d'Arbia Vin Santo d'Altesi - Doc

ARGIANO ♟♟♟♟
Località Sant'Angelo in Colle, tel. 0577864037
www.argiano.net
r • Brunello di Montalcino - Docg
r • Rosso di Montalcino - Doc
r • Solengo Toscana Rosso - Igt

BANFI - CASTELLO DI POGGIO ALLE MURA ♟♟♟
Località Sant'Angelo Scalo, tel. 0577840111
r • Brunello di Montalcino Poggio alle Mura - Docg
r • Brunello di Montalcino Riserva Poggio all'Oro - Docg
r • Rosso di Montalcino - Doc
r • Excelsus - Igt
s • Moscadello di Montalcino B - Doc

CAMIGLIANO ♟♟♟♟
Località Camigliano, via d'Ingresso 2, tel. 0577844068
www.camigliano.it
r • Brunello di Montalcino - Docg
r • Rosso di Montalcino - Doc
r • Sant'Antimo Cabernet Sauvignon - Doc
r • Poderuccio Rosso Toscana - Igt
s • Moscadello di Montalcino - Doc

CAMPOGIOVANNI ♟♟♟
Località Sant'Angelo in Colle, tel. 057739911
r • Brunello di Montalcino - Docg
r • Brunello di Montalcino Riserva Quercione - Docg

CANALICCHIO DI SOPRA ♟♟♟
Località Canalicchio di Sopra, tel. 0577848316
www.canalicchiodisopra.com
r • Brunello di Montalcino - Docg
r • Brunello di Montalcino Riserva - Docg
r • Rosso di Montalcino - Doc

CANALICCHIO DI SOTTO ♟♟♟♟
Podere Canalicchio di Sotto 8, tel. 0577848476
r • Brunello di Montalcino - Docg
r • Rosso di Montalcino - Doc

CANTINA COSTANTI ♟♟♟
Località Colle al Matrichese, tel. 0577848195
r • Brunello di Montalcino - Docg
r • Brunello di Montalcino Riserva - Docg
r • Rosso di Montalcino Calbello - Doc
r • Ardingo Calbello Toscana Rosso - Igt
r • Vermiglio - Vdt

CANTINA DI MONTALCINO ♟♟♟
Località Val di Cava, tel. 0577848704

www.cantinadimontalcino.it
r • Brunello di Montalcino - Docg
r • Villa di Corsano Toscana Rosso - Igt

CAPANNA ♟♟♟
Località Capanna 333, tel. 0577848298
r • Brunello di Montalcino - Docg
r • Brunello di Montalcino Riserva - Docg
r • Rosso di Montalcino - Doc

CASANOVA DI NERI ♟♟♟♟♟
Località Torrenieri, podere Casanova,
tel. 0577834455
giacner@tin.it
r • Brunello di Montalcino - Docg
r • Brunello di Montalcino Cerretalto - Docg
r • Brunello di Montalcino Tenuta Nuova - Docg
r • Rosso di Montalcino - Doc
r • Sant'Antimo Rosso Pietradonice - Doc

CASE BASSE SOLDERA ♟♟♟♟
Villa S. Restituta, tel. 02461544
www.soldera.it
r • Brunello di Montalcino Riserva - Docg
r • Brunello di Montalcino Riserva Intistieti - Docg

CASTELLO ROMITORIO ♟♟♟
Località Romitorio 279, tel. 0577897220
www.castelloromitorio.com
r • Brunello di Montalcino - Docg
r • Sant'Antimo Rosso Romito del Romitorio - Doc
r • Donna di Rango - Igt

CASTIGLION DEL BOSCO ♟♟♟
Località Castiglione del Bosco, tel. 0577807078
r • Brunello di Montalcino - Docg
r • Rosso di Montalcino - Doc
r • Bernaia n. 1 Cuvée Manfredi Rosso Toscana - Igt

CENTOLANI ♟♟♟
Località Friggiali, tel. 0577849314
agricolacentolani@libero.it
r • Brunello di Montalcino Tenuta Friggiali - Docg
r • Brunello di Montalcino Tenuta Pietranera - Docg
r • Rosso di Montalcino Tenuta Friggiali - Doc
r • Rosso di Montalcino Tenuta Pietranera - Doc
r • Pietrafocaia Rosso Toscana - Igt

CERBAIA ♟♟ ★10%
Via Moglio 45, tel. 0577848301
r • Brunello di Montalcino Vigna Cerbaia - Docg

CERBAIONA ♟♟♟♟
Località Cerbaiona, tel. 0577848660
r • Brunello di Montalcino - Docg
r • Cerbaiona - Vdt

CIACCI PICCOLOMINI D'ARAGONA ♟♟♟
Località Castelnuovo dell'Abate,
via Borgo di Mezzo 62, tel. 0577835616
www.ciaccipiccolomini.com
r • Brunello di Montalcino Riserva Vigna di Pianrosso - Docg
r • Brunello di Montalcino Vigna di Pianrosso - Docg
r • Rosso di Montalcino Vigna della Fonte - Doc
r • Sant'Antimo Rosso Fabius - Doc
r • Ateo Rosso Toscano - Igt

COLDISOLE ♟♟♟
Località I Verbi, tel. 0577355789
r • Brunello di Montalcino Coldisole - Docg
r • Rosso di Montalcino Coldisole - Doc

COLOMBINI CINELLI DONATELLA - CASATO PRIME DONNE ♟♟♟
Località Casato Prime Donne, tel. 0577662108
www.cinellicolombini.it
r • Brunello di Montalcino - Docg
r • Brunello di Montalcino Progetto Prime Donne - Docg
r • Chianti Superiore Fattoria Il Colle - Docg
r • Rosso di Montalcino - Doc
r • Leone Rosso Toscana - Igt

DUE PORTINE - GORELLI ♟♟♟
Via Cialdini 53, tel. 0577848098
r • Brunello di Montalcino - Docg
r • Rosso di Montalcino - Doc

EREDI FULIGNI ♟♟♟♟
Via Soccorso Saloni 33, tel. 0577848039
r • Brunello di Montalcino Vigneti dei Cottimelli - Docg
r • Rosso di Montalcino Ginestreto - Doc
r • Fuligni San Jacopo - Igt

FATTORIA CASISANO COLOMBAIO ♟♟♟
Località Casisano 52, tel. 0577835540
www.brunello.org
r • Brunello di Montalcino - Docg
r • Brunello di Montalcino Vigna del Colombaiolo - Docg
r • Rosso di Montalcino - Doc

FATTORIA DEI BARBI ♟♟♟
Località Podernovi, tel. 0577841111
www.fattoriadeibarbi.it
r • Brunello di Montalcino - Docg
r • Brunello di Montalcino Vigna del Fiore - Docg
r • Morellino di Scansano Colombini - Doc
r • Rosso di Montalcino - Doc
r • Birbone Toscana Rosso - Igt

FATTORIA LA FIORITA ♟♟♟♟
Località Castelnuovo dell'Abate,
via Piaggia della Porta 3, tel. 0577835657
www.fattorialafiorita.it
r • Brunello di Montalcino - Docg
r • La Quadratura del Cerchio - Igt
r • Laurus Toscana Rosso - Igt

FATTORIA LA GERLA ♟♟♟♟
Località Canalicchio, tel. 0577848599
r • Brunello di Montalcino - Docg
r • Brunello di Montalcino Riserva - Docg
r • Brunello di Montalcino Vigna degli Angeli - Docg
r • Rosso di Montalcino - Doc
r • Birba Toscana - Igt

FATTORIA LISINI ♟♟♟♟
Località Sant'Angelo in Colle,
tel. 0577844040
r • Brunello di Montalcino - Docg
r • Brunello di Montalcino Ugolaia - Docg
r • Rosso di Montalcino - Doc

FATTORIA POGGIO DI SOTTO - PALMUCCI ♟♟
Località Castelnuovo dell'Abate, tel. 0577835502
palmuccipds@libero.it
r • Brunello di Montalcino - Docg
r • Rosso di Montalcino - Doc

IL GRAPPOLO ♟♟♟
Località Sant'Angelo in Colle,
via Traversa dei Monti, tel. 0574813730
www.ilgrappolofortius.it
r • Sassocheto Toscana - Igt

IL GREPPONE MAZZI 🍷🍷🍷
Località Greppone, tel. 05583605
ruffino@ruffino.it
r • Brunello di Montalcino Greppone Mazzi - Docg
IL MARRONETO 🍷🍷🍷
Località Madonna delle Grazie, tel. 057745340
r • Brunello di Montalcino Il Marroneto - Docg
r • Brunello di Montalcino Riserva - Docg
IL POGGIOLO 🍷🍷🍷
Località Poggiolo 259, tel. 0577848412
info@ilpoggiolo.com
r • Brunello di Montalcino Beato - Docg
r • Brunello di Montalcino Sassello - Docg
r • Rosso di Montalcino Sassello - Doc
r • Rosso di Montalcino Terra Rossa - Doc
r • Sant'Antimo In Riva al Fosso - Doc
LA CAMPANA 🍷🍷🍷
Via Monti 13, tel. 0577847178
r • Brunello di Montalcino - Docg
r • Brunello di Montalcino Riserva - Docg
r • Rosso di Montalcino - Doc
LA CERBAIOLA 🍷🍷🍷🍷🍷
Piazza Cavour 20, tel. 0577848499
r • Brunello di Montalcino - Docg
r • Rosso di Montalcino - Doc
LA RASINA 🍷🍷🍷
Località Rasina 132, tel. 0577848536
r • Brunello di Montalcino - Docg
r • Rosso di Montalcino - Doc
LA TORRE 🍷🍷🍷
Località la Torre, tel. 068083258
r • Brunello di Montalcino - Docg
r • Brunello di Montalcino Riserva - Docg
r • Rosso di Montalcino - Doc
LE CHIUSE 🍷🍷🍷
Località Pullera 228, tel. 055597052
r • Brunello di Montalcino - Docg
r • Brunello di Montalcino Riserva - Docg
r • Rosso di Montalcino - Doc
LE PRESI 🍷🍷🍷
Località Castelnuovo dell'Abate, via Pantaneto 15, tel. 0577835541
lepresi@libero.it
r • Brunello di Montalcino - Docg
r • Brunello di Montalcino Riserva - Docg
r • Rosso di Montalcino - Doc
LUCE 🍷🍷🍷🍷🍷
Località Geografica A 369, tel. 05527141
r • Luce della Vite Rosso Toscana - Igt
r • Lucente La Vite Rosso Toscana - Igt
MASTROJANNI 🍷🍷🍷🍷🍷
Località Castelnuovo dell'Abate, podere Loreto, tel. 0577835681
www.mastrojanni.com
r • Brunello di Montalcino - Docg
r • Brunello di Montalcino Schiena d'Asino - Docg
r • Rosso di Montalcino - Doc
r • San Pio Rosso Toscana - Igt
s • Botrys Bianco Toscana - Igt
MOCALI 🍷🍷🍷🍷
Località Mocali, tel. 0577849485
r • Brunello di Montalcino - Docg
r • Rosso di Montalcino - Doc
s • Moscadello di Montalcino V.T. - Doc
PACENTI FRANCO 🍷🍷🍷
Località Canalicchio di Sopra 6, tel. 0577849277
r • Brunello di Montalcino - Docg
r • Brunello di Montalcino Riserva - Docg
r • Rosso di Montalcino - Doc
PALAZZO 🍷🍷🍷
Podere Palazzo, tel. 0577848479
az.palazzo@tin.it
r • Brunello di Montalcino - Docg
r • Rosso di Montalcino - Doc
r • Alcineo Toscana Rosso - Igt
PIAN DELL'ORINO 🍷🍷
Località Pian dell'Orino 189, tel. 03355250115
caroline@piandellorino.it
r • Piandorino Rosso Toscana - Igt
PIANCORNELLO 🍷🍷🍷
Località Piancornello, tel. 0577844105
r • Brunello di Montalcino - Docg
r • Rosso di Montalcino - Doc
PIEVE SANTA RESTITUTA 🍷🍷🍷🍷
Località Chiesa di Santa Restituta, tel. 0577848610
r • Brunello di Montalcino Rennina - Docg
r • Brunello di Montalcino Sugarille - Docg
r • Promis - Igt
PODERE BRIZIO - FONTEANTICA 🍷🍷🍷🍷
Località Podere Brizio 67, tel. 0577846004
poderebrizio@inwind.it
r • Podere Brizio Colli della Toscana Centrale Rosso - Igt
r • Pupà Pepu Colli della Toscana Centrale Rosso - Igt
PODERE CANNETA 🍷🍷🍷
Località Canneta 290, tel. 0558784452
www.i-mori.it
r • Brunello di Montalcino - Docg
PODERE CERRINO 🍷🍷🍷
Località Cerrino I, tel. 0577848187
r • Brunello di Montalcino - Docg
r • Rosso di Montalcino - Doc
PODERE SALICUTTI 🍷🍷🍷🍷
Località Podere Salicutti 174, tel. 0577847003
www.poderesalicutti.it
r • Brunello di Montalcino - Doc
r • Rosso di Montalcino - Doc
r • Dopoteatro Rosso Toscano - Igt
POGGIO ANTICO 🍷🍷🍷
Località I Poggi, tel. 0577848044
r • Brunello di Montalcino - Docg
r • Brunello di Montalcino Altero - Docg
r • Rosso di Montalcino - Doc
RASA - LA SERENA 🍷🍷
Podere Rasa, tel. 0577848659
laserena@virgilio.it
r • Brunello di Montalcino - Docg
r • Rosso di Montalcino - Doc
SAN FILIPPO - FANTI 🍷🍷🍷🍷
Località Castelnuovo Abate, via Borgo di Mezzo 16, tel. 0577835628
r • Brunello di Montalcino - Docg
r • Rosso di Montalcino - Doc
r • Sant'Antimo Rosso - Doc
r • Svoltone - Vdt
s • Vin Santo - Vdt
SAN FILIPPO ROSI 🍷🍷🍷
Località San Filippo 134, tel. 0577848705
azsanfilippo@libero.it
r • Brunello di Montalcino - Docg

r • Rosso di Montalcino - Doc
r • Rosiano Toscana Rosso - Igt

Sassetti Livio - Pertimali ♟♟♟♟
Località Pertimali, tel. 0577848721
r • Brunello di Montalcino - Docg
r • Rosso di Montalcino - Doc
r • Vigna dei Fili di Seta - Igt

Sassetti Vasco ♟♟♟
Località Castelnuovo dell'Abate, via Bassomondo 1, tel. 0577835619
r • Brunello di Montalcino - Docg
r • Brunello di Montalcino Bellavista - Docg
r • Brunello di Montalcino Colombaiolo - Docg
r • Brunello di Montalcino Riserva - Docg
r • Rosso di Montalcino - Doc

Scopetone ♟♟♟
Località Scopetone, tel. 0577848713
r • Brunello di Montalcino - Docg
r • Brunello di Montalcino Riserva - Docg
r • Rosso di Montalcino - Doc

Talenti ♟♟♟
Località Pian di Conte, tel. 0577844064
az-talenti@tin.it
r • Brunello di Montalcino Podere Pian di Conte - Docg
r • Rosso di Montalcino Podere Pian di Conte - Doc
r • Talenti Toscana Rosso - Igt

Tenimenti Angelini - Val di Suga ♟♟♟♟♟
Località Val di Cava, tel. 057780411
r • Brunello di Montalcino - Docg
r • Brunello di Montalcino Vigna del Lago - Docg
r • Brunello di Montalcino Vigna Spuntali - Docg
r • Rosso di Montalcino - Doc
r • Motuproprio Toscana Rosso - Igt

Tenuta Caparzo ♟♟♟♟♟
Località Caparzo, S.P. del Brunello al km 1.7, tel. 0577848390
www.caparzo.com
r • Brunello di Montalcino - Docg
r • Brunello di Montalcino Vigna La Casa - Docg
r • Chianti Classico Borgo Scopeto - Docg
r • Chianti Classico Riserva Vigna Misciano Borgo Scopeto - Docg
r • Rosso di Montalcino Vigna La Caduta - Doc
r • Sant'Antimo Rosso Cà del Pazzo - Doc
w • Sant'Antimo Bianco Le Grance - Doc

Tenuta Col d'Orcia ♟♟♟♟
Località Sant'Angelo in Colle, tel. 0577808001
www.coldorcia.it
r • Brunello di Montalcino - Docg
r • Brunello di Montalcino Riserva Poggio al Vento - Docg
r • Olmaia Cabernet Toscana - Igt
w • Ghiaie Bianche Toscana - Igt
s • Moscadello di Montalcino V. T. Pascena - Doc

Tenuta di Castelgiocondo ♟♟♟♟
Località Castelgiocondo, tel. 0577848492
r • Brunello di Montalcino Castel Giocondo - Docg
r • Brunello di Montalcino Riserva Ripe al Convento Castel Giocondo - Docg
r • Lamaione - Vdt

Tenuta di Collosorbo ♟♟♟
Località Castelnuovo dell'Abate, via Villa Sesta 25, tel. 0577835534
tenutadicollosorbo@libero.it
r • Brunello di Montalcino - Docg
r • Rosso di Montalcino - Doc
r • Sorbus Rosso Toscano - Igt

Tenuta di Sesta ♟♟♟
Località Sesta 25, tel. 0577835612
giovanni.ciacci@tin.it
r • Brunello di Montalcino - Docg
r • Rosso di Montalcino - Doc
r • Poggio d'Arna Rosso Toscana - Igt

Tenuta Greppo ♟♟♟
Località Greppo, tel. 0577848087
r • Brunello di Montalcino - Docg
r • Brunello di Montalcino Riserva - Docg
r • Rosso di Montalcino - Doc

Tenuta Il Poggione ♟♟♟
Località Sant'Angelo in Colle, tel. 0577844029
www.tenutailpoggione.it
r • Brunello di Montalcino - Docg
r • Rosso di Montalcino - Doc
r • San Leopoldo Rosso Toscana - Igt

Tenuta La Fuga ♟♟♟♟♟
Località La Fuga, tel. 0577816039
r • Brunello di Montalcino - Docg
r • Brunello di Montalcino Riserva - Docg
r • Rosso di Montalcino - Doc

Tenuta La Poderina - Saiagricola ♟♟♟♟♟
Località Poderina, tel. 0577835737
www.saiagricola.it
r • Brunello di Montalcino - Docg
r • Brunello di Montalcino Riserva - Docg
r • Brunello di Montalcino Selezione Poggio Banale - Docg
r • Rosso di Montalcino - Doc
s • Moscadello di Montalcino V.T. - Doc

Tenuta Le Potazzine - Gorelli ♟♟♟♟
Località Le Prata, tel. 0577849406
r • Brunello di Montalcino Le Potazzine - Docg
r • Rosso di Montalcino Le Potazzine - Doc

Tenuta Oliveto ♟♟♟
Località Oliveto, tel. 0577807170
oliveto.amachetti@tin.it
r • Brunello di Montalcino - Docg
r • Rosso di Montalcino Il Roccolo - Doc
r • Il Leccio Rosso di Toscana - Igt

Tenuta Pian delle Vigne ♟♟♟♟
Località Pian delle Vigne, tel. 0577816066
r • Brunello di Montalcino Pian delle Vigne - Docg

Tenuta Valdicava ♟♟♟♟
Località Valdicava, tel. 0577848261
r • Brunello di Montalcino - Docg
r • Brunello di Montalcino Riserva Madonna del Piano - Docg
r • Rosso di Montalcino - Doc

Tenute Donna Olga ♟♟♟
Località Friggiali, tel. 0577849314
r • Brunello di Montalcino - Docg
r • Rosso di Montalcino - Doc

Tenute Nardi Silvio ♟♟♟♟
Casale del Bosco, tel. 0577808269
r • Brunello di Montalcino - Docg
r • Brunello di Montalcino Manachiara - Docg
r • Rosso di Montalcino - Doc

Verbena ♟♟
Località Verbena, tel. 0577848432
r • Brunello di Montalcino - Docg
r • Rosso di Montalcino - Doc

VIGNETI PACENTI SIRO ♟♟♟
Podere Pelagrilli, tel. 0577848662
r • Brunello di Montalcino - Docg
r • Brunello di Montalcino Riserva - Docg
r • Rosso di Montalcino - Doc

VILLA LE PRATA ♟♟
Località Leprata, tel. 0577848325
r • Brunello di Montalcino - Docg
r • Rosso di Montalcino Tirso - Doc

VILLA POGGIO SALVI ♟♟♟
Località Poggio Salvi, tel. 0577848486
www.sienanet.it/biondi_santi
r • Brunello di Montalcino - Docg
r • Rosso di Montalcino - Doc
s • Moscadello di Montalcino Aurico - Doc

VITANZA ♟♟♟
Podere Renaione, tel. 0577846031
www.tenutavitanza.it
r • Brunello di Montalcino - Docg
r • Rosso di Montalcino - Doc
r • Sant'Antimo Rosso Quadrimendo - Doc

MONTECARLO

Lucca km 15 • m 162

WINERIES

CARMIGNANI G. FUSO ♟♟♟♟
Località Cercatoia, via della Tinaia 7, tel. 058322381
r • Montecarlo Rosso Sassonero - Doc
r • For Duke Rosso Toscana - Igt
r • Merlot della Topanera Rosso Toscana - Igt

FATTORIA DEL BUONAMICO ♟♟♟
Località Cercatoia, via Provinciale di Montecarlo 43, tel. 058322038
www.sole.it
r • Montecarlo Rosso - Doc
r • Cercatoja Rosso Toscana - Igt
r • Il Fortino Rosso Toscana - Igt
w • Vasario Bianco Toscano - Igt
s • Oro di Re Vendemmia Tardiva - Vdt

FATTORIA DEL TESO ♟♟♟
Via Poltroniera, tel. 0583286288
www.fattoriadelteso.com
r • Montecarlo Rosso - Doc
r • Anfidiamante Toscana - Igt
w • Montecarlo Bianco - Doc

FATTORIA DI MONTECHIARI ♟♟♟♟
Via Montechiari 27, tel. 058322189
r • Montecarlo Rosso - Doc
r • Montechiari Cabernet - Igt
r • Montechiari Pinot Nero - Igt
r • Montechiari Rosso - Igt
w • Montechiari Chardonnay - Igt

FATTORIA LA TORRE ♟♟♟
Via Provinciale 7, tel. 058322981
www.fattorialatorre
r • Stringaio Rosso Toscano - Igt
w • Montecarlo Bianco - Doc
w • Altair Bianco di Toscana - Igt

FATTORIA MAZZINI ♟♟
Via Roma 39, tel. 058322010
r • Montecarlo Rosso - Doc
r • Montecarlo Rosso Casalta - Doc
w • Montecarlo Bianco Vigna La Salita - Doc

VIGNA DEL GREPPO ♟♟
Via del Molinetto 24, tel. 058322593
w • Montecarlo Bianco - Doc

WANDANNA ♟♟♟
Via del Molinetto, tel. 0583228989
wandanna@libero.it
r • Terre de' Cascinieri Rosso Toscana - Igt
r • Virente Rosso Toscana - Igt
w • Montecarlo Bianco Terre de' Cascinieri - Doc
w • Labirinto Toscana - Igt
w • Roussanne Toscana - Igt

MONTECATINI VAL DI CECINA

Pisa km 62 • m 416

WINERIES

FATTORIA SORBAIANO ♟♟♟
Località Sorbaiano, tel. 058830243
r • Montescudaio Rosso delle Miniere - Doc
r • Pian del Conte Sangiovese di Toscana - Igt
w • Montescudaio Bianco Lucestraia - Doc

MONTELUPO FIORENTINO

Florence km 25 • m 35

WINERIES

FATTORIA DI PETROGNANO ♟♟♟
Via Bottinaccio 116, tel. 0571913795
www.petrognano.it
r • Chianti - Docg
r • Montevago Rosso Colli della Toscana Centrale - Igt
w • Petrognano Bianco Colli della Toscana Centrale - Igt

FATTORIA DI SAMMONTANA ♟♟♟
Località Sammontana, tel. 0571542003
fatt.sammontana@tin.it
r • Chianti Superiore Sanfirenze - Docg
r • Vigna del Maestro Rosso di Toscana - Igt

TENUTA SAN VITO IN FIOR DI SELVA ♟♟
Località Camaioni, tel. 057151411
r • Chianti dei Colli Fiorentini - Docg
r • Fior di Selva - Igt

MONTEMURLO

Prato km 28 • m 45/976

WINERIES

MARCHESI PANCRAZI - TENUTA DI BAGNOLO ♟♟♟♟
Località Bagnolo, via Montalese 156, tel. 0574652439 www.pancrazi.it
r • Villa di Bagnolo Pinot Nero Rosso Toscano - Igt

MONTEPULCIANO

Siena km 68 • m 605

WINERIES

AVIGNONESI ♟♟♟♟♟
Via Gracciano del Corso 91, tel. 0578724304
r • Vino Nobile di Montepulciano - Docg
r • Vino Nobile di Montepulciano Riserva Grandi Annate - Docg
r • Rosso di Montepulciano - Doc
r • Desiderio Rosso di Toscana - Igt
r • 50 & 50 - Vdt
s • Vin Santo - Vdt
s • Vin Santo Occhio di Pernice - Vdt

BINDELLA ♟♟♟
Via delle Tre Berte 10/A, tel. 0578767777
www.bindella.it
r • Vino Nobile di Montepulciano - Docg
r • Rosso di Montepulciano Fossolupaio - Doc
r • Vallocaia Toscana Rosso - Igt

Canneto ♟♟♟
Via dei Canneti 14, tel. 0578757737
r • Vino Nobile di Montepulciano - Docg
r • Rosso di Montepulciano - Doc

Contucci ♟♟♟
Via del Teatro 1, tel. 0578757006
www.contucci.it
r • Vino Nobile di Montepulciano - Docg
r • Vino Nobile di Montepulciano Riserva - Docg
r • Rosso di Montepulciano - Doc

Dei ♟♟♟
Via di Martiena 35, tel. 0578716878
r • Vino Nobile di Montepulciano - Docg
r • Rosso di Montepulciano - Doc
r • Sancta Catharina Rosso Toscana - Igt

Fassati - Fazi Battaglia ♟♟♟ ★15%
Località Gracciano, via di Graccianello 3/A,
tel. 0578708708
r • Chianti Gaggiole - Docg
r • Vino Nobile di Montepulciano Gersemi - Docg
r • Vino Nobile di Montepulciano Riserva Salarco - Docg
r • Rosso di Montepulciano Selciaia - Doc
r • Torre al Fante Rosso Toscana - Vdt

Fattoria del Cerro - Saiagricola ♟♟♟♟♟
Località Acquaviva, via Grazianella 5,
tel. 0578767722
www.saiagricola.it
r • Vino Nobile di Montepulciano - Docg
r • Vino Nobile di Montepulciano Vigneto Antica Chiusina - Docg
r • Rosso di Montepulciano - Doc
w • Braviolo Bianco Toscana - Igt
s • Vin Santo di Montepulciano Antonio da Sangallo - Doc

Fattoria di Palazzo Vecchio ♟♟♟
Località Valiano, tel. 0578724170
www.vinonobile.it
r • Vino Nobile di Montepulciano - Docg
r • Vino Nobile di Montepulciano Riserva - Docg
r • Rosso dell'Abate Chiarini - Igt

Fattoria di Paterno ♟♟♟
Località Sant'Albino, via di Fontelellera,
tel. 0578798174
r • Vino Nobile di Montepulciano - Docg
r • Vino Nobile di Montepulciano Riserva - Docg

Fattoria Le Casalte ♟♟♟
Località Sant'Albino, via del Termine 2,
tel. 0578798246
lecasalte@libero.it
r • Vino Nobile di Montepulciano - Docg
r • Vino Nobile di Montepulciano Riserva - Docg
r • Rosso di Montepulciano - Doc

Il Cavalierino ♟
Via di Poggiano 17, tel. 0578758733
r • Poggiano di Montepulciano - Vdt

La Braccesca ♟♟♟♟
Via Stella di Valiano 10, tel. 0578724252
www.antinori.it
r • Vino Nobile di Montepulciano - Docg
r • Rosso di Montepulciano Sabazio - Doc
r • La Braccesca Merlot Toscana - Igt

La Calonica ♟♟♟
Località Capezzine, via della Stella 27,
tel. 0578724119
r • Vino Nobile di Montepulciano - Docg
r • Cortona Rosso Girifalco - Doc
r • Rosso di Montepulciano - Doc
r • Il Signorelli Toscana Merlot - Igt
s • Vin Santo Toscana - Igt

La Ciarliana ♟♟♟
Località Gracciano, via della Ciarliana 31,
tel. 0578758423
r • Vino Nobile di Montepulciano - Docg
r • Vino Nobile di Montepulciano Riserva - Docg
r • Rosso di Montepulciano - Doc

Nottola ♟♟♟
Località Gracciano 15, S.S. 326, tel. 0577684711
r • Vino Nobile di Montepulciano - Docg
r • Vino Nobile di Montepulciano Vigna Fattore - Docg
r • Rosso di Montepulciano - Doc

Podere Corte alla Flora ♟♟
Via di Cervognano 23, tel. 0578766003
corteflora@tin.it
r • Vino Nobile di Montepulciano - Docg
r • Rosso di Montepulciano - Doc

Podere Il Macchione ♟♟♟
Località Caggiole, via Provinciale 12,
tel. 0578758595
r • Vino Nobile di Montepulciano - Docg
r • Vino Nobile di Montepulciano Riserva Le Caggiole - Docg

Poderi Boscarelli ♟♟♟♟♟
Località Cervognano, via di Montenero 28,
tel. 0578767277
www.poderiboscarelli.com
r • Vino Nobile di Montepulciano Vigna del Nocio - Docg
r • Boscarelli - 35° - Rosso Toscana - Igt
r • De Ferrari Toscana Rosso - Igt

Poderi Sanguineto I e II ♟♟
Località Acquaviva, via Sanguineto 2/4,
tel. 0578767782
www.sanguineto.com
r • Vino Nobile di Montepulciano - Docg
r • Vino Nobile di Montepulciano Riserva - Docg
r • Rosso di Montepulciano - Doc

Poliziano ♟♟♟♟♟
Località Montepulciano Stazione, via Fontago 1,
tel. 0578738171
www.carlettipoliziano.com
r • Vino Nobile di Montepulciano - Docg
r • Vino Nobile di Montepulciano Asinone - Docg
r • Rosso di Montepulciano - Doc
r • Le Stanze del Poliziano - Igt

Redi ♟♟♟ ★10%
Via di Collazzi 5, tel. 0578716092
www.cantinadelredi.com
r • Vino Nobile di Montepulciano - Docg
r • Vino Nobile di Montepulciano Briareo - Docg
r • Rosso di Montepulciano - Doc
r • Argo Sangiovese di Toscana - Igt
s • Vin Santo - Vdt

Romeo ♟♟♟
Via di Totona 29, tel. 0578708599
r • Vino Nobile di Montepulciano - Docg
r • Vino Nobile di Montepulciano Riserva dei Mandorli - Docg
r • Rosso di Montepulciano - Doc
r • Lipitiresco - Igt

SALCHETO ♟♟♟♟
Località Sant'Albino, via di Villa Bianca 15, tel. 0578799031
- *r* • Chianti dei Colli Senesi - Docg
- *r* • Vino Nobile di Montepulciano - Docg
- *r* • Vino Nobile di Montepulciano Salco - Docg
- *r* • Rosso di Montepulciano - Doc

TENIMENTI ANGELINI - TREROSE ♟♟♟♟
Località Valiano, via della Stella 3, tel. 0578724018
- *r* • Vino Nobile di Montepulciano La Villa - Docg
- *r* • Vino Nobile di Montepulciano Simposio - Docg
- *r* • Vino Nobile di Montepulciano Trerose - Docg
- *w* • Busillis - Igt
- *s* • Vin Santo - Igt

TENUTA DI GRACCIANO - DELLA SETA ♟♟♟
Località Gracciano, via Umbria 59/61, tel. 0552335313
- *r* • Vino Nobile di Montepulciano - Docg
- *r* • Rosso di Montepulciano - Doc

TENUTA DI GRACCIANO SVETONI ♟♟
Località Gracciano, via Umbria 63, tel. 0578707097
- *r* • Vino Nobile di Montepulciano Calvano - Docg

TENUTA LODOLA NUOVA ♟♟♟
Località Valiano, via Lodola 1, tel. 0578724032
www.ruffino.com
- *r* • Vino Nobile di Montepulciano Lodola Nuova - Docg
- *r* • Rosso di Montepulciano Alauda - Doc

TENUTA VALDIPIATTA ♟♟♟♟ ★10%
Località Gracciano, via della Ciarliana 25/A, tel. 0578757930
- *r* • Vino Nobile di Montepulciano - Docg
- *r* • Rosso di Montepulciano - Doc
- *r* • Trefonti Toscana - Igt
- *r* • Trincerone Rosso Toscana - Igt
- *w* • Nibbiano Toscana Bianco - Igt

VILLA SANT'ANNA ♟♟♟
Località Abbadia, villa Sant'Anna, tel. 0578708017
- *r* • Chianti dei Colli Senesi - Docg
- *r* • Vino Nobile di Montepulciano - Docg
- *r* • Rosso di Montepulciano - Doc
- *r* • I Valloni Rosso Toscana - Igt

MONTERIGGIONI
Siena km 15 • m 274

WINERIES

LORNANO ♟♟
Località Lornano, tel. 0577309059
- *r* • Chianti Classico - Docg

MONTEROTONDO MARITTIMO
Grosseto km 69 • m 539

WINERIES

SERRAIOLA ♟♟♟
Località Serraiola, tel. 0566910026 www.serrariola.it
- *r* • Monteregio di Massa Marittima Rosso Lentisco - Doc
- *r* • Campo Montecristo Maremma Toscana Rosso - Igt
- *w* • Monteregio di Massa Marittima Bianco Violina - Doc

SUVERAIA ♟♟♟♟
Località Campetroso, tel. 050564428
- *r* • Monteregio di Massa Marittima Rosso Bacucco di Suveraia - Doc
- *r* • Monteregio di Massa Marittima Rosso Suveraia - Doc

MONTE SAN SAVINO
Arezzo km 20 • m 330

WINERIES

MARENGO GIACOMO ♟♟♟
Località Palazzuolo, tel. 0575847083
www.marengo.it
- *r* • Chianti Castello di Rapale - Docg
- *r* • Chianti Le Tornaie - Docg
- *r* • Chianti Riserva Castello di Rapale - Docg
- *r* • Chianti Riserva La Commenda - Docg
- *r* • Stroncoli Tenuta del Fondatore Rosso Toscana - Igt

SAN LUCIANO ♟♟
Via S. Luciano, tel. 0575848518
- *r* • Boschi Salviati Toscana Rosso - Igt
- *r* • Colle Carpito Colli della Toscana Centrale Rosso - Igt
- *r* • D'Ovidio Toscana Rosso - Igt

MONTESCUDAIO
Pisa km 62 • m 242

WINERIES

FATTORIA POGGIO GAGLIARDO ♟♟♟
Località Poggio Gagliardo, tel. 0586630661
- *r* • Montescudaio Rosso Gobbo ai Pianacci - Doc
- *r* • Montescudaio Rosso Rovo - Doc
- *w* • Montescudaio Bianco Vignalontana - Doc

MERLINI ♟♟♟♟
Via delle Basse 2, tel. 0586680354
- *r* • Montescudaio Rosso Guadi Piani - Doc
- *r* • Montescudaio Rosso Le Colline - Doc

MONTESPERTOLI
Florence km 27 • m 257

WINERIES

FATTORIA CASTELLO SONNINO ♟♟♟
Via Volterrana Nord 10, tel. 0571609198
www.castellosonnino.it
- *r* • Cantinino Toscana Sangiovese - Igt
- *r* • Sanleone Toscana Rosso - Igt

FATTORIA LE CALVANE ♟♟♟
Località Montagnana, via Castiglioni 1/3/5, tel. 0571671073
- *r* • Chianti dei Colli Fiorentini Il Quercione - Docg
- *r* • Chianti dei Colli Fiorentini Riserva Il Trecione - Docg
- *r* • Borro del Boscone Colli della Toscana Centrale - Igt

FATTORIA POGGIO A POPPIANO ♟♟♟
Via di Poppiano 19, tel. 055213084
fezileri@tin.it
- *r* • Calamita Toscana - Igt
- *r* • Flocco Toscana - Igt

FATTORIA POGGIO CAPPONI ♟♟♟
Località Poggio Capponi, via Montelupo 184, tel. 0571671914
www.poggiocapponi.it
- *r* • Chianti Montespertoli Petriccio - Docg
- *r* • Chianti Poggio Capponi - Docg
- *r* • Tinorso Rosso Toscana - Igt

I CASCIANI ♟♟♟
Via Casciani 9, tel. 0571609093
- *r* • Villa Gaia Toscana Rosso - Igt

Tenuta La Cipressaia ♟♟♟
Via Romita 38, tel. 0571670868
lacipressaia@leonet.it
r • Chianti - Docg
r • Chianti Colli Fiorentini - Docg
r • Borgoricco Toscana Rosso - Igt

MONTEVARCHI
Arezzo km 31 • m 144
Wineries
I Selvatici - Fratelli Sala ♟♟
Via Ricasoli 61, tel. 055901146
www.iselvatici.it
r • Cardisco Sangiovese di Toscana - Igt
s • Vin Santo del Chianti Colli Aretini - Docg
La Rendola ♟♟♟♟
Località Mercatale Valdarno, tel. 0559707594
www.renideo.com
r • La Pineta Toscana - Igt
r • L'Incanto Toscana - Igt
r • Merlot Toscana - Igt
Podere Il Carnasciale ♟♟♟♟♟
tel. 055991142
r • Il Caberlot di Carnasciale Rosso Toscana - Igt
Tenuta di Petrolo ♟♟♟♟
Località Mercatale Valdarno, via Petrolo 30,
tel. 0559911322 www.petrolo.it
r • Galatrona Rosso Toscana - Igt
r • Terre di Galatrona Rosso Toscana - Igt
r • Torrione Rosso Toscana - Igt

MONTIGNOSO
Massa-Carrara km 5 • m 1087
Wineries
La Caloma ♟♟
Località Zamparina, tel. 0585309074
www.lacaloma.it
w • Candia dei Colli Apuani Secco Calomino Bianco - Doc

MONTOPOLI IN VAL D'ARNO
Pisa km 33 • m 98
Wineries
Fattoria Varramista ♟♟♟♟
Via Ricavo 31, tel. 0571468121
r • Frasca Toscana Rosso - Igt
r • Varràmista Rosso Toscana - Igt

MURLO
Siena km 25 • m 107/503
Wineries
Campriano ♟♟ ★10%
Località Campriano, tel. 0577814232
www.campriano.com
r • Chianti Colli Senesi Campriano - Docg
r • Chianti Colli Senesi Riserva Campriano - Docg
w • Campriano Bianco Toscana - Igt
Fattoria Casabianca ♟♟
Località Casabianca, tel. 0577811033
www.fattoriacasabianca.it
r • Chianti Colli Senesi Poggio Cenni - Docg
r • Chianti Riserva Poggio Cenni - Docg
r • Tenuta Casabianca Rosso di Toscana - Igt
Fattoria La Borsa - Pieralisi ♟♟
Località Casciano, piazza Gen. A. Dalla Chiesa 7,
tel. 0577818002
r • Chianti Superiore Pieralisi - Docg
r • Crevole Barrique Toscana Rosso - Igt
r • Crevole Toscana Rosso - Igt

ORBETELLO
Grosseto km 44 • m 3
Wineries
La Selva ♟♟♟
Località La Selva, tel. 0564885669
www.bioselva.it
r • Morellino di Scansano Colli dell'Uccellina - Doc
Rascioni e Cecconello ♟♟♟
Località Poggio Sugherino, tel. 0564885642
r • Il Dono Maremma Rosso - Igt
r • Poggio Ciliegio Maremma Rosso - Igt
Santa Lucia ♟♟
Località Fonteblanda, via Aurelia Nord 66,
tel. 0564885474
www.azsantalucia.it
r • Capalbio Rosso Losco - Doc
r • Morellino di Scansano Tore del Moro - Doc
w • Capalbio Vermentino Brigante - Doc
Tenuta La Parrina ♟♟♟
Località La Parrina, tel. 0564862636
parrina@dada.it
r • Parrina Rosso Muraccio - Doc
r • Radaia Maremma Toscana - Igt
w • Costa dell'Argentario Ansonica - Doc

PALAIA
Pisa km 41 • m 240
Wineries
San Gervasio ♟♟♟♟ ★10%
Località San Gervasio, tel. 0587483360
www.sangervasio.com
r • Chianti delle Colline Pisane Le Stoppie - Docg
r • Colli dell'Etruria Centrale Rosso A Sirio - Doc
s • Vin Santo di San Torpè Recinaio - Doc

PECCIOLI
Pisa km 38 • m 144
Wineries
Tenuta di Ghizzano ♟♟♟♟
Via della Chiesa 1, tel. 0587630096
www.tenutadighizzano.com
r • Nambrot Rosso Toscana - Igt
r • Veneroso Rosso Toscana - Igt
s • Vin Santo del Chianti San Germano - Doc

PELAGO
Florence km 23 • m 309
Wineries
Travignoli ♟♟♟
Via Travignoli 78, tel. 0558361098
r • Chianti Rufina - Docg
r • Calice del Conte Rosso dei Colli della Toscana Centrale - Igt
r • Tegolaia Rosso dei Colli della Toscana Centrale - Igt

PIETRASANTA
Lucca km 30 • m 14
Wineries
Metati - Hattenschwiler ♟♟♟
Via Metati Rossi Bassi 37, tel. 0584799323
r • Metati Toscana Rosso - Igt

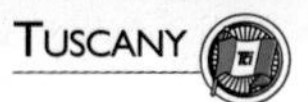

PIOMBINO

Livorno km 82 • m 21

WINERIES

PODERE SAN LUIGI ♟♟♟♟♟
Corso Vittorio Emanuele II nr. 75, tel. 0565220578
r • San Luigi Toscana - Igt
r • Fidenzio Toscana - Igt

SAN GIUSTO ♟♟♟
Località Salivoli 16, tel. 056541198
r • Bontesco Rosso Toscana - Igt
r • Rosso degli Appiani - Igt
w • Val di Cornia Bianco - Doc

TENUTA DI VIGNALE ♟♟♟
Località Vignale, tel. 056520812
r • Val di Cornia Rosso Vinivo - Doc
w • Val di Cornia Bianco Piaggia San Giovanni - Doc
w • Val di Cornia Vermentino Campo degli Albicocchi - Doc

PITIGLIANO

Grosseto km 74 • m 313

WINERIES

TENUTA ROCCACCIA ♟♟♟
Località Roccaccia, tel. 056416256
r • Fontenova Toscana Rosso - Igt
r • Poggio Cavalluccio Toscana Rosso - Igt
w • Bianco di Pitigliano - Doc

POGGIBONSI

Siena km 27 • m 116

WINERIES

FATTORIA LE FONTI ♟♟♟♟
Località San Giorgio le Fonti, tel. 0577935690
fattoria.lefonti@tin.it
r • Chianti Classico Fattoria Le Fonti - Docg
r • Chianti Classico Riserva Fattoria Le Fonti - Docg
r • Vito Arturo Toscana - Igt

FATTORIE MELINI ♟♟
Località Gaggiano, tel. 0577989001
www.giv.it
r • Chianti Classico Riserva Massovecchio - Docg
r • Chianti Classico Riserva Vigneti La Selvanella - Docg
w • Vernaccia di San Gimignano Le Grillaie - Docg

POGGIO A CAIANO

Prato km 8 • m 45

WINERIES

LA PIAGGIA ♟♟♟♟
Via Cegoli 47, tel. 0558705401
r • Carmignano Riserva - Docg
r • Il Sasso - Vdt

PONTASSIEVE

Florence km 18 • m 108

WINERIES

FATTORIA CASTELLO DEL TREBBIO ♟♟♟♟
Via S. Brigida 9, tel. 0558304900
r • Chianti Rufina Riserva Lastricato - Docg
r • Pazzesco Toscana - Igt
r • Rosso della Congiura Toscana - Igt

GRIGNANO ♟♟♟
Via di Grignano 22, tel. 0558398490
www.fattoriadigrignano.com
r • Chianti Rufina Fattoria di Grignano - Docg
r • Chianti Rufina Riserva Poggio Gualtieri Fattoria di Grignano - Docg
r • Pietromaggio Rosso dei Colli della Toscana Centrale - Igt

LAVACCHIO ♟♟♟
Via Montefiesole 55, tel. 0558317472
r • Chianti Rufina - Docg
r • Cortigiano Colli della Toscana Centrale - Igt
s • Oro del Cedro V.T. - Vdt

MARCHESI GONDI - TENUTA BOSSI ♟♟♟
Via dello Stracchino 32, tel. 0558317830
r • Chianti Rufina Riserva Pian dei Sorbi - Docg
r • Chianti Rufina Riserva Villa Bossi - Docg
r • Chianti Rufina San Giuliano - Docg
r • Mazzaferrata Colli della Toscana Centrale Rosso - Igt
s • Vin Santo del Chianti Rufina Riserva Cardinal de Retz - Doc

TENIMENTI RUFFINO ♟♟♟♟
Via Aretina 42/44, tel. 05583605
www.ruffino.com
r • Chianti Classico Aziano - Docg
r • Chianti Classico Riserva Ducale Oro - Docg
r • Chianti Classico Santedame - Docg
r • Modus Toscana - Igt
r • Nero del Tondo Rosso Toscana - Igt
r • Romitorio di Santedame Toscana - Igt
w • La Solatia Chardonnay di Toscana - Igt

PORCARI

Lucca km 10 • m 32

WINERIES

IL COLLE ♟♟♟
Via Torre 17, tel. 0583298062
www.vinimontrasio.com
r • Colline Lucchesi Merlot Montrasio - Doc
r • Colline Lucchesi Rosso Montrasio - Doc
w • Colline Lucchesi Bianco Montrasio - Doc

PORTOFERRAIO

Livorno km 82 • m 4

WINERIES

LA CHIUSA ♟
Località Magazzini 93, tel. 0565933046
s • Elba Aleatico Passito - Doc

RADDA IN CHIANTI

Siena km 31 • m 530

WINERIES

BORGO SALCETINO ♟♟♟
Località Lucarelli 5, tel. 0577733541
r • Chianti Classico Borgo Salcetino - Docg
r • Chianti Classico Riserva Lucarello - Docg
r • Rossole - Vdt

CASTELLO DI ALBOLA ♟♟♟
Via Pian d'Albola 31, tel. 0577738019
r • Chianti Classico - Docg
r • Acciaiolo Toscana Rosso - Igt
r • Le Marangolle Toscana Rosso - Igt

CASTELLO DI VOLPAIA ♟♟♟
Località Volpaia, tel. 0577738066
r • Chianti Classico - Docg
r • Chianti Classico Riserva Coltassala - Docg
r • Balifico Toscana - Igt
s • Vinsanto del Chianti Classico - Doc

Fattoria di Montemaggio ♟♟♟
Località Montemaggio 58, tel. 0577738323
www.montemaggio.it
r • Chianti Classico - Docg
r • Chianti Classico Riserva - Docg

Fattoria di Terrabianca ♟♟♟♟
Località San Fedele a Paterno,
tel. 0577738544
www.terrabianca.com
r • Chianti Classico Riserva Croce - Docg
r • Campaccio Rosso Toscana - Igt
r • Campaccio Selezione Speciale Toscana - Igt
r • Ceppate Rosso Toscana - Igt
s • Il Fior di Fino Toscana - Igt

Fattoria Vignavecchia ♟♟♟
Località Sdrucciolo di Piazza 7,
tel. 0577738090
r • Chianti Classico Vignavecchia - Docg
r • Canvalle - Igt
r • Raddese - Igt

La Brancaia ♟♟♟♟
Località Poppi 42/B, tel. 0577742007
www.brancaia.com
r • Chianti Classico Brancaia - Docg
r • Brancaia Il Blu Toscana - Igt
r • Brancaia Tre Toscana - Igt

Livernano ♟♟♟♟
Località Livernano, tel. 0577738353
r • Livernano Toscana Rosso - Igt
r • Purosangue Toscana Rosso - Igt
w • Anima Toscana Bianco - Igt

Montevertine ♟♟♟♟♟
Località Montevertine, tel. 0577738009
r • Il Sodaccio di Montevertine Toscana - Igt
r • Montevertine Toscana - Igt
r • Le Pergole Torte Toscana - Igt

Podere Capaccia ♟♟♟♟
Località Capaccia, tel. 0574582426
www.poderecapaccia.com
r • Chianti Classico Riserva - Docg
r • Querciagrande - Igt
s • Spera di Sole - Vdt

Poggerino ♟♟♟
Via Poggerino 6, tel. 0577738958
www.poggerino.com
r • Chianti Classico - Docg
r • Chianti Classico Riserva Bugialla - Docg
r • Primamateria Rosso di Toscana - Igt

Pruneto ♟♟
Località Pruneto 37, tel. 0577738013
r • Chianti Classico Riserva - Docg

RAPOLANO TERME

Siena km 27 • m 334

Wineries

Castello di Modanella ♟♟♟♟
Località Serre di Rapolano,
tel. 0577704604
www.modanella.com
r • Le Voliere Toscana Cabernet Sauvignon - Igt
r • Poggio L'Aiole Toscana Rosso - Igt
r • Poggio Montino Toscana Rosso - Igt

Villa Buoninsegna ♟♟ ★10%
Località Buoninsegna 111, tel. 0577724380
www.buoninsegna.it
r • Villa Buoninsegna Toscana Rosso - Igt

RIPARBELLA

Pisa km 59 • m 216

Wineries

Podere La Regola ♟♟♟
Via A. Gramsci 1, tel. 0586699216
www.laregola.com
r • Montescudaio Rosso La Regola - Doc
r • Montescudaio Rosso Vallino delle Conche - Doc
w • Montescudaio Bianco Steccaia - Doc

ROCCALBEGNA

Grosseto km 44 • m 522

Wineries

Villa Patrizia ♟♟♟
Località Cana, tel. 0564982028
r • Morellino di Scansano - Doc
r • Le Valentane - Igt
w • Alteta - Igt

ROCCASTRADA

Grosseto km 34 • m 475

Wineries

I Campetti ♟♟
Località Ribolla, via Collacchia 2,
tel. 0564579663
r • Monteregio di Massa Marittima Rosso Baccio - Doc
w • Monteregio di Massa Marittima Bianco Nebbiaie - Doc
w • Almabruna Maremma Toscana - Igt

Meleta ♟♟♟
Località Roccatederighi, tel. 0564567155
r • Massaio Rosso Toscana - Igt
r • Pietrello d'Oro Rosso Toscana - Igt
r • Rosso della Rocca Rosso Toscana - Igt

RUFINA

Florence km 25 • m 115

Wineries

Colognole ♟♟♟ ★10%
Via del Palagio 15,
tel. 0558319870
www.colognole.it
r • Chianti Rufina Cològnole - Docg
r • Chianti Rufina Riserva del Don - Docg
w • Quattro Chiacchiere Bianco Toscano - Igt

Fattoria di Basciano ♟♟♟♟
Viale Duca della Vittoria 159, tel. 0558397034
masirenzo@virgilio.it
r • Chianti Rufina - Docg
r • Erta e China Toscana - Igt
r • I Pini Rosso dei Colli della Toscana Centrale - Igt
r • Vigna Il Corto Rosso dei Colli della Toscana Centrale - Igt
s • Vin Santo del Chianti Rufina - Doc

Fattoria Selvapiana ♟♟♟♟
Via Selvapiana 3, tel. 0558369848
r • Chianti Rufina - Docg
r • Chianti Rufina Riserva Fornace - Docg
r • Chianti Rufina Riserva Vigneto Bucerchiale - Docg
r • Pomino Rosso - Doc
s • Vin Santo dei Colli della Toscana Centrale - Vdt

Fattorie di Galiga e Vetrice ♟♟♟
Località Montebonello, via Trieste 30,
tel. 0558397008
r • Chianti Rufina - Docg
r • Chianti Rufina Riserva Campo al Sorbo - Docg
r • Chianti Rufina Riserva Villa di Vetrice - Docg

SAN CASCIANO DEI BAGNI

Siena km 85 • m 582

Wineries

Giacomo Mori - Palazzone ♟♟♟
Piazza Pertini 8, tel. 0578227005
giacomo.mori@libero.it
r • Chianti Castelrotto - Docg
r • Chianti Giacomo Mori - Docg

SAN CASCIANO IN VAL DI PESA

Florence km 16 • m 310

Wineries

Antica Fattoria Niccolò Machiavelli ♟♟♟
Località Sant'Andrea in Percussina,
tel. 055828471
www.giv.it
r • Chianti Classico - Docg
r • Chianti Classico Riserva Vigna di Fontalle - Docg
r • Il Principe Pinot Nero Toscana - Igt

Castello Il Palagio ♟♟♟
Località Mercatale, via Campoli 130/4,
tel. 055821630
r • Chianti Classico - Docg
r • Apotheosis - Igt
r • Curtifreda Cabernet Sauvignon di Toscana - Igt
r • Montefolchi Merlot di Toscana - Igt
s • Vin Santo del Chianti Classico Amabile - Doc

Fattoria Cigliano ♟♟
Via Cigliano 15, tel. 055820033
fattoriacigliano@libero.it
r • Chianti Classico - Docg
r • Chianti Classico Riserva - Docg

Fattoria Corzano e Paterno ♟♟♟♟
Via Paterno 10, tel. 0558249114
r • Chianti Riserva I Tre borri Terre di Corzano - Docg
r • Chianti Terre di Corzano - Docg
r • Il Corzano - Igt

Fattoria Le Corti Corsini ♟♟♟♟
Via S. Piero di Sotto 1, tel. 055820123
www.principecorsini.com
r • Chianti Classico Don Tommaso - Docg
r • Chianti Classico Le Corti - Docg
r • Chianti Classico Riserva Cortevecchia - Docg

Il Mandorlo ♟♟♟
Via Borromeo 130, tel. 0558228211
www.il-mandorlo.it
r • Chianti Classico Il Mandorlo - Docg
r • Chianti Classico Riserva Il Rotone - Docg
r • Terrato Toscana Rosso - Igt

La Sala ♟♟♟
Via Sorripa 34, tel. 055828111
www.lasala.it
r • Chianti Classico La Sala - Docg
r • Chianti Classico Riserva La Sala - Docg
r • Campo all'Albero Colli della Toscana Centrale Rosso - Igt

Massanera ♟♟♟
Località Chiesanuova, via di Faltignano 74/76,
tel. 0558242360
www.agriturismo.net/massanera
r • Chianti Classico Massanera - Docg
r • Per Me - Igt
r • Prelato di Massanera - Igt

Poggiopiano ♟♟♟♟
Via di Pisignano 29, tel. 0558229629
poggiopiano@fton.it
r • Chianti Classico Poggiopiano - Docg
r • Rosso di Sera Toscana - Igt

Produttori Associati Castelli del Grevepesa ♟♟♟
Località Ponte di Gabbiano, via Grevigiana 34,
tel. 055821911
info@castellidelgravepesa.it
r • Chianti Classico Panzano - Docg
r • Chianti Classico Vigna Elisa - Docg
r • Coltifredi Rosso Toscana - Igt
r • Gualdo al Luco Rosso Toscana - Igt
r • Syrah di Toscana - Igt

San Nicolò a Pisignano ♟♟♟
Via Pisignano 36, tel. 055828834
www.marcofelluga.it
r • Sorripa Toscana Rosso - Igt

Solatione ♟♟♟
Località Mercatale, via Valigondoli 53/A,
tel. 055821623
solatione@virgilio.it
r • Chianti Classico Solatione - Docg
r • Chianti Classico Riserva Solatione - Docg
s • Vin Santo del Chianti Classico Solatione - Doc

Tenuta Castello Il Corno ♟♟♟
Via Malafrasca 64, tel. 0558248009
r • Chianti Classico - Docg
r • Chianti Colli Fiorentini San Camillo - Docg
r • Colorino del Corno Toscana Rosso - Igt

SAN GIMIGNANO

Siena km 38 • m 324

Wineries

Baroncini ♟♟
Località Casale 43, tel. 0577941961
r • Morellino di Scansano Riserva Terranera Aia della Macina - Doc
w • Vernaccia di San Gimignano Vigneto Poggio ai Cannicci Fattoria Sovestro - Docg

Cà del Vispo ♟♟♟
Via di Fugnano 31, tel. 0577943053
r • Chianti Colline Senesi - Docg
r • Poggio Solivo Rosso di Toscana - Igt
w • Vernaccia di San Gimignano Vigna in Fiore - Docg

Cappella Sant'Andrea ♟♟
Località Casale 26,
tel. 0577940456
a.leoncini@cyber.dada.it
r • San Gimignano Rosso Serreto - Doc

Casale - Falchini ♟♟♟♟
Via di Casale 40, tel. 0577941305
www.falchini.com
r • Chianti dei Colli Senesi Titolato Colombaio - Docg
r • Campora Toscana - Igt
r • Paretaio Toscana - Igt

w • Vernaccia di San Gimignano Riserva Vigna a Solatio - Docg
w • Vernaccia di San Gimignano Titolato Castel Selva - Docg

Castello di Montauto ♟♟
Località Montauto, tel. 0577743024
www.castellodimontauto.it
w • Vernaccia di San Gimignano - Docg

Cesani Vincenzo ♟♟♟
Località Pancole 82/D, tel. 0577955084
cesanivini@novamedia.it
r • Chianti dei Colli Senesi Cesani - Docg
r • Luenzo Rosso Toscano - Igt
w • Vernaccia di San Gimignano Cesani - Docg
w • Vernaccia di San Gimignano Sanice - Docg

Fattoria Cusona - Guicciardini Strozzi ♟♟♟♟
Località Cusona 5, tel. 0577950028
www.guicciardinistrozzi.it
r • Chianti dei Colli Senesi Titolato Strozzi - Docg
r • Millanni Rosso Toscana - Igt
r • Sòdole Toscana - Igt
w • Vernaccia di San Gimignano Perlato - Docg
w • Vernaccia di San Gimignano Titolato Strozzi - Docg

Fattoria di Pietrafitta ♟♟♟ ★10%
Località Cortennano, tel. 0577943200
r • Chianti dei Colli Senesi - Docg
w • Vernaccia di San Gimignano Borghetto - Docg
w • Vernaccia di San Gimignano Riserva La Costa - Docg

Fontaleoni ♟♟♟
Località Santa Maria 39/A, tel. 0577950193
r • Rosso di San Gimignano La Cerreta - Doc
w • Vernaccia di San Gimignano - Docg
w • Vernaccia di San Gimignano Vigna Casanuova - Docg

Fratelli Vagnoni ♟♟♟
Località Pancole 82, tel. 0577955077
r • Chianti Colline Senesi - Docg
w • Vernaccia di San Gimignano - Docg
w • Vernaccia di San Gimignano I Mocali - Docg

Il Paradiso ♟♟♟♟
Località Strada 21/A, tel. 0577941500
r • Chianti Colli Senesi - Docg
r • Bottaccio Toscana - Igt
r • Paterno II Toscana - Igt
r • Saxa Calida Toscana - Igt
w • Vernaccia di San Gimignano Biscondola - Docg

La Rampa di Fugnano ♟♟♟
Località Fugnano 55, tel. 0577941655
www.rampadifugnano.it
r • Chianti dei Colli Senesi Via dei Franchi - Docg
r • Gisèle Colli della Toscana Centrale - Igt
w • Vernaccia di San Gimignano Alata - Docg

Le Solive ♟♟♟
Via di S. Benedetto, tel. 0577944840
www.lesolive.com
r • Connubio Rosso Toscana - Igt
r • Rubiroso Rosso Toscana - Igt
w • Vernaccia di San Gimignano Vigna Aprico - Docg

Montenidoli ♟♟♟
Località Montenidoli, tel. 0577941565
r • Chianti dei Colli Senesi Montenidoli - Docg
r • Sono Montenidoli - Vdt
w • Vernaccia di San Gimignano - Docg

Palagetto ♟♟♟
Via Monteoliveto 46, tel. 0577943090
palagetto@iol.it
r • Brunello di Montalcino - Docg
w • Vernaccia di San Gimignano Riserva - Docg
w • Vernaccia di San Gimignano Vigna Santa Chiara - Docg

Panizzi ♟♟♟ ★10%
Località Santa Margherita 34, tel. 0577941576
panizzi@eyber.dada.it
r • Chianti dei Colli Senesi Vertunno - Docg
r • Ceraso Rosso Toscana - Igt
w • Vernaccia di San Gimignano - Docg

Pietraserena ♟♟
Località Casale 5, tel. 0577940083
r • Chianti dei Colli Senesi Caulio - Docg
r • Chianti dei Colli Senesi Poggio al Vento - Docg
w • Vernaccia di San Gimignano Vigna del Sole - Docg

Rubicini Italo ♟♟
Località San Benedetto 17/C, tel. 0577944816
www.rubicini.com
r • Chianti Colline Senesi - Docg
r • Chianti Colline Senesi Tripudio - Docg
w • Vernaccia di San Gimignano - Docg

Tenuta Le Calcinaie ♟♟♟
Località Santa Lucia 36, tel. 0577943007
r • Chianti dei Colli Senesi - Docg
r • Teodoro - Igt
w • Vernaccia di San Gimignano Vigna ai Sassi - Doc

Tenuta Mormoraia ♟♟♟
Località S. Andrea, tel. 0577940096
r • Neitea Rosso Toscana - Igt
w • Vernaccia di San Gimignano - Docg
w • Ostrea Grigia Bianco Toscano - Igt

Teruzzi E. & Puthod C. - Ponte a Rondolino ♟♟♟
Località Casale 19, tel. 0577940143
w • Vernaccia di San Gimignano - Docg
w • Carmen Puthod Bianco di Toscana - Igt
w • Terre di Tufi Bianco di Toscana - Igt

San Miniato

Pisa km 42 • m 140

Wineries

Fattoria di Sassolo ♟♟♟
Località La Serra, via Bucciano 59, tel. 0571460001
w • Bianco Pisano di San Torpè - Doc
s • Bianco Pisano di San Torpè Vin Santo - Doc
s • Bianco Pisano di San Torpè Vin Santo Fiorile - Doc

San Vincenzo

Livorno km 60 • m 5

Wineries

Podere San Michele ♟♟♟♟
Località Caduta 3/A, tel. 0565798038
r • Allodio Rosso - Igt
w • Allodio Bianco - Igt

Sarteano

Siena km 87 • m 573

Wineries

Tenuta di Trinoro ♟♟♟♟♟
Via Val d'Orcia 15, tel. 0578267110
www.tenutaditrinoro.it

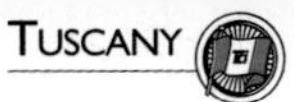

r • Cincinnato Rosso di Toscana - Igt
r • Le Cupole Toscana Rosso - Igt
r • Tenuta di Trinoro Toscana Rosso - Igt

SCANDICCI

Florence km 6 • m 47

WINERIES

FATTORIA BAGGIOLINO ♟♟♟
Località La Romola, via della Poggiona 4, tel. 055768916
r • Chianti dei Colli Fiorentini Titolato - Docg
r • Poggio Brandi - Vdt
s • Vin Santo Toscano - Vdt

FATTORIA SAN MICHELE A TORRI ♟♟♟
Via S. Michele 36, tel. 055769111
r • Chianti Classico - Docg
r • Murtas Colli della Toscana Centrale - Igt
s • Vin Santo del Chianti Classico - Doc

UGGIANO ♟♟
Località San Vincenzo a Torri, via Empolese, tel. 055769087
r • Chianti Riserva - Docg
r • Falconeri Toscana - Igt
r • Petraia Merlot di Toscana - Igt

VIGLIANO ♟♟♟♟
Località San Martino alla Palma, via Carcheri 309, tel. 0558727006
www.vigliano.com
r • Vigliano Toscana Rosso - Igt
r • Vigna dell'Erta Toscana - Igt
w • Bricoli Chardonnay Toscana - Igt

SCANSANO

Grosseto km 29 • m 500

WINERIES

BANTI ERIK ♟♟♟ ★10%
Località Fosso dei Molini, tel. 0564508006
r • Morellino di Scansano Ciabatta - Doc
r • Annosecondo Rosso Toscano - Igt
r • Aquilaia Toscana - Igt

CANTINA COOPERATIVA DEL MORELLINO DI SCANSANO ♟♟♟
Località Saragiolo, tel. 0564507288
r • Morellino di Scansano - Doc
r • Morellino di Scansano Riserva Roggiano - Doc
r • Morellino di Scansano Riserva San Rabano - Doc

CASTELLO DI MONTEPÒ ♟♟♟
Località Montepò, tel. 0564580231
www.sienanet.it/biondi_santi
r • Morellino di Scansano Riserva - Doc
r • Montepaone Toscana Rosso - Igt
r • Sassoalloro Toscana Rosso - Igt
r • Schidione Toscana Rosso - Igt

PROVVEDITORE ♟♟
Località Salaiola 174, tel. 0564599237
www.poderelafonte.it
r • Morellino di Scansano Provveditore - Doc

SELLARI FRANCESCHINI ♟♟
Via Marconi 65, tel. 0564507138
r • Morellino di Scansano Morello - Doc
w • Biondello dei Gaggioli - Vdt

SCARLINO

Grosseto km 45 • m 229

WINERIES

BOTRONA ♟♟♟♟
Località Botrona, tel. 0566866129
r • Monteregio di Massa Marittima Rosso - Doc

SIENA

m 322

WINERIES

CASTEL DI PUGNA ♟♟♟
Strada Val di Pugna 12/14, tel. 057746547
www.castelpugna.com
r • Chianti Colline Senesi Ellera - Docg
r • Chianti Superiore Poderina - Docg
r • Castelpugna Toscana Rosso - Igt

SAN GIORGIO A LAPI ♟♟♟
Strada Colle Pinzuto 30, tel. 0577356836
www.sangiorgioalapi.it
r • Chianti Classico - Docg
r • L'Eremo Toscana Rosso - Igt

SIGNA

Florence km 13 • m 46

WINERIES

FOSSI ♟♟♟♟
Via degli Arrighi 4, tel. 0558732174
agrifossi@libero.it
r • Sassoforte Toscana - Igt
r • Syrah Toscana - Igt
w • Primopreso Toscana - Igt

SINALUNGA

Siena km 45 • m 364

WINERIES

CASTELLO DI FARNETELLA ♟♟♟♟
Strada Siena-Bettolle al km 37, tel. 0577355117
felsina@dada.it
r • Lucilla Toscana Rosso - Igt
r • Nero di Nubi Pinot Nero Toscana - Igt
r • Poggio Granoni Toscana - Igt

TENUTA FARNETA ♟♟♟
Località Farneta 161, tel. 0577631025
r • Chianti dei Colli Senesi - Docg
r • Bentivoglio Rosso Toscana - Igt
r • Bongoverno Vigneto Casai Rosso Toscana - Igt

SORANO

Grosseto km 83 • m 379

WINERIES

RIPA ♟♟♟♟
Località Sovana, podere Sopra La Ripa, tel. 0564616885
www.sopralaripa.com
r • Ripa EA Toscana Rosso - Igt
r • Ripa Toscana Rosso - Igt

SASSOTONDO ♟♟♟
Località Sovana, tel. 0564614218
sassotondo@ftbcc.it
r • Sovana Rosso Superiore Franze - Doc
r • San Lorenzo Toscana Rosso - Igt
r • Sassotondo Toscana Rosso - Igt

SOVICILLE

Siena km 13 • m 265

WINERIES

POGGIO SALVI ♟♟♟
Località Poggio Salvi 251, tel. 0577349045

www.poggiosalvi.it
r • Chianti Colline Senesi - Docg
r • Campo del Bosco Rosso Toscana - Igt
s • Vin Santo di Toscana - Igt

Tenuta di Trecciano ♟♟♟
Località Trecciano, tel. 0577314357
trecciano@libero.it
r • Chianti dei Colli Senesi Terra di Siena - Docg
r • Daniello Rosso di Toscana - Igt
r • I Campacci Rosso Toscano - Igt

SUVERETO

Livorno km 78 • m 90

Wineries

Ambrosini Lorella ♟♟♟♟
Località Tabarò 96, tel. 0565829301
r • Val di Cornia Rosso Suvereto Subertum - Doc
r • Val di Cornia Rosso Suvereto Tabarò - Doc
r • Riflesso Antico - Igt

Bulichella ♟♟♟
Località Bulichella, tel. 0565829892
r • Val di Cornia Suvereto Rosso Rubino - Doc
r • Val di Cornia Suvereto Rosso Tuscanio - Doc
w • Val di Cornia Suvereto Bianco Tuscanio - Doc

Gualdo del Re ♟♟♟♟
Località Notri 77, tel. 0565829888
www.gualdodelre.it
r • Val di Cornia Suvereto Gualdo del Re - Doc
r • Federico Primo Rosso Toscana - Igt
r • l'Rennero Rosso Toscana - Igt
w • Lumen Bianco Toscana - Igt
w • Valentina Vermentino di Toscana - Igt

Il Bruscello ♟♟♟♟
Località Tabarò, tel. 0565829025
bruscello@interfree.it
r • Val di Cornia Loco dei Frati - Doc
r • Quarzo di Rocca Toscana Sangiovese - Igt

Il Falcone ♟♟
Località Falcone 186-187, tel. 0565829294
il.falcone@tin.it
r • Val di Cornia Suvereto Falcorosso - Doc
r • Val di Cornia Sangiovese Safeno - Doc
w • Val di Cornia Bianco Iliaco - Doc

Incontri ♟♟♟
Località Fossoni 38, tel. 0565829401
blocloko@hotmail.com
r • Val di Cornia Rosso Lorenzo degli Incontri - Doc
r • Val di Cornia Rosso Lago Bruno - Doc
w • Val di Cornia Bianco Ildobrandino - Doc

Le Pianacce ♟♟
Località Pianacce, tel. 0565828027
r • Diavolino Rosso - Vdt

Montepeloso ♟♟♟♟
Località Montepeloso 82, tel. 0565828180
r • Eneo - Igt
r • Gabbro - Igt
r • Nardo - Igt

Petra ♟♟♟
Località San Lorenzo Alto 131, tel. 0565845308
www.terramoretti.it
r • Val di Cornia Suvereto Rosso Petra - Doc
r • Petra Toscana Rosso - Igt

Petricci e Del Pianta ♟♟♟♟
Località San Lorenzo 20, tel. 0565845140
r • Val di Cornia Suvereto Rosso Albatrone - Doc
r • Val di Cornia Suvereto Rosso Buca di Cleonte - Doc
r • Cerosecco Rosso di Toscana - Igt

Russo ♟♟♟♟
Via Forni 71, tel. 0565845105
r • Val di Cornia Rosso Riserva Barbicone - Doc
r • Val di Cornia Rosso Suvereto Ceppitaio - Doc
r • Sassobucato Toscana - Igt

Tua Rita ♟♟♟♟♟
Località Notri 81, tel. 0565829237
r • Giusto di Notri - Igt
r • Redigaffi - Igt
w • Lodano - Igt

Villa Monte Rico ♟♟♟
Località Poggio Cerro, tel. 0565829550
reichenberg@dplanet.ch
r • Val di Cornia Rosso - Doc
r • Val di Cornia Rosso Il Grappolo - Doc

TAVARNELLE VAL DI PESA

Florence km 30 • m 378

Wineries

Fattoria Poggio Romita ♟♟♟
Via Commenda 10, tel. 0558077253
r • Chianti Classico Frimaio - Docg
r • Chianti Colli Fiorentini - Docg
r • La Sassaia - Vdt

Il Poggiolino ♟♟♟
Località Sambuca, via Chiantigiana 32, tel. 0558071635
www.ilpoggiolino.com
r • Chianti Classico - Docg
r • Chianti Classico Riserva - Docg
r • Le Balze del Poggiolino Toscana - Igt

Montecchio ♟♟♟
Località San Donato in Poggio, via Montecchio 4, tel. 0558072907
r • Chianti Classico - Docg
r • Chianti Classico Riserva - Docg
r • Pietracupa Colli della Toscana Centrale - Igt

Podere La Cappella ♟♟♟♟
Località San Donato in Poggio, via Cerbaia 10 A, tel. 0558072727
r • Chianti Classico Riserva Querciolo - Docg
r • Cantico - Igt
r • Corbezzolo - Vdt

Poggio al Sole ♟♟♟
Località Badia a Passignano, tel. 0558071504
r • Chianti Classico - Docg
r • Chianti Classico Casasilia - Docg
r • Seraselva - Igt

Tracolle ♟♟
Località Sambuca, strada in Greve 5, tel. 0558071234
r • Chianti Classico Tracolle - Docg
r • Chianti Classico Riserva Cetinale - Docg

TERRANUOVA BRACCIOLINI

Arezzo km 34 • m 156

Wineries

Tenuta Sette Ponti ♟♟♟♟♟
Località Oreno, tel. 055977443
www.tenutasetteponti.com
r • Crognolo Toscana Rosso - Igt
r • Oreno Toscana Rosso - Igt

TERRICCIOLA
Pisa km 39 • m 180

WINERIES

BADIA DI MORRONA ♟♟♟
Località Morrona, tel. 0587658505
r • Chianti I Sodi del Paretaio - Docg
r • Colli dell'Etruria Centrale Rosso Vignaalta - Doc
r • N'Antia Toscana - Igt

MOOS ♟♟♟
Località Soiana, via Pier Capponi 98, tel. 0587654180
r • Fontestina - Igt
r • Soianello - Igt

SORELLE PALAZZI ♟♟♟
Località Morrona, via del Chianti 34, tel. 0587654003
r • Chianti delle Colline Pisane Riserva - Docg
s • Bianco Pisano di San Torpé Vin Santo - Doc

VALLORSI ♟♟♟
Località Marrona, via della Cascina 19, tel. 0587658470
www.vallorsi.it
r • Chianti - Docg
r • San Bartolomeo Toscana Rosso - Igt
w • Bianco Pisano di San Torpè - Doc

TORRITA DI SIENA
Siena km 51 • m 325

WINERIES

INNOCENTI VITTORIO ♟♟
Località Montefollonico, via Landucci 10/12, tel. 0577669537
r • Vino Nobile di Montepulciano - Docg
r • Vino Nobile di Montepulciano Riserva - Docg
s • Vin Santo Toscana - Igt

VAGLIA
Florence km 18 • m 290

WINERIES

CAMPOSILIO DI RUSTIONI ♟♟♟
Località Pratolino, via di Basciano 805, tel. 055696456
www.camposilio.it
r • Camposilio Toscana Rosso - Igt
r • I Venti di Camposilio Toscana Rosso - Igt

VINCI
Florence km 42 • m 97

WINERIES

FATTORIA DI FALTOGNANO ♟♟♟
Via di Faltognano 158, tel. 057176936
r • Chianti Montalbano - Docg
r • Merizzo - Igt

LEONARDO DA VINCI ♟♟♟
Via Provinciale di Mercatale 291, tel. 0571902444
www.cantineleonardo.it
r • Chianti Leonardo - Docg
r • Sant'Ippolito Rosso Toscana - Igt
r • San Zio Rosso Toscano - Igt

THE MARCHES

ANCONA
m 16

WINERIES

LANARI ♟♟♟
Località Varano, via Pozzo 142, tel. 0712861343
r • Rosso Conero - Doc
r • Rosso Conero Fibbio - Doc

MARCHETTI MAURIZIO ♟♟
Via Pontelungo 168, tel. 071897386
r • Rosso Conero Villa Bonomi - Doc
w • Verdicchio dei Castelli di Jesi Classico - Doc
w • Verdicchio dei Castelli di Jesi Classico Tenuta del Cavaliere - Doc

MORODER ♟♟♟♟ ★10%
Località Montacuto 112, tel. 071898232
r • Rosso Conero - Doc
r • Rosso Conero Dorico - Doc
s • Oro Bianco Marche - Igt

SERENELLI ALBERTO ♟
Via Bartolini 2, tel. 07135505
r • Rosso Conero Trave - Doc
r • Rosso Conero Varano - Doc
w • Verdicchio dei Castelli di Jesi Classico Sora Elvira - Doc

APIRO
Macerata km 40 • m 516

WINERIES

CANESTRARI ♟♟
Via S. Francesco 18, tel. 0733611315
w • Verdicchio dei Castelli di Jesi Classico Lapiro - Doc
w • Verdicchio dei Castelli di Jesi Classico Moja Cupa - Doc

APPIGNANO
Macerata km 17 • m 199

WINERIES

FATTORIA DI FORANO ♟♟♟
Contrada Forano, 40, tel. 073357102
villaforano@libero.it
r • Rosso Piceno - Doc
r • Rosso Piceno Bulciano - Doc
w • Colli Maceratesi Bianco Monteferro - Doc

ASCOLI PICENO
m 154

WINERIES

VELENOSI ERCOLE ♟♟♟
Via dei Biancospini 11, tel. 0736341218
www.velenosivini.com
r • Rosso Piceno Superiore Brecciarolo - Doc
r • Rosso Piceno Superiore Roggio del Filare - Doc
r • Ludi Marche Rosso - Igt
w • Falerio Vigna Solaria - Doc
w • Rêve di Villa Angela Marche Chardonnay - Igt

BARBARA
Ancona km 51 • m 219

Wineries

Santa Barbara
Borgo Mazzini 35, tel. 0719674249
www.vinisantabarbara.it
r • Rosso Piceno Maschio da Monte - Doc
r • Pathos Marche Rosso - Igt
r • Pignocco Marche Rosso - Igt
r • Stefano Antonucci Marche Rosso - Igt
r • Vigna San Bartolo Marche Rosso - Igt
w • Verdicchio dei Castelli di Jesi Classico Le Vaglie - Doc
w • Verdicchio dei Castelli di Jesi Classico Stefano Antonucci - Doc

CAMERANO
Ancona km 12 • m 231

Wineries

Spinsanti
Via Galletto 29, tel. 071731797
agaggiotti@tiscali.it
r • Sassone Marche Rosso - Igt

Strologo Silvano
Via Loretana 114, tel. 071732359
s.strologo@libero.it
r • Rosso Conero Julius - Doc
r • Rosso Conero Traiano - Doc

CASTEL DI LAMA
Ascoli Piceno km 15 • m 65/233

Wineries

Tenuta De Angelis
Via S. Francesco 10, tel. 073687429
info@tenutadeangelis.it
r • Rosso Piceno Superiore Etichetta Oro - Doc
r • Rosso Piceno Superiore - Doc
r • Anghelos - Vdt

CASTELPLANIO
Ancona km 47 • m 305

Wineries

Fazi Battaglia ★15%
Via Roma 117, tel. 0731813444
r • Rosso Conero Riserva Passo del Lupo - Doc
w • Verdicchio dei Castelli di Jesi Classico Riserva San Sisto - Doc
w • Verdicchio dei Castelli di Jesi Classico Superiore Le Moie - Doc
s • Arkezia Muffo di San Sisto Marche Bianco - Igt

CINGOLI
Macerata km 29 • m 631

Wineries

Lucangeli Aymerich di Laconi - Tenuta di Tavignano ★10%
Località Tavignano, tel. 0733617303
tavignano@libero.it
w • Verdicchio dei Castelli di Jesi Classico Superiore Misco - Doc
w • Verdicchio dei Castelli di Jesi Classico Superiore Tavignano - Doc

CIVITANOVA MARCHE
Macerata km 27 • m 3

Wineries

Boccadigabbia
Contrada Castelletta 56, tel. 073370728
www.boccadigabbia.com
r • Rosso Piceno - Doc
r • Akronte Marche Cabernet Sauvignon - Igt
r • Pix Marche Merlot - Igt
r • Saltapicchio Marche Sangiovese - Igt
w • Montalperti Marche Chardonnay - Igt

CUPRA MARITTIMA
Ascoli Piceno km 41 • m 4

Wineries

Oasi degli Angeli
Contrada S. Egidio 50, tel. 0735778569
mora.r@siscom.it
r • Kurni Marche Rosso - Igt

CUPRA MONTANA
Ancona km 47 • m 505

Wineries

Colonnara - Viticultori in Cupramontana
Via Mandriole 6, tel. 0731780273
www.colonnara.it
r • Tornamagno Marche Rosso - Igt
w • Verdicchio dei Castelli di Jesi Classico Lyricus - Doc
w • Verdicchio dei Castelli di Jesi Classico Superiore Riserva Romitello delle Mandriole - Doc
w • Verdicchio dei Castelli di Jesi Classico Superiore Tufico V. T. - Doc
w • Verdicchio dei Castelli di Jesi Classico Superiore Vigna San Marco - Doc

Vallerosa - Bonci
Via Torre 13, tel. 0731789129
r • Rosso Piceno Casanostra - Doc
w • Verdicchio dei Castelli di Jesi Classico Riserva Barré - Doc
w • Verdicchio dei Castelli di Jesi Classico Superiore Le Case - Doc
w • Verdicchio dei Castelli di Jesi Classico Superiore San Michele - Doc
s • Verdicchio dei Castelli di Jesi Passito Rojano - Doc

FABRIANO
Ancona km 73 • m 325

Wineries

Mecella Enzo
Via Dante 112, tel. 073221680
r • Rosso Conero Rubelliano - Doc
r • Braccano Marche Rosso - Igt
r • Longobardo Marche Rosso - Igt
w • Verdicchio di Matelica Antico di Casa Fosca - Doc

FANO
Pesaro e Urbino km 12 • m 12

Wineries

Morelli Claudio
Viale Romagna 47, tel. 0721823352
clamoro@libero.it
r • Colli Pesaresi Sangiovese La Vigna delle Terrazze - Doc
r • Colli Pesaresi Sangiovese Sant'Andrea in Villis - Doc
r • Magliano Marche Rosso - Igt
r • Suffragium Marche Rosso - Igt
w • Bianchello del Metauro Borgo Torre - Doc

JESI
Ancona km 29 • m 97

WINERIES

BRUNORI MARIO E GIORGIO ♟♟
Viale della Vittoria 103, tel. 0731207213
brunorivini@libero.it
r • Lacrima di Morro d'Alba - Doc
w • Verdicchio dei Castelli di Jesi Classico Le Gemme - Doc
w • Verdicchio dei Castelli di Jesi Classico Superiore San Nicolò - Doc

MONTECAPPONE COLLI DI JESI ♟♟
Via Colle Olivo 2, tel. 0731205761
www.agrivinicola.it
r • Rosso Piceno Montesecco - Doc
w • Esino Bianco Tabano - Doc
w • Verdicchio dei Castelli di Jesi Classico Montesecco - Doc

LORETO
Ancona km 26 • m 127

WINERIES

GAROFOLI GIOACCHINO ♟♟♟♟♟
Via Arno 9, tel. 0717820162 mail@garofolivini.it
r • Rosso Conero Riserva Grosso Agontano - Doc
r • Rosso Conero Vigna Piancarda - Doc
w • Verdicchio dei Castelli di Jesi Classico Riserva Serra Fiorese - Doc
w • Verdicchio dei Castelli di Jesi Classico Superiore Podium - Doc
s • Verdicchio dei Castelli di Jesi Passito Le Brume - Doc

MACERATA
m 315

WINERIES

VILLAMAGNA FLORIANI ♟♟♟
Contrada Montanello 5, tel. 0733492236
www.boccadigabbia.com
r • Rosso Piceno - Doc
w • Mont'Anello Marche Bianco - Igt

MAIOLATI SPONTINI
Ancona km 47 • m 405

WINERIES

MANCINI ♟♟
Località Mote, via S. Lucia 7, tel. 0731702975
www.manciniwines.it
w • Verdicchio dei Castelli di Jesi Classico Superiore Villa Talliano - Doc

MONTE SCHIAVO ♟♟♟ ★10%
Località Monteschiavo, via Vivaio, tel. 0731700385
www.monteschiavo.it
r • Lacrima di Morro d'Alba - Doc
r • Rosso Conero Adeodato - Doc
r • Rosso Piceno Superiore Sassaiolo - Doc
w • Verdicchio dei Castelli di Jesi Classico Riserva Le Giuncare - Doc
w • Verdicchio dei Castelli di Jesi Classico Superiore Palio di San Floriano - Doc

MATELICA
Macerata km 45 • m 354

WINERIES

BELISARIO - CANTINA SOCIALE DI MATELICA E CERRETO D'ESI ♟♟♟ ★10%
Via Aristide Merloni 12, tel. 0737787247
www.belisario.it
w • Verdicchio di Matelica Riserva Cambrugiano - Doc
w • Verdicchio di Matelica Terre di Valbona - Doc
w • Verdicchio di Matelica Vigneti Belisario - Doc

BISCI ♟♟♟
Via Fogliano 120, tel. 0737787490
bisciwines@libero.it
r • Villa Castiglioni Rosso Marche - Igt
w • Verdicchio di Matelica Riserva - Doc
w • Verdicchio di Matelica Vigneto Fogliano - Doc

FATTORIA LA MONACESCA ♟♟♟
Contrada Monacesca, tel. 073381 2602
monacesca@tin.it
r • Camerte Marche Rosso - Igt
w • Verdicchio di Matelica La Monacesca - Doc
w • Verdicchio di Matelica Riserva La Monacesca - Doc
w • Ecclesia Marche Chardonnay - Igt
w • Mirum Marche Bianco - Igt

SAN BIAGIO ♟♟
Via S. Biagio 32, tel. 073783997
r • Bragnolo Marche Rosso - Igt
r • Grottagrifone Marche Cabernet Sauvignon - Igt
w • Verdicchio di Matelica Vigneto Braccano - Doc

MONDAVIO
Pesaro e Urbino km 39 • m 280

WINERIES

FATTORIA LAILA ♟♟♟
Via S. Filippo sul Cesano, tel. 0721979353
r • Rosso Piceno - Doc
r • Lailum Marche Rosso - Igt
w • Verdicchio dei Castelli di Jesi Lailum - Doc

MONTECAROTTO
Ancona km 48 • m 380

WINERIES

LAURENTINA ♟♟♟
Contrada S. Pietro 19/A, tel. 073189435
laurentina@katamail.com
r • Rosso Piceno - Doc
r • Rosso Piceno Talliano - Doc

SAN LORENZO ♟♟
Via S. Lorenzo 6, tel. 073189656
w • Verdicchio dei Castelli di Jesi Vigna delle Oche - Doc

TERRE CORTESI MONCARO ♟♟♟
Via Piandole 7/A, tel. 073189245
www.moncaro.com
r • Rosso Conero Riserva Cimerio - Doc
r • Barocco Marche Rosso - Igt
w • Rosso Piceno Superiore Rocca di Acquaviva - Doc
w • Verdicchio dei Castelli di Jesi Classico Riserva Vigna Novali - Doc
s • Verdicchio dei Castelli di Jesi Passito Tordiruta - Doc

MONTEFANO
Macerata km 17 • m 242

WINERIES

DEGLI AZZONI AVOGADRO CARRADORI ♟♟
Corso Carradori 13, tel. 0733850002

www.degliazzoni.it
r • Passatempo - Vdt

MONTEGRANARO
Ascoli Piceno km 77 • m 279
Wineries
Rio Maggio ♟♟♟
Contrada Vallone 41, tel. 0734889587
info@riomaggio.it
r • Rosso Piceno Granarijs - Doc
w • Falerio dei Colli Ascolani Telusiano - Doc
w • Artias Sauvignon - Vdt

MORRO D'ALBA
Ancona km 29 • m 199
Wineries
Mancinelli Stefano ♟♟♟
Via Roma 62, tel. 073163021
www.mancinelli-wine
r • Lacrima di Morro d'Alba Podere Santa Maria del Fiore - Doc
r • San Michele Marche Rosso - Igt
r • Terre dei Goti Marche Rosso - Igt
w • Verdicchio dei Castelli di Jesi Classico Superiore Podere Santa Maria del Fiore - Doc
w • Terre dei Goti Marche Bianco - Igt
Marotti Campi ♟♟♟ ★10%
Località Sant'Amico 14, tel. 0731618027
r • Lacrima di Morro d'Alba Orgiolo - Doc
s • Verdicchio dei Castelli di Jesi Passito Onyr - Doc

MORROVALLE
Macerata km 16 • m 245
Wineries
Capinera ♟
Contrada Crocette 12,
tel. 0733222444
www.capinera.com
r • Rosso Piceno Duca Guarnerio - Doc
w • La Capinera Selezione Marche Chardonnay - Igt

NUMANA
Ancona km 22 • m 56
Wineries
Conte Leopardi Dittajuti ♟♟♟
Via Marina II 26, tel. 0717390116
r • Rosso Conero Pigmento V.T. - Doc
r • Rosso Conero Vigneti del Coppo - Doc
w • Calcare Marche Sauvignon - Igt
Fattoria Le Terrazze ♟♟♟♟♟
Via Musone 4, tel. 0717390352
a.terni@fastnet.it
r • Rosso Conero - Doc
r • Rosso Conero Sassi Neri - Doc
r • Chaos Marche Rosso - Igt
w • Le Cave Marche Chardonnay - Igt

OFFAGNA
Ancona km 18 • m 306
Wineries
Malacari ♟♟♟♟
Via E. Malacari 6, tel. 0717207606
malacari@tin.it
r • Rosso Conero - Doc
r • Rosso Conero Grigiano - Doc

OFFIDA
Ascoli Piceno km 24 • m 293
Wineries
Aurora ♟♟♟
Via Ciafone 98, tel. 0736810007
www.viniaurora.it
r • Barricadiero Marche Rosso - Igt
San Giovanni ♟♟♟
Contrada Ciafone 41, tel. 0736889032
www.vinisangiovanni.it
r • Rosso Piceno Ophites - Doc
r • Rosso Piceno Superiore Leo Guelfus - Doc
r • Rosso Piceno Superiore Rosso del Nonno - Doc
w • Falerio dei Colli Ascolani Leo Guelfus - Doc
w • Falerio dei Colli Ascolani V. T. Marta - Doc
Villa Pigna ♟♟♟
Contrada Ciafone 63, tel. 073687525
www.villapigna.com
r • Rosso Piceno Superiore Vergaio - Doc
r • Briccaio Marche Rosso - Igt
r • Cabernasco Marche Rosso - Igt
r • Rozzano Marche Rosso - Igt
r • Vellutato Marche Rosso - Igt

OSIMO
Ancona km 18 • m 265
Wineries
Umani Ronchi ♟♟♟♟♟
S.S. 16 al km 310.4, tel. 0717108019
www.umanironchi.it
r • Rosso Conero Cùmaro - Doc
r • Medoro Marche Sangiovese - Igt
r • Pelago Marche Rosso - Igt
w • Verdicchio dei Castelli di Jesi Classico Riserva Plenio - Doc
w • Verdicchio dei Castelli di Jesi Classico Superiore Casal di Serra - Doc
w • Le Busche Marche Bianco - Igt
s • Maximo Botrytis Cinerea Marche Bianco - Igt

OSTRA VETERE
Ancona km 47 • m 250
Wineries
Fratelli Bucci ♟♟♟♟
Via Cona 30, tel. 071964179
www.villabucci.com
r • Rosso Piceno Tenuta Pongelli - Doc
w • Verdicchio dei Castelli di Jesi Classico - Doc
w • Verdicchio dei Castelli di Jesi Classico Riserva Villa Bucci - Doc

PEDASO
Ascoli Piceno km 50 • m 4
Wineries
Castello Fageto ♟♟
Via Valdaso 52,
tel. 0734931784
www.castellofageto.it
r • Rosso Piceno Rusus - Doc
w • Tristo di Elisena Marche Bianco - Igt
s • Alido Vino Passito - Vdt

PERGOLA
Pesaro e Urbino km 61 • m 265

Wineries

Fattoria Villa Ligi ♟♟
Via Zoccolanti 25/A, tel. 0721734351
villaligi@libero.it
r • Vernaculum Vigna La Rosa - Vdt

PESARO

m 11

Wineries

Fattoria Mancini ♟♟♟
Strada dei Colli 35, tel. 072151828
r • Colli Pesaresi Sangiovese - Doc
r • Blu Marche Rosso - Igt
r • Impero Marche Rosso - Igt
r • Montebacchino Marche Rosso - Igt
w • Impero Marche Bianco - Igt

POGGIO SAN MARCELLO

Ancona km 50 • m 385

Wineries

Marconi Maurizio ♟♟
Via Melano 23, tel. 0731267223
info@vinoearte.it
r • Lacrima di Morro d'Alba Casato - Doc
w • Verdicchio dei Castelli di Jesi Classico Superiore - Doc
w • Verdicchio dei Castelli di Jesi Classico Superiore Corona Reale - Doc

Sartarelli ♟♟♟♟
Contrada Costa del Molino, tel. 073189732
www.sartarelli.it
w • Verdicchio dei Castelli di Jesi Classico - Doc
w • Verdicchio dei Castelli di Jesi Classico Contrada Balciana - Doc
w • Verdicchio dei Castelli di Jesi Classico Tralivio - Doc

POTENZA PICENA

Macerata km 18 • m 237

Wineries

Santa Cassella ♟♟
Contrada S. Cassella 7, tel. 0733671507
santacassella@tiscalinet.it
r • Rosso Piceno - Doc
r • Conte Leopoldo Marche Cabernet Sauvignon - Igt
w • Colli Maceratesi Bianco - Doc

RIPATRANSONE

Ascoli Piceno km 38 • m 494

Wineries

La Cantina dei Colli Ripani ♟♟
Contrada Tosciano 28, tel. 07359505
r • Rosso Piceno Superiore Castellano - Doc
r • Rosso Piceno Superiore Leo Ripanus - Doc
w • Falerio dei Colli Ascolani Brezzolino - Doc

Le Caniette ♟♟♟♟
Contrada Canali, 23, tel. 07359200
r • Rosso Piceno Morellone - Doc
r • Rosso Piceno Riserva Nero di Vite - Doc
r • Sibilla Eritrea - Vdt
w • Falerio Lucrezia - Doc
w • Offida Pecorino Isomogaia - Doc

Poderi San Savino ♟♟♟
Località San Savino, contrada S. Maria in Carro 13, tel. 073590107
cantina.sansavino@libero.it
r • Rosso Piceno Campo alle Mura - Doc
r • Rosso Piceno Superiore Picus - Doc
w • Offida Pecorino Ciprea - Doc

Tenuta Cocci Grifoni ♟♟
Località San Savino, contrada Messieri 12, tel. 073590143
info@tenutacoccigrifoni.it
r • Rosso Piceno Superiore Il Grifone - Doc
w • Offida Pecorino Podere Colle Vecchio - Doc
w • Podere Colle Vecchio Marche Bianco - Igt

ROSORA

Ancona km 49 • m 380

Wineries

Cavallaro ♟♟
Via Tassanare 4, tel. 0731814158
r • Rosso Piceno Furtarello - Doc

SAN PAOLO DI JESI

Ancona km 44 • m 224

Wineries

Ceci Enrico ♟♟
Via S. Maria d'Arco 7, tel. 0731779033
cecienrico@virgilio.it
w • Verdicchio dei Castelli di Jesi Classico Superiore Santa Maria d'Arco - Doc

Piersanti & C. ♟♟
Via Borgo S. Maria 60, tel. 0731703214
www.piersantivini.com
w • Verdicchio dei Castelli di Jesi Classico Superiore Ori di Verdicchio - Doc

SERRA DE' CONTI

Ancona km 52 • m 216

Wineries

Casalfarneto ♟♟♟
Via Farneto 16, tel. 0731889001
www.casalfarneto.it
w • Verdicchio dei Castelli di Jesi Classico Superiore Cimaio - Doc
w • Verdicchio dei Castelli di Jesi Classico Superiore Fontevecchia - Doc
w • Verdicchio dei Castelli di Jesi Classico Superiore Grancasale - Doc

SERRA SAN QUIRICO

Ancona km 53 • m 300

Wineries

Accadia Angelo ♟♟
Via Ammorto 19, tel. 0731859007
www.assivip.it
w • Verdicchio dei Castelli di Jesi Classico Superiore Cantorì - Doc
w • Verdicchio dei Castelli di Jesi Classico Superiore Conscio - Doc

SERVIGLIANO

Ascoli Piceno km 47 • m 215

Wineries

Romolo e Remo Dezi ♟♟♟
Contrada Fontemaggio 14, tel. 0734750408
r • Dezio Vigneto Beccaccia Marche Rosso - Igt
r • Regina del Bosco Marche Rosso - Igt
w • Solo Marche Rosso - Igt

SPINETOLI

Ascoli Piceno km 20 • m 177

Wineries

Conte Saladini Pilastri Saladino ♟♟♟♟

Via Saladini 5, tel. 0736899534
saladpil@tin.it

- *r* • Rosso Piceno Superiore Montetinello - Doc
- *r* • Rosso Piceno Superiore Vigna Monteprandone - Doc
- *r* • Pregio del Conte Marche Rosso - Vdt
- *w* • Falerio Vigna Palazzi - Doc
- *w* • Pregio del Conte Marche Bianco - Vdt

STAFFOLO

Ancona km 48 • m 441

Wineries

Fattoria Coroncino ♟♟♟

Contrada Coroncino 7, tel. 0731779494

- *w* • Verdicchio dei Castelli di Jesi Classico Il Bacco - Doc
- *w* • Verdicchio dei Castelli di Jesi Classico Superiore Gaiospino - Doc
- *w* • Verdicchio dei Castelli di Jesi Classico Superiore Gaiospino Fumé - Doc
- *w* • Verdicchio dei Castelli di Jesi Classico Superiore Il Coroncino - Doc
- *w* • Le Lame Marche Bianco - Igt

Fonte della Luna ♟♟♟

Via S. Francesco 1/A, tel. 0731779307

- *r* • Rosso Piceno Grizio - Doc
- *w* • Verdicchio dei Castelli di Jesi - Doc
- *w* • Verdicchio dei Castelli di Jesi Fra Moriale - Doc

Zaccagnini ♟♟

Via Salmagina 9/10, tel. 0731779892
www.zaccagnini.it

- *r* • Rosso Conero - Doc
- *w* • Verdicchio dei Castelli di Jesi Classico Pier delle Vigne - Doc
- *w* • Verdicchio dei Castelli di Jesi Classico Salmàgina - Doc

UMBRIA

AMELIA

Terni km 24 • m 370

Wineries

Cantina Colli Amerini ♟♟♟ ★10%

Località Fornole, tel. 0744989721

- *r* • Colli Amerini Rosso Superiore Carbio - Doc
- *r* • Olmeto Merlot Umbria - Igt
- *r* • Torraccio Rosso Umbria - Igt

Castello delle Regine ♟♟

Località Le Regine, via di Castelluccio, tel. 0744702005
castellodelleregine@virgilio.it

- *r* • Merlot Umbria - Igt
- *r* • Podernovo Umbria Sangiovese - Igt
- *r* • Princeps Umbria Rosso - Igt

BASCHI

Terni km 58 • m 165

Wineries

Barberani - Vallesanta ♟♟♟

Località Cerreto, S.S. Todi-Baschi, tel. 0763341820
www.barberani.it

- *w* • Orvieto Classico Superiore Secco Castagnolo - Doc
- *s* • Orvieto Classico Superiore Dolce Calcaia Muffa Nobile - Doc
- *s* • Villa Monticelli Umbria Moscato Passito - Igt

Vaglie ♟♟

Via Amelia 48, tel. 0744957425
a.lumini@tiscali.it

- *r* • Masseo Umbria Rosso - Igt
- *r* • Momenti Umbria Rosso - Igt
- *r* • Vaglie Umbria Rosso - Igt

BEVAGNA

Perugia km 38 • m 210

Wineries

Adanti ♟♟

Vocabolo Arquata, tel. 0742360295

- *r* • Montefalco Sagrantino Arquata - Docg
- *r* • Arquata Rosso dell'Umbria - Igt
- *s* • Arquata Vin Santo dell'Umbria - Igt

Eredi Benincasa ♟♟

Località Capro 99, tel. 0742361307
www.aziendabenincasa.com

- *r* • Montefalco Rosso - Doc
- *w* • Colli Martani Poggio dell'Annunziata - Doc

Fattoria Antano Milziade ♟♟

Località Colle Allodole, tel. 0742360371

- *r* • Montefalco Sagrantino - Docg
- *r* • Montefalco Sagrantino Colle delle Allodole - Docg

CASTEL VISCARDO

Terni km 85 • m 507

Wineries

Cantina Monrubio - Vi.C.Or ♟♟♟

Località Le Prese di Monterubiaglio, tel. 0763626064
cantina.monrubio@tiscalinet.it

- *r* • Monrubio Umbria Rosso - Igt
- *w* • Orvieto Classico Salceto - Doc
- *w* • Orvieto Classico Superiore Soana - Doc

CASTIGLIONE DEL LAGO

Perugia km 44 • m 304

Wineries

Duca della Corgna ♟♟♟

Via Roma 236, tel. 0759653210
ducacorgna@libero.it

- *r* • Colli del Trasimeno Rosso Baccio del Rosso - Doc
- *w* • Colli del Trasimeno Bianco Baccio del Bianco - Doc
- *w* • Colli del Trasimeno Grechetto Nuricante - Doc

Fanini ♟♟♟

Località Petrignano, vocabolo I Cucchi, tel. 0755171141
www.fanini.net

- *r* • Merlot Umbria - Igt

r • Vigna La Pieve Umbria Sangiovese - Igt
w • Robbiano Chardonnay Umbria - Igt

POGGIO BERTAIO ♟♟♟♟
Località Frattavecchia 29, tel. 075956921
poggiobertaio@tiscalinet.it
r • Cimbolo Sangiovese dell'Umbria - Igt
r • Crovèllo Merlot-Cabernet dell'Umbria - Igt

CORCIANO
Perugia km 12 • m 408
WINERIES

PIEVE DEL VESCOVO ♟♟♟♟
Via Leopardi 82, tel. 0756978874
r • Colli del Trasimeno Rosso Pieve del Vescovo - Doc
r • Colli del Trasimeno Rosso Lucciaio - Doc
w • Colli del Trasimeno Bianco Etesiaco - Doc

FICULLE
Terni km 87 • m 437
WINERIES

TENUTA CASTELLO DELLA SALA ♟♟♟♟♟
Castello della Sala, tel. 076386051
antinori@antinori.it
r • Pinot Nero Umbria - Igt
w • Orvieto Classico Campogrande - Doc
w • Cervaro della Sala Bianco dell'Umbria - Igt
w • Conte della Vipera Bianco dell'Umbria - Igt
s • Muffato della Sala Umbria Bianco Passito - Igt

FOLIGNO
Perugia km 36 • m 234
WINERIES

CANTINA TERRE DE' TRINCI ♟♟
Via Fiamenga 57, tel. 0742320165
www.terredetrinci.com
r • Montefalco Sagrantino - Docg
r • Montefalco Rosso Riserva - Doc
r • Cajo Umbria Rosso - Igt

SAN LORENZO ♟♟♟
Località San Lorenzo Vecchio 30, tel. 074222553
r • Sagrantino di Montefalco Secco - Docg
r • Il Chiostro Sangiovese dell'Umbria - Igt
r • San Lorenzo Rosso Umbria - Igt

GUALDO CATTANEO
Perugia km 44 • m 446
WINERIES

COLPETRONE - SAIAGRICOLA ♟♟♟♟
Località Marcellano, via della Collina 4, tel. 0578767722
www.saiagricola.it
r • Sagrantino di Montefalco - Docg
r • Montefalco Rosso - Doc
s • Sagrantino di Montefalco Passito - Docg

MONTECASTRILLI
Terni km 24 • m 391
WINERIES

FATTORIA LE POGGETTE ♟♟♟♟
Località Le Poggette, tel. 0744940338
r • Colli Amerini Rosso Superiore - Doc
w • Canaiolo dell'Umbria - Igt
w • Grechetto Bianco dell'Umbria - Igt

MONTEFALCO
Perugia km 44 • m 472
WINERIES

ANTONELLI - SAN MARCO ♟♟♟
Località San Marco 59, tel. 0742379158
r • Montefalco Sagrantino - Docg
r • Montefalco Rosso - Doc
w • Colli Martani Grechetto - Doc

ROCCA DI FABBRI ♟♟♟♟
Località Fabbri, tel. 0742399379
www.roccadifabbri.com
r • Sagrantino di Montefalco - Docg
r • Rosso di Montefalco - Doc
s • Sagrantino di Montefalco Passito - Docg

SCACCIADIAVOLI ♟♟♟
Località Scacciadiavoli, tel. 0742371210
scacciadiavoli@tin.it
r • Sagrantino di Montefalco - Docg
r • Sagrantino di Montefalco Passito - Docg
r • Montefalco Rosso - Doc

VAL DI MAGGIO A. CAPRAI ♟♟♟♟♟
Località Torre, tel. 0742378802
www.arnaldocaprai.it
r • Montefalco Sagrantino Collepiano - Docg
r • Montefalco Sagrantino 25 anni - Docg
r • Montefalco Rosso - Doc
r • Montefalco Rosso Riserva - Doc
w • Grechetto dei Colli Martani Grecante - Doc

ORVIETO
Terni km 72 • m 325
WINERIES

CANTINA BIGI ♟
Località Ponte Giulio, tel. 0763316291 www.giv.it
w • Est Est Est di Montefiascone Graffiti - Doc
w • Orvieto Classico Torricella - Doc

CO.VI.O. VINI CARDETO ♟♟♟
Località Cardeto, tel. 0763341286
cardecom@tin.it
r • Pinot Nero Umbria - Igt
w • Orvieto Classico Cardeto - Doc
w • Grechetto Umbria - Igt

DECUGNANO DEI BARBI ♟♟
Località Fossatello, tel. 0763308255
r • Lago di Corbara Decugnano Rosso - Doc
r • "IL" Rosso Umbria - Igt
w • Orvieto Classico Superiore Decugnano "IL" - Doc
s • Orvieto Classico Superiore Pourriture Noble - Doc

LA CARRAIA ♟♟♟
Località Tordimonte 56, tel. 0763304013
r • Fobiano Umbria Rosso - Igt
w • Orvieto Classico La Carraia - Doc
w • Orvieto Classico Poggio Calvelli - Doc

PALAZZONE ♟♟♟♟
Località Rocca Ripesena 68, tel. 0763344921
www.palazzone.com
w • Orvieto Classico Campo del Guardiano - Doc
w • Orvieto Classico Terre Vineate - Doc
s • Muffa Nobile Umbria - Igt

TENUTA LE VELETTE ♟♟
Località Le Velette 23, tel. 076329090
levelette@tin.it
r • Rosso Orvietano Rosso di Spicca - Doc

PANICALE
Perugia km 34 • m 431
Wineries
Tenuta La Fiorita Lamborghini ♟♟♟♟
Via Soderi 1,
tel. 0758350029
www.lamborghinionline.it
r • Campoleone Umbria Rosso - Igt
r • Trescone Umbria Rosso - Igt

PENNA IN TEVERINA
Terni km 36 • m 302
Wineries
Rio Grande ♟♟
Località Montecchie, tel. 0744993102
r • Casa Pastore Umbria Rosso - Igt
w • Colle delle Montecchie Umbria Chardonnay - Igt

SPELLO
Perugia km 31 • m 280
Wineries
Sportoletti Ernesto & Remo ♟♟♟♟♟
Località Capitanloreto,
via Lombardia 1,
tel. 0742651461
www.sportoletti.com
r • Villa Fidelia Rosso - Igt
w • Assisi Grechetto - Doc
w • Villa Fidelia Bianco - Igt

STRONCONE
Terni km 9 • m 450
Wineries
La Palazzola ♟♟♟♟
Località Vascigliano,
tel. 0744272357
r • Merlot Umbria - Igt
r • Pinot Nero Umbria - Igt
w • La Palazzola Vendemmia Tardiva Umbria Bianco - Igt

TORGIANO
Perugia km 14 • m 219
Wineries
Lungarotti Giorgio ♟♟♟
Via Angeloni 16,
tel. 0759880348
www.lungarotti.it
r • Torgiano Rosso Riserva Rubesco Vigna Monticchio - Docg
r • Torgiano Rosso Rubesco - Doc
r • San Giorgio Rosso dell'Umbria - Igt
w • Torgiano Chardonnay Palazzi - Doc
w • Aurente Chardonnay dell'Umbria - Igt

UMBERTIDE
Perugia km 34 • m 247
Wineries
I Girasoli di Sant'Andrea ♟♟♟
Vocabolo Molino Vitelli,
tel. 0759410897
igirasolidisantandrea@tiscalinet.it
r • Cà Andrea Umbria Rosso - Igt
r • Il Doge Umbria Rosso - Igt
r • Muda Umbria Rosso - Igt

LATIUM

ACUTO
Frosinone km 33 • m 724
Wineries
Perinelli - Casale della Ioria ♟♟
Piazza Regina Margherita 1, tel. 077556031
r • Cesanese del Piglio Casale della Ioria - Doc
r • Cesanese del Piglio Torre del Piano - Doc
w • Passerina del Frusinate - Igt

ANAGNI
Frosinone km 22 • m 424
Wineries
Colacicchi ♟♟♟
Località Romagnano,
tel. 064469661
r • Romagnano Rosso - Vdt
r • Torre Ercolana - Vdt

CASTIGLIONE IN TEVERINA
Viterbo km 39 • m 228
Wineries
D'Amico Paolo ♟♟♟
Località Palombaro, tel. 0668134079
w • Calanchi di Vaiano Chardonnay Lazio - Igt
w • Falesia Chardonnay Lazio - Igt
Trappolini ♟♟
Via del Rivellino 65, tel. 0761948381
r • Cenereto Lazio Rosso - Igt
r • Paterno Lazio Sangiovese - Igt
w • Est! Est! Est! di Montefiascone - Doc
w • Brecceto Grechetto dell'Umbria - Igt
s • Idea Lazio - Igt
Vaselli Christine ♟♟♟♟
Via Pizza del Poggetto 12, tel. 0761947008
r • Le Pòggere Lazio Rosso - Igt
r • Torre Sant'Andrea Lazio Rosso - Igt

CERVETERI
Rome km 43 • m 81
Wineries
Cantina Sociale Cooperativa di Cerveteri ♟♟♟
Via Aurelia al km 42.7, tel. 069905697
r • Cerveteri Rosso Secco Vigna Grande - Doc
r • Tertium Rosso del Lazio - Igt
w • Cerveteri Bianco Vigna Grande - Doc

CIVITELLA D'AGLIANO
Viterbo km 29 • m 262
Wineries
Mottura Sergio ♟♟♟
Località Poggio della Costa 1,
tel. 0761914533
www.motturasergio.it
r • Civitella Rosso Lazio - Igt
r • Magone Lazio - Igt
w • Orvieto Vigna Tragugnano - Doc

w • Latour a Civitella Lazio Grechetto - Igt
s • Muffo Lazio - Igt

CORI

Latina km 26 • m 384

WINERIES

TENUTA PIETRA PINTA ♟♟♟ ★10%
Via Gramsci 52,
tel. 069678001
collesanlorenzo@libero.it
r • Cori Rosso Costavecchia - Doc
r • Colle Amato Lazio - Igt
w • Chardonnay Lazio - Igt

FRASCATI

Rome km 21 • m 320

WINERIES

CASALE MARCHESE ♟♟
Via di Vermicino 68, tel. 069408932
www.casalemarchese.it
r • Casale Marchese Rosso - Vdt
r • Vigna del Cavaliere - Vdt
w • Frascati Superiore - Doc

GROTTAFERRATA

Rome km 20 • m 320

WINERIES

CASTEL DE PAOLIS ♟♟♟♟
Via Val de Paolis, tel. 069413648
www.casteldepaolis.it
r • Quattro Mori Lazio - Igt
w • Frascati Superiore Campo Vecchio - Doc
w • Selve Vecchie Lazio - Igt
w • Vigna Adriana Lazio Bianco - Igt
s • Frascati Superiore Cannellino - Doc

STRADE VIGNA DEL SOLE ♟♟
Località Valle Mana, vicolo della Mola 45,
tel. 069387261 www.vinicugini.it
r • Grugnale Lazio Rosso - Igt
r • Morato Lazio Rosso - Igt

LATINA

m 21

WINERIES

CASALE DEL GIGLIO ♟♟♟♟
Località Le Ferriere, strada Cisterna-Nettuno
al km 13, tel. 0692902530
casaledelgiglio@tin.it
r • Cabernet Sauvignon Lazio Rosso - Igt
r • Madreselva Lazio Rosso - Igt
r • Mater Matutua Lazio Rosso - Igt
r • Petit Verdot Lazio Rosso - Igt
r • Shiraz Lazio Rosso - Igt
w • Antinoo Lazio Bianco - Igt
w • Chardonnay Lazio - Igt

MARINO

Rome km 22 • m 360

WINERIES

DI MAURO PAOLA - COLLE PICCHIONI ♟♟♟♟♟
Località Frattocchie,
via di Colle Picchioni 46,
tel. 0693546329
r • Colle Picchioni Lazio Rosso - Igt
r • Colle Picchioni Vigna del Vassallo Lazio Rosso - Igt
w • Marino Etichetta Verde - Doc
w • Marino Selezione Oro - Doc
w • Le Vignole Lazio Bianco - Igt

LIMITI DINO ♟
Corso Vittoria Colonna 170, tel. 069385051
www.dinolimiti.it
r • Colle del Turchetto - Vdt
w • Marino Campo Fattore - Doc

MONTEFIASCONE

Viterbo km 17 • m 590

WINERIES

FALESCO ♟♟♟♟♟
Zona artigianale Le Guardie, tel. 0761825669
falesco@leone.it
r • Merlot Umbria - Igt
r • Montiano Lazio - Igt
w • Est Est Est di Montefiascone Poggio dei Gelsi - Doc
w • Ferentano Lazio - Igt
s • Est Est Est di Montefiascone Poggio dei Gelsi Vendemmia Tardiva - Doc

MONTE PORZIO CATONE

Rome km 25 • m 451

WINERIES

COSTANTINI PIERO - VILLA SIMONE ♟♟♟
Via Frascati-Colonna 29, tel. 069449717
www.pierocostantini.it
r • La Torraccia - Vdt
w • Frascati Cannellino Vigneto Torricella - Doc
w • Frascati Superiore Villa Simone - Doc

FONTANA CANDIDA ♟
Via Fontana Candida 11, tel. 069420066
r • Kron Lazio Rosso - Igt
w • Frascati Superiore Vigneto Santa Teresa - Doc
w • Terre de' Grifi Malvasia del Lazio - Igt

ROME

m 20

WINERIES

CONTE ZANDOTTI ♟♟♟
Via Vigne Colle Mattia 8, tel. 0620609000
w • Frascati Cannellino - Doc
w • Frascati Superiore - Doc
w • Rumon Malvasia del Lazio - Igt

SERRONE

Frosinone km 42 • m 738

WINERIES

TERENZI GIOVANNI ♟♟
Località La Forma, via Prenestina 134,
tel. 0775594286
terenzigiovanni@libero.it
r • Cesanese del Piglio Colle Forma - Doc
r • Cesanese del Piglio Vajoscuro - Doc

VELLETRI

Rome km 38 • m 332

WINERIES

COLLE DI MAGGIO ♟♟
Via Fienili, tel. 0696453072
colledimaggio@colledimaggio.it
r • Le Anfore - Vdt
w • Porticato Bianco - Vdt
w • Villa Tulino Bianco - Vdt

ABRUZZO

ATESSA
Chieti km 59 • m 433

Wineries

Terra d'Aligi ♟
Località Piazzano, via Piana La Fara 90, tel. 0872897916
www.terradaligi.it
- r • Montepulciano d'Abruzzo - Doc
- r • Montepulciano d'Abruzzo Tatone - Doc
- rs • Montepulciano d'Abruzzo Cerasuolo - Doc
- w • Trebbiano d'Abruzzo - Doc

BOLOGNANO
Pescara km 40 • m 276

Wineries

Zaccagnini Ciccio ♟♟♟ ★10%
Contrada Pozzo, tel. 0858880195
www.cantinazaccagnini.it
- r • Montepulciano d'Abruzzo Riserva Sallis Castrum - Doc
- r • Montepulciano d'Abruzzo Riserva Il Tralcetto - Doc
- r • Montepulciano d'Abruzzo San Clemente - Doc
- rs • Montepulciano d'Abruzzo Cerasuolo Myosotis - Doc
- w • Trebbiano d'Abruzzo Castello di Salle - Doc

CASTILENTI
Teramo km 49 • m 272

Wineries

San Lorenzo ♟♟
Contrada Plaviniano 2, tel. 0861999325
sanlorenzovini@tiscali.net
- r • Montepulciano d'Abruzzo Antàres - Doc
- w • Trebbiano d'Abruzzo Antàres - Doc
- w • Alhena Colline Pescaresi Chardonnay - Igt

COLONNELLA
Teramo km 44 • m 303

Wineries

Lepore ♟♟
Contrada Civita, tel. 086170860
vinilepore@iol.it
- r • Montepulciano d'Abruzzo Riserva Luigi Lepore Colline Teramane - Doc
- r • Montepulciano d'Abruzzo RE Colline Teramane - Doc
- rs • Montepulciano d'Abruzzo Cerasuolo - Doc
- w • Controguerra Passerina DO - Doc

CONTROGUERRA
Teramo km 38 • m 267

Wineries

Illuminati Dino - Fattoria Nicò ♟♟♟
Contrada S. Biagio 18, tel. 0861808008
- r • Controguerra Rosso Riserva Lumen - Doc
- r • Montepulciano d'Abruzzo Zanna - Doc
- w • Controguerra Bianco Daniele - Doc
- s • Controguerra Passito Nicò - Doc
- s • Lorè Muffa Nobile - Vdt

Monti Antonio e Elio ♟♟♟♟
Contrada Pignotto, tel. 086189042
emilmon@tin.it
- r • Montepulciano d'Abruzzo - Doc
- r • Montepulciano d'Abruzzo Pignotto - Doc

Montori Camillo ♟♟
Via Piane Tronto 65, tel. 0861809900
- r • Controguerra Rosso Leneo Moro - Doc
- r • Montepulciano d'Abruzzo Fonte Cupa - Doc
- w • Controguerra Bianco Leneo d'Oro - Doc
- w • Trebbiano d'Abruzzo Fonte Cupa - Doc

FRANCAVILLA AL MARE
Chieti km 16 • m 3

Wineries

Fattoria Pasetti Franco ♟♟ ★10%
Contrada Pretaro, via S. Paolo 21, tel. 08561875
vignetipasetti@hotmail.com
- r • Montepulciano d'Abruzzo Fattoria Pasetti - Doc
- r • Montepulciano d'Abruzzo Tenuta di Testarossa - Doc

LORETO APRUTINO
Pescara km 24 • m 294

Wineries

Torre dei Beati ♟♟
Contrada Poggioragone 56, tel. 0854916069
- r • Montepulciano d'Abruzzo - Doc
- rs • Montepulciano d'Abruzzo Cerasuolo - Doc

Valentini ♟♟♟♟♟
Via del Baio 2, tel. 0858291138
- r • Montepulciano d'Abruzzo - Doc
- rs • Montepulciano d'Abruzzo Cerasuolo - Doc
- w • Trebbiano d'Abruzzo - Doc

NOCCIANO
Pescara km 26 • m 301

Wineries

Bosco Nestore ♟
Contrada Casali 7, tel. 085847345
www.nestorebosco.com
- r • Montepulciano d'Abruzzo Pan - Doc
- r • Linfa Colline Pescaresi Rosso - Igt
- w • Pan Colline Pescaresi Chardonnay - Igt

NOTARESCO
Teramo km 21 • m 267

Wineries

Fattoria Bruno Nicodemi ♟♟♟
Via Veniglio 29, tel. 085895493
fattoria.nicodemi@tin.it
- r • Montepulciano d'Abruzzo Colline Teramane Riserva Nicodemi - Doc
- r • Montepulciano d'Abruzzo Colli Venia Fattoria Nicodemi - Doc
- w • Trebbiano d'Abruzzo Colli Venia Fattorie Nicodemi - Doc
- w • Trebbiano d'Abruzzo Selezione Nicodemi - Doc

OFENA
L'Aquila km 48 • m 531

Wineries

Cataldi Madonna Luigi ♟♟♟
Località Piano di Ofena, tel. 0854911680

r • Montepulciano d'Abruzzo Tonì - Doc
r • Malandrino Alto Tirino - Doc
r • Occhiorosso Alto Tirino - Igt
rs • Montepulciano d'Abruzzo Cerasuolo - Doc
w • Trebbiano d'Abruzzo - Doc

ORTONA

Chieti km 29 • m 72

WINERIES

AGRIVERDE ♟♟
Località Caldari, via Monte Maiella 118, tel. 0859032101
www.agriverde.it
r • Montepulciano d'Abruzzo - Doc
r • Montepulciano d'Abruzzo Riseis - Doc

CITRA VINI ♟
Contrada Cucullo, tel. 0859031342
www.citra.it
r • Montepulciano d'Abruzzo Citra - Doc

FARNESE VINI ♟♟♟
Località Castello Caldora, via dei Bastioni, tel. 0859067388
www.farnese-vini.com
r • Montepulciano d'Abruzzo Casale Vecchio - Doc
r • Montepulciano d'Abruzzo Colline Teramane Riserva Opis - Doc
w • Trebbiano d'Abruzzo Casale Vecchio - Doc

SARCHESE DORA ♟♟
Contrada Caldari Stazione 65, tel. 0859031249
r • Montepulciano d'Abruzzo Pietrosa - Doc
r • Montepulciano d'Abruzzo Rosso di Macchia - Doc

POPOLI

Pescara km 51 • m 254

WINERIES

VALLE REALE ♟♟♟♟
Località San Calisto, tel. 0859808025
info@vallereale.it
r • Montepulciano d'Abruzzo - Doc
r • Montepulciano d'Abruzzo San Calisto - Doc

ROSCIANO

Pescara km 29 • m 242

WINERIES

MARRAMIERO ♟♟♟
Contrada S. Andrea 1, tel. 0858505766
r • Montepulciano d'Abruzzo Inferi - Doc

ROSETO DEGLI ABRUZZI

Teramo km 32 • m 5

WINERIES

ORLANDI CONTUCCI PONNO ♟♟♟
Contrada Voltarrosto, via Piana degli Ulivi 1, tel. 0858944049
www.orlandocontucci.com
r • Montepulciano d'Abruzzo Podere Regia Specula - Doc
r • Montepulciano d'Abruzzo Riserva - Doc
r • Liburnio Bourgeois Colli Aprutini - Igt
w • Trebbiano d'Abruzzo Podere Colle della Corte - Doc
w • Roccesco Colli Aprutini Chardonnay - Igt

VILLA SCIALLETTI ♟♟
Contrada Tanesi 10, tel. 0858091010
r • Montepulciano d'Abruzzo Sammarco Anniversary - Doc
r • Sammarco Colli Aprutini Rosso - Igt
r • Sammarco Oro Colli Aprutini Rosso - Igt
w • Trebbiano d'Abruzzo Villa Scialletti - Doc
w • Sammarco Colli Aprutini Bianco - Igt

SAN MARTINO SULLA MARRUCINA

Chieti km 26 • m 420

WINERIES

MASCIARELLI ♟♟♟♟♟
Via Gamberale 1, tel. 087185241
r • Montepulciano d'Abruzzo San Martino Rosso Marina Cvetic - Doc
r • Montepulciano d'Abruzzo Villa Gemma - Doc
w • Trebbiano d'Abruzzo Marina Cvetic - Doc
w • Chardonnay Marina Cvetic - Vdt
w • Villa Gemma Bianco - Vdt

SANT'OMERO

Teramo km 25 • m 209

WINERIES

VALORI LUIGI ♟♟♟
Via Torquato al Salinello 8, tel. 086188461
r • Montepulciano d'Abruzzo - Doc
r • Montepulciano d'Abruzzo Vigna Sant'Angelo - Doc
w • Trebbiano d'Abruzzo Preludio - Doc

SPOLTORE

Pescara km 8 • m 185

WINERIES

FATTORIA LA VALENTINA ♟♟♟
Via Colle Cesi 10, tel. 0854478158
www.fattorialavalentina.it
r • Montepulciano d'Abruzzo Binomio - Doc
r • Montepulciano d'Abruzzo Spelt - Doc
w • Trebbiano d'Abruzzo - Doc

TOCCO DA CASAURIA

Pescara km 44 • m 356

WINERIES

FILOMUSI GUELFI LORENZO ♟♟ ★12%
Via Filomusi Guelfi 11, tel. 08598353
r • Montepulciano d'Abruzzo - Doc
r • Montepulciano d'Abruzzo Riserva Vigna Fonte Dei - Doc
w • Le Scuderie del Cielo - Vdt

TOLLO

Chieti km 21 • m 152

WINERIES

CANTINA TOLLO ♟♟
Via Garibaldi 68, tel. 087196251
produzione@cantinatollo.it
r • Montepulciano d'Abruzzo Aldiano - Doc
r • Montepulciano d'Abruzzo Cagiolo - Doc
rs • Montepulciano d'Abruzzo Cerasuolo Valle d'Oro - Doc

TORANO NUOVO

Teramo km 31 • m 237

WINERIES

BARONE CORNACCHIA ♟♟
Località Le Torri, tel. 0861887412
barone.cornacchia@tin.it

r • Montepulciano d'Abruzzo Poggio Varano - Doc
r • Montepulciano d'Abruzzo Vigna Le Coste - Doc
w • Trebbiano d'Abruzzo - Doc

VACRI
Chieti km 17 • m 310
Wineries
Fattoria Buccicatino ♟♟ ★10%
Contrada Sterpara, tel. 0871720273
buccicatino@libero.it
r • Montepulciano d'Abruzzo Don Giovanni - Doc
r • Montepulciano d'Abruzzo Stilla Rubra - Doc
rs • Montepulciano d'Abruzzo Cerasuolo - Doc

VILLAMAGNA
Chieti km 13 • m 255
Wineries
Torre Zambra ♟♟
Viale Margherita 20,
tel. 0871300121
r • Montepulciano d'Abruzzo Brume Rosse - Doc

MOLISE

CAMPOMARINO
Campobasso km 69 • m 52
Wineries
Borgo di Colloredo ♟
Contrada Zezza 8/C, tel. 087557453
www.borgodicolloredo.com
r • Biferno Rosso Gironia - Doc
Cantina Cooperativa Cliternia ♟
Contrada Nuova Cliternia, tel. 087557106
www.cliternia.it
r • Biferno Rosso Trabucco - Doc
r • Molise Rosso - Doc
w • Biferno Bianco Trabucco - Doc
Masseria di Majo Norante ♟♟♟♟♟
Contrada Ramitello 4,
tel. 087557208
www.dimajonorante.com
r • Biferno Rosso Ramitello - Doc
r • Molise Aglianico Contado - Doc
r • Molise Montepulciano Don Luigi - Doc
w • Biblos Terra degli Osci Bianco - Igt
s • Molise Moscato Reale Passito Apianae - Doc

CAMPANIA

ATRIPALDA
Avellino km 4 • m 294
Wineries
Mastroberardino Michele ♟♟♟♟
Via Manfredi 75-81, tel. 0825614111
www.mastroberardino.com
r • Taurasi Radici - Docg
r • Lacryma Christi del Vesuvio Rosso - Doc
r • Avellanio Rosso Aglianico Irpinia - Igt
r • Naturalis Historia Irpinia - Igt
w • Fiano di Avellino Vignadora - Doc
w • Greco di Tufo Vignadangelo - Doc
w • Avalon Pompeiano Bianco - Igt

AVERSA
Caserta km 18 • m 39
Wineries
Terra di Lavoro ♟
Via Ettore Corcioni 75, tel. 0815033955
r • Lacryma Christi del Vesuvio Bianco Sessa - Doc

BACOLI
Naples km 23 • m 30
Wineries
Farro ♟♟
Località Fusaro, via Virgilio 30/36, tel. 0818545555
r • Campi Flegrei Piedirosso Per'e Palummo - Doc
w • Campi Flegrei Falanghina - Doc
w • Campi Flegrei Falanghina Le Cigliate - Doc

CAIAZZO
Caserta km 17 • m 200
Wineries
Tommasina Vestini Campagnano ♟♟♟♟♟
Località SS. Giovanni e Paolo, tel. 0823862770
vestinicampagnano@inwind.it
r • Casavecchia Terre del Volturno - Igt
r • Pallagrello Nero Terre del Volturno - Igt
w • Pallagrello Bianco Terre del Volturno - Igt
w • Pallagrello Bianco Terre del Volturno Le Ortole - Igt

CASTEL CAMPAGNANO
Caserta km 25 • m 58
Wineries
Castello Ducale ♟♟
Via Chiesa 35, tel. 0924972460
www.castelloducale.com
r • Contessa Ferrara Irpinia Aglianico - Igt
w • Sannio Falanghina - Doc

CASTELLABATE
Salerno km 66 • m 356
Wineries
Maffini Luigi ♟♟♟♟
Località Cenito, tel. 0974966345
r • Cenito Paestum Rosso - Igt
r • Kleos Paestum Rosso - Igt
w • Kratos Paestum Bianco - Igt

CASTELVENERE
Benevento km 29 • m 119
Wineries
Antica Masseria Venditti ♟♟♟
Via Sannitica 122, tel. 0824940306
www.venditti.it
r • Sannio Barbera Barbetta Vàndari - Doc
r • Sannio Rosso Masseria Venditti - Doc

r • Solopaca Rosso Bosco Caldaia - Doc
w • Sannio Falanghina Vàndari - Doc
w • Solopaca Bianco Bacalàt - Doc

FORESTA ♟
Via Nazionale Sannitica 31/33, tel. 0824940355
www.agricoleforesta.it
r • Safineis Piedirosso del Beneventano - Igt

CELLOLE
Caserta km 52 • m 19

WINERIES

FATTORIA VILLA MATILDE ♟♟♟♟♟ ★10%
S.S. Domitiana 18, tel. 0823932088
r • Falerno del Massico Rosso - Doc
r • Cecubo Rosso - Igt
r • Vigna Camarato - Igt
w • Falerno del Massico Bianco Vigna Caracci - Doc
s • Eleusi - Igt

CESINALI
Avellino km 5 • m 380

WINERIES

SARNO - CANTINA DEL BARONE ♟♟♟
Via Nocelleto 17, tel. 0825666751
www.cantinadelbarone.it
r • Nocelleto Aglianico Irpinia - Igt
w • Fiano di Avellino - Doc

CHIANCHE
Avellino km 25 • m 356

WINERIES

MACCHIALUPA ♟♟
Località San Pietro Irpino, via Fontana, tel. 0825996396
www.macchialupa.it
r • Aglianico Irpinia - Igt
w • Greco di Tufo - Doc
s • Esotica - Vdt

FOGLIANISE
Benevento km 15 • m 350

WINERIES

CANTINA DEL TABURNO ♟♟♟♟
Via Sala, tel. 0824871338
www.cantinadeltaburno.it
r • Bue Apis Aglianico del Beneventano - Igt
r • Delius Aglianico del Beneventano - Igt
w • Taburno Coda di Volpe Amineo - Doc
w • Taburno Falanghina Folius - Doc
w • Serra Docile Coda di Volpe del Beneventano - Igt

FORIO
Naples km 10 • m 18

WINERIES

D'AMBRA VINI D'ISCHIA ♟♟♟
Località Panza, via Mario D'Ambra 16, tel. 081907246
www.dambravini.com
r • Ischia Per'e Palummo - Doc
r • Ischia Rosso Dedicato a Mario D'Ambra - Doc
w • Ischia Biancolella Tenuta Frassitelli - Doc
w • Ischia Forastera - Doc
w • Kime Epomeo Bianco - Igt

PIETRATORCIA ♟♟♟ ★10%
Via Provinciale Panza 267, tel. 081908206
r • Ischia Rosso Vigne di Ianno Piro - Doc
r • Scheria Rosso - Vdt
w • Ischia Bianco Superiore Vigne del Cuotto - Doc
w • Ischia Bianco Superiore Vigne di Chignole - Doc
s • Meditandum - Vdt

FURORE
Salerno km 31 • m 656

WINERIES

GRAN FUROR DIVINA COSTIERA ♟♟♟♟♟
Via G.B. Lama 14, tel. 089830348
www.granfuror.it
r • Costa d'Amalfi Furore Rosso Riserva - Doc
r • Costa d'Amalfi Ravello Rosso Riserva - Doc
w • Costa d'Amalfi Furore Bianco Fior d'Uva - Doc

GALLUCCIO
Caserta km 56 • m 61/900

WINERIES

COOPERATIVA LAVORO E SALUTE - TELARO ♟♟
Via Cinque Pietre, tel. 0823925841
www.vinitelaro.it
r • Galluccio Aglianico Montecaruso - Doc
r • Galluccio Rosso Riserva Ara Mundi - Doc
w • Roccamonfina Falanghina Vendemmia Tardiva - Igt

GUARDIA SANFRAMONDI
Benevento km 28 • m 428

WINERIES

CORTE NORMANNA ♟
Località Sapenzie 20, tel. 0824817008
r • Sannio Aglianico Tre Pietre - Doc
w • Sannio Falanghina Palombaia - Doc

DE LUCIA ♟♟
Contrada Starze, tel. 0824864259
c.delucia@tin.it
r • Sannio Aglianico Adelchi - Doc
r • Sannio Aglianico Vigna La Corte - Doc
w • Sannio Falanghina - Doc

LAPIO
Avellino km 19 • m 500

WINERIES

COLLI DI LAPIO ♟♟♟
Contrada Azianiello 43, tel. 0825982184
w • Fiano di Avellino - Doc

ROMANO NICOLA ♟♟
Località Casale Arianiello, tel. 0825982040
w • Fiano di Avellino Apianum - Doc

MANOCALZATI
Avellino km 7 • m 450

WINERIES

D'ANTICHE TERRE - VEGA ♟
Contrada Lo Piano, S.S. 7/bis, tel. 0825675689
www.danticheterre.it
r • Taurasi - Docg

MONDRAGONE
Caserta km 44 • m 10

WINERIES

MOIO MICHELE FU LUIGI ♟♟♟♟
Via Margherita 6, tel. 0823978017
www.moio.it
r • Falerno del Massico Primitivo Maiatico - Doc

w • Falerno del Massico Falanghina - Doc
w • Villa dei Marchi Falanghina di Roccamonfina - Igt

MONTECORVINO PUGLIANO
Salerno km 20 • m 27/604
WINERIES
MONTE PUGLIANO ♟♟
Via S. Vito,
tel. 3283412515
cesare.cavallo@tiscalinet.it
r • Castellaccio Colli di Salerno Rosso Riserva - Igt
w • Aurum Colli di Salerno Fiano - Igt
w • Nebula Colli di Salerno Bianco - Igt

MONTEFREDANE
Avellino km 10 • m 593
WINERIES
VADIAPERTI ♟♟
Via Vadiaperti,
tel. 0825607270
www.vadiaperti.it
r • Aglianico d'Irpinia - Igt
w • Fiano di Avellino Vigna Arechi - Doc
w • Greco di Tufo Vigna Federico II - Doc
VILLA DIAMANTE ♟♟
Via Toppole 16, tel. 082530777
www.villadiamante.it
w • Fiano di Avellino Vigna della Congregazione - Doc
w • Fiano di Avellino Vigna della Congregazione barrique - Doc

MONTEFUSCO
Avellino km 21 • m 705
WINERIES
TERREDORA DI PAOLO ♟♟♟
Via Serra, tel. 0825968215
www.terredora.com
r • Taurasi Fatica Contadina - Docg
r • Aglianico Irpinia - Igt
r • Pompeiano Piedirosso - Igt
w • Fiano di Avellino V.T. Campo Re - Doc
w • Greco di Tufo Terre degli Angeli - Doc
w • Pompeiano Coda di Volpe - Igt
s • Fiano Passito Irpinia - Igt

MONTEMARANO
Avellino km 24 • m 820
WINERIES
MOLETTIERI SALVATORE ♟♟♟♟
Contrada Musanni 19/B,
tel. 082763424
www.italywines.com
r • Taurasi Vigna Cinque Querce - Docg
r • Cinque Querce Irpinia Rosso - Igt

MONTEMILETTO
Avellino km 20 • m 600
WINERIES
COLLI IRPINI ♟♟
Via Canale 13,
tel. 0825963972
www.colliirpini.com
r • Taurasi - Docg
w • Fiano di Avellino Sirios - Doc
w • Greco di Tufo Serapis - Doc

PONTE
Benevento km 15 • m 147
WINERIES
OCONE AGRICOLA DEL MONTE ♟♟
Località La Madonnella, via Monte, tel. 0824874040
www.oconevini.it
r • Aglianico del Taburno Diomede - Doc
w • Taburno Falanghina Vigna del Monaco - Doc
w • Taburno Greco - Doc

PRIGNANO CILENTO
Salerno km 59 • m 410
WINERIES
DE CONCILIIS ♟♟♟♟ ★10%
Località Querce 1, tel. 0974831090
r • Donnaluna Paestum Aglianico - Igt
r • Naima Paestum Aglianico - Igt
r • Zero Paestum Rosso - Igt
w • Donnaluna Paestum Fiano - Igt
w • Perella Paestum Fiano - Igt

QUARTO
Naples km 16 • m 55
WINERIES
GROTTA DEL SOLE ♟♟♟
Via Spinelli 2, tel. 0818762566
www.grottadelsole.it
r • Penisola Sorrentina Gragnano - Doc
r • Penisola Sorrentina Lettere - Doc
w • Campi Flegrei Falanghina Coste di Cuma - Doc

RUTINO
Salerno km 63 • m 371
WINERIES
ROTOLO ♟♟♟
Via S. Cesario 18, tel. 0974830050
r • Cilento Aglianico - Doc
w • Cilento Bianco - Doc
w • Valentina Paestum Bianco - Igt

SALZA IRPINA
Avellino km 11 • m 540
WINERIES
DI MEO ♟♟♟
Contrada Coccovoni 1, tel. 0825981419
www.dimeo.it
r • Taurasi Riserva - Docg
r • Irpinia Aglianico - Igt
w • Fiano di Avellino Colle dei Cerri - Doc

SAN CIPRIANO PICENTINO
Salerno km 16 • m 364
WINERIES
MONTEVETRANO ♟♟♟♟
Località Nido, via Montevetrano, tel. 089882285
www.montevetrano.com
r • Montevetrano Colli di Salerno Rosso - Igt

SAN SEBASTIANO AL VESUVIO
Naples km 11 • m 175
WINERIES
CANTINA DE FALCO ♟♟
Via Figliola Traversa I nr. 2, tel. 0815745510
defalcovini@tin.it
w • Fiano di Avellino - Doc
w • Greco di Tufo - Doc

SANT'AGATA DE' GOTI
Benevento km 35 • m 159

WINERIES

MUSTILLI ♟♟

Via dei Fiori 20, tel. 0823717433
info@mustilli.com
- *r* • Sant'Agata dei Goti Aglianico Vigna Cesco di Nece - Doc
- *r* • Sant'Agata dei Goti Piedirosso - Doc
- *r* • Briccone Rosso - Vdt
- *w* • Sant'Agata dei Goti Falanghina - Doc
- *w* • Sant'Agata dei Goti Greco - Doc

SERINO
Avellino km 12 • m 359/1806

WINERIES

VILLA RAIANO ♟♟

Via Pescatore 19, tel. 0825592826
www.villaraiano.it
- *r* • Raiano Irpinia Aglianico - Igt
- *w* • Fiano di Avellino - Doc
- *w* • Greco di Tufo - Doc

SESSA AURUNCA
Caserta km 44 • m 203

WINERIES

GALARDI ♟♟♟♟♟

Località Galardi, S.P. Sessa Mignano,
tel. 0823925003
galardi@napoli.com
- *r* • Terra di Lavoro Roccamonfina Rosso - Igt

MASSERIA FELICIA ♟♟♟♟

Località San Terenzano, via Provinciale Appia,
tel. 081736220
www.masseriafelicia.it
- *r* • Falerno del Massico Rosso Etichetta Bronzo - Doc
- *r* • Falerno del Massico Rosso Etichetta Senape - Doc

SORBO SERPICO
Avellino km 10 • m 480

WINERIES

FEUDI DI SAN GREGORIO ♟♟♟♟♟

Località Cerza Grossa,
tel. 0825986266
www.feudi.it
- *r* • Taurasi Riserva Piano di Montevergine - Docg
- *r* • Taurasi Selve di Luoti - Docg
- *r* • Pàtrimo Irpinia Rosso - Igt
- *r* • Serpico Irpinia Rosso - Igt
- *w* • Fiano di Avellino - Doc
- *w* • Greco di Tufo - Doc
- *w* • Campanaro Irpinia Bianco V.T. - Igt
- *s* • Privilegio Irpinia Bianco - Igt

TAURASI
Avellino km 26 • m 398

WINERIES

CAGGIANO ANTONIO ♟♟♟♟♟

Contrada Sala, tel. 082774043
www.cantinecaggiano.it
- *r* • Taurasi Vigna Macchia dei Goti - Docg
- *w* • Fiano di Avellino Béchar - Doc
- *s* • Mel - Vdt

TEVEROLA
Caserta km 17 • m 25

WINERIES

CAPUTO ♟♟♟♟

Via Garibaldi 64,
tel. 0815033955
www.caputo.it
- *r* • Lacryma Christi del Vesuvio Rosso - Doc
- *r* • Sannio Aglianico Clanius - Doc
- *r* • Zicorrà Aglianico Terre del Volturno - Igt
- *w* • Greco di Tufo Vignola - Doc
- *w* • Sannio Falanghina Frattasi - Doc

CICALA 1886 - WINE CELLARS TERREFERTILIA ♟

Via Roma 268, tel. 0818118103
winecicala@libero.it
- *w* • Sannio Falanghina - Doc
- *w* • Sannio Greco - Doc

TORRECUSO
Benevento km 20 • m 420

WINERIES

FATTORIA LA RIVOLTA ♟♟♟

Contrada Rivolta,
tel. 0824872921
www.fattorialarivolta.com
- *r* • Taburno Aglianico - Doc
- *r* • Taburno Aglianico Riserva Terra di Rivolta - Doc
- *w* • Taburno Coda di Volpe - Doc
- *w* • Taburno Falanghina - Doc

FONTANAVECCHIA ♟♟♟

Via Fontanavecchia,
tel. 0824876275
orerillo@tin.it
- *r* • Taburno Aglianico - Doc
- *r* • Taburno Aglianico Riserva Vigna Cataratte - Doc
- *r* • Orazio Rosso del Beneventano - Igt
- *w* • Facetus Bianco del Beneventano - Igt

TORRE LE NOCELLE
Avellino km 22 • m 420

WINERIES

I CAPITANI ♟♟ ★10%

Via Bosco Faiano,
tel. 082522624
www.icapitani.com
- *r* • Emé Irpinia Rosso - Igt
- *r* • Jumara Irpinia Aglianico - Igt

TUFO
Avellino km 16 • m 250

WINERIES

DI MARZO ♟♟

Via Gaetano di Marzo,
tel. 0825998022
- *r* • Irpinia Rosso - Igt
- *w* • Greco di Tufo San Michele - Doc

FERRARA BENITO ♟♟♟

Località San Paolo 14/A,
tel. 0825998194
www.benitoferrara.it
- *r* • Irpinia Aglianico - Igt
- *w* • Greco di Tufo - Doc
- *w* • Greco di Tufo Vigna Cicogna - Doc

APULIA

ALEZIO

Lecce km 37 • m 75

Wineries

Rosa del Golfo ♟♟♟

Via Garibaldi 56, tel. 0833281045

- *r* • Quarantale Riserva Mino Calò Rosso del Salento - Igt
- *r* • Scaliere Salento Rosso - Igt
- *rs* • Rosa del Golfo Salento Rosato - Igt

ANDRIA

Bari km 58 • m 151

Wineries

Conte Spagnoletti ♟♟

Contrada S. Domenico, S.S. 98 al km 21, tel. 0883569511

- *r* • Castel del Monte Pezza La Ruca - Doc
- *r* • Castel del Monte Riserva del Conte - Doc

Rivera ♟♟♟ ★10%

Contrada Rivera, tel. 0883569501
www.rivera.it

- *r* • Castel del Monte Aglianico Riserva Cappellaccio - Doc
- *r* • Castel del Monte Nero di Troia Puer Apuliae - Doc
- *r* • Castel del Monte Rosso Riserva Il Falcone - Doc
- *r* • Triusco Primitivo Puglia - Igt
- *w* • Castel del Monte Chardonnay Preludio N. 1 - Doc

BRINDISI

m 13

Wineries

Rubino Luigi ♟♟♟

Via Medaglie d'Oro 15/A, tel. 0831502912

- *r* • Brindisi Rosso Iaddico - Doc
- *r* • Marmorelle Salento Rosso - Igt
- *r* • Visellio Salento Primitivo - Igt

CAROSINO

Taranto km 15 • m 72

Wineries

Feudo di Santa Croce ♟

Località Curezza, tel. 0457235394
www.tinazzi.it

- *r* • Negroamaro Salento - Igt

CELLINO SAN MARCO

Brindisi km 21 • m 58

Wineries

Due Palme ♟♟♟♟

Via S. Marco 130, tel. 0831617865
www.cantineduepalme.it

- *r* • Brindisi Rosso - Doc
- *r* • Salice Salentino Rosso Riserva Selvarossa - Doc
- *r* • Canonico Salento Negroamaro - Igt
- *r* • Primitivo Salento - Igt
- *r* • Tenuta Albrizzi Salento Rosso - Igt

Tenute Carrisi Albano ♟♟♟

Contrada Bosco 13, tel. 0831619211
tenute@albanocarrisi.com

- *r* • Don Carmelo Salento Rosso - Igt
- *r* • Nostalgia Salento Rosso - Igt
- *r* • Platone Salento Rosso - Igt
- *r* • Taras Salento Rosso - Igt

CERIGNOLA

Foggia km 37 • m 120

Wineries

Torre Quarto ♟♟

Contrada Quarto 5, tel. 0885418453
www.torrequartocantine.it

- *r* • Torre Quarto Rosso Puglia - Igt
- *rs* • Torre Quarto Rosato Puglia - Igt
- *w* • Torre Quarto Bianco Puglia - Igt

COPERTINO

Lecce km 14 • m 34

Wineries

Cantina Sociale Cooperativa Copertino ♟♟

Via Martiri del Risorgimento 6, tel. 0832947031

- *r* • Copertino Rosso Riserva - Doc
- *rs* • Cigliano Salento Rosato - Igt
- *w* • Cigliano Salento Bianco - Igt

Masseria Monaci ♟♟♟

Località Tenuta Monaci, tel. 0832947512

- *r* • Copertino Rosso Eloquenzia - Doc
- *r* • Le Braci Salento Rosso Vendemmia Tardiva - Igt
- *r* • Simposia Salento Rosso - Igt

CORATO

Bari km 45 • m 232

Wineries

Santa Lucia ♟♟♟ ★10%

Strada comunale S. Vittore 1, tel. 0808721168
www.vinisantalucia.com

- *r* • Castel del Monte Rosso Riserva Le More - Doc
- *r* • Castel del Monte Rosso Vigna del Melograno - Doc
- *w* • Castel del Monte Bianco Vigna Tufaroli - Doc

Torrevento ♟♟♟ ★10%

Località Castel del Monte, S.S. 170 al km 28, tel. 0808980929

- *r* • Castel del Monte Rosso Riserva Vigna Pedale - Doc
- *w* • Castel del Monte Bianco - Doc
- *s* • Moscato di Trani Dulcis in Fundo - Doc

GALATINA

Lecce km 20 • m 75

Wineries

Valle dell'Asso ♟♟

Via Guidano 18, tel. 0836561470

- *r* • Galatina Rosso - Doc
- *r* • Piromàfo Salento Rosso - Igt
- *r* • Vigna San Giovanni Primitivo del Salento - Igt

GIOIA DEL COLLE

Bari km 39 • m 360

Wineries

Petrera Pasquale ♟♟

Vicolo Spinomarino 291, tel. 0803448037

- *r* • Gioia del Colle Primitivo Riserva Fatalone - Doc
- *w* • Spinomarino Fatalone Murgia Bianco - Igt

GRAVINA DI PUGLIA
Bari
Wineries
Cantina Cooperativa Botromagno ♟
Via Fratelli Cervi 12, tel. 0803265865
www.botromagno.it
r • Pier delle Vigne Rosso Murgia - Igt
rs • Silvium Murgia Rosato - Igt

GUAGNANO
Lecce km 20 • m 44
Wineries
Antica Masseria del Sigillo ♟♟
Via Provinciale 143, tel. 0832706331
r • Sigillo Primo Primitivo del Salento - Igt
r • Terre del Guiscardo Salento Rosso - Igt
Cantele ♟♟
S.P. Salice Salentino-S. Donaci al km 35.8, tel. 0832240962
www.cantele.it
r • Salice Salentino Rosso Riserva - Doc
r • Amativo Salento Rosso - Igt
r • Teresa Manara Salento Rosso - Igt
Eredi Taurino Cosimo ♟♟♟♟♟
S.S. 605, tel. 0832706490
www.taurinovini.it
r • Salice Salentino Rosso Riserva - Doc
r • Patriglione Rosso Salento - Igt
r • Notarpanaro Salento Rosso - Vdt
rs • Scaloti Salento Rosato - Igt
w • I Sierri Salento Bianco - Igt

LATIANO
Brindisi km 24 • m 97
Wineries
Lomazzi & Sarli ♟♟
Contrada Partemio, S.S. 7 Br-Ta, tel. 0831725898
www.vinilomazzi.it
r • Latias Salento Primitivo - Igt
r • Brindisi Rosato Solise - Doc
w • Imperium Chardonnay Salento - Igt

LECCE
m 49
Wineries
Vallone ♟♟♟♟♟
Via XXV Luglio 5, tel. 0832308041
www.agricolevallone.com
r • Brindisi Rosso Vigna Flaminio - Doc
r • Graticciaia Salento Rosso - Igt
rs • Brindisi Rosato Vigna Flaminio - Doc
w • Corte Valesio Salento Bianco - Igt
s • Passo de Le Viscarde Salento Bianco - Igt

LEVERANO
Lecce km 18 • m 39
Wineries
Conti Zecca ♟♟♟♟ ★10%
Via Cesarea, tel. 0832925613
www.contizecca.it
r • Leverano Rosso Vigna del Saraceno - Doc
r • Salice Salentino Rosso Cantalupi - Doc
r • Conti Zecca Primitivo Salento - Igt
r • Nero Rosso del Salento - Igt
r • Zinfandel Primitivo del Salento - Igt

LOCOROTONDO
Bari km 65 • m 410
Wineries
Cantina Sociale di Locorotondo ♟♟
Via Madonna della Catena 99, tel. 0804311644
r • Primitivo di Manduria Terre di Don Peppe - Doc
r • Casale San Giorgio Puglia Rosso - Igt
r • Cummerse Rosso di Puglia - Igt
rs • Cummerse Rosato di Puglia - Igt
w • Locorotondo Vigneti in Tallinaio - Doc
Cardone Vini Classici ♟♟♟
Località Martiri della Libertà 28, tel. 0804312561
www.cardonevini.com
r • Primaio Primitivo di Puglia - Igt
r • Salento Primitivo - Igt
w • Placeo Salento Chardonnay Barricato - Igt
I Pastini ♟♟
Via Alberobello 232, tel. 0808980923
www.torrevento.it
r • Murgia Rosso - Igt
r • Primitivo del Tarantino - Igt

MANDURIA
Taranto km 36 • m 79
Wineries
Casale Bevagna ♟♟♟
Via Santo Stasi I, zona industriale, tel. 0999711660
www.accademiadeiracemi.it
r • Salice Salentino Te Deum Laudamus - Doc
Felline ♟♟♟♟
Via Santo Stasi I, zona industriale, tel. 0999711660
www.accademiadeiracemi.it
r • Primitivo di Manduria - Doc
r • Alberello Rosso del Salento - Igt
r • Vigna del Feudo Rosso Puglia - Igt
Masseria Pepe ♟♟♟♟
Via Santo Stasi I, zona industriale, tel. 0999711660
www.accademiadeiracemi.it
r • Primitivo di Manduria Dunico - Igt
Pervini ♟♟♟
Via Santo Stasi I, zona industriale, tel. 0999738929
www.accademiadeiracemi.it
r • Primitivo di Manduria Archidamo - Doc
r • Bizantino Salento Rosso - Igt
w • Grelise Puglia Moscato - Igt
Sinfarosa ♟♟♟♟
Via Santo Stasi I, zona industriale, tel. 0999711660
www.accademiadeiracemi.it
r • Primitivo di Manduria Zinfandel - Doc
Torre Guaceto ♟♟♟
Via Santo Stasi I, zona industriale, tel. 0999711660
www.accademiadeiracemi.it
r • Sum Rosso del Salento - Igt

NOVOLI
Lecce km 11 • m 37
Wineries
La Corte ♟♟♟♟
Via Trepuzzi, tel. 0559707594
www.renideo.com
r • Anfora Zinfandel Puglia Rosso - Igt
r • La Corte Negroamaro Salento - Igt
r • La Corte Zinfandel Tarantino Rosso - Igt

ORSARA DI PUGLIA
Foggia km 44 • m 635

WINERIES

CANTINA IL TUCCANESE ♟
Via Di Vittorio 15, tel. 0881964660
r • Magliano - Vdt

SALICE SALENTINO
Lecce km 18 • m 48

WINERIES

LEONE DE CASTRIS ♟♟ ★10%
Via Senatore De Castris 50,
tel. 0832733608
www.leonedecastris.com
r • Primitivo di Manduria Santera - Doc
r • Salice Salentino Rosso Riserva Donna Lisa - Doc
r • Illemos Salento Rosso - Igt
rs • Five Roses Salento Rosato - Igt
w • Messapia Salento Bianco - Igt

SAN DONACI
Brindisi km 26 • m 42

WINERIES

CANDIDO FRANCESCO ♟♟♟
Via Armando Diaz 46, tel. 0831635674
r • Salice Salentino Rosso Riserva - Doc
r • Immensum Salento Rosso - Igt
r • Duca d'Aragona - Vdt
rs • Salice Salentino Rosato Le Pozzelle - Doc
w • Vigna Vinera Salento Bianco - Igt

SAN PIETRO VERNOTICO
Brindisi km 18 • m 36

WINERIES

COOPERATIVA AGRICOLA SANTA BARBARA ♟♟
Via Maternità e Infanzia 23, tel. 0831652749
r • Barbaglio Rosso del Salento - Igt
r • Ursa Major Salento Rosso - Igt
w • Ursa Major Salento Bianco - Igt

RESTA ♟♟♟
Via Maternità e Infanzia 4, tel. 0831671182
vinicolaresta@libero.it
r • Salice Salentino Rosso - Doc
r • Squinzano Rosso - Doc

VIGNETI DEL SUD ♟♟♟♟♟
Via Maternità e Infanzia 21, tel. 0831671035
www.tormaresca.it
r • Castel del Monte Bocca di Lupo - Doc
r • Masseria Maine Salento - Igt
r • Tormaresca Rosso Puglia - IGT
w • Castel del Monte Pietrabianca - Doc
w • Tormaresca Chardonnay Puglia - Igt

SAN SEVERO
Foggia km 29 • m 86

WINERIES

D'ALFONSO DEL SORDO ♟♟♟♟
Contrada S. Antonino, tel. 0882221444
www.dalfonsodelsordo.it
r • San Severo Rosso Montero - Doc
r • Cava del Re Tenuta Cappuccini Daunia Cabernet Sauvignon - Igt
r • Guado San Leo Tenuta Cappuccini Daunia Uva di Troia - Igt

SCORRANO
Lecce km 31 • m 95

WINERIES

DUCA CARLO GUARINI ♟♟ ★10%
Largo Frisari 1,
tel. 0836460288
r • Accardo Salento Rosso - Igt
r • Vigne Vecchie Salento Primitivo - Igt
w • Murà Salento Sauvignon - Igt

TUGLIE
Lecce km 36 • m 74

WINERIES

CALÒ MICHELE & FIGLI ♟♟♟
Via Masseria Vecchia 1,
tel. 0833596242
www.mjere.it
r • Mjère Salento Rosso - Igt
r • Spano Salento Rosso - Igt
rs • Alézio Rosato Mjère - Doc

MOTTURA - CAPOLEUCA ♟
Piazza Melica 4, tel. 0833596601
capoleu@tin.it
r • Primitivo di Manduria Villa Mottura - Doc
r • Squinzano Rosso Villa Mottura - Doc
s • Moscato di Trani Villa Mottura - Doc

VEGLIE
Lecce km 18 • m 47

WINERIES

CANTINA VITICULTORI ASSOCIATI ♟
Via Salice, tel. 0832969057
www.cva.it
r • Salice Salentino Rosso Riserva Rooster Blood - Doc
r • Rapture Salento Rosso - Igt

BASILICATA

ACERENZA
Potenza km 41 • m 833

WINERIES

BASILIUM ♟♟
Contrada Pipoli, tel. 0971741449
basilium@freenet.it
r • Aglianico del Vulture Alle Porte del Trono - Doc
r • Aglianico del Vulture Le Gastaldie Sicone - Doc
w • I Portali Basilicata Greco - Igt

BARILE
Potenza km 44 • m 600

WINERIES

ELENA FUCCI ♟♟♟♟
Contrada Solagna del Titolo,
tel. 09722770736
r • Aglianico del Vulture Titolo - Doc

PATERNOSTER ♟♟♟♟♟
Via Nazionale 23, tel. 0972770224
paternoster.vini@tiscalinet.it

r • Aglianico del Vulture Riserva Don Anselmo - Doc
r • Aglianico del Vulture Synthesi - Doc
r • Aglianico del Vulture Vigneto Villa Rotondo - Doc
w • Bianco di Corte Basilicata Bianco - Igt

SASSO ♟♟♟♟
Contrada Le Querce, tel. 0971470709
r • Aglianico del Vulture Minorco - Doc
r • Aglianico del Vulture Pian dell'Altare - Doc

TENUTA DEL PORTALE ♟♟
Contrada Le Querce, tel. 0972724691
r • Aglianico del Vulture Le Vigne a Capanno - Doc
r • Aglianico del Vulture Riserva - Doc

TENUTA LE QUERCE ♟♟♟♟♟
Contrada Le Querce, tel. 0971470709
www.tenutalequerce.com
r • Aglianico del Vulture Il Viola - Doc
r • Aglianico del Vulture Rosso di Costanza - Doc
r • Aglianico del Vulture Vigna della Corona - Doc

MATERA
m 401

WINERIES

PROGETTO DIVINO DI SANTE LOMURNO & C. ♟♟
Via Nazionale 76, tel. 0835262851
r • San Biagio Basilicata Rosso - Vdt

RIONERO IN VULTURE
Potenza km 41 • m 656

WINERIES

BASILISCO ♟♟♟
Via Umberto I nr. 129,
tel. 0972720032
basilisco@interfree.it
r • Aglianico del Vulture Basilisco - Doc

CANTINE DEL NOTAIO ♟♟♟♟♟ ★10%
Via Roma 159, tel. 0972717111
www.cantinedelnotaio.com
r • Aglianico del Vulture Il Repertorio - Doc
r • Aglianico del Vulture La Firma - Doc
w • L'Autentica - Igt

D'ANGELO ♟♟♟
Via Provinciale 8, tel. 0972721517
r • Aglianico del Vulture Riserva Vigna Caselle - Doc
r • Canneto Basilicata Rosso - Igt
r • Serra delle Querce Basilicata Rosso - Igt
w • Vigna dei Pini Basilicata Bianco - Igt

DI PALMA ♟
Via Potenza 13, tel. 0972722515
cantinedipalma@tin.it
r • Aglianico del Vulture Il Nibbio Grigio - Doc

EUBEA - SASSO ♟♟
Via Roma 209, tel. 0972723574
r • Aglianico del Vulture Il Covo dei Briganti - Doc
s • Seduzione - Vdt

MARTINO ARMANDO ♟♟
Via Lavista 2/A, tel. 0972721422
r • Aglianico del Vulture - Doc
r • Aglianico del Vulture Oraziano - Doc
r • Aglianico del Vulture Riserva Bel Poggio - Doc

VENOSA
Potenza km 59 • m 415

WINERIES

TERRE DEGLI SVEVI ♟♟♟
Località Pian di Camera,
tel. 0972374175
n.capurso@giv.it
r • Aglianico del Vulture Re Manfredi - Doc

CALABRIA

CASIGNANA
Reggio di Calabria km 83 • m 342

WINERIES

LA CANTINA DI STELITANO ♟
Contrada Palazzi 1, tel. 096491 3023
stelitano@interfree.it
s • Greco di Bianco - Doc

CIRÒ
Crotone km 40 • m 351

WINERIES

FATTORIA SAN FRANCESCO ♟♟♟♟
Località Quattromani,
tel. 096232228
r • Cirò Rosso Classico Ronco dei Quattro Venti - Doc
r • Cirò Rosso Classico Superiore Donna Madda - Doc
r • Martà - Vdt
rs • Cirò Rosé - Doc
w • Pernicolò Calabria Bianco - Igt

CIRÒ MARINA
Crotone km 36 • m 5

WINERIES

CANTINA COOPERATIVA CAPARRA & SICILIANI ♟♟
S.S.106, tel. 0962371435
www.cirol.it/caparra&siciliani/
r • Cirò Rosso Classico Superiore Volvito - Doc
r • Mastro Giurato Val di Neto Rosso - Doc
w • Cirò Bianco Curiale - Doc

IPPOLITO 1845 ♟♟
Via Tirone 118, tel. 096231106
ippolito1845@ippolito1845.it
r • Cirò Rosso Classico Superiore Riserva Colli del Mancuso - Doc
rs • Cirò Rosato - Doc
w • Cirò Bianco - Doc

LIBRANDI ANTONIO CATALDO E NICODEMO ♟♟♟♟♟
Contrada S. Gennaro, S.S. 106, tel. 096231518
www.librandi.it
r • Cirò Rosso Riserva Duca San Felice - Doc
r • Melissa Rosso Asylia - Doc
r • Gravello Rosso Val di Neto - Igt
r • Magno Megonio - Igt
rs • Terre Lontane Val di Neto Rosato - Igt
w • Efeso Val di Neto Bianco - Igt
s • Le Passule Passito Val di Neto - Igt

Malena ♟♟
Contrada Pirainetto,
tel. 096231758
info@malena.it
r • Cirò Rosso Classico Superiore - Doc
r • Cirò Rosso Classico Superiore Riserva Pian della Corte - Doc

LAMEZIA TERME
Catanzaro km 35 • m 216

Wineries

Lento ♟♟♟
Via del Progresso 1, tel. 096828028
lento@cantinelento.it
r • Lamezia Rosso Riserva - Doc
r • Federico II - Vdt
w • Contessa Emburga - Vdt

Statti Cantine e frantoio ♟♟ ★10%
Tenuta Lenti, tel. 0968456138
www.statti.com
r • Arvino Calabria Rosso - Igt
r • Cauro Calabria Rosso - Igt
w • Ligeia Calabria Bianco - Igt
s • Nosside Passito di Mantonico - Igt

MONTALTO UFFUGO
Cosenza km 21 • m 430

Wineries

Tenuta Terre Nobili ♟
Contrada Cariglialto, tel. 0984934005
r • Cariglio Terre Nobili Valle del Crati Rosso - Igt

NOCERA TERINESE
Catanzaro km 59 • m 240

Wineries

Odoardi ♟♟♟♟
Contrada Campodorato, tel. 098429961
odoardi@tin.it
r • Savuto Superiore Vigna Mortilla - Doc
r • Scavigna Rosso Garrone - Doc
w • Scavigna Bianco - Doc
w • Pian della Corte Blu - Vdt
s • Valeo - Vdt

SARACENA
Cosenza km 70 • m 606

Wineries

Viola Luigi ♟
s • Moscato di Saracena - Vdt

STRONGOLI
Crotone km 96 • m 342

Wineries

Ceraudo ♟♟♟
Contrada Dattilo,
tel. 0962865613
www.dattilo.it
w • Imyr Val di Neto Bianco - Igt
w • Petelia Val di Neto Bianco - Igt

SICILY

ACATE
Ragusa km 34 • m 199

Wineries

Torrevecchia ♟♟
Contrada Torrevecchia,
tel. 0932990951
www.torrevecchia.it
r • Cerasuolo di Vittoria Mont Serrant - Doc

Valle dell'Acate ♟♟♟♟ ★10%
Contrada Biddini 48, tel. 0932874166
www.valledellacate.com
r • Cerasuolo di Vittoria - Doc
r • N.N. Nero d'Avola Sicilia - Igt
w • Bidis Bianco Sicilia - Igt

ALCAMO
Trapani km 52 • m 258

Wineries

Ceuso - Melia Antonino ♟♟
Via Enea 18, tel. 0924507860
www.ceuso.it
r • Ceuso Custera Rosso Sicilia - Igt
r • Fastaia Sicilia Rosso - Igt

BUTERA
Caltanissetta km 55 • m 402

Wineries

Feudo Principi di Butera ♟♟♟♟
Contrada Deliella, tel. 0934347726
info@feudobutera.it
r • Calat Merlot Sicilia - Igt
r • Deliella Nero d'Avola Sicilia - Igt
r • San Rocco Cabernet Sauvignon Sicilia - Igt

CALTAGIRONE
Catania km 68 • m 608

Wineries

Antica Tenuta del Nanfro ♟
Contrada Nanfro S. Nicola Le Canne,
tel. 093360525
www.nanfro.com
w • Nanfro Inzolia Sicilia - Igt
w • Tenuta Nanfro Sicilia Bianco - Igt

CAMPOREALE
Palermo km 46 • m 425

Wineries

Fattorie Azzolino ♟♟
Contrada Azzolino, tel. 0464834195
www.trentinodoc.it/cantinadinomi
r • Di'more Sicilia Rosso - Igt
r • Nero d'Avola Sicilia Rosso - Igt
w • Chardonnay Sicilia - Igt

Tenuta Rapitalà ♟♟♟
Contrada Rapitalà, tel. 092437233
www.giv.it
r • Hugonis Sicilia Rosso - Igt
r • Solinero Syrah Sicilia - Igt
w • Grand Cru Chardonnay Sicilia - Igt

CASTELBUONO
Palermo km 89 • m 423

Wineries

Abbazia Santa Anastasia ♟♟♟♟♟
Contrada S. Anastasia,
tel. 0921671959
www.abbaziasantanastasia.it
r • Litra Rosso Sicilia - Igt
r • Montenero Rosso Sicilia - Igt
r • Passomaggio Rosso Sicilia - Igt
r • Nero d'Avola Sicilia - Igt
w • Passomaggio Bianco Sicilia - Igt

CASTELDACCIA

Palermo km 21 • m 79

Wineries

Duca di Salaparuta ♟♟♟♟♟
Via Nazionale, tel. 091945111
r • Eloro Bennoto - Doc
r • Duca Enrico Sicilia - Igt
r • Triskelè Sicilia - Igt
w • Bianca di Valguarnera Sicilia - Igt
w • Kados Sicilia - Igt

CASTIGLIONE DI SICILIA

Catania km 58 • m 621

Wineries

Cottanera - Fratelli Cambria ♟♟♟♟♟
Contrada Jannazzo, tel. 0942963601
staff@cottanera.it
r • Barbazzale Sicilia Rosso - Igt
r • Fatagione Sicilia Rosso - Igt
r • Grammonte Rosso Sicilia - Igt
r • L'Ardenza Rosso Sicilia - Igt
r • Sole di Sesta Sicilia Rosso - Igt

CATANIA

m 7

Wineries

Dô Zenner ♟♟
Via P. Mascagni 72, tel. 095530560
terradellesirene@sicilyonline.it
r • Terra delle Sirene Nero d'Avola Sicilia - Igt

CHIARAMONTE GULFI

Ragusa km 19 • m 668

Wineries

Gulfi - Ramada ♟♟♟♟
Contrada Passo Guastella, tel. 0932921654
www.gulfi.it
r • Rosso Ibleo Sicilia Rosso - Igt
w • Caricanti Sicilia Bianco - Igt
w • Valcanziria Sicilia Bianco - Igt

COMISO

Ragusa km 17 • m 209

Wineries

Avide ♟♟
Strada Comiso-Chiaramonte, tel. 0932967456
r • Cerasuolo di Vittoria Barocco - Doc
r • Sigillo Rosso Sicilia - Igt
w • Vigne d'Oro Sicilia - Igt

GROTTE

Agrigento km 21 • m 516

Wineries

Morgante ♟♟♟♟♟
Contrada Racalmare-Grotte, tel. 0922945579
morgante_vini@virgilio.it
r • Don Antonio Sicilia Rosso - Igt
r • Morgante Sicilia Rosso - Igt

ISPICA

Ragusa km 33 • m 170

Wineries

Curto Giovanbattista ♟
Via Galilei 4, tel. 0932950161
r • Curto Rosso Sicilia - Igt

MARSALA

Trapani km 31 • m 12

Wineries

Baglio Hopps ♟♟
Contrada Biesina 2, tel. 0923967020
www.infohopps.com
r • Incantari Sicilia Rosso - Igt
r • Nero d'Avola Sicilia - Igt
w • Grillo Sicilia Bianco - Igt

De Bartoli Marco - Vecchio Samperi ♟♟♟♟
Contrada Fornara-Samperi 292, tel. 0923962093
s • Marsala Superiore - Vdt
s • Vecchio Samperi Ventennale Vino Liquoroso Secco - Vdt
s • Vigna La Miccia Vino Liquoroso - Vdt

Florio ♟♟♟♟
Via Vincenzo Florio 1, tel. 0923781111
www.cantineflorio.com
s • Baglio Florio Marsala Vergine Oro - Vdt
s • Targa Riserva 1840 Marsala Superiore Riserva Semisecco Ambra - Vdt
s • Terre Arse Marsala Vergine Oro Secco - Vdt
s • Vecchioflorio Marsala Superiore Riserva Ambra Semisecco - Vdt
s • Vecchioflorio Marsala Vergine Oro Secco - Vdt

Pellegrino ♟♟
Via del Fante 37/39, tel. 0923719911
r • Gorgo Tondo Sicilia Rosso - Igt
s • Marsala Superiore Riserva Dom Pellegrino - Doc
s • Moscato Passito di Pantelleria Nes - Doc

Rallo ♟♟♟
Via Vincenzo Florio 2, tel. 0923721633
r • Vesco Sicilia Rosso - Igt
s • Marsala Vergine Soleras Riserva 12 anni - Doc
s • Passito di Pantelleria Mare d'Ambra - Doc

Tenuta di Donnafugata ♟♟♟♟
Via Sebastiano Lipari 18, tel. 0923724200
www.donnafugata.it
r • Contessa Entellina Rosso Mille e Una Notte - Doc
r • Contessa Entellina Rosso Tancredi - Doc
w • Contessa Entellina Bianco Vigna di Gabri - Doc
w • Contessa Entellina Chiarandà del Merlo - Doc
s • Moscato Passito di Pantelleria Ben Ryé - Doc

MENFI

Agrigento km 79 • m 119

Wineries

Cantina Settesoli ♟♟
S.S. 115, tel. 092577111
www.mandrarossa.it
r • Mandrarossa Beddicò Nero d'Avola Sicilia - Igt
w • Mandrarossa Furetta Sicilia Bianco - Igt
w • Mandrarossa Chardonnay Sicilia - Igt

Planeta 🍷🍷🍷🍷
Contrada Dispensa, tel. 092580079
www.planeta.it
r • Cerasuolo di Vittoria - Doc
r • La Segreta Rosso Sicilia - Igt
r • Merlot Sicilia - Igt
r • Santa Cecilia Sicilia Rosso - Igt
r • Syrah Sicilia Rosso - Igt
w • Cometa Bianco Sicilia - Igt
w • La Segreta Bianco Sicilia - Igt

MESSINA

m 3

Wineries

Colosi 🍷🍷🍷
Via Militare Ritiro 23, tel. 09053852
www.cantinecolosi.com
r • L'Incontro Sicilia Rosso - Igt
w • Malvasia delle Lipari Naturale di Salina - Doc
s • Malvasia delle Lipari Passito di Salina - Doc
s • Moscato di Pantelleria - Doc
s • Passito di Pantelleria - Doc

Palari 🍷🍷🍷🍷🍷
Località Santo Stefano Briga, contrada Barna, tel. 090694281
r • Faro Palari - Doc
r • Rosso del Soprano Sicilia - Igt

MONREALE

Palermo km 8 • m 310

Wineries

Pollara 🍷🍷
Contrada Malvello, S.P. 4/bis al km 2, tel. 0918462922
r • Il Rosso Principe di Corleone Sicilia - Igt
r • Principe di Corleone Nero d'Avola Sicilia - Igt
w • Principe di Corleone Inzolia Sicilia - Igt

Spadafora 🍷🍷🍷🍷🍷
Contrada Virzì, tel. 091514952
www.spadafora.com
r • Don Pietro Rosso Sicilia - Igt
r • Schietto Cabernet Sauvignon Sicilia - Igt
r • Schietto Chardonnay Sicilia - Igt
r • Schietto Syrah Sicilia - Igt
r • Sole dei Padri Sicilia Rosso - Igt

PACECO

Trapani km 7 • m 36

Wineries

Firriato 🍷🍷🍷🍷
Via Trapani 4, tel. 0923882755
www.firriato.it
r • Camelot Sicilia Rosso - Igt
r • Chiaramonte Catarratto Sicilia - Igt
r • Chiaramonte Nero d'Avola Sicilia - Igt
r • Harmonium Sicilia Rosso - Igt
w • Santagostino Baglio Soria Bianco Sicilia - Igt

PALERMO

m 14

Wineries

Abraxas 🍷🍷🍷
Via Enrico Albanese 29, tel. 0916110051
www.winesabraxasa.com
w • Kuddia del Gallo Sicilia Bianco - Igt
s • Passito di Pantelleria - Doc

Miceli 🍷🍷
Via Denti di Piraino Ammiraglio 9, tel. 0916396111
www.midmiceli.it
r • Majo San Lorenzo Sicilia Rosso - Igt
r • Syrah Sicilia Rosso - Igt
w • Initio Bianco Sicilia - Igt
w • Yrnm Bianco Sicilia - Igt
s • Passito di Pantelleria Nun - Doc

PANTELLERIA

Trapanim 5

Wineries

Bukkuram 🍷🍷🍷🍷
Contrada Kamma 276, tel. 0923918344
s • Moscato Passito di Pantelleria Bukkuram - Doc
s • Pietra Nera Sicilia - Igt

Case di Pietra 🍷🍷🍷
Contrada Nicà, tel. 0923916152
www.casedipietra.it
s • Passito di Pantelleria Nikà - Doc

Cooperativa Nuova Agricoltura 🍷🍷 ★10%
Via Napoli 22, tel. 0923915712
s • Moscato Passito di Pantelleria Le Lave del Kuttinar - Doc

Minardi Andrea 🍷🍷
Contrada Karuscia 6, tel. 0923911160
www.viniminardi.com
s • Passito di Pantelleria Karuscia - Doc

Murana Salvatore 🍷🍷🍷🍷🍷
Contrada Kamma 276, tel. 0923915231
s • Moscato di Pantelleria Mueggen - Doc
s • Moscato Passito di Pantelleria Khamma - Doc
s • Moscato Passito di Pantelleria Martingana - Doc

PARTINICO

Palermo km 29 • m 175

Wineries

Cusumano 🍷🍷🍷🍷
Contrada S. Carlo, S.S. 113, tel. 0918903456
www.cusumano.it
r • Benuara Sicilia Rosso - Igt
r • Noà Sicilia Rosso - Igt
r • Sàgana Sicilia Rosso - Igt
w • Cubìa Sicilia Bianco - Igt
w • Jalé Chardonnay Sicilia - Igt

PIAZZA ARMERINA

Enna km 34 • m 697

Wineries

Tenuta di Budonetto 🍷🍷🍷🍷
Contrada Budonetto, tel. 091321788
info@maurigi.it
r • Terre di Maria Sicilia Rosso - Igt
w • Coste all'Ombra Sicilia Bianco - Igt
w • Terre di Sofia Sicilia Bianco - Igt

SALAPARUTA

Trapani km 75 • m 171

Wineries

Palermo Antonino - Bruchicello 🍷🍷🍷
Via Pietro Nenni 27, tel. 092475717
www.bruchicello.it
r • Bruchicello Nero d'Avola Sicilia - Igt

SAMBUCA DI SICILIA

Agrigento km 90 • m 350

WINERIES
DI PRIMA ♟♟♟
Via Guasto 27, tel. 0925941201
www.diprimavini.it
r • Villamaura Syrah Sicilia - Igt
w • Sambuca di Sicilia Bianco Pepita - Doc

SAN CIPIRELLO
Palermo km 31 • m 394
WINERIES
CALATRASI ♟♟
Contrada Piano Piraino, tel. 0918576767
r • D'Istinto Magnifico Sicilia Rosso - Igt
r • D'Istinto Nero d'Avola Sicilia - Igt
r • D'Istinto Syrah Sicilia - Igt
r • Terre di Ginestra Nero d'Avola Sicilia - Igt
w • Terre di Ginestra Catarratto Sicilia - Igt

SAN GIUSEPPE JATO
Palermo km 30 • m 467
WINERIES
FEOTTO DELLO JATO ♟♟
Contrada Feotto, tel. 0918572650
www.feottodellojato.com
r • Rosso di Turi Sicilia Rosso - Igt
r • Syrae Sicilia Rosso - Igt
r • Terra di Giulia Sicilia Rosso - Igt

SANTA MARINA SALINA
Messina km 41 • m 25
WINERIES
HAUNER CARLO ♟♟♟
All'Isola Salina, via Umberto I, lingua di Salina, tel. 0909843141
r • Antonello Salina Rosso - Igt
w • Salina Bianco - Igt
s • Malvasia delle Lipari Passita - Doc

SANTA VENERINA
Catania km 23 • m 337
WINERIES
TENUTA SAN MICHELE ♟♟
Via Zafferana 13, tel. 095950520
r • Etna Rosso Murgo - Doc
r • Tenuta San Michele Sicilia Rosso - Igt

SCLAFANI BAGNI
Palermo km 75 • m 813
WINERIES
CONTE TASCA D'ALMERITA ♟♟♟♟♟
Contrada Regaleali, tel. 0921544011
www.tascadalmerita.it
r • Contea di Sclafani Cabernet Sauvignon - Doc
r • Regaleali Rosso di Sicilia - Igt
r • Rosso del Conte Sicilia Rosso - Igt
w • Contea di Sclafani Bianco Nozze d'Oro - Doc
w • Contea di Sclafani Chardonnay - Doc

SIRACUSA
m 17
WINERIES
PUPILLO ♟♟♟
Contrada Targia 5, tel. 0931494029
solacium@tin.it
s • Moscato di Siracusa Pollio - Doc
s • Moscato di Siracusa Solacium - Doc
s • Moscato di Siracusa Vigna di Mela - Doc

TRAPANI
m 3
WINERIES
CANTINA SOCIALE DI TRAPANI ♟♟
Contrada Ospedaletto, tel. 0923539349
www.cantinasocialetrapani.com
r • Forti Terre di Sicilia Nero d'Avola Sicilia - Igt
r • Forti Terre di Sicilia Rosso - Igt
w • Forti Terre di Sicilia Bianco Sicilia - Igt
FAZIO WINES ♟♟♟ ★10%
Località Fulgatore, via Cap. Rizzo 39, tel. 0923811700
www.faziowines.it
r • Pietrasacra Sicilia Rosso - Igt
r • Torre dei Venti Sicilia Rosso - Igt
w • Torre dei Venti Inzolia Chardonnay Sicilia - Igt
w • Torre dei Venti Inzolia Sicilia - Igt
s • Ky Moscato Passito Sicilia - Igt

VIAGRANDE
Catania km 14 • m 410
WINERIES
BENANTI ♟♟♟♟
Via Garibaldi 475, tel. 0957893438
www.vinicolabenanti.it
r • Etna Rosso Rovittello - Doc
r • Lamorémio Rosso Sicilia - Igt
w • Etna Bianco Superiore Pietramarina - Doc
w • Edélmio Bianco Sicilia - Igt
s • Passito di Pantelleria Coste di Mueggen - Doc

VITTORIA
Ragusa km 25 • m 168
WINERIES
COS ♟♟♟
Piazza del Popolo 34, tel. 0932864042
r • Contrade Dedalo Rosso Sicilia - Igt
r • Contrade Labirinto Rosso Sicilia - Igt
r • Contrade Licata Rosso Sicilia - Igt
r • Contrade Victoria Rosso Sicilia - Igt
rs • Cerasuolo di Vittoria Vigna di Bastonaca - Doc

SARDINIA

ALGHERO
Sassari km 36 • m 7
WINERIES
CANTINA SOCIALE SANTA MARIA LA PALMA ♟ ★10%
Località Santa Maria La Palma, tel. 079999008
www.vini.santamarialapalma.com
r • Alghero Cagnulari - Doc
r • Cannonau di Sardegna - Doc
w • Vermentino di Sardegna I Papiri - Doc

Tenute Sella & Mosca ♣♣♣
Località I Piani, tel. 079997700
- *r* • Alghero Marchese di Villamarina - Doc
- *r* • Cannonau di Sardegna Riserva - Doc
- *w* • Vermentino di Gallura Monteoro - Doc
- *w* • Vermentino di Sardegna La Cala - Doc
- *s* • Alghero Monteluce - Doc

ARZACHENA
Sassari km 113 • m 85

Wineries

Capichera ♣♣♣♣♣
S.S. Arzachena-S.Antonio al km 6, tel. 078980612
capichera@tiscalinet.it
- *r* • Capichera Assajè - Vdt
- *r* • Capichera Mantènghja - Vdt
- *w* • Capichera Classico - Vdt
- *w* • Capichera Vendemmia Tardiva - Vdt
- *w* • Capichera Vigna 'Ngena - Vdt

BERCHIDDA
Sassari km 70 • m 300

Wineries

Cantina Sociale del Giogantinu ♣♣♣
tel. 079704163
- *r* • Terra Mala Vigne Storiche Colli del Limbara Rosso - Igt
- *w* • Vermentino di Gallura Superiore Vigne Storiche del Giogantinu - Docg
- *w* • Vermentino di Gallura Vigne Storiche del Giogantinu - Docg

CABRAS
Oristano km 8 • m 6

Wineries

Contini Attilio ♣♣♣
Via Genova 48, tel. 0783290806
www.vinicontini.it
- *r* • Cannonau di Sardegna Riserva - Doc
- *r* • Nieddera Rosso della Valle del Tirso - Igt
- *w* • Vernaccia di Oristano Antico Gregori - Doc
- *w* • Vernaccia di Oristano Riserva Speciale - Doc
- *s* • Karmis Vernaccia della Valle del Tirso - Igt

CARDEDU
Nuoro km 98 • m 40

Wineries

Loi Alberto ♣♣
S.S. 125 al km 124.2, tel. 070240866
www.cantina.it/albertoloi
- *r* • Tuvara Isola dei Nuraghi Rosso - Igt
- *w* • Cepola Isola dei Nuraghi Bianco - Igt

DOLIANOVA
Cagliari km 21 • m 212

Wineries

Dolianova ♣♣
Località Sant'Esu, S.S. 387 al km 17.150, tel. 070744101
cantinedolianova@tiscalinet.it
- *r* • Cannonau di Sardegna - Doc
- *r* • Monica di Sardegna - Doc
- *w* • Vermentino di Sardegna Naeli - Doc

DORGALI
Nuoro km 32 • m 390

Wineries

Cantina Sociale di Dorgali ♣♣
Via Piemonte 11, tel. 078496143
www.csdorgali.com
- *r* • Cannonau di Sardegna Vigna di Isalle - Doc
- *r* • Fùili Rosso dei Baroni Provincia di Nuoro - Igt
- *r* • Noriolo Provincia di Nuoro - Igt

FLORINAS
Sassari km 19 • m 417

Wineries

Tenute Soletta ♣♣ ★10%
Via Sassari 77, tel. 079438160
www.tenutesoletta.it
- *r* • Cannonau di Sardegna Riserva - Doc
- *w* • Vermentino di Sardegna Prestizu - Doc
- *w* • Vermentino di Sardegna Soletta - Doc

JERZU
Nuoro km 96 • m 427

Wineries

Soc. Cooperativa Vitivinicola di Jerzu ♣♣♣
Via Umberto I nr. 1, tel. 078270028
www.jerzuantichipoderi.it
- *r* • Cannonau di Sardegna Marghìa - Doc
- *r* • Cannonau di Sardegna Riserva Chuerra - Doc
- *r* • Cannonau di Sardegna Riserva Jostu Migliore - Doc

MOGORO
Oristano km 35 • m 132

Wineries

Cantina Sociale Il Nuraghe ♣♣
S.S. 131 al km 62, tel. 0783990285
cantina@ilnuraghe.it
- *r* • Cannonau di Sardegna Vigna Ruja - Doc
- *r* • Monica di Sardegna Superiore Nabui - Doc
- *w* • Vermentino di Sardegna Dongiovanni - Doc

MONTI
Sassari km 81 • m 300

Wineries

Cantina Sociale del Vermentino ♣♣
Via S. Paolo 2, tel. 078944012
www.vermentinomonti.it
- *w* • Vermentino di Gallura Superiore Aghiloia - Docg
- *w* • Vermentino di Gallura Funtanaliras - Docg
- *w* • Vermentino di Gallura S'Eleme - Docg

Pedra Majore ♣♣
Via Roma 106, tel. 078943185
- *w* • Vermentino di Gallura Hyonj - Docg
- *w* • Vermentino di Gallura I Graniti - Docg
- *w* • Vermentino di Sardegna Le Conche - Doc

NUORO
m 549

Wineries

Gabbas Giuseppe ♣♣♣♣
Via Trieste 65, tel. 078431351
- *r* • Cannonau di Sardegna Lillové - Doc
- *r* • Arbeskia - Igt
- *r* • Dule Rosso della Barbagia - Igt

OLBIA
Sassari km 103 • m 15

WINERIES

CANTINA DELLE VIGNE ♟♟♟
Località Cala Saccaia, tel. 078950717
www.pieromancini.it
r • Cannonau di Sardegna - Doc
w • Vermentino di Gallura Cucaione - Docg
w • Vermentino di Gallura Saraina - Docg

SANTADI
Cagliari km 65 • m 135

WINERIES

CANTINA SOCIALE SANTADI ♟♟♟♟♟
Via Su Pranu 12,
tel. 0781950127
www.cantinadisantadi.it
r • Carignano del Sulcis Riserva Rocca Rubia - Doc
r • Carignano del Sulcis Superiore Terre Brune - Doc
w • Vermentino di Sardegna Villa Solais - Doc
w • Villa di Chiesa Valli di Porto Pino Bianco - Igt
s • Latinia Valli di Porto Pino Nasco Vendemmia Tardiva - Igt

SAN VERO MILIS
Oristano km 14 • m 10

WINERIES

CANTINA DELLA VERNACCIA PUDDU JOSTO ♟♟♟
Via S. Lussorio 1, tel. 078353329
www.cantinapuddu.it
r • Cannonau di Sardegna Antares - Doc
r • Monica di Sardegna Torremora - Doc
w • Vermentino di Sardegna Marìs - Doc
w • Armonie Valle del Tirso Bianco - Igt
s • Vernaccia di Oristano Riserva - Doc

SENNORI
Sassari km 10 • m 277

WINERIES

TENUTE DETTORI ♟♟♟♟
Località Badde Nigolosu, S.P. 29 al km 10,
tel. 079514711
www.tenutedettori.it
r • Dettori Romangia Rosso - Igt
r • Tenores Romangia Rosso - Igt
r • Tuderi Romangia Rosso - Igt
s • Moscadeddu - Vdt

SENORBÌ
Cagliari km 41 • m 199

WINERIES

CANTINA TREXENTA ♟♟
Viale Piemonte 28, tel. 0709808863
r • Cannonau di Sardegna Baione - Doc
r • Tanca Su Conti Isola dei Nuraghi Rosso - Igt
w • Nuragus di Cagliari Tenute San Mauro - Doc
w • Vermentino di Sardegna Tanca Sa Contissa - Doc
s • Monica di Sardegna Duca di Mandas - Doc

SERDIANA
Cagliari km 20 • m 171

WINERIES

ARGIOLAS ♟♟♟♟♟
Via Roma 56/58, tel. 070740606
r • Cannonau di Sardegna Costera - Doc
r • Korem Isola dei Nuraghi - Igt
r • Turriga Isola dei Nuraghi - Igt
w • Vermentino di Sardegna Costamolino - Doc
s • Monica di Sardegna Perdera - Doc

FRATELLI PALA ♟♟♟
Via Verdi 7, tel. 070740284
cantinapala@tiscali.it
r • Cannonau di Sardegna Triente - Doc
r • Monica di Sardegna Elima - Doc
w • Nuragus di Cagliari Sàlnico - Doc

TEMPIO PAUSANIA
Sassari km 69 • m 566

WINERIES

CANTINA SOCIALE GALLURA ♟♟♟
Via Val di Cossu 9, tel. 079631241
r • Dolmen Rosso Colli del Limbara - Igt
w • Vermentino di Gallura Gemellae - Docg
w • Balajana Bianco Colli del Limbara - Igt

USINI
Sassari km 12 • m 200

WINERIES

CHERCHI GIOVANNI MARIA ♟♟♟
Via Ossi 18/20, tel. 079380273
vinicolacherchi@tiscali.it
r • Cannonau di Sardegna - Doc
r • Cagnulari Isola dei Nuraghi Rosso - Igt
w • Vermentino di Sardegna Tuvaoes - Doc

U.S. Wine Importers

Banfi Vintners
1111 Cedar Swamproad
Old Brookville,
NY 11545
Tel.: 516-626-9200
Fax: 516-686-2621

Opici Import Company
25 De Boer Drive
Glen Rock, NJ 07452
Tel.: 201-689-1200
Fax: 201-251-8081

Empson USA
719 Prince Street
Alexandria, VA 22314
Tel.: 703-684-0900
Fax: 703-684-2065

Palm Bay Imports
343 Underhill Blvd.
Syosset, NY 11791
Tel.: 516-921-9005
Fax: 516-921-8405

Wine Wave Inc.
100 Jericho Quadrangle -
Suite 343
Jericho, NY 11750
Tel.: 516-433-1121
Fax: 516-433-1207

Remy Amerique, Inc.
1350 Ave. of Americas,
7th Fl.
New York, NY 10019
Tel.: 212-399-4200
Fax: 212-399-6909

Prestige Wine Imports Corp.
5 West 19th Street
Fourth Floor
New York, NY 10011
Tel.: 212-229-0080
Fax: 212-229-0051

William Grant & Son
130 Fieldcrest Avenue -
Raritan Center
Edison, NJ 08837
Tel.: 732-225-9000
Fax: 732-225-3458

Frederick Wildman & Sons, Ltd.
307 East 53rd Street
New York, NY 10022
Tel.: 212-355-0700
Fax: 212-355-4723

Brown-Forman Bev. Co.
850 Dixie Highway
Louisville, KY 40201
Tel.: 502-585-1100
Fax: 502-774-7185

Paterno Wines International
900 Armour Drive
Lake Bluff, IL 60044
Tel.: 847-604-5774
Fax: 847-604-5849

Kobrand Corporation
134 East 40th Street
New York, NY 10016
Tel.: 212-490-9300
Fax: 212-983-0774

Vias Imports
875 6th Avenue
New York, NY 10001
Tel.: 212-629-0200
Fax: 212-629-0262

Schieffelin & Somerset Co.
2 Park Avenue
New York, NY 10003
Tel.: 212-696-9310
Fax: 212-251-8385

Selected Estates of Europe Ltd.
620 Concord Avenue
Mamaroneck, NY 10534
Tel.: 914-698-7202
Fax: 914-698-7204

A.V. Imports Inc.
6450-6 Dobbin Road
Columbia, MD 21045
Tel.: 410-884-9463
Fax: 410-884-9470

Fedway Imports Co.
1900 Hempstead Tpke.
East Meadow, NY 11554
Tel.: 516-794-6850
Fax: 516-794-6855

Tri-Vin Imports, Inc.
1 Park Avenue
Mt. Vernon, NY 10550
Tel.: 914-664-3155
Fax: 914-664-3319

Five Star Fine Products, Inc.
1500 Old Country Road
Plainview, NY 11803
Tel.: 516-524-2646
Fax: 516-414-4607

Admiral Wine Imports
603 South 21st Street
Irvington, NJ 07111
Tel.: 973-371-2211
Fax: 973-371-8521

Mionetto USA Inc.
55 Washington St., Suite 657
Brooklyn, NY 11201
Tel.: 718-596-3339
Fax: 718-596-5355

Parliament Wine Co.
3303 Atlantic Avenue
Atlantic City, NJ 08401
Tel.: 609-348-1100
Fax: 609-348-3690

Skyy Spirits
381 Park Avenue South
1413
New York, NY 10016
Tel.: 212-213-9777
Fax: 212-213-8236

Campari International
381 Park Avenue South
1413
New York, NY 10016
Tel.: 212-213-9777
Fax: 212-213-8236

Panebianco LLC
1140 Broadway - Suite 504
New York, NY 10001
Tel.: 212-685-7560
Fax: 212-685-7566

Shaw-Ross International Import
233 East 69th St. Apt. 6C
New York, NY 10021
Tel.: 212-223-8088
Fax: 212-753-8635

Chatham Imports
257 Park Avenue South
New York, NY 10010
Tel.: 212-473-1100
Fax: 212-473-2956

Bacchus Imports inc.
250 East 63rd Street, Ste 902
New York, NY 10021
Tel.: 212-758-5820
Fax: 212-758-4122

Barton Brands
55 East Monroe - Suite 2600
Chicago, IL 60603
Tel. 312-346-9200
Fax: 312-855-1220

Laird Importers
1 Laird Rd.
Scobeyville, NJ 07724
Tel.: 732-542-0312
Fax: 732-542-2244

Domaine Select Wine Estates
555 8th Avenue # 2302
New York, NY 10018
Tel.: 212-279-0799
Fax: 212-279-0499

House of Burgundy
36 Midland Avenue
Port Chester, NY 10574
Tel.: 914-937-6330
Fax: 914-937-8824

Star Industries
PO Box 9004
Syosset, NY 11791-9004
Tel.: 516-921-9300
Fax: 516-921-0567

La Gioiosa USA, Inc.
The Lucerne at Lenox
Ste. 280 - 3391 Peachtree Rd.
Atlanta, GA 30326
Tel.: 404-364-3470
Fax: 404-364-3471

Marie Brizard
Wines & Spirits
11900 Biscayne Blvd. 600
North Miami, FL 33181
Tel.: 305-893-3394
Fax: 305-891-6577

Michael Skurnik Wines Inc.
575 Underhill Blvd, Ste 216
Syosset, NY 11791
Tel.: 516-677-9300
Fax: 516-677-9301

Dreyfus Ashby & Company
630 3rd Avenue, # 15
New York, NY 10017
Tel.: 212-818-0770
Fax: 212-953-2366

Ecco Domani
E&J Gallo Winery
600 Yosemite Blvd.
Modesto, CA 95354-2760
Tel.: 209-341-7698
Fax: 209-341-4919

Wilson Daniels, Ltd.
P.O. Box 440 B
St. Helena, CA 94574
Tel.: 707-963-9661
Fax: 707-963-8566

Tricana Imports
1120 Old Country Road
Plainview, NY 11803
Tel.: 516-935-4080
Fax: 516-933-1755

The Wine Emporium
209 North 11th Street
Brooklyn, NY 11211
Tel.: 718-486-3913
Fax: 718-486-3915

Merlin-Montgomery Imports, Ltd.
3104 Central Avenue
Union City, NJ 07087
Tel.: 201-865-3505
Fax: 201-865-1086

Robert Mondavi Winery
80 Varick Street, #10D
New York, NY 10013
Tel.: 212-965-0007
Fax: 707-265-5126

Beringer Blass Wine Estates
1000 Pratt Avenue
St. Helena, CA 94574
Tel.: 707-963-8989
Fax: 707-963-1735

Baron Francois Collection
236 West 26th Street,
Suite 304
New York, NY 10001
Tel.: 212-924-1414
Fax: 212-924-3768

Charmer Sales Company
48-11 20th Avenue
Astoria, NY 11105
Tel.: 718-545-7400
Fax: 718-726-9183

Leonard Kreusch, Inc.
2971 Pines Brook Road
Walton, NY 13856
Tel.: 607-865-6994
Fax: 201-784-0951

Supreme Wines
420 Lexington Avenue
Suite 1639
New York, NY 10170
Tel.: 212-404-7904
Fax: 212-404-7910

Italian Wine Growers
18 Wayne Avenue
West Haverstraw,
NY 10993
Tel.: (845) 942-5384
Fax: (845) 942-5385

A.I.M.C. Co., Inc.
16 Taunton Rd. East
Scarsdale, NY 10583
Tel.: 914-472-2577
Fax: 914-472-2828

USA Wine Imports
285 West Broadway,
Suite 340
New York, NY 10013
Tel.: 212-941-7133
Fax: 212-941-7174

Tastings Import Company
910 West Van Buren,
Suite 5000
Chicago, IL 60607
Tel.: 312-226-9438
Fax: 312-226-7858

Distillerie Stock USA
58-58 Lauriel Hill Blvd.
Woodside, NY 11377
Tel.: 718-651-9800
Fax: 718-651-7806

Zonin USA, Inc.
630 Peter Jefferson Parkway
Ste 110
Charlottesville, VA 22911
Tel.: 434-979-6180
Fax: 434-979-6188

District Manager Vini Corvo
35 Herrick Avenue
Staten Island, NY 10309
Tel.: 718-605-1878
Fax: 718-605-1222

World Wines Classics, Ltd.
35 Portman Road
New Rochelle, NY 10801
Tel.: 914-235-2500
Fax: 914-576-2037

Cliquot Inc.
717 Fifth Avenue
New York, NY 10022
Tel.: 212-888-7575
Fax: 212-888-7551

Premier Wine Company
1091 Essex Avenue
Richmond, CA 94804
Tel.: 650-364-8544
Fax: 650-364-4687

Vinifera Imports, Ltd.
205 13th Avenue
Ronkonkoma, NY 11779
Tel.: 631-467-5907
Fax: 631-467-6516

Martin Scott Wines, Ltd.
1981 Marcus Avenue-Suite
E-117

Lake Success, NY 11042
Tel.: 516-327-0808
Fax: 516-327-9495

Trebon Wines & Spirits Corp.
18-02 131st Street
College Point, NY 11356
Tel.: 718-886-7310
Fax: 718-886-7313

Dufour & Company
17 High Street
Brookline, MA 01446
Tel.: 617-734-6488
Fax: 617-731-8599

Lauber Imports Ltd
24 Columbia Rd.
Somerville, NJ 08876
Tel.: 908-725-2100
Fax: 908-725-0317

U.S.A. Wine Imports Inc.
285 West Broadway
New York, NY 10013
Tel.: 212-941-7133
Fax: 212-941-7174

Monsieur Touton Selections Ltd.
129 West 27th Street
New York, NY 10001
Tel.: 212-255-0674
Fax: 212-255-2628

Terranova Imports Corp.
5301 Tacony St. -
Box 323
Philadelphia, PA 19137
Tel.: 215-744-8565
Fax: 215-744-8564

Monsieur Henri Wines Ltd.
6125 King Road
Loomis, CA 95650
Tel.: 916-652-3791
Fax: 916-630-3110

Frank M. Hartley Inc.
P.O. Box 263 - 82
Village Drive
Mahwah, NJ 07430
Tel.: 201-760-0020
Fax: 201-760-0250

Moore Brothers Wine Co.
7200 Northg Park Drive
Pennsauken, NJ 08109
Tel.: 856-317-1177
Fax: 856-317-0055

A & E Trading, Inc,
P.O. Box 492
Shrub Oak, NY 10588
Tel.: 845-528-4330
Fax: 845-528-0156

A.G. Wines
352 Seventh Avenue
New York, NY 10001
Tel.: 212-396-9077
Fax: 212-961-9195

Athenee Importers
P.O. Box 2039
Hempstead, NY 11551
Tel.: 516-505-4800
Fax: 516-505-4876

Bedford International
30 Lake Street
White Plains, NY 10603
Tel.: 914-761-4321
Fax: 914-761-7454

Biagio Cru & Estate Wines
73 Powerhouse Road
Roslyn Heights, NY 11577
Tel.: 516-299-4344
Fax: 516-299-4348

David Milligan Selections
P.O. Box 790
Sagaponack, NY 11962
Tel.: 631-537-7126
Fax: 631-537-6512

De-Vine Imports, Inc.
7210 20th Avenue
Brooklyn, NY 11204
Tel.: 718-621-4000
Fax: 718-621-4710

Embassy Wine Company
106-15 Foster Avenue
Brooklyn, NY 11236
Tel.: 718-272-0600
Fax: 718-272-7845

Italian Quality Standards Inc.
111 John Street
New York, NY 10038
Tel.: 212-791-2187
Fax: 212-791-2196

Jeroboam Wines
285 West Broadway
New York, NY 10013
Tel.: 212-625-2505
Fax: 212-625-2511

Metropolis Wine Merchants Inc.
527 West 45tgh Street
New York, NY 10036
Tel.: 212-686-3686
Fax: 212-581-4872

Metrowine Distribution Co.
1565 Franklin Avenue
Mineola, NY 11501
Tel.: 516-746-4488
Fax: 516-746-4149

Romano Brands, Inc.
400 South Oyster Bay
Road - Ste 302
Hicksville, NY 11801
Tel.: 516-681-5159
Fax: 516-932-9463

Calita Imports
537 4th St. - Suite B
Santa Rosa, CA 95401
Tel.: 707-568-7701
Fax: 707-568-0774

Dalla Terra & Amp./Uve Enterprises
520 California Blvd., Suite 6
Napa, CA 94559
Tel.: 707-259-5405
Fax: 707-259-5419

J.K. Imports
P.O. Box 946
Pasadena, CA 91102
Tel.: 626-793-4660
Fax: 626-793-4667

M.R. Downey Slections Inc.
138 South Garfield Street
Arlington, VA 22204
Tel.: 703-920-5690
Fax: 703-685-4669

Premier Imports, LLC
164 Old Gate Lane
Milford, CT 06460
Tel.: 203-878-4433
Fax: 203-761-9911

Wine Cellars Ltd.
314 Chappaqua Road
Briarcliff Manor, NY 10510
Tel.: 914-762-6540
Fax: 914-762-6515

Vin Divino
1811 West Bryn Mawr
Chicago, IL 60660
Tel.: 773-334-6700
Fax: 773-271-8263

Nicholas Minicucci & Sons LLC
65 Ramapo Valley Road,
Suite Two
Mahwah, NJ 07430
Tel.: 201-512-3399
Fax: 201-512-9992

Padania Corporation
816 Long Beach Blvd.
Ship Bottom, NJ 08008
Tel.: 609-361-9600
Fax: 609-361-9696

Verdoni Wine Imports
532 Lafayette
Hawthorne, NJ 07506

Tel.: 973-636-0800
Fax: 973-636-0488

Mr. David Bittone
Castellar Imports, Inc.
P.O. Box 6601
Bridgewater, NJ 08807-0601
Tel.: 908-342-1800

Noble Harvest Ltd.
P.O. Box 1008
Paoli, PA 19301
Tel.: 610-518-9229
Fax: 610-518-1994

Priore Wine Company
901 Tonne Road
Elk Grove, IL 60007
Tel.: 847-690-9315

Villa Italia Imports
175 Utah Avenue
So. San Francisco,
CA 94083
Tel.: 650-872-6060
Fax: 650-873-2574

Vinity Wine Company
5950 Doyle Street
Emeryville, CA 94608
Tel.: 510-601-6010
Fax: 510-601-7021

Vinum International
1345 Henry Road
Napa, CA 94559
Tel.: 707-224-9601
Fax: 707-224-1672

Citadel Trading Corp.
25 Central Park West
New York, NY 10023
Tel.: 212-245-2844
Fax: 212-258-2644

Gabriella Importers
481 Johnson Avenue, Unit D
Bohemia, NY
Tel.: 631-563-0400
Fax: 631-563-0400 (same)

Bartolomeo Pio, Inc.
260 New York Drive,
Fort Washington, PA 19034
Tel.: (215) 641-1600
Fax: (215) 641-0235

Sapori Italiani, Inc.
24 Third Street
New Rochelle, NY 10085
Tel.: 914-961-3703
Fax: 914-779-9440

Vinvino Wine Co., Inc.
56 King Street
New York, NY 10014
Tel.: 212-463-7880
Fax: 212-463-7311

Rossback & Company
196 East 75th Street
New York, NY 10021
Tel.: 212-988-8475
Fax.: 212-988-8559

Abruzzi Imports
27 Greenway Street
Stamford, CT 06907
Tel.: 203-316-9397
Fax: 1-888-316-9398

Montevideo Importers, Inc.
8 South Main Street,
Suite 6
Port Chester, NY 10573
Tel.: 1-914-934-2288
Fax: 1-914-937-8270

Vintage Trading, Inc.
516 Fifth Avenue, 11th Fl.
New York, NY 10036
Tel.: 212-764-1255
Fax: 212-302-6063

Eagle Wine Inc.
1235 Alton Road
Miami Beach, FL 33139
Tel.: 305-293-0248
Fax: 305-293-9551

Italian Wine Importer
145 S. Roxbury Drive,
Suite 10
Beverly Hills, CA 90212
Tel.: 310-789-1520
Fax: 310-788-7616

Elizabeth Imports
6500 Stapleton Drive
- South A
Denver, CO 80216
Tel.: 303-394-0691
Fax.: 303-394-0693

Regal Wine Imports, Inc.
20 West Stow Street,
Suite 2
Marlton, NJ 08053
Tel.: 856-985-6388
Fax: 856-985-5848

D'Aquino Italian Imports
1850 Business Center Drive
Duarte, CA 91010
Tel.: 626-359-1988
Fax.: 626-358-6387

Masciarelli Wines
65 East Mathewson Drive
Westmouth, MA 02189
Tel.: 781-335-6620
Fax.: 781-335-6620

Fiume Wines
864 S. Robertson Blvd -
Suite 303
Los Angeles, CA 90035
Tel.: 310-360-0373
Fax.: 310-360-0895

Angelini Wine Ltd.
22 Industrial Park Rd.
Center-brook, CT 06409
Tel.: 860-767-9463
Fax: 860-767-3988

Tempo Wine Imports
5505 43rd Street
Maspeth, NY 11378
Tel.: 718-260-8200
Fax: 718-260-8135

Podere San Luigi
160 Broadway, Suite 12 East
New York, NY 10038
Tel.& Fax: 212-693-1417

Royal Wine Company
63 Lafante Lane
Bayonne, NJ 07002
Tel.: 718-534-0212
Fax: 718-486-8943

Branca Products Corporation
Fratelli Branca Building
12-14 Desbrosses Street
New York, NY 10013
Tel.: 212-925-7525
Fax: 212-226-8316

Trinacria Imports, Inc.
275 Main Street
Mount Kisko, NY 10549
Tel.: 914-242-5499
Fax: 914-242-5499

Bouvignon International
12400 Ventura Blvd. - Suite 227
Ventura, CA 91604
Tel.: 818-324-7932

Apollo Fine Spirits
55 Northern Blvd. Suite 201
Great Neck, NY 11021
Tel.: 516-482-6656
Fax: 516-482-6614

Atlantic Wines & Spirits
16 Bridgewater Street
Brooklyn, NY 11222
Tel.: 1-800-382-3820
Fax: 1-800-441-5596

Medco Atlantic Inc. MHW Ltd
272 Plandom Road,
Suite 100
Manhasset, NY 11030
Tel.: 1-877-668-2490
Fax: 1-877-516-869-9171

Nestor Imports, Inc.
225 Broadway, Suite 2911
New York, NY 10007
Tel.: 212-267-1133
Fax: 212-267-2233

Omni Wines
29-16 120th Street
Linden Hill, NY 11354
Tel.: 718-353-8700
Fax: 718-353-3741

Testa Wines of the World, Ltd.
20 East Vanderventer Avenue
Port Washington,
NY 11050
Tel.: 516-883-6313
Fax: 516-767-2024

Vignaioli Selection
18 West 27th Street,
11th Fl. Front
New York, NY 10001
Tel.: 212-686-3095
Fax: 212-686-3097

Vintage Wines, Inc.
360 Broadway
Staten Island, NY 10310
Tel.: 718-818-0808
Fax: 718-818-0807

Vintwood International
40 Prospect Street
Huntington, NY 11743
Tel.: 631-424-9777
Fax: 631-424-9749

Wines for Food, Ltd.
161 West 75th Street
New York, NY 10023
Tel.: 212-769-1300
Fax: 212-501-0717

Wines We Are Importers & Distributor
104 Sackett Street
Brooklyn, NY 11231
Tel.: 718-680-4500
Fax: 718-680-3488

Famiglia di Gatti Imports
P.O. Box 1767
Montague, NJ 07827
Tel.: 973-293-3626
Fax: 973-293-8745

Vineyard Brands Inc.
2000 Resource Dr.
Birmingham, AL 35242
Tel.: (205) 980-8802
Fax: (205) 980-1682

Genova Imports
80 Pratt
Glen Cove (NY) 11542
Tel.: (516) 676-8151
Fax: (516) 676-5439

Imports Inc. Chicago
1850 North Levitt Street
Chicago, IL 60647
Tel.: 773-227-9463
Fax: 773-227-7827

Chartrand Imports
PO Box 1319
Rockland, Maine 04841
Tel.: 207-594-7300
Fax: 207-594-8098

De-Vine
7210 20th Avenue
Brooklyn, NY 11204
Tel.: 718-621-4000
Tel.: 718-621-4710

Rolar Imports
10 Cutter Mill Road
Great Neck, NY 11021
Tel.: 516-466-9222
Fax: 516-466-9564

Bacchanal Wine Imports, Inc.
224 West 35th Street - Ste 1402/A
New York, NY 10001
Tel.: 212-290-9515
Fax: 212-290-2322

Faropian Wine Importers
98 Kean Street
West Babylon, NY
Tel.: (631) 643-3281
Fax: n.a.

Tramici Wine Inc.
4474 Pearl Road
Cleveland, OH 44109
Tel.: 216-351-5675
Fax: 216-351-6312

Dal Wine Imports
2269 65th Street
Brooklyn, NY 11204
Tel.: 718-256-8092
Fax: 718-256-1932

Cadet Importers Ltd.
PO Box 3140
Mt. Vernon, NY 10553
T.: 914-961-2763
Fax: 914-961-0702

Ronac Wine Importers Inc.
575 Lexington Avenue, 4th Fl.
New York, NY 10022
Tel.: 212-572-8308
Fax: 212-535-6304

Tenuta di Arceno
185 Clinton Avenue # 10C
Brooklyn, NY 11205
Tel.: 718-596-8819
Fax: N.A.

Monti Rossi Imports, Ltd.
232 Union Avenue
New Rochelle, NY 10801
Tel.: 914-235-5635
Fax: 914-712-7737

Olana Wine Imports
2 Carillon Road
Brewster, NY 10509
Tel.: 845-279-8077
Fax: 845-279-8246

DeMarco/Blue Sky
1088 Central Park Avenue
Scarsdale, NY 10583
Tel.: 888-421-6546
Fax: 914-723-5850

Jacquin International Ltd.
2633 Trenton Avenue
Philadelphia, PA 19125

Index of Great Wines

All the following wines are included in Denominazione di Origine Controllata (DOC) or Denominazione di Origine Controllata e Garantita (DOCG) productions.

INDEX OF PLACES

All the following places appear in this book as individual entries.

PICTURE CREDITS

Front Cover: *Sime Photo*; Back Cover: T. Spagone. – G. *Andreini*: 205, 225. – T. Nicolini: 80; Orcorte: 234 bottom. – G. *Carfagna*: 201. – *Enoteca Italiana-Siena*: 178, 182. – *Grazia Neri*: Mairani: 300. – *Laura Ronchi*: V. Lombardo: 337. – *Mairani*: 24, 27, 31 center and bottom, 32/33, 41, 43, 47, 54, 55, 62 top, 68, 70, 76, 83 bottom, 88, 93, 96, 101, 106, 118, 124 top and center, 132, 134-135, 136, 137 top, bottom and center, 139, 146, 162, 186, 187, 192, 194, 196, 198, 200, 209 bottom, 215, 222 top and center, 227, 228/229, 232, 235, 240, 244 bottom, 248 top and center, 258 bottom, 263, 264, 269 bottom, 270, 272, 276, 281, 282, 290, 293, 294, 297 top, 304, 308, 309, 310 top, 312 bottom, 320/321, 323, 324 top, 328 bottom, 329, 332 bottom, 338. – *Realy Easy Star*: 56, 95, 148 center, 328 center; C. Concina: 74, 83 top, 91, 142; M. Di Paolo: 244 top; B. Evola: 312 top; G. Furghieri: 63; A. Garozzo: 298; Guidorlando: 313; G. Iacono: 310 center and bottom; F. Iorio: 273, 286; M. La Tona: 326; L. Pessina: 59, 281 bottom; A. Picone: 297 bottom; A. Pitrone: 321; G. Pontari: 297 center; N. Reitano: 318; C. Rizzi: 99 center; V. Rossato: 245, 246, 334; M. Rubino: 52, 82, 234 top and center, 239; L. Samperi: 109 bottom; L.A. Scatola: 262 bottom; T. Spagone: 8, 9, 12, 22 center and bottom, 29, 35, 38, 46, 49, 62 center, 72, 148 bottom, 205, 209 center, 213, 216, 217, 219, 220, 223, 230, 241, 242, 249, 253, 254, 258 top, 281 center, 278, 279, 283, 289, 291, 302 top, 372 bottom; M. Vicinanza: 262 center; P. Viola: 335; C.A. Zabert: 145; A. Zaven: 324. – *Scala*: 6, 7. – *Soletti*: 22 top, 66, 79, 83 center, 89, 99 top and bottom, 109 top, 111, 112, 114, 116, 117 top and bottom, 120, 121, 122, 123, 124 bottom, 128, 130, 148 top, 154, 155 bottom, 156, 158, 169, 172 top, 174/175, 184, 190, 311, 317 – *White Star*: G. Veggi: 45.

The other pictures have been supplied by the wineries and firms mentioned in the guide.

Notes

Notes